T0185728

Mastering GitHub Enterprise Management and Administration

A Guide for Seamless Management and Collaboration

Balu Nivrutti Ilag
AjayKumar P. Baljoshi
Ganesh J. Sangale
Yogesh Athave

Apress®

Mastering GitHub Enterprise Management and Administration: A Guide for Seamless Management and Collaboration

Balu Nivrutti Ilag
Tracy, CA, USA

AjayKumar P. Baljoshi
Bengaluru, Karnataka, India

Ganesh J. Sangale
Irving, TX, USA

Yogesh Athave
Bengaluru, Karnataka, India

ISBN-13 (pbk): 979-8-8688-0368-0
https://doi.org/10.1007/979-8-8688-0369-7

ISBN-13 (electronic): 979-8-8688-0369-7

Managing Director, Apress Media LLC: Welmoed Spahr
Acquisitions Editor: Smriti Srivastava
Development Editor: Laura Berendson
Editorial Project Manager: Kripa Joseph

Cover designed by eStudioCalamar

Distributed to the book trade worldwide by Springer Science+Business Media New York, 1 New York Plaza, Suite 4600, New York, NY 10004-1562, USA. Phone 1-800-SPRINGER, fax (201) 348-4505, e-mail orders-ny@springer-sbm.com, or visit www.springeronline.com. Apress Media, LLC is a California LLC and the sole member (owner) is Springer Science + Business Media Finance Inc (SSBM Finance Inc). SSBM Finance Inc is a **Delaware** corporation.

For information on translations, please e-mail booktranslations@springernature.com; for reprint, paperback, or audio rights, please e-mail bookpermissions@springernature.com.

Apress titles may be purchased in bulk for academic, corporate, or promotional use. eBook versions and licenses are also available for most titles. For more information, reference our Print and eBook Bulk Sales web page at http://www.apress.com/bulk-sales.

Any source code or other supplementary material referenced by the author in this book is available to readers on GitHub. For more detailed information, please visit https://www.apress.com/gp/services/source-code.

If disposing of this product, please recycle the paper

Table of Contents

Chapter 9: Secure Software Development Lifecycle Through GitHub Advanced Security 693

Chapter 10: GitHub Troubleshooting, Monitoring, and Reporting 743

Index ....

About the Authors

Balu Nivrutti Ilag is a former Microsoft Certified Trainer (MCT), Former MVP, Microsoft 365 Certified Teams Administrator Associate, and Microsoft Certified Solutions Expert (MCSE) for communication and productivity. He has written several blog posts on unified communication and collaboration technologies including subjects ranging from a how-to guide to best practices and troubleshooting.

He is currently working as an Office 365 and collaboration specialist at Juniper networks. Balu has over 15 years of experience in messaging, telecom, and unified communications and collaboration and focuses on Microsoft Teams and Microsoft Office 365 collaboration. His role is a combination of product administration, product development, and strategic guidance for enterprise customers.

AjayKumar P. Baljoshi is a Site Reliability Engineer at Juniper Networks with ten years of IT experience. As a Site Reliability Engineer, he has experience in orchestrating seamless integration and continuous delivery pipelines for different types of applications that are hosted on various platforms.

Ganesh J. Sangale is a Senior Software Developer at Mphasis Corp, bringing over a decade of expertise in designing and developing applications. With a primary focus on cloud-based applications, he excels in crafting scalable, high-quality solutions. Ganesh skillfully manages his responsibilities while simultaneously developing top-notch applications and leading teams to surpass client expectations.

ABOUT THE AUTHORS

Yogesh Athave, a Principal Engineer at Sasken Technologies Limited, boasts 15 years of expertise in technology, specializing in telecommunications and mobile technology. He excels in NetAdapter-based Windows driver development for 5G modems and Android application design with a focus on the Radio Interface Layer. With a comprehensive understanding of the mobile telephony stack, from design to development, Yogesh is also adept in utilizing version control tools effectively.

About the Technical Reviewer

Vikas Sukhija has nearly two decades of IT infrastructure experience. He is certified in and has worked on various Microsoft and related technologies.

He has been awarded eight times with the Microsoft Most Valuable Professional title.

Vikas is a lifelong learner, always eager to explore new technologies and expand his knowledge. He keeps himself up to date with the latest trends and developments in the field, ensuring that his reviews reflect the current best practices and industry standards. His commitment to continuous improvement and his passion for sharing knowledge make him an invaluable resource for technical content creators and readers alike.

With a strong foundation in Microsoft technologies, Vikas has continuously expanded his knowledge and skills throughout his career, adapting to the ever-evolving landscape of the cloud. His deep understanding of the Microsoft ecosystem, including Windows Server, SQL Server, Exchange Server, Active Directory, and other technologies, allows him to provide comprehensive and insightful reviews of technical materials.

Vikas's passion for automation and scripting led him to specialize in PowerShell and Python, where he has honed his skills in developing efficient and robust scripts for various administrative tasks. His expertise in PowerShell/Python ranges from simple automation scripts to complex solutions, empowering organizations to streamline their processes and enhance productivity.

ABOUT THE TECHNICAL REVIEWER

His contributions can be browsed here:

`http://TechWizard.cloud` and `http://SysCloudPro.com` blog site
(owner and author)
`www.facebook.com/TechWizard.cloud` facebook page (owner and author)

Acknowledgments

We extend our sincerest gratitude to those who have been instrumental in guiding us through the intricate world of GitHub administration and management. Foremost, we are deeply grateful to our mentor, whose wisdom and encouragement have been the beacon guiding us through challenges and toward success. Your mentorship has been invaluable, and this work stands as a testament to the impact of your guidance.

We are profoundly thankful to the GitHub documentation team and Microsoft for crafting comprehensive and detailed documentation. Your efforts have provided us with the foundational knowledge and resources necessary to navigate GitHub's complexities and have significantly contributed to the content of this book. The dedication to excellence and commitment to supporting users that your work demonstrates is truly inspiring.

Additionally, our heartfelt thanks go to the vibrant GitHub support community. Your valuable support and insights have been a cornerstone of our learning and growth. The community's willingness to share knowledge, solve problems collaboratively, and foster a supportive environment has been instrumental in our journey. Your contributions have not only enriched this book but have also strengthened the GitHub ecosystem as a whole.

To all mentioned, your collective wisdom, support, and dedication have been the driving forces behind this work. This book is a tribute to your contributions to the field of GitHub administration and management, and we are honored to share this journey with you.

Introduction

Welcome to *Mastering GitHub Enterprise Management and Administration*, a comprehensive guide designed to navigate the complexities of GitHub, the world's leading platform for software development collaboration and version control. This book is tailored for IT professionals, system administrators, and developers looking to deepen their understanding of GitHub's vast capabilities, specifically within an enterprise setting. Whether you're new to GitHub or seeking to enhance your existing skills, this book offers valuable insights into effectively managing and securing GitHub repositories, optimizing workflows, and leveraging GitHub's advanced features to streamline your development processes.

Structure of the Book

The book is structured into ten detailed chapters, each focusing on a critical aspect of GitHub Enterprise management:

1. **Chapter 1, Introduction to GitHub:** Lays the foundation by exploring GitHub's significance in collaborative software development and version control

2. **Chapter 2, GitHub Enterprise Account and Organization Setup and Administration:** Guides you through setting up and managing GitHub Enterprise accounts and organizations

3. **Chapter 3, GitHub Repository Management and Best Practices:** Offers strategies for securing repositories and adhering to best practices in repository management

4. **Chapter 4, GitHub Identity and Access Management (IAM):** Discusses managing user identities, access, and the lifecycle of user accounts within GitHub

5. **Chapter 5, GitHub Actions and GitHub Packages Management:** Delves into automating workflows with GitHub Actions and managing software packages

6. **Chapter 6, GitHub Enterprise Organization Management and Administration:** Focuses on the nuances of managing GitHub organizations effectively

7. **Chapter 7, GitHub Copilot Management:** Introduces GitHub Copilot and how to manage this AI-powered code assistant

8. **Chapter 8, Automate Development Tasks and Workflow with GitHub Actions:** Explores advanced uses of GitHub Actions for automating development tasks

9. **Chapter 9, Secure Software Development Lifecycle Through GitHub Advanced Security:** Examines integrating security practices throughout the software development lifecycle with GitHub's security features

10. **Chapter 10, GitHub Troubleshooting, Monitoring, and Reporting:** Concludes with strategies for troubleshooting common issues, monitoring GitHub operations, and generating insightful reports

Who This Book Is For

This book is intended for a wide range of readers, from IT professionals tasked with managing GitHub Enterprise environments to developers interested in leveraging GitHub's advanced features for project management and collaboration. System administrators looking to implement robust security practices and streamline development workflows will also find this book invaluable.

Why GitHub?

GitHub's central role in facilitating team collaboration, regardless of geographical location, makes it an indispensable tool for modern software development projects. It not only enhances efficiency but also ensures high-quality outcomes through comprehensive version control, integration capabilities, and support for open source contributions. This book underscores GitHub's importance in fostering collaboration, maintaining code quality, and meeting compliance requirements, particularly within large organizations.

Can Organizations Thrive Without GitHub?

While GitHub is a powerful tool for many developers and organizations, it's not the sole solution for source code management and collaboration. This book acknowledges the existence of alternatives like GitLab and Bitbucket and explores scenarios where other solutions might better align with an organization's specific needs and preferences.

Understanding GitHub and Repositories

At its core, GitHub serves as a platform for hosting and collaborating on code projects, with repositories acting as containers for these projects. This book delves into the symbiotic relationship between GitHub and repositories, highlighting how to maximize the platform's features for project management, issue tracking, and collaboration.

As you embark on this journey through *Mastering GitHub Enterprise Management and Administration*, you'll gain the knowledge and skills necessary to effectively manage GitHub environments, ensuring your projects are secure, efficient, and aligned with best practices in software development.

CHAPTER 1

Introduction to GitHub

This chapter provides a comprehensive overview of the essential components and functions related to Version Control Systems (VCS), a vital technology indispensable for modern organizations across various industries. This chapter serves as a gateway for understanding the role, significance, and application of VCS within the context of organizational needs. Specifically, the chapter is structured around the following focal areas:

- **Introduction to Version Control Systems:** An exploration of the fundamental principles and mechanics of VCS, setting the groundwork for understanding its importance

- **Version Control Systems' Importance for Organization:** An examination of why VCS is critical for organizational functionality, collaboration, and efficiency

- **Introduction to GitHub:** A detailed look into GitHub, one of the leading platforms in the VCS landscape, familiarizing readers with its features and capabilities

- **GitHub History:** A historical perspective on GitHub's evolution and how it has become an integral part of the software development ecosystem

© Balu Nivrutti Ilag, AjayKumar P. Baljoshi, Ganesh J. Sangale and Yogesh Athave 2024
B. N. Ilag et al., *Mastering GitHub Enterprise Management and Administration*,
https://doi.org/10.1007/979-8-8688-0369-7_1

- **Why GitHub Is Required:** An insight into the specific needs that GitHub addresses, underscoring its relevance and indispensability

- **Overview of GitHub Repositories**

- **Overview of Secure Management in Software Development Lifecycle with GitHub**

Together, these sections form a cohesive understanding of how GitHub, as a prominent VCS, shapes and facilitates the complex dynamics of software development, collaboration, and management within organizations. Whether you are a developer, IT manager, or someone interested in the technological infrastructure of modern business, this chapter serves as a valuable guide.

Organizations across various industries require Version Control Systems (VCS) to manage and safeguard their development processes. VCS provides a structured mechanism to track changes, facilitating collaboration among team members and ensuring that overlapping work doesn't lead to conflicts. By maintaining a detailed history of modifications, it enhances accountability, enabling precise tracing of when, why, and by whom changes were made. This historical record also serves as a vital disaster recovery tool, allowing teams to revert to previous versions in case of errors or system failures. Moreover, in industries with stringent compliance standards, VCS aids in adhering to regulatory requirements through meticulous recordkeeping. Whether it's enhancing teamwork, ensuring data integrity, or complying with legal obligations, VCS stands as an indispensable asset in an organization's technological toolkit. The implementation of Version Control Systems (VCS), and more specifically Distributed Version Control Systems (DVCS), is vital for organizations in various industries.

Introduction to Version Control Systems

Version Control Systems are the cornerstone of software development, allowing for efficient tracking of changes, managing issues, and reverting to previous versions if needed. There are three major types of VCS, and each comes with unique characteristics and challenges.

1. Local Version Control Systems (VCS)

Local VCS stores changes on an individual's local machine, managing versions through folders or basic databases.

Limitations

- **Limited Collaboration:** No collaboration across different machines

- **Risk of Errors:** Potential for mistakes, such as saving in the wrong directory

- **Security Concerns:** Vulnerabilities due to local storage without centralized access control

2. Centralized Version Control Systems (CVCS)

CVCS employs a central server to store all versions of files. Developers check out and commit changes to this central repository.

Challenges

- **Single Point of Failure:** If the central server fails, it halts collaboration.

- **Network Dependency:** Constant network connection is required.

Examples: Subversion (SVN), Perforce (Helix Core), IBM Rational ClearCase

3. Distributed Version Control Systems (DVCS)

DVCS, on the other hand, provides each developer with a complete clone of the repository, including its full history.

Advantages

- **Offline Work Capability:** Developers can commit changes locally and sync later.

- **Enhanced Data Redundancy:** Every copy acts as a full backup.

- **Flexible Collaboration:** More decentralized, allowing collaboration without a central server.

- **Advanced Branching and Merging:** More robust handling of branching and merging.

Examples: Git, Mercurial, Bazaar

Where GitHub Stands Out

GitHub is a platform that leverages Git, which is a Distributed Version Control System. Here's why GitHub stands out:

- **Collaboration:** It enhances collaboration by providing tools for code review, comments, issue tracking, and more.

- **Integration:** GitHub offers integration with various third-party tools, enabling automation, continuous integration, and more.

- **Open Source Community:** With its strong community focus, GitHub hosts numerous open source projects, encouraging community contributions.

- **Forking and Pull Requests:** It allows users to fork repositories, make changes, and then propose those changes via pull requests, thus encouraging community-driven development.

- **Security and Access Control:** GitHub adds layers of security with features like two-factor authentication and detailed access control on repositories.

In conclusion, GitHub leverages the strengths of Distributed Version Control Systems, especially Git, and adds layers of collaboration, security, and community engagement. Its versatility and comprehensive feature set make it a preferred platform for individual developers, open source projects, and enterprise-level development. Let's understand more on what GitHub is and its detailed introduction in the following topic.

Need for VCS in Organizations

Here's a detailed breakdown of why this is the case:

- **Traceability and Accountability:** VCS provides a detailed history of changes, enabling organizations to track who made a change, when it was made, and why. This fosters accountability and provides valuable insight during troubleshooting and auditing.

- **Collaboration:** It allows multiple developers or teams to work simultaneously without overwriting each other's changes. This parallel development boosts productivity and facilitates teamwork.

- **Disaster Recovery:** By maintaining historical versions, VCS acts as a safety net, enabling organizations to revert to previous versions if a critical error occurs or if there's a need to review earlier stages of the development.

- **Compliance and Governance:** Many industries have regulatory requirements that necessitate detailed recordkeeping of changes. VCS helps in compliance by maintaining these detailed records.

Emphasizing DVCS

DVCS takes these benefits further, providing specific advantages:

- **Offline Accessibility:** Developers can work offline, making changes locally and then syncing with the central repository, enabling remote and flexible work arrangements.

- **Enhanced Data Redundancy:** Each developer's copy of the repository acts as a full backup, providing an extra layer of security against data loss.

- **Scalability:** As every developer has a complete copy of the repository, DVCS scales well with growing teams, avoiding the bottlenecks that can occur with a central server.

- **Advanced Branching and Merging:** DVCS supports complex branching and merging workflows, which is essential for large projects with multiple teams working in parallel.

Industries That Need GitHub and Why

Many industries can benefit from GitHub, particularly those that rely on agile development and collaboration:

- **Technology and Software Development:** For software companies, continuous innovation and collaboration are key. GitHub offers a platform that supports these needs.

- **Financial Services:** With stringent compliance requirements, financial institutions can leverage GitHub for secure development, traceability, and robust access controls.

- **Healthcare and Life Sciences:** In developing applications for diagnostics, treatment, and data analysis, GitHub can facilitate collaboration across multidisciplinary teams.

- **Education:** Academic institutions and researchers can use GitHub for collaborative research, code sharing, and educational purposes.

Example: Bloguc Technology Corporation

Let's consider an example of a tech company, Bloguc Technology Corporation. As a growing organization dealing with multiple projects across different teams, XYZ needed a robust VCS to handle their complex development landscape.

By implementing GitHub, they leveraged the strengths of DVCS. The company found GitHub essential in facilitating collaboration across globally dispersed teams, integrating with continuous integration tools, and managing different project branches effectively. The ability to review code, comment, and track issues within a single platform made the development process more streamlined and efficient.

Introduction to GitHub

GitHub is a global platform that has revolutionized the way developers work, collaborate, and share code. Founded in 2008, it has become the largest host of source code in the world, providing a space where millions of developers can contribute to open source projects, manage their own repositories, and connect with like-minded individuals. GitHub, Inc. is a platform and cloud-based service for software development and version control using Git, allowing developers to store and manage their code.

At its core, GitHub leverages Git, the Distributed Version Control System created by Linus Torvalds. This allows developers to efficiently track changes, branch off to work on new features, and merge updates, all while maintaining the integrity of the code. GitHub takes these powerful functionalities and wraps them in an intuitive web interface, making it accessible to both seasoned developers and newcomers alike.

But GitHub is more than just a tool for version control. It's a community where developers can discover projects that inspire them, contribute to others' work, and showcase their own creations. With features like issues, pull requests, and GitHub Actions, it fosters a collaborative environment that transcends geographical boundaries.

From individual hobbyists to large corporations, GitHub serves as a vital hub for software development. Its impact on the industry is evident in the vast array of projects hosted on the platform, including some of the most prominent open source projects in technology today.

Whether you're looking to contribute to existing projects, manage your code, or learn from others, GitHub stands as a central figure in the modern development landscape, driving innovation, collaboration, and continuous learning. It's not just a service; it's a thriving ecosystem that embodies the spirit of the open source movement.

GitHub History

GitHub's history is an exciting example of how collaboration and version control have become essential in modern software development.

When and How GitHub Was Born

GitHub was founded on April 10, 2008, by Tom Preston-Werner, Chris Wanstrath, and P.J. Hyett. The idea behind GitHub originated from the need to provide a platform where developers could collaborate on code and manage changes without the complexities associated with traditional Version Control Systems.

GitHub's emergence has had a significant impact on how developers collaborate and manage code. By building on the robust foundation of Git, it simplified the process, made it more accessible, and fostered a vibrant community that continues to drive innovation in software development. Its acquisition by Microsoft in 2018 for $7.5 billion further solidified its position as a central platform in the tech industry. Whether for individual developers or large enterprises, GitHub continues to be an indispensable tool in modern software development.

The Transition from Git to GitHub

The relationship between Git and GitHub is essential to understanding the platform:

- **Git:** Created by Linus Torvalds in 2005, Git is a Distributed Version Control System. It allows developers to track changes in their code, collaborate with others, and work on multiple versions of a project simultaneously. Git is the core technology that GitHub builds upon.

- **GitHub:** It is a web-based hosting service for Git repositories. While Git is a command-line tool, GitHub provides a graphical interface. It adds many collaboration features, such as bug tracking, feature requests, task management, and wikis for every project.

How the Git to GitHub Transaction Happened

- **Utilizing Git's Power:** GitHub took the fundamental concepts of Git (branching, merging, committing) and wrapped them in a user-friendly web interface. This made it more accessible to a broader audience of developers, not just those comfortable with command-line interfaces.

- **Adding Value:** Beyond merely hosting Git repositories, GitHub introduced social features, like following users, starting projects, and more. It became a social network for developers.

- **Continuous Growth:** Since its inception, GitHub has continued to grow, adding new features, expanding its community, and becoming a central hub for open source development.

Why GitHub Is Required

GitHub, being a central repository, makes it easy for teams to collaborate on software development projects. Regardless of geographical location, teams can work together in real time, increasing efficiency and ensuring a more seamless workflow. With GitHub, teams can review, comment on, and merge changes to the codebase, ensuring everyone is on the same page, and the final product is of the highest quality.

GitHub is also essential for version control. It allows developers to track changes, understand the history of a project, and revert changes if needed. This makes debugging easier and reduces the risk of catastrophic mistakes.

Why GitHub Is Required for Source Code Version Management

- **Collaboration:** GitHub provides a platform where multiple developers can work on the same project simultaneously without overriding each other's changes.

- **Version Control:** Utilizing Git, GitHub helps in tracking changes and maintaining different versions of the code, making it easier to revert to previous states if needed.

- **Integration:** GitHub integrates with various tools and technologies, making it easier for developers to use other services like continuous integration, code testing, and more.

- **Open Source Contributions:** For projects that are open source, GitHub offers a community and tools to facilitate contributions from developers all over the world.

- **Accessibility and Security:** GitHub provides secure remote access to code repositories, enabling distributed teams to collaborate with ease.

Is GitHub Essential for Organizations?

While GitHub offers many conveniences, it may not be essential for every organization. The necessity of GitHub depends on the organization's size, project complexity, collaboration needs, and specific workflow preferences.

- **Large Organizations:** Many large organizations find GitHub essential due to the robust features it offers for collaboration, version control, and integration with other tools. It helps in maintaining code quality and facilitates agile development practices.

- **Small and Medium Organizations:** Even small and medium businesses can benefit from GitHub's features, but they might also consider alternatives depending on their budget, needs, and preferences.

Can an Organization Survive Without GitHub?

Absolutely. While GitHub has become a standard tool for many developers and organizations, it's not the only solution out there. Alternatives like GitLab, Bitbucket, and others provide similar functionalities for source code management. Organizations can also opt to host their Git repositories on-premises if they prefer.

Choosing whether to use GitHub or another solution depends on various factors, such as the organization's specific requirements, budget considerations, and the nature of the projects they're handling. Some might find GitHub's community and extensive toolset to be irreplaceable, while others might prefer a different solution that aligns better with their unique needs.

In summary, GitHub has indeed become a significant tool for source code version management, especially for collaborative projects. But it's not the only pathway, and organizations can certainly find success using other tools or platforms tailored to their particular needs and preferences.

Understand GitHub and Repository (Repo) Relationship

The relationship between GitHub and repositories is central to understanding how GitHub functions as a platform for code collaboration and version control. Consider GitHub as a platform whereas a repository is a container for projects that reside on GitHub.

> **GitHub:** GitHub is a web-based platform that provides hosting for software development and a robust set of collaboration tools built around Git, a Distributed Version Control System. It's widely used by developers to collaborate on code, manage projects, track issues, and contribute to open source projects.

> **Repository (Repo):** A repository, or "repo," is essentially a container for a project. It includes all of the project files and stores each file's revision history. Repositories can also contain folders, links to related data, and metadata about the project such as access controls, issues, and project boards.

The Relationship Between GitHub and Repositories

- **Hosting Repositories:** GitHub hosts repositories, making them accessible to team members, collaborators, or even the public if it's an open source project. Hosting repositories on GitHub allows developers from different locations to access and work on the same codebase easily.

- **Version Control with Git:** GitHub uses Git for version control, meaning that it keeps track of changes made to files within a repository. Every time a change is made, a new "commit" is created in the repository's history, allowing you to see what was changed, who changed it, and why.

- **Collaboration:** GitHub repositories provide a collaborative environment where multiple users can work on a project simultaneously. Features like branching and merging allow developers to work on separate aspects of a project without interfering with each other's work.

- **Access Control:** Within a GitHub repository, you can set different access levels, allowing certain users to modify code, while others might only have read access. This enables better control and security over who can make changes to the project.

- **Integration and Automation:** GitHub repositories can be integrated with various tools and services, enabling automated testing, continuous integration and deployment (CI/CD), issue tracking, and more.

- **Forking and Contributing:** In open source projects hosted on GitHub, users can "fork" a repository, creating a personal copy that they can modify. They can then submit their changes back to the original repository via a "pull request," facilitating community contributions.

- **Documentation and Issues:** Repositories on GitHub often include documentation like README files, wikis, and issue tracking, all aiding in the clear communication and management of a project's goals and problems.

In summary, repositories are central to GitHub's functionality, serving as the containers for projects, while GitHub provides the platform and tools to collaborate, control versions, secure, and automate processes related to those repositories. The synergy between GitHub and repositories creates an efficient and collaborative environment for software development.

How GitHub Is Helpful for Business Processes and Use Cases

For businesses, GitHub offers a powerful platform to streamline software development. Some use cases include

- **Collaborative Coding:** GitHub enables real-time collaboration among developers, allowing teams to work together even when dispersed globally.

- **Documentation:** Beyond just code, GitHub can also host documentation, ensuring it is version-controlled and accessible to the team.

- **Continuous Integration/Continuous Deployment (CI/CD):** GitHub can integrate with various CI/CD tools, automating the process of testing and deploying code.

- **Open Source Projects:** Businesses can use GitHub to manage open source projects, inviting contributions from the broader developer community.

Overview of GitHub Repositories

In the context of GitHub, one of the most fundamental and powerful concepts is that of repositories. This section offers a brief overview, setting the stage for an in-depth exploration in Chapter 3.

What Is a Repository?

A GitHub repository, often simply referred to as a "repo," is a storage space where your project lives. It can have folders, files, images, spreadsheets, datasets, and all relevant documentation for the project. Repositories enable collaboration by organizing and tracking changes to your project over time.

Types of Repositories

There are three main types of repositories on GitHub:

- **Public Repositories:** It is accessible to anyone and often used for open source projects.

- **Private Repositories:** It has restricted access to the owner, until explicitly shared with the users.

- **Internal Repositories:** It will be accessible to all enterprise members.

Why Repositories Are Crucial

GitHub repositories act as the central hub for project collaboration. They enable multiple contributors to work simultaneously, manage version histories, and ensure that changes are transparently tracked and managed.

- **Connection with Distributed Version Control Systems (DVCS):** GitHub repositories use the power of Distributed Version Control Systems, allowing for advanced features like branching and merging, offline work, and robust backup strategies.

- **GitHub Repositories in Action:** Almost every action on GitHub revolves around repositories. From initiating a new project to making incremental updates or downloading the latest version of a project, repositories are at the core of the GitHub experience.

This overview touches upon the essential aspects of GitHub repositories, providing an insight into their purpose, functionality, and importance in the collaborative workflow. As repositories are central to the operation and collaboration within GitHub, Chapter 3 will delve into more specific details, exploring advanced features, best practices, and real-world applications of GitHub repositories. Whether new to GitHub or seeking to deepen understanding, the upcoming chapter promises to enrich your knowledge on this key element of GitHub's ecosystem.

Overview of Secure Management in Software Development Lifecycle with GitHub

In the intricate world of software development, managing the lifecycle of a project with security and efficiency is paramount. This section presents a brief overview of how GitHub enables secure software development lifecycle management (SDLC), a topic that will be explored in detail in Chapter 8.

What Is Secure SDLC?

Secure software development lifecycle management integrates security practices within the SDLC process. It ensures that security considerations are not an afterthought but are embedded throughout the design, development, testing, and deployment phases.

GitHub's Role in Secure SDLC

GitHub, as a platform, brings powerful tools and methodologies that facilitate a secure and transparent SDLC process.

- **Security from the Start:** GitHub enables security checks from the early stages of development, encouraging a "shift left" approach in security considerations.

- **Collaboration and Code Review:** By using GitHub's collaborative environment, code reviews become more robust, enabling team members to identify and rectify security vulnerabilities early on.

- **Automated Security Features:** GitHub offers integration with various automated testing and security tools, providing continuous feedback and automated vulnerability scanning.

- **Access Control and Permissions:** With detailed control over permissions and access, GitHub ensures that only authorized individuals can make changes, enhancing the security of the codebase.

- **Audit and Compliance:** GitHub's tracking and logging capabilities facilitate a comprehensive audit trail, essential for regulatory compliance and understanding security incidents.

Key Features for Secure SDLC on GitHub

- **Issues:** Issues on GitHub serve as a secure way to identify and track bugs, enhancements, tasks, and other kinds of questions that are intended for software projects. They provide a collaborative space where team members can easily share the latest updates, thereby ensuring that no critical security issues are overlooked.

- **Discussions:** This feature enables a forum-like environment within a GitHub repository to hold more structured and threaded conversations. This is especially helpful for discussing security approaches and strategies without cluttering the Issues list.

- **Pull Requests:** Pull requests provide a way to notify project maintainers about changes you'd like them to consider. This feature offers a platform for code review, which is crucial for detecting security vulnerabilities before the code is merged.

- **Notifications:** GitHub provides notification features to keep you updated on activities that concern you. Setting up notifications for security alerts can help the team respond to vulnerabilities as soon as they are discovered.

- **Labels:** Using labels can help categorize issues and pull requests related to security. Labels like "Security Bug" or "Vulnerability" can prioritize security concerns within the development process.

- **Actions:** GitHub Actions automates all your software workflows. Security scans can be automated so that any code you submit is automatically reviewed for vulnerabilities.

- **Forks:** Forks allow you to freely experiment with changes without affecting the original project. This is particularly useful for testing security patches and updates before applying them to the main project.

- **Projects:** This feature allows you to manage your work within GitHub. You can set up boards with columns like "To Do," "In Progress," and "Done" to track the progress of security-related tasks in your SDLC.

Secure Workflow with GitHub

Here's a general guide for integrating these features into a secure SDLC workflow:

- **Planning:** Use issues and projects to outline the security requirements of your project.

- **Development:** Utilize forks to create separate environments for developing security features.

- **Code Review:** Implement pull requests to ensure that each line of code is scrutinized for potential security vulnerabilities.

- **Testing:** Automate security tests using GitHub Actions.

- **Deployment:** Use GitHub Actions to automate secure deployment processes.

- **Monitoring:** Leverage notifications to stay aware of any security vulnerabilities or necessary updates.

Integration with Industry Standards

GitHub's secure SDLC practices align with well-established industry standards, such as ISO/IEC 27001 and NIST SP 800-64, ensuring a robust and internationally recognized approach to secure development.

Real-World Applications

Many organizations, ranging from small startups to Fortune 500 companies, leverage GitHub's secure SDLC features to protect intellectual property, comply with regulations, and build trust with customers.

This overview provides a glimpse into how GitHub addresses the critical aspect of security within the software development lifecycle. Through a combination of built-in features, integration capabilities, collaboration, and alignment with industry standards, GitHub offers a compelling solution for secure SDLC. For a comprehensive understanding of how to implement and leverage these features, Chapter 8 will offer in-depth insights, practical guidance, and examples tailored to various organizational needs. It's a vital component for any developer, security professional, or organization striving to create software with integrity, reliability, and confidence.

Additional Features of GitHub

GitHub, in addition to Version Control Systems, also offers several features and tools that enhance collaboration and streamline development processes. These added features include

1. **Teams:** It supports creating teams, which makes it easier to manage access control and permissions for repositories. Teams help in organizing and categorizing developers based on their roles or responsibilities within the project, easing efficient collaboration.

2. **Projects:** It provides an effective way to organize and manage tasks and issues associated with a project. It offers features like customizable boards, automated workflows, and a visual way to track the progress of various tasks.

3. **Actions:** It is an automation platform that enables developers to create custom workflows for their repositories, which can be executed based on use cases. These workflows can automate tasks such as building, testing, and deploying code. It's a powerful tool for continuous integration and continuous deployment (CI/CD) and can help streamline the development and release processes.

4. **Packages:** It is a package registry that helps to publish and share packages within the organization. It supports various package managers like npm,

Docker, RubyGems, and more. This feature allows us to manage and distribute code dependencies across your projects.

5. **Security:** It comes with various security features to help protect your code and data. This includes code scanning for identifying vulnerabilities, dependency analysis to check for known security issues, and token scanning to detect and revoke exposed credentials.

Further exploration of these features will be covered comprehensively in the upcoming chapters.

Programmatically Access GitHub

It provides the following options to communicate, generate, and capture required information:

- GitHub's API (Application Programming Interface) provides powerful tools for automating and managing various tasks within GitHub repositories, organizations, and enterprises.

- GitHub's GraphQL API is a versatile and efficient way to interact with the platform and perform tasks or gather information about GitHub repositories, organizations, and enterprises.

Difference Between the REST API and GraphQL

GraphQL is a query language for APIs that allows you to request specific data from GitHub. Unlike traditional REST APIs, GraphQL enables you to specify precisely what data you need, reducing overfetching and underfetching of information.

Summary

This chapter offered a comprehensive exploration of Version Control Systems (VCS) and their pivotal role in modern organizational frameworks. It serves as a foundational resource, delving into the fundamental principles and mechanics of VCS to elucidate its significance. The chapter underscored the imperative nature of VCS for organizational functionality, collaboration, and efficiency, highlighting its indispensable role in contemporary workflows. Central to the discussion was an in-depth examination of GitHub, a leading platform in the VCS landscape, which was meticulously dissected to familiarize the readers with its features and capabilities. By tracing GitHub's historical evolution and elucidating its transformative impact on software development practices, the chapter contextualized its importance within the broader ecosystem. Furthermore, it elucidated the specific needs addressed by GitHub, emphasizing its relevance and indispensability in facilitating streamlined collaboration and version control management. The chapter culminated in an overview of GitHub repositories and the secure management of software development lifecycle (SDLC) with GitHub, offering a comprehensive understanding of its practical application in organizational settings.

Resources

- GitHub foundational information: https://docs. github.com/en/get-started/learning-about- github/githubs-plans

- What is GitHub and source control system information: https://learn.microsoft.com/en-us/training/ modules/introduction-to-github/2-what-is-github

- Software development lifecycle using GitHub: https://resources.github.com/security/software-development-strategy-essentials/

- GitHub details: https://docs.github.com/en/get-started/quickstart/hello-world

- REST information: https://docs.github.com/en/rest/quickstart?apiVersion=2022-11-28

- GraphQL information: https://docs.github.com/en/graphql/overview/about-the-graphql-api

CHAPTER 2

GitHub Enterprise Account and Organization Setup and Administration

This chapter delves into the setup and administration of GitHub Enterprise accounts and organizations. It focuses on how to effectively create and manage these entities while also emphasizing the best practices to ensure efficient operations.

Topics covered in this chapter include

- Introduction
- Understanding GitHub Personal, Enterprise, and Organization Accounts
- Setting Up a GitHub Enterprise Account
- Setting Up and Managing Organizations in GitHub Enterprise Cloud
- Overview of GitHub Billing

© Balu Nivrutti Ilag, AjayKumar P. Baljoshi, Ganesh J. Sangale and Yogesh Athave 2024
B. N. Ilag et al., *Mastering GitHub Enterprise Management and Administration*,
https://doi.org/10.1007/979-8-8688-0369-7_2

- Understanding Different Roles and Their Management on GitHub

- Overview of Enterprise Managed User (EMU)

- GitHub Administration and Management

- Best Practices for GitHub Enterprise Account and Organization Administration

Introduction

Navigating the complex landscape of software development requires more than just coding skills; it's also about ensuring that your tools and platforms are configured optimally. One such indispensable tool for modern enterprises is GitHub. With its ability to foster collaboration and streamline code management, setting up GitHub efficiently becomes pivotal.

In this chapter, we aim to be your compass, guiding you through the meticulous process of setting up and administering GitHub Enterprise accounts and organizations. We don't stop at just the mechanics; our focus is also on imparting strategies and best practices. Whether you're a fledgling startup or a large conglomerate, the methodologies detailed here will enable you to harness the full potential of GitHub, ensuring fluid operations and efficient collaboration.

From account creation to organization management, this chapter serves as a comprehensive blueprint. We'll unveil the nuances, provide insights, and equip you with the knowledge to establish a robust GitHub presence for your enterprise. So, buckle up and let's embark on this journey of optimizing your GitHub setup and administration.

Understanding GitHub Personal, Enterprise, and Organization Accounts

GitHub Enterprise is the self-hosted version of GitHub that provides an environment for businesses to manage their source code privately. It is a powerful tool that combines the workflow capabilities of GitHub with the security, high availability, and performance needs of an enterprise environment.

GitHub organizations, on the other hand, allow businesses to consolidate and manage multiple repositories that belong to a single project or business unit. They provide a space where businesses can provide access to multiple collaborators and control their permissions at different granularity levels.

Understanding GitHub Account Types

While delving into the realm of GitHub, it's crucial to grasp the differentiation between GitHub account types and the plans they offer. GitHub categorizes its accounts into three main types:

1. Personal

2. Organization

3. Enterprise

In this topic, we will dive deep into each of these account types, offering insights, features, and practical examples to help you get a comprehensive understanding:

1. **GitHub Personal Accounts**

    Every individual navigating through GitHub.com logs in using a personal account, which is also commonly known as a user account. It represents your identity on GitHub, distinguished by a unique username called GitHub handle and profile. Always choose a GitHub username or GitHub handle meaningfully so that you can remember it and it identifies you correctly.

Key Features

- Using a personal account, you can own resources, including repositories, packages, and projects.

- Actions like raising issues or reviewing pull requests are directly linked to your personal account.

For example: Balu has a personal account on GitHub with the username Balu_dev28. He manages his projects, participates in discussions, and contributes to open source repositories under this account.

Plan Variations

- **GitHub Free:** Offers unlimited public and private repositories with a limited feature set for private repositories

- **GitHub Pro:** Provides a more expansive range of features for both public and private repositories

2. **Organization Accounts**

Unlike the individual-centric personal accounts, organization accounts act as collaborative platforms where multiple participants can work across various projects simultaneously.

Key Features

- Offer a multitiered permission system.

- Can own a multitude of resources like repositories, packages, and projects.

- Members don't log in to the organization directly; they access it via their personal accounts.

For example: A software company named "Bloguc" might set up an organization account. Team members, developers, and collaborators will be part of this organization, working together on different projects.

Roles and Permissions

- **Organization Owners and Security Managers:** Possess the capability to adjust settings for the organization, handle access permissions and application integration, and implement advanced security features

- **Members:** Can actively collaborate within repositories and projects

3. **Enterprise Accounts**

   Enterprise accounts are custom-made for a more centralized management approach; enterprise accounts on GitHub.com let administrators uniformly manage policies, identity access, billing, and more for various organizations under their enterprise umbrella.

Key Features

- Manage policies across all owned organizations at the enterprise level or organization level

- Facilitate inner sourcing between organizations within the enterprise

For example: A Bloguc corporation with multiple tech subsidiaries might opt for an enterprise account. This allows them to maintain a centralized GitHub presence, with each subsidiary possibly having its own organization account under the main enterprise.

Organizational Management

- **Invite:** Existing organizations can be invited to the enterprise account.

- **Transfer:** Organizations can be moved between enterprise accounts.

- **Create:** New organizations can be initiated within the enterprise.

By understanding these account differences, users can bind the full potential of GitHub, ensuring a seamless collaboration and development experience tailored to their needs. The next topics explain the GitHub product plans.

GitHub Product Plans

Navigating through GitHub's vast array of functionalities can seem overwhelming, especially when trying to pinpoint the exact plan that fits your or your organization's requirements. This topic aims to demystify GitHub's product offerings, ranging from free plans to enterprise solutions. Figure 2-1 shows the available plans.

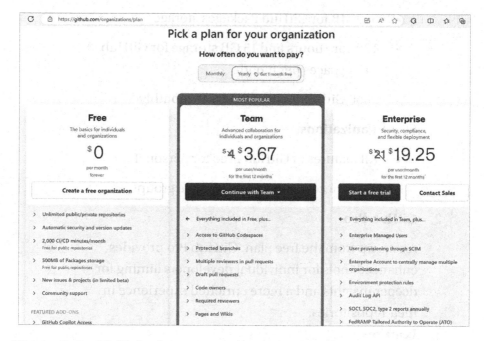

Figure 2-1. *GitHub plans*

1. **GitHub Free**

   The starting point for both individuals and
   organizations, GitHub Free offers a foundational
   set of features that cater to those starting out or
   requiring basic collaborative tools.

   For Personal Accounts

   - Unlimited public and private repositories

   - Collaborate with an unlimited number of
     collaborators

   - Community support

   - Dependabot alerts and two-factor authentication

- 500 MB for GitHub Packages storage

- 120 core hours and 15 GB storage for GitHub Codespaces per month

- 2000 GitHub Actions minutes monthly

For Organizations

- All features of GitHub Free for personal

- Team access controls to manage groups

2. **GitHub Pro**

A step-up from the free plan, GitHub Pro provides enhanced tools for individual developers aiming for deeper insights and a more enriched experience in their repositories.

Features

- All offerings of GitHub Free

- Email support

- Enhanced GitHub Actions minutes and Packages storage

- 3000 GitHub Actions minutes per month

- 2 GB GitHub Packages storage

- 180 GitHub Codespaces core hours per month

- 20 GB GitHub Codespaces storage per month

- Advanced tools and insights in private repositories

  - Required pull request reviewers

  - Multiple pull request reviewers

  - Protected branches

- Code owners

- Autolinked references

- GitHub Pages

- Wikis

- Repository insight graphs for pulse, contributors, traffic, commits, code frequency, network, and forks

3. **GitHub Team**

Tailored for organizations, the GitHub Team bridges the gap between individual developers and larger teams, offering collaborative tools that foster seamless team-oriented workflows.

Features

- All provisions of GitHub Pro

- Optionality on GitHub Codespaces

- GitHub Support via email

- 3000 GitHub Actions minutes per month

- 2 GB GitHub Packages storage

- Advanced tools and insights in private repositories

  - Required pull request reviewers

  - Multiple pull request reviewers

  - Draft pull requests

  - Team pull request reviewers

  - Protected branches

- Code owners

- Scheduled reminders

- GitHub Pages

- Wikis

4. **GitHub Enterprise**

   For organizations seeking a top-tier experience
   with maximized support, security, and advanced
   features, GitHub Enterprise stands out as the most
   comprehensive offering.

   Features

   - Everything in GitHub Team, complemented by

     - Enhanced support

     - Advanced security, compliance, and
       deployment controls

     - SAML (Security Assertion Markup Language)
       Single Sign-On and SCIM (System for Cross-
       domain Identity Management) for access
       provisioning

     - GitHub Connect

     - Option to purchase GitHub Advanced
       Security

   For example: Imagine a large corporation "Bloguc" with various
   tech divisions spread globally. Opting for GitHub Enterprise
   ensures that they benefit from reinforced security protocols,
   access management, and specialized support, ensuring
   streamlined operations.

GitHub Enterprise Options

GitHub Enterprise, while designed to cater to larger organizations with extensive demands, is not a one-size-fits-all solution. It provides two distinct offerings to cater to varied organizational needs:

1. **GitHub Enterprise Server (GHES):** GHES stands as a self-hosted solution, granting organizations autonomy over their infrastructure. It is tailored for those who prioritize having a hands-on approach, with complete control over their environment.

2. **GitHub Enterprise Cloud:** While retaining the core essence of GitHub Enterprise, the Cloud variant brings added functionalities and resources:

   - A whopping 50,000 GitHub Actions minutes monthly

   - A generous allocation of 50 GB storage for GitHub Packages

   - A commitment to reliability with a 99.9% monthly uptime service-level agreement

   - Centralized management capabilities, allowing oversight of policy and billing across multiple GitHub.com organizations via an enterprise account

   - Enhanced user management through the provision of Enterprise Managed Users, streamlining the user account processes for developers

Key Difference: The primary distinction between GHES and GitHub Enterprise Cloud lies in their deployment. GHES is suited for organizations preferring an on-premise, controlled setup. In contrast, GitHub Enterprise Cloud offers enhanced resources, especially in the realm of GitHub Actions and Packages storage, designed for organizations seeking scalability and cloud advantages.

Understanding GitHub Enterprise and GitHub Organizations

GitHub Enterprise is a self-hosted version of GitHub designed for use within an organization's internal network. It provides all the features of GitHub but allows you to host your repositories, code, and data on your own infrastructure. This is particularly useful for organizations that require additional security, compliance, and control over their development workflows.

GitHub organizations, on the other hand, is a way to manage and organize GitHub users and repositories within a collective group. Organizations can be used by teams, open source projects, businesses, or any group of GitHub users working together. Here are the key points to understand:

- **Repositories:** An organization can have multiple repositories, and each repository can have its own access control and settings.

- **People (Members):** Members of an organization can have varying roles, such as owners (with administrative privileges), collaborators (with read/write access to repositories), and outside collaborators (users who contribute to specific repositories).

- **Teams:** Organizations can create teams for group members and manage repository access more easily.

- **Billing:** Organizations can choose different billing plans, including free plans for open source projects and paid plans for businesses.

- **Project:** It is a digital tool that helps in planning and managing work effectively; it also allows us to adapt it according to requirements.

- **Packages:** It is a place where we can store, manage, and share software components you need for your projects. It helps keep everything organized and accessible, making it easier for developers to work together on building software.

Refer to Figure 2-2 for GitHub Enterprise and organization structure.

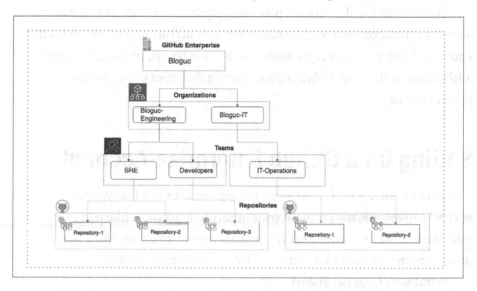

Figure 2-2. *GitHub Enterprise and organization*

- **GitHub Enterprise:** The top-level environment, such as "Bloguc," represents your GitHub Enterprise instance, which serves as the overarching platform for your repositories and user accounts.

- **Organizations:** Within GitHub Enterprise, organizations act as containers for grouping repositories and users based on departments, projects, or other organizational needs. For instance, "Bloguc-Engineering" is an organization dedicated to engineering teams.

37

- **Teams:** Organizations can be further organized into teams based on functionality or projects. These teams facilitate the management of permissions and collaboration. For example, you can create teams dedicated to SRE teams called SRE to control access to specific repositories for engineering-related functions.

This hierarchical structure provides a systematic way to manage access permissions and organization within GitHub Enterprise. It enables you to control access to repositories at various levels, maintain security, and promote efficient collaboration among different departments or project teams.

Setting Up a GitHub Enterprise Account

On GitHub Enterprise Cloud, your enterprise account lets you oversee several organizations. Think of your enterprise account like a big umbrella. Just like any other account on GitHub, your enterprise account needs a unique name, known as a "handle." Here's a simpler breakdown.

What's an Organization?

It's like a shared workspace for members of an enterprise. Everyone can work on various projects in this space. The heads of these organizations (organization owners) can decide who gets access to what data and project. They also have advanced tools to ensure the organization's data is safe and organized.

What Can You Do in Enterprise Settings?

If you're the big boss (enterprise owner), you can ask other organizations to join your enterprise account. Need to shift organizations around? You can do that, too – moving them from one enterprise account to another. Starting from scratch? You can set up a new organization within your enterprise account.

Setting Rules with Enterprise Policies

Your enterprise account gives you the power to set rules for all the organizations under it. These rules or policies help ensure everyone follows the same best practices.

You can either set a particular rule or let organization owners decide what's best for them.

Starting with GitHub Enterprise Cloud?

If you're new and using GitHub Enterprise Cloud for just one organization, it's a good idea to set up an enterprise account. Setting up a GitHub Enterprise account is like setting up a dedicated space for your team's coding projects, but it comes with more advanced features tailored for businesses and larger teams. Let's break down the process step by step in straightforward terms.

1. **Choose Your Enterprise Option:**

   Before you begin, decide which GitHub Enterprise option suits your needs:

   - **GitHub Enterprise Server:** This is like having your own special version of GitHub, but it's hosted on your servers. It's great if you want more control over your infrastructure.

   - **GitHub Enterprise Cloud:** This is hosted by GitHub itself on the cloud. Think of it as renting space from GitHub where your team can work without worrying about server maintenance.

2. **Create an Enterprise Account:**

   Head over to the GitHub Enterprise page. Choose the appropriate plan (Server or Cloud) and click "Start a free trial" if you want to try it out first or "GitHub Contact Sales" to discuss pricing and get

started. Follow the prompts to set up your account.
This will include basic details like your name, email,
and password. For illustration purposes, we are
setting up the trial Enterprise account.

GitHub Enterprise Account: A Step-by-Step Guide

If you're looking to expand your organization's collaboration
capabilities on GitHub, creating an enterprise account on GitHub
Enterprise Cloud is the way to go. This account lets you bring multiple
organizations together and offers a unified point for managing them.
Here's a step-by-step guide to help you set up an enterprise account:

Understanding the Basics

- **What's an Enterprise Account?** It's an account
  type on GitHub Enterprise Cloud designed for
  larger organizations and collaborations across
  multiple teams.

- **Cost Implications:** Setting up an enterprise account
  doesn't add extra charges to your bill.

- **Existing Users:** If you're already using GitHub
  Enterprise Cloud for a single organization and pay by
  invoice, the process to transition is streamlined. You
  can initiate the transition through your billing page.

Steps to Create an Enterprise Account

1. **Log In to GitHub (`https://github.com/`):** Begin by
   logging in to your GitHub account.

2. **Access Settings:** On the top right-hand corner of
   any GitHub page, click your profile photo, and from
   the dropdown menu, select "Settings." Figure 2-3
   shows the Settings option.

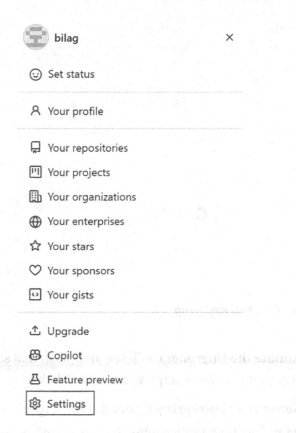

Figure 2-3. *GitHub settings*

3. **Go to Organizations:** In the "Access" section on the sidebar, find and click "Organizations."

4. **Select Your Organization:** Next to your organization name, click "Settings."

5. *Access Billing:* If you're an organization owner, in the "Access" section of the sidebar, click "Billing and plans." Figure 2-4 shows the upgrade option.

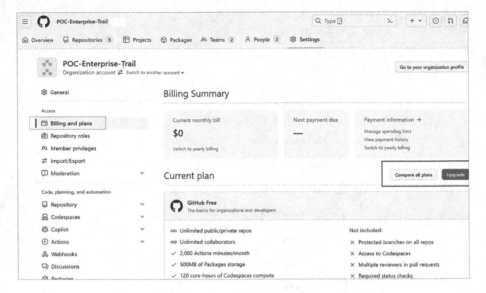

Figure 2-4. *GitHub org upgrade*

6. **Initiate the Upgrade:** You'll see an option that says "Upgrade" to the enterprise account. Click it.

7. **Name Your Enterprise:** Under the "Enterprise name" section, input a name for your new enterprise account. On the setup enterprise account page, select the enterprise URL, Industry, Number of employees, and organization information. Under "Enterprise URL slug," type out a unique slug. This will form part of your enterprise URL. For instance, if you choose "Bloguc," your URL will be `https://github.com/enterprises/Bloguc`. Figure 2-5 shows the GitHub account setup.

Note   You may visit `https://github.com/account/` `enterprises/new` and then log in with your GitHub account and password to create a new enterprise account.

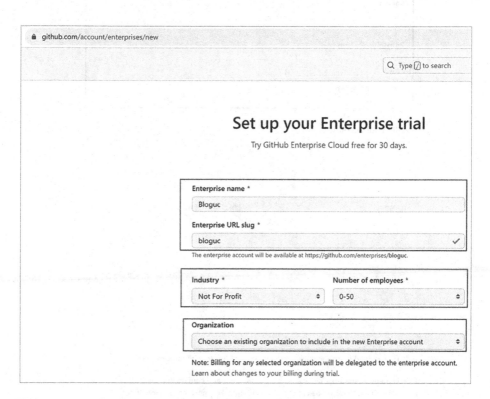

Figure 2-5. *Creating an Enterprise trial*

8. Then, update the contact information and click "Create your enterprise." Refer to Figure 2-6 for creating an enterprise.

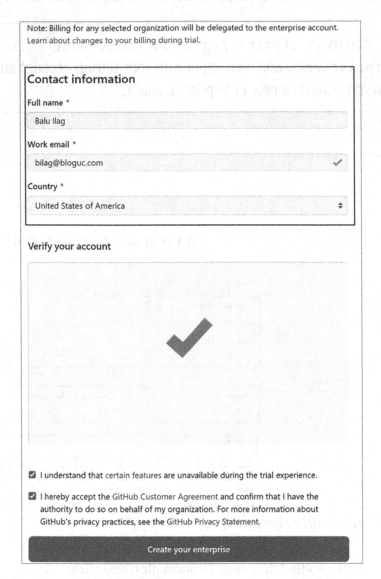

Figure 2-6. *Creating an Enterprise account*

9.   Once the account is created, you can continue with
     the trial or buy an enterprise. Refer to Figure 2-7 for
     the billing page.

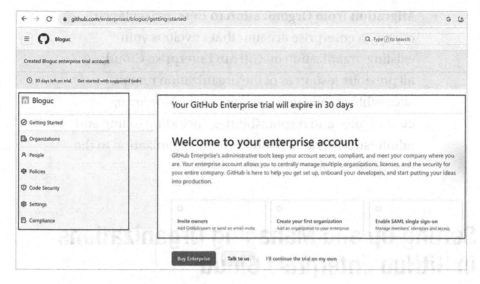

Figure 2-7. *You can buy an enterprise*

Billing and Payment

Finally, set up the billing details by choosing a subscription plan and then adding the payment details. It is important to keep an eye on your billing settings to understand your usage and costs.

> **Finalize the Upgrade:** Click "Confirm and upgrade." A set of warnings and notices will appear. Make sure to read them carefully.
>
> **Complete the Process:** Once you've read and understood the warnings, click "Create enterprise account."

Important Notes

- **Free Trial:** If you're not sure about committing just yet, consider setting up a free trial of GitHub Enterprise Cloud. However, note that trials are capped at 50 seats.

45

- **Migration from Organization to Enterprise:** If you create an enterprise account that envelops your existing organization on GitHub Enterprise Cloud, all previous resources of the organization remain accessible at the same web addresses. Moreover, certain roles and responsibilities, including billing and administrative rights, shift from the organization to the enterprise level.

Setting Up and Managing Organizations in GitHub Enterprise Cloud

Managing large-scale software projects requires seamless collaboration across teams. GitHub Enterprise Cloud facilitates this by letting you manage multiple organizations under one umbrella: the enterprise account. Let's break down how to create, invite, and transfer organizations within the GitHub Enterprise Cloud realm.

1. **About Organizations in Your Enterprise Account:** Your enterprise account can house multiple organizations, making collaboration easy. Organizations are collaborative spaces where members can work on multiple projects simultaneously.

   You can bring existing organizations from GitHub. com into your enterprise. However, organizations from an enterprise with managed user management can't be transferred to another enterprise.

2. **Creating a New Organization**

Within your enterprise account settings, any newly
created organization will be part of your GitHub
Enterprise Cloud subscription.

Steps

1. Click your profile photo (top right on GitHub.
    com) and select "Your enterprises."

2. Choose the enterprise you wish to view.

3. Navigate to the "Organizations" tab and click
    "New organization." Refer to Figure 2-8 for
    creating the new organization.

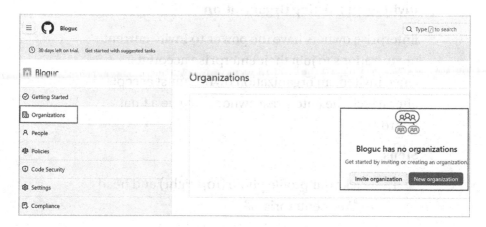

Figure 2-8. *Create a new organization*

4. Provide a name for your new organization.

5. Click "Create organization." Optionally, you
    can invite others to be organization owners.

Figure 2-9. *GitHub new org*

> 6. For instance, "Bloguc-Engineering," created and shown in Figure 2-9.

3. **Inviting an Existing Organization**

   Enterprise owners have the power to invite current organizations to join their enterprise accounts. Once invited, an organization owner must accept, after which the enterprise owner can give a final approval.

   Steps

   1. Click your profile photo (top right) and head to "Your enterprises."

   2. Pick the enterprise you want to see.

   3. Go to the "Organizations" tab and choose "Invite organization."

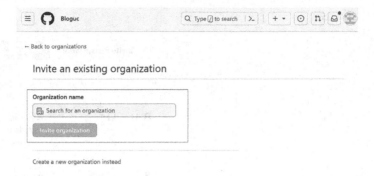

Figure 2-10. *Invite organization*

4. Type and select the desired organization's name.

5. Click "Invite organization." Owners of that organization will get an invitation email.

6. Once accepted, return to the "Organizations" tab.

7. Under "Organizations," there'll be a pending section. Click it and approve the transfer.

4. **Transferring Organizations Between Enterprise Accounts**

    An enterprise owner can transfer organizations between different enterprise accounts. However, you must be an owner of both enterprises to do this.

    Steps

    1. Click your profile photo (top right) and navigate to "Your enterprises."

    2. Select the enterprise you wish to view.

    3. Next to the organization to be transferred, open the dropdown menu and select "Transfer organization." Refer to Figure 2-11 for GitHub org transfer.

49

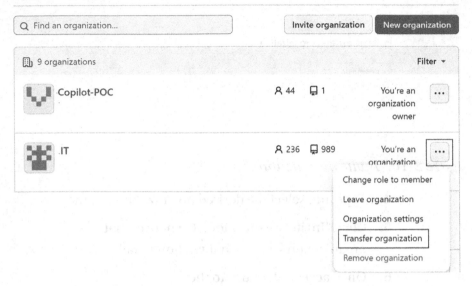

Figure 2-11. *GitHub org transfer*

4. Pick the target enterprise from the dropdown.

5. Review the details and confirm the transfer.

Important Considerations

- If your enterprise requires two-factor authentication (2FA), members not using 2FA will be removed from the organization.

- Transferring an organization might involve changes in billing, ownership roles, applied policies, SAML configurations, and more.

- If your organization uses billed GitHub Marketplace apps, post-transfer, the organization must directly pay the app vendor.

By understanding and leveraging these features, you can optimize the collaboration and management of multiple organizations under your GitHub Enterprise Cloud account.

Overview of GitHub Billing

Understanding GitHub Enterprise Billing

Navigating the billing landscape for enterprise software can be complex. When it comes to GitHub Enterprise, understanding how billing works can help you make informed decisions that align with your budget and operational goals. Here's a detailed overview of the billing structure for GitHub Enterprise accounts.

Centralized Billing Point

When you create or manage an enterprise account on GitHub.com, that account serves as the central hub for all billing-related matters. This includes billing for all the organizations that fall under the enterprise account. If you are running a stand-alone organization on GitHub Enterprise Cloud without an enterprise account, billing occurs at the organization level.

Monthly Billing

GitHub calculates your monthly bill based on the total number of licensed seats within your enterprise account. This also includes charges for any additional services you might be using with GitHub Enterprise Cloud, like GitHub Actions minutes. Detailed insights on how per-user pricing affects your bill can be found in the section "About per-user pricing" in the GitHub documentation.

Invoice and Subscription

If you are an invoiced customer, your invoice will include a single bill charge that accounts for all your paid services on GitHub.com and any GitHub Enterprise Server instances. To keep track of your subscription and usage, you can refer to these sections in the GitHub documentation:

- "Viewing the subscription and usage for your enterprise account"

- "Managing invoices for your enterprise"

Administrative Access

Administrators of the enterprise account have the privilege to access and manage billing details. Various roles within the enterprise can perform these actions, and more information on the roles can be found in the section "Roles in an enterprise" in the GitHub documentation.

Azure Integration

If your enterprise utilizes Azure, you can link an Azure Subscription ID to your GitHub Enterprise account. This enables you to manage usage-based billing for GitHub services like GitHub Codespaces, GitHub Actions, or GitHub Packages beyond the allocated amounts included with your account. Refer to Figure 2-12 for billing information and Azure subscription.

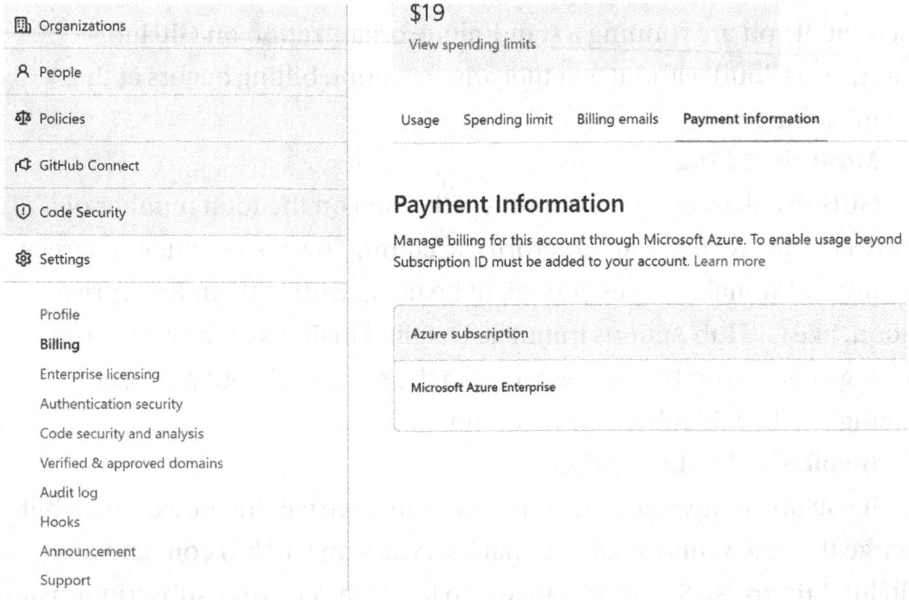

Figure 2-12. *GitHub Enterprise planning*

Additional Considerations

If you're using GitHub Enterprise Cloud with a single organization and haven't transitioned to an enterprise account yet, you can do so for consolidated billing. For more information, see "Creating an enterprise account."

GitHub Per-User Licensing and Pricing

Understanding GitHub's per-user licensing model is pivotal for both organizations and enterprises, especially for efficient cost management and resource allocation. This guide provides an elaborate overview of how GitHub's per-user pricing system functions, which is an essential component of your billing framework.

Basics of Per-User Pricing

The core aspect of your GitHub bill is determined by the number of standard licensed seats that you allocate for your organization or enterprise. GitHub operates on a unique-user licensing model, meaning the number of licensed seats is calculated based on the total number of unique users across all your GitHub deployments.

One License per User

A user will only consume one license, irrespective of

- How many GitHub Enterprise Server instances they use

- How many organizations they are a part of on GitHub Enterprise Cloud

This is designed to provide cost-efficiency and flexibility, allowing individuals to engage with multiple GitHub Enterprise deployments without incurring additional costs.

Synchronized Licensing

For enterprises utilizing both GitHub Enterprise Server and GitHub Enterprise Cloud, you can synchronize license usage between these environments to ensure that a single user isn't consuming more than one license. For more information, refer to "About licenses for GitHub

Enterprise" in the GitHub documentation `https://docs.github.com/en/enterprise-cloud@latest/billing/managing-your-license-for-github-enterprise/about-licenses-for-github-enterprise`.

Additional Billing Components

Beyond the cost of licensed seats, your bill may include other charges such as GitHub Advanced Security. Details can be found in "About billing for your enterprise."

Who Consumes a License?

On GitHub Enterprise Cloud

- Enterprise owners who are members or owners of at least one organization within the enterprise

- All organization members, including owners

- Outside collaborators on private or internal repositories owned by your organization, excluding forks

- Dormant users

- Anyone with a pending invitation to become an organization owner, member, or an outside collaborator on private or internal repositories

On GitHub Enterprise Server

Each user account on GitHub Enterprise Server will consume a seat license.

Note

- Suspended users do not count toward the license consumption.

- Dormant users do occupy a seat, but you have the option to suspend these users to free up licenses.

Exceptions: GitHub does not bill for

- Suspended managed user accounts

- Enterprise owners who are not part of at least one organization

- Billing managers at both enterprise and individual organization levels

- Pending invitations to become billing managers

- Users of Visual Studio subscriptions with GitHub Enterprise whose GitHub.com accounts are not linked

Managing Subscription Changes

You can modify the number of licensed seats anytime, according to your needs. Upgrades and downgrades in the subscription can be managed depending on the type of your GitHub account. For further assistance, you can contact GitHub's Sales team or GitHub Support.

By understanding the finer details of GitHub's per-user licensing model, organizations and enterprises can better align their GitHub usage with budgetary constraints and operational requirements.

Understanding Different Roles and Their Management on GitHub

Working with GitHub Enterprise? Knowing the different roles can help you manage your projects more efficiently. Here's an easy-to-understand rundown of the roles you might come across.

1. **Enterprise Owners**

   What They Do

   - They are the bosses! They control everything related to the enterprise account.

   - They can add or remove organizations and even people.

   - They can tweak settings, manage billing, and make rules across the enterprise.

What They Can't Do

- They can't see individual organization settings or content unless they join that organization.

Need to Know

- They use up one license, but only if they're part of at least one organization in the enterprise.

- It's smart to have only a few enterprise owners to keep things secure.

2. **Enterprise Members**

What They Do

- They're part of the team but have less power than enterprise owners.

- They can work within organizations but can't change enterprise-level settings or billing.

What They Can't Do

- They can't mess with overall enterprise settings.

Need to Know

- You can check what each member can access. For more info, look up "Viewing people in your enterprise."

3. **Billing Managers**

What They Do

- They handle the money side of things.

- They can see and change billing settings, like user licenses.

What They Can't Do

- They can't add or remove enterprise owners or mess with organizations or their content.

Need to Know

- Like enterprise owners, they use up one license if they're part of at least one organization.

Special Cases

- **Enterprise Managed Users:** If your enterprise uses a special system for managing identities (known as IdP), the roles are set there and can't be changed on GitHub.

- **Outside Collaborators:** These are folks who can work on certain projects but aren't actually members of the enterprise.

- **Support Entitlements:** Want to get tech help? Enterprise owners and billing managers automatically can. They can also allow enterprise members to get this kind of support.

Remember, you can always find more details by checking out sections like "Roles in an organization" or "Managing support entitlements for your enterprise" in the GitHub documentation.

Overview of Enterprise Managed User (EMU)

Enterprise Managed Users facilitate centralized control over user accounts in your GitHub Enterprise via an identity provider (IdP). By linking your IdP to GitHub Enterprise, you gain the capability to manage user roles, access permissions, and profile details directly from your IdP. This model encompasses several roles, such as users, enterprise owners, and billing managers, offering fine-grained control over organizational and team memberships.

Authentication and Conditional Access Policies

Employing OpenID Connect Single Sign-On (OIDC SSO) allows your enterprise to harness your IdP's conditional access policies. This feature safeguards interactions when users change IP addresses or use personal access tokens and SSH keys.

Capabilities and Constraints

Managed users can access and contribute to repositories within the enterprise but cannot engage with GitHub's broader user base or produce public content. Users can't alter their usernames or profile data as these are dictated by the IdP. Comprehensive auditing features are available for enterprise owners.

Account Types

Utilizing EMU necessitates a specialized enterprise account that enables this feature. The choice between EMU and other Identity and Access Management options should be carefully considered.

Membership Management in Organizations

You can either manually manage organization memberships or automate them using IdP groups. The method employed for adding a member dictates how they can be removed.

Identity Providers Supported

Supported IdPs include Azure Active Directory, Okta, and PingFederate. Both SAML and SCIM must be supported by the chosen IdP.

Specifics on Abilities and Restrictions

Managed accounts are restricted to private and internal enterprise repositories. They can only authenticate via the IdP, bypassing GitHub's two-factor authentication and password requirements. The accounts are also limited in terms of interaction with public repositories and cannot fork repositories from outside the enterprise.

Configuration Steps

Before implementing EMU, you must undergo a series of setup processes. The GitHub Sales team will assist you in creating an enterprise account designed for managed users.

Authentication for Managed Users

Users can authenticate via their IdP's application portal or GitHub's login page. Several policies, including security settings and recovery codes, are in place for enhanced security.

Usernames and Profile Constraints

Usernames are automatically generated based on an identifier from your IdP. Conflicts can arise if multiple users have similar identifiers, requiring manual intervention. Managed user profiles, including names and email addresses, are read-only and sourced from the IdP.

By reorganizing the information into a more structured format, the preceding summary provides a detailed yet concise overview of GitHub Enterprise Managed Users.

GitHub Administration and Management

GitHub administration and management are very important for creating a secure, efficient, and collaborative development environment that can adapt to changing needs and scale as per the growth of the organization or the project. It provides the backbone that allows development teams to focus on what they do best: writing quality code. GitHub administration and management cannot be overstated, particularly in a technology-driven environment where collaboration, security, and efficiency are paramount. The following are some key reasons why effective GitHub administration is crucial:

Security

- **Access Control:** Through proper administration, you can specify who has access to what within your repositories. GitHub provides granular control over code, issues, pull requests, and more.

- **Authentication:** The use of multiple authentication methods, like two-factor authentication (2FA) and Single Sign-On (SSO), adds additional layers of security to protect sensitive information.

- **Code Integrity:** Administrators can enforce policies such as code reviews, ensuring that no code gets merged without proper oversight.

Collaboration

- **Team Management:** GitHub makes it easy to organize contributors into teams and assign permissions, thereby streamlining workflow.

- **Notification and Mentions:** An administrator can set up notification policies that ensure that the right people are informed about changes or issues in a timely manner.

- **Branch Policies:** Administrators can enforce specific branch policies to ensure that collaborators adhere to best practices, further improving code quality.

Efficiency and Productivity

- **Automated Workflows:** GitHub Actions and other CI/
  CD integrations make it possible to automate testing
  and deployment, reducing the time-to-market and
  human error.

- **Documentation:** Through wikis and READMEs,
  administrators can ensure that all documentation is
  centrally located and up to date, facilitating smoother
  project onboarding and reference.

- **Analytics and Insights:** GitHub offers detailed insights
  into repository activity, code contributions, and
  more. These metrics are valuable for evaluating team
  performance, tracking project health, and planning
  future sprints.

Compliance and Audit

- **Legal Compliance:** GitHub enables administrators to
  enforce license compliance and ensures that the code
  meets the legal prerequisites.

- **Audit Trails:** The ability to look back through detailed
  logs and histories allows administrators to understand
  who did what and when, a feature essential for internal
  audits and compliance checks.

Scalability

- **Organization and Enterprise Level Management:**
  As your projects grow, you may need to manage
  multiple teams and even entire organizations. GitHub
  administration scales seamlessly from small teams to
  large enterprises.

- **Resource Optimization:** Effective GitHub administration allows you to optimize the use of resources both in terms of human input and server capabilities, making your operations more cost-effective.

Best Practices and Culture

- **Code Reviews and Quality Assurance:** GitHub administration enables the institutionalization of code review and QA practices.

- **Community Building:** Through the use of features like discussions and issues, GitHub can serve as a community-building platform, essential for open source projects.

What Is GitHub Administration?

As someone responsible for GitHub administration, your primary aim is to ensure an effortless experience for all users involved. This tutorial will introduce you to the hierarchical structure of GitHub organizations and the administrative responsibilities at each level.

Team-Level Administration

In the GitHub ecosystem, each user is considered an organizational member who can be added to various teams. Creating teams within your organization allows for a tiered approach to permissions and mentions, thereby reflecting your organization's actual structural needs. Teams serve as the building blocks for setting precise repository permissions and enhancing intra-team communication and notifications.

Moreover, GitHub offers integration with identity provider (IdP) services such as Microsoft Entra ID. Synchronizing a GitHub team with an IdP service enables automatic updates, eliminating the necessity for laborious manual interventions and tailor-made scripts. This simplifies administrative chores like inducting new team members, setting new permissions, and revoking existing access rights. Figure 2-13 shows the GitHub Team level administration.

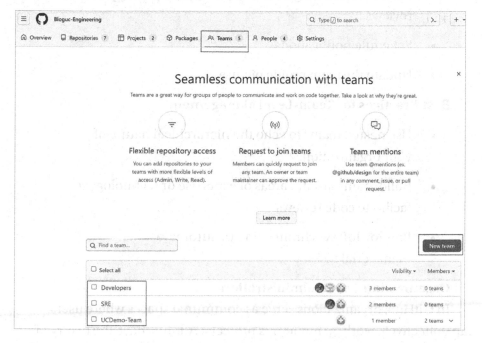

Figure 2-13. *Bloguc-Engineering Organization and Teams for Communication*

Team Administrators and Repository Admins Can

- Instantiate a new team and define its parent team.

- Delete or rename existing teams.

- Modify team membership manually or sync it with an IdP service.

- Manage external contributors for team repositories.

- Enable or deactivate team discussions.

- Alter the team's visibility settings within the organization.

- Utilize GitHub's algorithm for automatic pull request reviews.

- Schedule notifications.

- Update the team profile picture.

Best Practices for Team-Level Management

- Use nested teams to echo the hierarchical nature of your organization.

- Build teams around areas of expertise or technology to facilitate code reviews.

- Employ IdP synchronization to automate managerial tasks.

Organization-Level Administration

In GitHub, organizations serve as communal spaces where users can collectively work on numerous projects. Admins have the luxury of advanced features to control member access to organizational data and repositories.

Organization Owners Can

- Invite or expel organization members.

- Assemble users into teams and assign "team maintainer" roles.

- Manage external collaborators for organization repositories.

- Regulate repository permissions and set default access levels.

- Establish security protocols.

- Oversee billing details or delegate a billing manager.

- Execute custom scripts for data extraction or mass changes.

Points to Consider for Multiple Organizations

- Duplication or shared configurations across organizations are not feasible.

- Additional costs might arise depending on software provider agreements.

- Managing multiple organizations increases complexity and error potential.

Enterprise-Level Administration

Enterprise accounts, which include both GitHub Enterprise Cloud and Enterprise Server, allow for centralized policy and billing oversight across multiple organizations.

Enterprise Owners Can

- Enable SAML-based Single Sign-On (SSO) for the enterprise account.

- Add or remove organizations under the enterprise umbrella.

- Designate a billing manager for the entire enterprise.

- Formulate repository, project board, and team policies that are globally applicable.

- Use custom scripts for data analytics or large-scale changes.

Through this structured approach, GitHub administration not only becomes easier but also more effective, benefiting the entire organization.

GitHub Authentication Mechanisms

Username and Password: The most straightforward method of authentication involves the use of a username and password. However, this method, often termed "basic" HTTP authentication, is increasingly considered insecure for handling sensitive data. Therefore, it's highly advised to employ one or more of the other more secure options enumerated as follows.

Personal Access Tokens (PATs)

Personal access tokens act as substitutes for passwords when interfacing with GitHub through its API or the command line. Users create these tokens via GitHub settings and allocate permissions tied to specific repositories or organizations. When interacting with GitHub via git, the token can be used as an authentication credential instead of the usual username and password.

SSH Keys

SSH keys are a more secure alternative for authentication. Upon setting up SSH, a user generates an SSH key, adds it to the ssh-agent for extra passphrase security, and then attaches it to their GitHub account. This method obviates the need to provide a username and personal access token for each operation.

SSH keys can also be used within organizations that enforce SAML Single Sign-On. Certain organizations may offer SSH certificates for additional layers of security.

Deploy Keys

Deploy keys function as a special set of SSH keys that offer read-only access to a single repository. Unlike other keys that are tied to individual accounts, these keys are attached directly to the repository in question. Write access can be enabled when adding them to a repository.

Additional Security Layers on GitHub

Two-Factor Authentication (2FA)

Also known as multifactor authentication (MFA), 2FA offers an additional layer of security by requiring a second form of verification besides the username and password. The second form is often a code generated by an app on the user's mobile device or sent via text message (SMS).

Organizations and enterprise owners can mandate 2FA for their members, external collaborators, and billing managers, thus enhancing organizational security.

SAML Single Sign-On (SSO)

SAML SSO provides centralized identity management via an identity provider (IdP). It offers organization and enterprise owners a robust way to secure access to resources such as repositories, issues, and pull requests. Users are redirected to the organization's SAML IdP for authentication and, upon successful verification, gain access to the organization's GitHub resources.

GitHub supports all IdPs that adhere to the SAML 2.0 standard, including but not limited to

Active Directory Federation Services (AD FS)

- Microsoft Entra ID

- Okta

- OneLogin

- PingOne

LDAP (Lightweight Directory Access Protocol)

LDAP is an industry-standard protocol for accessing and managing directory information. It enables GitHub Enterprise Server to authenticate against your existing user accounts and manage repository access centrally. Compatible LDAP services include

- Active Directory

- Oracle Directory Server Enterprise Edition

- OpenLDAP

- Open Directory

Through a combination of these authentication and security options, GitHub allows organization owners to fine-tune access controls, thereby ensuring robust security mechanisms are in place.

Best Practices for GitHub Enterprise Account and Organization Administration

The administration of a GitHub Enterprise account or organization is no small feat, especially when the stakes involve multiple teams, projects, and compliance requirements. The following are some best practices that can help you administer your GitHub Enterprise account effectively.

Access Control and Permissions

1. **Role-Based Access Control (RBAC):** Make use of roles such as owners, maintainers, and members to divide responsibilities within the organization. Assign these roles based on the principle of least privilege – give users only the permissions they need to fulfill their tasks.

2. **Repository Permissions:** Assign repository-level permissions carefully. You can provide read, write, or admin access depending on what the user needs to perform.

3. **Use Teams for Permission Management:** Create teams that mirror your organizational structure and assign repository permissions to these teams instead of individual users. This makes it easier to manage and track permissions.

Security

1. **Enforce Two-Factor Authentication (2FA)**: Require all users to enable 2FA to add an additional layer of security.

2. **Single Sign-On (SSO)**: Utilize SSO for centralized authentication. This allows you to manage users more effectively and often offers additional security benefits.

3. **Audit Logs**: Regularly review the audit logs for suspicious activities. GitHub Enterprise accounts offer more detailed logs that can be integrated into SIEM solutions.

Collaboration

1. **Branch Protection**: Use branch protection rules to enforce code reviews and to prevent direct pushes to critical branches like main or master.

2. **Code Review Guidelines**: Establish a code review process and document it. Make sure every contributor understands how to perform and receive code reviews.

3. **Issue and Pull Request Templates**: Use templates to standardize the creation of issues and pull requests, making it easier to collate information and understand context.

Workflow Automation

1. **Continuous Integration/Continuous Deployment (CI/CD)**: Use GitHub Actions or integrate with third-party CI/CD solutions to automate testing and deployment tasks.

2. **Automate Stale Branch Removal**: Implement automation to remove stale branches to reduce clutter and confusion.

3. **Automated Assignments**: Use GitHub bots or GitHub Actions to automate the assignment of issues and pull requests to appropriate teams or individuals.

Compliance and Governance

1. **License Compliance**: Ensure that all repositories contain a LICENSE file that complies with your organization's legal requirements.

2. **Contribution Guidelines**: Include a CONTRIBUTING.md file in all repositories to guide internal and external contributors.

3. **Data Retention Policies**: Set policies for data backup and retention, especially for repositories that have been forked, archived, or deleted.

Monitoring and Insights

1. **Activity Dashboard**: Regularly check the GitHub Enterprise dashboard for a high-level overview of activities, including active repositories and the most active contributors.

2. **Repository Insights**: Use GitHub's repository insights to keep track of code frequency, commit activities, and other performance metrics.

3. **Notifications**: Customize notification settings so that key personnel are immediately alerted about critical events like security vulnerabilities or operational issues.

Miscellaneous

1. **Documentation**: Keep all your administrative procedures, policies, and FAQs documented. This will help in the onboarding process and will serve as a reference.

2. **Community Building**: If your organization also hosts open source projects, consider building a community around it. Use discussions, README files, and GitHub Pages to provide useful information and to engage with the community.

By adhering to these best practices, you can ensure that your GitHub Enterprise account is not only secure and compliant but also an effective and efficient platform for development and collaboration.

Summary

This chapter offered an in-depth exploration of GitHub Enterprise account and organization setup and administration, aimed at equipping users to effectively establish and manage these critical elements. From an introductory understanding of GitHub's various account types to the intricacies of setting up and managing organizations within the GitHub Enterprise Cloud, the chapter provided a comprehensive guide. Key operational aspects like billing, role management, and the concept of Enterprise Managed Users (EMU) were elucidated, along with an extensive discussion on general administration and management tasks. Importantly, the chapter underscored best practices that should be adhered to for maintaining an efficient and secure GitHub Enterprise environment.

Resources

- Understanding GitHub Personal, Enterprise, and Organization Accounts: https://docs.github.com/en/get-started/learning-about-github/types-of-github-accounts

- Creating an enterprise account: https://docs.github.com/en/enterprise-cloud@latest/admin/overview/creating-an-enterprise-account

- Organization's addition to the enterprise: https://docs.github.com/en/enterprise-cloud@latest/admin/managing-accounts-and-repositories/managing-organizations-in-your-enterprise/adding-organizations-to-your-enterprise

- GitHub billing and their plans: https://docs.github.com/en/billing/managing-the-plan-for-your-github-account/about-billing-for-plans

- Roles in an organization: https://docs.github.com/en/organizations/managing-peoples-access-to-your-organization-with-roles/roles-in-an-organization

- GitHub Enterprise Managed Users: `https://`
  `docs.github.com/en/enterprise-cloud@latest/`
  `admin/identity-and-access-management/using-`
  `enterprise-managed-users-for-iam/about-`
  `enterprise-managed-users`

- Best practices for enterprises: `https://docs.github.`
  `com/en/enterprise-cloud@latest/admin/overview/`
  `best-practices-for-enterprises`

CHAPTER 3

GitHub Repository Management and Best Practices

GitHub repository management refers to the practices and measures taken to ensure the security of your GitHub repositories. This involves protecting your code, data, and collaboration processes from unauthorized access, data breaches, and other security threats. In this chapter, we will cover in-depth insight into secure management practices for GitHub repositories. This also underlines industry-standard methodologies to handle repositories while maintaining security and achieving optimal outcomes. More precisely, this chapter is organized based on the following central themes:

1. **Overview of GitHub Repositories:** This highlights the pivotal role of repositories in overseeing code on GitHub. They serve as core hubs for version control, collaboration tools, and project structuring, collectively shaping the landscape of software development and collaborative work.

B. N. Ilag et al., *Mastering GitHub Enterprise Management and Administration*,
https://doi.org/10.1007/979-8-8688-0369-7_3

2. **Understanding Repository Permissions and Collaborator Roles:** This clarifies the distinct permission levels and how these roles provide defined actions to users. It underscores the significance of allocating suitable permissions and collaborator roles to uphold both code security and efficient teamwork.

3. **Secure Coding Practices:** This emphasizes the importance of writing secure code to mitigate vulnerabilities and protect applications and data from potential attacks.

4. **Repository Maintenance Best Practices:** This involves implementing practices such as consistent code review, automated testing, careful dependency management, and the creation of thorough documentation.

Before engaging with a GitHub repository and repository secure management, it's crucial to grasp the necessary requirements. Familiarity with these prerequisites is vital before delving into GitHub. Here are the foundational aspects you need to be acquainted with:

Prerequisite

Git Installation

- **Git Installation:** Ensure Git is installed on your local machine. You can download and install Git from https://git-scm.com/downloads. Please refer to https://git-scm.com/book/en/v2/Getting-Started-The-Command-Line for a detailed setup of the command line.

GitHub Account

- **Create a GitHub Account:** You need a GitHub account to create and manage repositories. You can sign up for a GitHub account at `https://github.com/signup`.

SSH Key (Optional, but Recommended)

- **Generate SSH Key:** To securely interact with your GitHub repository, it's recommended to set up SSH keys. You can generate an SSH key on your local machine using the **ssh-keygen** command.

  - To generate a new SSH key pair on your local machine, you can use the ssh-keygen command as follows:

    ```
    $ ssh-keygen -t ed25519 -C "emailid@example.com"
    ```

    where

    - The **-t** flag is used to specify the type of key to create, in this case, an ed25519, which is a popular type of public-key cryptography.

    - The **-C** flag is used to provide additional information about the key, such as its purpose or the user who generated it.

    - Emailid@example.com can be replaced with actual emailid.

  - When prompted with this question, simply press ENTER to validate the recommended file path the key pair will be saved at, or type in another path if a similar file already exists in the .ssh directory.

Generating public/private ed25519 key pair.

Enter file in which to save the key (/c/Users/ganes/. ssh/id_ed25519):

- To the following questions, type in a passphrase to secure your key, and press ENTER once again to complete the process.

Enter passphrase (empty for no passphrase):

Enter same passphrase again:

- You should now see a similar output in your terminal window confirming that the key was successfully generated:

Your identification has been saved in /c/Users/ ganes/.ssh/id_ed25519

Your public key has been saved in /c/Users/ganes/. ssh/id_ed25519.pub

The key fingerprint is:

SHA256:bGTogwWsWyFKfABjzxUo70Sq8VfEKkB6C DlH03iWlZk emailid@example.com

The key's randomart image is:

```
+--[ED25519 256]--+
|B*++o*o+         |
|B**=O.E.         |
|+=BB +o o        |
|ooooo+.+         |
|.oo+..o S        |
|. o.. o          |
| .               |
```

```
|                        |
|                        |
+----[SHA256]-----+
```

- And you should be able to find the following files in your .ssh directory:

```
$ ls ~/.ssh
id_ed25519  id_ed25519.pub
```

where

- The id_ed25519 file is your private key whose content should be kept confidential.

- The id_ed25519.pub file is your public key that we'll use in the next step.

- **Add SSH Key to GitHub:** Add your SSH public key to your GitHub account. This establishes a secure connection between your local machine and your GitHub account without the need for a username and password every time you interact with GitHub.

  - To add a public key to your GitHub account, first display the content of the **public** key file you've just created using the cat command and copy it to your clipboard using Ctrl+C (or CMD+C on macOS).

  ```
  $ cat ~/.ssh/id_ed25519.pub
  ```

  - Alternatively, you can use the pbcopy command on macOS as follows:

  ```
  $ pbcopy < ~/.ssh/id_ed25519.pub
  ```

- Once you've done that

    - Log in to your GitHub account.

    - Navigate to "Settings."

    - Click "SSH and GPG keys" in the left menu.

    - Click the "New SSH key" button.

    - Or directly follow this link: `https://github.com/settings/ssh/new`.

- Then here

    - Add a short descriptive title in the Title field.

    - Paste the public key in the Key field.

    - Click the "Add SSH key" button to finalize the process. Figure 3-1 shows the screen for adding the SSH key.

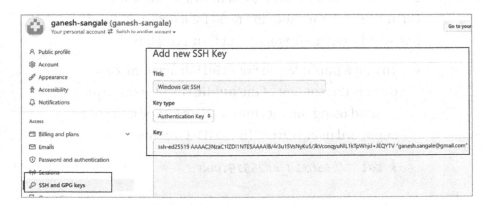

Figure 3-1. *Add SSH key*

Note   If you encounter any issues while using SSH to connect and authenticate to GitHub, you can refer to the official GitHub documentation for troubleshooting SSH-related problems. The provided link contains detailed information and steps to help you resolve unexpected SSH issues. Here is the link for your reference: `https://docs.github.com/en/authentication/troubleshooting-ssh`.

Internet Connection

- **Internet Connection:** Ensure a stable Internet connection. Git operations, especially when pushing and pulling changes, require Internet connectivity to interact with remote repositories on GitHub.

Overview of GitHub Repositories

GitHub repositories are like magic spell books for developers, where you can store, manage, and collaborate on your code projects. A GitHub repository, often called a "repo," is a container that holds all the files, folders, and history of a project. It's a central hub for collaboration, version control, and code management. Each developer can work on their own copy of the repository, making changes and committing them independently. Repositories are equipped with tools to track changes, manage issues, run workflows, merge, and synchronize the work of multiple contributors. Figure 3-2 shows the native functionality of GitHub repo.

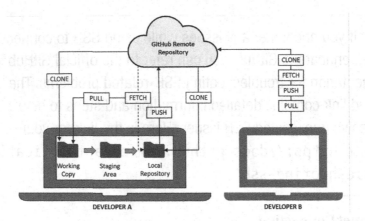

Figure 3-2. *GitHub repo (Reference:* `www.git-tower.com/learn/` `git/ebook/en/command-line/remote-repositories/introduction`*)*

Here is an overview of key concepts and the need for GitHub repositories, illustrated with an example:

- **Repository:** A GitHub repository is a folder or directory where your project's files and version history are stored. It contains all the information needed to track changes to your project.

- **Commit:** A commit represents a specific snapshot of your project at a given point in time. It includes changes made to files and a commit message describing those changes.

- **Branch:** A branch is a separate line of development in a GitHub repository. It allows you to work on features or fixes or adding content independently, without affecting the main codebase.

- **Merge:** Merging is the process of combining changes from one branch into another. It is used to integrate the work of different developers on the team or to bring feature branches into the main branch.

- **Remote:** A remote is a GitHub repository hosted on a server. It allows multiple developers to collaborate on the same project. Common remote hosting services include GitHub, GitLab, and Bitbucket.

Why GitHub Repository Is Required

A GitHub repository is required for several reasons, primarily related to version control and collaboration in software development and other file-based projects. You can refer to Chapter 1 topic, "Overview of GitHub Repositories."

Here are some key reasons why GitHub repositories are essential:

- **Version Control**

  - GitHub repositories are the core of Git's version control system. They allow you to track changes in your code or project files over time.

  - Each commit in a GitHub repository represents a snapshot of your project at a specific point in time, making it easy to review and revert changes.

- **Collaboration**

  - GitHub repositories facilitate collaboration among multiple developers or team members. They provide a centralized place to store and share code and project files.

  - Collaborators can work on their own copies of the repository, make changes, and then merge their work back into the main repository.

- **Branching and Parallel Development**

  - GitHub allows you to create branches within a repository. Each branch can represent a new feature, bug fix, or experiment.

  - Branches enable parallel development, allowing team members to work on unique features simultaneously without interfering with each other's work.

- **Conflict Resolution**

  - When multiple contributors make changes to the same code or file, conflicts can arise. GitHub repositories provide tools to identify and resolve these conflicts efficiently.

- **Code History and Auditing**

  - GitHub repositories maintain a detailed history of all changes made to the project. This historical record is valuable for auditing, debugging, and understanding how the code evolved over time.

- **Code Backup and Disaster Recovery**

  - GitHub repositories serve as a backup of your code and project files. In case of data loss or system failures, you can recover your work by cloning the repository from a remote server or another local copy.

- **Remote Collaboration**

  - GitHub repositories can be hosted on remote servers, such as GitHub, GitLab, or Bitbucket. This allows distributed teams to collaborate seamlessly, even if team members are geographically dispersed.

- **Continuous Integration and Deployment (CI/CD)**

  - GitHub repositories integrate seamlessly with CI/CD pipelines, enabling automated testing, building, and deployment of code changes. This is crucial for maintaining a consistent and reliable development workflow.

- **Code Review**

  - GitHub repositories support code review processes. Team members can review each other's changes through pull requests or merge requests before they are incorporated into the main codebase.

- **Open Source Development**

  - For open source projects, GitHub repositories provide a transparent and accessible way for contributors from around the world to collaborate and submit contributions.

- **Documentation and Project Management**

  - GitHub repositories often include project documentation, issue tracking, and project management tools. These features help maintain structured and organized development processes.

  - Git repositories are indispensable for effective version control, collaboration, and project management in software development and other file-based projects. They enable teams to work together, track changes, maintain code quality, and ensure the reliability of software projects.

Types of GitHub Repositories

There are two types of repositories; they are as follows:

- **Bare Repository**

  - A bare repository is a type of repository that does not contain a working directory. It means it does not store the actual project files like a regular repository does. Instead, it has the versioned data, GitHub history, and repository configuration files.

  - They serve as a pivotal point where developers can share their changes. These repositories are often hosted on servers and function as destinations for developers to push their changes to and pull changes from.

  - It can be created using the **"git init –bare"** command.

- **Non-bare Repositories**

  - Non-bare repositories, also known as working repositories, have versioned data with a working directory. This working directory is used by developers to interact with project files directly, making modifications and conducting code testing.

  - Non-bare repositories are the dynamic workspace where active development occurs. They are usually cloned from either a bare repository or another non-bare repository, helping smooth teamwork and the exchange of updates among developers.

  - It can be created using the **"git init"** command.

Connect to a Remote Repository

To begin, you will want to establish a remote repository. On GitHub, initiate the creation of a new, blank repository. Provide it with a name and specify whether it should be public or private. This process typically appears as follows:

- **Log In to GitHub:**

    - Go to `https://github.com/` and log in to your account. If you don't have an account, you will need to sign up.

- **Create a New Repository:**

    - Click the "+" sign in the top-right corner of the GitHub page.

    - Select "New repository" from the dropdown menu. Figure 3-3 shows the New repository option.

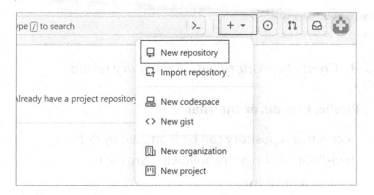

Figure 3-3. *New repository*

- **Configure Your Repository:**

  Fill in the following details for your new repository:

  - **Repository Name:** Enter a name for your
    repository. This will also be the project's URL.

  - **Description:** Optionally, provide a brief description
    of your project. Figure 3-4 shows Create Repository
    with Repository name.

Create a new repository

A repository contains all project files, including the revision history. Already have a project repository elsewhere?
Import a repository.

Required fields are marked with an asterisk (*).

Owner *   Repository name *

🔘 Bloguc-Engineering ▾ / Bloguc-repository

                              ✅ Bloguc-repository is available.

Great repository names are short and memorable. Need inspiration? How about curly-happiness ?

Description (optional)

This is Demo repository for blog uc

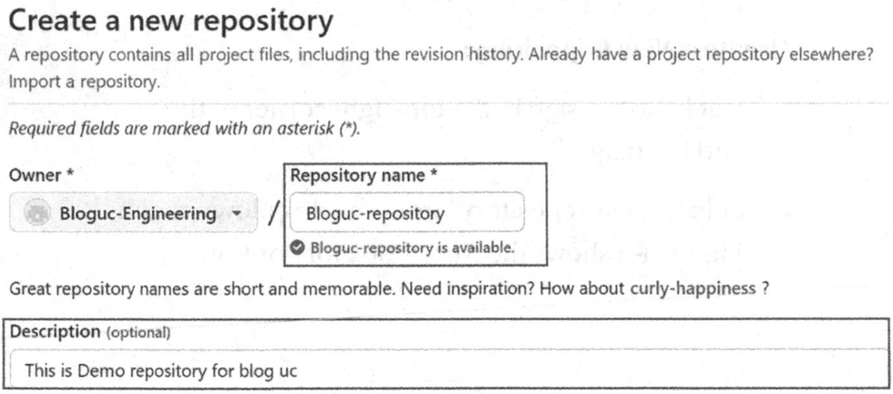

Figure 3-4. *Create Repository with Repository name*

- **Public, Private, or Internal:**

  Access to a repository can be managed by defining
  its visibility settings; the following are the three
  types of repositories:

  - **Public Repositories:** These repositories are made
    available publicly. Users have access to clone or
    fork the repository by initiating a pull request and
    obtaining approval from the owner; these changes
    can be incorporated.

88

- **Private Repositories:** These repositories have controlled access, allowing only authorized users or teams to access to view and collaborate on the repository's content; unless the owner provides access to the repository, nobody else has access to it.

- **Internal Repositories:** These repositories' visibility is restricted to members within a particular organization. Figure 3-5 shows the Repository types.

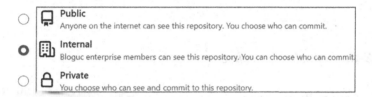

Figure 3-5. Repository types

- **Initialize This Repository with a README:** You can check this option if you want to create an initial README file. This is often a good way to provide information about your project.

- **Add .gitignore:** Optionally, you can select a programming language or framework to generate a suitable .gitignore file, which helps exclude specific files and directories from version control. Detailed information about .gitignore can be found at https://github.com/github/gitignore.

- **Add a License:** You can choose an open source
  license if you want others to be able to use, modify,
  and distribute your code legally. Figure 3-6 shows the
  Repository license options.

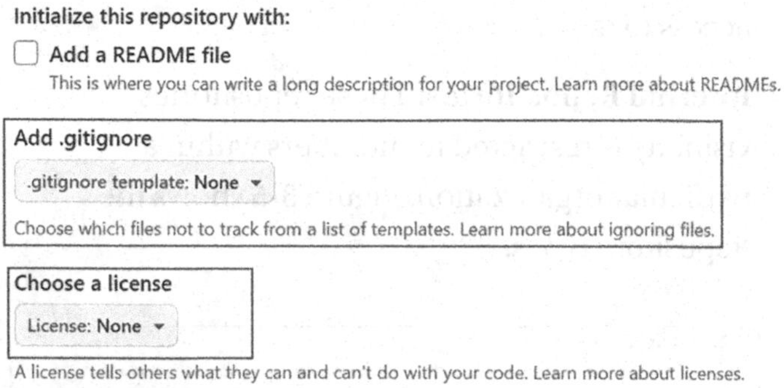

Initialize this repository with:

☐ **Add a README file**
This is where you can write a long description for your project. Learn more about READMEs.

Add .gitignore

.gitignore template: None ▾

Choose which files not to track from a list of templates. Learn more about ignoring files.

Choose a license

License: None ▾

A license tells others what they can and can't do with your code. Learn more about licenses.

Figure 3-6. *Repository license*

- **Create Repository**

  - Click the "Create repository" button to create
    your new repository. Figure 3-7 shows the Create
    repository options.

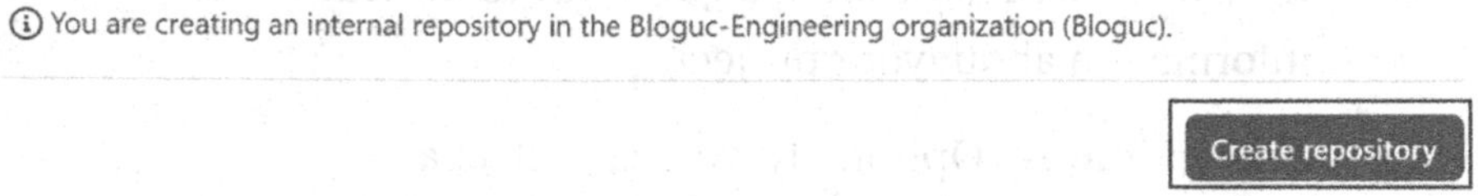

ⓘ You are creating an internal repository in the Bloguc-Engineering organization (Bloguc).

Create repository

Figure 3-7. *Create repository*

Now you have successfully created a new remote repository on GitHub.
Let's see how we can clone the repository on a local desktop.

Cloning a GitHub Repository

Cloning a GitHub repository means creating a local copy of a repository from GitHub onto your own computer. This is an essential step when you want to work on an existing project, collaborate with others, or contribute to an open source project hosted on GitHub. Here is how you can clone a GitHub repository:

Using HTTPS

- **Copy the Repository URL:**

  - Go to the GitHub repository you want to clone.

  - Click the "Code" button, and then click the HTTPS tab to get the repository URL.

- **Open Terminal or Command Prompt:**

  - Open your terminal or command prompt on your local machine.

- **Navigate to the Directory Where You Want to Clone the Repository:**

  - Use the **cd** command to navigate to the directory where you want to store the local copy of the repository:

    $ cd BlogUc-Repository

- **Clone the Repository:**

  - Use the following command to clone the repository:

    - *$ git clone https://github.com/Bloguc-Engineering/Bloguc-repository.git*

91

- Replace `https://github.com/Bloguc-Engineering/Bloguc-repository.git` with the actual repository URL you copied from GitHub.

- **Enter Your GitHub Credentials (If Required):**

  - If it is a private repository, Git may prompt you to enter your GitHub username and password to authenticate.

- **Cloning Is Complete:**

  - Git will download the repository files and create a local copy in the specified directory.

    ```
    $ git clone https://github.com/Bloguc-
    Engineering/Bloguc-repository.git

    Cloning into 'Bloguc-repository'...
    ```

Using SSH (If You Have Set Up SSH Keys with GitHub)

- **Copy the Repository URL:**

  - Go to the GitHub repository you want to clone.

  - Click the "Code" button, and then click the SSH tab to get the repository URL.

- **Open Terminal or Command Prompt:**

  - Open your terminal or command prompt on your local machine.

- **Navigate to the Directory Where You Want to Clone the Repository:**

  - Use the **cd** command to navigate to the directory where you want to store the local copy of the repository.

    ```
    $ cd BlogUc-Repository
    ```

- **Clone the Repository:**

  - Use the following command to clone the repository using SSH:

    ```
    $ git clone git@github.com:ganesh.
    sangale/Bloguc-repository.git
    ```

  - Replace **git@github.com:ganesh.sangale/repository.git** with the actual SSH repository URL you copied from GitHub.

- **Cloning Is Complete:**

  - Git will download the repository files and create a local copy in the specified directory.

Now you have successfully cloned a GitHub repository to your local machine. You can start working on the project.

Creating a New Repository Locally/Initializing Git Repository

git init is a Git command used to initialize a new Git repository in your project directory. When you run git init, Git sets up the necessary files and data structures required for version control in the current directory, turning it into a repository. To create a new Git repository locally, follow these steps in your command-line interface (such as Terminal on macOS or Command Prompt/PowerShell on Windows):

- **Open Terminal:**

  - **macOS:** You can open Terminal on macOS by searching for it in Spotlight (CMD+Space, then type "Terminal") or by navigating to Applications ➤ Utilities ➤ Terminal.

  - **Linux:** You can open the terminal by searching for it in the application menu or by using the shortcut keys (often **Ctrl+Alt+T**).

- **Windows:** You can press Windows+R to start the Windows Run dialog. Type PowerShell in the Run dialog, and press Enter to get into PowerShell in Windows.

Note   In the following example, we will be using the Windows PowerShell tool.

- **Navigate to the Desired Directory:**
  - Use the **cd** command to navigate to the directory where you want to create your new repository:

    $ cd BlogUc-Repository

- **Create a New Directory for Your Project:**
  - Use the **mkdir** command to create a new folder for your project. Replace **your-project-name** with the desired name of your project:

    $ mkdir BlogUc-Demo

- **Initialize a Git Repository:**
  - Use the following command to initialize a Git repository in the current directory:

    $ git init

    Initialized empty Git repository in C:/ Users/ganes/blogUC-Repository/BlogUc-Demo/.git/

  - This command initializes an empty Git repository in your project folder.

- **Create and Add Files:**

  - Create files for your project within this directory using any text editor or IDE.

  - Use the git add command to stage all files in the directory for the initial commit.

- **Commit Your Changes:**

  - Commit the staged files with a commit message.

  - Replace **"Initial commit"** with an appropriate message describing your initial changes.

Now you have successfully created a new Git repository locally in your specified directory, and your project directory is a Git repository, and you can start adding files, staging changes, making commits, and managing your version control using Git commands. Remember that you only need to run git init once in your project directory because it will create a **.git** hidden folder in the repository. After that, you can use other Git commands like git add, git commit, and git push to work with your repository.

Contents of the .git Folder

The **.git** directory, situated at the root of a GitHub repository, contains all the essential internal data and metadata needed for version control. The following are some of the important contents of .git:

- **branches:** This directory contains references to branch heads in your repository.

- **hooks:** GitHub allows you to set up custom scripts that run at various points in the GitHub workflow.

  ```
  $ ls .git/hooks
  ```

- **info:** This directory contains various global and repository-specific configuration files.

  `$ ls .git/info`

- **objects:** This directory stores all the data for your project, including commits, trees (directory structures), and blobs (file contents).

  `$ ls .git/objects`

- **refs:** Like the branch's directory, the refs directory stores references to commits, tags, and other objects.

  - To list references to branch heads:

    `$ ls .git/refs/heads`

  - To list references to tags:

    `$ ls .git/refs/tags`

  - To list references to remote branches:

    `$ ls .git/refs/remote`

- **config:** The config file contains configuration settings for the repository, including user information, remote repository URLs, and more.

  `$ cat .git/config`

- **description:** This file is a human-readable description of the repository. It's often used by GitHub hosting services like GitHub.

  `$ cat .git/description`

- **HEAD:** This file points to the currently checked-out branch or commit in the repository. It's used to keep track of your current working state.

  ```
  $ cat .git/HEAD
  ```

- **index:** The index file, also known as the staging area, keeps track of changes that have been added but not committed.

  ```
  $ git ls-files --stage
  ```

- **logs:** This directory contains log files, including reflogs, which record changes to references (branches and tags).

  ```
  $ ls .git/logs
  ```

These are some of the key contents you'll find inside the **.git** directory and how you can interact with them using GitHub commands. Keep in mind that manually manipulating the contents of the **.git** directory can lead to data corruption or other issues, so it's generally not recommended to modify these files and directories directly unless you have a deep understanding of Git's internal workings. Instead, you should use GitHub commands and tools to interact with your repository. If you want to delve deeper into Git commands and learn more about its extensive capabilities, the official Git website is an excellent resource. It provides comprehensive documentation, tutorials, and guides that cover various Git commands and workflows in detail. Here is the link to the official Git website: `https://git-scm.com/`. Now that we have successfully cloned and initialized a Git repository, let's explore the process of committing new changes to the repository.

Committing Changes to GitHub Repository

In Git, a commit is a snapshot of your changes at a specific point in time. It records changes to the repository and allows you to track your project's history effectively. When you make changes to your files, you first stage them, and then you commit those staged changes.

Here are the steps to perform a commit in Git:

- **Stage Your Changes:**

    - Before you commit, you need to stage the changes you want to include in the commit. You can stage specific files or all changes in your working directory.

        - To stage specific files, use

          ```
          $ git add readme.txt help.txt
          ```

        - To stage all changes, use

          ```
          $ git add
          ```

- **Commit Your Changes:**

    - After staging your changes, you commit them along with a commit message describing what changes you made.

    - Use the following command to commit your changes:

      ```
      $ git commit -m "Initial Commit"
      ```

      Replace "Initial Commit" with a concise and descriptive message summarizing the changes you made in this commit. A good commit message explains why the change was made, not just what was changed.

- **View Commit History:**

  - You can view the commit history of your repository using

  ```
  $ git log
  ```

This shows a chronological list of commits, including commit hash, author, date, and commit message.

Commit Best Practices

- **Commit Frequently:**

  - Commit small, focused changes frequently to ensure a clear and logical commit history.

- **Write Descriptive Commit Messages:**

  - Commit messages should be clear, concise, and meaningful. They help others (and your future self) understand the purpose of the change.

- **Keep Commits Atomic:**

  - Each commit should represent a single logical change. Avoid mixing unrelated changes in a single commit.

- **Review Changes Before Committing:**

  - Use git status to check which files are staged and which changes are pending. Review your changes before committing.

- **Use Branches:**

  - Consider creating feature branches. Make changes in the branch and merge it back into the main branch (or another target branch) once the feature is complete.

Remember, commits are the building blocks of your project's history. Well-crafted commits make collaboration smoother and help in maintaining a clean and understandable project history. Once you've made your commits, you can push these changes to your GitHub remote repository. The next topic will cover the process of pushing changes.

Pushing Changes to the GitHub Repository

In Git, git push is a command used to upload the changes you made locally to a remote repository. It is a way to share your changes with others or store them in a central repository. When you git push, you are essentially sending your committed changes to a remote repository, making them accessible to others who have access to that repository. Here is a breakdown of the **git push** command:

- **Pushing Changes:** When you work on a local Git repository and make changes (such as editing files, adding new files, or committing changes), those changes are only stored locally on your machine. To share these changes with others or store them on a remote server (like GitHub, GitLab, or Bitbucket), you need to push them.

- **To Which Repository:** The **git push** command specifies the remote repository where you want to send your changes. By default, Git knows which remote repository your local repository was cloned from or associated with. You can also specify a remote repository and a branch explicitly if needed.

- **Branches:** When you push, you usually push a specific branch (like **master** or **main**). This allows you to update the branch on the remote repository with the changes you made locally.

- **Synchronization: git push** not only uploads your changes but also synchronizes your branches with the remote repository. It updates the branch on the remote server to match the branch in your local repository.

Here are some common scenarios with examples:

- **Pushing to the Default Remote Repository:** If you've cloned a repository, Git remembers the URL of the remote repository. You can simply push your changes to the default remote repository:

  `$ git push`

- **Pushing Changes to a Specific Branch:** You might want to push changes to a specific branch. In this case, you specify the branch name after the remote repository:

  `$ git push origin feature/first-commit`

- **Pushing a New Branch to the Remote Repository:** If you've created a new branch locally and want to push it to the remote repository, use

  `$ git push origin feature/first-commit:feature/first-commit`

- **Pushing All Branches to the Remote Repository:** To push all branches to the remote repository, use

  `$ git push -all origin`

- **Force-Pushing Changes:** Sometimes, you might
  need to force-push changes (use with caution, as it
  overwrites history).

  ```
  $ git push –force origin feature/first-commit
  ```

- **Pushing Tags:** To push tags to the remote
  repository, use

  ```
  $ git push –tags origins
  ```

Remember to be careful when using git push --force, as it can rewrite history and cause issues if collaborators have based their work on the old history. Always communicate with your team before force pushing.

Pulling Changes from a Remote Repository

In Git, **git pull** is a command used to update your local repository with changes from a remote repository. It's essentially a combination of two other commands: **git fetch**, which downloads the changes from the remote repository, and **git merge**, which integrates those changes into your current branch. Here is how the git pull command works:

- **Downloading Changes:** When you run **git pull**, Git
  first contacts the remote repository specified (usually
  origin if you cloned the repository) and downloads any
  changes (commits, branches, etc.) that you don't have
  in your local repository. This is done using **git fetch**.

- **Merging Changes:** After downloading the changes,
  Git merges them into your current branch. If you
  have changes in your branch that aren't in the
  remote branch you're pulling, Git performs a merge
  to integrate the changes. If there are no conflicting
  changes, the merge is automatic. If there are conflicts,
  you need to resolve them manually.

Here's the basic syntax of the git pull command:

```
git pull <remote> <branch>
```

- **<remote>:** The name of the remote repository (usually origin by default)

- **<branch>:** The branch from the remote repository that you want to pull changes from

For example, if you want to pull changes from the **master** branch of the **origin** remote repository, use

```
$ git pull origin master
```

This command will download changes from the **master** branch of the remote repository specified as **origin** and merge them into your current local branch.

It's important to note that git pull is a convenient way to update your local repository, but it automatically performs a merge. If you prefer to review changes before merging, you can use git fetch followed by git merge or git rebase to integrate the changes manually.

The Git operations mentioned earlier provide insights into how GitHub repositories function among team members. In the next section, we will delve into repository permissions and collaborator roles.

Understanding Repository Permissions and Collaborator Roles

GitHub stands out as a powerful version control tool tailored to facilitate collaborative development. Nevertheless, effectively monitoring and controlling individuals' access to modify your code can sometimes be a challenge. GitHub permissions provide you with the means to oversee and regulate the actions people are permitted to take on your repositories, projects, and branches, particularly when dealing with sensitive codebases.

What Are GitHub Permissions?

Within GitHub, you have the freedom to make numerous modifications to your source code and account. This includes actions like creating new repositories, modifying files, or updating billing information for your organization. Nevertheless, the extent of your capabilities on GitHub is contingent upon the permissions granted to you. GitHub permissions refer to the level of access a GitHub user needs to control a specific account or resource. For example, the ability to open and merge a pull request is a type of permission. Furthermore, administrators have the authority to allocate distinct permissions to individuals or teams, allowing them to manage various GitHub resources and functionalities. This collection of permissions is commonly referred to as a "role."

How GitHub Permissions Work?

It is not necessary for everyone to possess full access to your source code or be authorized to modify it extensively. Take, for example, an external collaborator like a DevOps freelancer; it's not advisable for them to be granted access to the entirety of your organization's repositories. Ideally, this collaborator should be restricted to accessing only the specific repository they are actively working on. Furthermore, it is crucial to provide the freelancer with the bare minimum access required for them to carry out their assigned tasks effectively. This access typically includes the ability to commit code, create issues, and submit pull requests. However, it should not encompass privileges like adding new members to the repository, altering the organization's billing details, or deleting repositories.

Similarly, a project manager might require access to the repository to monitor progress. They do not need to engage in code alterations. Hence, their permissions should be limited to viewing the project's status and advancement, without enabling them to directly modify or contribute to the project. GitHub offers administrators the means to exercise control over what actions users can perform and what they can access. Administrators possess this control by virtue of the permissions settings they can configure.

GitHub provides three primary permission levels for repositories, which are essential for controlling access and collaboration within your projects. These primary permission levels are

- **Read**

  - Users with read access can view the contents of a repository.

  - They can clone the repository to their local machines; browse files, commits, and branches; and access the entire commit history.

  - Additionally, users with read access can create issues, review pull requests, and initiate new pull requests.

  - This access level is typically granted to individuals who need to observe and interact with the project but do not require write or administrative privileges.

- **Write**

  - Write access includes all the permissions of read access.

  - Users with write access can also make changes to the repository.

- They can create new branches, push commits to existing branches, and make modifications to the codebase.

- Write access is suitable for active contributors who actively contribute to the project's development.

- **Admin**

  - Admin access encompasses all the permissions of write and read access.

  - Users with admin access have full control over the repository.

  - They can manage collaborators, change repository settings, and perform all actions, including deleting the repository.

  - Admin access is typically granted to repository owners and administrators who need to manage the repository's configuration and security.

  - These three primary permission levels are fundamental to controlling access and defining roles within a GitHub repository. Depending on a user's role and responsibilities in a project, they can be assigned the appropriate permission level to ensure they have the necessary access without granting unnecessary privileges. Additionally, GitHub offers more nuanced permissions such as triage and maintain for more specific access control when needed.

GitHub indeed provides a range of nuanced permissions that fall between the basic access levels of read, write, and admin. These intermediate permissions offer more fine-grained control over what users can do within a repository. Some of these permissions include

- **Triage:** This permission level offers more access
  than read but less than write. It's like giving someone
  a backstage pass at a concert. Users with triage
  permission can do things like apply or dismiss labels on
  issues and pull requests, which read-level users cannot
  do. However, they cannot create, edit, or delete labels, a
  privilege reserved for write-level users and above.

- **Maintain:** Maintain seats between write and admin
  access levels. It is like being an assistant manager at a
  store. Users with maintain permissions can perform
  actions like editing a repository's description, like
  what an admin can do but unlike write-level users.
  However, maintain users do not have the authority
  to delete an issue; that privilege remains reserved for
  administrators.

These nuanced permissions provide more flexibility for assigning responsibilities within a repository or organization. It allows you to grant users specific capabilities based on their roles and responsibilities, ensuring that they have precisely the right level of access needed to contribute effectively without overextending their permissions.

GitHub Permissions for Personal GitHub

GitHub's personal account allows you to manage your development projects. You are assigned the Owner role once you create your account. However, the personal account comes with three permission levels, including

1. Admin

2. Write

3. Read

You will be assigned admin permission as the repository's owner. This permission level gives you complete access to all GitHub Actions and resources, including creating and deleting repositories.

For example, you would like to collaborate with other developers on your project. GitHub allows you to invite them to contribute to your repository. Additionally, you can assign the collaborators write access. This permission level allows your partners to pull and push changes to your repository. Finally, you would like to share your open source project with others. However, you do not want the public to contribute directly to your code. GitHub allows you to grant read access in these kinds of situations. Now, anyone with a link to your project can see what you have been working on. GitHub users with read permission can only view your project. They cannot perform any action, including creating pull requests or commenting on commits.

It is worth reiterating that your admin status gives you total control of your GitHub account and projects. For instance, you can rename the default branch any time you wish. However, this privilege does not extend to your collaborators with write access. Instead, they can rename any other branch except the default. Similarly, collaborators cannot invite others to join your repository. Only you can do this. Collaborators can only remove themselves from the repository.

Limiting Access to Repositories

You can control and restrict access to GitHub repositories to maintain security and privacy within your organization. By managing repository settings, you can limit who can view, clone, commit, or merge changes. These access restrictions ensure that only authorized individuals have the appropriate permissions, enhancing the overall security of your GitHub repositories.

Here is how you can limit access to the GitHub repository:

- Navigate to Repository settings.

- Scroll to the bottom of the page; you will see **Danger Zone**.

- Click Change visibility under "**Change repository visibility.**"

- Based on the requirement, select the appropriate visibility and provide your acknowledgment on confirmations. Figure 3-8 shows about limiting repository access.

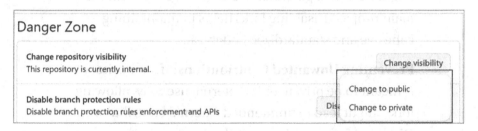

Figure 3-8. Limiting repository access

Disable Forking of Repositories

Disabling forking of repositories on GitHub might be necessary in certain situations to enhance security, maintain control over the codebase, or protect sensitive information. Here are a few reasons why someone might choose to disable forking of repositories:

- **Security Concerns:** If a repository contains sensitive or proprietary code, disabling forking ensures that the code remains within the organization, reducing the risk of unauthorized access or leaks.

- **Intellectual Property Protection:** Companies or individuals who want to protect their intellectual property might disable forking to prevent others from creating derivative works based on their code.

- **Maintaining Control:** Disabling forking ensures that contributors can't create personal copies of the repository, maintaining control over who has access to the code and who can make changes.

- **Code Stability:** In some cases, particularly for projects that need to maintain a stable codebase, allowing forks might lead to fragmentation and divergence from the main project. Disabling forks helps in maintaining a cohesive and standardized codebase.

- **Preventing Unwanted Contributions:** If a repository is meant to be private or for internal use only, allowing forks might lead to unintended external contributions. Disabling forks restricts contributions to a select group of individuals or team members.

- **Compliance Requirements:** Certain industries or organizations have strict compliance requirements regarding code access and modification. Disabling forking ensures adherence to these regulations.

- **Avoiding Code Fragmentation:** For projects that need to be maintained collaboratively, disabling forking can prevent code fragmentation. It ensures that everyone works on a central repository, reducing confusion and integration challenges.

However, it is essential to balance security and control with collaboration. Disabling forking might limit collaboration opportunities, so organizations should carefully evaluate their needs before making a decision. If collaboration is essential, managing permissions and code review processes might be more suitable than outright disabling forking.

How to Disable Forking

- **Navigate to Repository Settings**

  - Go to the main page of your GitHub repository.

  - Click the "Settings" tab, located on the right side of the menu bar below your repository's name.

- **Access Repository Options**

  - In the left sidebar, click the "Options" tab under the "Settings" category.

- **Disable Forking**

  - Scroll down to the "Danger Zone" section at the bottom of the Options page.

  - Look for the "Forking" option.

  - Uncheck the box that says, "Allow forks of this repository."

- **Confirm and Save**

  - GitHub will prompt you to confirm this action since it is a critical setting.

  - Confirm your choice to disable forking.

  - Scroll down to the bottom of the page and click the green button that says, "Save repository settings."

After following these steps, forking will be disabled for your GitHub repository. Remember that only users with administrative privileges can change this setting.

Restricting and Monitoring Permissions for Outside Collaborators

Restricting and monitoring permissions for outside collaborators on GitHub is crucial for several reasons, primarily focused on security, intellectual property protection, and maintaining the integrity of the codebase. Here is why it is important:

- **Security:** By restricting permissions, especially for external collaborators, you limit the actions they can perform within the repository. This prevents accidental or malicious changes that could compromise the security of the codebase.

- **Data Protection:** Restricting permissions helps in safeguarding sensitive data. Outside collaborators might not be privy to all internal policies and data protection measures. Limiting their access ensures that confidential information remains secure.

- **Intellectual Property Protection:** Organizations need to protect their intellectual property. Limiting the actions of outside collaborators reduces the risk of code theft, plagiarism, or unauthorized use of proprietary algorithms or technologies.

- **Code Quality Control:** By restricting permissions, organizations can enforce code review processes. Changes made by external collaborators can be closely monitored and reviewed before they are merged into the main codebase, ensuring high code quality standards.

- **Compliance:** Many industries have strict compliance regulations. Controlling who can access and modify the code ensures adherence to these regulations and prevents unintentional breaches.

- **Preventing Unwanted Contributions:** External collaborators may not always be aligned with the project's goals or coding standards. Restricting permissions helps in preventing unwanted contributions that might not align with the project's vision.

- **Maintaining Project Focus:** Restricting permissions ensures that only authorized individuals can make decisions about the project's direction. It prevents unnecessary discussions or changes that can distract the team from their primary goals.

- **Monitoring and Accountability:** By restricting permissions, it becomes easier to monitor the actions of external collaborators. If an issue arises, it's clear who had the authority to make specific changes, ensuring accountability and facilitating issue resolution.

- **Code Consistency:** External collaborators might not be aware of the project's coding guidelines. Restricted permissions prevent them from making changes that deviate from the established coding standards, ensuring consistency in the codebase.

Restricting and monitoring permissions for outside collaborators is essential for protecting the organization's assets, maintaining code quality, and ensuring that the project remains focused, secure, and compliant with industry standards and regulations. Here is how to restrict and monitor permissions for outside collaborators on GitHub with an example:

- **Access Repository Settings**

  - Go to the repository where you want to manage outside collaborators.

  - Click the "Settings" tab at the top right of the repository's main page.

- **Collaborators and Teams**

  - In the left sidebar, select "Collaborators & teams."

- **Add or Edit Collaborator**

  - To add an outside collaborator, start typing their GitHub username or email address in the "Add a collaborator" field.

  - Select the collaborator from the dropdown list.

  - Choose the appropriate role for the collaborator:

    - **Read:** Allows read-only access to the repository

    - **Write:** Grants write access to the repository, enabling them to push code

    - **Admin:** Provides administrative privileges, including the ability to add or remove collaborators, manage settings, and access sensitive information

  - Click the "Add [Collaborator]" button.

- **Adjust Permissions**

  - To edit permissions for an existing collaborator:

    - Find the collaborator's name in the list of collaborators.

    - Click the collaborator's name.

- Use the dropdown menu next to their name to change their role to read, write, or admin.

- Click the "Save changes" button.

- **Monitoring and Restrictions**

  Now, let's explore how to monitor and restrict outside collaborator permissions with an example:

  For example, suppose you have an open source project on GitHub with outside collaborators contributing code. You want to restrict and monitor their permissions to ensure code quality and security.

- **Monitoring and Restricting Permissions**

  - **Code Review:** Enforce a code review process for changes made by outside collaborators. This ensures that all code contributions are reviewed and approved by repository maintainers before being merged.

  - **Branch Protections:** Configure branch protections to restrict who can push to specific branches. For instance, protect the "main" branch and require that code changes receive approval (via code review) before they can be merged.

  - **Status Checks:** Implement status checks using GitHub Actions or other CI/CD tools to verify the quality and security of code changes. For example, require that all tests pass before allowing merges.

- **Security Scanning:** Set up code scanning and dependency scanning to automatically check for security vulnerabilities and coding errors in pull requests. Automatically require fixes for identified issues.

- **Issue Templates:** Use issue templates to guide collaborators, including outside collaborators, in reporting issues effectively. For instance, create templates for bug reports and feature requests to ensure that all necessary information is provided.

- **Issue and Pull Request Templates:** Implement templates for issues and pull requests to standardize the information required for each. This helps maintain consistency and ensures that changes are properly documented.

- **Audit Logs**

  - Regularly review the audit logs for the repository to monitor actions taken by outside collaborators. You can access audit logs by going to the "Settings" tab, selecting "Audit log," and reviewing the recorded activities.

- **Removing Collaborators**

  - If you need to remove an outside collaborator's access, go to the "Collaborators & teams" section, find the collaborator's name, and click the "Remove" button.

- **Regularly Review Permissions**

  - It's essential to regularly review and update the permissions and access of outside collaborators based on project needs and security considerations.

By following these steps and implementing these strategies in the example scenario, you can effectively restrict and monitor permissions for outside collaborators on GitHub while maintaining control over your repository's security and code quality.

Removing Inactive Members

Removing inactive members from a GitHub repository is essential for several reasons:

- **Security:** Inactive members might still have access to sensitive information within the repository. If their accounts are compromised, it could lead to unauthorized access, data breaches, or malicious activities.

- **Access Control:** By removing inactive members, you maintain a clear and updated list of collaborators who should have access to the repository. This ensures that only authorized individuals can contribute to the project.

- **Resource Management:** GitHub often charges based on the number of collaborators in private repositories. Removing inactive members helps optimize costs by ensuring you're not paying for unused accounts.

- **Project Management:** Inactive members can clutter collaboration tools and discussions, making it difficult to engage with active contributors effectively. Keeping the team focused on active members helps streamline project-related communications.

117

- **Compliance:** In certain organizations or projects, there might be compliance requirements or policies stating that access should be promptly revoked for individuals who no longer actively contribute.

- **Workflow Efficiency:** Active contributors need a clear understanding of who else is actively involved in the project. Removing inactive members from team lists and discussions helps maintain clarity in team communications and decision-making processes.

- **Ownership and Responsibility:** Clear ownership of repositories is crucial. Inactive members might have administrative privileges, making it important to transfer ownership or remove them to maintain a responsible and accountable repository management structure.

Remember, before removing any member, it's good practice to communicate with them. They might be inactive temporarily due to personal reasons, and it's respectful to inform them about the removal and provide an opportunity to retain access if they plan to contribute again. Here is how you can remove inactive members:

- **Access Repository Settings**

  - Navigate to the repository where you want to manage members.

  - Click the "Settings" tab, located on the right side of the repository's main page.

- **Access Collaborators and Teams**

  - In the left sidebar, select "Collaborators & teams."

- **Remove Inactive Members**

  - Scroll down to the "Outside collaborators" section to see a list of all collaborators.

  - Identify the inactive member(s) you want to remove.

  - To the right of the member's name, click the gear icon (⚙) to access the options.

  - Select "Remove [Member's Name]."

  - Confirm the removal when prompted.

- **Remove Inactive Members in Bulk**

  If you have multiple inactive members to remove, GitHub provides an option to remove them in bulk. Here's how:

  - Go to the "Collaborators & teams" section of your repository.

  - Click the "Manage access" tab.

  - On the right side, you'll find a "Bulk actions" dropdown menu.

  - Select "Remove from [Repository Name]."

  - Check the members you want to remove from the list.

  - Click the "Remove" button to confirm.

Note   When removing collaborators, ensure that they no longer require access to the repository. Always communicate with team members before removing them to avoid accidental removals.

Please be aware that to avoid continued charges, you must downgrade your organization's paid seats after removing users. Otherwise, you'll still be billed for the removed users. Additionally, you can reinstate a user anytime if their contribution is needed. Furthermore, it's essential that the user deletes all local copies of the repository on their end. Merely removing them from your repository does not erase any local copies. GitHub retains their data for up to three months after removal, simplifying the process if you decide to reinstate their permissions.

Secure Coding Practices

Recognizing the significance of Git security is of utmost importance because neglecting it can lead to severe consequences, including data breaches, financial losses, data corruption, reputation damage, and even declines in stock prices. When a company conducts a comprehensive assessment of the risks associated with using GitHub and proactively implements preventive measures to mitigate these risks, it not only protects its critical and sensitive information but also ensures the stability of its business operations. In this section, we will explore the complexities of establishing GitHub Advanced Security.

Why We Need GitHub Security Practices

Implementing digital security measures is a well-known necessity for software development teams, yet it often becomes a neglected aspect, sometimes entirely overlooked. Careless practices and routines can lead to significant consequences, jeopardizing your infrastructure and data integrity. GitHub stands as a symbol of code version control and the application development process. While competitors like Azure Pipelines and AWS Code Commit exist, they lack GitHub's widespread adoption, community support, and market dominance.

A study conducted by North Carolina State University underscored the magnitude of the issue. A continuous six-month scan of over a million GitHub accounts revealed alarming findings: publicly accessible text strings containing sensitive information like usernames, passwords, API tokens, database snapshots, cryptographic keys, and configuration files. Among the exposed data were over 212,000 Google API keys, 26,000 AWS Access Keys, and 28,000 social media access tokens.

Of concern were the 542 publicly available Stripe Standard API keys on GitHub. Possession of these keys grants a malicious user direct access to financial accounts, enabling them to make fraudulent charges. This not only damages the business's reputation but also compromises data integrity.

Never Store Credentials and Sensitive Data on GitHub

The primary function of GitHub is to serve as a host for code repositories. Apart from the permissions you establish on your account, there are no additional security measures to guarantee the protection of your secret keys, private credentials, and sensitive data within a controlled and secure environment. Every git code commit records a comprehensive history of additions and deletions, making your sensitive data a permanent part of a branch. The risk of a potential data or infrastructure breach significantly rises, especially when branches are merged or forked.

To address this challenge, GitHub has implemented preventive measures to enhance security – GitHub secret scanning. This service meticulously scans your complete Git history across all branches in your GitHub repository, actively seeking leaked login credentials. If it detects any usernames or passwords within code or commit metadata, it automatically resets this sensitive information and promptly alerts you via email. This proactive approach ensures data protection and peace of mind.

GitHub's secret scanning feature performs a thorough scan of your entire Git history across all branches in your GitHub repository, meticulously searching for these secrets. It doesn't stop there; the scanning process also extends to issue descriptions and comments, actively looking for any exposed secrets. Furthermore, secret scanning meticulously examines titles, descriptions, and comments within both open and closed historical issues, promptly flagging any leaked secrets as alerts on GitHub. This comprehensive approach ensures that no stone is left unturned in safeguarding your sensitive information.

Secrets

We all have our secrets regardless of their size. What truly matters is that we each keep these secrets hidden from the world for reasons. However, there is one commonality, among all secrets. Nobody wants them to be exposed!

As per IBM website:

A secret refers to information such as an API key, password or any form of credentials used to access systems.

As evident, from the explanation, the repercussions of losing secrets within information systems are far-reaching. Data loss can result in setbacks and erosion of trust and even lead to the demise of businesses. Therefore, it is imperative that we exercise caution! Safeguarding secrets holds importance.

GitHub Secret Scanning

When your project interacts with an external service, authentication often involves using tokens or private keys issued by the service provider. These tokens and keys are sensitive pieces of information. If mistakenly included in a repository, anyone with read access to that repository can misuse them, gaining unauthorized access to the external service with your privileges. To avoid this risk, it's crucial to store secrets in a dedicated, secure location outside of the repository. GitHub's secret scanning feature is designed to enhance security. It meticulously examines your entire Git history across all branches within your GitHub repository, scanning for these sensitive secrets. Secret scanning does not just stop at code, it also delves into issue descriptions and comments, ensuring a comprehensive search.

We will be covering secret scanning as a part of the upcoming section "Repository Maintenance Best Practices."

Disable Forking

Disabling forking in the context of secure coding practices refers to restricting the ability of users to fork repositories within a GitHub organization. Forking allows users to create personal copies of repositories, which can sometimes lead to security risks, especially if sensitive code or data is involved. Disabling forking ensures better control over who can access and modify the repository content. By disabling forking, organizations can prevent unintended access to their codebase, reducing the risk of unauthorized modifications, data breaches, or accidental leaks. This practice is especially relevant when dealing with proprietary or sensitive software. To disable forking on GitHub, organization owners or administrators can configure repository settings to restrict forking permissions. This helps enforce security policies and ensures that code remains within the controlled environment of the organization.

As explained previously, in this chapter, we can make use of **disable forking for secure coding practices**.

Disable Visibility Changes

Disabling visibility changes in the context of secure coding practices means preventing users from altering the visibility settings of repositories within a GitHub organization. GitHub allows repositories to have different visibility levels, such as public, private, or internal. Public repositories can be accessed and viewed by anyone, private repositories restrict access to authorized users, and internal repositories are accessible only within the same enterprise. Disabling visibility changes ensures that the visibility settings of repositories remain consistent and secure. This is particularly important when dealing with sensitive or proprietary code. By restricting the ability to change visibility, organizations can prevent accidental exposure of sensitive information to unauthorized users.

To disable visibility changes for secure coding practices on GitHub, you can follow these steps:

- **Organization Settings**
  - Navigate to the organization's main page on GitHub.
  - Click the Settings tab (it may require administrative privileges).

- **Repository Settings**
  - Under the organization settings, select Repositories in the left sidebar.

- **Visibility Settings**
  - Find the Visibility section in the Repositories settings.
  - Disable the option that allows members to change repository visibility. The exact wording may vary but look for settings related to repository visibility.

- **Save Changes**
  - After making the necessary changes, make sure to save your settings.

By disabling the ability to change repository visibility, you ensure that repositories within the organization maintain a consistent and secure visibility level, following your organization's secure coding practices.

Tightly Manage External Contributor Permissions

Tightly managing external contributor permissions is vital for safeguarding data, ensuring code integrity, and maintaining compliance. By restricting access, organizations prevent unauthorized actions, protect against insider threats, and enforce coding standards. It also promotes accountability, prevents unauthorized forking, and aligns with security best practices, enhancing overall repository security and integrity. Here are some best practices and steps to tightly manage external contributor permissions:

- **Limit External Contributions:**

    - Restrict repository access to a select group of trusted external contributors.

    - Avoid granting write access to external contributors unless necessary.

- **Use Collaborator Roles:**

    - Assign external contributors the appropriate collaborator role based on their level of contribution:

        - **Read Access:** Allows contributors to view the repository but not make any changes

        - **Write Access:** Permits contributors to make changes, create issues, and submit pull requests

        - **Admin Access:** Grants full control, including repository settings and access management

- **Leverage Teams:**

    - Organize external contributors into teams with specific access levels and responsibilities.

    - Apply team-based permissions to multiple repositories, ensuring consistency and ease of management.

- **Regularly Review Access:**

  - Periodically review the list of external contributors and their permissions.

  - Remove access for contributors who are no longer active or required for the project.

- **Require Two-Factor Authentication (2FA):**

  - Encourage or mandate external contributors to enable two-factor authentication for added security.

  - GitHub provides options to enforce 2FA requirements for specific roles or all users.

- **Utilize Repository Settings:**

  - Explore repository settings to enforce specific restrictions, such as branch protection rules, required reviews, and status checks before merging.

- **Educate Contributors:**

  - Provide guidelines and best practices to external contributors regarding code submissions, issue reporting, and security considerations.

  - Ensure contributors are aware of your organization's code of conduct and security policies.

- **Automate Security Checks:**

  - Implement automated security scanning tools to detect vulnerabilities in code submitted by external contributors.

- Utilize GitHub Actions or other CI/CD pipelines to run tests and security checks before merging external contributions.

- **Regularly Update Dependencies:**

  - Keep project dependencies up to date to minimize security vulnerabilities.

  - Utilize Dependabot or similar tools to automate dependency updates and security vulnerability notifications.

- **Establish a Response Plan:**

  - Have a response plan in place for handling security incidents or breaches involving external contributors.

  - Clearly define the steps to be taken and the responsible parties in case of a security incident.

By following these practices, you can ensure that external contributors are tightly managed, reducing security risks and maintaining a secure development environment on GitHub.

Revoke Permissions in a Timely Manner

Revoking permissions in a timely manner is crucial for maintaining the security and integrity of a GitHub repository. When users no longer require access, prompt revocation ensures they cannot inadvertently or maliciously compromise the codebase. This proactive measure reduces the risk of unauthorized access, prevents potential security breaches, and upholds data confidentiality. By promptly revoking permissions, organizations can maintain a robust security posture and prevent unintended access to sensitive information.

How to Revoke Permissions in a Timely Manner on GitHub

To revoke permissions in a timely manner on GitHub, follow these steps:

- **Organization Owners/Admins**

  - For organizations, go to your organization's main page.

  - Click "Settings" (the gear icon in the upper-right corner).

  - Select "People" from the left sidebar.

  - Find the user whose permissions you want to revoke.

  - Click the user's name.

  - Scroll down to the "Repository access" section.

  - Click "Remove" next to the repositories you want to revoke access to.

- **Repository Owners/Admins**

  - For individual repositories, go to the repository's main page.

  - Click "Settings" (the gear icon on the right side, just above the list of files).

  - Select "Collaborators."

  - Find the user you want to remove.

  - Click the user's name.

  - Click "Remove access."

- **Command Line (for Repository Owners/Admins)**

  - Use the following Git command to remove a user's access:

    $ git remote remove ganesh.sangale

Remember, it's crucial to revoke permissions as soon as they are no longer necessary to minimize security risks.

Require Commit Signing

Requiring commit signing is a security measure in Git that ensures every commit is associated with a verified identity. This means the commits cannot be forged or tampered with, providing a higher level of trust and integrity to the codebase. Here is how you can require commit signing on GitHub:

- **For an Individual Repository**

  - Go to your repository on GitHub.

  - Click "Settings" (the gear icon).

  - In the left sidebar, click "Branches."

  - Under the "Branches" section, click "Branch protection rules."

  - Click "Add rule" or edit an existing rule.

  - Enable the option "Require signed commits."

- **For an Organization (Enterprise Account)**

  - Go to your organization's main page on GitHub.

  - Click "Settings" (the gear icon).

  - In the left sidebar, click "Policies."

  - Under "Policies," click "Protected branches."

- Click "Add branch rule" or edit an existing rule.

- Enable the option "Require signed commits."

After enabling this option, contributors will have to sign their commits with their GPG key before they can be merged into protected branches. This ensures the authenticity and integrity of the code changes.

Enforce Code Review Before Commit

Enforcing code review before commits is a crucial practice in software development workflows. It ensures that changes made to the codebase are thoroughly examined, promoting code quality, consistency, and adherence to project standards. Here is how you can enforce code review before commits on GitHub:

- **Pull Requests**

  - Developers create feature branches for their changes.

  - Once changes are implemented, they create a pull request (PR) to merge these changes into the main branch.

  - Project collaborators or team members review the changes within the PR.

  - Reviews might include discussions, feedback, and suggestions for improvements.

  - A pull request can only be merged if it receives approval from the required number of reviewers.

- **Branch Protection Rules**

  - GitHub allows you to set up branch protection rules for specific branches (usually main or master branches).

- Within these rules, you can enforce status checks, requiring all status checks to pass before a pull request can be merged.

- One of these status checks can be a code review, ensuring that a pull request has been reviewed and approved before merging.

By enforcing code review through pull requests and branch protection rules, teams can maintain a high standard of code quality, catch potential issues early, and ensure that every change is validated by team members before becoming a permanent part of the codebase.

Repository Maintenance Best Practices

Ensuring software security is a crucial concern that encompasses the entire software development lifecycle. While much attention is given to writing secure code and securing infrastructure, safeguarding the processes at every stage of software development is equally vital.

Imagine you are overseeing a significant GitHub repository. You aim to maintain top-notch security while fostering a collaborative and inclusive environment for contributors. However, enhancing security measures often comes with a trade-off, potentially hindering productivity for everyone involved. To strike a balance, GitHub provides a range of automated features. These tools empower you to efficiently manage a secure repository, minimizing disruptions and streamlining the development process for all contributors.

Security

Embedding security into an application or system isn't a task that can be tacked on later; it must be an integral part of every phase in the software development lifecycle. This is especially critical for applications handling sensitive or highly confidential data. In practical terms, holding development teams accountable necessitates shifting security processes to earlier stages in the development lifecycle. By moving security steps from a final checkpoint at deployment to an earlier phase, errors are reduced, enabling developers to work more swiftly.

Historically, application security has not been a primary focus for developers, partly due to training challenges and partly due to organizational emphasis on rapid feature development. The advent of DevOps practices has made integrating security testing into the pipeline much simpler. Instead of being a task exclusively handled by security experts, security testing should seamlessly blend into day-to-day delivery operations. When factoring in the time for potential rework, incorporating security into your DevOps practices earlier in the development process enables teams to identify issues sooner, potentially reducing the overall time required to develop high-quality software.

Shifting left involves a change in processes; it is not about a singular control or a specific tool. Rather, it is about making all security measures more developer-centric and providing developers with security feedback in their natural workflow. GitHub offers security features that help keep data secure in repositories and across organizations. To locate the security tab

- On GitHub.com, go to the main page of the repository.

- Under the repository name, select **Security**. Figure 3-9 shows the tab option for repository security.

Figure 3-9. *Repository security*

From the Security tab, you can add features to your GitHub workflow to help avoid vulnerabilities in your repository and codebase. These features include

- **Security policies** that allow you to specify how to report a security vulnerability in your project by adding a SECURITY.md file to your repository

- **Dependabot alerts** that notify you when GitHub detects that your repository is using a vulnerable dependency or malware

- **Security advisories** that you can use to privately discuss, fix, and publish information about security vulnerabilities in your repository

- **Code scanning** that helps you find, triage, and fix vulnerabilities and errors in your code

Security Policies

If you want to provide guidelines for reporting security vulnerabilities in your project, you have the option to include a SECURITY.md file in your repository's root, docs, or .github folder. When someone raises an issue in your repository, they will find a direct link to your project's security policy. Once a security vulnerability in your project has been reported, GitHub Security Advisories can be utilized to reveal, address, and share details about the vulnerability. For additional details on the procedures for reporting and disclosing vulnerabilities on GitHub, please refer to the provided information. To add security policy to your repository, follow these steps:

- On GitHub.com, navigate to the main page of the repository.

- Under the repository name, click Security. If you cannot see the "Security" tab, select the dropdown menu, and then click Security, as shown in Figure 3-9.

- In the left sidebar, under "Reporting," click Policy. Figure 3-10 shows the screen for setting up security policy.

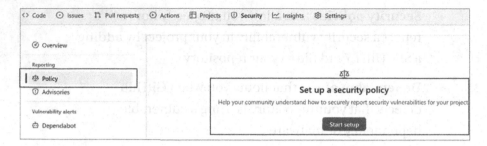

Figure 3-10. *Setting up security policy*

- Click Start setup.

- In the new SECURITY.md file, add information about supported versions of your project and how to report a vulnerability. Figure 3-11 shows the screen about documenting security.md file.

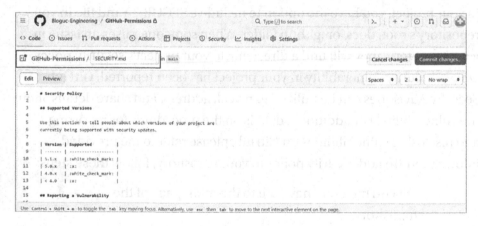

Figure 3-11. *Security.md file sample*

- Then click Commit changes. Figure 3-12 shows the screen for committing changes.

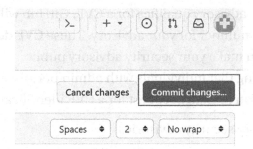

Figure 3-12. *Committing changes*

GitHub Security Advisories

GitHub Security Advisories provide a platform for repository maintainers to confidentially address and resolve security vulnerabilities in their projects. After collaborating on a solution, maintainers can release the security advisory to openly inform the project's community about the identified vulnerability. Sharing these advisories simplifies the process for the community to update package dependencies and assess the potential impact of the security issues. GitHub archives these published advisories in the Common Vulnerabilities and Exposures (CVE) list, ensuring automatic notifications to affected repositories utilizing software with listed vulnerabilities.

GitHub Security Advisories build upon the foundation of the CVE list. The security advisory form on GitHub is a standardized form that matches the CVE description format. GitHub is a CVE Numbering Authority (CNA) and is authorized to assign CVE identification numbers. When creating a security advisory for a public repository on GitHub, you can opt to include an existing CVE identification number for the security vulnerability. If your project lacks a CVE identification number and you require one, you can request it from GitHub. The request is typically reviewed within 72 hours. Importantly, requesting a CVE identification number does not automatically make your security advisory public.

If your security advisory qualifies for a CVE, GitHub will reserve a CVE identification number for your advisory. These CVE details will be published after you make your security advisory public.

It is worth noting that individuals with admin permissions for a security advisory can initiate a request for a CVE identification number.

- Repository security advisories

  - Repository security advisories enable repository maintainers to address security vulnerabilities in their projects privately. Once a solution is collaborated upon and implemented, maintainers can publish the security advisory, openly sharing the details with the project's community. This practice streamlines the process for the community to update package dependencies and assess the impact of the security vulnerabilities.

  - With repository security advisories, you can

    - Create a draft security advisory and use the draft to privately discuss the impact of the vulnerability on your project.

    - Privately collaborate to fix the vulnerability in a temporary private fork.

    - Publish the security advisory to alert your community of the vulnerability once a patch is released.

Creating a Repository Security Advisory

Creating a repository security advisory on GitHub involves informing your community about a security vulnerability in your project and providing guidance on how to address it. Here are the steps to create a repository security advisory:

- **Identify the Security Vulnerability:**

  - Detect and confirm the security vulnerability within your project. Understand its scope, impact, and potential risks.

- **Collaborate on a Fix:**

  - Work with your team or contributors to develop a solution for the identified vulnerability. Ensure the fix effectively resolves the issue.

- **Prepare the Security Advisory:**

  Draft a detailed security advisory. Include the following information:

  - **Title:** Clearly describe the vulnerability in the title.

  - **Description:** Explain the nature of the vulnerability, its impact, and how it was discovered.

  - **Affected Versions:** Specify the versions of the software or components affected by the vulnerability.

  - **Fix:** Describe the steps taken to fix the vulnerability.

  - **CVE Identifier (Optional):** If applicable, include the CVE identifier for the vulnerability.

  - **Credit (Optional):** Acknowledge the person or team who reported the vulnerability if desired.

  - **Mitigation:** Provide temporary measures or workarounds for users until they can update their installations.

  - **References:** Include links to relevant resources or related issues.

- **Publish the Security Advisory:**

  - Go to your GitHub repository on the GitHub website.

  - Navigate to the "Security" tab in the repository menu.

  - Select "Advisories" from the submenu.

  - Click the "Create advisory" button. Figure 3-13 shows the screen for security advisory.

Figure 3-13. *Security advisory*

- Fill out the advisory form with the prepared information.

- Review the advisory to ensure accuracy and clarity.

- Click the "Publish advisory" button to make the advisory public. Figure 3-14 shows the published security advisory.

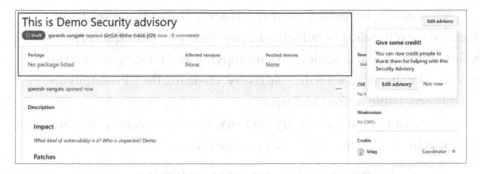

Figure 3-14. *Published security advisory*

- **Notify the Community:**
  - Inform your community about the security advisory through the repository's README, project documentation, or dedicated security channels. Encourage users to update their installations or follow the provided mitigation steps.

- **Monitor and Respond:**
  - Keep an eye on the advisory for any community feedback or questions. Be responsive to user inquiries and provide assistance if needed.

By creating a repository security advisory, you contribute to a safer and more secure open source ecosystem, ensuring that users are informed about vulnerabilities and can take appropriate actions to protect their installations.

Publish a Security Advisory

Publishing a security advisory serves as a crucial notification to your community, informing them about a specific security vulnerability and the steps taken to address it. This practice facilitates your community in promptly updating package dependencies and understanding the implications of the vulnerability.

Additionally, repository security advisories provide a convenient method for reiterating details about a previously disclosed security vulnerability. You can achieve this by copying and pasting the relevant information into a new security advisory, ensuring that the details are readily accessible to your audience.

Before you publish a security advisory, you can privately collaborate to fix the vulnerability in a temporary private fork.

- Collaborating in a temporary private fork is a prudent approach to resolving a repository security vulnerability while ensuring confidentiality and security. Here is how you can collaborate effectively in such a scenario:

  - **Create a Private Fork:**

    - Create a private fork of the repository where the security vulnerability exists. This ensures that the collaboration and fixes are contained within a secure environment.

  - **Invite Collaborators:**

    - Invite trusted collaborators, developers, or security experts to join the private fork. Ensure they have the necessary permissions to contribute to the repository.

  - **Discuss the Vulnerability:**

    - Use the fork's issue tracker or a private communication channel to discuss the details of the security vulnerability. Clearly document the issue, its impact, and potential fixes.

- **Collaborate on a Solution:**

  - Work collaboratively on developing a solution
    to the security vulnerability. Implement best
    practices and security measures to address the
    issue comprehensively.

- **Code Review and Testing:**

  - Conduct thorough code reviews within the
    private fork. Test the proposed changes
    rigorously to ensure they effectively resolve the
    vulnerability without introducing new issues.

- **Maintain Confidentiality:**

  - Keep all discussions, code changes, and testing
    within the private fork. Avoid public discussions
    or disclosures to prevent unauthorized access
    to sensitive information.

- **Prepare the Advisory:**

  - Once the solution is verified and confirmed,
    prepare a detailed security advisory outlining
    the vulnerability, its impact, and the steps taken
    to resolve it.

- **Publish the Advisory:**

  - Publish the security advisory as per the
    established procedures. Ensure that all
    necessary details are included while
    maintaining a responsible disclosure approach.

- **Merge Changes and Monitor:**

  - Merge the changes back into the main
    repository once the vulnerability is resolved.
    Monitor the repository for any feedback or
    issues reported by users after the changes are
    deployed. Figure 3-15 shows the screen about
    starting a temporary fork.

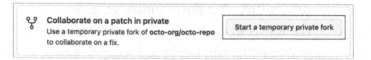

Figure 3-15. Start a temporary fork

By collaborating in a temporary private fork, you can effectively
address the security vulnerability, maintain confidentiality, and ensure
a responsible and secure resolution process. When you publish a draft
advisory from a public repository, the following details become visible to
everyone:

- The current version of the advisory data

- Any advisory credits that the credited users have
  accepted

Note   The public will never have access to the edit history of the
advisory; they will only see the published version.

Once a security advisory is published, its URL remains unchanged.
Anyone with read access to the repository can view the security advisory.
Collaborators involved in the advisory can access previous discussions,

including the entire comment thread, within the security advisory, unless an individual with admin permissions removes a collaborator from the advisory.

Editing a Repository Security Advisory

Anyone with admin permissions to a repository security advisory, or with a security manager role within the repository, can edit the security advisory.

- On GitHub.com, navigate to the main page of the repository.

- Under the repository name, click Security. If you cannot see the "Security" tab, select the dropdown menu, and then click Security.

- In the left sidebar, under "Reporting," click **Advisories**.

- In the "Security Advisories" list, click the name of the security advisory you would like to edit.

- In the upper-right corner of the details for the security advisory, click **Edit advisory**. This will open the security advisory form in edit mode. Figure 3-16 shows the screen for editing security advisory.

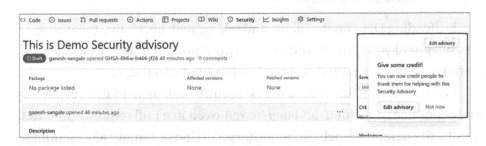

Figure 3-16. *Editing security advisory*

Dependabot Alerts

Dependabot alerts are crucial notifications that inform you about potential security vulnerabilities within the packages your code relies on. Addressing these vulnerabilities promptly is essential to maintaining the security and reliability of your project. Dependabot alerts serve as vital notifications, indicating if your code relies on a package that has security vulnerabilities. Such vulnerabilities can pose significant risks to your project and its users. Immediate action is necessary in these situations:

- **Upgrading to Secure Versions:** If your code depends on a package with a security vulnerability, it is imperative to upgrade to a secure version of the package promptly. These upgrades often contain patches and fixes that address the vulnerabilities, enhancing your project's security.

- **Replacing Malware or Compromised Packages:** In cases where your code relies on a package contaminated with malware or other malicious content, replacing the compromised package with a secure alternative is essential. This action ensures that your project is not inadvertently distributing harmful software to its users.

By heeding Dependabot alerts and taking swift corrective measures, you safeguard your project and its users from potential security threats, fostering a secure environment for development and usage.

In addition, GitHub offers a robust security mechanism that reviews any dependencies added, updated, or removed in a pull request submitted against the default branch of a repository. GitHub automatically identifies changes that might compromise the security of your project. By flagging alterations that could introduce vulnerable dependencies or malware, this proactive approach enables you to detect and address potential security threats before they infiltrate your codebase. This preemptive measure ensures a vigilant defense against security vulnerabilities, allowing you to maintain a secure and resilient project environment. Within the Dependabot alerts tab, you can

- **Filter Alerts**

  - Filter alerts based on specific packages, ecosystems, or manifests, streamlining your search for relevant information.

- **Sorting Options**

  - Utilize sorting options to arrange the list of alerts according to your preferences, enhancing readability and organization.

- **Detailed Alert Views**

  - Click into individual alerts to access detailed information, gaining insights into the nature and impact of each vulnerability.

- **Dismiss or Reopen Alerts**

  - Take action by dismissing or reopening alerts. You have the flexibility to handle alerts one by one or manage multiple alerts simultaneously.

The Dependabot alerts tab provides a robust interface for managing your project's security posture, allowing you to stay informed, take prompt actions, and ensure the continuous security of your codebase.

Configuration of Dependabot alerts

Configuring Dependabot alerts involves setting up security policies for your repository to receive notifications about security vulnerabilities in your project's dependencies. Here are the steps to configure Dependabot alerts:

- **Navigate to Repository Settings:**

  - Go to your GitHub repository.

  - Click the **Settings** tab located near the right end of the menu bar.

- **Security and Analysis Settings:**

  - In the left sidebar, click **Security and Analysis** or **Security**. Figure 3-17 shows the screen for security and analysis.

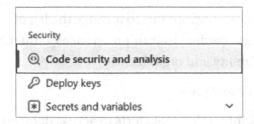

Figure 3-17. *Code security and analysis*

- **Configure Dependabot Alerts:**

  - Scroll down to the **Dependency graph** section or a similar section related to security settings.

  - Look for options related to Dependabot alerts. GitHub provides options to enable or disable security alerts for vulnerable dependencies and security advisories. Figure 3-18 shows the Dependabot configuration screen.

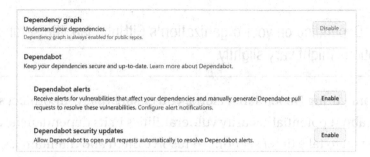

Figure 3-18. *Dependabot configuration*

- **Select Notification Recipients:**
  - Configure the email addresses or GitHub usernames that should receive notifications about Dependabot alerts. You can choose to send alerts to repository administrators, maintainers, or custom email addresses. Figure 3-19 shows the screen for setting up default notification email configuration.

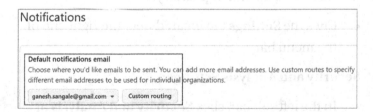

Figure 3-19. *Setting up default notification email*

- **Save Changes:**
  - Once you have configured the desired settings, save your changes.

Note   Depending on your organization's GitHub plan, the settings and options might vary slightly.

By configuring Dependabot alerts, you ensure that your project stays updated about potential security vulnerabilities in its dependencies, allowing you to take timely actions to resolve them and maintain a secure codebase.

Viewing and Updating Dependabot Alerts

In your repository, the Dependabot alerts tab serves as a central hub, displaying a comprehensive list of both open and closed Dependabot alerts, along with corresponding security updates. This tab offers powerful filtering capabilities, allowing you to sort alerts by package, ecosystem, or manifest, enabling precise navigation through your project's dependencies.

Viewing Dependabot Alerts

- **Navigate to Repository Settings:**

  - Go to your GitHub repository.

  - Click the **Settings** tab located near the right end of the menu bar.

- **Security and Analysis Settings:**

  - In the left sidebar, click **Security and Analysis** or **Security** (depending on your GitHub version).

- **View Dependabot Alerts:**

  - Look for the section related to Dependabot alerts or security advisories.

  - GitHub will display a list of security alerts indicating any vulnerable dependencies in your project.

Updating Dependabot Alerts

- **Review the Alerts:**

  - Examine the list of security alerts to understand which dependencies are affected and the severity of the vulnerabilities.

- **Update Vulnerable Dependencies:**

  - For each vulnerable dependency, update your project's configuration files (such as **package.json**, **Gemfile**, etc.) to use a version that contains the security fixes.

  - Alternatively, check if there is a patch or update provided by the package maintainer. Apply the necessary changes to your project.

- **Create Pull Requests:**

  - Once you have made the necessary changes, create pull requests for your updates. Ensure your pull requests are carefully reviewed and tested.

- **Merge Pull Requests:**

  - After your pull requests have been reviewed and pass all checks, merge them into your default branch (usually **main** or **master**).

- **Confirm Alerts Are Resolved:**

  - GitHub will automatically mark Dependabot alerts as resolved when the vulnerable dependency versions are no longer in use in your repository.

- **Continuous Monitoring:**

  - Regularly review Dependabot alerts, especially after adding or updating dependencies, to ensure your project stays secure.

By following these steps, you can effectively view, address, and update Dependabot alerts, ensuring your project remains secure and up to date with the latest security patches and fixes.

Code Scanning

GitHub's code scanning feature empowers developers to meticulously analyze the code within a GitHub repository, aiming to identify security vulnerabilities and coding errors. The analysis scrutinizes the codebase comprehensively, flagging any problems encountered during the process, and presents these findings directly within GitHub's interface. With code scanning, developers can

- **Detect, Triage, and Prioritize Fixes:**

  - Identify existing problems within the code and prioritize them based on severity. Developers can effectively triage and address these issues to enhance the overall security posture of the project.

- **Prevent Introduction of New Problems:**

  - Code scanning acts as a proactive measure, preventing developers from inadvertently introducing new vulnerabilities or errors as they work on the code. By identifying issues before they become part of the codebase, developers can maintain code integrity.

- **Flexible Scheduling and Triggers:**

  - Developers have the flexibility to schedule code
    scans for specific days and times, ensuring regular
    checks for vulnerabilities. Additionally, scans
    can be triggered by specific events, such as code
    pushes, ensuring timely analysis whenever changes
    occur in the repository.

- **Alerts and Issue Resolution:**

  - When code scanning identifies potential
    vulnerabilities or errors, GitHub generates alerts
    within the repository. Once developers address
    the problematic code, GitHub automatically closes
    the corresponding alert, providing a streamlined
    workflow for issue resolution.

GitHub's code scanning feature thus plays a pivotal role in bolstering
the security of software projects, offering developers a robust toolset to
maintain code quality and robustness.

Managing Code Scanning Alerts for Your Repository

In the security view, you can easily review, resolve, or dismiss alerts
pertaining to potential vulnerabilities or errors detected in your project's
code. Who can utilize this feature? Individuals with write permissions to a
repository have the ability to manage code scanning alerts specific to that
repository.

Viewing Code Scanning Alerts for a Repository

Within a GitHub repository, you can access a dedicated section called
"Security" or "Security and Analysis." Here, you will find an "Alerts" or
"Vulnerability Alerts" tab, which provides a comprehensive overview of

all security-related notifications. These alerts include information about potential vulnerabilities, coding errors, and other security issues identified in the repository's codebase. To view these alerts:

- **Navigate to the Repository:**

  - Go to the GitHub repository you want to inspect.

- **Access the Security Tab:**

  - Click the "Security" or "Security and Analysis" tab, typically located in the repository's menu bar.

- **Explore the Alerts Section:**

  - Within the "Security" tab, find the "Alerts" or "Vulnerability Alerts" section. This area lists all the identified issues with detailed descriptions.

- **Review Alert Details:**

  - Click individual alerts to explore more information, including the nature of the problem, affected files, and potential fixes.

By following these steps, you can thoroughly examine and understand the security alerts associated with the repository, enabling you to take necessary actions to address the identified issues.

Filtering Code Scanning Alerts

In the code scanning alerts view on GitHub, you have the flexibility to filter alerts, enabling a more focused analysis, especially when dealing with numerous alerts. GitHub offers predefined filters and a variety of keywords to help you narrow down the list of displayed alerts. When you choose a keyword from the dropdown list or enter it in the search field, only values with relevant results are shown, preventing you from setting filters that yield no results and optimizing your search process.

If you apply multiple filters, the view will display alerts that match all specified criteria. For instance, using filters like "is:closed severity:high branch:main" will show only closed high-severity alerts present on the main branch. However, filters related to refs (ref, branch, and pr) work differently; for example, "is:open branch:main branch:next" displays open alerts from both the main and next branches.

It is essential to note that if you filter alerts on a non-default branch, but the same alerts exist on the default branch, the alert page for any specific alert will still reflect its status on the default branch, even if it conflicts with the status on a non-default branch. For instance, an alert listed in the "Open" section for branch-x might show a "Fixed" status on the alert page if it's already fixed on the default branch. You can check the alert's status for the filtered branch in the "Affected branches" section on the right side of the alert page. Moreover, you can exclude specific tags by prefixing the tag filter with "-". For instance, "-tag:style" displays alerts without the "style" tag, and "-tag:experimental" excludes all experimental alerts from the results.

Searching Code Scanning Alerts

In the code scanning alerts view on GitHub, you can search through the alert list. This feature proves handy when dealing with a substantial number of alerts in your repository or when you are not certain about the exact name of a specific alert. GitHub allows free-text search across two crucial aspects:

- **Alert Name:** This includes the specific name assigned to the alert.

- **Alert Details:** This encompasses all the information related to the alert, including the details initially hidden from view, accessible by expanding the "Show more" collapsible section.

This search functionality ensures you can efficiently locate and manage alerts, even in repositories with extensive alert lists.

Supported Search	Syntax Example	Results
Single word search	injection	Returns all the alerts containing the word injection
Multiple word search	sql injection	Returns all the alerts containing sql or injection
Exact match search (use double quotes)	"sql injection"	Returns all the alerts containing the exact phrase sql injection
OR search	sql OR injection	Returns all the alerts containing sql or injection

Tracking Code Scanning Alerts in Issues

Tracking code scanning alerts in issues is an effective way to centralize communication, collaboration, and resolution efforts within your development team. By integrating code scanning alerts with GitHub Issues, you can create a systematic process to address security vulnerabilities and ensure timely responses.

Here is how you can track code scanning alerts using GitHub Issues:

- **Create an Issue:** Whenever a code scanning alert is generated, create a new GitHub Issue dedicated to addressing that specific alert. Include relevant details such as the alert description, affected file paths, and any other contextual information that can aid developers in understanding the problem.

- **Assign Owners:** Assign the issue to the appropriate team member or team responsible for resolving the code scanning alert. Clearly define the owner(s) to ensure accountability and prevent confusion about who is addressing the issue.

- **Prioritize the Issue:** Evaluate the severity of the code scanning alert and prioritize the GitHub Issue accordingly. Critical vulnerabilities should be addressed with higher priority, ensuring they are resolved promptly to minimize potential risks.

- **Discuss Solutions:** Use the GitHub Issue as a platform for discussing potential solutions. Team members can collaborate, share insights, and propose fixes within the comments section of the GitHub Issue. Encourage open communication to foster a collaborative environment.

- **Implement Fixes:** Once a suitable solution is agreed upon, developers can implement the necessary code changes to address the vulnerability. Document the changes made and reference the GitHub Issue number in the commit messages for traceability.

- **Link Commits:** Link the specific commits that resolve the code scanning alert to the GitHub Issue. This linkage provides a clear connection between the code changes and the associated issue, enabling easier tracking of the resolution process.

- **Perform Code Reviews:** If applicable, conduct code reviews for the changes made to address the code scanning alert. Code reviews help ensure the quality and correctness of the fixes before they are merged into the main codebase.

- **Test the Fixes:** Thoroughly test the implemented
  fixes to validate that the code scanning alert has been
  effectively addressed. Use automated tests, manual
  testing, and any relevant testing methodologies to
  confirm the resolution.

- **Close the GitHub Issue:** Once the code scanning alert
  is resolved and the fixes have been successfully merged
  and tested, close the GitHub Issue. Provide a summary
  of the changes made and any additional context to
  document the resolution process.

- **Learn and Prevent:** After resolving the code scanning
  alert, conduct a brief retrospective to understand
  the root cause and identify preventive measures.
  Implement best practices, coding guidelines, or
  automated checks to prevent similar vulnerabilities in
  the future.

By tracking code scanning alerts in GitHub Issues, you establish a
structured workflow that promotes collaboration, transparency, and
accountability within your development team, leading to more secure and
resilient software projects.

Fixing an Alert

Individuals with write permissions for a repository have the ability
to rectify an alert by committing the necessary corrections directly to the
codebase. If the repository is configured to run code scanning during
pull requests, it's advisable to submit a pull request containing your
fixes. This action triggers a comprehensive code scanning analysis of the
changes, ensuring that your solution doesn't introduce any new issues. For
additional guidance, please refer to the resources on "Customizing your
advanced setup for code scanning" and "Triaging code scanning alerts in
pull requests."

Users with write permissions can review resolved alerts by accessing the summary of alerts and selecting the "Closed" tab. The "Closed" list displays both fixed alerts and those that users have dismissed. To efficiently manage alerts, you can employ the free-text search or utilize filters to narrow down the displayed alerts. Subsequently, you can mark all corresponding alerts as closed.

It's important to note that fixes applied to alerts in one branch may not necessarily extend to other branches. To confirm whether an alert has been resolved in a specific branch, utilize the "Branch" filter available in the summary of alerts.

Dismissing an Alert

Dismissing alerts allows repository maintainers to acknowledge and dismiss specific alerts, indicating that they have been reviewed and don't require immediate action. This feature is particularly useful when dealing with false positives, alerts that are not relevant to the current context, or issues that have been addressed through other means. To dismiss an alert, follow these steps:

- **Access the Alert:** Navigate to the summary of alerts in your repository, where you can see a list of all active alerts.

- **Review the Alert:** Click the specific alert you want to dismiss to view its details and context.

- **Dismiss the Alert:** Within the alert details, locate the "Dismiss" or "Resolve" button, usually found at the bottom of the alert. Click it to initiate the dismissal process. Figure 3-20 shows a screen for dismissing code scanning alert.

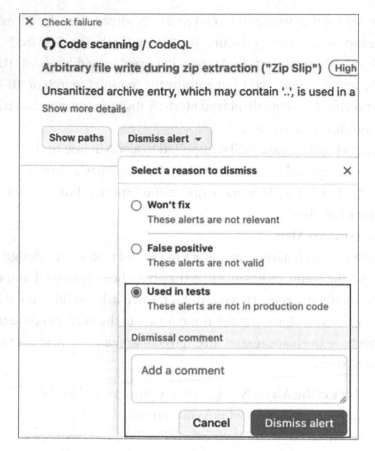

Figure 3-20. *Dismissing code scanning alert*

- **Provide a Reason (Optional):** GitHub might prompt
  you to provide a reason for dismissing the alert. This
  optional step allows you to document the rationale
  behind the dismissal, providing clarity for other
  contributors.

- **Confirm the Dismissal:** After providing a reason (if
  required), confirm the dismissal. The alert will be
  marked as dismissed and will no longer appear on the
  active alert list.

It is essential to use the dismissal feature responsibly, ensuring that only appropriate alerts are dismissed. Dismissing alerts does not fix the underlying issues; it simply acknowledges that the alert has been reviewed and deemed noncritical at the moment.

Please note that the ability to dismiss alerts might be restricted based on repository permissions and settings, ensuring that this feature is utilized judiciously.

Dismissing Multiple Alerts at Once

If your project has multiple alerts that you wish to dismiss for the same reason, you can efficiently handle this task by dismissing them in bulk from the summary of alerts. This approach is especially useful when dealing with several alerts that share a common reason for dismissal. Here is how you can do it:

- **Access the Summary of Alerts:** Navigate to the summary of alerts in your project, where you can view the list of all active alerts.

- **Filter the Alerts (Optional):** If you have specific criteria, you can use filters to narrow down the list. For instance, you might want to filter alerts tagged with a particular Common Weakness Enumeration (CWE) vulnerability.

- **Select Multiple Alerts:** After filtering, select all the alerts that you want to dismiss in bulk. GitHub usually provides checkboxes next to each alert for selection.

- **Initiate Bulk Dismissal:** Look for the "Dismiss" or "Bulk Dismiss" option, usually located at the top or bottom of the list. Click it to initiate the bulk dismissal process.

- **Provide a Common Reason (Optional):** GitHub might prompt you to provide a common reason for dismissing the selected alerts. If required, enter the reason to document why these alerts are being dismissed together.

- **Confirm the Bulk Dismissal:** After providing the reason (if prompted), confirm the bulk dismissal. The selected alerts will be marked as dismissed, and they will no longer appear in the active alert list.

By bulk dismissing alerts, you can efficiently manage multiple notifications that share a common dismissal rationale, streamlining the process and ensuring consistent handling of similar issues.

Branch Protection

Branch protection on GitHub is a powerful feature that allows repository administrators to enforce certain rules and restrictions on branches. By enabling branch protection, you can ensure that changes to critical branches go through a controlled process, including code review, status checks, and other requirements, before they are merged. This helps maintain the integrity and stability of your codebase. Here are the key aspects of branch protection:

- **Pull Request Reviews**

  - With branch protection, you can require that all changes be made via pull requests (PRs). This means that contributors must create a branch, make their changes, and then submit a pull request for review.

- **Code Review Approval**

  - You can enforce code review by requiring a certain number of approvals from designated reviewers before a PR can be merged. This ensures that changes are scrutinized by peers.

- **Status Checks**

  - You can set up status checks to ensure that automated tests (like continuous integration) pass before a PR can be merged. This prevents merging code that might break the build or fail tests.

- **Branch Protection Rules**

  - Branch protection rules allow you to specify conditions that must be met before changes can be made to a branch.

  - Rules can include requiring status checks to pass, specific people to review the code, or even specific files to be modified or left unmodified in the PR.

- **Restrictions on Pushing Directly to Branches**

  - Once a branch is protected, contributors cannot directly push changes to it. All changes must go through pull requests, which are subject to the defined rules.

Creating a Branch Protection Rule

1. **Navigate to Repository Settings:**

   - Go to your repository on GitHub.

   - Click "Settings" (or select it from the dropdown menu if you do not see it). Figure 3-21 shows the screen for navigating to repository settings.

Figure 3-21. *Repository settings*

2. **Access Branch Protection Settings:**

   - In the "Code and automation" section of the sidebar, click "Branches."

   - Click "Branch protection rules." Figure 3-22 shows the screen for branch protection rules.

Figure 3-22. *Branch protection rules*

3. **Create a New Rule:**

   - Click "Add branch protection rule."

   - Specify the branch name or pattern you want to protect under "Branch name pattern."

- Specify protect matching branches.

  - Require a pull request before merging. When enabled, all commits must be made to a non-protected branch and submitted via a pull request before they can be merged into a branch that matches this rule.

  - Require status checks to pass before merging. Choose which <u>status checks</u> must pass before branches can be merged into a branch that matches this rule. When enabled, commits must first be pushed to another branch, then merged or pushed directly to a branch that matches this rule after status checks have passed.

  - Require conversation resolution before merging. When enabled, all conversations on code must be resolved before a pull request can be merged into a branch that matches this rule.

  - Require signed commits. Commits pushed to matching branches must have verified signatures.

  - Require linear history. Prevent merge commits from being pushed to matching branches.

  - Require deployments to succeed before merging. Choose which environments must be successfully deployed to before branches can be merged into a branch that matches this rule.

  - Lock branch. Branch is read-only. Users cannot push to the branch.

- Do not allow bypassing the preceding settings. The preceding settings will apply to administrators and custom roles with the "bypass branch protections" permission.

- Restrict who can push to matching branches. Specify people, teams, or apps allowed to push to matching branches. Required status checks will still prevent these people, teams, and apps from merging if the checks fail.

- Additionally, you can specify rules applied to everyone, including administrators:

  - **Allow Force Pushes:** Permit force pushes for all users with push access.

  - **Allow Deletions:** Allow users with push access to delete matching branches.

- Click "Create." Figure 3-23 shows the screen for additional branch protection rules settings.

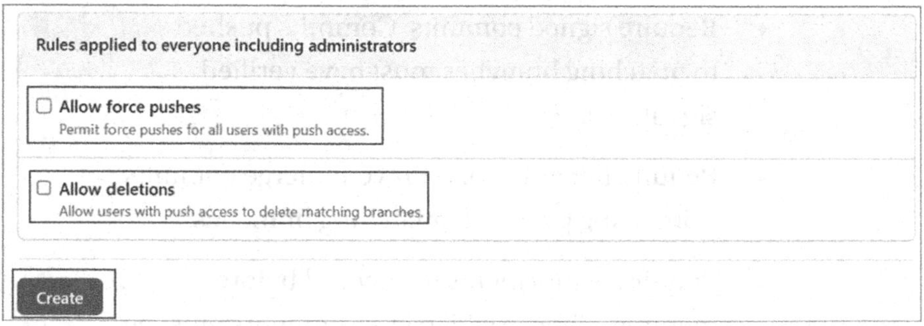

Rules applied to everyone including administrators

☐ Allow force pushes
Permit force pushes for all users with push access.

☐ Allow deletions
Allow users with push access to delete matching branches.

Create

Figure 3-23. *Additional options for all users while creating a branch protection rule*

Editing a Branch Protection Rule

1. **Access Branch Protection Settings:**

   - Navigate to the repository settings and click "Branches."

   - Locate the branch protection rule you want to edit.

2. **Edit the Rule:**

   - Click "Edit" next to the branch protection rule.

   - Make the desired changes to the rule, such as modifying branch name patterns, adding/removing requirements, or changing access controls.

   - Click "Save changes." Figure 3-24 shows the screen for editing branch protection rules.

Figure 3-24. *Editing branch protection rules*

Deleting a Branch Protection Rule

1. **Access Branch Protection Settings:**

   - Navigate to the repository settings and click "Branches."

   - Locate the branch protection rule you want to delete.

2. **Delete the Rule:**

   - Click "Delete" next to the branch protection rule.

   - Confirm the deletion. Figure 3-25 shows the screen for deleting a branch protection rule.

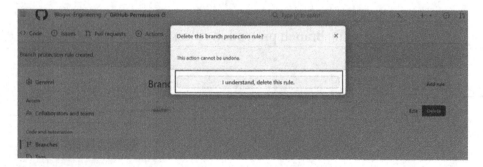

Figure 3-25. *Deleting a branch protection rule*

These actions allow repository administrators to manage the protection rules for branches, ensuring that code changes are reviewed, tested, and meet specific criteria before being merged into protected branches. These practices help maintain code quality, security, and collaboration standards within the repository.

Code Scanning

Code scanning on GitHub refers to a security feature that automatically analyzes the code in repositories to find security vulnerabilities, bugs, and other issues. It helps developers identify and fix potential problems in their codebase, enhancing overall software security and reliability.

GitHub's code scanning works by integrating security tools directly into the development workflow. When developers push code changes to a repository, GitHub automatically triggers various security analysis tools, such as CodeQL and other third-party scanners, to scan the new code. These tools search for known security vulnerabilities, coding errors, and other issues by analyzing the code syntax, dependencies, and patterns. If any issues are found during the scanning process, GitHub creates alerts for the repository owners and contributors. These alerts provide detailed information about the problem, including the affected code files and specific lines of code. Developers can then review the alerts, understand the issues, and take appropriate actions to fix them.

Code scanning on GitHub is a proactive approach to security, enabling developers to catch potential problems early in the development process. It helps prevent security vulnerabilities and bugs from making their way into the final product, ultimately improving the overall security posture of software projects. To monitor results from code scanning across your repositories or your organization, you can use webhooks and the code scanning API.

- Enable code scanning to automatically find vulnerabilities in your code using static analysis. You can configure workflows to run these scans regularly.

- Code scanning alerts can be found in the "Security" tab of your repository.

There are three main methods to utilize CodeQL analysis for code scanning:

- **Default Setup:** GitHub offers a convenient default setup option that quickly configures CodeQL analysis for code scanning in your repository. This setup automatically selects the languages to analyze, the

query suite to run, and the events that trigger scans. If
you prefer more control, you can manually choose the
query suite and languages to analyze. Once CodeQL
is enabled, GitHub Actions will execute workflow runs
to scan your code. For detailed instructions, refer to
"Configuring default setup for code scanning" in the
GitHub documentation.

- **Advanced Setup:** For more customization, you can opt
  for the advanced setup. This method involves adding
  the CodeQL workflow to your repository, generating a
  customizable workflow file. This file uses the GitHub/
  codeql-action to run the CodeQL command-line
  interface (CLI). This approach gives you greater
  flexibility in tailoring the scanning process according to
  your specific requirements.

- **Integration with External CI Systems:** If your project
  uses an existing continuous integration (CI) system,
  you can run the CodeQL CLI directly within that
  system. After analyzing your code, upload the results
  to GitHub to view code scanning alerts. This approach
  allows seamless integration with your current CI setup.

CodeQL

CodeQL revolutionizes the way we approach code analysis by
treating code as data, ensuring more robust identification of potential
vulnerabilities compared to traditional static analyzers. Here is how
CodeQL works:

- **Generate CodeQL Database:** Start by generating a
  CodeQL database that accurately represents your
  codebase.

- **Run CodeQL Queries:** Execute CodeQL queries on the generated database. These queries pinpoint issues within your codebase.

- **Code Scanning Alerts:** The results of these queries manifest as code scanning alerts directly on GitHub when CodeQL is integrated with code scanning.

CodeQL is versatile, supporting both compiled and interpreted languages. It excels in identifying vulnerabilities and errors in code written in the following supported languages:

C/C++, C#, Go, Java/Kotlin, JavaScript/TypeScript, Python, Ruby, Swift

---

Note

- CodeQL analysis for Swift is currently in beta. During this beta phase, the analysis of Swift might be less comprehensive than that of other languages. Additionally, support for Swift 5.8 is not yet available.

- CodeQL analysis for Kotlin is also in beta, with potential limitations compared to the analysis of other languages.

- To analyze code written in Java, Kotlin, or both, you can use the "java-kotlin" option.

- Similarly, for code written in JavaScript, TypeScript, or both, you can use the "javascript-typescript" option.

- By utilizing CodeQL, you can ensure a higher degree of confidence in identifying vulnerabilities, making your codebase more secure and robust.

CodeQL Database

A CodeQL database is a structured representation of source code that enables static analysis to be performed on the codebase. CodeQL databases are used on GitHub's CodeQL analysis to identify security vulnerabilities, bugs, and other issues in software projects. Here are the key components of a CodeQL database:

- **Code Representation**

  - **Abstract Syntax Tree (AST):** Represents the syntactic structure of the source code, capturing the hierarchical arrangement of code elements.

  - **Data-Flow Graph (DFG):** Represents how data flows between variables in the code, helping track the flow of values and information.

  - **Control-Flow Graph (CFG):** Represents the control flow in the code, showing the possible paths the program can take during execution.

- **Database Schema**

  - **Tables:** CodeQL databases consist of tables that store information about various code constructs. For example, there might be tables for expressions, statements, functions, variables, etc.

  - **Relations:** Define the connections between different tables, allowing complex queries to be formulated.

- **Database Generation**

  - **Extraction Process:** The process of creating a CodeQL database involves extracting code from source files and transforming it into a format suitable for analysis.

- **Language Support:** CodeQL supports a variety
  of programming languages, including but not
  limited to C/C++, C#, Java, JavaScript, Python,
  Ruby, and Go.

- **Querying**

  - **CodeQL Query Language (QL):** CodeQL provides
    a query language that allows users to write queries
    to analyze the data stored in the database. Queries
    are used to identify patterns, vulnerabilities, and
    other issues in the codebase.

  - **Standard Queries:** GitHub provides standard
    CodeQL queries written by GitHub researchers
    and the community. Users can also create custom
    queries tailored to their specific analysis needs.

- **Customization**

  - **Query Suites:** CodeQL query suites allow users to
    organize and select queries based on file names,
    locations, or metadata properties. Query suites
    help manage and categorize multiple queries for
    analysis.

  - **Language Packs:** Language-specific CodeQL packs
    contain rules and queries tailored for a particular
    programming language, aiding in language-specific
    code analysis.

- **Usage**

  - **Automated Analysis:** CodeQL databases are
    utilized in automated security checks performed
    by GitHub Actions and other CI/CD systems. These
    checks help identify security vulnerabilities and
    code quality issues.

  - **Manual Analysis:** Security researchers and
    developers can manually write and execute
    CodeQL queries against databases to perform
    in-depth analysis and identify specific issues in
    the code.

CodeQL databases play a crucial role in automating security checks
and enabling developers to perform variant analysis, ensuring the
software's security and reliability.

CodeQL Queries

CodeQL queries are written in the CodeQL query language and
are used to perform static code analysis on software projects. These
queries allow developers and security researchers to identify patterns,
vulnerabilities, and other issues within a codebase. CodeQL queries
are particularly powerful for finding security vulnerabilities and bugs in
software. The following are some key aspects of CodeQL queries:

- **Syntax**

  - CodeQL queries are written in a declarative
    language that resembles SQL. They consist of
    predicates, expressions, and logical operators.
    Here's a basic structure of a CodeQL query:

    from ... where ... select ...

- **Components**

  - **From Clause:** Specifies the data source, such as variables, functions, classes, etc., that the query will analyze

  - **Where Clause:** Contains conditions and filters that narrow down the scope of the analysis

  - **Select Clause:** Determines what information to retrieve as the query result

- **Predicates**

  - Predicates are reusable code patterns defined in CodeQL libraries. They encapsulate common coding patterns, security vulnerabilities, or best practices. Developers can use existing predicates or create custom ones.

- **Data Flow and Control Flow**

  - CodeQL allows tracking data flow (how data moves between variables) and control flow (how the program executes) in the queries. This enables the analysis of how data is used, manipulated, and propagated through the code.

- **Taint Analysis**

  - Taint analysis in CodeQL focuses on identifying sources of untrusted data (tainted data) and tracking how this data propagates through the code. This is crucial for identifying security vulnerabilities related to user input.

- **Result Presentation**

  - When a query is executed, the results are presented as a list of code locations or instances where the query pattern matches the code. These results typically include file names, line numbers, and descriptions of the issues found.

- **Standard Queries**

  - GitHub provides a set of standard CodeQL queries covering common security vulnerabilities. These queries are continuously updated and improved by GitHub and the open source community. They serve as a starting point for code analysis.

- **Custom Queries**

  - Developers and security experts can create custom CodeQL queries tailored to specific projects or requirements. These queries can focus on project-specific coding patterns, business rules, or security policies.

- **Integrations**

  - CodeQL queries can be integrated into CI/CD pipelines, IDEs, and code review tools. This allows developers to receive feedback on potential issues directly within their development workflows.

CodeQL queries are an essential tool for identifying and addressing security vulnerabilities and improving the overall code quality of software projects. Developers often use a combination of standard and custom queries to comprehensively analyze their codebases.

Configuring Default Setup for Code Scanning

The default setup for code scanning is the fastest and simplest way to enable code scanning for your repository. It automatically generates a tailored code scanning configuration based on your repository's code. Once enabled, your repository's code will be scanned:

- Whenever there's a push to the repository's default branch or any protected branch

- When creating or committing to a pull request based on the repository's default branch or any protected branch

- On a weekly basis

Note   If no push or pull requests occur in a repository for 60 days, the weekly schedule will be disabled to conserve your GitHub Actions minutes.

You can swiftly enable the automatically chosen default setup configuration to start scanning your code promptly. Alternatively, you have the option to customize certain aspects of the configuration to align it with your specific code scanning requirements. If you opt for customization, you can specify

- The programming languages that the default setup will analyze.

- The query suite that the default setup will employ. For further details, refer to "Built-in CodeQL query suites" in the GitHub documentation.

Additionally, you can apply the default setup across multiple or all repositories within an organization simultaneously. To qualify for the default setup for code scanning, your repository must meet the following criteria:

- It includes at least one programming language supported by CodeQL.

- GitHub Actions are enabled for the repository.

- The repository is publicly visible.

Even if your repository includes languages not supported by CodeQL (such as R), you can still use the default setup.

Configuring a Default Setup for a Repository

- **Access Repository Settings:**

  - Go to the main page of your repository on GitHub.com.

- **Enable GitHub Actions for Forks (If Applicable):**

  - If you're configuring a default setup for a fork, you must first enable GitHub Actions. Under your repository name, click **Actions**.

  - Click "**I understand my workflows, go ahead and enable them**." Please note that enabling this will activate all existing workflows in your fork.

- **Navigate to Repository Settings:**

  - Under your repository name, click **Settings**. If you can't find the "Settings" tab, click the dropdown menu, and then select Settings.

- **Access Code Scanning Settings:**

  - In the left sidebar, find and click "**Code security and analysis**" under the "Security" section.

- **Initiate Default Setup:**

  - In the "Code scanning" section, click "**Set up**," then choose "**Default.**"

- **Review Default Configuration:**

  - A dialog will appear, summarizing the "CodeQL default configuration" automatically created by the default setup.

  - If your repository includes only compiled CodeQL-supported languages (e.g., Java), you'll need to select the languages you want to add to your default setup configuration.

- **Customize Your Setup (Optional):**

  - To customize your code scanning setup, click "**Edit.**"

  - Add or remove languages from the analysis by selecting or deselecting them in the "Languages" section. Choose the compiled languages you wish to analyze with the default setup.

  - Specify your preferred CodeQL query suite in the "Query suites" section.

- **Enable CodeQL:**

  - Review your setup settings, then click "**Enable CodeQL.**" This action will initiate a workflow to test the newly generated configuration automatically.

- **Handle Switch from Advanced Setup (Optional):**

  - If you're transitioning from an advanced setup to a default setup, a warning will inform you that the default setup will override existing code scanning configurations. This means the existing workflow file will be disabled, and any CodeQL analysis API uploads will be blocked.

- **View Your Configuration (Optional):**

  - If you want to view your default setup configuration after enabling it, click "**View CodeQL configuration.**"

Once you've set up code scanning using the default configuration and it runs successfully at least once, you can begin reviewing and addressing the generated code scanning alerts.

Configuring Advanced Setup for Code Scanning with CodeQL

To tailor your code scanning process, you have the option to create and modify a workflow file. If you select the advanced setup, GitHub provides a basic workflow file that you can customize according to your needs.

Note   You can configure code scanning for any public repository where you have write access.

Here's how to set it up:

- **Navigate to Your Repository Settings:**

  - Go to the main page of your repository on GitHub.com.

  - Click **Settings**. If you can't see the "Settings" tab, click the dropdown menu and then select Settings.

- **Access Code Scanning Settings:**

  - In the sidebar, locate and click **Code security and analysis** under the "Security" section.

- **Switch to Advanced Setup:**

  - Scroll down to the "Code scanning" section.

  - Click **Set up**, then select **Advanced**. Figure 3-26 shows the screen for code scanning configuration for a repository.

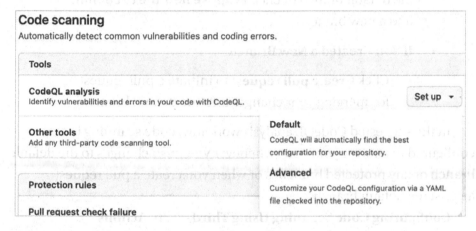

Figure 3-26. *Code scanning configuration*

- **Customize Code Scanning by Editing the Workflow:**

  - Modify the workflow as needed. Usually, you can commit the provided CodeQL analysis workflow without alterations. However, certain third-party workflows might require additional configuration. Be sure to read the comments within the workflow file before committing.

- **Commit Your Changes:**

  - Click **Commit changes...** to open the commit changes form.

- Enter a commit message in the designated field.

- Decide whether you want to commit directly to the default branch or create a new branch and initiate a pull request.

- Click **Commit new file** to commit the workflow file to the default branch or click **Propose new file** to commit it to a new branch.

- **If You Created a New Branch**

  - Click **Create pull request** to initiate a pull request for merging your changes into the default branch.

In the suggested CodeQL analysis workflow, code scanning is configured to analyze your code whenever you push changes to the default branch or any protected branches or when you create a pull request against the default branch.

Configuring Code Scanning Using Third-Party Actions

GitHub provides preconfigured starter workflows for security features like code scanning, streamlining the process of setting up your code scanning workflows without having to create them from scratch. Here is how to access and customize these starter workflows:

- **Access Starter Workflows:**

  - Go to the main page of your repository on GitHub.com.

  - Click the "Actions" tab under your repository name.

- **Select a New Workflow:**

  - If your repository already has at least one workflow configured, click "New workflow" to explore starter workflows. If there are no existing workflows, proceed to the next step.

- **Choose a Security Workflow:**

  - In the "Choose a workflow" or "Get started with GitHub Actions" view, scroll down to the "Security" category.

  - Click "Configure" under the specific security workflow you want to set up. If needed, click "View all" to find more security workflows.

- **Customize the Workflow:**

  - Follow the instructions provided within the workflow to customize it according to your requirements. You can modify the workflow parameters and settings.

  - If you need more general assistance with workflows, click "Documentation" on the right pane of the workflow page for detailed guidance.

By using these starter workflows, you can efficiently configure your security-related workflows, ensuring your repository is protected without the hassle of creating workflows entirely from the ground up.

Customizing Your Advanced Setup for Code Scanning

Customizing your advanced setup for code scanning allows you to tailor the scanning process to your specific needs and requirements. Here is how you can customize your advanced setup for code scanning on GitHub:

- **Access Repository Settings:**

  - On GitHub.com, navigate to the main page of your repository.

  - Under your repository name, click **Settings**. If you don't see the "Settings" tab, click the dropdown menu next to your repository name and select **Settings**.

- **Navigate to Code Scanning Settings:**

  - In the "Security" section of the sidebar, click **Code security and analysis**.

- **Switch to Advanced Setup:**

  - Scroll down to the "Code scanning" section.

  - Click **Set up**, then select **Advanced**.

- **Customize the Workflow:**

  - Edit the workflow to match your specific requirements. You can modify various aspects of the workflow, such as

    - **Languages:** Choose the programming languages you want to scan for vulnerabilities.

    - **Queries:** Select the CodeQL query suites you want to use for the analysis.

    - **Workflow File:** Edit the workflow file directly to add custom steps, actions, or conditions.

- **Commit Changes:**

  - After customizing the workflow, scroll down to the bottom of the page.

  - Provide a commit message explaining the changes you made.

  - Choose whether to commit directly to the default branch or create a new branch and start a pull request.

  - Click **Commit changes** to apply your customized code scanning setup.

By customizing your advanced setup for code scanning, you ensure that the scanning process aligns perfectly with your project's needs, enhancing security and identifying vulnerabilities effectively.

Editing a Code Scanning Workflow

GitHub stores workflow files in the .github/workflows directory within your repository. To locate a specific workflow file, you can simply search for its file name. For instance, the default workflow file for CodeQL code scanning is named codeql-analysis.yml. Here are the steps to edit a workflow file in your repository:

- Navigate to the workflow file you wish to modify within your repository.

- In the top-right corner of the file view, click the pencil icon to access the workflow editor.

- After making the necessary changes, click "Start commit" and fill out the "Commit changes" form. You can either commit the changes directly to the current branch or create a new branch and initiate a pull request.

By editing a code scanning workflow, you can customize the scanning process, add additional steps, integrate with other tools, and ensure the workflow aligns with your project's specific requirements.

Configuring Frequency

You have the flexibility to set up the CodeQL analysis workflow to scan code either on a scheduled basis or in response to specific events occurring within a repository. Scanning code each time someone pushes a change or creates a pull request is crucial for preventing the introduction of new vulnerabilities and errors into the codebase. Additionally, scheduling regular scans ensures that you stay informed about the latest vulnerabilities and errors identified by GitHub, security researchers, and the community. This proactive approach helps maintain the repository's security, even during periods when developers are not actively working on it.

Scanning on Push

By default, the CodeQL analysis workflow is configured to activate upon the on:push event. This setting initiates a code scan whenever there's a push to the default branch of the repository or any protected branches. To ensure code scanning triggers on a specific branch, the workflow file must be present in that particular branch. When code scanning is set to activate on push events, the scan results are displayed in the Security tab of your repository.

Moreover, if a scan triggered by the on:push event generates results that can be linked to an open pull request, these alerts will automatically be visible on the pull request. These alerts appear in the same locations as other pull request alerts. The system identifies these alerts by comparing the existing analysis of the head of the branch with the analysis conducted for the target branch.

Scanning Pull Requests

The default CodeQL analysis workflow is designed to utilize the pull_request event, which activates code scanning for pull requests targeted at the default branch. However, for pull requests originating from private forks, the pull_request event will only be triggered if you've enabled the "Run workflows from fork pull requests" option in the repository settings. If you configure code scanning for pull requests, the results will be presented as alerts within a pull request check.

By using the pull_request trigger, configured to scan the pull request's merge commit instead of the head commit, you can achieve more efficient and accurate results compared to scanning the head of the branch with each push. Nevertheless, in cases where you're using a CI/CD system that cannot be configured to trigger on pull requests, you can still employ the on:push trigger.

Avoiding Unnecessary Scans of Pull Requests

To prevent specific pull requests targeted against the default branch from triggering a code scan, regardless of the changed files, you can configure this behavior by utilizing **on:pull_request:paths-ignore** or **on:pull_request:paths** in the code scanning workflow. For instance, if the changes in a pull request are limited to files with the extensions .md or .txt, you can use the **paths-ignore** array. Figure 3-27 shows a yaml file example.

```
on:
  pull_request:
    paths-ignore:
      - '**/*.md'
      - '**/*.txt'
```

Figure 3-27. *yaml file for ignoring paths for avoiding scans*

Scanning on a Schedule

To schedule regular code scans in your GitHub repository, you can configure the CodeQL analysis workflow to run on a specific schedule. Here are the steps to set up scanning on a schedule:

- **Create or Edit the Workflow File:**

  - Navigate to the **.github/workflows** directory in your repository.

  - Create a new workflow file (e.g., **codeql-analysis. yml**) or edit an existing one if available.

- **Configure the Workflow Trigger:**

  - Use the **schedule** event in the workflow file to define the schedule. Figure 3-28 shows a schedule file example.

```
on:
    schedule:
      - cron: '0 5 * * *'
```

Figure 3-28. codeql-analysis.yml file example

- In this example, the **cron** syntax **0 5 * * *** specifies the schedule as 5 AM UTC daily.

- **Define the Rest of the Workflow:**

  - Configure the rest of your CodeQL analysis workflow steps, including setting up the CodeQL analysis, defining the languages to analyze, specifying query suites, etc.

- **Commit and Push the Workflow File:**

  - After configuring the workflow, save the changes to the file.

  - Commit the changes and push them to your repository.

Once committed, the workflow will be triggered based on the defined schedule. GitHub Actions will automatically run the workflow at the specified time and frequency, allowing you to perform regular code scans on your repository.

Code Scanning with Your Existing CI System

Instead of running code scanning within GitHub using GitHub Actions, an alternative approach is to analyze code in an external continuous integration or continuous delivery/deployment (CI/CD) system and then upload the results to GitHub. To implement this, you can either integrate the CodeQL CLI into your third-party system or use another third-party static analysis tool capable of producing results in the Static Analysis Results Interchange Format (SARIF) 2.1.0 data format.

The CodeQL CLI serves as a stand-alone, command-line tool for analyzing code. Alerts generated through external code scanning are displayed in the same manner as those generated within GitHub. If code scanning is performed using multiple configurations, the same alert might be generated by more than one setup. In such cases, you can check the status of the alert for each configuration on the alert page.

Setting Up Your Analysis Tool

Setting up the CodeQL CLI involves installing the CLI tools and configuring them to analyze code in your repositories. Here are the general steps to set up the CodeQL CLI:

Prerequisites

- **GitHub Account:** Ensure you have a GitHub account and access to the repository you want to analyze.

- **CodeQL CLI Installation:** Install the CodeQL CLI tools on your local machine. You can download them from GitHub: `https://github.com/github/codeql-cli-binaries/releases`.

187

Steps to Set Up the CodeQL CLI

- **Install the CodeQL CLI:**

  - Download the appropriate version of the CodeQL CLI for your operating system.

  - Follow the installation instructions provided in the CodeQL CLI documentation or the README file.

- **Set Up the CodeQL Database:**

  - Initialize a CodeQL database for your repository. Run the following command in your repository directory:

    ```
    codeql database create <database-path>
    --language=<language>
    ```

    - Replace **<database-path>** with the path where you want to store the database and **<language>** with the programming language of your repository (e.g., **javascript**).

- **Extract Data for Analysis:**

  - Extract data from your codebase into the CodeQL database. Run the following command:

    ```
    codeql database analyze <database-path>
    --source-root=<path-to-source>
    ```

    - Replace **<path-to-source>** with the root path of your source code.

- **Run CodeQL Queries:**

  - Write or use existing CodeQL queries to analyze your code for vulnerabilities.

- Run CodeQL queries against the database. For
  example:

  ```
  codeql query run <query-file>.ql
  --database=<database-path>
  ```

  - Replace **<query-file>.ql** with the path to your
    CodeQL query file.

- **View Results:**

  - Review the results of the queries. CodeQL will
    output potential vulnerabilities and issues found in
    your code.

- **Automate the Process (Optional):**

  - Integrate CodeQL CLI commands into your CI/CD
    pipelines to automate code scanning on every push
    or pull request.

Remember to refer to the official https://codeql.github.com/docs/
for detailed information and specific commands related to your use case
and programming language.

Analyzing Code

Analyzing code with the CodeQL CLI or any other analysis tool
involves several steps. Here is a generic process that you can follow,
considering the CodeQL CLI as the analysis tool:

- **Clone the Repository:**

  - Clone the repository that contains the code you
    want to analyze. Use Git to clone the repository to
    your local machine:

    ```
    $ git clone <repository-url>
    $ cd <repository-directory>
    ```

- **Set Up the Environment:**

  - Make sure you have the necessary dependencies installed for the codebase. This may include libraries, compilers, or interpreters specific to your project.

- **Find Build Commands (Optional):**

  - If you are using a specific build system, locate the build commands. This information is often present in the project's configuration files (such as **package.json** for Node.js projects, **pom.xml** for Maven projects, etc.).

  - For example, in a Node.js project, the build command might be

    ```
    $ npm install
    ```

- **Create a CodeQL Database:**

  - As shown in **Steps to Set Up the CodeQL CLI**

- **Extract Data for Analysis:**

  - As shown in **Steps to Set Up the CodeQL CLI**

- **Run CodeQL Queries:**

  - As shown in **Steps to Set Up the CodeQL CLI**

- **Review the Results:**

  - The SARIF file contains the analysis results. You can use various tools to visualize and interpret these results.

- **Integrate into CI/CD (Optional):**
  - Integrate these commands into your CI/CD
    pipelines to automate code scanning on every push
    or pull request.

Remember, the specific commands and steps might vary based on your project's structure, language, and the analysis tool you are using.

Generating a Token for Authentication with GitHub

For any continuous integration (CI) server to upload analysis results to GitHub, it requires authorization in the form of a GitHub App or a personal access token. This applies whether you are utilizing the CodeQL CLI, the REST API, or any other method. The crucial permission needed is **security_events write**.

If your CI servers are already utilizing a token with this specific scope to fetch repositories from GitHub, you can potentially use the same token for uploading results. However, if such a token doesn't exist, it's advisable to create a new one with the necessary **security_events write** permission. This new token should be stored securely within the CI system's secret store for secure access and usage.

Uploading Your Results to GitHub

After analyzing your code, generating SARIF results, and ensuring authentication with GitHub, you can proceed to upload the results. By default, code scanning expects a single SARIF results file per analysis in a repository. Therefore, if you upload a second SARIF results file for a commit, it replaces the original data. However, there might be scenarios where you need to upload multiple SARIF files for one analysis.

For instance, your analysis tool might generate distinct SARIF files for different languages it analyzes or for different rule sets it employs. If you intend to upload more than one set of results for a commit, each set must be uniquely identified. The method to specify a category for a SARIF upload varies based on the analysis approach you're using.

Uploading Results to GitHub

To upload SARIF results to GitHub, follow these general steps:

- **Ensure Authentication:** Make sure you have authentication credentials such as a personal access token or GitHub App token with the **security_events** write permission. If your CI server doesn't have such a token, create a new one and store it securely in your CI system's secret store.

- **Generate SARIF Files:** Use your code analysis tool or the CodeQL CLI to generate SARIF results files. Ensure that each analysis produces a separate SARIF file if you're analyzing multiple languages or using different rule sets.

- **Upload SARIF Files:**
  - **Using the CodeQL CLI:** If you're using the CodeQL CLI, you can use the **codeql** command-line tool to upload SARIF results to GitHub. Here's a general command template:

    codeql upload sarif -r <repository>
    -c <commit_sha> <sarif_file_path>

    - Replace **<repository>** with your repository name, **<commit_sha>** with the commit SHA where the analysis was performed, and **<sarif_file_path>** with the path to your SARIF file.

  - **Using the REST API:** If you're using a different analysis tool, you can use the GitHub REST API to upload SARIF results. Make a POST request to the following endpoint:

    POST /repos/:owner/:repo/code-scanning/sarifs

- Include your SARIF data in the request body.

- Ensure that you specify unique identifiers for each set of results if you're uploading multiple sets for a single commit. The way to specify a category for a SARIF upload varies based on your analysis method.

- **Verify Results:** After uploading, verify the results on the GitHub Security tab or the specific pull request associated with the analysis. Ensure that the uploaded results are accurately reflected in the GitHub interface.

Please refer to the documentation specific to your analysis tool or the GitHub API documentation for detailed and tool-specific instructions on uploading SARIF results. By using GitHub code scanning, developers can proactively identify and address security vulnerabilities, ensuring the overall security and reliability of their software projects.

Secret Scanning

GitHub performs automatic scans on repositories to detect known types of secrets. The primary goal of this process is to prevent the unauthorized or fraudulent use of secrets that may have been unintentionally committed to repositories. The secret scanning alerts for partners operate by automatically scanning public repositories and public npm packages. The purpose of this scanning is to notify service providers about any exposed secrets found on GitHub.com. Users also have access to secret scanning alerts at no cost on all public repositories. Organizations that use GitHub Enterprise Cloud, with a license for GitHub Advanced Security, can extend this feature to private and internal repositories.

Regarding the secret scanning process, it's essential to recognize that when your project interacts with external services, you often employ tokens or private keys for authentication. These tokens and keys are considered secrets, which should be kept secure. If you inadvertently commit a secret into a repository, anyone with read access to the repository can misuse it to gain access to the external service with your privileges. For security reasons, it's advisable to store secrets in a dedicated, protected location external to your project's repository. The secret scanning functionality comprehensively scans your entire Git history, including all branches in your GitHub repository, in search of secrets. It also extends its search to issue descriptions and comments for potential secret exposure. Moreover, secret scanning covers the titles, descriptions, and comments within both open and closed historical issues. Any discovered secrets are reported as alerts on GitHub.

GitHub's secret scanning feature is available in two forms:

- **Secret Scanning Alerts for Partners:** This automated scanning is applied to all public repositories and public npm packages. Service providers collaborate with GitHub to define specific secret patterns for scanning. Whenever a string matches these patterns, the relevant partner is directly informed.

- **Secret Scanning Alerts for Users:** Users in the following categories have the ability to enable and configure additional scanning:

  - Owners of public repositories on GitHub.com

  - Organizations that own public repositories

  - Organizations utilizing GitHub Enterprise Cloud for public repositories (free) and private or internal repositories with a GitHub Advanced Security license

Any strings matching predefined patterns from secret scanning partners, other service providers, or patterns defined by you or your organization are reported as alerts in the Security tab of repositories.

If a string in a public repository matches a partner's pattern, it is also reported to the partner. To track the actions taken in response to secret scanning alerts, GitHub provides auditing tools like historical timelines, security overview, audit logs, the API, and webhooks. Additionally, you can enable secret scanning as a push protection feature for a repository or organization. This feature prevents contributors from pushing code that contains detected secrets. Contributors must either remove the secret(s) from the push or bypass the protection to proceed. Admins can specify a custom link with resources specific to the organization to help contributors. For individuals, you can enable push protection for yourself, ensuring protection when pushing to any public repository.

Note   When forking a repository with secret scanning or push protection enabled, these features are not automatically activated on the fork. You can enable secret scanning or push protection on the fork in the same manner as you would on a stand-alone repository.

Secret Scanning Alerts for Partners

When you make a repository public on GitHub or push changes to a public repository, GitHub automatically scans the code for secrets that match specific patterns defined by partner organizations. This scanning also extends to public packages available on the npm registry. Additionally, secret scanning actively searches through issue descriptions and comments for any potential secrets. If secret scanning detects a potential secret, GitHub notifies the service provider who issued that secret. The service provider then validates the identified string and assesses the associated risks to both you and them. Based on this evaluation, they may choose to revoke the secret, issue a new one, or directly contact you to address the situation. It's important to note that the specific actions taken by the service provider depend on the perceived risks involved.

For public repositories, it's essential to understand that you cannot modify the configuration of secret scanning for partner patterns. GitHub handles this process automatically to enhance security measures for public codebases. GitHub employs distinct sets of default secret scanning patterns to enhance security across different scenarios:

- **Partner Patterns:** These patterns identify potential secrets in all public repositories and public npm packages. GitHub collaborates with partners to enhance the effectiveness of these patterns, contributing to a more secure coding environment. More details about the partner program can be found in the "Secret Scanning Partner Program."

- **User Alert Patterns:** These patterns are designed to identify potential secrets specifically in public repositories where secret scanning alerts for users have been enabled. GitHub users can leverage these alerts to enhance security in their public repositories.

- **Push Protection Patterns:** These patterns are utilized in repositories where secret scanning is enabled as a push protection mechanism. They help detect potential secrets, preventing contributors from pushing sensitive information accidentally.

Owners of public repositories and organizations using GitHub Enterprise Cloud with GitHub Advanced Security have the option to enable secret scanning alerts for users on their repositories, ensuring an added layer of security. If you encounter situations where you believe a secret should have been detected but was not, it's crucial to verify whether GitHub supports the specific secret in question.

Secret Scanning Partner Program

GitHub actively scans repositories to identify common secret formats, preventing accidental exposure of sensitive credentials. This scanning is automatic for public repositories and public npm packages. Additionally, repository administrators and organization owners can enable secret scanning for private repositories. As a service provider, you have the option to collaborate with GitHub by including your secret formats in their scanning process. Here is how it works:

- **Automatic Scanning**

  - GitHub automatically scans public repositories and public npm packages for known secret formats.

  - Repository administrators and organization owners can activate secret scanning for private repositories.

- **Collaboration Opportunity**

  - Service providers can partner with GitHub by adding their secret formats to GitHub's scanning algorithms.

- **Detection and Alerts**

  - When a match is found in a public repository, GitHub sends the detected secret information to an HTTP endpoint specified by the service provider.

  - In private repositories with secret scanning enabled, both repository administrators and the person who committed the secret are promptly alerted. They can then review and manage the detected secret on GitHub.

This partnership ensures swift detection of accidental credential exposures, allowing for proactive management and protection of sensitive data. Joining the secret scanning partner program provides a valuable layer of security for both service providers and GitHub users.

Partner Alerts

Partner alerts are notifications sent to secret providers whenever a leak involving one of their secrets is reported. GitHub actively scans public repositories and public npm packages for secrets issued by specific service providers. When a secret is detected within a commit, GitHub alerts the respective service provider. Notably, if accessing a resource requires paired credentials, GitHub generates an alert only when both parts of the pair are found in the same file. This approach ensures that crucial security breaches are not obscured by partial leak information. Pair matching also reduces false positives, as both elements of a pair must be used together to access the provider's resource.

User Alerts

User alerts are notifications provided to GitHub users. These alerts are generated when secret scanning alerts for users are enabled. GitHub scans repositories for secrets issued by various service providers and creates user alerts. Users can view these alerts on the Security tab of the repository. Like partner alerts, user alerts are created only when both parts of a paired credential are detected in the same file. This method prevents vital security issues from being overshadowed by partial leaks and minimizes false positives.

Push Protection Alerts

Push protection alerts are user alerts triggered by push protection. Secret scanning, functioning as push protection, scans repositories for secrets issued by specific service providers. However, push protection alerts are not generated for secrets bypassed with user-based push protection.

For scenarios where accessing a resource demands paired credentials, alerts are created only when both parts of the pair are identified in the same file. This practice ensures that significant security risks are not concealed behind partial leak information and reduces the occurrence of false positives. It's important to note that older versions of certain tokens might not be supported by push protection due to a higher likelihood of generating false positives. Push protection may not apply to legacy tokens, such as Azure Storage Keys. GitHub exclusively supports recently created tokens that do not match legacy patterns.

Supported Secrets

GitHub supports several types of secrets for secret scanning. These secrets are scanned within repositories to prevent fraudulent use and enhance security. Here are some types of the supported secrets:

- **Access Tokens:** Access tokens are used for authenticating with GitHub APIs. They grant specific permissions for various operations. GitHub scans repositories for exposed access tokens to prevent unauthorized access.

- **API Keys:** API keys are alphanumeric strings used by applications to authenticate external services. GitHub scans for API keys that might have been mistakenly committed to the repository, ensuring they are not misused.

- **Service Tokens:** Service tokens are issued by services like AWS or Azure and are used for secure communication between services. GitHub scans for leaked service tokens to prevent unauthorized interactions.

- **Encryption Keys:** Encryption keys are used to encode and decode sensitive data. If encryption keys are exposed, it could lead to data breaches. GitHub scans repositories for leaked encryption keys to safeguard sensitive information.

- **SSH Private Keys:** SSH (Secure Shell) private keys are used for secure communication between remote repositories and users' machines. GitHub checks for exposed SSH private keys to prevent unauthorized access to repositories.

- **GPG Keys:** GPG (GNU Privacy Guard) keys are used for signing commits and tags, providing a way to verify the authenticity of code changes. GitHub scans for exposed GPG keys to ensure the integrity of commits.

- **Azure Application Credentials:** Azure application credentials are used for authenticating with Azure services. GitHub scans repositories for leaked Azure credentials to prevent unauthorized access to Azure resources.

- **AWS Access Keys:** AWS (Amazon Web Services) access keys are used for interacting with AWS services. GitHub scans for exposed AWS access keys to enhance AWS security and prevent unauthorized usage.

- **Firebase Tokens:** Firebase tokens are used for authentication and accessing Firebase services. GitHub scans for leaked Firebase tokens in repositories to prevent unauthorized access to Firebase resources.

- **Google Cloud Platform (GCP) Service Account JSON:** JSON files containing GCP service account credentials are scanned. These credentials are used for authenticating with Google Cloud Platform services. GitHub ensures the security of GCP resources by detecting potential leaks.

GitHub continuously monitors public repositories and public npm packages for these secrets. If any of these secrets are detected, GitHub alerts the relevant parties, ensuring timely action is taken to prevent security breaches and maintain the confidentiality of sensitive information.

Configuring Secret Scanning for Your Repositories

Configuring secret scanning for your repositories on GitHub involves setting up the scanning process to detect and respond to potential secrets within your codebase. Here are the general steps to configure secret scanning:

- **Enable Secret Scanning:**

  - Make sure you have the necessary permissions within the repository.

  - Go to the repository on GitHub.

  - Click the **Settings** tab.

  - In the left sidebar, click **Security and analysis**.

  - Under "Secret scanning," check if it's enabled. If not, click **Set up secret scanning** and enable it.

- **Configure Secret Scanning Alerts:**

  - GitHub automatically scans for known secret formats. Configure alerts to be notified when secrets are found.

  - You can set up email notifications and integrate with other communication tools using webhooks or GitHub Actions.

- **Configure Push Protection (Optional):**

  - Push protection prevents contributors from pushing code that contains detected secrets.

  - You can configure push protection rules to block or allow certain actions when secrets are found.

- **Integrate Secret Scanning with Your Workflow (Optional):**

  - GitHub secret scanning can integrate with other security tools and workflows.

  - Set up actions based on the results of secret scanning, such as triggering automated responses or sending notifications to specific channels.

- **Review and Respond to Alerts:**

  - Regularly review secret scanning alerts in the "Security" tab of your repository.

  - Take immediate actions to remediate any detected secrets, such as rotating credentials, revoking tokens, or updating configurations.

- **Customize Secret Scanning (Optional):**

  - GitHub allows you to customize secret scanning further by adding your own secret patterns.

  - You can specify custom patterns to search for specific secrets relevant to your project.

- **Monitor and Improve:**

  - Continuously monitor secret scanning alerts.

  - Analyze any false positives and adjust patterns if needed to reduce them.

  - Keep your team informed about best practices to avoid accidentally committing sensitive information.

By following these steps, you can effectively configure secret scanning for your repositories, enhancing security and ensuring sensitive information is not accidentally exposed.

Enabling Secret Scanning Alerts for Users for All Your Public Repositories

To enable secret scanning alerts for users for all your public repositories through your personal account settings on GitHub, follow these steps:

- **Access Your Account Settings:**

  - Click your profile photo in the upper-right corner of any page on GitHub.

  - From the dropdown menu, click **Settings**.

- **Access Code Security and Analysis Settings:**

  - In the left sidebar, click **Code security and analysis** under the "Security" section.

- **Enable Secret Scanning:**

  - Under "Code security and analysis," locate the "Secret scanning" section.

  - To the right of "Secret scanning," click **Enable all**. This will enable secret scanning alerts for all your existing public repositories.

- **Optional: Automatically Enable for New Repositories:**

  - Below "Secret scanning," there might be an option to "**Automatically enable for new public repositories**."

  - If available, select the checkbox if you want secret scanning to be automatically enabled for any new public repositories you create in the future.

- **Save Changes:**

  - Scroll to the bottom of the page and click "**Save changes**" to apply the changes.

By following these steps, you've enabled secret scanning alerts for users for all your public repositories. This helps in detecting and responding to potential secrets and sensitive information exposed in your codebase across all your public repositories.

Excluding Directories from Secret Scanning Alerts for Users

To configure a **secret_scanning.yml** file to exclude directories from secret scanning, follow these steps:

- **Navigate to the Repository's Main Page:**

  - Go to the main page of your repository on GitHub.com.

- **Create a New secret_scanning.yml File:**

  - Above the list of files, click the "**Add file**" dropdown menu, then select "**Create new file**."

  - Alternatively, you can click the "+" button in the file tree view on the left.

- **Specify the File Name and Exclusions:**

  - In the file name field, type **.github/secret_ scanning.yml**.

  - Under "**Edit new file**," type **paths-ignore:** followed by the paths you want to exclude from secret scanning. Figure 3-29 shows yaml file configuration.

```
paths-ignore:
  - "BlogUc-Repository/Sample-Workflow/*.txt"
```

Figure 3-29. *yaml file for ignoring secret scanning*

- You can use special characters such as * to filter paths. For more information about filter patterns, refer to the "Workflow syntax for GitHub Actions" documentation.

- **Save Your Changes:**

  - Scroll down and click the "**Commit new file**" button to save your changes.

Notes

- If there are more than 1000 entries in paths-ignore, secret scanning will only exclude the first 1000 directories from scans.

- If secret_scanning.yml is larger than 1 MB, secret scanning will ignore the entire file. Be mindful of the file size to ensure it is within the acceptable limit.

Enabling a Feature for All Repositories for an Organization

To enable a security feature for all repositories in your organization, follow these steps:

- **Navigate to Organization Settings:**

  - Go to the main page of your organization on GitHub.com.

  - Under your organization name, click "**Settings**."

  - If you don't see the "Settings" tab, click the **dropdown menu** (represented by three dots) and then select "**Settings**."

- **Access Code Security and Analysis Settings:**

  - In the left sidebar, click "Code security and analysis."

- **Enable the Feature for All Repositories:**

  - Locate the feature you want to enable for all repositories.

  - Next to the name of the feature, click "**Enable all**" to enable the feature in all repositories where it is supported.

Please note that enabling a feature for all repositories can have a significant impact. Ensure you understand the implications of enabling the feature globally, especially if it involves resource allocation, notifications, or other interactions within your organization.

Enabling a Feature for New Repositories

To ensure immediate protection for all newly created repositories in your organization, you have the option to automatically enable specific security features. Enabling these features upon repository creation ensures swift protection and early identification of any vulnerabilities. However, for a more tailored approach, you might prefer to review and configure each new repository individually.

Here is how to enable this feature:

- Go to your organization's main page on GitHub.com.

- Under your organization's name, click "**Settings**." If you don't see the "Settings" tab, click the dropdown menu and then select "**Settings**."

- In the left sidebar, find and click "**Code security and analysis**."

- Look for the specific security feature you want to enable automatically in future repositories.

- Below the feature's name, select the option to enable it in all applicable future repositories. Figure 3-30 shows the feature for enabling alerts for a new repository.

Dependabot
Keep your dependencies secure and up-to-date. Learn more about Dependabot.

Dependabot alerts
Receive alerts for vulnerabilities that affect your dependencies and manually generate Dependabot pull requests to resolve these vulnerabilities. Configure alert notifications.

☑ **Automatically enable for new repositories**

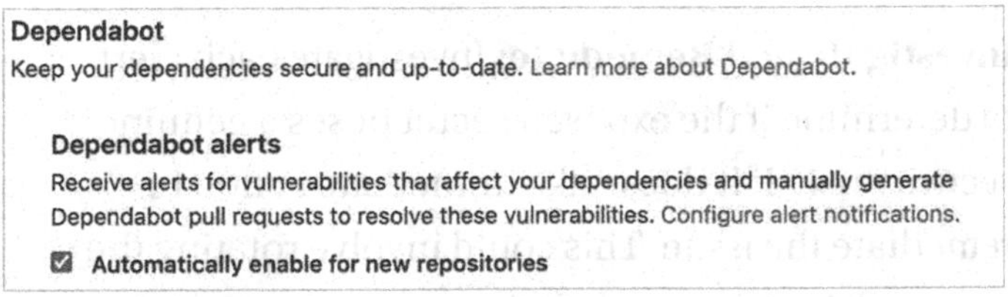

Figure 3-30. *Dependabot alerts for a new repository*

By following these steps, the chosen security feature will be automatically activated in all new repositories created within your organization.

Managing Alerts from Secret Scanning

Managing alerts from secret scanning involves handling notifications and addressing potential security risks related to exposed secrets within your codebase. When secret scanning identifies sensitive information, such as API keys or credentials, it generates alerts that prompt actions to mitigate these risks.

Here is how you can manage alerts from secret scanning:

- **Notification:** When secret scanning detects exposed secrets, it generates alerts. GitHub will notify repository administrators and the repository's secret management team. Notifications are sent through various channels, such as email or GitHub's user interface.

- **Review Alerts:** Repository administrators should review the alerts to understand the nature of the exposed secrets. Each alert provides information about the type of secret found and the location in the code where it was detected.

- **Investigate and Remediate:** Investigate each alert to determine if the exposed secret poses a genuine security risk. If it does, take immediate action to remediate the issue. This could involve rotating the compromised secret, updating access controls, or modifying the code to remove the exposed information.

- **False Positives:** Sometimes, alerts might be false positives, indicating a secret where none exists. It's essential to confirm the validity of each alert. If an alert is a false positive, mark it as such to prevent unnecessary actions.

- **Security Policies:** Establish and enforce security policies within your organization. Clearly define how exposed secrets are handled, ensuring a consistent and secure approach across all projects.

- **Education and Training:** Educate developers and team members about best practices for managing secrets securely. Regular training can help prevent accidental exposure of sensitive information.

- **Integration with Security Tools:** Integrate secret scanning with other security tools and workflows. For example, automatically create issues or tickets in your project management system when new alerts are generated.

- **Continuous Monitoring:** Implement continuous monitoring to detect new secrets added to the codebase. Regular scans can help identify and address potential security issues before they escalate.

By following these steps, organizations can effectively manage alerts from secret scanning, enhance their security posture, and protect sensitive information from unauthorized access.

Managing Secret Scanning Alerts

The following are the steps on how to manage secret scanning alerts in a GitHub repository:

- **Navigate to the Repository:**

  - Go to the main page of your repository on GitHub.com.

- **Access the Security Tab:**

  - Under the repository name, click **Security**. If you don't see the "Security" tab, click the dropdown menu and select **Security** from there.

- **Select Secret Scanning:**

  - In the left sidebar, under "Vulnerability alerts," click **Secret scanning**.

- **View the Alert:**

  - Under "Secret scanning," click the specific alert that you want to view.

  - If the leaked secret is a GitHub token, you can also review the token metadata by following the appropriate link.

- **Dismiss the Alert:**

  - To dismiss the alert, select the "**Close as**" dropdown menu.

  - Choose a reason for resolving the alert from the options provided.

  - Optionally, you can add a dismissal comment in the "**Comment**" field. This comment will be added to the alert timeline and can serve as justification during auditing and reporting.

- **Close the Alert:**

  - After providing the necessary information, click "**Close alert**" to dismiss the alert.

By following these steps, you can effectively manage and dismiss secret scanning alerts in your GitHub repository.

Configuring Notifications for Secret Scanning Alerts

The following setup explains about notifications for incremental scans and historical scans in GitHub secret scanning:

- **Incremental Scans**

  When a new secret is detected, GitHub notifies all
  users with access to security alerts for the repository
  according to their notification preferences.

  These users include

  - **Repository Administrators:** Users with
    administrative privileges for the repository

  - **Security Managers:** Users designated as security
    managers for the repository

  - **Users with Custom Roles:** Users assigned custom
    roles with read/write access to the repository

  - **Organization Owners and Enterprise Owners:**
    If they are administrators of repositories where
    secrets were leaked

Note   Commit authors who've accidentally committed secrets will
be notified, regardless of their notification preferences.

Email Notifications

You receive email notifications if

- You are a watcher on the repository.

- You have enabled notifications for "All Activity" or
  custom "Security alerts" on the repository.

- Under your notification settings, you have selected
  to receive notifications by email for activities you
  are watching.

To enable email notifications:

- Navigate to the main page of the repository on GitHub.com.

- Click Watch and select All Activity to subscribe to all notifications. Alternatively, for security alerts only, choose Custom, then click Security alerts.

- Go to your notification settings (`https://github.com/settings/notifications`).

- Under Subscriptions and Watching, select the Notify me dropdown.

- Choose Email as a notification option and click Save.

- **Historical Scans**

  For historical scans, GitHub notifies the following users:

  - **Organization Owners, Enterprise Owners, and Security Managers:** They are notified whenever a historical scan is complete, even if no secrets are found.

  - **Repository Administrators, Security Managers, and Users with Custom Roles:** They are notified whenever a historical scan detects a secret, and notifications are sent according to their notification preferences.

Note   Commit authors are not notified in the case of historical scans.

These notifications ensure that relevant stakeholders are informed about potential security concerns detected through both incremental and historical scans.

Removing Stale Configurations and Alerts from a Branch

Cleaning up your repository periodically is essential to maintain a streamlined and organized development environment. One aspect of this cleanup process involves removing stale configurations and alerts from specific branches. Outdated configurations and alerts might clutter your repository and create confusion. Here is how you can remove them:

- **Review Branch Configurations:** Start by reviewing the configurations specific to the branch you want to clean. This could include outdated workflows, redundant settings, or unnecessary access permissions. Identify configurations that are no longer relevant to the branch's current development status.

- **Identify Stale Alerts:** Similarly, identify alerts associated with the branch. GitHub's alert system might have flagged certain issues in the past. Check if these issues have been resolved or if they are no longer applicable. Stale alerts can be removed to keep your repository's security information up to date.

- **Access Repository Settings:** Navigate to the repository settings on GitHub. Look for options related to branch configurations, security settings, or alerts. These options are generally available in the repository's settings menu.

- **Locate Branch-Specific Configurations:** Within the settings, find the section related to branch-specific configurations. This section allows you to manage branch protection rules, security policies, and alert settings.

213

- **Edit or Remove Configurations:** For each outdated configuration or alert, edit the settings to bring them up to date or remove them entirely if they are no longer necessary. GitHub's interface typically provides options to edit or delete configurations directly from the settings page.

- **Confirm Changes:** After editing or removing the configurations, GitHub might ask for confirmation. Review the changes you are about to make to ensure they align with your cleanup goals. Confirm the changes to apply them.

- **Documentation (Optional):** If you are removing configurations that were previously documented, update your repository's documentation to reflect the changes. This ensures that all team members are aware of the modifications made.

By periodically reviewing and removing stale configurations and alerts from branches, you maintain a cleaner repository, reducing clutter and ensuring that your development environment is well organized and up to date.

Auditing Responses to Code Scanning Alerts

Auditing responses to code scanning alerts is crucial for maintaining the security and integrity of your codebase. Properly handling these alerts ensures that vulnerabilities are addressed promptly, minimizing potential risks. Here is a systematic approach to auditing responses to code scanning alerts:

- **Review Alert Details:** Start by thoroughly reviewing the details of each code scanning alert. Understand the nature of the vulnerability, its potential impact, and the affected code paths. GitHub provides detailed information about each alert, including the file, line numbers, and a description of the issue.

- **Identify Responsible Team Members:** Determine the team members or individuals responsible for the code where the alert originated. GitHub's notification system typically assigns alerts to specific contributors or teams based on the code ownership and the configuration in the repository.

- **Assign Ownership:** If the alert is unassigned or unclear about its ownership, assign it to the appropriate team or developer. Clearly defining ownership ensures that someone takes responsibility for investigating and addressing the issue.

- **Evaluate Severity:** Assess the severity of the alert. Critical vulnerabilities require immediate attention, while minor issues may be prioritized differently. Use GitHub's severity indicators to gauge the urgency of the alert.

- **Coordinate Fixes:** Collaborate with the responsible team members to develop a fix for the identified vulnerability. Discuss potential solutions, implement necessary code changes, and test the fixes thoroughly to prevent regressions.

- **Document Fixes:** Document the fixes made to address the alert. Provide clear explanations of the changes made, including code modifications, security patches, or configuration adjustments. Documentation helps team members understand the issue and the applied solution.

- **Implement Preventive Measures:** Identify patterns in the types of vulnerabilities reported. Implement preventive measures, such as coding guidelines, secure coding practices, and automated tests, to avoid similar issues in the future. Learning from past vulnerabilities strengthens your codebase's overall security posture.

- **Verify Fixes:** After implementing the fixes, conduct rigorous testing to validate the changes. Use automated tests, manual testing, and code reviews to ensure that the vulnerability has been effectively resolved without introducing new issues.

- **Close the Alert:** Once the fix has been verified and the vulnerability is resolved, close the code scanning alert on GitHub. Provide a concise summary of the fix implemented for future reference.

- **Continuous Improvement:** Conduct periodic reviews of resolved alerts to identify any recurring issues or areas for improvement. This feedback loop helps teams enhance their coding practices and prevent similar vulnerabilities in the future.

By following these steps, you can systematically audit and respond to code scanning alerts, fostering a secure and resilient codebase for your project.

Managing Sensitive Information Out of GitHub Repository with .gitignore

Developers often miss files when making commits, sometimes innocuous ones like build files. However, there is always a chance that sensitive data, like API keys or private configurations, might be inadvertently committed, creating a potential security risk. To mitigate this risk, developers can utilize .gitignore files. These files guide client tools like the git command line, instructing them to ignore specific paths and patterns when consolidating files for a commit.

The following example highlights typical scenarios where files are ignored. Figure 3-31 shows an example of .gitignore.

Figure 3-31. *.gitignore file*

Now all .log files and anything in temp folders will be ignored by Git.

Within your repository, there might be several .gitignore files. The settings are inherited from parent directories, and if there are overriding fields in new .gitignore files within specific folders or subfolders, those settings take precedence over the parent ones. Typically, the primary focus is on managing the root .gitignore file. However, adding a .gitignore file in a project directory can be beneficial, especially when the project has unique requirements that are easier to manage separately from the parent file. This is particularly useful for specifying files that should not be ignored.

Removing Sensitive Data from a GitHub Repository

If you mistakenly commit sensitive information like passwords or SSH keys into a Git repository, it is possible to remove this data from the repository's history. To eliminate unwanted files from a repository's history, there are tools available, such as the git filter-repo tool or the BFG Repo-Cleaner open source tool. These tools offer the capability to scrub sensitive data from your Git history, ensuring that it does not remain in the repository's record of changes.

Note   Here, we will see instructions for BFG, and to install BFG, you will need to have Java installed on your local machine.

To demonstrate the functionality of git filter-repo, we will see the process of removing a file containing sensitive data from your repository's history. Additionally, you can go with the .gitignore file to exclude files from the GitHub repository. The following are the instructions for BFG Repo-Cleaner:

- The BFG Repo-Cleaner, maintained by the open source community, offers a quicker and simpler alternative to git filter-repo for eliminating unwanted data from repositories.

- For instance, to delete a file containing sensitive information while keeping your latest commit intact, execute the following command:

  $ java -jar bfg.jar –delete-files help.txt

- To replace all occurrences of text listed in passwords.txt throughout your repository's history, run

  $ java -jar bfg.jar –replace-text password.txt

Password.txt can have content like Figure 3-32 to replace passwords. Figure 3-32 shows an example of a file used in BFG Repo-Cleaner.

```
PWD2==>EnterPwdHere        # replace with 'EnterPwdHere' instead
PWD3==>                    # replace with the empty string
```

Figure 3-32.   password.txt used in BFG Repo-Cleaner

- Once the sensitive data has been removed, it's essential
  to force-push your changes to GitHub. Force pushing
  rewrites the repository history, effectively erasing
  sensitive data from the commit history. However, be
  cautious, as force pushing might overwrite commits
  upon which others have based their work:

```
$ git push --force
```

Branch Protection Rules

On GitHub, you have the capability to establish branch protection rules
to enforce specific workflows for one or more branches. This enforcement
might include requirements like obtaining an approving review or
ensuring that all pull requests merged into the protected branch have
passed certain status checks. These branch protection rules can be utilized
to facilitate various essential workflows, such as

- **Running Builds:** Ensuring that the code changes can
  be successfully built and compiled.

- **Linter Checks:** Verifying code for typographical
  errors and confirming adherence to internal coding
  conventions.

- **Automated Testing:** Executing automated tests to
  identify any alterations in the code's behavior.

- **And More:** Branch protection rules can encompass a
  wide range of checks and validations tailored to your
  specific project requirements.

By implementing these protection rules, you enhance the reliability
and quality of your codebase, promoting a seamless and error-free
development process.

Add a CODEOWNERS File

By incorporating a CODEOWNERS file into your repository, you gain the ability to designate specific team members or entire teams as code owners for paths within your repository. These designated code owners become mandatory reviewers for any changes made to files within the specified paths.

For example, consider the configuration within a CODEOWNERS file, as shown in Figure 3-33.

```
# Changes to files with the '.sql' extension must be reviewed by the 'sql-owner' user or group:
*.sql     @sql-owner

# Changes to files in the 'Api' folder must be reviewed by the 'bilag' user or group:
/api/ @bilag
```

Figure 3-33. CODEOWNERS file

In this setup, any alterations to files ending with ".sql" necessitate review and approval from the "sql-owner" user or group. Similarly, modifications made within the "api" folder mandate review from the "bilag" user or group. You have the flexibility to create the CODEOWNERS file either at the root level of the repository or within specific folders such as "docs" or ".github".

Automated Security

Analyze and Update Outdated Dependencies

Identifying and resolving outdated dependencies with security vulnerabilities is essential to uphold the security and reliability of your projects. Keeping your dependencies up to date ensures that your software remains resilient against potential threats and exploits. Here are the steps to detect and address outdated dependencies with security vulnerabilities:

- **Dependency Analysis:** Regularly scan your project's dependencies to identify outdated packages. Dependency management tools, like Dependabot, can automate this process by notifying you about available updates.

- **Security Alerts:** Leverage tools and services that provide security alerts for your dependencies. Platforms like GitHub automatically alert you if your repository contains vulnerable dependencies, allowing you to take prompt action.

- **Upgrade Dependencies:** Once you receive notifications about outdated dependencies, promptly upgrade them to the latest secure versions. Most package managers offer commands to update dependencies easily.

- **Automated Pull Requests:** Utilize automation tools, such as Dependabot, to create automated pull requests for updating dependencies. These tools can create a pull request with the updated dependency version, making it convenient for you to review and merge the changes.

- **Continuous Integration (CI) Pipeline:** Integrate dependency checks into your CI pipeline. Tools like OWASP Dependency-Check can be integrated into CI systems to scan for vulnerabilities automatically during the build process.

- **Regular Audits:** Conduct regular security audits of your dependencies. Periodically review the list of dependencies, even those that aren't part of your active development, to ensure that no vulnerabilities are introduced over time.

- **Documentation and Change Logs:** Stay informed about security updates by reading documentation and change logs provided by the dependency authors. This helps you understand the changes, especially security-related ones, introduced in newer versions.

By following these practices, you can proactively detect, manage, and fix outdated dependencies with security vulnerabilities, safeguarding your projects against potential security risks.

Repository Dependency Graphs

Repository dependency graphs are visual representations of the dependencies between different packages and libraries used in a software project. They help developers understand the relationships between various components within a repository. Let's break down the concept with an example.

Example: A Node.js Web Application

Imagine you are working on a Node.js web application. Your application relies on external packages (also known as dependencies) to function properly. These dependencies are specified in the **package.json** file, which is a standard configuration file used in Node.js projects.

Figure 3-34 shows a sample package.json file.

```
{
    "name": "weather-api",
    "version": "1.0.0",
    "dependencies": {
        "express": "^4.17.1",
        "body-parser": "^1.19.0"
    }
}
```

Figure 3-34. package.json

In this package.json file, express and body-parser are the external packages your web application depends on.

- **Dependency Graph**

    - Your repository's dependency graph, in this case, would look something like Figure 3-35, which shows a dependency graph of a weather-api application.

```
weather-api
├── express@4.17.1
│   └── body-parser@1.19.0
├── body-parser@1.19.0
```

Figure 3-35. *Dependency graph for weather-api*

- weather-api depends on express@4.17.1, body-parser@1.19.0.

- express@4.17.1 further depends on body-parser@1.19.0.

- This graphical representation showcases the relationships between the main project (weather-api) and its direct dependencies (express and body-parser), as well as the dependencies of the express package (body-parser).

- **Understanding the Graph**

  - weather-api directly depends on two packages: express and body-parser.

  - express depends on body-parser.

- **Benefits**

  - **Visual Clarity:** The graph provides a clear visual representation of how different packages are interlinked within your project.

  - **Dependency Analysis:** Developers can quickly analyze which packages are critical for the project and which ones are dependencies of the main packages.

  - **Version Management:** It helps in tracking the versions of packages being used, ensuring compatibility and security.

Repository dependency graphs are especially valuable when dealing with larger projects and complex dependency trees, offering developers an organized way to understand and manage their project's dependencies.

Automated Dependency Alerts

Automated dependency alerts on GitHub notify repository maintainers about known vulnerabilities in their dependencies. These alerts help developers identify and fix security vulnerabilities and keep their projects secure. Figure 3-36 shows automated dependency alerts.

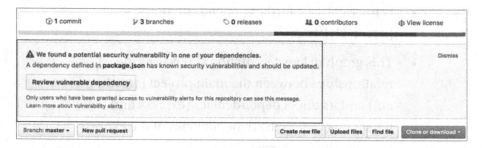

Figure 3-36. *Automated dependency alert*

Here is how it works:

- **Dependency Scanning**

  - GitHub automatically scans the dependencies of repositories for security vulnerabilities.

  - It checks the repository's dependencies against a database of known vulnerabilities.

- **Alert Generation**

  - If a vulnerable dependency is detected, GitHub generates an automated dependency alert.

  - The alert provides information about the vulnerability, including its severity level, affected versions, and possible fixes.

- **Notification to Repository Maintainers**
    - The repository maintainers receive notifications about these alerts.
    - The notifications appear in the repository's "Security" tab and are also sent via email to repository administrators.

- **Taking Action**
    - Repository maintainers can review the alerts to understand the nature of the vulnerabilities.
    - They can then update their dependencies to versions that do not contain the vulnerabilities or apply patches if available.
    - Maintainers can dismiss the alert if they believe the vulnerability doesn't apply to their project or if they have mitigated it through other means.

- **Automatic Pull Requests (Dependabot)**
    - GitHub can also automatically create pull requests to update vulnerable dependencies.
    - This is facilitated by Dependabot, a GitHub feature that helps maintainers keep their dependencies up to date by opening pull requests when new versions are available.

- **Monitoring and Resolution**
    - Repository maintainers can continuously monitor their dependencies for new vulnerabilities and receive alerts as new issues are discovered.
    - By promptly addressing these alerts, developers can enhance the security of their projects.

Automated dependency alerts play a crucial role in maintaining the security of software projects by keeping developers informed about potential vulnerabilities in their codebase. They enable proactive measures to be taken to address security issues promptly.

Automated Code Scanning

Code scanning on GitHub serves as a crucial security tool for identifying and addressing issues in your codebase. Code scanning is a feature on GitHub designed to perform in-depth analysis of your code to discover security vulnerabilities, errors, and coding issues. It is a valuable tool for maintaining code quality, security, and reliability in your projects. Code scanning can be accessed through the security tab of a GitHub repository. Figure 3-37 shows the configuration option for enabling code scanning.

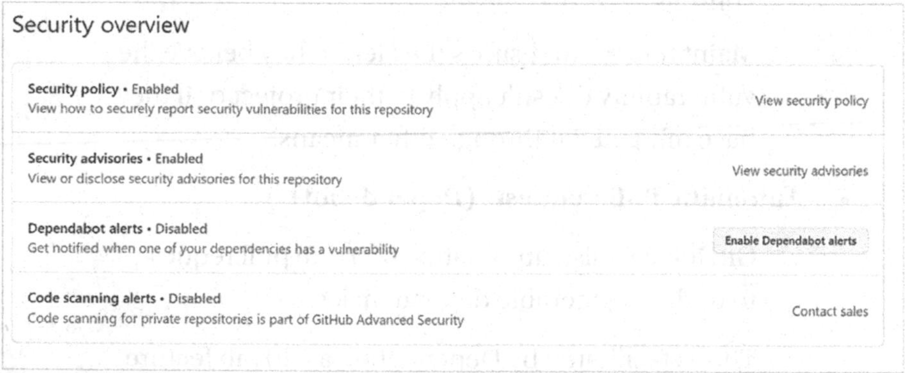

Security overview

Security policy • Enabled
View how to securely report security vulnerabilities for this repository
View security policy

Security advisories • Enabled
View or disclose security advisories for this repository
View security advisories

Dependabot alerts • Disabled
Get notified when one of your dependencies has a vulnerability
Enable Dependabot alerts

Code scanning alerts • Disabled
Code scanning for private repositories is part of GitHub Advanced Security
Contact sales

Figure 3-37. *Code scanning alert configuration*

Key Benefits of Code Scanning

- **Vulnerability Detection:** Code scanning scans your codebase to identify known security vulnerabilities and coding errors.

- **Issue Triage:** It helps prioritize issues, allowing you to address critical problems first and providing a clear view of the severity of each issue.

- **Preventing New Issues:** By integrating code scanning into your workflow, you can prevent new security problems from being introduced into your codebase with each code change.

- **Customizable Queries with CodeQL:** CodeQL is a powerful query language that treats code as data. This enables you to create custom queries tailored to your specific codebase or use prebuilt queries from the open source community.

Enabling Code Scanning

- Go to the **Security tab** of your GitHub repository.

- Click **Code scanning alerts and workflows** to activate the feature.

- GitHub will perform automated scans on your repository code using default settings, highlighting identified issues in the Security tab.

- You can enhance the scanning process by creating custom CodeQL queries to target specific areas of concern or meet your project's unique requirements.

Customization and Maintenance

Code scanning offers the flexibility to adapt to your project's evolving needs. Developers can create, customize, and maintain their scanning rules, ensuring that code analysis remains effective over time. By utilizing code scanning and CodeQL, GitHub provides developers with a comprehensive solution for code quality and security. This proactive approach not only helps detect and address existing vulnerabilities but also mitigates the risk of introducing new security issues during the development process. It empowers developers to maintain a high level of code security and reliability in their projects.

Secret Scanning

Secret scanning is a vital security feature on GitHub, providing automated detection of known secrets or credentials committed within a repository. Secret scanning is a security mechanism employed by GitHub to automatically identify and alert users about sensitive data like API keys, passwords, or other credentials accidentally committed in the codebase. These secrets, if exposed, could lead to security breaches, data theft, or other malicious activities. Please refer to the previous section for detailed information on secret scanning.

Summary

This chapter delved into the secure management and best practices for GitHub repositories, likening them to the bustling epicenter of a programmer's universe where version control and collaboration converge. An understanding of repository permissions and collaborator roles was emphasized, portrayed as the tickets that allocate specific actions to users, crucial for safeguarding code and promoting effective teamwork. The section on "Secure Coding Practices" served as a clarion call for developers, urging them to be the superheroes of cybersecurity, writing code that is as resilient as a fortress against potential threats. Completing the narrative are repository maintenance best practices, presented as the vigilant caretakers who ensure the code remains as timeless as a classic novel, advocating for practices like consistent code reviews, automated testing, and comprehensive documentation. In this intricate web of GitHub management, administrators and organization owners act as the maestros, orchestrating the flow with advanced security options to create a harmonious and secure coding environment.

Resources

- GitHub code security: `https://docs.github.com/en/code-security`

- GitHub repositories: `https://docs.github.com/en/repositories`

- Microsoft learnings: `https://learn.microsoft.com/en-us/training/`

- Configure and use secret scanning in your GitHub repository:

- `https://learn.microsoft.com/en-us/training/modules/configure-use-secret-scanning-github-repository/`

- Dependabot: `https://github.com/dependabot`

- Gitignore: `https://github.com/github/gitignore`

- Code scanning with GitHub CodeQL: `https://learn.microsoft.com/en-us/training/modules/code-scanning-with-github-codeql/`

- Manage repository settings: `https://docs.github.com/en/repositories/managing-your-repositorys-settings-and-features`

- Git-SCM: `https://git-scm.com/docs`

- Warp: `www.warp.dev/terminus`

- GitHub permissions: `https://nira.com/github-permissions/`

CHAPTER 4

GitHub Identity and Access Management (IAM)

In this chapter, we dig into the comprehensive mechanisms of Identity and Access Management (IAM) on GitHub, specifically focusing on SAML Single Sign-On (SSO), Enterprise Managed Users (EMU), and user onboarding and offboarding procedures.

Topics covered in this chapter include

- Structuring Your GitHub Organization

- Introduction to IAM on GitHub

- SAML SSO Setup for Enterprise and Organization Levels

- Implementing SAML SSO in GitHub Organizations

- Understanding and Managing GitHub EMU

- GitHub User Onboarding and Offboarding Process

- Best Practices for Managing Access to GitHub

© Balu Nivrutti Ilag, AjayKumar P. Baljoshi, Ganesh J. Sangale and Yogesh Athave 2024
B. N. Ilag et al., *Mastering GitHub Enterprise Management and Administration*,
https://doi.org/10.1007/979-8-8688-0369-7_4

Structuring Your GitHub Organization

When structuring your enterprise on GitHub, there are five main organizational structures to consider, each supporting different company sizes, trust levels, and access control needs.

For small- or medium-sized companies where there is a high level of trust among members, a single organization with direct repository access is ideal. In this structure, all members have direct access to every repository. Teams are primarily used for coordination and communication rather than access control. The base permissions in this setup are typically set to "write" or "read," allowing for a more open and collaborative environment.

Alternatively, if your company requires more stringent control over repository access, a **single organization with teams for repository access** might be more suitable. This approach is often adopted by medium-sized or smaller companies where trust levels might be lower. Here, the base permissions are set to "none," and specific teams are granted access to particular repositories. This setup allows for more controlled and restricted access to sensitive or critical repositories.

For larger companies, where different groups may not need to collaborate or share resources, multiple organizations with direct repository access is a fitting choice. In this structure, each organization operates independently, with members having access to all repositories within their respective organizations. The base permissions for each organization are typically set to "write" or "read," similar to the single organization structure, but with a clear separation between different organizational units.

Very large companies often require even more granular control over repository access within multiple organizations. This need is addressed by the multiple organizations with teams for repository access structure. Similar to the single organization with teams, the base permissions are set to "none," and access to specific repositories is managed through teams. This structure allows for finely tuned access control within a larger, more complex organizational framework.

Lastly, there are the multiple organizations with different access methods structures. This hybrid approach is beneficial for companies that want the collaborative benefits of a single organization for most of their employees and repositories, typically setting base permissions to "write" or "read." Concurrently, they create a separate organization for more sensitive repositories, where access is more restricted. In this second organization, base permissions are set to "none," and access to these sensitive repositories is tightly controlled through team memberships.

Each of these structures offers different benefits and can be tailored to fit the unique needs and characteristics of your enterprise, ensuring efficient management and collaboration within your GitHub environment.

Considerations for the Number of Organizations: Minimize the number of organizations. Generally, it's better to have fewer organizations. This approach encourages more collaboration and inner sourcing, leading to increased efficiency. Often, a single organization is sufficient because it simplifies finding resources.

Communication is easier within one organization.

A single, larger organization can promote collaboration and loyalty, while multiple smaller ones might lead to isolation.

- **When to Have Multiple Organizations:** If your company is large and you don't want every owner to access all repositories, multiple organizations might be necessary. This allows for different policies and settings, like SAML configurations, for each organization.

- **Avoid One-to-One Mapping:** Don't create an organization for every team or business unit. Instead, group entities with similar policies into one organization. This maximizes collaboration while meeting regulatory needs.

- **Start Small:** It's easier to add organizations later than to remove them. Begin with a few and expand as needed. Reducing the number of organizations later can be challenging and disruptive.

Introduction to IAM on GitHub

This topic provides a foundational understanding of Identity and Access Management (IAM) on GitHub, focusing on its importance and how it works to manage user identities, permissions, and access within GitHub organizations and repositories.

GitHub user login process flow: Here is the sequence diagram that explains the process of a user logging in to GitHub.com using GitHub Enterprise Cloud, GitHub organization with multiple repositories, Azure Identity, and multifactor authentication.

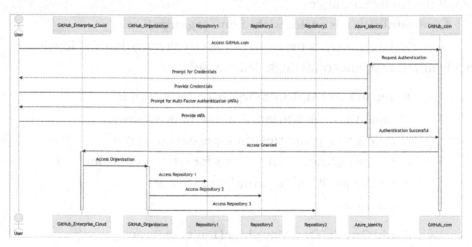

Figure 4-1. *User login process*

This diagram captures the sequence of interactions starting from the user accessing GitHub.com; going through authentication with Azure Identity, including multifactor authentication; and finally accessing repositories within a GitHub organization through GitHub Enterprise Cloud.

GitHub Identity and Access Management is an essential security and administrative framework designed to manage access to GitHub resources effectively. At its core, IAM encompasses the processes of identifying, authenticating, and authorizing individuals or teams to interact with applications, networks, and databases. It involves associating specified user rights and restrictions with the identities that have been established within the GitHub environment.

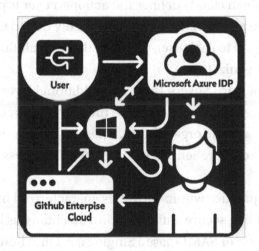

Figure 4-2. *The user connected to GitHub via IdP*

The importance of IAM on GitHub can't be overstated, especially considering the potentially sensitive nature of the code and data hosted on the platform. A robust IAM system ensures that only authorized individuals have access to manipulate these resources, thus mitigating risks, safeguarding intellectual property, and ensuring compliance with various regulatory standards. Figure 4-2 shows the user connected to the GitHub Enterprise Cloud through Azure IdP.

At the heart of GitHub's IAM are user accounts, which represent the individual identities within GitHub. These can range from actual users to service accounts designed for automation tasks. Organizations and teams within GitHub allow for collaborative work where multiple users can simultaneously collaborate across projects. Managing access within these groups is a crucial aspect of IAM.

The cornerstone of IAM is authentication, which verifies user identity. GitHub supports a multitude of authentication methods, including traditional passwords, personal access tokens, SSH keys, and more sophisticated mechanisms like SAML Single Sign-On for enhanced security.

Once authenticated, a user's actions within GitHub are governed by authorization. This is primarily facilitated through role-based access control (RBAC), which clearly defines the actions a user is permitted to perform within the platform. This is complicatedly tied to the roles and permissions assigned to each user, dictating their capabilities within a repository or an organization.

For GitHub Enterprise users, there's an additional layer of IAM features that manage user access across a broader corporate environment rather than within a single organization. These enterprise-level accounts necessitate a more comprehensive IAM strategy to address the larger scale of operations.

A robust IAM practice within GitHub is characterized by a few key approaches, including secure authentication mechanisms like two-factor authentication or SAML-based Single Sign-On. There's a significant emphasis on providing minimum privilege access, ensuring users have just enough access to perform their roles. Regular access reviews and audit logging are critical for maintaining security and visibility over who is doing what within the platform.

However, with the scaling of operations and the increasing number of contributors, IAM can present challenges. Manual management of access rights becomes inefficient, and automation, along with integration with identity providers, becomes a necessity. Compliance with industry standards poses its own set of challenges, requiring meticulous access control that can be audited and reported on demand.

To navigate these challenges, consistent IAM policies across all repositories and teams are essential. Integrating GitHub with an organization's identity provider simplifies access management. It's also crucial to educate users about IAM policies and security practices regularly.

Why Is GitHub IAM Important?

GitHub, being a repository hosting service, contains potentially sensitive code and data. IAM helps mitigate risks, protecting intellectual property and complying with various regulations by ensuring that only authorized individuals can access and manipulate resources within GitHub.

GitHub IAM Components

- **User Accounts:** These are individual identities on GitHub. They can represent actual users or can be service accounts for automation.

- **Organizations:** This is a grouping within GitHub where multiple users can collaborate across many projects at once. IAM here involves managing access to these organizations.

- **Teams:** Within organizations, teams allow a group of user accounts to manage access to several repositories.

- **Authentication:** This is the process of verifying who a user is. GitHub supports various authentication methods, such as passwords, personal access tokens, SSH keys, and SAML Single Sign-On.

- **Authorization:** Once a user is authenticated, they must be authorized. GitHub uses role-based access control (RBAC) to define what actions a user can perform.

- **Roles and Permissions:** GitHub assigns specific roles to users with different levels of permissions, determining what actions they can perform within a repository or an organization.

- **Enterprise Accounts:** For GitHub Enterprise, additional IAM features are provided to manage users across an entire corporate entity rather than a single organization.

Authentication Methods in GitHub Enterprise Cloud

In GitHub Enterprise Cloud, you have the flexibility to choose how people authenticate to access your enterprise's resources. This choice revolves around whether to allow the use of personal GitHub.com accounts or to exercise more control through Enterprise Managed Users.

Authentication Through GitHub.com: This method is straightforward, where individuals within your enterprise create and manage their personal accounts on GitHub.com. Once granted access to your enterprise, they can sign in with their GitHub.com account to access enterprise resources. This approach allows members to manage their accounts independently and contribute to a wide array of projects and repositories on GitHub.com. It's an ideal choice for enterprises that prefer to give their members more autonomy and the ability to engage with the broader GitHub community.

Authentication with Additional SAML Access Restriction: If you choose to add SAML access restrictions, users still need to manage personal accounts on GitHub.com. However, accessing enterprise resources requires successful authentication via both their GitHub.com account and a SAML identity provider (IdP). This dual authentication enhances security and ensures that access to your enterprise's resources is tightly controlled. It's particularly suited for enterprises looking to balance user autonomy with enhanced security measures.

Authentication with Enterprise Managed Users and Federation: For enterprises requiring more control over member accounts, Enterprise Managed Users is the way to go. In this setup, user accounts are provisioned and managed through your IdP. Each member signs in to a managed account, with your enterprise overseeing account management. This approach restricts contributions to the rest of GitHub.com, offering a higher degree of control and security. It is ideal for enterprises with stringent security requirements or those that need to manage user activity and access closely.

About Provisioning

With SAML access restriction, individuals create personal accounts on GitHub.com, and you can grant these accounts access to enterprise resources. This method does not involve provisioning accounts on your end.

In contrast, Enterprise Managed Users require configuring your IdP to provision user accounts within your enterprise on GitHub.com using SCIM. This approach is more involved but provides tighter control over account creation and management.

Supported Identity Providers

For SAML SSO, GitHub is compatible with IdPs adhering to the SAML 2.0 standard, and some IdPs are officially supported and tested by GitHub. With Enterprise Managed Users, GitHub has partnerships with certain identity management system developers, offering streamlined integration. If you use a partner IdP, you can set up one application on your IdP for both authentication and provisioning. If your IdP is not a partner or is used only for authentication, you can still integrate it with GitHub, provided it supports SAML 2.0 and SCIM 2.0 standards. Each of these authentication methods has its advantages and suits different enterprise needs and workflows. Whether it's the independence offered by personal accounts, the enhanced security of SAML access restriction, or the tight control of Enterprise Managed Users, GitHub Enterprise Cloud provides a range of options to align with your enterprise's security posture and operational preferences.

Best Practices for GitHub IAM

Elaborating on GitHub Identity and Access Management (IAM) best practices, it's crucial to understand that effective IAM within GitHub is foundational to maintaining security, compliance, and operational efficiency in software development. Here's a detailed look at the key practices based on the provided points:

1. **Consistent IAM Policies**

   - Establishing and enforcing clear IAM policies is paramount. This involves defining who has access to what within your GitHub environment. Consistency in these policies across all repositories and teams ensures that there are no ambiguities or loopholes that could lead to security breaches.

- For instance, you might have policies that dictate who can merge pull requests, who can push to the main branch, or who can access certain private repositories. These policies should be uniformly applied across the entire organization to maintain a secure and orderly environment.

2. **Integrating with Identity Providers (IdPs)**

- Integrating GitHub with an organization's identity provider (IdP) streamlines access management significantly. By using Single Sign-On (SSO), you can manage GitHub user accounts and permissions through your central IdP, which might be a service like Azure AD, Okta, or Google Workspace.

- This integration not only simplifies the user onboarding and offboarding processes but also enhances security. With SSO, users don't need to manage separate credentials for GitHub, reducing the risk of password-related security issues.

3. **Education and Training**

- Regular training and education of users on IAM policies and security best practices are vital. This includes making sure that all team members understand the importance of following established protocols and are aware of the potential risks associated with poor security practices.

- Training sessions might cover topics like recognizing phishing attempts, using strong passwords, and understanding the implications of granting repository access. This education helps in building a security-conscious culture within the organization.

4. **Utilizing GitHub's IAM Tools**

   GitHub offers a range of built-in tools that can be leveraged to manage access effectively. These include

   - **Organization Audit Logs:** These logs provide a record of significant actions across the organization, helping in monitoring and auditing user activities.

   - **Repository Access Settings:** These settings allow you to control who has access to each repository. You can define teams or individuals who have read, write, or admin access to repositories.

   - **Branch Protection Rules:** These rules help in safeguarding important branches. For example, you can enforce code reviews and status checks or restrict who can push to specific branches.

By implementing these best practices, organizations can create a robust and secure environment on GitHub. This environment not only protects sensitive code and data but also supports a culture of security and efficiency, which is essential in today's fast-paced and security-conscious software development landscape.

How do I identify the best authentication method for your GitHub Enterprise?

Choosing the right authentication method for your GitHub organization or enterprise involves careful consideration of your specific security requirements, user management preferences, and workflow considerations. This topic provides a detailed analysis to guide you through the decision-making process:

> **Control Over User Accounts:** If the autonomy of user accounts is a critical factor for your organization, then Enterprise Managed Users (EMUs) might be the suitable choice. EMUs allow the enterprise to provision and directly manage user accounts. This gives you greater control over usernames, associated email addresses, and the overall identity conformity of your enterprise members on GitHub. For example, if your company policy requires strict adherence to identity norms or if you're currently mandating new GitHub accounts for enterprise access, EMUs would align well with these requirements.
>
> Conversely, SAML Single Sign-On (SSO) allows users to utilize their personal GitHub accounts linked to their corporate identity via the identity provider. This approach may be more appropriate if your enterprise values flexibility and if developers are already accustomed to using their personal GitHub accounts in a professional capacity.
>
> **Identity Provider Compatibility:** The choice between SAML SSO and EMUs can also be influenced by the identity provider (IdP) your

enterprise uses. SAML SSO is widely compatible with IdPs that support the SAML 2.0 standard, and GitHub has official support for some of the most common IdPs. This means if your IdP is SAML 2.0 compliant, you could set up SAML SSO relatively easily. For example, an enterprise using Okta or Azure Active Directory would find SAML SSO to be a convenient and secure authentication method.

For EMUs, the integration process can be streamlined if you use an IdP that GitHub has partnered with, as this allows for a combined authentication and provisioning setup. If your IdP is not a GitHub partner or you only use it for authentication without SCIM support, then configuring EMUs might involve a more complex integration process.

Public Repository and External Collaboration:
Another critical consideration is the nature of your developers' work. If your developers frequently use public repositories, gists, or GitHub Pages sites for their projects, EMUs may impose too many restrictions, as they limit visibility and collaboration strictly within the enterprise. Such restrictions may be a hindrance if public engagement or open source contributions are integral to your workflows.

In contrast, SAML SSO allows for a broader scope of collaboration, permitting work on both internal and external repositories, which could be essential for enterprises that engage with wider open source communities or need to collaborate with external partners.

Workflow Complexity and Migration Costs: Lastly, the complexity of your developers' workflows and the potential migration costs are significant factors. For enterprises already using GitHub with personal accounts, switching to EMUs would necessitate a migration to a new enterprise account. This transition could introduce costs associated with the migration effort, retraining staff, and potential disruptions to current operations.

For new GitHub Enterprises, both SAML SSO and EMUs are viable starting points with no inherent advantage in terms of adoption ease. However, if migration costs and changes to existing workflows are a concern, SAML SSO might be the preferable option as it enables a more straightforward addition of SSO capabilities to existing GitHub workflows without the need for significant changes.

In summary, when deciding between SAML SSO and Enterprise Managed Users, consider the level of account control and identity conformity you desire, your current IdP's compatibility with GitHub's systems, the nature of your developers' public and external collaborations, and the potential impact of migration efforts. For example, a large enterprise with strict identity policies and internal collaboration focus may lean toward EMUs, while a more flexible, open source–oriented organization might opt for SAML SSO to support a wider range of collaborative engagements. The decision should align with your operational priorities, security policies, and the desired balance between control and flexibility.

SAML SSO Setup for Enterprise and Organization Levels

This topic will walk you through configuring SAML SSO at both the enterprise and organization levels, ensuring secure and seamless user authentication across GitHub. By integrating GitHub with a SAML identity provider (IdP), you'll enable users to authenticate through their enterprise credentials, strengthening security while improving user experience.

Setting up SAML Single Sign-On (SSO) on GitHub at the enterprise and organization levels is a process designed to centralize and secure user authentication across corporate resources. This method leverages the Security Assertion Markup Language (SAML), which is an open standard for exchanging authentication and authorization data between an identity provider and a service provider – in this case, GitHub.

For an enterprise using GitHub, integrating SAML SSO enables the organization to manage user access to both their GitHub organization and other enterprise resources seamlessly. The process begins with choosing an identity provider that supports SAML 2.0 – many enterprises opt for well-known solutions like Okta, Microsoft's Azure Active Directory, or Google's Identity Platform.

Once an IdP is chosen, the GitHub Enterprise owner or organization owner initiates the SSO setup by registering GitHub as a new application within the IdP's console. This involves configuring SAML settings such as assertion consumer service URLs and entity IDs, which are provided by GitHub. The IdP, in turn, generates metadata containing information like the IdP's entity ID and SSO URL, which the enterprise owner then inputs back into GitHub's SSO configuration page.

The next step involves establishing a trust relationship between GitHub and the IdP by exchanging certificates. This ensures that the SAML assertions used during the authentication process are secure and trusted on both ends. With the necessary configurations in place, the enterprise owner can then enforce SSO authentication for all users within the enterprise account, requiring them to authenticate via the IdP to access GitHub resources.

For users, the experience of accessing GitHub post-SAML SSO setup is straightforward. When they attempt to access GitHub, they are redirected to their IdP's login page. Upon successful authentication, the IdP sends a SAML assertion back to GitHub, which grants the user access. This means that users no longer need to manage a separate GitHub-specific password, thus reducing the number of credentials they need to remember and significantly improving security.

From an administrative perspective, SAML SSO simplifies user management and enhances security. It allows enterprise and organization owners to manage user permissions in a centralized location and enforce consistent access policies across all integrated applications. This centralization also extends to security measures, such as multifactor authentication (MFA), which can be mandated at the IdP level.

Moreover, the integration of SAML SSO can streamline the onboarding and offboarding processes. When a new team member joins, they can be granted access to GitHub and other enterprise resources through the IdP. Conversely, when someone leaves the organization, access can be revoked in one place, immediately denying entry to all connected services.

In essence, GitHub's SAML SSO setup for enterprises and organizations not only fortifies security by centralizing authentication but also provides a more convenient and unified login experience for users. It aligns with modern security best practices, offering an efficient way to control access to corporate resources while maintaining compliance with security standards.

Supported Identity Providers

GitHub Enterprise Cloud is compatible with IdPs that adhere to the SAML 2.0 standard. This includes, but is not limited to, the following officially supported and internally tested IdPs:

- Active Directory Federation Services (AD FS)

- Azure Active Directory (Azure AD)

- Okta

- OneLogin

- PingOne

- Shibboleth

For an in-depth understanding of the SAML 2.0 standard, you can refer to the SAML wiki on the OASIS website.

Understanding of the SAML 2.0 Standard

Understanding the SAML 2.0 standard is crucial for implementing modern authentication and authorization processes, especially in enterprise environments. SAML, which stands for Security Assertion Markup Language, is an open standard that allows identity providers (IdPs) to pass authorization credentials to service providers (SPs). What makes SAML 2.0 particularly significant is its widespread adoption for web-based Single Sign-On (SSO) applications.

At its core, SAML 2.0 is about securely exchanging user authentication and authorization data between domains. It uses XML-based protocol messages to facilitate these exchanges. The process typically begins when a user attempts to access a service or application (the SP). If the user is not already authenticated, the service provider redirects them to the IdP. The IdP then authenticates the user and sends a SAML assertion back to the SP, which contains the authentication and authorization information necessary to grant the user access.

One of the key strengths of SAML 2.0 is its ability to enable SSO, thereby enhancing user experience by reducing the number of times a user has to log in. This is not only convenient for users but also strengthens security by minimizing password fatigue and the risks associated with managing multiple credentials.

Moreover, SAML 2.0 supports a range of authentication methods, making it versatile for various security requirements. It also allows the secure transfer of attributes or pieces of data about the user, which can include their name, role, or email address, among others.

Organizations often use SAML 2.0 to streamline access to cloud applications and services. For instance, a company might use SAML 2.0 to authenticate employees for access to a suite of online tools like GitHub, ensuring that access control policies are consistently enforced across all platforms. This standard is widely supported by many software vendors, making it a go-to choice for businesses seeking a reliable, secure, and user-friendly authentication solution.

Important   You have the option to configure SAML Single Sign-On (SSO) at the level of each individual GitHub organization, allowing for separate SSO configurations for each organization. Alternatively, you can set up SAML SSO at the GitHub Enterprise account level, which enforces a uniform SSO configuration across all organizations within the enterprise.

Switching Your SAML SSO Configuration from a GitHub Organization to an Enterprise Account

Are you considering upgrading your GitHub SAML SSO setup from the organization level to the enterprise level? It's a significant move that can streamline and secure access across your entire enterprise, but it comes with some important considerations and steps.

Understanding SAML SSO for Enterprise Accounts

SAML SSO is a powerful tool for controlling access to your GitHub resources, like repositories, issues, and pull requests. When you enable it at the enterprise level, it applies to all organizations under your enterprise account. This means every member, including enterprise owners, will use SAML SSO for authentication across all organizations.

Special Considerations

If you already have SAML SSO set up at the organization level, remember that each organization is linked to a unique SSO identity in your identity provider (IdP). Switching to an enterprise-level SAML SSO means consolidating these identities, so each member has just one SAML identity for all organizations in the enterprise.

What Happens When You Switch?

Once you activate SAML SSO for your enterprise account, your new setup overrides any existing organization-level SAML configurations. Team synchronization settings at the organization level will be removed (remember to note down these settings if you plan to re-enable them). Members won't get a notification about this change, but they'll need to authenticate via SAML as usual. They'll also need to use the new enterprise-level app on their IdP dashboard to access organization resources.

Additionally, all previously authorized personal access tokens, SSH keys, OAuth apps, and GitHub Apps will remain authorized. However, any that weren't authorized for SAML SSO at the organization level will need new authorization.

Note   SCIM provisioning won't be supported with enterprise-level SAML SSO. If you're using SCIM at the organization level, you'll lose this functionality.

Should You Remove Organization-Level SAML Configurations?

It's not mandatory to remove these configurations before switching, but it's worth considering. If SAML is ever disabled at the enterprise level, the organization-level configurations will kick back in, which could lead to confusion or security gaps.

Making the Switch

- Enforce SAML SSO for your enterprise account and ensure all members are linked to the enterprise's IdP app.

- Optionally, remove existing organization-level SAML configurations to avoid future complications.

- If you keep any organization-level configurations, consider hiding their apps in your IdP to prevent confusion.

- Inform your enterprise members about the change. They'll need to use the new enterprise-level app for access and may need to reauthorize some tools for SAML SSO.

Switching to an enterprise-level SAML SSO configuration on GitHub is a strategic move that can enhance security and simplify access management across your enterprise. Just remember to plan carefully, communicate clearly with your team, and consider the implications for existing configurations and tools.

Enforcing SAML Single Sign-On for Your GitHub Enterprise Using Azure AD

You can configure SAML SSO at the organization level (for each GitHub organization), or you can set SAML SSO at the enterprise level. When you opt to enforce SAML SSO at the enterprise level, it replaces any SAML configurations set at the organization level within that enterprise. This is crucial to consider, especially if any of your enterprise's organizations are already using SAML SSO.

Upon enforcing SAML SSO for an organization, GitHub will remove any members who haven't successfully authenticated via your SAML IdP. However, for enterprise-level enforcement, members who haven't authenticated successfully are not removed but will be required to authenticate via the SAML IdP upon their next access to the enterprise's resources.

Here is a step-by-step guide on enabling SAML using Azure:

Steps to Enable SAML SSO

1. Navigate to your profile photo in the top-right corner of GitHub.com and select Your enterprises. Figure 4-3 shows the enterprise option.

Figure 4-3. *Your enterprises*

2. Choose the enterprise account you wish to configure.

3. In the enterprise account sidebar, select Settings, then click Authentication Security. Figure 4-4 shows the settings option.

Figure 4-4. *Enterprise settings*

4. To review current configurations for all organizations in your enterprise account before making changes, select View your organizations' current configurations.

5. Under "SAML Single Sign-On," choose to Require SAML authentication. Figure 4-5 shows the SAML authentication enable option.

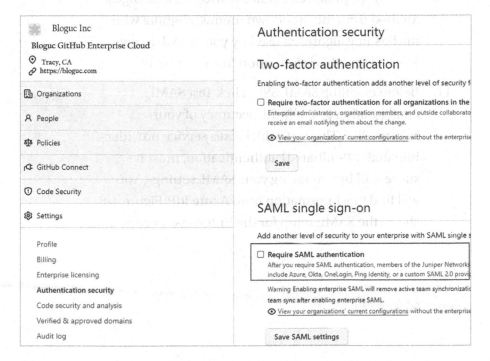

Figure 4-5. *Enterprise account SAML authentication*

6. In the Sign-on URL field, input the HTTPS endpoint of your IdP for Single Sign-On requests. This information is found in your IdP configuration.

7. Optionally, in the Issuer field, input your SAML issuer URL to validate the authenticity of messages. You will find this information from Azure IdP.

8. Under Public Certificate, paste the certificate to verify SAML responses.

9. To the right of the current signature and digest methods, click the pencil icon to edit.

10. Select your preferred Signature Method and Digest Method from the dropdown menus, aligning with the hashing algorithm used by your SAML issuer. You will find this information from Azure IdP.

11. Before enabling SAML SSO, click Test SAML configuration to verify the accuracy of your information. This test, which uses service provider–initiated (SP-initiated) authentication, must be successful before saving your SAML settings. You will find this information from Azure IdP. Figure 4-6 shows the SAML setup for the Enterprise account.

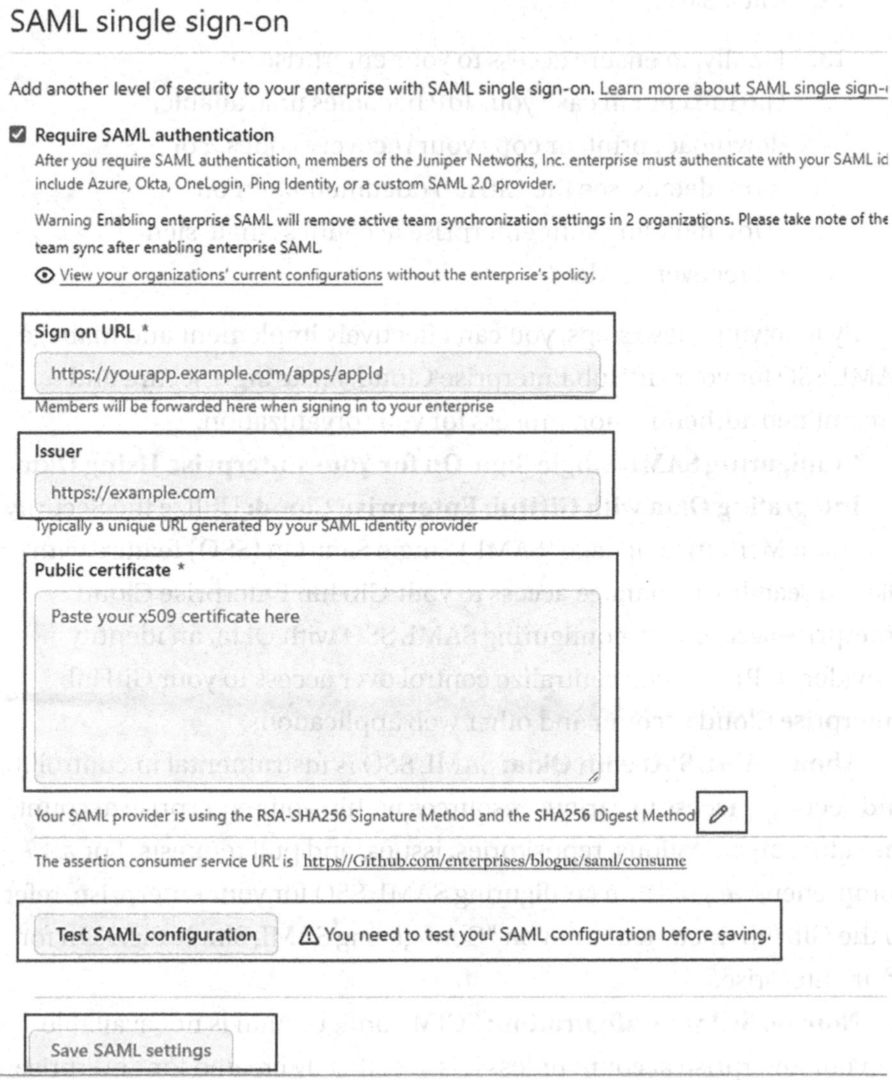

SAML single sign-on

Add another level of security to your enterprise with SAML single sign-on. Learn more about SAML single sign-

☑ **Require SAML authentication**

After you require SAML authentication, members of the Juniper Networks, Inc. enterprise must authenticate with your SAML id include Azure, Okta, OneLogin, Ping Identity, or a custom SAML 2.0 provider.

Warning Enabling enterprise SAML will remove active team synchronization settings in 2 organizations. Please take note of the team sync after enabling enterprise SAML.

⊙ View your organizations' current configurations without the enterprise's policy.

Sign on URL *

https://yourapp.example.com/apps/appId

Members will be forwarded here when signing in to your enterprise

Issuer

https://example.com

Typically a unique URL generated by your SAML identity provider

Public certificate *

Paste your x509 certificate here

Your SAML provider is using the RSA-SHA256 Signature Method and the SHA256 Digest Method ✎

The assertion consumer service URL is https://Github.com/enterprises/bloguc/saml/consume

| Test SAML configuration | ⚠ You need to test your SAML configuration before saving. |

Save SAML settings

Figure 4-6. *Enterprise account SAML authentication setup*

12. Click Save.

13. Finally, to ensure access to your enterprise on GitHub.com in case your IdP becomes unavailable, download, print, or copy your recovery codes. For more details, see the GitHub documentation on "Downloading your enterprise account's single sign-on recovery codes."

By following these steps, you can effectively implement and manage SAML SSO for your GitHub Enterprise Cloud, ensuring a secure and streamlined authentication process for your organization.

Configuring SAML Single Sign-On for Your Enterprise Using Okta

Integrating Okta with GitHub Enterprise Cloud: Utilize the Security Assertion Markup Language (SAML) Single Sign-On (SSO) feature with Okta to seamlessly manage access to your GitHub Enterprise Cloud enterprise account. By configuring SAML SSO with Okta, an identity provider (IdP), you can centralize control over access to your GitHub Enterprise Cloud account and other web applications.

About SAML SSO with Okta: SAML SSO is instrumental in controlling and securing access to various resources within your enterprise account, including organizations, repositories, issues, and pull requests. For a comprehensive guide on configuring SAML SSO for your enterprise, refer to the GitHub documentation on "Configuring SAML Single Sign-On for your enterprise."

Note on SCIM Configuration: SCIM configuration is not available for your enterprise account unless it is specifically created for Enterprise Managed Users. For enterprises not using Enterprise Managed Users but wishing to use SCIM provisioning, SAML SSO must be configured at the organization level, not the enterprise level. More details can be found in the GitHub documentation on "About identity and access management with SAML Single Sign-On."

Special Considerations: If any organizations within your enterprise account are already using SAML SSO, special considerations are required when enabling SAML SSO for your enterprise account. For more information, see the GitHub documentation on "Switching your SAML configuration from an organization to an enterprise account."

SAML SSO can also be configured using Okta for individual organizations using GitHub Enterprise Cloud.

Adding GitHub Enterprise Cloud Application in Okta

1. Log in to your Okta account.

2. Find the GitHub Enterprise Cloud – Enterprise Accounts application in the Okta Integration Network and select Add Integration.

3. In the Applications section, click Applications from the left sidebar.

4. Optionally, next to "Application label," input a descriptive name for the application.

5. Next to "GitHub Enterprises," enter the name of your enterprise account (e.g., for `https://github.com/enterprises/bloguc`, enter bloguc).

6. Click Done.

Enabling and Testing SAML SSO

1. Sign in to your Okta account.

2. Navigate to Applications using the dropdown in the left sidebar and select Applications.

3. Click the label of the application you created for your enterprise account.

4. Assign the application to your user in Okta (see Okta documentation for "Assign applications to users" for guidance).

5. Under the application name, click Sign on, then Edit next to Settings.

6. In "Configured SAML Attributes," next to "groups," select Matches regex from the dropdown menu and type …

7. Click Save.

8. Under "SIGN ON METHODS," select View Setup Instructions.

9. Follow these setup instructions to enable SAML for your enterprise account. For more detailed guidance, refer to "Configuring SAML Single Sign-On for your enterprise" in the GitHub documentation.

By following these steps, you can effectively integrate Okta with your GitHub Enterprise Cloud, ensuring a secure and streamlined access management system for your enterprise.

Implementing SAML SSO in GitHub Organizations

SAML SSO can be a game changer for organizations using GitHub Enterprise Cloud, offering a seamless and secure authentication experience. Here's a detailed look at how to implement and configure SAML SSO for your GitHub organization. SAML SSO can be enabled in your organization on GitHub Enterprise Cloud without making it mandatory for all members immediately. This gradual approach aids in the smooth adoption of SAML SSO. Initially, members who do not opt for SAML SSO can still retain their membership in the organization. It's worth noting, however, that SAML authentication isn't required for outside collaborators. Once most members are comfortable with SAML SSO, you can enforce it across your organization. You can set up a trial to get started with GitHub Enterprise Cloud.

Note   When SAML SSO is disabled at any point, all external identities linked to GitHub Enterprise Cloud are removed.

Configuring SAML SSO for GitHub Organization

Initial Setup: Before enforcing SAML SSO, ensuring your organization is ready for this shift is important. You can find more information on preparation steps in the GitHub documentation.

Identity Providers (IdPs): GitHub supports various IdPs for SAML SSO. Information on connecting your IdP to your GitHub organization is available on GitHub's guidelines. We are using Azure IdP for this book topic; you are free to use any supported IdP.

Enabling SAML SSO for the Organization

1. Access your organization settings by clicking your profile photo in the upper-right corner of GitHub. com and selecting "Your organizations."

2. Navigate to the "Authentication security" section in the "Security" sidebar.

3. Select "Enable SAML authentication" under the SAML Single Sign-On section. Figure 4-7 shows the org SAML setup.

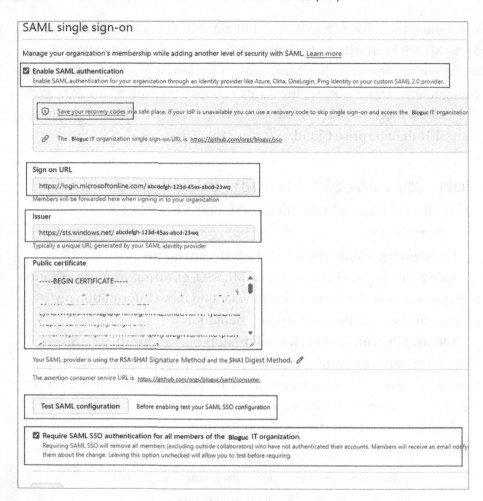

Figure 4-7. *Enable SAML for the GitHub org*

4. Enter the sign-on URL from your IdP configuration. Refer to Figure 4-7 for an example URL.

5. Optionally, specify your SAML issuer's name in the "Issuer" field for message authenticity verification. This is required for team synchronization.

6. Paste your public certificate to verify SAML responses.

7. Choose the appropriate Signature Method and Digest Method as used by your SAML issuer.

Testing the Configuration

Before fully enabling SAML SSO, conduct a test to verify the accuracy of the setup. This involves a service provider–initiated authentication test and should be successful before saving the SAML settings. Figure 4-8 shows the test SAML configuration.

> Test SAML configuration   ⚠ You need to test your SAML configuration before saving.

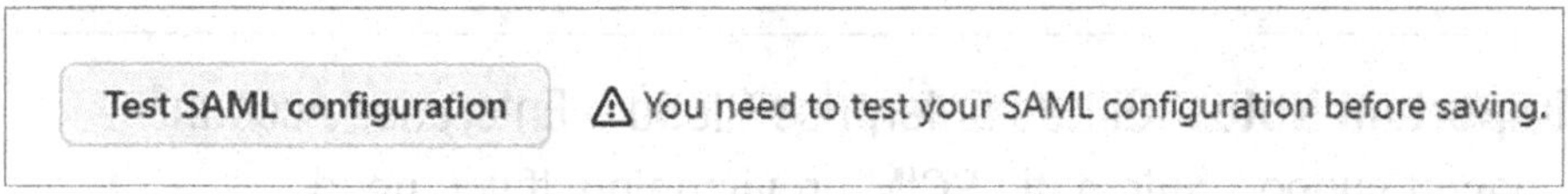

Figure 4-8. *Test SAML configuration*

Enforcement

To enforce SAML SSO and exclude members not authenticated via your IdP, select the option "Require SAML SSO authentication for all members of the Bloguc organization." Then, save your settings to apply these changes. Figure 4-9 shows the SAML enforcement.

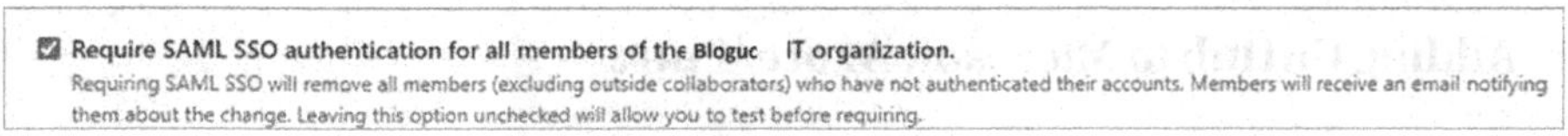

> ☑ Require SAML SSO authentication for all members of the Bloguc   IT organization.
> Requiring SAML SSO will remove all members (excluding outside collaborators) who have not authenticated their accounts. Members will receive an email notifying them about the change. Leaving this option unchecked will allow you to test before requiring.

Figure 4-9. *Enforce SAML SSO*

Additional Important Considerations

After enabling SAML SSO, it may be necessary to revoke and reauthorize OAuth and GitHub App authorizations for them to access the organization. Downloading Single Sign-On recovery codes is recommended post enabling SAML SSO. These codes ensure access to your organization even if the IdP is unavailable.

Implementing SAML SSO in your GitHub organization not only enhances security but also streamlines the authentication process. While the setup requires careful configuration and testing, the result is a more controlled and secure environment for your team's collaborative efforts.

Setting Up SSO with GitHub Enterprise Cloud Using Microsoft Azure/Entra

This topic will show you how to set up Microsoft Entra SAML integration with a GitHub Enterprise Cloud – Enterprise Account. By doing this, you can control who in Microsoft Entra ID has access to your GitHub Enterprise Account and its organizations.

Important Note   GitHub Enterprise Cloud – Enterprise Account doesn't support automatic SCIM provisioning. If you need provisioning, set up SAML at the organization level using the GitHub Enterprise Cloud – Organization Microsoft Entra application. For Enterprise Managed Users (EMUs), use the GitHub Enterprise Managed User Microsoft Entra application.

GitHub Enterprise Cloud – Enterprise Account supports both SP- and IdP-initiated SSO.

Adding GitHub to Microsoft Azure/Entra

1. Log in to the Microsoft Azure/Entra admin center (https://portal.azure.com/#home) as a Global Admin or Cloud Admin.

2. Go to Enterprise applications ➤ New application. Figure 4-10 shows the new enterprise application.

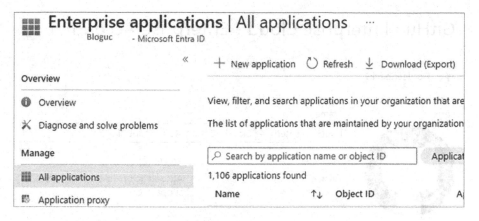

Figure 4-10. *New enterprise application*

3. In the gallery, search for and add GitHub Enterprise
   Cloud – Enterprise Account.

4. Alternatively, use the Enterprise App Configuration
   Wizard for a more guided setup.

Configuring and Testing Microsoft Azure/Entra SSO
Configure Microsoft Azure/Entra SSO:

1. Sign in to the Microsoft Azure/Entra admin center.

2. Go to Enterprise applications. Refer to Figure 4-10,
   which shows the new application.

3. GitHub Enterprise Cloud – Enterprise Account.
   Figure 4-11 shows the enterprise account setup.

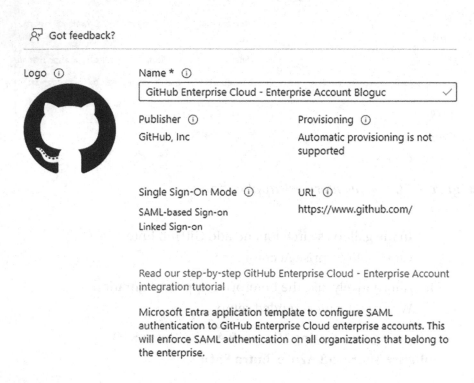

Figure 4-11. *New enterprise account setup*

4. Then choose Single Sign-On and then choose SAML
    as your Single Sign-On method.

5. Edit the Basic SAML Configuration:

    a. For the Identifier (Entity ID), use this pattern:
        `https://github.com/enterprises/<YOUR-`
        `ENTERPRISE-NAME>`.

    b. For the Reply URL, use `https://github.com/`
        `enterprises/<YOUR-ENTERPRISE-NAME>/saml/`
        `consume`.

    c. If setting up SP-initiated mode, add a Sign-on URL.

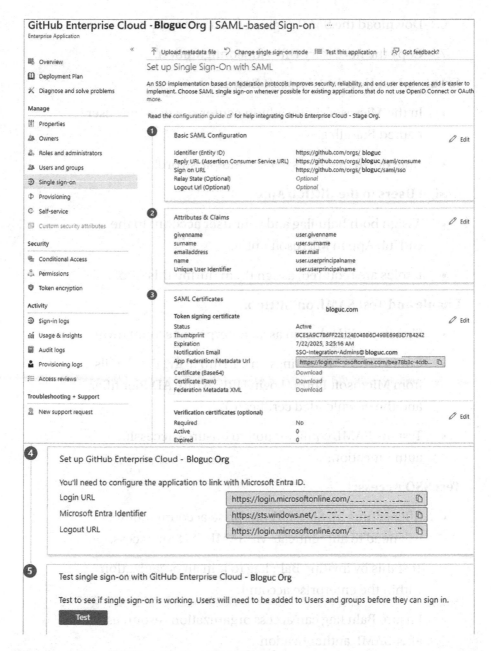

Figure 4-12. *GitHub Enterprise Cloud*

6. Download the SAML Signing Certificate and save it.

7. Copy the necessary URLs for configuration.

Create a Test User in Microsoft Entra:

- In the Microsoft Entra admin center, create a new user named Balu.Ilag.

- Note down the user's details and password.

Assign Users to the GitHub App:

- Assign both Balu.ilag and your user account to the GitHub App in Microsoft Entra.

- If roles are required, assign them during this step.

Enable and Test SAML on GitHub:

- Sign in to GitHub.com as an enterprise account owner.

- Configure SAML settings on GitHub using the details from Microsoft Entra (Login URL, Azure AD Identifier, and the downloaded certificate).

- Test the SAML configuration to ensure successful authentication.

Test SSO Access:

- After setting up SSO, all enterprise account members will need to authenticate via SAML SSO for access.

- Test this by inviting Balu Ilag to join an organization within the enterprise account.

- Ensure Balu Ilag can access organization resources after SAML authentication.

By following these steps, you'll successfully integrate SSO using Microsoft Entra with your GitHub Enterprise Cloud – Enterprise Account, allowing for secure and streamlined access management.

Understanding and Managing GitHub EMU

Enterprise Managed Users (EMUs) are accounts that belong to an enterprise account instead of being directly linked to an individual. This section covers the ins and outs of EMUs, explaining how to create, manage, and use them effectively to streamline your GitHub IAM strategy.

GitHub Enterprise Managed Users – Centralized Identity and Access Management: With EMUs, GitHub allows you to centrally manage the lifecycle and authentication of your enterprise members on GitHub.com from your identity provider (IdP). This system enables you to integrate GitHub Enterprise Cloud with existing identities and group memberships in your IdP, streamlining user access and management.

Key Features of Enterprise Managed Users

User Account Management

- Your IdP provisions new user accounts on GitHub.com.

- Control over usernames, profile data, team membership, and repository access lies with your IdP.

- Managed user accounts can own organizations within your enterprise and manage other user accounts.

Role Assignment

- Assign roles like member, enterprise owner, or guest collaborator in your IdP.

- See "Roles in an enterprise" and "About organizations" in the GitHub documentation for more details.

Security and Compliance

- When using OIDC SSO, GitHub automatically applies your IdP's Conditional Access Policy (CAP) IP conditions.

- This enhances security, especially when IP addresses change or when using personal access tokens or SSH keys.

Content Creation and Collaboration Restrictions

- Managed users can access and contribute to enterprise repositories.

- They cannot create public content or collaborate outside the enterprise on GitHub.

- Usernames and profile information are set through your IdP and are not changeable by the users.

Audit and Compliance

- Enterprise owners can audit all actions of managed user accounts on GitHub.

Prerequisites for Using EMUs

- This requires a specific type of enterprise account with EMUs enabled.

- For setup, contact GitHub's Sales team.

Authentication and User Provisioning
IdP Integration

- GitHub partners with several IdP developers for seamless integration.

- Supported authentication methods include SAML and OIDC (Azure AD).

- User provisioning is handled via SCIM (System for Cross-domain Identity Management).

Supported IdPs

The following are the supported IdPs for GitHub:

- Azure Active Directory

- Okta

- PingFederate

- Other IdPs adhering to SAML 2.0 and SCIM 2.0 specifications

Provisioning and Authentication

- GitHub's public SCIM schema is in public beta.

- It's recommended to test provisioning in an isolated environment.

Getting Started with EMUs

1. **Initial Setup**

   - Contact GitHub's Sales team to create a new enterprise with managed users.

   - Provide necessary details like email for setup user and a unique short code for usernames (GitHub Account).

2. **Configuration**

   - The setup user, created during the initial process, is used to configure SSO and SCIM.

   - Enable two-factor authentication for added security.

   - Choose between OIDC and SAML for authentication, depending on your IdP.

271

3. **Managing Organization Membership**

- Sync IdP groups with GitHub teams for automatic membership management.

- Manual removal is required for members added manually.

4. **Authentication Process for Managed Users**

- Managed users must authenticate through their IdP.

- GitHub displays a 404 error by default for unauthenticated users, but enterprises can opt for automatic redirects to SSO.

- In case of SAML configuration errors, recovery codes can be used for access.

5. **Support for Multiple GitHub Accounts**

- Users needing to contribute to resources outside the managed enterprise can maintain separate personal accounts.

- Git configurations and account switching features on GitHub.com can simplify managing multiple accounts.

Enterprise Managed Users offer a robust, centralized system for managing GitHub access and identities, aligning with enterprise security and compliance standards. For detailed guidance on each aspect, refer to the specific GitHub documentation sections mentioned earlier.

Setting Up SAML Single Sign-On for GitHub Enterprise Managed Users

What is SAML SSO for Enterprise Managed Users? SAML (Security Assertion Markup Language) Single Sign-On (SSO) is a way for you to control access to your GitHub Enterprise account. Instead of using a GitHub username and password, your team members will sign in through your identity provider (IdP), which is an external service that manages your team's identities.

Why Use SAML SSO for GitHub?

- It makes signing in to GitHub simpler and more secure.

- It centralizes the management of your enterprise's access on GitHub.com.

Important Steps and Recommendations

After setting up SAML SSO, save your recovery codes. These are important if you can't access your IdP. If you're already using SAML SSO and want to switch to OIDC (OpenID Connect) for extra features like CAP (Conditional Access Policy), there's a way to migrate.

Prerequisites

- Before you start, it is important to understand Your IdP: Make sure you know how your IdP works with GitHub. Your IdP should support SAML 2.0. You can learn more about SAML 2.0 on the OASIS website's SAML wiki.

- **Access Requirements:** You should have a tenant (a dedicated instance in the IdP service) and administrative access to your IdP.

- **Avoid Unnecessary Changes:** Once you set up SAML SSO and user provisioning, it's best not to switch to a different platform. If you really need to change, talk to your account manager at GitHub's Sales team.

How to Set Up SAML SSO?

Configure Your IdP

If you're using a partner IdP (like Azure AD, Okta, or PingFederate), you'll need to install the GitHub Enterprise Managed User application. You can find these applications in their respective marketplaces or directories:

- For Azure AD, go to the Azure Marketplace (`https://azuremarketplace.microsoft.com/en-us/marketplace/apps/aad.githubenterprisemanageduser?tab=Overview`).

- For Okta, check Okta's integration directory (`www.okta.com/integrations/github-enterprise-managed-user/`).

- For PingFederate, visit their downloads website and look for the GitHub EMU Connector 1.0 under the Add-ons tab (`www.pingidentity.com/en/resources/downloads/pingfederate.htm`).

If your IdP is not a partner, you'll need to create and set up a generic SAML 2.0 application on your IdP.

Configure Your Enterprise on GitHub.com

Assign yourself or another user who will set up SAML SSO for your enterprise on GitHub.com to the application you configured on your IdP.

Find and note down important information from your IdP application:

- **IdP Sign-On URL:** This is the application's URL on your IdP.

- **IdP Identifier URL:** Also known as the Issuer, this is your IdP's identifier for SAML authentication.

- **Signing Certificate (Base64-Encoded):** This is a public certificate your IdP uses for signing authentication requests.

Setting Up SAML SSO for Your GitHub Enterprise
Initial Steps

- Once you've set up SAML SSO with your IdP, the next step is to configure your enterprise on GitHub.com.

- Remember, after this initial setup, the only thing you can change on GitHub.com is the SAML certificate. If you need to update the sign-on URL or issuer URL, you'll have to disable SAML SSO first and then redo the setup with the new details.

Logging In

- Sign in to GitHub.com using your enterprise's setup user account. The username will be something like @YOUR_SHORT-CODE_admin (replace YOUR_SHORT-CODE with your actual enterprise's short code).

- If you've forgotten the setup user's password, you'll need to contact GitHub Support to reset it.

Accessing Enterprise Settings

- Once logged in, click your profile photo in the top-right corner, then select "Your enterprises."

- Choose the enterprise you want to configure.

- In the enterprise account sidebar, select "Settings."

Configuring Authentication Security

- Under "Settings," go to "Authentication security."

- Select "Require SAML authentication" under "SAML Single Sign-On."

- Enter the Sign-on URL, Issuer, and Public Certificate details you noted from your IdP. These are crucial for verifying the authenticity of messages and responses.

- Choose the appropriate Signature Method and Digest Method as used by your SAML issuer.

Testing and Saving Your Configuration

- Before enabling SAML SSO, test your configuration by clicking "Test SAML configuration." This step is important to ensure all details are correct.

- Once the test is successful, click "Save."

Note   After enabling SAML SSO, the setup user will lose access to the enterprise settings but will remain signed in to GitHub. Only user accounts managed by your IdP will have access to the GitHub Enterprise.

Important Note   Keep recovery codes securely; as to prepare for any future issues with your IdP, download, print, or copy your recovery codes for safekeeping.

Enabling User Provisioning

After setting up SAML SSO, you should enable user provisioning. This is how new users get added to your GitHub Enterprise system.

Setting Up Guest Collaborators

Guest collaborators are useful for giving limited access to vendors and contractors. They can access only specific repositories or organizations you assign them to. If you're using Azure AD or Okta, you might need to update your IdP application settings to include guest collaborators.

For Azure AD Users: Perform the following steps.

1. Log in to the Azure portal.

2. Go to "Enterprise applications" ➤ "All applications."

3. Check your Enterprise Managed Users application for "Restricted User" or "Guest Collaborator" roles.

4. If these roles aren't there, go to "App registrations" and find your application.

5. Click "Manifest" and add the "Guest Collaborator" role with the specified details.

6. Save your changes.

For Okta Users: Perform the following steps.

1. Go to your Enterprise Managed Users application on Okta.

2. Click "Provisioning" and then "Go to Profile Editor."

3. Find "Roles" and edit it.

4. Add "Guest Collaborator" as a new role with the specified display name and value.

5. Save your changes.

Adding Guest Collaborators

Once you've set up the guest collaborator role, you can start adding them to your enterprise.

Basically, configuring your GitHub Enterprise on GitHub.com involves setting up SAML SSO, testing and saving your configuration, preparing recovery codes, enabling user provisioning, and setting up guest collaborators if needed. This process ensures a secure and streamlined way to manage access to your enterprise's resources on GitHub.

GitHub User Onboarding and Offboarding Process

This section provides detailed guidelines on how to smoothly and securely onboard new users onto GitHub, granting them appropriate access and resources, and likewise, how to offboard users when they no longer require access, ensuring that all associated data and access permissions are handled properly.

Onboarding Process

Account Creation and Setup

- New users create a GitHub account, selecting a username and providing essential details like email addresses.

- They then configure their profile, adding information such as their name, bio, and profile picture to personalize their account.

Introduction to GitHub Interface

- Users are introduced to the GitHub interface, including repositories, branches, commits, pull requests, and issues.

- They learn how to navigate the dashboard, explore repositories, and understand the basic layout of GitHub.

Repository Management

- Users learn how to create and manage repositories. This includes initializing a new repository, setting up a README, and understanding repository settings.

- They also learn about branch management and the importance of the main/master branch.

Version Control Basics

- Essential Git commands (like git clone, git pull, git push) are introduced.

- Users learn how to make changes, commit them, and push these changes to GitHub.

Collaboration Tools

- Users are taught how to collaborate using GitHub. This includes understanding pull requests, code reviews, and issue tracking.

- They learn how to fork repositories, make changes, and submit pull requests.

Security and Permissions

- Understanding of user roles, permissions, and repository access levels is provided.

- Introduction to security features like two-factor authentication and SSH keys.

Integrations and Advanced Features

- Users are introduced to GitHub integrations with other tools and platforms.

- Advanced features like GitHub Actions, GitHub Pages, and webhooks are also covered.

Offboarding Process
Access Revocation

- The user's access to company repositories and data is revoked. This includes removing them from organization teams and repositories.

- Their administrative privileges, if any, are also removed.

Transfer of Ownership

- Repositories, issues, and pull requests owned by the departing user are transferred to another team member.

- This ensures continuity and that no critical information or processes are lost.

Review of Contributions

- A review of the user's contributions and ongoing work is conducted to ensure a smooth transition.

- This includes checking for any open pull requests or unresolved issues that need attention.

Security Audit

- A security audit is performed to ensure no sensitive data is leaving with the user.

- This includes checking for any SSH keys or personal access tokens that need to be revoked.

Final Steps

- The user's account is either completely removed from the GitHub organization or downgraded to a read-only state, depending on company policy.

- A final communication is sent to the user, confirming the completion of the offboarding process.

Importance of Onboarding and Offboarding Processes

- **Ensures Security and Compliance:** Proper onboarding and offboarding processes are crucial for maintaining security. They ensure that only authorized personnel have access to sensitive data and systems. Compliance with data protection regulations is also ensured by controlling access to information.

- **Facilitates Knowledge Transfer:** Onboarding helps new users quickly get up to speed with the tools and processes. This leads to a more productive and efficient workforce. Offboarding ensures that the departing user's knowledge and responsibilities are transferred, preventing any disruption in workflows.

- **Maintains Organizational Efficiency:** Streamlined onboarding processes help new users integrate quickly into teams, reducing the time it takes for them to become productive. Effective offboarding ensures that there are no loose ends when an employee leaves, maintaining the organization's operational efficiency.

- **Protects Intellectual Property:** Offboarding processes help in safeguarding the company's intellectual property by ensuring that access to sensitive information is revoked when an employee leaves.

- **Promotes a Positive Work Culture:** A smooth onboarding process can significantly improve a new employee's experience, fostering a positive work culture. Respectful offboarding shows that the company values its employees and their contributions, even as they exit, which can positively impact current employee morale.

The onboarding and offboarding processes on GitHub are essential for operational efficiency, security, compliance, and maintaining a positive work environment. They ensure that new users are quickly brought up to speed and that the organization's assets and information remain secure when users depart.

Best Practices for Managing Access to GitHub

Managing access and identity on GitHub is a critical component of maintaining a secure and efficient software development environment. Here's a comprehensive approach to achieving this.

Firstly, integrating GitHub with a centralized identity provider (IdP), such as Azure AD, Okta, or LDAP, is essential. This integration not only centralizes user management and simplifies access control but also enhances overall security through Single Sign-On (SSO) capabilities. For instance, when a new developer joins the team, they can be seamlessly added to the IdP, automatically granting them access to the necessary GitHub repositories.

Another crucial step is the implementation of two-factor authentication (2FA). This security measure adds an extra layer of protection, ensuring that even if a user's password is compromised, unauthorized access is still prevented unless the attacker also possesses the second factor. GitHub supports various 2FA methods, including Time-based One-Time Password (TOTP) apps and hardware security keys, offering flexibility and enhanced security.

Regularly reviewing access permissions is also vital. This involves conducting periodic audits of repository access, team memberships, and organization roles to ensure that only the right people have access to sensitive data and systems. For example, a quarterly review could be conducted to verify if all members with write access to critical repositories still require this level of permission.

Organizing users into teams based on their role or function and assigning repository access to these teams is an effective way to manage permissions. This not only simplifies permission management but also fosters collaboration. For example, a "front-end" team might be given access to front-end repositories, while a "back-end" team has access to back-end repositories.

Implementing branch protection rules is another best practice. These rules help prevent unauthorized changes and maintain code quality by enforcing code reviews, status checks, and restricting who can push to important branches, like the "main" branch.

For automation tasks, it's advisable to use separate bot accounts. This practice ensures a clear distinction between human and automated actions, enhancing clarity and security. These bot accounts should be assigned only the necessary permissions for tasks like CI/CD pipelines.

Educating team members on security best practices is equally important. Regular training sessions on topics like phishing awareness and secure password practices can significantly reduce the risk of human error, which is a major security threat.

Monitoring and auditing activities through GitHub's audit logs is a proactive way to detect suspicious activities and ensure compliance. Integrating with a SIEM system for advanced monitoring can provide additional security layers, allowing for alerts on unusual repository access patterns. Defining and enforcing contribution policies is critical for maintaining code quality and legal compliance. Clear contribution guidelines, coupled with automated checks, ensure adherence to these policies.

Finally, having a clear offboarding process is crucial. This process should include steps for revoking access and transferring ownership of repositories and code when a team member leaves. Prompt action in these situations is key to maintaining security.

Use a Centralized Identity Provider (IdP)

- **Why:** It centralizes user management, simplifies access control, and enhances security.

- **How:** Integrate GitHub with an IdP like Azure AD, Okta, or LDAP. This allows for Single Sign-On (SSO) and easier user management.

- **Example:** When a new developer joins your team, they are added to the IdP, automatically granting them access to the necessary GitHub repositories.

Implement Two-Factor Authentication (2FA)

- **Why:** It adds an extra layer of security beyond just usernames and passwords.

- **How:** Enforce 2FA for all users. GitHub supports several 2FA methods, including TOTP apps and hardware security keys.

- **Example:** Even if a developer's password is compromised, the account remains secure unless the attacker also has access to the second factor.

Regularly Review Access Permissions

- **Why:** It ensures that only the right people have access to sensitive data and systems.

- **How:** Conduct periodic audits of repository access, team memberships, and organization roles.

- **Example:** Quarterly reviews where you check if all members with write access to critical repositories still require it.

Use Teams for Repository Access Management

- **Why:** It simplifies permission management and enhances collaboration.

- **How:** Organize users into teams based on their role or function and assign repository access to these teams.

- **Example:** A "front-end" team might have access to front-end repositories, while a "back-end" team has access to back-end repositories.

Implement Branch Protection Rules

- **Why:** It prevents unauthorized changes and maintains code quality.

- **How:** Use branch protection rules to enforce code review and status checks and restrict who can push to important branches.

- **Example:** Protect the "main" branch so that changes can only be made via pull requests reviewed by senior developers.

Use Bot Accounts for Automation

- **Why:** It separates human from automated actions for clarity and security.

- **How:** Create separate bot accounts for automated tasks like CI/CD pipelines and assign them only the necessary permissions.

- **Example:** A bot account that only has access to deploy code to production from the main branch.

Educate Team Members

- **Why:** Human error is a significant security risk.

- **How:** Regularly train your team on security best practices, including phishing awareness and secure password practices.

- **Example:** Conducting workshops on recognizing and reporting phishing attempts.

Monitor and Audit Activities

- **Why:** It detects suspicious activities and ensures compliance.

- **How:** Use GitHub's audit logs to monitor activities. Consider integrating with a SIEM system for advanced monitoring.

- **Example:** Setting up alerts for unusual repository access patterns.

Define and Enforce Contribution Policies

- **Why:** It maintains code quality and legal compliance.

- **How:** Create clear contribution guidelines and use automated checks to enforce them.

- **Example:** Requiring all commits to be signed for verification.

Plan for Offboarding

- **Why:** It ensures that access is revoked when no longer needed.

- **How:** Have a clear offboarding process that includes revoking access and transferring ownership of repositories and code.

- **Example:** When a developer leaves, their access is immediately revoked, and their responsibilities are reassigned.

By adopting these practices, organizations can create a robust framework for managing access and identity on GitHub, ensuring that their development processes are secure, compliant, and efficient.

Summary

The structure you choose should facilitate the kind of collaboration and efficiency you aim for in your enterprise. It's important to balance ease of access with security and control and to be willing to adjust your structure as your organization grows and evolves.

The chapter concluded by consolidating the best practices for managing access to GitHub. This includes setting up strong authentication methods, implementing least privilege principles, maintaining an updated access inventory, regular audits, and more.

By the end of this chapter, readers will have a clear understanding of how GitHub's Identity and Access Management works, including setting up SAML SSO, managing EMUs, and effectively handling the onboarding and offboarding of users while adhering to the best practices to ensure maximum security and efficiency.

Resources

- EMU information and configuration details:
  https://docs.github.com/en/enterprise-cloud@
  latest/admin/identity-and-access-management/
  configuring-authentication-for-enterprise-
  managed-users/configuring-saml-single-sign-on-
  for-enterprise-managed-users

- Azure AD apps: https://azuremarketplace.
  microsoft.com/en-us/marketplace/apps/aad.github
  enterprisemanageduser?tab=Overview

- Okta: www.okta.com/integrations/github-
  enterprise-managed-user/

- PingFederate: www.pingidentity.com/en/resources/
  downloads/pingfederate.html

- SAML metadata: https://docs.github.com/en/
  enterprise-cloud@latest/admin/identity-and-
  access-management/iam-configuration-reference/
  saml-configuration-reference

CHAPTER 5

GitHub Actions and GitHub Packages Management

This chapter provides a comprehensive guide on GitHub Actions and GitHub Packages – powerful features of GitHub that allow for the automation of workflows and management of software dependencies in a project.

Topics covered in this chapter include

- Introduction to GitHub Actions and GitHub Packages

- Understanding GitHub Actions

- Workflow Configuration and Management

- Understanding Variables and Secrets in GitHub Actions

- Understanding Environments

- Using Containers in GitHub Actions

- GitHub Actions Usage Billing, Limits, and Administration

- Installing and Publishing Packages

© Dalu Nivrutti Ilag, AjayKumar P. Baljochi, Ganesh J. Sangale and Yogesh Athave 2024
B. N. Ilag et al., *Mastering GitHub Enterprise Management and Administration*,
https://doi.org/10.1007/979-8-8688-0369-7_5

- Using GitHub Actions to Automate Publishing Packages

- Best Practices for Using GitHub Actions and GitHub Packages

Introduction to GitHub Actions and GitHub Packages

The chapter begins with an overview of GitHub Actions and GitHub Packages, explaining what they are and their role in software development and project management. The topic of "Introduction to GitHub Actions and GitHub Packages to Automate Development Tasks and Workflow" delves into the powerful capabilities of GitHub as a platform for not only hosting and managing code but also for automating various aspects of the software development process. At the heart of this automation are GitHub Actions, a feature that enables developers to create custom software development lifecycle (SDLC) workflows directly in their GitHub repositories.

GitHub Actions are pivotal in automating repetitive tasks and workflows, thereby streamlining development processes and enhancing productivity. This automation can range from simple tasks like code linting and running tests to more complex workflows such as deploying applications to production environments. By leveraging GitHub Actions, developers can respond to events within their repositories – such as a push or pull request – and execute a series of commands in response, all defined in a YAML file within the repository.

The integration of GitHub Packages with GitHub Actions further enhances this automation. GitHub Packages serves as a package hosting service, allowing developers to publish, version, and consume packages as part of their GitHub workflows. This integration means that software packages can be automatically published or updated as part of the CI/CD pipeline, ensuring that dependencies are always up to date and reducing the manual effort required in package management.

In addition to automating standard development tasks, GitHub Actions can also be used for automating GitHub Administration. This includes tasks like managing branch protections, enforcing coding standards, and automating the management of issues and pull requests. These administrative workflows ensure that the repository remains organized and that the codebase adheres to predefined quality standards.

Examples of GitHub Actions in practice could include setting up workflows to automatically deploy a web application to a cloud service provider whenever the main branch is updated or workflows that send notifications to a Slack channel when a new pull request is created or an issue is opened. The possibilities are vast and can be tailored to the specific needs of a project or team. Overall, GitHub Actions and GitHub Packages represent a significant shift in how development workflows are managed, moving toward a more automated, efficient, and integrated approach. This not only saves time and reduces the potential for human error but also allows developers to focus more on writing code and less on the administrative and operational aspects of software development. Let's learn more about GitHub Actions and Packages.

Understanding GitHub Actions

GitHub Actions emerges as a formidable tool in the realm of automation and workflow management within the GitHub ecosystem. This feature is ingeniously designed to automate a wide array of tasks and processes directly within your GitHub environment, thereby revolutionizing the way developers interact with their code repositories.

At its core, GitHub Actions allows you to create custom workflows that automatically trigger in response to specific events within your GitHub repositories. These events can range from a push or pull request to more specific activities like creating a tag or releasing a new version. The flexibility of GitHub Actions lies in its ability to respond to these events with a series of predefined steps, which are executed in an automated fashion. These steps are defined in YAML files within the repository, making them easily accessible and modifiable.

The power of GitHub Actions is not just limited to automating routine development tasks such as building, testing, and deploying code. It extends to a broader range of possibilities, allowing for the automation of virtually any process that can be scripted. This includes tasks like updating dependencies, sending notifications to other platforms (like Slack or email), and even synchronizing with external databases or cloud services.

One of the key strengths of GitHub Actions is its deep integration with the GitHub platform. This integration ensures seamless interaction with GitHub's features and data, allowing workflows to leverage the full spectrum of GitHub's capabilities. For instance, an action can be set up to automatically merge pull requests after passing certain checks, label issues based on their content, or even assign reviewers to pull requests based on the code's complexity or area.

Moreover, GitHub Actions supports a marketplace where developers can share and discover custom actions created by the community. This marketplace fosters a collaborative environment, enabling developers to leverage the collective expertise of the GitHub community to find solutions that meet their specific workflow needs. The following are some of the important concepts related to GitHub Actions:

1. **Workflow Automation:** GitHub Actions allows users to create custom workflows for automating a variety of tasks. The following are some of the common examples:

- **Automated Testing:** We can set up automated tests for code to ensure that new changes don't introduce bugs or issues.

- **Issue and Mention Responses:** It also helps us to respond to new issues or mentions in your repositories, making it easier to manage and communicate with contributors.

- **Code Reviews:** Actions can be triggered to perform code review tasks, like checking coding standards or identifying issues.

- **Pull Request (PR) Handling:** Workflows can also be used to automate tasks related to PRs, such as running tests and even automatically merging or closing PRs based on specific criteria.

- **Branch Management:** Actions can automate branch management tasks, such as creating new branches for feature development, enforcing naming conventions, and applying branch protection rules.

2. **YAML-Based Configuration:** GitHub Actions are defined using YAML files. These files specify the workflows, events, and actions to execute when specific conditions are met. YAML is a human-readable format that allows you to define and version-control your automation workflows alongside your code; it needs to be saved in .github/workflows/workflow.yaml.

3. **Execution Environments (Runners):** GitHub Actions run on execution environments known as "Runners." There are two types; they are as follows:

   - **GitHub-Hosted Runners:** These are provided and maintained by GitHub, offering a range of preconfigured environments like Ubuntu, Windows, and macOS. They work well for many use cases.

   - **Self-Hosted Runners:** Organizations can set up their own Runners on their infrastructure. This provides greater control over the execution environment and can be tailored to specific needs.

4. **Event-Driven:** Actions are triggered by events such as code pushes to a repository, the creation of a new issue or PR, or scheduled tasks. We can specify when and how actions should be executed based on these events.

5. **Reusable Actions:** GitHub Actions can be packaged as reusable components called "actions." These actions can be shared with the GitHub community through the GitHub Marketplace. This allows developers to easily integrate existing actions into their workflows or create their own custom actions.

6. **Security and Isolation:** GitHub Actions prioritize security. They run in isolated environments with access only to the resources and permissions defined in the workflow configuration. This ensures that your automation is secure and doesn't interfere with your codebase.

In summary, GitHub Actions stands as a versatile and powerful tool that significantly enhances the automation capabilities within the GitHub environment. Its ability to automate complex workflows, coupled with its deep integration with GitHub, makes it an invaluable asset for developers looking to streamline their development processes, enhance productivity, and focus more on creating and less on the repetitive tasks that can be automated. It can be testing, code reviews, or PR management, we can use GitHub Actions to automate tasks and enhance your development workflow while maintaining a human-readable configuration.

Runners

In the context of GitHub Actions, the concept of Runners plays a crucial role in the execution of workflows. When you establish a workflow in GitHub Actions, it typically comprises various jobs. These jobs can be likened to a series of tasks or operations that need to be executed. In a real-world analogy, these jobs are akin to assignments that you would delegate to workers in a workplace.

Runners in GitHub Actions are essentially the workers that carry out these jobs. They are servers – either hosted by GitHub or set up in your own environment – that listen for available jobs, run one job at a time, and report the results back to GitHub. When a specific event triggers a workflow in your repository, the jobs defined in that workflow are queued. The GitHub Runner then picks up these jobs and executes them based on the instructions provided in the workflow file.

Each job within a workflow runs in a fresh instance of the Runner, ensuring that the environment is clean and isolated from previous jobs. This is crucial for maintaining the integrity and consistency of the workflow execution. The Runner environment contains all the necessary tools and dependencies to execute the jobs, whether it's running scripts, compiling code, or deploying applications.

The steps within each job are the specific actions that these workers need to perform. These actions can be like following a set of instructions or scripts.

There are two types of Runners are there, they are as follows GitHub-hosted Runners and self-hosted Runners.

GitHub-Hosted Runners

- **GitHub-Hosted Runners:** GitHub-hosted Runners are provided by GitHub and offer a range of virtual environments for different operating systems, such as Windows, Linux, and macOS. These are ideal for standard use cases and simplify the setup process since GitHub manages and maintains these Runners. The following are the properties of GitHub-hosted Runners:

  - **Preconfigured Environments:** These hosted Runners come with various operating systems and software preinstalled.

    For example, you can ask for an "ubuntu-latest" Runner, and GitHub will provide a worker with the latest version of Ubuntu and commonly used tools.

  - **No Setup Required:** You don't need to worry about setting up or maintaining these Runners. GitHub takes care of everything, including keeping them up to date.

- **Easy to Use:** You can easily request a hosted Runner for your workflows in GitHub Actions without any hassle. Just specify the type of Runner you want, and GitHub handles the rest.

- **Limited Time:** There is a time limit for how long a workflow can run on a hosted Runner. Typically, it's 6 hours for a job and 72 hours (about 3 days) for an entire workflow.

Self-Hosted Runners

- **Self-Hosted Runners:** Self-hosted Runners provide more control and flexibility. They allow you to use your own machines for running jobs, which can be beneficial if you require a specific configuration, need to access private networks, or want to use hardware that GitHub does not provide. Self-hosted Runners can be set up in your local environment, in a private data center, or even in the cloud, depending on your requirements. These are the Runners which are managed by users, which can be customized to fit your exact needs; some of the properties are as follows:

  - **Customized Environments:** With self-hosted Runners, you have full control over the worker's environment. You can install any software, set up any configuration, and use any operating system that your project requires.

  - **Your Responsibility:** Unlike hosted Runners, self-hosted Runners require you to set them up and maintain them.

- **Versatility:** Self-hosted Runners are highly versatile and can be used in various scenarios, especially when your project has unique requirements or needs to interact with your own infrastructure.

- Self-hosted Runners can be added at various levels within an Enterprise:

    - Repository level (single repository)

    - Organizational level (multiple repositories in an organization)

    - Enterprise level (multiple organizations across an Enterprise)

Steps required to configure self-hosted Runners will be discussed in the later part of the chapter.

Note   GitHub strongly advises against using self-hosted Runners in public repositories; the following are some of the concerns about using self-hosted Runners in public repositories.

- **Security Concerns:** When you use self-hosted Runners, you're essentially allowing a connection between your repository and a computer within your own network. If your repository is public, anyone on the Internet can potentially trigger actions on your self-hosted Runner.

- **Code Execution Risk:** Allowing code execution on a computer within your network from external sources can be a significant security risk. It's like inviting a stranger to run programs on your computer without knowing their intentions. This could lead to unintended consequences, including security breaches.

- **Prefer Hosted Runners:** GitHub offers hosted Runners that are specifically designed for public repositories. They are isolated from your network and have security measures in place to protect your infrastructure. It's like having a security team handle potential threats before they reach your computer.

Exploring Actions Flow

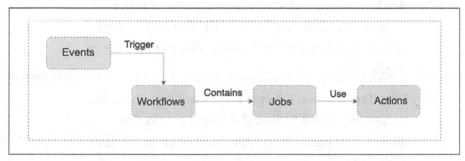

Figure 5-1. *GitHub Actions flow*

A flow can be explained as follows:

1. **GitHub Tracks Events:** GitHub acts as a watchful eye that keeps an eye on things which are happening in the projects. It pays attention to various activities, like code changes or issues being created.

2. **Events Trigger Workflows:** When a specific event happens, like a code change or a new issue, it can set off a series of actions called workflows. These

workflows are like a set of instructions for GitHub to follow.

3. **Scheduled and External Triggers:** Sometimes, workflows do not need an event to start. They can also be scheduled to run at specific times, like clockwork. Plus, they can be kicked off by things happening outside of GitHub, like an external system.

4. **Manual Triggers:** You, as a user, can also start a workflow manually. This can be helpful when you want to run a specific task without waiting for an event or a schedule.

5. **Workflows and Jobs:** Workflows are like the big picture plan, and they contain smaller tasks called jobs. Each job has a specific role, like testing code or deploying it.

6. **Jobs Use Actions:** Jobs get their work done by using something called "actions." Actions are like little helpers that perform specific tasks, such as sending notifications or running scripts.

To summarize, GitHub keeps an eye on what is happening, and when some event occurs, it follows a set of instructions (workflow) to perform various tasks (jobs), with the help of specialized helpers (actions). These workflows can start automatically on a schedule or when you decide it is time.

Understanding GitHub Actions

Below is the sample of a GitHub workflow.

```
1    name: Sample-Workflow
2    on: [push]
3    jobs:
4      Running-jobs:
5        name: executing-jobs
6        runs-on: ubuntu-latest
7        steps:
8          - name: Checkout repo
9            uses: actions/checkout@v4
10         - name: Set up Python
11           uses: actions/setup-python@v4
12           with:
13             python-version: '3.10'
14         - name: Display Python version
15           run: python -c "import sys; print(sys.version)"
16         - name: Executing python code
17           run: |
18             python3 sample.py
```

Figure 5-2. *Sample workflow [Refer to the sample-workflow-main/*
.github/workflows/sample.yml file for code]

Workflows include several standard syntax elements; they are as
follows:

- **Name:** This is the name of the workflow. It is optional
  but is highly recommended. It will appear in several
  places within the GitHub UI; in the example in
  Figure 5-2, it is Sample-Workflow.

- **On:** This is the event or list of events that will trigger
  the workflow; in the example in Figure 5-2, it runs on
  push event.

- **Jobs:** This is the list of jobs to be executed. Workflows
  can have one or more jobs, and it has a property called
  name, which will be used to identify in GitHub UI.

- **Runs-on:** It tells Actions which Runner to use.

- **Steps:** It is the list of steps for the job. Steps within a job execute on the same Runner.

- **Uses:** It tells Actions which predefined action needs to be retrieved. For example, you might have an action that installs Python.

- **Run:** It tells the job to execute a command on the Runner.

Evaluating Execution

In your repository, you can find a section called "Actions" where you can check the status of actions being executed.

Figure 5-3. *Repository options*

To check the output of GitHub workflow, click on "Actions", output looks as below.

Figure 5-4. *GitHub Actions output*

Here, you can see the status of workflows and the total time taken for execution, and to get more details about a specific job, just click its name [executing-jobs]. It will look like Figure 5-5.

Figure 5-5. *GitHub Actions job view*

In this view, you can find information about the individual steps and how much time they took to execute. To access the logs of these steps, simply click them. The view will be something like Figure 5-6.

Figure 5-6. *GitHub Actions job logs*

If you are using GitHub-hosted Runners, it is important to note that you will be billed based on the time your actions take to execute.

To monitor your usage and billing details, click "Run details." Under this section, you can see your usage, and it will look like Figure 5-7.

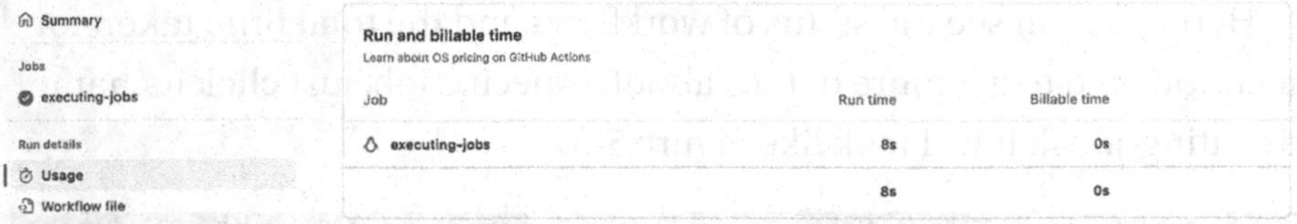

Figure 5-7. *GitHub Actions Runner's minutes usage*

This way, you can keep track of your actions, understand their status, review their execution details, and monitor usage and billing when using GitHub-hosted Runners.

Workflow Configuration and Management

Workflow Name

As discussed earlier, every workflow file will start with a keyword "name" which indicates the name of the workflow.

In the workflow file, we can control the execution based on events using the "on" keyword in the workflow we can define the action execution based on that event; some of the common use cases are as follows.

Events That Trigger Workflows

In GitHub Actions, you can create workflows that run at specific times or on a regular schedule. This type of trigger is often referred to as a "scheduled workflow," using scheduled events.

To set up a scheduled workflow, we need to provide a cron schedule. A cron schedule is like a timetable that specifies when your workflow should start running. It uses a special syntax to define the schedule; in the workflow file, it looks like this:

```
on:
   schedule:
      - cron: '0 0 * * *'   # This schedule means the workflow
                              will run every day at midnight
                              (00:00).
```

Cron schedules are based on five values:

- Minute (0–59)

- Hour (0–23)

- Day of the month (1–31)

- Month (1–12)

- Day of the week (0–6)

The breakdown of the schedule goes like this:

- The first 0 represents the minute (0–59).

- The second 0 represents the hour (0–23).

- The * in the other positions means "every" for that unit of time.

- So, * * * * * would mean "every minute of every hour, every day, every month, every day of the week."

We can also customize the schedule to match our specific needs. For example, if you want a workflow to run every weekday at 8 AM, you might use a schedule like 0 8 * * 1–5, where 1–5 represents Monday through Friday.

Some of the examples where we can use scheduled events are for nightly build, report generation, and other recurring tasks.

Understanding Code Events

When working with the GitHub repository, some of the interactions with the GitHub repository are considered as events which can be used as triggers that kick off various actions. Some common examples of code events include "pull_request" and "push."

Example for a Specific Event

Let us say you want to trigger a workflow whenever a "pull_request" is created. You can set it up like this:

```
on:
    - pull_request
```

Example for Multiple Events

You can also be flexible and respond to multiple events. For instance, you might want your workflow to activate both when there is a "push" and a "pull_request." Here's how you can do it:

```
on:
  - push
  - pull_request
```

Example for Branch Filters

Based on the branching policy setup, you might want your workflow to run only when there's a "push" to a particular branch, like "develop." You can set it up like this:

```
on:
  push:
       branches:
            - develop
```

You can specify a list of branches or even use wildcards to match patterns, for example, to match any branch that starts with "feature/":

```
on:
   push:
        branches:
              - develop
              - 'feature/**'
```

Using "Ignore" to Exclude

If you want to exclude specific branch patterns, you can use the "branches-ignore" filter. However, it's important to note that you can't use both "branches" and "branches-ignore" filters for the same event in a workflow. Here's how you might use it:

```
on:
   push:
        branches-ignore:
              - develop
              - 'feature/**'
```

So, with these configurations, you can control when and how your workflow responds to different code events in your repository.

Understanding Manual Events

When you want to run a workflow manually, such as when you need to perform a specific action that is not covered by automated triggers, follow these steps to ensure the action is completed accurately.

To do this, GitHub provides a special event called "workflow_dispatch." This event acts like a button you can press to start your workflow manually; the configuration looks like this:

```
on:
  workflow_dispatch:
```

Default Branch Requirement

Now, there is a rule you should be aware of before using manual trigger: To use "workflow_dispatch" to trigger a workflow manually, that workflow must be set up in the default branch of your repository. The default branch is typically the main branch of your project, like "main" or "master."

Think of it like this: the "workflow_dispatch" button is only available when you are on the main stage (the default branch). You cannot press it from the side stages (other branches).

So, if you want to manually trigger a workflow, make sure it is set up in your repository's default branch. This way, you can use "workflow_dispatch" to run it whenever you need to, even if it is not automatically triggered by events. It gives you extra control over your automation.

This can be used when we want to have on-demand execution, such as terminating an environment or generating a report.

Figure 5-8 shows an example of using workflow_dispatch in a GitHub Actions workflow. This example demonstrates how to create a workflow that can be manually triggered from the GitHub Actions UI.

```
1    name: Manual Workflow Trigger
2    on:
3      workflow_dispatch:
4    jobs:
5      build:
6        runs-on: ubuntu-latest
7        steps:
8          - name: Checkout code
9            uses: actions/checkout@v4
10         - name: Run a command
11           run: echo "Runs manual trigger"
```

Figure 5-8. *Workflow for a manual trigger [Refer to the sample-workflow-main/.github/workflows/manual-workflow.yml file for code]*

In the example workflow

We have defined a workflow named "Manual Workflow Trigger."

- The "on" section specifies that this workflow listens for the workflow_dispatch event, which will enable manual triggering.

- Inside the job section, there is a single job named "build" that runs on the latest version of the Ubuntu Runner.

- In the job steps, we first check out your repository's code using the actions/checkout action. Then, we run a simple command (in this case, echoing a message).

Follow these steps to trigger the workflow:

Go to the "Actions" tab in your GitHub repository.

- Click the workflow you want to trigger (in this case, "Manual Workflow Trigger").

- On the right-hand side, you'll see a "Run workflow" button. Click it. It looks like Figure 5-9.

Figure 5-9. *Manual trigger workflow option*

You can optionally provide input values depending on your workflow configuration.

- Click the "Run workflow" button to trigger the workflow manually.

Understanding Webhook Events

GitHub webhooks is a way of telling GitHub, "Hey, if this happens, let my workflows know so they can start working automatically."

So, when a GitHub webhook is "called" or triggered by an event (like someone making a change to your repository), it tells your workflows, "Time to trigger the workflow."

```
on:
    gollum
```

This event would fire when someone updates (or first creates) a wiki page.

Understanding External Events

When you want to kick off the workflows not based on events within GitHub, but when an event occurs outside of GitHub, such as updating a database or uploading a new file to your server, follow these steps to trigger the workflow accurately.

This is where the "GitHub API" comes in handy. It acts as a remote control for your GitHub repository. You can use it to send a special signal, called a "webhook event," to your repository, which will trigger the workflow; the configuration looks like this:

1. **GitHub Repository Setup**

   - Create a GitHub repository where you want to set up this workflow.

   - In your repository, navigate to the "Actions" tab and create a new workflow file (e.g., .github/workflows/dispatch-workflow.yml).

2. **Define the Workflow File**

Here's an example workflow file that listens for the "repository_dispatch" event and runs a simple job, as shown in Figure 5-10.

```
1   name: Example for External Event Workflow
2   on:
3     repository_dispatch:
4       types:                    # Define the event types to trigger the workflow
5         - custom_event          # Replace with your custom event type
6   jobs:
7     external-job:
8       name: Exteranljob
9       runs-on: ubuntu-latest
10      steps:
11        - name: Checkout code
12          uses: actions/checkout@v4
13        - name: Run custom action
14          run: |
15            echo "This workflow was triggered by an external event."
```

Figure 5-10. Trigger workflow from an external event. [Refer to the sample-workflow-main/.github/workflows/external-dispatch.yml file for code]

In the example

- We have defined a workflow named "Example for External Event Workflow."

- We have also specified that it should run only when a "repository_dispatch" event with a specific event type, in this case, "custom_event," is dispatched.

- The workflow contains a single job called "Externaljob" that runs on the latest version of Ubuntu.

- In the job steps, we check out the code and perform a simple action, which could be more complex depending on your requirements.

Trigger the Workflow Using the GitHub API

To trigger this workflow externally, you can use the GitHub API to send a "repository_dispatch" event with the specified "event_type" ("custom_event" in this case). Here's a simplified example using curl:

```
curl -X POST -H "Authorization: token YOUR_GITHUB_TOKEN" \
                    -H "Accept: application/vnd.github.
                    everest-preview+json" \
-d '{"event_type": "custom_event"}' \
  https://api.github.com/repos/YOUR_USERNAME/YOUR_REPO_NAME/
  dispatches
```

Replace YOUR_GITHUB_TOKEN, YOUR_USERNAME, and YOUR_REPO_NAME with your GitHub credentials and repository information.

Once you execute the preceding command, there will not be any response printed by default.

Jobs

Jobs are like individual tasks within a workflow plan. They are sets of actions or steps that need to be executed in a specific order.

Steps Within a Job

- Each job is made up of multiple steps. Think of steps as the actions you need to take to complete a job.

  For example, if a job is like "bake a cake," the steps could be "mix ingredients," "put in the oven," and "decorate."

- All the steps within a job run on the same computer, called a "Runner."

  It's like having a dedicated worker who follows your instructions for that specific job.

  Because all steps share the same Runner, they also share the same computer space or "filesystem."

Logs and Artifacts

- While the jobs are running, they produce information about the execution; it is called logs.

  You can search through these logs to see what happened during each job, which is helpful for debugging or understanding the workflow.

- In some scenarios, we want to save the output of step or file generated in step for future reference. These outputs are called artifacts and can also be used in subsequent jobs.

Job Execution

When you set up a workflow in GitHub Actions and it includes multiple jobs, these jobs will run simultaneously by default.

Think of it like this: imagine you have a list of tasks to do, and these tasks do not depend on each other. In the real world, you might assign different people to work on each task at the same time. That way, you get things done faster.

In GitHub Actions, each job in your workflow is like one of these tasks. If they do not rely on the outcome of each other, they can start running as soon as there is a Runner available. This parallel execution can speed up your workflow and make your automation more efficient.

Jobs with Dependencies

It is used when we want to execute the jobs where we have dependency, for example, build the code and then deploy; in such scenario, we will use the "needs" keyword to control the execution.

Figure 5-11 shows an example of a Python workflow with job dependencies; here, we will do code static analysis, then perform a unit test, and then deploy the code.

```
Code    Blame    36 lines (33 loc) · 896 Bytes

1     name: Workflow with Job Dependencies
2     on:
3       push:
4         branches:
5           - main  # You can customize the branch as needed
6     jobs:
7       build:
8         runs-on: ubuntu-latest
9         defaults:
10          run:
11            working-directory: app
12        steps:
13          - name: Checkout code
14            uses: actions/checkout@v4
15
16          - name: Set up Python
17            uses: actions/setup-python@v4
18            with:
19              python-version: '3.10'
20          - name: Install dependencies
21            run: pip install -r requirements.txt
22
23          - name: Run static code analysis
24            run: pylint app.py
25
26          - name: Run tests
27            run: python -m unittest discover
28      deploy:
29        needs: build  # Specifies that this job depends on the 'build' job
30        runs-on: ubuntu-latest
31        steps:
32          - name: Checkout code
33            uses: actions/checkout@v4
34          - name: Deploy to production
35            run: |
36              echo "Deploying to production..."
```

Figure 5-11. *Job dependencies [Refer to the sample-workflow-main/ .github/workflows/job-dependency.yml file for code]*

In the example

- We define a workflow named "Workflow with Job Dependencies."

- The workflow is triggered on pushes to the main branch. You can adjust the branch name to match your project's default branch.

- There are two jobs: build and deploy.

  - The build job sets up the Python environment, installs project dependencies, runs static code analysis, and run tests.

  - The deploy job is set to run only when the build job successfully completes. It deploys your code to production, and you can customize the deployment steps as needed.

The "needs" keyword in the deploy job specifies that it depends on the successful completion of the build job. This ensures that the deployment only happens when the "build" is successful.

Note   If the startup job in the preceding example fails, the deploy job will not execute.

If we want to use a commit ID or pass credentials in the workflow, GitHub Action provides two options. They are variables where values will be visible to the users and secrets that can be used for storing sensitive values and use them in workflows.

In the next section, we will discuss in detail and see variables and secrets in the GitHub Actions workflow.

Understanding Variables and Secrets in GitHub Actions

Variables

Think of variables such as containers or boxes where you can keep useful information. This information could be anything from the name of a server to special settings for a program.

Now, why do we use these containers (variables)? Well, imagine you have a list of things you need to remember when you are doing a task, like building a website. Instead of typing those things repeatedly, you can put them in a box (variable). When you need one of those things, you can open the box and use it.

There are two types of variables available in the GitHub Actions workflow; they are as follows:

1. **Default Variables:** GitHub sets default variables for each GitHub Actions workflow run; these can also be referred to in the workflow.

2. **Custom Variables:** These are the variables defined by users at different levels based on the use case.

Using Default Variables

We can use the following list of variables in the workflow; let's create a workflow to demonstrate using default variables.

In the workflow, we will use GITHUB_RUN_ID to pass the input script; it looks like this:

```
- name: Building package using run_id
  run: |
    bash build.sh $GITHUB_RUN_ID
```

On execution, we can see the logs as shown in Figure 5-12.

```
  ∨  ✓  Building package using run_id

   1   ▸ Run bash build.sh $GITHUB_RUN_ID
   4    Script uses github GITHUB_RUN_ID to build package
   5    Printing GITHUB_RUN_ID: 6879165737
   6     adding: package/ (stored 0%)
```

Figure 5-12. *Job logs*

We can use these default GitHub environment variables in multiple ways based on use cases, for example, if we are building a docker image as part of a pipeline and we want to know which commit has built the docker image, in that case we can use the following.

Here, the workflow will have two steps; they are as follows:

1. Get the short sha using a GitHub environment variable, that is, GITHUB_SHA; cut the first five characters from it and save it in GITHUB_ENV; to do it, we can use the following step:

   ```
   - name: Add SHORT_SHA env property with commit
   short sha
       run: |
         echo "SHORT_SHA=`echo ${GITHUB_SHA} |
         cut -c1-5`" >> $GITHUB_ENV
   ```

2. In the preceding step, we have a new environment variable called **SHORT_SHA**, which will be accessible inside the job, so in this step we can use it as follows:

   ```
   - name: Build image using short sha
     run: |
         docker build . --tag sample/demo-app:${SHORT_SHA}
   ```

317

Once the job executed logs, here we can see SHORT_SHA used as an environment; on inspecting job logs, we can see the docker image built using the same sha.

```
✓  Build docker image using SHORT_SHA value
   1   ▼ Run docker build . --tag sample/demo-app:${SHORT_SHA}
   2     docker build . --tag sample/demo-app:${SHORT_SHA}
   3     shell: /usr/bin/bash -e {0}
   4     env:
   5       SHORT_SHA: bf6ca
```

Figure 5-13. *Environment variable*

```
#9 naming to docker.io/sample/demo-app:bf6ca done
```

Figure 5-14. *Docker image tag*

Using Custom Variables

It is used when we want to store and reuse nonsensitive configuration information. We can store any configuration data such as compiler flags, usernames, or server names or region as variables.

These variables can be defined at different levels; they are as follows:

- **Single Workflow:** To define environment variables specific to a workflow, you can use the **env** key in the workflow file; it can be set in the following levels:

  - The entire workflow, by using env at the top level of the workflow file.

  - The contents of a job within a workflow, by using jobs.<job_id>.env.

  - At the step level, we can also define variables and use them in the next steps.

A sample workflow looks like this:

```
name: Variable Demo
on:
  push:
    branches:
      - main
env:
  WORKFLOW_VARIABLE: "This is a workflow-level
variable"
jobs:
  my-job:
    runs-on: ubuntu-latest
    env:
      JOB_VARIABLE: "This is a job-level variable"
    steps:
      - name: Print Workflow Variable
        run: echo $WORKFLOW_VARIABLE

      - name: Print Job Variable
        run: echo $JOB_VARIABLE
```

If we want to assign variables at the step level in a workflow, it will have two steps; they are as follows:

Step 1: Define the variable.

```
- name: Set Mode
  id: run-mode
  run: echo "RUN-MODE=debug" >> "$GITHUB_OUTPUT"
```

- Set Mode is the name of the step.

- It has a unique identifier (id: run-mode) that allows us to reference it later.

- The run command is like a script that executes something. Here, it's adding a line to a file named $GITHUB_OUTPUT.

- The line being added is "RUN-MODE=debug," which suggests that the execution mode is set to "debug."

Step 2: Refer the variable.

```
- name: Get mode
  run: echo "The selected mode is $EXECUTION_MODE"
  env:
    EXECUTION_MODE: ${{ steps.run-mode.outputs.
    RUN-MODE }}
```

- Get mode is the step name.

- It uses the env key to define an environment variable named EXECUTION_MODE.

- The value of EXECUTION_MODE is obtained from the output of the earlier step (${{ steps.run-mode.outputs. RUN-MODE }}).

- The run command echoes a message that includes the selected execution mode.

- **Multiple Workflows**

  We can create configuration variables for use across multiple workflows and can define them at either the organization, repository, or environment level.

  Creating Configuration Variables for a Repository

  To create secrets or variables on GitHub for your personal repository, you need to be the owner. For organization repositories, you must have admin access.

If you want to create secrets using the GitHub REST API, you need collaborator access for personal or organization repositories.

Here are the steps to create:

- Step 1: On GitHub.com, navigate to the main page of the repository; under your repository name, click **Settings**.

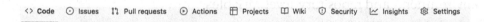

Figure 5-15. *Setting option*

- Step 2: In the "Security" section of the sidebar, select Secrets and variables, then click Actions. Click the **Variables** tab.

Figure 5-16. *Variable option*

- Step 3: Click **New repository variable**. In the **Name**
  field, enter a name for your variable, and in the **Value**
  field, enter the value for your variable and click **Add**
  variable.

To add variables at the environment level, we must select
Environments under settings and follow the preceding steps.

All these created variables can be accessed across the workflow using
the "vars" context; the following is a sample workflow which uses both
environment- and repository-level variables.

```
1    name: repo-env-variables-demo
2    on:
3      push:
4        branches:
5          - main
6    jobs:
7      demo-variables:
8        runs-on: ubuntu-latest
9        environment: dev
10       steps:
11       - name: Use variables
12         run: |
13           echo "repository variable : $REPOSITORY_VAR"
14           echo "variable from shell environment : $env_var"
15         env:
16           REPOSITORY_VAR: ${{ vars.REPO_VAR }}
17           ENV_VAR: ${{ vars.DEV_VAR }}
```

Figure 5-17. *Workflow with variables [Refer to the gh-actions-demo-
main/.github/workflows/repo-env.yaml file for code]*

In the workflow in Figure 5-17, the "Use variables" step prints the
values of two variables:

- **$REPOSITORY_VAR:** A repository-level variable
  sourced from a variable named REPO_VAR

- **$ENV_VAR:** An environment-level variable sourced
  from a variable named DEV_VAR

Variable Precedence

If you have a variable with the same name set at different levels on GitHub (like organization, repository, and environment), the one set at the lowest level is the one that's used. So, if you set a variable at the repository level and organization level with the same name, the repository-level one will be used. If there's an environment-level variable too, it takes precedence over both organization and repository levels. The environment will be discussed in upcoming topics.

Secrets

Secrets are variables defined at the organization, repository, or repository environment level on GitHub. Workflows should have a reference of secrets, and it must be referred to in the workflow based on the use case; we can use secrets defined at any level.

When we have secrets stored at an organization, we can use access rules to decide which projects can use these secrets. These organization-level secrets help us avoid repeating the same secrets for different projects. If we need to change a secret, we must do it once, and it automatically applies to all the projects using it.

For secrets tied to a specific environment, we can set up a system where certain people need to approve before any project in that environment can use those secrets. This means that a task in a project can't access those secrets until the right people give their approval.

Naming Standard Secrets

The following are the naming standards defined by GitHub to be followed when using secrets and accessing them in a workflow:

If we want a specific task to use a secret, we must tell it where to find it. We do this by adding the secret as part of the instructions in the workflow file, either as an input or as a special kind of information the task can use.

Note   If a secret was used in the job, GitHub automatically redacts secrets printed to the log. You should avoid printing secrets to the log intentionally.

Creating Secrets

Repository Secret

When creating a secret, you should be the owner of the repo for personal repositories; for an organization repository, you should have admin access.

Follow these steps to create a secret at the repository level:

- On GitHub.com, navigate to the main page of the repository.

- Under your repository name, click **Settings**. If you cannot see the "Settings" tab, select the dropdown menu, then click **Settings**.

<> Code   ⊙ Issues   ⛛ Pull requests   ⊙ Actions   ⊞ Projects   ⬚ Wiki   ⊙ Security   ⬚ Insights   ⬚ Settings

Figure 5-18.   *Settings option*

- In the "Security" section of the sidebar, select **Secrets and variables,** then click **Actions**.

- Click the **Secrets** tab.

Actions secrets and variables   [New repository secret]

Secrets and variables allow you to manage reusable configuration data. Secrets are encrypted and are used
for sensitive data. Learn more about encrypted secrets. Variables are shown as plain text and are used for
non-sensitive data. Learn more about variables.

Anyone with collaborator access to this repository can use these secrets and variables for actions. They are
not passed to workflows that are triggered by a pull request from a fork.

| Secrets | Variables |

Figure 5-19. *Actions secrets and variables*

- Select **New repository secret**.

- In the **Name** field, enter the name for your secret.

- In the **Secret** field, enter the value for your secret.

- Click **Add secret**.

Organization Secret

To create a secret at the organization level, the user must be an organization owner. The secret should be created under the organization's name.

Once an organization secret is created, it will be available for all the repositories.

Sample Workflow Using Secrets

Based on the use case, we can create secrets at the repository level or at the organization level; to use it in a workflow, a reference can be found in Figure 5-19.

Imagine you have a specific job in your workflow that requires a secret should be available at different steps; you can set up an environment variable for that job at the top level, that is, at the job level.

If a specific step requires a secret, then we can refer to the required secret for that task and use it.

The following is a sample workflow where we are using secrets at different levels of the workflow; here, at line number 9, we can see the secret referred to as the environment level at the job level, and at line number 19, we can see the secret referred to at the step level.

On execution, we can see the job log does not print the actual value; it will be replaced with * in Figure 5-20.

```
1    name: Sec-Workflow
2    on:
3      push:
4        branches:
5          - main
6    jobs:
7      build:
8        runs-on: ubuntu-latest
9        env:
10          JOB_SECRET: ${{ secrets.JOB_SECRET }}
11          REPO_SECRET: ${{ secrets.GH_REPO_SECRET }}
12        steps:
13          - name: Checkout Repository
14            uses: actions/checkout@v3
15          - name: Use Organization Secret
16            run: |
17              echo "Organization Secret: $ORG_SECRET"
18              echo "Using job secert: $JOB_SECRET"
19            env:
20              ORG_SECRET: ${{ secrets.GH_ORG_SECRET }}
21          - name: Use Repository Secret
22            run: |
23              echo "Repository Secret: $REPO_SECRET"
24              echo "Running step using job secert: $JOB_SECRET"
```

Figure 5-20. *Secret workflow [Refer to the sec.yaml file for code]*

Figure 5-21. *Job log*

Understanding Environments

As we understood using variables and secrets now, we can combine these and use them together to have a more controlled way of deployment using the GitHub environment; we will learn how to use it effectively, which will help us to deploy applications on different environments easily.

Environments

GitHub environments can be considered as stages in an application deployment process.

Think of them as different places where your code can be deployed, such as development, staging, and production. Each environment can have its own set of rules and secrets, which provide better control over the deployment.

Some of the considerations are as follows.

This feature is available only for public repositories on all current GitHub plans, but not on older plans like **Bronze**, **Silver**, or **Gold**. To use this feature for private or internal repositories, you'll need GitHub Pro, GitHub Team, or GitHub Enterprise.

Once we understand environments, the following components are part of an environment:

Deployment Protection Rules

These are rules with conditions that must be met before a task, such as updating website or app code, can proceed. These rules allow us to set up controls like manual approval from the code owner, delaying a task, or restricting deployment to specific branches. We can also configure these rules using GitHub Apps.

We can have many GitHub Apps–based deployment protection rules installed on a repository. However, a maximum of six deployment protection rules can be enabled in any environment.

Defining Reviewer Process

GitHub allows you to enforce a review process for workflow jobs linked to a specific environment using required reviewers. This feature mandates approval from a designated person or team, with the flexibility to list up to six individuals or teams as reviewers.

Importantly, only one of the required reviewers needs to be approved for the workflow job to continue, streamlining the approval process. Additionally, GitHub provides an option to prevent self-reviews for deployments to protected environments, ensuring that even if the person initiating the deployment is a required reviewer, they cannot self-approve. This precaution ensures that deployments to secure environments undergo scrutiny from multiple reviewers, enhancing the overall quality control process.

Wait Timer

We can delay the deployment using a wait timer. The time (in minutes) must be an integer between 0 and 43,200 (30 days).

It's important to note that if you're using GitHub and have a Free, Pro, or Team plan, the wait timer feature is only accessible for public repositories.

Managing Deployments Using Branches and Tags

We can control limiting deployment branches and tags in GitHub environments, explained in detail as follows:

1. **No Restriction**

   There is no restriction; we can use any branch and tag for deployment without limitations.

2. **Protected Branches Only**

   Only branches with branch protection rules can deploy to environment.

   If no rules exist, all branches are allowed for deployment.

Note Tags with the same name as a protected branch and forks with matching branch names can't deploy.

---

3. **Selected Branches and Tags**

   Define specific name patterns for branches and tags allowed for deployment.

   For instance, using a pattern like releases/* allows only branches or tags starting with releases/ to deploy.

   Wildcard characters won't match /, so for names like release/xyz, use release/*/*.

   Each branch or tag requires its own configured name pattern.

Managing Admin Privileges

By default, administrators can override protection rules and manually trigger deployments to specific environments. If you want to prevent administrators from bypassing these rules for all deployments in an environment, you can configure the environment settings accordingly.

It's important to note that the option for administrators to bypass protection rules is restricted to public repositories and is applicable for users on GitHub Free, GitHub Pro, and GitHub Team plans.

Using Custom Deployment Protection Rules

There's a new feature called **custom deployment protection rules**, and it's currently being tested in a public beta, which means they're trying it out, and it might change a bit in the future.

These rules allow you to add extra checks before deployment execution. The idea is to automatically approve code deployments to GitHub.com.

Note that this feature is only available for public repositories, and it works for users on GitHub Free, GitHub Pro, and GitHub Team plans.

Managing Secrets and Variables

When you store secrets in an environment for GitHub Actions, these secrets are only accessible to workflow jobs that specifically use that environment. If the environment requires approval, then a job cannot access these secrets until it gets approved.

Here are some important points to keep in mind.

Self-hosted Runners are used for workflows; they don't run in an isolated container, even if they use environments. So we should treat environment secrets with the same level of security as repository and organization secrets.

Environment secrets are only available in public repositories if you are using GitHub Free. To access environment secrets in private or internal repositories, you'll need GitHub Pro, GitHub Team, or GitHub Enterprise.

Regarding environment variables, they follow a similar concept. Variables stored in an environment are only visible to workflow jobs linked to that environment and can be accessed using the vars context.

If you're working with public repositories, environment variables are accessible to everyone. For GitHub Pro or GitHub Team plans, these environment variables are also available for private repositories.

Creating an Environment and Managing a Workflow

Here, we will first understand how we can create an environment on GitHub, then create a workflow where the environment will be used.

Create a GitHub Environment

To set up an environment in a repository within your personal account, you need to be the owner of that repository. If it's an organization's repository, you must have administrative access to configure an environment.

Note

- Creating an environment in a private repository is possible for organizations with GitHub Team plans and individual users with GitHub Pro.

- Note that certain features related to environments may have restrictions or limited availability for private repositories.

Once logged in to GitHub.com, navigate to the main page of the repository; under your repository name, click Settings.

Figure 5-22. *Repository settings*

In the left sidebar, click **Environments**, then click "**New environment**."
Enter a name for the environment, then click **Configure environment**.
Environment names are not case sensitive. An environment name may not
exceed 255 characters and must be unique within the repository.

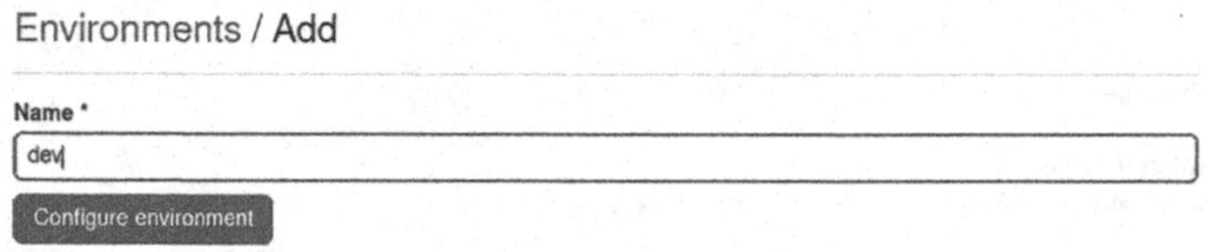

Environments / Add

Name *

dev|

Configure environment

Figure 5-23. *Create an environment*

Configure Reviewers (Optional)

Here, we have an optional setting, where we can specify people or teams
that must approve workflow jobs that use this environment. Select
Required reviewers; we can enter up to six people or teams.

Only one of the required reviewers needs to approve the job.

Optionally, you can prevent users from approving workflow runs that
they triggered; select **Prevent self-review**.

Once all the configurations are checked, click **Save protection rules**.

Deployment protection rules

Configure reviewers, timers, and custom rules that must pass before deployments to this environment can proceed.

☑ **Required reviewers**

Specify people or teams that may approve workflow runs when they access this environment.

Add up to 5 more reviewers

| Search for people or teams... |

🐾 ganesh-sangale   ✕

☐ **Prevent self-review**

Require a different approver than the user who triggered the workflow run.

☐ **Wait timer**

Set an amount of time to wait before allowing deployments to proceed.

Enable custom rules with GitHub Apps (Beta)

Learn about existing apps or create your own protection rules so you can deploy with confidence.

☑ **Allow administrators to bypass configured protection rules**

Save protection rules

Figure 5-24. Environment protection rules

There is another optional configuration where you can specify the amount of time to wait before allowing workflow jobs that use this environment to proceed.

Select **Wait timer**.

Enter the number of minutes to wait.

Click **Save protection rules**.

We can restrict administrators from bypassing configuration; it can be done by deselecting **Allow administrators to bypass configured protection rules**.

Click **Save protection rules**.

Specify Deployment Branches and Tags (Optional)

Decide which branches and tags can deploy to the environment; in the "Deployment branches" dropdown, select your preferred option.

- If you choose "Selected branches and tags," click "Add deployment branch or tag rule."

- Choose whether it's a Branch or Tag rule in the dropdown.

- Enter the name pattern for the branch or tag you want to allow.

Click "Add rule."

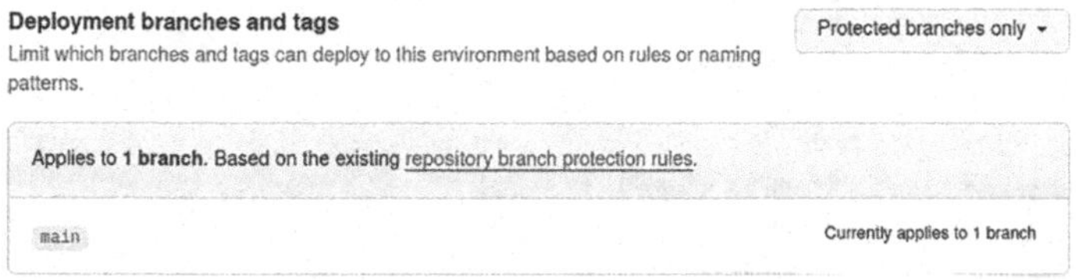

Deployment branches and tags

Limit which branches and tags can deploy to this environment based on rules or naming patterns.

Protected branches only ▾

Applies to **1 branch**. Based on the existing repository branch protection rules.

```
main
```
Currently applies to 1 branch

Figure 5-25. *Branch protect rules*

Add Environment Secrets (Optional)

Environment secrets are only available to workflow jobs using the environment.

Jobs can access these secrets after passing any configured rules (e.g., required reviewers).

- Under "Environment secrets," click "Add Secret."

- Enter the secret name and value.

- Click "Add secret."

Add Environment Variables (Optional)

Environment variables are exclusive to workflow jobs using the environment; they are accessible only through the `vars` context.

- Under "Environment variables," click "Add Variable."

- Enter the variable name and value.

- Click "Add variable."

Sample Workflow

Before we create a workflow, make sure the environment is created in "dev" and has a secret called DEV_API_KEY, and then we can use the sample workflow in Figure 5-26.

```
1    name: Deploy-env
2    on:
3      push:
4        branches: [ main ]
5      pull_request:
6        branches: [ main ]
7    jobs:
8      Build:
9        runs-on: ubuntu-latest
10       steps:
11         - uses: actions/checkout@v3
12         - name: Compile
13           run: echo "Running code compile"
14     DeployDev:
15       name: Deploy to Dev
16       needs: [Build]
17       runs-on: ubuntu-latest
18       environment: dev
19       steps:
20         - name: Deploy
21           run: |
22             echo "Current Environment: ${{ github.event_name }}"
23             echo "Starting deployment on dev"
24           env:
25             API-KEY: ${{ secrets.DEV_API_KEY }}
```

Figure 5-26. *Sample env workflow [Refer to the env-workflow.yml file for code]*

In the sample workflow, you can see the second job called DeployDev; there is a keyword called "environment" which is used to define the environment where it will be deployed.

Once executed, we can inspect the deployment details at the environment level; to check, navigate to Actions; under that, you will see an option called Deployments, as shown in Figure 5-27.

Figure 5-27. Deployment option

Once we click Deployments, it will redirect to the Deployments page where we can see all environments exist and the deployment status, as shown in Figure 5-28.

Figure 5-28. Deployment status

Deleting an Environment

When an application or environment is decommissioned, then the respective environment will be deleted; deleting an environment removes all its secrets and protection rules; any jobs awaiting approval due to rules from the deleted environment will automatically fail.

Perform the following steps to delete an environment.

Navigate to settings under the repository which environment needs to be deleted, then in the left sidebar, click **Environments**.

Next to the environment you want to delete, click the delete icon.

Click **I understand, delete this environment**.

In the next section, we will discuss a feature of GitHub which will let us save packages and container images on GitHub.

So far in the chapter, we are using GitHub-hosted Runners; in the next section, we will discuss how to configure a self-hosted Runner and use it in a workflow.

Understanding Self-Hosted Runners

We can configure self-hosted Runners at various levels on GitHub; they are as follows:

- Repository-level Runners are dedicated to a single repository.

- Organization-level Runners can process jobs for multiple repositories in an organization.

- Enterprise-level Runners can be assigned to multiple organizations in an Enterprise account.

Developing a Strategy for Managing Self-Hosted Runners

When it comes to managing self-hosted Runners, there are two primary approaches: centralized and decentralized.

In a centralized management setup, it's advisable to have a dedicated team overseeing the self-hosted Runners. In this case, the best practice is to add the Runners at the highest shared organization or Enterprise level. This way, your team can conveniently monitor and manage all Runners from a single location. If you're operating within a single organization, adding

Runners at the organization level is essentially the same, but it might pose challenges if you plan to introduce additional organizations in the future.

However, decentralized management involves each team taking charge of their own self-hosted Runners. In this scenario, it's recommended to add the Runners at the highest level of team ownership. For instance, if each team has its own organization, adding Runners at the organization level simplifies the process. While it's possible to add Runners at the repository level, this approach brings increased management complexity and requires more Runners since they cannot be shared between repositories.

Before proceeding to configure the self-hosted Runner, ensure you review the following links, as they contain information about the

Operating System and supported architectures:

`https://docs.github.com/en/actions/hosting-your-own-runners/managing-self-hosted-runners/about-self-hosted-runners#supported-architectures-and-operating-systems-for-self-hosted-runners`

Connectivity requirements:

`https://docs.github.com/en/actions/hosting-your-own-runners/managing-self-hosted-runners/about-self-hosted-runners#communication-requirements`.

Configuring Self-Hosted

Adding Self-Hosted at the Repository Level

To add self-hosted Runners to a specific repository, the user should be the owner of that repository. In the case of an organization's repository, being the organization owner or having administrative access to the repository is necessary for adding a self-hosted Runner.

The following are the steps:

- On GitHub.com, go to the main page of the repository. Below the repository name, click "Settings." If the "Settings" tab is not visible, access it by selecting the dropdown menu and then choosing "Settings."

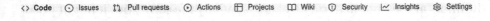

- Navigate to the left sidebar and choose "Actions," followed by selecting "Runners." Click "New self-hosted Runner." From there, pick the operating system image and architecture that align with your self-hosted Runner machine.

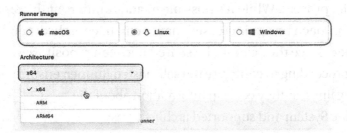

Figure 5-29. *Runner architecture*

- Instructions will be displayed, guiding you on how to download the Runner application and install it on your self-hosted Runner machine, which looks like Figure 5-30, for Linux.

Download

```
# Create a folder
$ mkdir actions-runner && cd actions-runner
# Download the latest runner package
$ curl -o actions-runner-linux-x64-2.311.0.tar.gz -L https://github.com/actions/runner/releases
/download/v2.311.0/actions-runner-linux-x64-2.311.0.tar.gz
# Optional: Validate the hash
$ echo "29fc8cf2dab4c195bb147384e7e2c94cfd4d4022c793b346a6175435265aa278  actions-runner-linux-
x64-2.311.0.tar.gz" | shasum -a 256 -c
# Extract the installer
$ tar xzf ./actions-runner-linux-x64-2.311.0.tar.gz
```

Figure 5-30. *Download section*

Configure

```
# Create the runner and start the configuration experience
$ ./config.sh --url https://github.com/Bloguc-Engineering/gh-actions-env --token
AHMF5XJBPUUOOA47F6H35ZDFT6S4I
# Last step, run it!
$ ./run.sh
```

Figure 5-31. *Configure section*

Configuration begins by downloading and extracting the self-hosted Runner application. Subsequently, run the configuration script, which not only configures the self-hosted Runner application but also registers it with GitHub Actions. During this configuration process, you'll need to provide the destination URL and use an automatically generated time-limited token for authentication.

On Windows, the configuration script also offers the option to install the self-hosted Runner application as a service. For Linux and macOS users, service installation can be performed after the initial Runner addition by following the guidance provided in "Setting up the self-hosted Runner application for service configuration."

Finally, run the self-hosted Runner application to establish a connection between your machine and GitHub Actions. These steps ensure the seamless integration of a self-hosted Runner into your GitHub Actions workflow, allowing for customized and efficient automation of your project tasks.

Setting up the self-hosted Runner application for service configuration on Linux involves the following steps.

Before configuring the self-hosted Runner application as a service, it is necessary to add a Runner to GitHub, which includes download, extract, and run config.sh script.

Access a shell on the Runner machine within the directory where the self-hosted Runner application is installed. Utilize the provided commands to install and handle the self-hosted Runner service.

Setting Up the Service

- Stop the self-hosted Runner application if it is currently running.

- Install the service with the following command:

  ```
  sudo ./svc.sh install
  ```

- Alternatively, the command takes an optional user argument to install the service as a different user.

  ```
  sudo ./svc.sh install USERNAME
  ```

- Start the service with the following command:

  ```
  sudo ./svc.sh start
  ```

- Check service status using the following command:

  ```
  sudo ./svc.sh status
  ```

Note   svc.sh also has a stop option to stop the service and an uninstall option to remove the self-hosted Runner.

Once the Runner is configured successfully, we can see it as idle, and it looks like Figure 5-32.

Figure 5-32. *Self-hosted Runner information*

If we click the Runner's name, it will redirect to the page as shown in Figure 5-33, where we can see the details, such as labels attached to the Runner and active job information.

Runners / k8s-runner-1   Remove

Configuration: Linux x64

Labels

Labels are values used with the r u n s - o n : key in your workflow's YAML to send jobs to specific runners. To copy a label, click on it. Learn more about labels.

self-hosted   Linux   X64   k8s-runner   ⚙

Active Job

There are currently no running jobs

Add `runs-on: self-hosted` to your workflow's YAML to send jobs to this runner.

Figure 5-33. *Self-hosted Runner status*

Adding Self-Hosted Runner at the Organization Level

At the organization level, organization owners can incorporate self-hosted Runners, which can then be used to execute tasks for many repositories within the organization. Adding a self-hosted Runner to an organization requires the permissions of an organization owner.

The steps are like adding Runners at the repository level; the only change is we need to add at the organization level. Here, let's assume we are adding a self-hosted Runner for the "Bloguc-Engineering" organization.

To add a Runner to the organization, navigate to the main page of the organization and select "Settings."

Navigate to the left sidebar and choose "Actions," followed by selecting "Runners." Click "New self-hosted Runner." From there, pick the operating system image and architecture that align with your self-hosted Runner machine, and when you check in the configure section, you will notice the org name, as shown in Figure 5-34.

Configure

```
# Create the runner and start the configuration experience
$ ./config.sh --url https://github.com/Bloguc-Engineering --token AHMF5XNXLDV7PJEDT7XJLKLFTJIYY
# Last step, run it!
$ ./run.sh
```

Figure 5-34. *Runner config org*

Other steps will remain the same, which are discussed in the preceding section where we have configured at the repository level.

Once successfully added, it will be visible under the "Actions" – "Runners" section.

Adding Self-Hosted Runner at the Enterprise Level

As an Enterprise owner, you have the authority to incorporate self-hosted Runners at the Enterprise level, allowing them to be allocated across multiple organizations. The organization owner retains control over specifying which repositories can leverage these Runners. To add a self-hosted Runner to an Enterprise, the requisite permission is ownership at the Enterprise level.

The steps are like adding Runners at the repository level; the only change is we need to add at the Enterprise level. Here, let's assume we are adding a self-hosted Runner for the "Bloguc" Enterprise.

To add a Runner to the Enterprise, navigate to the main page of the Enterprise and select "Settings" and follow the same steps to configure the Runners.

By default, self-hosted Runners within the "Default" Runner group of an Enterprise are accessible to all organizations within the Enterprise. However, they are not automatically accessible to every repository within each organization.

If you want to enable an Enterprise-level self-hosted Runner group for a specific organization repository, you may need to adjust the inherited settings of the Runner group within the organization. This involves making the necessary configuration changes to ensure the Runner becomes available for use in repositories within that organization.

Runners Status

Once a Runner is configured, it will be in one of the following statuses:

- **Idle:** The Runner is connected to GitHub and ready to perform jobs.

- **Active:** The Runner is presently executing a job.

- **Offline:** The Runner is not connected to GitHub, which might be due to the machine being offline, the self-hosted Runner application not running, or communication issues between the self-hosted Runner application and GitHub.

Labels in Self-Hosted Runners

You can utilize labels to categorize your self-hosted Runners based on their features or configuration. By using these labels, you can effectively manage self-hosted Runners and route jobs accordingly.

Here, we will discuss how to create and manage labels at different levels of self-hosted Runners.

A self-hosted Runner on GitHub can be placed in various locations, such as your repository, organization, or Enterprise account settings. To handle a self-hosted Runner effectively, specific permissions are required, depending on its placement.

If the self-hosted Runner is in a user repository, ownership of the repository is necessary. For an organization-level Runner, you need to be the owner of the organization. In the case of a self-hosted Runner within an organization's repository, either organization ownership or administrative access to the repository is required.

This hierarchical permission structure ensures that individuals with the appropriate authority can manage and configure self-hosted Runners based on their location.

Creating/Adding Custom Labels to Runners

At both the repository and organization levels, it's possible to create/add custom labels for Runners.

To create a custom label for a repository or organization self-hosted Runner on GitHub, follow these steps:

- **Creating a Custom Label**

  Navigate to the main page of the repository or organization where your self-hosted Runner group is registered.

  Click "Settings."

  In the left sidebar, select "Actions," then click "Runners."

  From the list of Runners, choose the specific Runner you want to configure.

  In the "Labels" section, click the symbol with a plus sign.

  In the "Find or create a label" field, enter the desired name for your new label and click "Create new label." The custom label is now created and assigned to the self-hosted Runner. Note that while custom labels can be removed, manual deletion is currently unavailable.

  Any unused labels not assigned to a Runner will be automatically deleted within 24 hours.

- **Assigning a Label to a Self-Hosted Runner**

  To assign a label to a repository or organization Runner, navigate to the corresponding main page.

Follow the steps mentioned earlier to create a custom label.

In the "Labels" section, select the label you want to assign to your self-hosted Runner.

By following these steps, you can effectively manage and customize the labels associated with your self-hosted Runners at both the repository and organization levels on GitHub.

Once labels are assigned to self-hosted Runners, they can be used in the workflow, as shown in Figure 5-35; in the below workflow, you can see in job section we have used the Runner label called "k8s-runner", which will be used for executing this job.

Note   These labels are case sensitive, so ensure the label added matches the case in the workflow.

```
1    name: helm-deploy
2    on:
3      workflow_run:
4        workflows: ["Docker-Build-Push"]
5        branches:
6          - "main"
7          - "develop"
8        types:
9          - completed
10   jobs:
11     helm-deploy:
12       runs-on: k8s-runner
13       steps:
14         - name: Checkout code
15           uses: actions/checkout@v3
```

Figure 5-35. *Workflow on a self-hosted Runner*

Removing Custom Labels to Runners

Whenever the Runners are removed or decommissioned or for some other reasons, if we want to remove the custom labels, we can do so by following these steps:

- **Removing a Custom Label**

  Navigate to the main page of the repository or organization where your self-hosted Runner group is registered.

  Click "Settings."

  In the left sidebar, select "Actions," then click "Runners."

  In the "Labels" section, click the symbol denoting label management.

  In the "Find or create a label" field, assigned labels are identified with an icon. To unassign a label from your self-hosted Runner, simply click the labeled icon.

- **Removing a Custom Label from an Organization Runner**

  Visit the main page of the organization where your self-hosted Runner group is registered.

  Click "Settings."

  In the left sidebar, select "Actions," then click "Runners."

  Access the "Labels" section and click the label management symbol.

  In the "Find or create a label" field, locate assigned labels marked with an icon. Click the labeled icon to unassign it from your self-hosted Runner.

Assigning Labels Programmatically

To programmatically assign labels to a self-hosted Runner, you have two options: one for an existing Runner and another during the initial configuration.

For an existing self-hosted Runner, the REST API must be utilized.

To programmatically assign labels during the initial configuration, you can pass label names to the configuration script using the label parameter. It's crucial to note that the configuration script cannot be used to assign labels to an already existing self-hosted Runner.

For instance, when setting up a new self-hosted Runner, you can use a command like this:

```
./config.sh --url <REPOSITORY_URL> --token <REGISTRATION_TOKEN>
--labels docker
```

This command creates the label "docker" if it doesn't already exist. Additionally, you can assign default labels like x64 or linux during configuration. GitHub Actions accepts these labels without validating if the Runner is using the specified operating system or architecture.

To assign multiple labels, use comma separation, as shown in this example:

```
./config.sh --url <REPOSITORY_URL> --token <REGISTRATION_TOKEN>
--labels docker, x64, linux
```

Note   If you replace an existing Runner, make sure to reassign any custom labels to maintain consistency.

Controlling Access to Self-Hosted Runners Through Groups

To regulate access to self-hosted Runners within an organization, policies can be employed. This feature is available to Enterprise accounts, organizations owned by Enterprise accounts, and organizations utilizing GitHub Team.

These entities can establish and oversee multiple Runner groups, providing a structured approach to managing access permissions for self-hosted Runners added to their repositories. With this capability, organizations can enhance security and tailor Runner access based on specific policies and requirements.

Introduction to Runner Groups

GitHub Team plan users can efficiently manage Runner access at the organization level by utilizing Runner groups. These groups organize sets of Runners and establish security boundaries, allowing organization owners to specify which repositories have permission to run jobs on these machines.

After granting access to a Runner group, it appears in the organization's Runner settings. Organization owners can further refine access by implementing repository-specific policies. Newly created Runners are automatically assigned to the default group, but they can be moved between groups as needed.

Creating and Managing Runner Groups

GitHub Team plan users can efficiently manage Runner groups to control repository access for self-hosted Runners. Initially, all organizations have a default Runner group, but GitHub Team plan users can create additional groups with specific access policies. To create a Runner group:

- Navigate to the organization's main page on GitHub.com.

- Click "Settings" (or access it through the dropdown menu if not directly visible).

- In the left sidebar, select "Actions," then choose "Runner groups."

- In the "Runner groups" section, click "New Runner group."

- Provide a name for the Runner group and assign a policy for repository access.

- Configure the group to be accessible to a specific list of repositories or all repositories in the organization. Click "Create group" to finalize the group and apply the policy.

To modify repository access for an existing Runner group:

- Navigate to the organization's main page.

- Click "Settings."

- In the left sidebar, select "Actions," then choose "Runner groups." From the list of groups, select the Runner group to configure. Under "Repository access," use the dropdown menu to choose "Selected repositories."

- Click the pencil icon next to the dropdown menu. In the pop-up, use checkboxes to select repositories that can access this Runner group.

- Click "Save group" to apply the changes.

- These steps ensure granular control over repository access for Runner groups, optimizing security and workflow efficiency.

Self-Hosted Runner Limits

There are specific limitations to be aware of when using self-hosted Runners in GitHub Actions, and these limits may change over time:

- **Workflow Runtime**

  Each workflow run has a maximum duration of 35 days, including execution time, waiting time, and approval time. If the limit is reached, the workflow run is automatically canceled.

- **Job Queue Time**

  Jobs for self-hosted Runners queued for more than 24 hours will be canceled. The actual queue time can extend up to 48 hours before cancellation. If the self-hosted Runner doesn't start executing the job within this timeframe, the job is terminated and marked as incomplete.

- **API Requests**

  There's a limit of 1000 requests to the GitHub API per hour for all actions within a repository. Exceeding this limit results in additional API calls failing, potentially causing job failures.

- **Job Matrix**

  A job matrix can generate a maximum of 256 jobs per
  workflow run, applicable to both GitHub-hosted and
  self-hosted Runners.

- **Workflow Run Queue**

  Repositories have a limit of 500 workflow runs queued
  in a ten-second interval. If this limit is reached, the
  workflow run is terminated and marked as incomplete.

- **Registering Self-Hosted Runners**

  The maximum number of self-hosted Runners allowed
  in one Runner group is 10,000. If this limit is reached,
  adding a new Runner to the group becomes impossible.

Using Containers in GitHub Actions

Containers in GitHub Actions

GitHub Actions allows running jobs in containers, offering a flexible and
isolated environment for workflows. With this feature, you can define
jobs to execute within specified containers, ensuring consistent and
reproducible builds. Containerized jobs provide a way to encapsulate
dependencies, making it easier to manage project dependencies and avoid
conflicts.

To utilize a container for running steps in a GitHub Actions job that
doesn't explicitly specify a container, you can employ `jobs.<job_id>.
container`. This is particularly useful when dealing with a mix of script
and container actions in a job, as the container actions will run as sibling
containers on the same network with shared volume mounts.

If you choose not to set a container explicitly, all steps will run directly on the specified host, unless a step refers to an action configured to run in a container. It's important to note that the default shell for run steps inside a container is `sh`, not `bash`. However, this default behavior can be overridden using `jobs.<job_id>.defaults.run` or `jobs.<job_id>.steps[*].shell`. This flexibility allows you to tailor the containerized execution environment according to your specific needs.

Executing a Job Inside a Container

Let's take a simple example where we want to execute a test case using a Python image; the workflow looks like Figure 5-36.

```
1   name: Docker-Actions
2   on:
3     push:
4   jobs:
5     docker-test:
6       runs-on: ubuntu-latest
7       container:
8         image: python:3.8
9         volumes:
10          - .:/app
11      steps:
12      - name: Checkout code
13         uses: actions/checkout@v3
14      - name: Running testing
15         run: |
16           python docker-test.py
```

Figure 5-36. *Workflow using a container*

The provided GitHub Actions workflow is named "Docker-Actions" and is triggered on a `push` event, indicating that it should run when changes are pushed to the repository.

The workflow includes a single job named "docker-test." This job is set to run on an Ubuntu latest environment and utilizes a Docker container with the Python 3.8 image. The container is configured with a volume, mapping the current directory (".") to the "/app" directory within the container.

The steps within the job involve checking out the code using the `actions/checkout` action, ensuring that the latest version is retrieved. Subsequently, a step named "Running testing" executes a Python script named "docker-test.py" in the mapped volume ("/app").

Examine the Output

When we check the output, we can see as part of initialization it will pull a docker image and mount the directory, as shown in Figure 5-37, then the actual steps will be executed.

Figure 5-37. *Job log*

Executing a Job Inside a Container Using a Private Registry

We have the option to utilize privately hosted Docker images for executing jobs. This approach becomes particularly useful when working with custom images containing all the required packages.

To employ a private image, authentication is necessary. In the workflow, we can pass the required credentials for authentication. The workflow setup, in this case, involves specifying the custom image with the authenticated credentials, ensuring a seamless and secure integration of the custom Docker image into the job execution process.

We can use GitHub secrets and pass a token or password and refer to the workflow when using GitHub Package; it looks as follows:

```
container:
  image: ghcr.io/owner/image
  credentials:
    username: ${{ github.actor }}
    password: ${{ secrets.github_token }}
```

The workflow using a private docker image looks like Figure 5-38.

```
1   name: Docker-CI
2   on:
3     push:
4   jobs:
5     test:
6       runs-on: ubuntu-latest
7       container:
8         image: ghcr.io/ajay253517/flask-app:v-064cd
9         credentials:
10          username: ${{ github.actor }}
11          password: ${{ secrets.GH_TOKEN }}
12        volumes:
13            - .:/app
14      steps:
15      - name: Checkout code
16        uses: actions/checkout@v3
17      - name: Running testing
18        run: |
19          python docker-test.py
```

Figure 5-38. *Workflow using a private registry*

The GitHub Actions workflow named "Docker-CI" is triggered on a push event, indicating that it should run whenever changes are pushed to the repository.

Within this workflow, there is a single job labeled "test." This job is configured to run on an Ubuntu latest environment, and it utilizes a Docker container with the specified image from the GitHub Container Registry (ghcr.io/ajay253517/flask-app:v-064cd). Importantly, this image is a privately hosted Docker image, and authentication is required for access.

To facilitate authentication, the workflow includes credential information, where the username is dynamically set as ${{ github.actor }}, and the password is retrieved from the GitHub repository secrets using ${{ secrets.GH_TOKEN }}. This ensures secure access to the private Docker image.

Furthermore, the job is set up with a volume mapping, linking the current directory (.) to the "/app" directory within the container. This is done to enable the seamless integration of the codebase into the Docker environment.

The actual steps of the job involve checking out the code using the actions/checkout action to ensure the latest version is obtained. Subsequently, a step named "Running testing" executes a Python script named "docker-test.py" in the mapped volume ("/app").

Environment Variables with a Container

In GitHub Actions, you can employ the jobs.<job_id>.container.env configuration to establish a set of environment variables within a container for a specific job. This allows you to define key-value pairs that are accessible by processes running inside the container during the execution of the specified job.

In a workflow, it looks as follows:

```
jobs:
  build:
    runs-on: ubuntu-latest
    container:
      image: python: 3.8
      env:
        server: test-ex.com
    steps:
      - name: Checkout repository
        uses: actions/checkout@v3
      - name:  Running tests
        run: |
            python test.py --destination ${server}
```

Exposing Network Ports on a Container

In GitHub Actions, the "jobs.<job_id>.container.ports" configuration allows you to specify an array of ports that should be exposed when running a job within a container. This is particularly useful when your workflow involves services that need to be accessible through specific ports.

We can utilize the jobs.test.container.ports syntax to define the necessary port mappings. Here's an example:

```
jobs:
  test:
    runs-on: ubuntu-latest
    container:
      image: my-custom-image:latest
```

```
    ports:
      - 8080
      - 9000
    steps:
```

Here, both 8080 and 9000 ports can be used within the job steps, enabling services or processes inside the container to communicate over the specified ports.

Using Volumes with Containers

In GitHub Actions, the "jobs.<job_id>.container.volumes" configuration allows you to define an array of volumes for a container within a specific job. Volumes play an important role in sharing data between services or different steps within a job, enabling efficient communication and data transfer during the workflow execution. You can utilize this feature to specify named Docker volumes or bind mounts on the host.

When specifying a volume, you provide the source and destination path in the format "<source>:<destinationPath>". The <source> can be either a volume name or an absolute path on the host machine, while <destinationPath> is an absolute path within the container; the example configuration looks as follows:

```
jobs:
  myJob:
    runs-on: ubuntu-latest
    container:
      image: my-custom-image:latest
      volumes:
        - my_named_volume:/data
        - /host/path:/container/path
```

In this example, the job named "myJob" utilizes two volumes: my_named_volume and a bind mount from /host/path on the host to /container/path within the container. These volumes can then be used within the job's steps to share data, files, or resources as needed during the workflow execution. This flexibility in volume configuration enhances the versatility of GitHub Actions workflows, especially when dealing with complex dependencies or data sharing requirements.

Container Options

In GitHub Actions, the jobs.<job_id>.container.options configuration provides a means to set additional Docker container resource options within a specific job. These options allow users to fine-tune various aspects of the container's behavior and resource utilization during the workflow execution. It serves as a way to customize the Docker container environment based on specific requirements.

The options specified using jobs.<job_id>.container.options align with the parameters available in the docker create command. These parameters cover a range of settings, including resource constraints, security configurations, and environment variables.

In the workflow, it will look as follows:

```
jobs:
  mem-Job:
    runs-on: ubuntu-latest
    container:
      image: my-custom-image:latest
      options: --memory 2g --env MY_VARIABLE=example_value
    steps:
```

In this example, the job named "mem-Job" includes container options such as setting a memory limit (--memory 2g) and defining an environment variable (--env MY_VARIABLE=example_value). These options provide a level of control over the container's behavior and configuration.

Limitations

It's crucial to note that there are some limitations and considerations. The **--network and --entrypoint options** are not supported within this context. Users should be mindful of these restrictions when configuring additional options for the Docker container.

GitHub Actions Usage Billing, Limits, and Administration

GitHub Actions workflows come with certain usage limits. If a repository exceeds the allotted free minutes and storage, usage charges will be incurred. These limits are in place to manage and regulate the resource utilization within GitHub Actions. It's essential for owners to be aware of these limits to avoid unexpected charges and ensure efficient use of GitHub Actions resources.

Overview About GitHub Actions Billing

For customers on a monthly billing cycle, there is a default spending limit of 0 US dollars (USD) imposed on the account. This limit prevents additional consumption of minutes or storage for private repositories beyond the included amounts. Conversely, if an account is billed via invoice, it enjoys an unlimited default spending limit.

Organization owners have the option to link an Azure Subscription ID to their organization account. This connection enables them to use and pay for GitHub Actions usage that goes beyond the predefined limits associated with the account. Further information on connecting an Azure subscription can be found in the guide titled "Connecting an Azure subscription."

It's worth noting that the usage limits, specifically minutes, reset monthly, while storage usage remains unaffected by these resets. This ensures a clear understanding of resource utilization and allows for effective management of GitHub Actions usage over time.

GitHub Actions Usage Limits

Usage of GitHub Actions with GitHub-hosted Runners is subject to certain limitations, which are subject to potential changes over time. Limitations related to self-hosted Runners have already been discussed in the self-hosted Runners' section.

In GitHub Actions, there are several usage limits and constraints to be aware of when utilizing GitHub-hosted Runners. These limits aim to manage and regulate the workflow execution effectively.

Firstly, each job within a workflow has a maximum execution time of six hours. If a job surpasses this limit, it is automatically terminated, leading to failed completion.

Workflow runs, encompassing both execution duration and time spent on waiting and approval, are capped at 35 days. If a workflow run extends beyond this period, it is canceled.

For API requests, a cap of 1000 requests to the GitHub API per hour is imposed across all actions within a repository. Exceeding this limit may result in job failures.

Concurrent job execution is determined by your GitHub plan and the type of Runner used. The number of concurrent jobs varies across plans, with Enterprise plans allowing customers to request higher limits if needed.

Job matrices have a maximum limit of 256 jobs per workflow run, applicable to both GitHub-hosted and self-hosted Runners.

Workflow run queues have a limit of 500 runs in a ten-second interval per repository. If this limit is reached, the workflow run is terminated.

For GitHub-hosted larger Runners, the concurrent job limits are determined based on your GitHub plan, without specific caps for macOS jobs.

Enterprise plan customers can request higher limits for concurrent jobs as needed, providing flexibility for organizations with specific requirements. For further details or to request higher limits, users can utilize the GitHub support portal.

Reusable Workflow Billing

When a workflow is reused, the associated billing is always tied to the calling workflow. The allocation of GitHub-hosted Runners is solely evaluated based on the context of the caller. It's important to note that the caller cannot use GitHub-hosted Runners from the repository being called.

Retention Policies for Artifacts and Logs

You have the flexibility to set the retention period for artifacts and log files in your repository, organization, or Enterprise account.

By default, any artifacts and log files generated by workflows are kept for 90 days (about 3 months) before being automatically removed. However, you can tailor this retention period based on your repository type:

- For public repositories, you have the option to adjust the retention period to be anywhere between 1 day and 90 days (about 3 months).

- For private repositories, the retention period can be customized within a range of 1 day to 400 days (about 1 year).

It's crucial to note that when you modify the retention period, the changes apply only to newly generated artifacts and log files. They do not retroactively impact existing objects. Additionally, for managed repositories and organizations, the maximum retention period cannot surpass the limit defined by the overseeing organization or Enterprise. This flexibility allows you to manage the storage duration of your workflow artifacts and logs in a way that aligns with your specific needs.

Controlling and Disabling GitHub Actions for Your Repository or Organization

You have the option to either disable or set limitations on GitHub Actions for your repository or organization. By default, GitHub Actions is enabled for all repositories and organizations. If needed, you can choose to disable it entirely or restrict its use to specific actions and reusable workflows within your organization; by following these steps, you can disable a workflow on a repository:

- Visit the repository's main page on GitHub.com.

- Click the "Actions" tab located beneath the repository name.

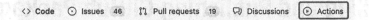

***Figure 5-39.** Actions options*

- On the left sidebar, select the workflow you wish to deactivate.

- Click the ellipsis icon (...) to unveil a dropdown menu, then choose the option to disable the workflow.

***Figure 5-40.** Disable actions*

- Clicking Disable workflow, it will immediately disable the workflow.

- If we want to enable again, we can follow the same steps; we can see the Enable workflow option in Figure 5-41.

***Figure 5-41.** Enable actions*

Now that we've got a good grasp of how GitHub Actions works, let's switch gears and dive into the exciting world of GitHub Packages. Get ready for an adventure as we explore and understand this new aspect!

Installing and Publishing GitHub Packages

GitHub Packages is like a centralized location for hosting different types of software packages, containers, and dependencies. It simplifies how you manage permissions and handle billing related to software development within the GitHub platform.

Let's say you have a project that relies on a specific version of a programming library. Instead of fetching it from various sources, you can store that library as a package in GitHub Packages. This not only centralizes your dependencies but also makes it easy for collaborators to access and use the same versions.

GitHub Packages can host the following packages:

- npm
- RubyGems
- Apache Maven
- Gradle
- Docker
- NuGet

Now as we understand what GitHub is, let's do a deep dive on other concepts related to packages.

Creating Packages

GitHub Packages relies on the standard commands of native package tools to both publish and install different versions of packages. This means that when you want to share your software package on GitHub Packages, you use the regular commands provided by the specific package manager associated with your programming language or framework.

Similarly, when others want to use or install your package, they can do so using the standard commands of their native package manager.

This approach ensures compatibility and ease of use with existing package management workflows.

Here is the list of package registries:

Language	Package Format	Package Client
JavaScript	package.json	npm
Ruby	Gemfile	gem
Java	pom.xml	mvn
Java	build.gradle or build.gradle.kts	gradle
.NET	Nupkg	dotnet CLI
N/A	Dockerfile	Docker

When you're developing a software package, it's beneficial to include a description, installation guidelines, and usage instructions on the package page. These details provide valuable information for users, helping them understand how to effectively use the package and its intended purposes.

In the event that a new version of your package addresses a security vulnerability, it's crucial to communicate this information to users. You can achieve this by publishing a security advisory directly to your repository. For instance, you might provide specifics about the security issue, the steps users need to take to update to the secure version, and any additional precautions they should be aware of.

This proactive communication helps maintain transparency and ensures that users are informed about potential security risks, empowering them to take the necessary steps to secure their systems. Also, you can connect a repository to more than one package. Ensure the README and description provide information about each package.

Publishing Packages

Steps can be summarized for publishing packages using any supported package:

- Generate or use an existing access token

  - Create a personal access token (PAT) with the necessary permissions for your specific task.

  - Personal access tokens can have specific scopes based on your requirements.

- Authentication

  - Use your access token to authenticate yourself to GitHub Packages.

  - Follow the instructions provided for your package client on how to carry out the authentication process.

- Package publication

  - Once authenticated, follow the instructions provided by your package client to publish your package.

The following are some of the examples where we will see how we can use the CLI and publish GitHub Packages.

npm Registry

The use case for the npm registry involves authenticating and publishing npm packages on GitHub.

To authenticate with the npm registry on GitHub, you have two options: either update your personal ~/.npmrc file with your personal access token (PAT) or use the npm login command in the terminal.

If you choose to edit the ~/.npmrc file manually, add the following line:

```
//npm.pkg.github.com/:_authToken=TOKEN
```

Create a new ~/.npmrc file if it doesn't already exist; alternatively, you can use the npm login command in the terminal:

```
$ npm login --scope=@OWNER --registry=https://npm.pkg.
github.com
```

When prompted, enter your GitHub username, PAT as the password, and your public email address.

Make sure to replace USERNAME with your GitHub username, TOKEN with your PAT, and PUBLIC-EMAIL-ADDRESS with your email.

Steps to Publish Packages

The GitHub Packages registry provides a space to store your npm packages, linked to your GitHub organization or personal account, and lets you associate them with repositories. You have the flexibility to decide whether to use the repository's permissions or set specific permissions for packages.

By default, when you publish a package for the first time, it is private. If you want to adjust visibility or manage access permissions, you can refer to the guide on "Configuring a package's access control and visibility." To connect a published package with a repository, you can include a repository field in the package.json file. This method allows you to link multiple packages to the same repository.

Note   When a package is linked to a repository, it automatically inherits the access permissions of that repository. GitHub Actions workflows in the linked repository also gain access to the package, unless automatic inheritance is disabled by your organization.

For setting up the scope mapping in your project, you can use a local .npmrc file or the publishConfig option in package.json. GitHub Packages exclusively supports scoped npm packages, identified by names like @ NAMESPACE/PACKAGE-NAME. These scoped packages always start with an @ symbol. If needed, update the name in your package.json to use the scoped format.

Publishing a Package

Prepare for Authentication:

- Ensure you're authenticated to GitHub Packages.

Create or Edit .npmrc:

- In the project directory, create or edit an .npmrc file to specify the GitHub Packages URL and the account owner's namespace for routing package requests:

```
@NAMESPACE:registry=https://npm.pkg.github.com
```

Add .npmrc to the Repository:

- Include the .npmrc file in your repository so GitHub Packages can locate your project.

Verify Package Details:

- Check your package.json.

- Ensure the "name" field includes the scope and name of the package (e.g., @my-org/test).

- Confirm the "repository" field matches your GitHub repository's URL.

Publish the Package:

- Execute the command `npm publish` to share your package on GitHub Packages.

Using publishConfig in package.json

Edit package.json:

> - In your package.json file, include a
> "publishConfig" entry:

```
"publishConfig": {
                    "registry": https://npm.pkg.github.com
    }
```

Verify the Repository Field:

> - Confirm that the "repository" field in package.json
> matches your GitHub repository's URL.

Publish the Package:

> - Execute the command `npm publish` to publish
> your package using the specified configuration.

Publishing Multiple Packages to the Same Repository

> - To link multiple packages to the same repository,
> include the repository URL in the "repository" field
> of each package.json file:

"repository": https://github.com/OWNER/REPOSITORY,

Installing a Package

Authenticate to GitHub Packages:

> - Make sure you're authenticated, using a
> GitHub PAT.

Create or Edit .npmrc:

> - In the project directory, create or edit an .npmrc file
> to route package requests through GitHub Packages:

```
@NAMESPACE:registry=https://npm.pkg.github.com
```

Add .npmrc to the Repository:

> - Include the .npmrc file in your repository.

Configure package.json:

> - In your project's package.json, specify
> dependencies using the full-scoped package name
> (e.g., @my-org/server).

Install the Package:

> - Execute the command `npm install` to install the
> specified package.

Installing Packages from Other Organizations

- If you need packages from different organizations, add additional lines to your .npmrc file:

```
@NAMESPACE:registry=https://npm.pkg.github.com
@NAMESPACE:registry=https://npm.pkg.github.com
```

Publishing NPM Packages Using GitHub Actions

We can use GitHub Actions to publish the npm packages; you need to have an account in the NPM registry; then you need to create a token with an automation token and save the token as a GitHub secret. Now you can create a GitHub Actions workflow which looks like Figure 5-42; based on the requirements, this workflow can be adjusted.

```
1    name: Publish-NPM
2    on:
3      release:
4        types: [created]
5    jobs:
6      build:
7        runs-on: ubuntu-latest
8        steps:
9          - name: Checkout
10             uses: actions/checkout@v4
11         - name: Setup Node
12             uses: actions/setup-node@v3
13             with:
14               node-version: '16.x'
15               registry-url: 'https://registry.npmjs.org'
16         - name: Install dependencies and build
17             run: npm ci && npm run build
18         - name: Publish package on NPM
19             run: npm publish
20             env:
21               NODE_AUTH_TOKEN: ${{ secrets.NPM_TOKEN }}
```

Figure 5-42. *NPM publish workflow. [Refer to the npm.yml file for code]*

Container Registry

The GitHub Container Registry is a feature that allows you to store and manage Docker and OCI (Open Container Initiative) images. It uses the package namespace: `https://ghcr.io`.

You can use GitHub Packages, including the Container Registry, with various GitHub plans, such as GitHub Free, GitHub Pro, GitHub Team, GitHub Enterprise Cloud, GitHub Enterprise Server 3.0 or higher, and GitHub AE.

However, it's not available for private repositories owned by accounts using legacy per-repository plans. Also, accounts with legacy per-repository plans can't access registries that support granular permissions.

The Container Registry lets you store container images within your organization or personal account and associate them with a repository. You have the flexibility to inherit permissions from a repository or set granular permissions independently. Additionally, you can access public container images anonymously.

In terms of supported container image formats, the Container Registry currently works with Docker Image Manifest V2, Schema 2, and follows the Open Container Initiative (OCI) Specifications. When installing or publishing a Docker image, the registry supports foreign layers, including those from Windows images.

Authenticating to the Container Registry

To use GitHub Packages, you need a personal access token for authentication. This token is required for tasks like publishing and installing packages. In GitHub Actions, you can use **"GITHUB_TOKEN"** to work with the repository's packages and a personal access token with **"read:packages"** scope for packages from other private repositories.

Authenticating the Container Registry in Workflow

This registry supports granular permissions. For registries that support granular permissions, if your GitHub Actions workflow is using a personal access token to authenticate to a registry, we highly recommend you update your workflow to use the GITHUB_TOKEN.

Note   The ability for GitHub Actions workflows to delete and restore packages using the REST API is currently in public beta and subject to change.

Once we generated a token, we can use it as follows:

```
export CR_PAT=YOUR_TOKEN
```

The preceding command will export the token as an environment variable.

echo $CR_PAT | docker login ghcr.io -u USERNAME --password-stdin
> Login Succeeded

The preceding command will log in using a token; on successful login, we will receive a succeeded login message.

Pushing Images

Once we build the image, we can use the following command to push it to the GitHub registry:

docker push ghcr.io/NAMESPACE/IMAGE_NAME:latest

Replace NAMESPACE with the name of the personal account or organization to which you want the image to be scoped.

When you publish a package for the first time, it is set to private by default; based on requirement permissions, it can be adjusted as per requirements.

Link a Repository with Packages

You can link a package to a repository using either the GitHub user interface or the command line. This provides a convenient way to associate your package with a specific code repository.

There are two ways of linking packages; they are as follows:

1. **Using the UI**

   Here, if it is a user-scoped package, then we can follow these steps:

   – On GitHub, navigate to the main page of your personal account.

   – In the top-right corner of GitHub.com, click your profile photo, then click **Your profile**.

– On your profile page, in the header, click the
   Packages tab.

– Search for and then click the name of the package that
   you want to manage.

– Under your package versions, click **Connect
   repository**.

– Select a repository to link to the package, then click
   Connect repository.

   Follow the same steps at the organizational level.

2. **Using the Command Line**

   You can use commands in the command-line
   interface (CLI) of your computer. GitHub provides
   command-line tools that allow you to perform
   various actions, including linking a package to a
   repository.

Dockerfile Changes

   In your Dockerfile, add this line, replacing OWNER
   and REPO with your details:

```
LABEL org.opencontainers.image.source=https://github.com/
OWNER/REPO
```

   For example, if you're the user demouser and own
   aap-repo, you would add this line to your Dockerfile:

```
LABEL org.opencontainers.image.source=https://github.com/
demouser/app-repo
```

Build and Push Image

Once the file is ready, we can use the following command to build a docker image:

```
docker build -t ghcr.io/NAMESPACE/IMAGE_NAME:Tag_Version .
```

On successful build, use the following command to push a docker image:

```
docker push ghcr.io/NAMESPACE/IMAGE_NAME:Tag_Version
```

Publishing Packages Using GitHub Actions

We can use GitHub Actions to publish docker images automatically using the GitHub workflow; it looks like Figure 5-43.

```
1    name: Docker-Image-CI
2    on:
3      push:
4        branches: [ "master" ]
5      pull_request:
6        branches: [ "master" ]
7    jobs:
8      build:
9        runs-on: ubuntu-latest
10       steps:
11       - uses: actions/checkout@v3
12       - name: Log in to the Container registry
13         uses: docker/login-action@65b78e6e13532edd9afa3aa52ac7964289d1a9c1
14         with:
15           registry: ghcr.io
16           username: ${{ github.actor }}
17           password: ${{ secrets.PAT_TOKEN }}
18       - name: Build the Docker image
19         run: |
20           echo "Runid is ${GITHUB_RUN_ID}"
21           docker build -t ghcr.io/ajay253517/py-flask:v-${GITHUB_RUN_ID} .
22       - name: Push the Docker image
23         run: docker push ghcr.io/ajay253517/py-flask:v-${GITHUB_RUN_ID}
```

Figure 5-43. *Docker publish workflow. [Refer to the docker.yml file for code]*

As we are at the end of the chapter now, you have a list of best practices for using GitHub Actions and GitHub Packages.

Best Practices for Using GitHub Actions and GitHub Packages

In previous sections, we have understood about GitHub Actions and GitHub Packages; now here are some of the best practices which will help us to use them effectively.

Organize Workflows

- **Workflow Separation:** Organize your workflows logically and separate them based on different tasks or stages of your development process; this makes it easier to understand and maintain workflows.

- **Workflow Triggers:** Clearly define triggers for workflows. Understand when and how workflows should be executed, such as on pull requests, pushes, or releases.

- **Use Tags for Releases:** Consider using Git tags to trigger specific workflows for releases.

  This helps automate tasks such as versioning, changelog generation, and deployment.

Security and Secret Management

- **Use Secrets:** Use GitHub secrets to securely store and manage sensitive data such as API keys and other credentials.

- **Limit Access to Secrets:** Control access to secrets by restricting who can view and edit them. This helps prevent unauthorized access to sensitive information.

Leverage GitHub Packages

- **Private Package Registry:** Utilize GitHub Packages as a private package registry to store and manage dependencies. This is especially useful for internal libraries and packages.

- **Scoped Registries:** Consider using scoped registries to organize group-related packages. This enhances discoverability and helps in maintaining a clean package registry.

Regularly Review and Update

- **Periodic Review:** Regularly review and update your workflows, dependencies, and configurations. This helps keep your workflows up to date with the latest best practices and improvements.

Summary

In the next chapter, we will discuss in detail the core components of a GitHub organization and provide detailed information about managing GitHub organizations effectively.

Resources

- GitHub provides certain free minutes based on the type of the plan: https://docs.github.com/en/billing/managing-billing-for-github-actions/about-billing-for-github-actions

- Hardware specifications: `https://docs.github.com/en/actions/using-github-hosted-runners/about-github-hosted-runners/about-github-hosted-runners#supported-runners-and-hardware-resources`

- Preinstalled software: `https://docs.github.com/en/actions/using-github-hosted-runners/about-github-hosted-runners/about-github-hosted-runners#preinstalled-software`

- Workflow syntax for GitHub actions: `https://docs.github.com/en/actions/using-workflows/workflow-syntax-for-github-actions`

- GitHub Actions workflow API dispatch event: `https://docs.github.com/en/rest/actions/workflows?apiVersion=2022-11-28#create-a-workflow-dispatch-event`

- Managing a complex workflow: `https://docs.github.com/actions/learn-github-actions/managing-complex-workflows`

- Environment variables: `https://docs.github.com/en/actions/learn-github-actions/variables#default-environment-variables`

- For naming convention to be followed while naming a variable: `https://docs.github.com/en/actions/learn-github-actions/variables#naming-conventions-for-environment-variables`

- Docker create options: `https://docs.docker.com/engine/reference/commandline/create/#options`

- Supported architecture and operating system: `https://docs.github.com/en/actions/hosting-your-own-runners/managing-self-hosted-runners/about-self-hosted-runners#supported-architectures-and-operating-systems-for-self-hosted-runners`

- Connectivity requirements: `https://docs.github.com/en/actions/hosting-your-own-runners/managing-self-hosted-runners/about-self-hosted-runners#communication-between-self-hosted-runners-and-github`

- Using secrets in GitHub Actions: `https://docs.github.com/en/actions/security-guides/using-secrets-in-github-actions#naming-your-secrets`

- About spending limits: `https://docs.github.com/en/billing/managing-billing-for-github-actions/about-billing-for-github-actions#about-spending-limits`"

- REST API documentation: `https://docs.github.com/en/rest/actions/self-hosted-runners?apiversion=2022-11-28`

- Security hardening: `https://docs.github.com/en/actions/security-guides/security-hardening-for-github-actions#hardening-for-self-hosted-runners`

- Proxy server information: `https://docs.github.com/en/actions/hosting-your-own-runners/managing-self-hosted-runners/using-a-proxy-server-with-self-hosted-runners`

- Troubleshoot information: `https://docs.`
  `github.com/en/actions/hosting-your-own-`
  `runners/managing-self-hosted-runners/`
  `monitoring-and-troubleshooting-self-hosted-`
  `runners#troubleshooting-network-connectivity`

- Automatic token authentication: `https://docs.`
  `github.com/en/actions/security-guides/`
  `automatic-token-authentication#using-the-`
  `github_token-in-a-workflow`

- Security hardening for GitHub Actions: `https://docs.`
  `github.com/en/actions/security-guides/security-`
  `hardening-for-github-actions#considering-cross-`
  `repository-access`

- Package configuration: `https://docs.github.com/en/`
  `packages/learn-github-packages/configuring-a-`
  `packages-access-control-and-visibility`

- Types of packages: `https://docs.github.`
  `com/en/packages/working-with-a-github-`
  `packages-registry`

CHAPTER 6

GitHub Enterprise Organization Management and Administration

This is a critical chapter for any team or enterprise aiming to leverage GitHub at scale. This chapter delves into the best practices, strategies, and tools necessary for effectively managing and administering GitHub organizations. It covers a range of essential topics, from setting up and configuring organizations and managing member access and permissions to implementing security policies and compliance checks. The importance of this chapter cannot be overstated; it serves as the foundation for creating a secure, efficient, and collaborative development environment within GitHub. By mastering organization management and administration, teams can ensure that their development practices are not only aligned with industry standards but also optimized for productivity and security. This knowledge enables organizations to fully harness the power of GitHub's collaborative features while maintaining control over their codebases, contributing to the overall success and agility of the

© Balu Nivrutti Ilag, AjayKumar P. Baljoshi, Ganesh J. Sangale and Yogesh Athave 2024
B. N. Ilag et al., *Mastering GitHub Enterprise Management and Administration*,
https://doi.org/10.1007/979-8-8688-0369-7_6

development process. It is crucial to cover a range of topics that cater to the needs and interests of GitHub administrators, support engineers, DevOps professionals, and similar audiences. These individuals often require a comprehensive understanding of both the strategic and technical aspects of managing GitHub at an enterprise level. Here are some suggested topics to include in the chapter:

- Introduction to GitHub Enterprise

- Setting Up a GitHub Enterprise Instance

- User Management and Access Control

- Repository Management

- Security and Compliance

- Integration with CI/CD Pipelines

- Backup and Disaster Recovery

- Advanced Features and Customization

- Troubleshooting and Support

- Best Practices for Enterprise Organization Management

Introduction to GitHub Enterprise

GitHub serves as a comprehensive developer platform designed to facilitate the entire software development lifecycle, offering tools and features to build, scale, and deliver secure software. Businesses leverage GitHub's suite of products to enhance development velocity and elevate code quality throughout the software development process. Developers can utilize GitHub repositories to store and version control their source code, employing issues and projects to efficiently plan and track their work. The platform provides a cloud-hosted development environment known as GitHub Codespaces, enabling developers to code collaboratively. Pull requests facilitate code review among team members, with additional code security features ensuring the protection of sensitive information and identification of vulnerabilities within the codebase. Automation of the build, test, and deployment pipeline is made possible through GitHub Actions, and software packages can be hosted using GitHub Packages.

The 2022 Total Economic Impact study of GitHub, conducted by Forrester Consulting, delves into the potential return on investment (ROI) for companies leveraging GitHub Enterprise over a span of three years. The findings are derived from an analysis of a composite organization, formed from insights gathered through interviews with GitHub Enterprise customers. This commissioned study aims to provide a comprehensive understanding of the economic impact and benefits that organizations can achieve by adopting GitHub Enterprise into their software development workflows. The results aim to highlight the tangible outcomes and advantages realized by businesses that integrate GitHub Enterprise into their operations.

To streamline administration across all stages of the software development lifecycle, GitHub offers enterprise accounts, providing a unified point of visibility and management. Enterprise accounts empower organizations to manage billing and settings, enforce policies, and conduct audits of individuals with access to the enterprise's resources. For enhanced code security, businesses have the option to incorporate GitHub Advanced Security, which introduces additional security features. Additionally, GitHub Premium Support offers enhanced support options to meet the specific needs of organizations leveraging GitHub Enterprise. This comprehensive ecosystem contributes to the efficiency, security, and success of software development initiatives within businesses. Upon acquiring GitHub Enterprise, users gain access to both GitHub Enterprise Cloud and GitHub Enterprise Server, offering flexibility in deployment options. GitHub Enterprise Cloud encompasses a set of advanced functionalities hosted on GitHub.com, providing users with a cloud-based solution that offers convenience and scalability. On the other hand, GitHub Enterprise Server serves as a self-hosted platform, allowing organizations to deploy and manage the GitHub Enterprise environment within their own infrastructure. This dual offering ensures that businesses can choose the deployment model that aligns with their specific requirements and preferences, whether it be leveraging the cloud-based capabilities of GitHub Enterprise Cloud or opting for self-hosted solutions with GitHub Enterprise Server.

GitHub Enterprise Cloud enhances GitHub.com by introducing advanced functionalities such as SAML authentication, additional GitHub Actions minutes, the capability to restrict email notifications to verified domains, and privately published GitHub Pages sites. These features contribute to an enriched user experience and increased versatility for organizations leveraging GitHub Enterprise Cloud. A key distinction between GitHub Enterprise Cloud and other plans for GitHub.com lies in the inclusion of an enterprise account. Enterprise accounts serve as a centralized hub, offering administrators a unified point of visibility and management across multiple organizations. This centralized administration facilitates streamlined control over various aspects of the software development lifecycle, including billing, setting enforcement, policy implementation, and auditing of individuals with access to enterprise resources. The availability of enterprise accounts adds an extra layer of efficiency and governance for organizations utilizing GitHub Enterprise Cloud. On the other hand, GitHub Enterprise Server serves as a self-hosted platform designed for software development within enterprise environments. This platform empowers teams to leverage Git version control, robust APIs, productivity tools, collaboration features, and integrations to facilitate the building and shipping of software. Developers familiar with GitHub.com can seamlessly onboard and contribute using familiar features and workflows within GitHub Enterprise Server. This self-hosted solution operates on your infrastructure, allowing organizations to enforce access and security controls defined by firewalls, network policies, Identity and Access Management (IAM), monitoring systems, and Virtual Private Networks (VPNs). GitHub Enterprise Server is particularly well suited for enterprises subject to regulatory compliance, providing a solution that mitigates potential issues associated with utilizing software development platforms in the public cloud.

GitHub distributes GitHub Enterprise Server as a self-contained virtual appliance. After provisioning a virtual machine and installing the appliance, the instance runs on a Linux operating system with a custom application stack. It's important to note that GitHub Enterprise Server does not support the installation of third-party software or modifications to the underlying operating system. Organizations have the flexibility to deploy GitHub Enterprise Server either on-premises or to a supported cloud environment, offering a choice that aligns with their specific infrastructure preferences and requirements. This adaptability ensures that businesses can tailor the deployment of GitHub Enterprise Server to suit their unique needs while adhering to security and compliance standards.

GitHub Enterprise Server provides flexibility in deployment options, allowing organizations to choose between on-premises data center deployment using virtualization hypervisors and deployment to public cloud services. GitHub supports various virtualization hypervisors for on-premises deployment, including

- Microsoft Hyper-V

- OpenStack KVM

- VMware ESXi

For cloud deployment, GitHub supports integration with popular cloud services, enabling organizations to leverage the scalability and features of these platforms. The supported cloud services include

- Amazon Web Services (AWS)

- Google Cloud Platform (GCP)

- Microsoft Azure

This diverse range of deployment options ensures that organizations can choose the infrastructure that best aligns with their preferences, requirements, and existing IT landscape. Whether on-premises or in the cloud, GitHub Enterprise Server provides a consistent and powerful environment for software development, collaboration, and version control.

GitHub Enterprise offers a comprehensive set of features tailored for larger organizations with specific requirements for security, collaboration, and control. Some key features of GitHub Enterprise include

- **Self-Hosted Deployment:** GitHub Enterprise allows organizations to deploy the platform on their own infrastructure, whether on-premises or in the cloud, providing greater control over security and compliance.

- **Advanced Access Controls:** Organizations can define and enforce access controls, including firewalls, network policies, IAM (Identity and Access Management), monitoring, and VPNs, ensuring secure collaboration.

- **Enterprise Accounts:** Introduction of enterprise accounts provides administrators with a centralized point of visibility and management across multiple organizations, streamlining administration tasks.

- **Advanced Security Features:** GitHub Enterprise includes advanced security features such as SAML authentication, additional GitHub Actions minutes, and domain-restricted email notifications, enhancing the security posture of the development environment.

- **GitHub Advanced Security:** Organizations can opt for GitHub Advanced Security as an add-on, providing features like code scanning, secret scanning, and dependency scanning to identify and address security vulnerabilities.

- **Deployment Flexibility:** GitHub Enterprise supports deployment to various virtualization hypervisors (Hyper-V, KVM, ESXi) for on-premises deployment and integrates with major cloud services (AWS, GCP, Azure) for cloud deployment.

- **Virtual Appliance Distribution:** GitHub Enterprise is distributed as a self-contained virtual appliance, simplifying the installation process and ensuring consistency across deployments.

- **Single Sign-On (SSO):** Support for SAML-based Single Sign-On (SSO) allows organizations to integrate GitHub Enterprise with their identity providers, enhancing authentication security.

- **Auditing and Compliance:** GitHub Enterprise provides audit logs and compliance features, allowing organizations to track user activities and demonstrate compliance with regulatory requirements.

- **Repository Insights and Analytics:** GitHub Enterprise offers detailed insights and analytics for repositories, helping organizations understand code frequency, contributors, and overall project health.

- **High Availability (HA) and Failover:** GitHub Enterprise supports high-availability configurations and failover mechanisms to ensure continuous availability of services.

- **Centralized Administration:** Centralized administration features enable administrators to manage billing, settings, and policies across multiple organizations within the enterprise account.

- **Premium Support:** GitHub Enterprise users have access to enhanced support options through GitHub Premium Support, providing prioritized assistance for critical issues.

- **Collaboration Tools:** GitHub Enterprise includes collaboration tools such as issues, pull requests, code reviews, and project boards to facilitate efficient teamwork.

- **Customizable Workflows:** GitHub Actions, available on GitHub Enterprise, enables organizations to create customizable workflows for automated build, test, and deployment processes.

GitHub Enterprise differs from standard GitHub offerings in several key aspects, primarily designed to cater to the specific needs of larger organizations with elevated requirements for security, compliance, and scalability. Let's delve into these differences with examples:

	Standard GitHub	GitHub Enterprise
Deployment Model	Users leverage GitHub's cloud-based service hosted at github.com	Organizations deploy GitHub Enterprise on their own infrastructure, either on-premises or in the cloud
Access Controls	Provides basic access controls and collaboration features	Offers enhanced access controls, allowing organizations to define and enforce security measures
Advanced Security Features	Offers standard security features available on github.com	Introduces advanced security features such as SAML authentication, GitHub Actions minutes, and domain-restricted email notifications
Enterprise Accounts	Organizations are managed independently	Introduces the concept of enterprise accounts for centralized management
GitHub Advanced Security	Basic security features available on github.com like authentication and authorization, repository visibility and access controls, webhooks and alerts, and dependency/code scanning	Offers GitHub Advanced Security as an additional option for more robust security capabilities like CodeQL analysis, dependency insights, and automated security fixes
Support Options	Standard support options available on github.com	Offers GitHub Premium Support for prioritized and enhanced support
Deployment Options	Limited to cloud-based deployment	Supports on-premises deployment using virtualization hypervisors and deployment to major cloud services
Virtual Appliance Distribution	No self-hosted deployment options	Distributed as a self-contained virtual appliance

The "The Introduction to GitHub Enterprise" section provides essential insights and guidance for administrators navigating GitHub Enterprise. Covering key aspects such as repository management, security configurations, and collaborative tools, the course equips administrators with the knowledge to efficiently manage and optimize GitHub Enterprise instances, ensuring a streamlined and secure development environment.

Setting Up a GitHub Enterprise Instance

Setting up a GitHub Enterprise instance involves configuring a private, self-hosted environment for collaborative software development. This process includes installing the GitHub Enterprise Server, configuring essential settings, securing communication with SSL/TLS, and customizing the instance to meet organizational needs. Additional steps include user authentication setup, integration with existing tools, implementing security measures, and establishing monitoring and backup strategies. The process ensures a secure, tailored, and efficient platform for teams to collaborate, manage repositories, and streamline development workflows. GitHub Enterprise Server supports various platforms for setting up instances, providing flexibility based on organizational preferences and infrastructure.

The supported platforms include

- **AWS (Amazon Web Services):** GitHub Enterprise can be deployed on AWS, utilizing the cloud infrastructure and services provided by Amazon.

- **Azure (Microsoft Azure):** GitHub Enterprise is compatible with Microsoft Azure, allowing organizations to set up their instances on Microsoft's cloud platform.

- **Google Cloud Platform (GCP):** GitHub Enterprise supports deployment on the Google Cloud Platform, leveraging Google's infrastructure and services.

- **Hyper-V:** Organizations using Microsoft Hyper-V virtualization can set up GitHub Enterprise instances on their Hyper-V infrastructure.

- **OpenStack KVM:** GitHub Enterprise is compatible with the KVM (Kernel-based Virtual Machine) virtualization platform within the OpenStack framework.

- **VMware:** Organizations utilizing VMware virtualization technology can deploy GitHub Enterprise instances on their VMware infrastructure.

These platform options accommodate to diverse organizational requirements, allowing GitHub Enterprise to seamlessly integrate with different cloud providers and virtualization environments. Organizations can choose the platform that aligns with their existing infrastructure and preferences for deployment. Let's consider AWS as an example for establishing a GitHub Enterprise instance.

Enabling GitHub Packages with AWS

To deploy the GitHub Enterprise Server on Amazon Web Services (AWS), you need to initiate an Amazon Elastic Compute Cloud (EC2) instance and establish a distinct Amazon Elastic Block Store (EBS) data volume, which should be created and attached.

Prerequisites

To proceed with setting up your GitHub Enterprise Server instance on AWS, you need to possess a GitHub Enterprise license file. Additionally, ensure that you have an active AWS account with the capability to launch EC2 instances and create EBS volumes. While many actions can be carried out through the AWS Management Console, it is advisable to install the AWS Command Line Interface (CLI) for the initial setup.

Hardware Considerations

We recommend different hardware configurations based on the number of user licenses for your GitHub Enterprise Server instance. Provisioning more resources than the minimum requirements can enhance the performance and scalability of your instance. The following table outlines the recommended configurations:

User Licenses	x86-64 vCPUs	Memory	Root Storage	Attached (Data) Storage
Trial, Demo, or 10 Light Users	4	32 GB	200 GB	150 GB
10 to 3000	8	48 GB	200 GB	300 GB
3000 to 5000	12	64 GB	200 GB	500 GB
5000 to 8000	16	96 GB	200 GB	750 GB
8000 to 10,000+	20	160 GB	200 GB	1000 GB

If you plan to enable GitHub Actions or Container registry for the users of your instance, additional resources are required.

Storage Recommendations

For GitHub Enterprise Server to perform optimally, GitHub suggests using high-performance SSDs known for their high IOPS and low latency. This is crucial due to the I/O-intensive nature of the server's workloads. For those utilizing a bare-metal hypervisor, direct attachment of the disk or employing a SAN disk is recommended. Ensure the use of a persistent data disk separate from the root disk for the instance. For GitHub Actions, external blob storage is required. Note that the root filesystem's available space will be 50% of the total disk size. You can adjust the root disk size by either setting up a new instance or modifying an existing one.

CPU and Memory Requirements

The CPU and memory needs for GitHub Enterprise Server depend on user, automation, and integration activity levels. It's important to use virtual machines (VMs) that support the x86-64 CPU architecture, as others like Aarch64 or arm64 are incompatible. Enabling GitHub Actions necessitates additional CPU and memory, with a recommendation of at least 6.5 GB of memory per vCPU for up to 16 vCPUs. Beyond 16 vCPUs, maintaining this memory-to-vCPU ratio isn't required, though monitoring for adequate memory is recommended. To maintain instance performance and scalability, it's advised to use webhook events for external system notifications instead of automated checks or polling.

Determining the Instance Type

Before launching your GitHub Enterprise Server instance on AWS, you'll need to determine the machine type that best fits the needs of your organization. To review the minimum requirements for GitHub Enterprise Server, please check the section "Hardware Considerations." You can always scale up your CPU or memory by resizing your instance. Changing the resources available to your instance requires downtime for your users, so GitHub recommends overprovisioning resources to account for scale. GitHub recommends a memory-optimized instance for GitHub Enterprise Server.

Selecting the GitHub Enterprise Server AMI

To choose an Amazon Machine Image (AMI) for GitHub Enterprise Server, you have the option to do so through the GitHub Enterprise Server portal or the AWS Command Line Interface (CLI). GitHub Enterprise Server offers AMIs in the AWS GovCloud region, specifically in US-East and US-West. This provision enables US customers with particular regulatory requirements to operate GitHub Enterprise Server within a cloud environment that aligns with federal compliance standards.

Using the GitHub Enterprise Server Portal to Select an AMI

Follow these steps to select an image for your new GitHub Enterprise Server instance on AWS:

- Navigate to the desired image.

- Visit the Release notes section of GitHub Enterprise.

  - In the right sidebar, choose the version you wish to download.

  - Click "Download GitHub Enterprise Server X.X.X."

- Under "GitHub in the Cloud," access the "Select your platform" dropdown menu, and choose Amazon Web Services.

- From the "Select your AWS region" dropdown menu, pick your preferred region.

- Take note of the displayed AMI ID.

Using the AWS CLI to Select an AMI

To choose an Amazon Machine Image (AMI) for your GitHub Enterprise Server instance using the AWS CLI, follow these steps:

- Open your terminal or command prompt.

- Use the "aws ec2 describe-images" command to list available AMIs. Specify filters to narrow down the results, such as the owner ("--owners github-enterprise"), the image name, or other relevant criteria.

- Identify the AMI ID for the GitHub Enterprise Server version you want to use.

- Make note of the selected AMI ID for use in launching your GitHub Enterprise Server instance.

Here's an example command:

```
aws ec2 describe-images --owners github-enterprise --filters
"Name=name,Values=GitHub Enterprise Server*" --query 'Images[].
[Name,ImageId]' --output table
```

The preceding command lists GitHub Enterprise Server images, displaying their names and corresponding Image IDs in a table format. Choose the Image ID that matches your desired version.

Creating a Security Group

To create a security group for GitHub Enterprise Server in AWS, you have the option to use either the AWS Management Console or the AWS Command Line Interface (CLI). Here are the steps to create a security group using the AWS Management Console:

- Using AWS Management Console:

  - Sign in to the AWS Management Console by navigating to the AWS Management Console and logging in to your AWS account.

  - Open the EC2 Dashboard by finding it in the AWS Management Console's navigation pane.

  - Navigate to the "Security Groups" section within the EC2 Dashboard.

  - Click the "Create Security Group" button.

  - Configure the security group by providing a name and description and selecting the VPC in which you want to create the security group.

  - Add inbound rules under the "Inbound rules" section, specifying the necessary ports for GitHub Enterprise Server, such as 22 for SSH, 80 for HTTP, and 443 for HTTPS.

- Add outbound rules under the "Outbound rules" section.

- Review your configurations and click "Create Security Group."

By following these steps in the AWS Management Console, you can efficiently create a security group tailored to the requirements of GitHub Enterprise Server.

Here's an example command:

```
aws ec2 create-security-group --group-name GitHubSecurityGroup
--description "Security group for GitHub Enterprise Server"
--vpc-id your-vpc-id
```

Remember to replace "your-vpc-id" with the actual VPC ID where you want to create the security group. After creating the security group, you may need to modify its inbound and outbound rules to allow the necessary traffic for GitHub Enterprise Server. Use the "authorize-security-group-ingress" and "authorize-security-group-egress" commands for this purpose.

Creating the GitHub Enterprise Server Instance

To create the instance for GitHub Enterprise Server on AWS, follow these steps, which include launching an EC2 instance and configuring storage:

- **Launch an EC2 Instance:**

  - Utilize the AWS CLI to launch an EC2 instance using the GitHub Enterprise Server AMI and the security group previously created.

- Ensure you attach a new block device to serve as a storage volume for your instance data. Adjust the size of the storage volume based on your user license count.

```
aws ec2 run-instances \
    --security-group-ids SECURITY_GROUP_ID \
    --instance-type INSTANCE_TYPE \
    --image-id AMI_ID \
    --block-device-mappings '[{"DeviceName":"/dev/
xvdf","Ebs":{"VolumeSize":SIZE,"VolumeType":
"TYPE"}}]' \
    --region REGION \
    --ebs-optimized
```

Note If you opt for data disk encryption, it adds an extra layer of security but may impact performance. It's advisable to encrypt the volume before starting the instance for the first time. Refer to the Amazon guide on EBS encryption for more details.

Warning Enabling encryption after configuring the instance requires migrating data to the encrypted volume, incurring some downtime for users. Plan accordingly to minimize disruptions.

Allocating an Elastic IP and Associating It with the Instance

For a production instance, it is highly advisable to allocate an Elastic IP (EIP) and associate it with the instance before configuring GitHub Enterprise Server. This step is crucial to retain the public IP address of the instance even after restarts. Failure to assign an EIP may result in changes to the public IP address, causing potential disruptions. In production high-availability configurations, it is essential to assign separate EIPs to both primary and replica instances for optimal performance and redundancy. This ensures a robust and reliable setup for GitHub Enterprise Server in a production environment.

Configuring the GitHub Enterprise Server Instance

Configuring the GitHub Enterprise Server instance involves several crucial steps to ensure proper setup and security. Follow these steps to configure the instance:

- **Access the Instance:**

    - Copy the virtual machine's public DNS name and paste it into a web browser.

    - Upload the GitHub Enterprise Server license file when prompted.

- **Set a Management Console Password:**

    - Set a secure root Management Console password during the setup process.

    - It is essential to personally set the root password to prevent potential security risks.

- **Configure Instance Settings:**

    - In the Management Console, navigate through the configuration options.

    - Set up desired settings, including network configurations, authentication methods, repository storage, and other preferences.

    - **Restart the Instance:** Save the configured settings, triggering an automatic restart of the GitHub Enterprise Server instance.

- **Visit Your Instance:** Once the instance restarts, click "Visit your instance" to verify that the configuration changes have been successfully applied.

Note   Promptly set the root Management Console password and create the first user to enhance security and prevent potential security vulnerabilities.

To summarize, setting up a GitHub Enterprise instance for GitHub administrators involves configuring a dedicated environment tailored to organizational needs. Administrators oversee user access, repository management, and security settings, ensuring a robust and tailored GitHub Enterprise setup for efficient and secure collaborative software development.

User Management and Access Control

User management and access control in GitHub Enterprise involve the administration of user accounts and defining permissions to regulate access within the platform. This encompasses creating, modifying, and deleting user accounts, as well as establishing roles and permissions for different users. Administrators can manage users through a centralized dashboard, where they can add or remove team members, assign specific roles, and control access to repositories and organizational resources. Access control mechanisms allow administrators to specify who can view, edit, or merge code, ensuring a secure and organized collaborative development environment. In GitHub Enterprise, user management and access control are vital components of maintaining a structured and secure platform, enabling organizations to customize and optimize user interactions while safeguarding sensitive code repositories and project assets.

Key aspects of user management and access control in GitHub Enterprise include

- **User Account Administration:** GitHub Enterprise provides tools for administrators to manage user accounts efficiently. This involves tasks such as adding or removing team members, updating user details, and handling account-related configurations.

- **Role Assignment:** Administrators can assign different roles to users based on their responsibilities and permissions. Common roles include owners, collaborators, and contributors, each with varying levels of access to repositories and organizational features.

- **Access Levels:** GitHub Enterprise allows administrators to configure access levels for individual repositories. This ensures that users have appropriate permissions for actions such as viewing, editing, merging code, and managing issues.

- **Team Management:** Users can be organized into teams, simplifying access control at a group level. Teams can be granted specific permissions and access to particular repositories, streamlining collaboration for larger groups.

- **Organizational Policies:** Administrators can establish policies that define how users interact with repositories and enforce standards within the organization. This includes setting rules for branch protection, code review requirements, and other governance measures.

Effective user management and access control are crucial for ensuring a secure and organized GitHub environment. These features empower organizations to tailor user interactions, maintain collaboration standards, and safeguard sensitive code repositories and project assets.

Accounts on GitHub Enterprise Server

GitHub Enterprise Server provides a platform for storing and collaborating on code, and user accounts play a crucial role in organizing and controlling access to this code. There are three main types of accounts on GitHub Enterprise Server:

- **Personal Accounts:** Every individual user who interacts with GitHub Enterprise Server has a personal account. Users sign in with their personal accounts to access the platform.

- **Organization Accounts:** Organization accounts facilitate collaboration among multiple personal accounts. They serve as a way to group users together, making it easier to manage and coordinate collaborative efforts.

- **Enterprise Accounts:** The enterprise account is associated with the GitHub Enterprise Server instance itself. It allows for centralized management of multiple organizations within the GitHub Enterprise Server environment. This centralization streamlines administrative tasks and provides a comprehensive overview of the entire GitHub ecosystem within the enterprise.

Administration of a GitHub Enterprise Account (Cloud Hosted)

Within a GitHub Enterprise Server instance, administrators play a pivotal role in overseeing various facets of the enterprise account. This includes managing enterprise membership, personal involvement in

403

organizations, and key functionalities like monitoring license usage, implementing security measures (SSH certificate authorities, two-factor authentication), and setting enterprise-wide policies. It's important to note that changing the enterprise display name does not affect the URL's enterprise name, and there is only one default enterprise account.

For GitHub Enterprise Cloud users, administrators have similar oversight capabilities, including managing memberships, billing, and security features like Single Sign-On and IP allow lists. Additionally, for those utilizing both GitHub Enterprise Cloud and Server, the enterprise account on GitHub.com provides comprehensive management over billing and usage for Server instances and support functionalities.

Roles Within an Enterprise

Roles are crucial for regulating access within an enterprise, with specific roles including enterprise owner, billing manager, enterprise member, and guest collaborator (exclusive to Enterprise Managed Users). Direct invitations are possible for roles like enterprise owner or billing manager, while enterprises using Enterprise Managed Users must provision roles through their identity provider (IdP), with role assignments being immutable within GitHub.

Enterprise Owners: Enterprise owners have broad control, capable of managing administrators, adding or removing organizations, managing settings, enforcing policies, and handling billing. They do not automatically access organization settings and must join organizations to do so. Licensing counts them as a single license regardless of multiple organization roles, emphasizing the need for a personal GitHub account and recommending a limited number of enterprise owners to minimize risk.

Billing Managers: Billing managers focus on billing settings, able to view and manage billing details, and add or remove other billing managers. They consume a license if part of an organization and lack access to organizational or repository settings. A personal GitHub account is required for this role.

Enterprise Members: Members of organizations under an enterprise are automatically enterprise members but lack access to enterprise settings. They can access all "internal" visibility repositories across the enterprise, facilitating cross-organization collaboration.

Guest Collaborators: For enterprises with Enterprise Managed Users, guest collaborators offer restricted access for vendors and contractors, provisioned through the IdP. They access only internal repositories within their organizations, with their role and access managed through SCIM. It's crucial to assign the guest collaborator role correctly in the IdP to avoid privilege conflicts.

Important points to remember:

- The administration of enterprise accounts involves comprehensive management of memberships, security, and policies.

- Roles within an enterprise are designed to explain access and responsibilities clearly.

- Enterprise owners wield extensive control but require careful management to minimize security risks.

- Billing managers and enterprise members have specific access rights, emphasizing the importance of role-based access control.

- Guest collaborators provide a flexible way to involve external parties securely, with their access tightly controlled through the IdP.

- This streamlined overview emphasizes the importance of structured administration and role management in securing and efficiently managing GitHub Enterprise environments.

Invite People to Manage the Enterprise

The ability to invite and remove enterprise owners and billing managers is a feature available for your enterprise account, and its usage depends on the nature of your GitHub setup. For enterprises not utilizing Enterprise Managed Users, GitHub Enterprise Cloud provides the flexibility to add or remove enterprise owners and billing managers directly through the platform. Enterprise owners, in particular, can extend invitations to other individuals, inviting them to assume additional responsibilities as enterprise administrators. However, if your enterprise employs Enterprise Managed Users, the process of adding or removing enterprise owners and billing managers follows a different protocol. In this scenario, such administrative changes must be carried out exclusively through your identity provider. GitHub defers to the identity provider for managing the roster of enterprise owners and billing managers within the context of Enterprise Managed Users.

Invite an Enterprise Administrator to an Enterprise Account

To invite an individual to become an enterprise administrator for your enterprise account, follow these steps. After extending the invitation, the invitee must accept it via email to gain access to the enterprise account. Keep in mind that any pending invitations will expire after a period of seven days. Here's how you can manage and send invitations:

- Go to GitHub.com and log in to your account.

- In the top-right corner, click your profile photo, then select "Your enterprises" from the dropdown menu.

- From the list of enterprises, click the specific enterprise you wish to manage.

- Within the enterprise account sidebar, navigate to "People."

- Under "People," click "Administrators."

- Above the list of administrators, you'll find an option to "Invite admin." Click this option.

- Enter the username, full name, or email address of the person you intend to invite as an enterprise administrator. Select the correct person from the search results.

- Choose the role you want to assign to the invited person – either "Owner" or "Billing Manager." Figure 6-1 shows the invite admin screen.

Figure 6-1. *Invite admin screen*

- Finally, click "Send invitation" to dispatch the invitation to the selected individual.

Remove an Enterprise Administrator from an Enterprise Account

To remove enterprise administrators from your enterprise account, only enterprise owners have the authority to do so. Follow these steps to manage administrators:

- On GitHub.com, click your profile photo in the top-right corner, then select "Your enterprises" from the dropdown menu.

- From the list of enterprises, choose the specific enterprise you wish to manage.

- In the enterprise account sidebar, go to "People."

- Under "People," navigate to "Administrators."

- Find the username of the administrator you want
  to remove.

- Next to the username, click the dropdown menu. Here,
  you have two options:

  - **Convert to Member:** This option removes their
    administrative role but retains their memberships
    in organizations owned by the enterprise.

  - **Remove from Enterprise:** This option removes
    both their administrative role and organization
    memberships. Figure 6-2 shows the screen for
    removing an enterprise administrator.

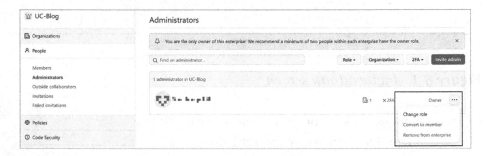

Figure 6-2. *Remove an enterprise administrator*

- Read the confirmation message and ensure you
  understand the consequences.

- Click "Yes, convert USERNAME to member" or "Yes,
  remove USERNAME" to confirm your decision.

It's important to consider the implications of either converting to a member or completely removing from the enterprise based on the specific requirements and circumstances.

Manage Invitations to Organizations Within an Enterprise Account

For invitation management, you have the flexibility to retry or cancel invitations to organizations within your enterprise, whether it's a single invitation or multiple invitations simultaneously. This feature is accessible to enterprise owners who have the authority to manage invitations to organizations within their enterprise. Whether you are dealing with invitations to your enterprise or specific organizations within it, the management process remains consistent. For expired invitations, which have a lifespan of seven days, you can retry or cancel them individually or in bulk. This includes the ability to handle failed invitations to outside collaborators within the same view. To engage with this functionality:

- On GitHub.com, navigate to the top-right corner and click your profile photo. From the dropdown menu, select "Your enterprises."

- Choose the specific enterprise you want to manage from the list of enterprises.

- In the enterprise account sidebar, click "People."

- Under "People," find and click "Failed invitations."

- Optionally, retry or cancel a single invitation:

  - To the right of the invitation you want to handle, select the dropdown menu and click "Retry invitation" or "Cancel invitation."

  - Confirm your choice by clicking "Yes, retry" or "Yes, cancel."

- Optionally, retry or cancel multiple invitations
  simultaneously:

  - Select the checkboxes next to the invitations you
    wish to handle.

  - At the top of the list, use the "X invitations selected"
    dropdown menu to click "Retry invitations" or
    "Cancel invitations." Figure 6-3 shows the screen for
    cancelling invite.

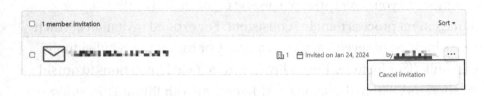

Figure 6-3. *Cancel invitation*

By following these steps, enterprise owners can efficiently manage
and organize invitations to organizations within their enterprise, ensuring
effective collaboration and streamlined administrative processes.

Manage Organization Members in an Enterprise Account

Enterprise owners have the capability to efficiently manage
organization memberships in bulk by adding or removing members
through a streamlined process. To use this feature:

- On GitHub.com, navigate to the top-right corner and
  click your profile photo. From the dropdown menu,
  select "Your enterprises."

- Choose the specific enterprise you wish to manage
  from the list.

- In the enterprise account sidebar, click "People."

- Select the checkbox next to each user you intend to add or remove.

- At the top of the member list, use the "X user(s) selected" dropdown menu. Then, click either "Add to organizations" or "Remove from organizations."

- In the ensuing pop-up, specify the organizations to which you want to add or remove the user. It's important to note that you can only select organizations where you hold the role of organization owner.

- To confirm your action, click either "Add user" or "Remove user." Figure 6-4 shows the screen to add/remove a user to/from organizations.

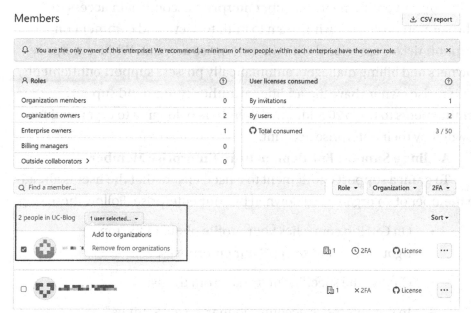

Figure 6-4. *Add/remove a user*

Additionally, if you need to process multiple users simultaneously, you can select multiple checkboxes and use the dropdown menu to choose between "Add to organizations" and "Remove from organizations." This bulk management feature is particularly useful for enterprise owners who want to efficiently control and organize the membership status of individuals within the organizations associated with their enterprise. Importantly, members added through this bulk method do not receive email invitations; they are promptly added as members to the selected organizations.

Managing Support Entitlements for an Enterprise

To empower enterprise members with the ability to manage support tickets for your enterprise account, it's essential to understand support entitlements and the process of granting or removing them. Individuals with support entitlements for your enterprise account gain access to the support portal, allowing them to initiate, view, and comment on support tickets associated with the enterprise account. While enterprise owners and billing managers automatically possess support entitlements, enterprise owners have the additional authority to extend support entitlements to up to 20 additional members belonging to organizations owned by their enterprise account.

Adding a Support Entitlement to an Enterprise Member

To grant a support entitlement to a user, ensure that the user is already a member of an organization owned by your enterprise. Follow these steps:

- On GitHub.com, click your profile photo in the top-right corner and select "Your enterprises."

- Choose the specific enterprise from the list.

- In the enterprise account sidebar, go to "Settings."

- Under "Settings," click "Support."

- In the search bar, type the name or username of the person you wish to grant a support entitlement. Click their name in the list of matches.

- Click "Add support entitlement."

Removing a Support Entitlement from an Enterprise Member

Support entitlements are automatically removed when a user is removed from the enterprise. However, if a user remains an enterprise member, and you need to manually remove their support entitlement, follow these steps:

- On GitHub.com, click your profile photo in the top-right corner and select "Your enterprises."

- Choose the specific enterprise from the list.

- In the enterprise account sidebar, navigate to "Settings."

- Under "Settings," click "Support."

- Under "Support members," to the right of the person from whom you want to remove a support entitlement, click the respective icon.

It's important to note that support entitlements cannot be removed from enterprise owners or billing managers. This process ensures efficient management of support-related responsibilities within the enterprise account. Please be aware that after adding a support entitlement, the enterprise member might need to sign out from the GitHub Support portal and then sign in again before gaining the ability to manage tickets. This step is crucial to ensure that the updated support entitlements take effect and that the members can fully utilize their newly granted ticket management capabilities within the GitHub Support portal.

View and Manage a User's SAML Access to an Enterprise

Enterprise owners have the capability to inspect and revoke an enterprise member's linked identity, active sessions, and authorized credentials, specifically in the context of SAML access to organizations within the enterprise account. This feature is accessible to enterprise owners who hold the authority to oversee and manage a member's SAML access to organizations within the enterprise. When SAML Single Sign-On is enabled for your enterprise account, each enterprise member has the option to link their external identity from the identity provider (IdP) to their existing account on GitHub.com. To access the resources of each organization on GitHub Enterprise Cloud, a member must have an active SAML session in their browser. Additionally, for accessing the organization's protected resources via API and Git, members must use a personal access token or SSH key that they have authorized for use with the organization. Enterprise owners retain the authority to review and revoke a member's linked identity, active sessions, or authorized credentials at any given time.

For enterprises using Enterprise Managed Users, it's important to note that members will utilize accounts provisioned through the IdP, and these managed user accounts will not rely on their existing user accounts on GitHub Enterprise Cloud.

View and Revoke a Linked Identity

To manage the Single Sign-On (SSO) identity linked to a member's account on GitHub.com, and potentially revoke it if needed, follow these steps:

- On GitHub.com, click your profile photo in the top-right corner, and select "Your enterprises" from the dropdown menu.

- From the list of enterprises, choose the specific enterprise you want to manage.

- In the enterprise account sidebar, click "People."

- Locate and click the name of the member whose linked identity you'd like to inspect or revoke.

- In the left sidebar, click "SAML identity linked."

- Under "Linked SSO identity," you can view the SSO identity that is currently linked for the member.

- To revoke the linked identity, navigate to the right of the displayed identity, and click "Revoke."

This process is especially useful if a member has linked the wrong identity to their GitHub.com account, allowing them to try linking the correct identity again. For enterprises using Enterprise Managed Users, it's important to note that the deprovisioning or removal of user accounts from the enterprise on GitHub Enterprise Cloud is not possible directly. Any modifications to managed user accounts should be handled through your IdP.

View and Revoke an Active SAML Session

To manage and potentially revoke an active SAML session for a member in your GitHub Enterprise account, follow these steps:

- On GitHub.com, click your profile photo in the top-right corner and select "Your enterprises" from the dropdown menu.

- From the list of enterprises, choose the specific enterprise you want to manage.

- In the enterprise account sidebar, click "People."

- Locate and click the name of the member whose SAML session you'd like to inspect or revoke.

- In the left sidebar, click "SAML identity linked."

- Under "Active SAML sessions," you can view the currently active SAML sessions for the member.

- To revoke a specific session, navigate to the right of the displayed session, and click "Revoke."

This process lets you monitor and act on the active SAML sessions associated with a member's account. Revoking a session is particularly useful in scenarios where you need to ensure the security and controlled access to GitHub Enterprise resources.

View and Revoke Authorized Credentials

To view and potentially revoke personal access tokens and SSH keys that a member has authorized for API and Git access in your GitHub Enterprise account, follow these steps:

- On GitHub.com, click your profile photo in the top-right corner and select "Your enterprises" from the dropdown menu.

- From the list of enterprises, choose the specific enterprise you want to manage.

- In the enterprise account sidebar, click "People."

- Locate and click the name of the member whose authorized credentials you'd like to inspect or revoke.

- In the left sidebar, click "SAML identity linked."

- Under "Authorized credentials," you can view the list of credentials that the member has authorized.

- To revoke specific credentials, navigate to the right of the displayed credentials, and click "Revoke."

- Read the information provided, and to confirm, click "I understand, revoke access for this token."

This process allows you to have visibility into and control over the credentials authorized by a member, ensuring security and proper access management within your GitHub Enterprise account. If necessary, collaborate with the member to determine which credentials should be revoked.

Export Membership Information for an Enterprise

To export information about all the members in your enterprise from GitHub's web UI, follow these steps:

- On GitHub.com, click your profile photo in the top-right corner and select "Your enterprises" from the dropdown menu.

- Choose the specific enterprise you want to manage from the list.

- In the enterprise account sidebar, click "People."

- To the right of "Members," click "CSV Report." Figure 6-5 shows the download CSV report option.

Members				⬇ CSV report

A Roles		User licenses consumed	
Organization members	0	By invitations	1
Organization owners	2	By users	2
Enterprise owners	1	⏻ Total consumed	3 / 50
Billing managers	0		
Outside collaborators >	0		

Figure 6-5. *Download CSV report option*

If your enterprise has less than 1000 members, the report will download immediately. However, if your enterprise has 1000 or more members, you'll receive an email shortly with a link to download the report. The membership information report includes various details about each member, such as username and display name details, two-factor authentication status, organization owner or member status, organizations with pending invitations, and optionally, additional information based on your enterprise's configuration. This could include email addresses for a verified domain, SAML NameID, GitHub Enterprise Server instance details, and more. This export feature is valuable for tasks like performing audits of your enterprise's current members. Additionally, note that GitHub's APIs can also be utilized to retrieve information about your enterprise's members. Organization owners can also export membership information for a specific organization within the enterprise.

Removing a Member from Your GitHub Enterprise Account

To remove a member from your GitHub Enterprise account, simply follow these straightforward steps:

1. Go to GitHub.com and click your profile photo located in the top-right corner. From the dropdown menu, select "Your enterprises."

2. From the list, pick the enterprise you wish to manage.

3. In the sidebar of the enterprise account, click "People."

4. Find the person you wish to remove. Click the dropdown menu next to their name and select "Remove from enterprise."

This action will remove the individual from your enterprise, which includes all organizations under your enterprise's umbrella. This means any administrative roles they held, such as owner or billing manager, will be revoked. Keep in mind the following:

- If the member you're removing is the last owner of an organization within your enterprise, you'll automatically be assigned as an owner of that organization.

- For enterprises or organizations using an IdP to manage memberships, the removed member might be re-added by the IdP. To avoid this, make sure to update your IdP settings accordingly.

- In cases where your enterprise employs Enterprise Managed Users, you'll need to remove members through your IdP using SCIM integration.

This streamlined process is designed to help you effectively manage your enterprise's membership, ensuring you have control over who has access and what roles they hold within your GitHub Enterprise account.

Manage Dormant Users

A user account is designated as dormant if it remains inactive for a continuous period of 90 days. User activity within an enterprise is determined based on various actions performed by the user within the enterprise's ecosystem. An active user is identified by engaging in activities such as authenticating to access the enterprise's resources via SAML SSO; creating or interacting with repositories, issues, or pull requests; and commenting, labeling, assigning, and participating in various other actions. Notably, pushing to a repository via SSH does not contribute to assessing user dormancy. When evaluating user dormancy, the focus is on organizations, repositories, or sign-on events associated with the enterprise. For instance, a user who recently engaged with a public repository outside the enterprise may be deemed dormant, while activity within the enterprise-associated repositories keeps a user classified as active. This assessment applies uniformly to both enterprise members and external collaborators. To obtain insights into dormant users, enterprise administrators can download a dormant user's report by navigating to the Compliance section in the enterprise account settings on GitHub. com. By selecting "Dormant Users" and opting to generate a new report, administrators can access valuable information about user dormancy. The generated report, available under "Recent reports," can be conveniently downloaded for further analysis and compliance management.

Suspending and Unsuspending Users

In the event that a user leaves the company or transitions to a different department, it is advisable to adjust their access permissions or entirely revoke their ability to access your GitHub Enterprise Server instance. For departing employees, a practical approach is to suspend their GitHub Enterprise Server accounts. This action not only frees up user licenses within your GitHub Enterprise license but also maintains the integrity of the content they contributed, such as issues, comments, repositories, gists, and other data. Suspended users are unable to log in to your instance, and their capacity to push or pull code is restricted. Upon suspending a user, the change takes immediate effect without providing any notification to the user. Should the suspended user attempt to interact with a repository, they will encounter an error message indicating their account suspension. This error prevents actions like cloning, pushing, or pulling code. An example of the error message is as follows:

```
$ git clone git@[hostname]:blog-uc/test-repo.git
Cloning into 'test-repo'...
ERROR: Your account is suspended. Please check with
your installation administrator.
fatal: The remote end hung up unexpectedly
```

It's essential to note that before suspending site administrators, it is necessary to demote them to regular user status to ensure a smooth transition in access management.

View Suspended Users in the Site Admin Dashboard

To view suspended users in the site admin dashboard of GitHub Enterprise Server, begin by logging in as a site administrator. Once logged in, navigate to the site admin dashboard, usually accessible through the administrative settings or a dedicated dashboard within your GitHub Enterprise Server installation. Look for a section related to user management or user accounts within the dashboard. In this section, you should find a list or table containing user accounts, with suspended users potentially marked or indicated differently, such as through a specific status icon or label. Identify and view the details of suspended users in this section, which may include usernames, display names, and relevant information. Some instances may offer filters or options to display only suspended users, streamlining the identification process.

Suspend a User from the Site Admin Dashboard

Suspending a user from the site admin dashboard on GitHub Enterprise Server involves a series of steps for managing user access. As a site administrator, log in to the GitHub Enterprise Server instance and navigate to the site admin dashboard. Locate the section related to user management or user accounts, where you should find a list or table of user accounts. Identify the user you intend to suspend and select the corresponding actions or options for that user. Typically, there will be a "Suspend" or similar option available. Confirm the suspension action, and the user's account will be immediately suspended. Suspended users lose access to the GitHub Enterprise Server instance, preventing them from logging in or performing actions like pushing or pulling code. It's crucial to note that before suspending site administrators, they must be demoted to regular user status to ensure a smooth transition in access management.

Unsuspend a User from the Site Admin Dashboard

Unsuspending a user from the site admin dashboard on GitHub Enterprise Server involves reversing the suspension action and restoring the user's access to the platform. As a site administrator, log in to the GitHub Enterprise Server instance and navigate to the site admin

421

dashboard. In the user management or user accounts section, locate the
list or table of user accounts, and identify the user you wish to unsuspend.
Select the appropriate actions or options for that user, typically labeled as
"Unsuspend" or a similar term. Confirm the unsuspension action, and the
user's account will be reinstated. Unsuspended users regain access to the
GitHub Enterprise Server instance, allowing them to log in and resume
activities such as pushing or pulling code. It's important to ensure that
unsuspension is carried out judiciously, and any necessary adjustments in
user roles or permissions are made to align with the organization's access
policies.

Viewing Suspended Users in the Site Admin Dashboard

To view suspended users on your GitHub Enterprise Server, start
by logging in as a site administrator. Once logged in, navigate to the
site admin dashboard. This is usually found through the administrative
settings or a dedicated dashboard section within your GitHub Enterprise
Server installation. Look for a user management or user accounts section
within the dashboard. Here, you should find a list or table of user accounts,
where suspended users are typically marked or indicated with a specific
status icon or label. This section allows you to identify and view details of
suspended users, which may include usernames, display names, and other
relevant information. Some instances may provide filters or options to
display only suspended users, making it easier to identify them.

Suspending a User from the Site Admin Dashboard

To suspend a user from the site admin dashboard on GitHub
Enterprise Server, follow these steps as a site administrator:

1.   Log in to your GitHub Enterprise Server instance
     and navigate to the site admin dashboard.

2.   Find the user management or user accounts section,
     where you'll see a list or table of user accounts.

3. Locate the user you wish to suspend and select the corresponding actions or options for that user, usually a "Suspend" or similar option.

4. Confirm the suspension action, and the user's account will be immediately suspended, losing access to the GitHub Enterprise Server instance and preventing them from logging in or interacting with repositories.

Note Before suspending a site administrator, ensure they are demoted to regular user status to manage access smoothly.

Unsuspending a User from the Site Admin Dashboard

To unsuspend a user and restore their access to the GitHub Enterprise Server, follow these steps:

1. As a site administrator, log in to the GitHub Enterprise Server instance and navigate to the site admin dashboard.

2. In the user management or user accounts section, find the list or table of user accounts and identify the user you wish to unsuspend.

3. Select the appropriate actions or options for that user, typically labeled as "Unsuspend" or similar.

4. Confirm the unsuspension action, and the user's account will be reinstated, allowing them to log in and resume their activities on the platform.

Ensure that unsuspension is conducted judiciously, with any necessary adjustments to user roles or permissions made in accordance with your organization's access policies.

Suspending a User from the Command Line

To suspend a user on your GitHub Enterprise Server instance, follow these steps:

- **SSH into Your GitHub Enterprise Server Instance:** If your instance has multiple nodes, SSH into the primary node. In case of a cluster, you can SSH into any node. Use the following command:

  ssh -p 122 admin@HOSTNAME

  Replace "HOSTNAME" with the appropriate hostname or IP address of your GitHub Enterprise Server instance. For more details on SSH access, refer to the documentation on "Accessing the administrative shell (SSH)."

- **Run ghe-user-suspend with the Username to Suspend:** Once logged in, use the "ghe-user-suspend" command along with the username you want to suspend. Execute the following command:

  ghe-user-suspend USERNAME

  Replace "USERNAME" with the actual username of the user you intend to suspend.

These commands will initiate the suspension process for the specified user on your GitHub Enterprise Server instance. It's important to note that suspending a user will restrict their access, preventing them from logging in or performing certain actions. Ensure you have the necessary administrative privileges and consider any organizational policies related to user management before executing these commands.

Creating a Custom Message for Suspended Users

Creating a custom message for suspended users on GitHub Enterprise Server involves providing clear and informative communication to users whose accounts have been suspended. This customized message serves as an explanation for the suspension and can include specific instructions or guidance for the affected users. To implement this, GitHub Enterprise Server administrators can leverage the platform's capabilities to customize user suspension messages. Typically, administrators have the option to define a standard message that suspended users will encounter when attempting to access the platform. This message can convey details about the reason for suspension, any necessary next steps, or contact information for support. The goal is to ensure that suspended users are informed about the status of their accounts and to guide them on the appropriate actions. Crafting a thoughtful and informative suspension message contributes to a transparent and user-friendly experience during periods of restricted access.

Unsuspending a User from the Command Line

To unsuspend a user on your GitHub Enterprise Server instance, follow these steps:

- **SSH into Your GitHub Enterprise Server Instance:** If your instance has multiple nodes, SSH into the primary node. In case of a cluster, you can SSH into any node. Use the following command:

  ssh -p 122 admin@HOSTNAME

  Replace "HOSTNAME" with the appropriate hostname or IP address of your GitHub Enterprise Server instance. Refer to the documentation on "Accessing the administrative shell (SSH)" for more information.

- **Run ghe-user-unsuspend with the Username to Unsuspend:** Once logged in, use the "ghe-user-unsuspend" command along with the username you want to unsuspend. Execute the following command:

ghe-user-unsuspend USERNAME

Replace "USERNAME" with the actual username of the user you intend to unsuspend.

These commands will initiate the unsuspension process for the specified user on your GitHub Enterprise Server instance. Unsuspending a user restores their access, allowing them to log in and resume normal activities on the platform. Ensure you have the necessary administrative privileges and consider any organizational policies related to user management before executing these commands.

Place a Hold on a User or Organization

To place a hold on a user or organization in GitHub Enterprise Server and ensure that repositories they own are available for restore indefinitely, follow these steps:

- **Sign In to GitHub Enterprise Server:** Access your GitHub Enterprise Server instance by navigating to http(s)://HOSTNAME/login. Log in with your administrative credentials.

- **Access the Site Admin Page:** From an administrative account, click the user icon (usually located in the upper-right corner of any page) and then click the "Site admin" option. If you are not on the "Site admin" page, click "Site admin" in the upper-left corner.

- **Search for the User or Organization:** Under "Search users, organizations, teams, repositories, gists, and applications," type the name of the user or organization in the provided text field. Click "Search" to retrieve the search results.

- **Navigate to the User or Organization Profile:** In the search results, click the name of the user or organization for which you want to place a hold.

- **Access the Admin Settings:** In the upper-right corner of the user or organization profile page, click "Admin."

- **Place a Hold:** Under "hold," click "Place hold" to initiate the hold process.

By following these steps, you will have placed a hold on the specified user or organization, ensuring that repositories they own are available for restore indefinitely. This measure is particularly useful in preserving important data and preventing the permanent deletion of repositories from your GitHub Enterprise Server instance.

Auditing SSH Keys

Site administrators have the ability to launch an instance-wide audit of SSH keys in GitHub Enterprise Server. This audit serves to disable all existing SSH keys, compelling users to either approve or reject them before they can engage in cloning, pulling, or pushing operations in repositories. This feature proves valuable in scenarios where an employee or contractor departs from the company, ensuring that all keys are verified.

Initiating an Audit

To initiate an SSH key audit, navigate to the "All users" tab within the site admin dashboard. Clicking the "Start public key audit" button will lead you to a confirmation screen, explaining that starting the audit will disable all public keys, preventing SSH-based pushing and pulling. Users will then be prompted to verify their public keys to restore SSH access. After clicking the "Begin audit" button, all SSH keys become invalidated, and a notification will confirm the commencement of the audit.

User Experience During Audit

If a user attempts any git operation over SSH during the audit, it will fail, displaying a message indicating the ongoing SSH key audit. The user is directed to a specific link to approve their keys, providing a fingerprint for verification. Once users approve or reject their keys, they regain the ability to interact with repositories as usual.

Adding an SSH Key

When a new user adds an SSH key, GitHub Enterprise Server prompts for authentication to confirm the user's access. A notification email is sent to the user with details of the added SSH key, including its fingerprint. Users receiving such notifications can visit a provided link to remove the key and disable access if they believe the key was added in error. By employing these features, GitHub Enterprise Server allows site administrators to maintain secure control over SSH key access and conduct periodic audits for enhanced security measures.

Rebuilding Contributions Data

In GitHub Enterprise Server, the process of linking existing commits to a user account may require rebuilding contributions data. This becomes necessary when a commit is pushed to the platform and needs to be associated with a user account that might have recently registered a new email address or created a new account. Here are the steps to rebuild commit contributions data:

- **Access GitHub Enterprise Server:** Log in with administrative credentials.

- **Navigate to Site Admin:** Click the user profile icon in the upper-right corner, and if not already on the "Site admin" page, select "Site admin" from the options.

- **Search for the User:** Under "Search users, organizations, teams, repositories, gists, and applications," enter the user's name in the text field. Click "Search" to find the relevant account.

- **Identify the User:** If there's no exact match, review the search results, particularly in the "Fuzzy matches" section, and click the user's name to ensure correct identification.

- **Access Admin Options:** In the upper-right corner of the user's details page, click "Admin."

- **Initiate Rebuilding:** Locate the option "Rebuild commit contributions data" and click "Rebuild" to trigger the process.

Upon initiating the rebuild, GitHub Enterprise Server will enqueue background jobs to relink commits with the specified user's account. A banner at the top of the screen will confirm that the "Rebuild commit contributions jobs" have been enqueued. This ensures that contributions data is accurately linked, resolving any discrepancies and maintaining a coherent record of user activity within the platform.

Role-Based Access Control

Role-based access control (RBAC) in GitHub Enterprise provides GitHub administrators with a powerful mechanism to manage and control access to repositories, organizations, and other resources based on predefined roles. GitHub Enterprise has several default roles, each with specific permissions, and administrators can also create custom roles to meet the organization's unique requirements. The following are key aspects of RBAC for GitHub administrators.

Default Roles

GitHub Enterprise comes with default roles that play a fundamental role in managing user access and permissions within the platform. These predefined roles are designed to provide a baseline structure for assigning specific capabilities to users based on their responsibilities and requirements. The key default roles in GitHub Enterprise include

- **Owner:** The owner role is the highest level of privilege within GitHub. Users assigned as owners have full administrative control over the entire organization or repository. This includes the ability to manage access, repositories, teams, billing, and other critical settings.

- **Member:** Members have elevated access rights, allowing them to contribute to repositories by pushing and pulling code. While they don't have the same administrative powers as owners, members can actively participate in projects, create issues, and collaborate with others.

- **Billing Manager:** Billing managers are responsible for managing the financial aspects of the organization, including subscription details and billing information. This role is crucial for organizations with paid GitHub plans, enabling designated users to oversee and handle billing-related tasks.

These default roles serve as the foundation for organizing and regulating user permissions. Owners have the highest level of control, members contribute to the development process, and billing managers handle financial aspects. However, GitHub Enterprise also provides the flexibility for administrators to create custom roles tailored to specific organizational needs. This allows for fine-tuning access controls and ensuring that users have precisely the right level of permissions for their roles within the GitHub Enterprise environment.

Creating Custom Roles

The creation of custom roles in GitHub Enterprise provides administrators with the flexibility to craft precise access controls aligned with the unique needs of their organization. This customization goes beyond the default roles, enabling a more nuanced management of user permissions. The process to create a custom role involves the following general steps:

- **Access GitHub Enterprise Settings:** Administrators log in with their administrative credentials and navigate to the specific organization or repository where custom roles are intended.

- **Navigate to Role Settings:** Within the "Settings" or "Access" section, which may vary in location based on the GitHub Enterprise version, administrators manage roles and permissions.

- **Choose Custom Roles:** In the role management interface, an option to create custom roles is typically available alongside default roles such as owners, members, and billing managers.

- **Define Role Permissions:** Administrators specify the permissions associated with the custom role. This involves detailing actions like repository creation, code pushing, merging pull requests, and other relevant activities while defining the scope and level of access for each permission.

- **Assign Users to Custom Roles:** Once the custom roles are established, administrators assign specific users or teams to these roles, ensuring individuals receive precise permissions tailored to their responsibilities.

- **Example – Custom Role for Release Managers:** As an illustrative example, envision the creation of a release manager role customized to grant permissions for tasks such as creating and managing releases, tagging versions, and engaging with deployment workflows. Administrators define these specific permissions and assign team members responsible for release management to this custom role.

- **Regular Review and Adjustment:** Custom roles undergo periodic reviews to align with evolving organizational needs. Administrators may need to adjust permissions or create new custom roles as the structure and requirements of the organization change over time. The creation of custom roles enhances access control precision, ensuring users have exact permissions needed for their roles within the GitHub Enterprise environment and fostering a tailored and secure collaboration environment for development teams.

By creating custom roles, GitHub administrators enhance the precision of access control, ensuring that users have the exact permissions needed for their roles within the GitHub Enterprise environment. This flexibility contributes to a more tailored and secure collaboration environment for development teams.

Repository-Level Access

RBAC allows GitHub administrators to control access at the repository level. In GitHub Enterprise, repository-level access is a critical aspect of access control managed by GitHub administrators, allowing them to define and regulate the permissions granted to users or teams for specific repositories within the organization. This level of granularity ensures that access is tailored to the needs of individual projects or codebases. GitHub administrators can manage repository-level access through the following steps:

- **Access Repository Settings:** Navigate to the specific repository for which you want to manage access. In the repository settings, administrators can find options related to access control.

- **Define Collaborator Roles:** GitHub Enterprise provides default collaborator roles such as "Read," "Write," and "Admin" with varying levels of permissions. Administrators can assign these roles based on the responsibilities of individuals or teams.

- **Adding Collaborators:** GitHub administrators can add users or teams as collaborators to the repository. This involves specifying their GitHub usernames or team names and assigning them the appropriate role.

- **Example – Collaborator Access for a Development Team:** For instance, consider a scenario where a development team needs access to a repository. The GitHub administrator navigates to the repository settings, adds the usernames of the team members, and assigns them the "Write" role for collaborative code contributions. Additionally, a release management team might be granted "Admin" access for overseeing version releases.

- **Removing Collaborators:** Administrators can also manage access by removing collaborators who no longer require permissions for a particular repository.

- **Branch Protection Rules:** GitHub administrators can further enhance access control by implementing branch protection rules. These rules define who can push to or merge changes into specific branches, safeguarding critical branches from unintended modifications.

- **Regular Review and Adjustment:** Regularly reviewing
  and adjusting repository-level access ensures that
  access permissions align with the evolving needs of
  the development projects. Administrators may modify
  access settings, add or remove collaborators, and adjust
  roles as the project requirements change.

By leveraging repository-level access in GitHub Enterprise,
administrators maintain precise control over who can interact with specific
repositories, facilitating a secure and organized collaborative development
environment.

Organization-Level Access

In GitHub Enterprise, organization-level access is a fundamental
aspect of access control that allows GitHub administrators to regulate
and customize permissions across multiple repositories within an
organization. This feature ensures a cohesive and centralized approach to
managing access for teams and individuals working on various projects
under the organization's umbrella. Key steps for GitHub administrators to
handle organization-
level access include the following:

- **Navigate to Organization Settings:** Access the
  organization settings from the GitHub Enterprise
  interface. This central hub provides administrators
  with tools to manage members, teams, and overall
  organization-level configurations.

- **Manage Members and Teams:** GitHub administrators
  can add users to the organization as members and
  organize them into teams. This structuring allows for
  more efficient access management, especially when
  dealing with larger teams or multiple projects.

- **Define Member Roles:** Assigning roles to organization members is crucial for regulating access. GitHub Enterprise offers default roles such as "member," "owner," and "billing manager," each with distinct permissions. Owners have full administrative control, while members have varying levels of access based on their role.

- **Team Permissions:** Teams within the organization can be configured with specific permissions, simplifying access management for a group of individuals. GitHub administrators can set team-level permissions to control actions like repository creation, deletion, and code modification.

- **Repository Access:** Organization-level access ensures consistency across repositories. GitHub administrators can define which teams or individuals have read, write, or administrative access to each repository within the organization.

- **Example – Development and QA Teams:** As an example, an organization may have a "Development" team with write access to repositories for active coding projects, while a separate "Quality Assurance (QA)" team may have read-only access to assess and test the code. GitHub administrators can customize these permissions to align with the responsibilities of each team.

- **Regular Review and Adjustment:** Regularly reviewing and adjusting organization-level access settings is crucial to accommodate changes in team structures, project requirements, or personnel. GitHub administrators can modify roles, permissions, and team compositions as needed.

Organization-level access in GitHub Enterprise provides a centralized and flexible mechanism for GitHub administrators to govern access permissions, fostering collaboration while ensuring security and adherence to organizational policies.

Two-Factor Authentication (2FA) Enforcement

GitHub administrators can use RBAC to enforce security policies such as mandatory two-factor authentication. This ensures an additional layer of security for users with elevated access. You, as an admin, can enable two different types of 2FA, one from GitHub.com as an application layer and another way to enable 2FA at an identity provider (IdP) layer. For more details, please visit the "Security and Compliance" section later in this chapter.

Audit Logs

GitHub Enterprise provides audit logs that GitHub administrators can review to track changes made to roles, permissions, and access control settings. This helps in monitoring and ensuring compliance with security policies. For more details, please visit the "Security and Compliance" section later in this chapter.

Enforcing Collaborator Invitations

In GitHub Enterprise, there's a feature called Collaborator Invite Enforcement that helps keep your repositories secure. It lets administrators decide who can invite collaborators to repositories. This is important because it stops people who shouldn't have access from getting it and makes sure that only certain people can manage who works on a repository. Here's a simple breakdown of how it works:

- **Who Can Invite Collaborators:** Only certain people, usually those with administrative rights, can invite others to collaborate on a repository. This stops just anyone from adding new collaborators without permission.

- **Centralized Control:** Administrators have a special dashboard where they can see and manage all the invitations. This makes it easier to keep track of who's being added to work on repositories.

- **Security Benefits:** By controlling who can send out invitations, you reduce the risk of letting the wrong person access sensitive or important project information. It's a way to make sure that adding new collaborators is done safely and according to the rules.

- **Keeping Track:** This feature also lets administrators monitor who's been invited and added as collaborators, which helps with keeping things transparent and accountable.

- **Custom Settings:** Administrators can change the settings to fit what the organization needs. This means they can decide who gets to invite collaborators, making sure it lines up with the organization's security policies.

In short, Collaborator Invite Enforcement in GitHub Enterprise is all about giving administrators the power to keep the development environment secure and well organized. By setting up who can invite collaborators, it ensures that the repository remains protected and only the right people can add new members. This is especially important for businesses that need to follow strict rules about who has access to their code and data.

Setting Up Teams in Enterprise

Setting up teams within your organization on GitHub is essential for managing access rights, streamlining notifications, and enhancing collaboration. Teams allow owners and maintainers to assign different levels of access – such as admin, read, or write – to organization repositories. By mentioning a team's name, organization members can quickly send notifications to the entire team, although it's important to note that only internal organization members can be included in a team. Owners and maintainers have the flexibility to disable team notifications if necessary. Additionally, organization members can highlight specific teams for review requests if those teams have read access to the relevant repository. Utilizing a CODEOWNERS file, teams can be designated as responsible for certain code areas, which aids in automatic notification for reviews. Team synchronization is another feature that automatically updates team membership based on the organization's identity provider settings.

Teams can be set as either visible or secret; visible teams are open to all organization members, while secret teams are only accessible to their members and those with owner permissions, making them ideal for sensitive collaborations. The hierarchical organization of teams, with parent and child teams, simplifies permission management and ensures that child teams inherit access permissions from their parent. This hierarchical structure is reflected on each team's page, which displays members, child teams, and linked repositories, and where owners and maintainers can update team details.

Before nesting teams, it's wise to audit each team's repository access permissions to identify necessary adjustments. Planning the desired team structure is crucial, with parent teams ideally assigned repository access permissions that are safe for every member of both parent and child teams. Removing all members from existing teams before reorganizing can provide a clean slate, allowing for a detailed review of permissions. Assigning a parent to each team based on the planned hierarchy and carefully selecting parents for any new teams ensures a well-organized and secure team structure. Adding individuals directly to teams, with consideration for their required access levels, finalizes the setup, creating a structured hierarchy that supports the organization's collaboration needs while maintaining optimal security and access control.

Creating a Team

Creating a team in GitHub Enterprise is a pivotal process for organizing and overseeing collaboration within an organization. GitHub offers a user-friendly interface that empowers administrators or team maintainers to establish teams aligned with the organizational structure. The process encompasses the following steps.

Begin by accessing team creation: log in to GitHub Enterprise and navigate to the organization where the team is to be created. Users with necessary administrative privileges can initiate the team creation process. Once within the organization's interface, locate the "Teams" section. This section may be found in the main navigation menu or under specific organizational settings, depending on the GitHub Enterprise version. Initiate the creation of a new team within the "Teams" section. This option typically prompts the user to enter essential details such as the team's name, description, and its visibility status (visible or secret). Visible teams are viewable and mentionable by all organization members, while secret teams are visible only to team members and those with owner permissions. Assign repository access permissions to the team based on its role and responsibilities. GitHub Enterprise provides options for teams to have admin, read, or write access to organization repositories. For those creating nested teams to mirror a hierarchical structure, the option to choose a parent team for the new team is available. This step, although optional, aids in establishing a hierarchical organization of teams. Utilize GitHub Enterprise's customization options for team settings. Administrators or team maintainers can tailor settings related to team mentions, notifications, and repository visibility. After defining the team's configuration, proceed to add members. Team members may include individuals from within the organization who will collaborate within the specified repositories. Review the configured settings to ensure alignment with the intended structure and access permissions. Once satisfied, confirm the creation of the team. Figure 6-6 shows the screen for creating a team.

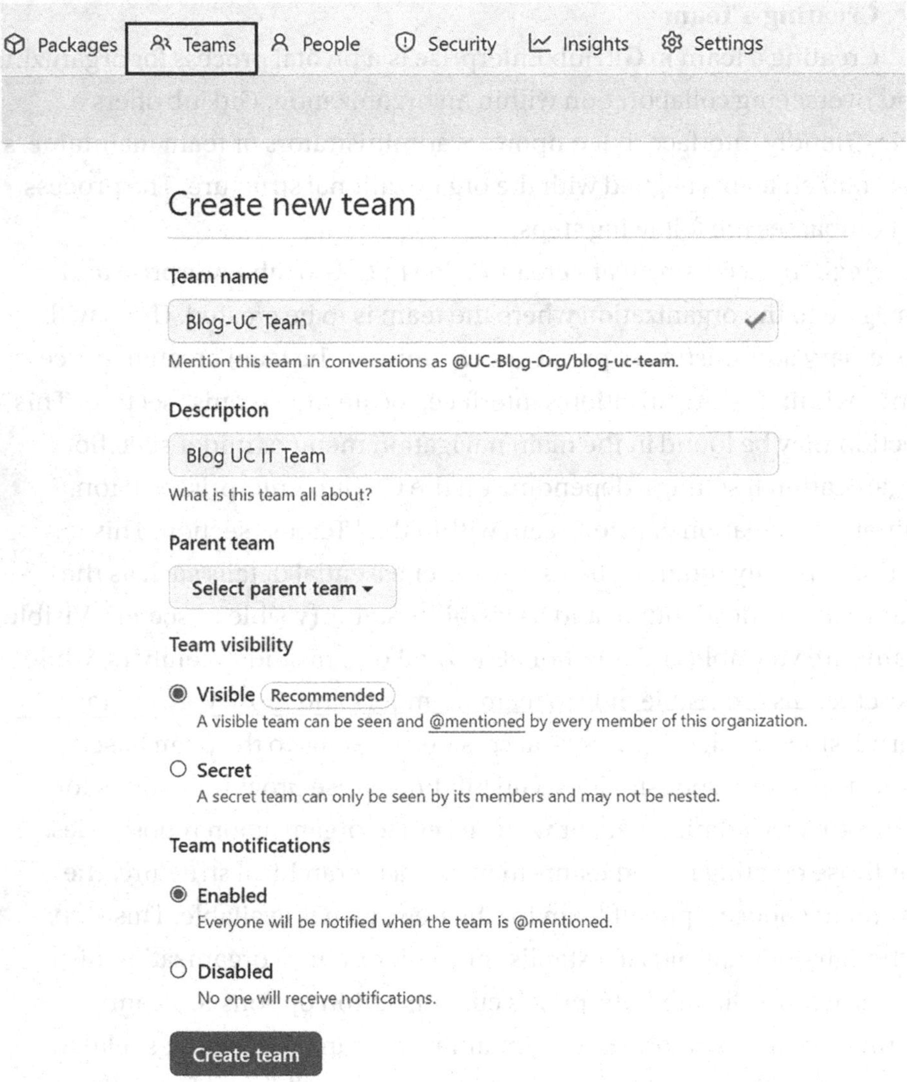

Figure 6-6. *Create a new team*

By following these steps, GitHub Enterprise users can adeptly create teams tailored to their organization's needs, playing a pivotal role in facilitating collaboration, managing access permissions, and enhancing communication within the GitHub environment.

Adding Organization Members to the Team

Adding organization members to a team in GitHub Enterprise is a crucial step in fostering collaboration and organizing roles within an organization. GitHub provides a straightforward process for administrators or team maintainers to include members in a team, allowing for efficient workflow management.

Start by logging in to GitHub Enterprise and navigating to the organization's interface. Locate the "Teams" section, where you can access the settings for the team to which you want to add members. Within the "Teams" section, identify and select the specific team to which you want to add organization members. Click the team's name to access its settings. Look for the "Members" tab within the team's settings. This tab provides an overview of existing members and allows for the addition of new members. In the "Members" tab, there should be an option to add members. This may involve typing the GitHub usernames of the individuals you want to add or selecting them from a list.

GitHub Enterprise allows you to specify the level of access or permissions for each member added to the team. This includes designations such as read, write, or admin access, depending on the responsibilities of the team members. After selecting and assigning permissions to the organization members, confirm the addition. GitHub Enterprise may prompt for confirmation to ensure that you intend to add the specified individuals to the team. Optionally, GitHub can send notifications to the added members, informing them about their inclusion in the team. This enhances transparency and ensures that team members are aware of their updated roles. Administrators or team maintainers can review the team's composition regularly and make adjustments as organizational needs evolve. This ensures that the right individuals have the necessary access for effective collaboration.

By following these steps, GitHub Enterprise users can seamlessly add organization members to a team, fostering a collaborative environment while maintaining control over access permissions. This process is integral to the effective utilization of GitHub Enterprise's team-based structure for streamlined and organized development workflows.

GitHub offers various permission levels tailored for organizations such as read, triage, write, maintain, and admin. To streamline GitHub permissions within an organization, it is beneficial to categorize employees into teams. GitHub facilitates the creation of custom teams, aligning with your organizational structure or project management framework. This approach enhances the organization, ensuring that the right individuals have appropriate access and fostering efficient collaboration and project management.

Here is how you can manage permissions in a GitHub organization with an example.

Let us consider an organization called "Bloguc-Engineering" with multiple repositories. The organization owner wants to manage permissions for developers and admins working on the "sample-workflow" repository.

Add Collaborators to the Organization:

- The organization owner invites developers Balu and Ram to the organization as members.

- Balu is given write access because she actively contributes code.

- Ram is given read access because he needs to review but not modify the code.

Create a Team for Admins:

- The organization owner creates a team called "Bloguc Admins."

- Admins, like Ganesh and Ajay, are added to this team.

- The team is given admin access to the "sample-workflow" repository.

Custom Permissions for a Specific Repository:

- The organization owner goes to the "sample-workflow" repository settings.

- In the "Collaborators & teams" section, the organization owner adds the "Bloguc Admins" team.

- The owner can create a custom permission level for this team.

- Custom permissions allow specific actions, such as pushing to certain branches, tagging releases, or managing issues.

Revoke Access:

- If a collaborator's role changes, the owner can modify their permissions.

- If a team member leaves the project, the owner can remove them from the team or the organization.

By following these steps and examples, the organization owner effectively manages permissions, ensuring that team members have appropriate access levels tailored to their roles and responsibilities within the organization's repositories.

By default, GitHub allows all organization members to create teams. To allow or restrict members from creating a new team, navigate to the organization settings and click "Member Privileges" and scroll all the way to the bottom. You will be able to see the option. Figure 6-7 shows about allowing access to team members to create teams.

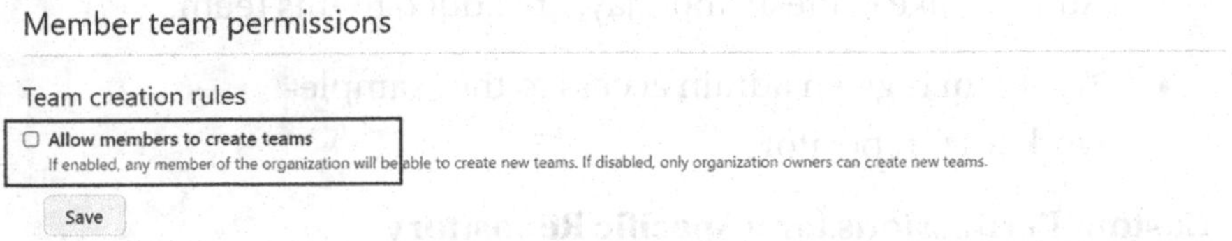

Member team permissions

Team creation rules

☐ **Allow members to create teams**
If enabled, any member of the organization will be able to create new teams. If disabled, only organization owners can create new teams.

Save

Figure 6-7. *Allowing access to team members to create teams*

User management and access control in GitHub Enterprise is a critical aspect of maintaining a secure and organized collaborative development environment. GitHub administrators have the responsibility of managing user accounts efficiently, which includes actions such as creating, suspending, and deleting accounts. Role-based access control (RBAC) is a key feature, allowing administrators to define and assign specific roles to users based on their responsibilities and permissions. Setting up teams further enhances collaboration by grouping individuals with shared responsibilities. Teams can be assigned specific access levels to repositories, streamlining permission management. This approach ensures that users, whether individually or as part of a team, have the appropriate access levels tailored to their roles within the organization.

Repository Management

Managing repositories in GitHub Enterprise involves overseeing the creation, organization, and access control of repositories within the GitHub environment. GitHub administrators play a key role in establishing and enforcing repository policies, ensuring adherence to security standards, and optimizing repository structures for efficient collaboration. This encompasses defining branching strategies, access controls, and repository templates to maintain consistency across projects. GitHub Enterprise provides features such as repository insights and dependency tracking, allowing administrators to monitor repository health and manage dependencies effectively. Administrators are also responsible for implementing and managing workflows related to code reviews, pull requests, and automated testing to uphold code quality standards. Regularly auditing and managing permissions, integrating with external systems, and ensuring comprehensive documentation contribute to the overall effectiveness of repository management. In essence, GitHub administrators focus on creating a well-organized and secure repository landscape aligned with the organization's development practices and policies.

A GitHub Enterprise repository serves as the foundational unit for storing code, files, and their revision history, offering a collaborative space for managing work. Repositories, fundamental to GitHub, can be public, internal, or private, accommodating multiple collaborators. Creating a new repository involves visiting `https://github.com/new`, and key repository-related terms include branches, clones, forks, merges, pull requests, remotes, and upstream branches.

Repository ownership can be individual or shared within an organization, with access managed through permissions. Collaborative features include using issues for feedback and bug reporting, GitHub Discussions for communication, pull requests for proposing changes, and projects for organizing tasks. GitHub Free allows unlimited collaboration on public repositories or limited collaboration on private repositories, while advanced tooling for private repositories is available through GitHub Pro, GitHub Team, or GitHub Enterprise Cloud.

Repository visibility options encompass public, private, and internal. Public repositories are accessible to everyone, private repositories have restricted access, and internal repositories are visible to all enterprise members. Organization owners always have access to every repository. Internal repositories, specific to organizations owned by an enterprise account, facilitate "innersource" collaboration without public exposure. These repositories are visible only to enterprise members, and forking is possible for enterprise members, except for managed user accounts, which cannot fork internal repositories. Enterprise account ownership enables centralized management, and internal repositories are the default setting for new repositories within such organizations. Forks of internal repositories are automatically removed if a user is no longer associated with the enterprise.

Efficient collaboration, organization, and security in GitHub Enterprise involve best practices during repository creation. These practices aim to establish a structured and secure environment for software development. When creating a repository, adopting clear and consistent naming conventions enhances discoverability. Defining ownership and communicating it clearly, selecting appropriate visibility, initializing a new repository with a README file, and enabling branch protection for the main branch contribute to a stable and secure codebase. Leveraging branching strategies, implementing access controls, creating a contribution guide, adding collaborators judiciously, enabling GitHub Actions, and providing comprehensive documentation ensure effective repository management.

For more detailed information on creating and managing GitHub repositories, please refer to Chapter 3. This documentation will provide comprehensive guidance and additional details on best practices, advanced features, and any updates to the repository management processes in the GitHub Enterprise environment.

Managing Repositories in Your Enterprise

Managing repositories in your enterprise involves implementing best practices to ensure effective collaboration, organization, and security within the GitHub environment. Key aspects of this management include adopting clear naming conventions for repositories, establishing ownership, choosing appropriate visibility settings, and initializing repositories with essential documentation.

Branch protection and the adoption of branching strategies contribute to code stability and organized development efforts. Access controls, such as defining permissions and following the principle of least

446

privilege, help secure repositories. Creating a contribution guide and adding collaborators judiciously facilitate external contributions while maintaining control.

Enabling GitHub Actions for automation, documenting repository purposes, and regularly reviewing and cleaning up inactive repositories contribute to efficient development processes. Integration with issue tracking enhances bug tracking and task management. Overall, effective repository management ensures a well-organized, secure, and collaborative GitHub Enterprise environment.

Viewing User-Owned Repositories in Your Enterprise

If your enterprise employs Enterprise Managed Users and has granted users permission to create repositories under their user accounts, you can review all repositories owned by individual users within the enterprise. Additionally, you have the option to temporarily access any user-owned repository. For detailed instructions, refer to the guide on "Accessing user-owned repositories in your enterprise." Follow these steps to view user-owned repositories within your enterprise:

1. Click your profile photo in the top-right corner of GitHub.com and select "Your enterprises."

2. From the list of enterprises, choose the specific enterprise you wish to examine.

3. In the enterprise account sidebar, navigate to "Policies."

4. Under "Policies," select "Repositories."

5. Within the "Repository creation" section, under "Repository Creation" click "View user namespace repositories in your enterprise."

Accessing User-Owned Repositories in Your Enterprise

As a GitHub Enterprise administrator has the capability to gain temporary access to a repository owned by a user within your enterprise.

Note   The temporary access feature for user-owned repositories is currently in beta for Enterprise Managed Users and is subject to potential changes.

If your enterprise employs Enterprise Managed Users and permits users to create repositories owned by their user accounts, you can gain temporary access to any user-owned repository within your enterprise. During the temporary access period, which lasts for two hours, you obtain administrative privileges over the repository. This allows you to perform all the same actions as the repository owner, such as editing the repository, modifying its settings, transferring ownership, and deleting the repository. The repository owner will be notified via email about your activation of temporary access to the repository. Additionally, a repo. temporary_access_granted event will be recorded in the audit log for both your enterprise and the user's security log.

To temporarily access a repository, start by navigating to the top-right corner of GitHub.com and clicking your profile photo. From there, select "Your enterprises" from the dropdown menu. In the list of enterprises, choose the specific enterprise you wish to view. Within the enterprise account sidebar, click "Policies." Under "Policies," locate and click "Repositories." In the "Repository creation" section, find "Block the creation of user namespace repositories," and click "View user namespace repositories in your enterprise." Next, identify the repository you intend to access, select the dropdown menu to the right of it, and then click "Enable temporary access." Be sure to read any warnings provided, and once ready, click "Yes, enable temporary access." This process allows you to gain temporary access to the selected repository within the specified enterprise.

Configure Git Large File Storage for an Enterprise

Git Large File Storage (Git LFS) is an open source extension designed for Git, providing a seamless way to handle large files in a manner similar to regular text files. Git LFS can be applied to a single repository, all personal or organizational repositories, or across every repository within an enterprise. However, before enabling Git LFS for specific repositories or organizations, it is essential to activate it for the entire enterprise. By default, the Git LFS client stores large assets on the same server hosting the Git repository. Once Git LFS is enabled on your GitHub Enterprise Server instance, these substantial assets are stored on the data partition, specifically in /data/user/storage.

It's crucial to note that users won't be able to push Git LFS assets to GitHub Enterprise Server if Git LFS is disabled at the enterprise or repository level. Enabling Git LFS provides a robust solution for effectively managing and version-controlling large files within the Git ecosystem.

To adjust the Git LFS access settings in GitHub Enterprise Server, begin by clicking your profile photo, situated in the top-right corner of GitHub Enterprise Server. From the ensuing dropdown menu, opt for "Enterprise settings." Once in the enterprise account sidebar, proceed to the "Policies" section. Inside the "Policies" section, specifically access the "Options" category. Within "Options," find the "Git LFS access" settings. In this section, utilize the dropdown menu to choose between "Enabled" and "Disabled" based on your desired configuration. These steps empower users to easily manage and customize Git LFS access settings, tailoring the handling of large files according to their preferences within GitHub Enterprise Server.

Configure Git Large File Storage for an Individual Repository

For administrative actions on GitHub Enterprise Server, initiate the process by clicking the profile icon located in the upper-right corner of any page. If not already on the "Site admin" page, navigate there by clicking "Site admin" in the upper-left corner. Utilize the search functionality under "Search users, organizations, teams, repositories, gists, and applications" by entering the repository's name in the text field. Click "Search" to proceed. Upon locating the repository under "Search results – Repositories," click its name. Once on the repository page, click "Admin" in the upper-right corner and then select "Admin" from the left sidebar. In the "Git LFS" section, situated next to "Toggle Git LFS access," choose to either enable or disable as needed. These steps empower administrators to efficiently manage Git LFS access settings on a repository level within the GitHub Enterprise Server.

Note   Each repository inherently adopts default settings from the organization or user that possesses it. Overriding these default configurations becomes impossible if the repository's owner has uniformly enforced the settings across all their repositories.

Configuring Git Large File Storage to Use a Third-Party Server

By default, the Git Large File Storage (LFS) client stores large assets on the same server that hosts the Git repository. However, when Git LFS is enabled on your GitHub Enterprise Server instance, large assets are stored on the data partition, specifically in the path /data/user/storage. If you need to disable Git LFS on your GitHub Enterprise Server instance, you can follow the steps outlined here. First, create a Git LFS configuration file pointing to a third-party server. Use the following commands to show the default configuration and create the .lfsconfig file:

```
# Show default configuration
$ git lfs env
> git-lfs/1.1.0 (GitHub; darwin amd64; go 1.5.1; git 94d356c)
> git version 2.7.4 (Apple Git-66)
 
> Endpoint=https://GITHUB-ENTERPRISE-HOST/path/to/repo/info/lfs
(auth=basic)
 
```

```
# Create .lfsconfig that points to a third-party server.
$ git config -f .lfsconfig remote.origin.lfsurl https://THIRD-
PARTY-LFS-SERVER/path/to/repo
$ git lfs env
> git-lfs/1.1.0 (GitHub; darwin amd64; go 1.5.1; git 94d356c)
> git version 2.7.4 (Apple Git-66)
 
> Endpoint=https://THIRD-PARTY-LFS-SERVER/path/to/repo/info/lfs
(auth=none)
 
# Show the contents of .lfsconfig
$ cat .lfsconfig
[remote "origin"]
lfsurl = https://THIRD-PARTY-LFS-SERVER/path/to/repo
```

To maintain consistent Git LFS configurations for each user, commit the custom .lfsconfig file to the repository:

```
git add .lfsconfig
git commit -m "Adding LFS config file"
```

Additionally, if there are existing Git LFS assets, migrate them as needed. These steps help customize Git LFS settings and ensure a smooth transition for users in a GitHub Enterprise Server environment.

Migrate to a Different Git Large File Storage Server

Migrating to a different Git Large File Storage (LFS) server involves configuring Git LFS to use a third-party server and then transferring LFS objects from the old remote to the new remote. Here's a step-by-step guide with an example.

Step 1: Configure the repository with a second remote.

```
$ git remote add NEW-REMOTE https://NEW-REMOTE-HOSTNAME/
path/to/repo
$ git lfs env
> git-lfs/1.1.0 (GitHub; darwin amd64; go 1.5.1; git 94d356c)
> git version 2.7.4 (Apple Git-66)
> Endpoint=https://GITHUB-ENTERPRISE-HOST/path/to/repo/info/lfs
(auth=basic)
> Endpoint (NEW-REMOTE)=https://NEW-REMOTE-HOSTNAME/path/to/
repo/info/lfs (auth=none)
```

In this example, we add a new remote named "NEW-REMOTE" with the URL pointing to the third-party LFS server. The `git lfs env` command verifies the configuration for both the existing and new remotes.

Step 2: Fetch all objects from the old remote.

```
$ git lfs fetch origin --all
> Scanning for all objects ever referenced...
> ✓ 16 objects found
> Fetching objects...
> Git LFS: (16 of 16 files) 48.71 MB / 48.85 MB
```

This step ensures that all LFS objects from the old remote (origin) are fetched.

Step 3: Push all objects to the new remote.

```
$ git lfs push NEW-REMOTE --all
> Scanning for all objects ever referenced...
> ✓ 16 objects found
> Pushing objects...
> Git LFS: (16 of 16 files) 48.00 MB / 48.85 MB,
879.10 KB skipped
```

Here, we push all LFS objects to the new remote (NEW-REMOTE). The `git lfs push` command transfers the LFS files to the specified remote.

By following these steps, you effectively migrate your repository's LFS objects to a different server. This process is useful when transitioning from one hosting environment to another or when consolidating repositories under a new LFS server. Ensure that you have the necessary permissions and access credentials for both the old and new LFS servers during this migration.

Migrating to Internal Repositories

As a GitHub Enterprise administrator, you have the option to migrate to internal repositories, providing a unified "innersource" experience for developers across GitHub Enterprise Server and GitHub Enterprise Cloud. Internal repositories, introduced in GitHub Enterprise Server 2.20+, enable innersource collaboration within your enterprise, allowing members to work together using open source methodologies while keeping proprietary information secure, even when private mode is disabled. In upcoming GitHub Enterprise Server releases, there will be adjustments to how repository visibility is handled, ensuring consistent meanings for public, internal, and private across both GitHub Enterprise Server and GitHub Enterprise Cloud.

To prepare for these changes, especially if private mode is enabled, you can initiate a migration on your instance to convert public repositories to internal. Currently optional, this migration allows testing on a nonproduction instance and will become mandatory in the future. During the migration, all public repositories owned by organizations on your instance will transition to internal repositories. Forks associated with these repositories will become private, while private repositories will retain their privacy settings. Public repositories owned by user accounts will also become private, with forks following suit. Fork owners will receive read permissions to their fork's parent. As a result of the migration, anonymous Git read access will be disabled for each public repository that transitions to internal or private. If your current default visibility is public, it will shift to internal; if private, the default will remain unchanged, and you have the flexibility to modify this default setting at any time.

The repository creation policy for the instance will be updated to disable public repositories while allowing private and internal repositories. This policy adjustment is customizable as needed. If private mode is not enabled, the migration script will have no impact on your repositories. To execute the migration, follow these steps:

- Connect to the administrative shell.

- Run the migration command in the administrative shell. Use the following command:

```
github-env bin/safe-ruby lib/github/
transitions/20191210220630_convert_public_ghes_repos_
to_internal.rb --verbose -w | tee -a /tmp/convert_
public_ghes_repos_to_internal.log
```

This command initiates the migration process. The `--verbose` flag provides detailed output, and the `-w` flag ensures that warnings are displayed during the migration. The `tee` command appends the output to a log file at `/tmp/convert_public_ghes_repos_to_internal.log`.

Ensure that you have the necessary permissions to execute administrative commands and that you are aware of the potential impact of this migration on your repositories.

Disable Git SSH Access on the Enterprise

To restrict Git over SSH access for specific repositories on your GitHub Enterprise Server, follow these steps:

1. From an administrative account, navigate to GitHub Enterprise Server and click the profile icon in the upper-right corner of any page.

2. If you are not already on the "Site admin" page, click "Site admin" in the upper-left corner.

3. Under "Search users, organizations, teams, repositories, gists, and applications," type the name of the repository in the text field. Then, to the right of the field, click "Search."

4. In the "Search results – Repositories," click the name of the repository you want to modify.

5. Once on the repository page, in the upper-right corner, click the profile icon again.

6. If you are not on the "Site admin" page, navigate to it by clicking "Site admin" in the upper-left corner.

7. In the upper-right corner of the page, click "Admin."

8. Under "Git SSH access," select the dropdown menu, and click "Disabled."

By following these steps, you disable Git SSH access for the specified repository, ensuring that users cannot use SSH for Git operations on that particular repository. Keep in mind that this action affects only the selected repository and does not alter the default settings inherited from the repository owner.

Disabling Git SSH Access to All Repositories Owned by a User or Organization

Disabling Git SSH access for all repositories owned by a user or organization in GitHub Enterprise Server involves following specific steps to ensure a uniform setting across multiple repositories. As an administrator, begin by accessing the administrative settings on GitHub Enterprise Server. In the upper-right corner of any page, click the profile icon, and if needed, navigate to the "Site admin" page by clicking "Site admin" in the upper-left corner. Utilize the search functionality under "Search users, organizations, teams, repositories, gists, and applications" to locate the desired user or organization.

Once you've identified the user or organization, click its name in the "Search results – Repositories." On the repository page, click the profile icon in the upper-right corner. If you're not on the "Site admin" page, go to it by clicking "Site admin" in the upper-left corner. From there, click "Admin" in the upper-right corner to access administrative settings.

Under the "Git SSH access" section, use the dropdown menu to select "Disabled." This action will enforce the disabling of Git SSH access for all repositories owned by the specified user or organization. It's important to note that this setting will override the defaults for each individual repository, ensuring a consistent access policy. This approach provides administrators with centralized control over SSH access, contributing to security and compliance measures across the entire GitHub Enterprise Server instance.

Disable Git SSH Access to All Repositories in the Enterprise

To disable Git over SSH access for all repositories within your GitHub Enterprise Server, administrators can take the following steps:

- Access the administrative features on GitHub Enterprise Server by clicking the profile icon in the upper-right corner of any page and selecting "Site admin" if not already on that page.

- In the "Site admin" section, navigate to the upper-right corner of the page and click "Admin."

- Under "Git SSH access," administrators will find a dropdown menu. Selecting this menu allows them to choose between "Enabled," "Disabled," or "Default."

- To disable Git SSH access for all repositories, choose "Disabled" from the dropdown menu.

By selecting "Disabled," administrators enforce the restriction on using Git over SSH for all repositories across the enterprise. It's essential to note that these changes will override any default settings that may have been inherited from the organization or user owning the repositories. Disabling Git SSH access enhances security measures, ensuring that users must rely on alternative access methods for their Git operations within the GitHub Enterprise Server environment.

Locking a Repository

Locking a repository in GitHub Enterprise involves a GitHub administrator taking specific actions to restrict certain activities within the repository. When a repository is locked, it prevents contributors from making changes, such as pushing new commits, creating pull requests, or merging branches. This feature is particularly useful in scenarios where you want to temporarily freeze development or stabilize the codebase. To lock a repository, the GitHub administrator navigates to the repository settings, usually accessible through the GitHub Enterprise interface. In the settings, there is an option to enable repository restrictions or set the repository status to "read-only" mode. Once activated, contributors will be unable to perform various write operations, preserving the repository in its current state. This capability is valuable for ensuring code stability during critical periods, such as releases or when addressing urgent issues. It provides administrators with a means to exert control over the development lifecycle and maintain the integrity of the codebase. Additionally, the locking feature aligns with best practices in version control and collaborative software development, contributing to a more controlled and organized development environment.

Unlocking a Repository

Unlocking a repository in GitHub Enterprise is a process that grants users the ability to make changes and execute various actions within a repository that was previously restricted or locked, limiting specific operations. This privilege is typically wielded by GitHub administrators and is exercised when there is a temporary need to lift imposed restrictions on a specific repository. The steps for unlocking a repository involve the following:

- Access the GitHub Enterprise Server and log in using administrator credentials.

- Navigate to the specific repository that requires unlocking.

- Click the repository to access its settings and configuration.

- Locate the section or settings related to repository access or permissions.

- Identify an option or toggle designed for administrators to unlock the repository.

- Enable or toggle the identified setting to unlock the repository, providing users with the flexibility to make changes and execute actions as required.

- Confirm and save the changes to implement the unlocking of the repository.

Unlocking a repository is a deliberate and controlled action undertaken by administrators to efficiently manage access and permissions. This process should be executed cautiously to ensure that the security and integrity of the repository are maintained while simultaneously offering the necessary flexibility for collaborative development. The ability to lock and unlock repositories is a pivotal feature in GitHub Enterprise, particularly in scenarios where temporary restrictions must be lifted to facilitate the development processes effectively.

Restore Deleted Repository

Repository restoration in GitHub Enterprise by a GitHub administrator involves the recovery and reinstatement of a previously deleted repository within the GitHub environment. This process becomes crucial in scenarios where a repository, due to various reasons, has been deleted or disabled, and there is a need to retrieve its contents and functionality. GitHub administrators, holding the necessary permissions, wield the authority to initiate the repository restoration process, following a series of systematic steps.

Firstly, the GitHub administrator accesses the GitHub Enterprise Server by logging in with their administrator credentials, obtaining the required privileges for repository restoration. Subsequently, within the GitHub Enterprise interface, the administrator navigates to the section or feature displaying deleted repositories or providing access to repository history. Here, the administrator selects the specific repository slated for restoration from the list of deleted repositories. The next step involves initiating the restoration process. GitHub administrators typically locate an option or action associated with repository restoration, which might include clicking a designated "Restore" button or a similar functionality. A confirmation step follows, where the administrator affirms the decision to restore the repository. Depending on the GitHub Enterprise configuration, additional prompts may be presented to ensure the administrator's intentional commitment to the restoration process.

Once confirmed, the restoration process is set in motion, with the system working to recover the repository and its contents. After completion, administrators can verify the successful restoration of the repository. If the repository had specific access controls or settings before deletion, the administrator may need to review and update these configurations based on the organization's requirements.

It is crucial to note that repository restoration should be executed judiciously, considering the reasons behind the repository's deletion and ensuring the mitigation of potential data loss. The ability to restore repositories serves as a safety net against accidental deletions, supporting data recovery efforts and maintaining the integrity of version-controlled code and collaborative work within the GitHub Enterprise environment.

Troubleshooting Service Hooks

When troubleshooting service hooks and addressing issues related to payload delivery, it is crucial to perform a systematic check for common problems. As an administrator on GitHub Enterprise Server, you can obtain information on the last response of all service hook deliveries for a specific repository by following these steps:

Begin by clicking the profile photo in the upper-right corner of any page. If not already on the "Site admin" page, navigate to it by selecting "Site admin" in the upper-left corner. Proceed to the repository under investigation and, in the navigation sidebar, choose "Hooks." Identify the service hook encountering issues and click "Latest Delivery." In the "Remote Calls" section, examine the headers utilized during the POST request to the remote server, along with the response received from that server.

To inspect the payload associated with a service hook experiencing problems, follow these steps:

From an administrative account, click the profile photo in the upper-right corner. If necessary, navigate to the "Site admin" page by clicking "Site admin" in the upper-left corner. Locate and browse to the repository under investigation, then select "Hooks" from the navigation sidebar. Choose the problematic service hook and click the "Latest Delivery" link. Click "Delivery" to access the details, including information about the payload.

For the review of past deliveries, it's important to note that deliveries are stored for 15 days. To access past deliveries, perform the following steps:

Click the profile photo in the upper-right corner from the administrative account. If not on the "Site admin" page, click "Site admin" in the upper-left corner. Navigate to the repository in question and select "Hooks" from the navigation sidebar. Under the problematic service hook, click the "Latest Delivery" link. To explore additional deliveries for that specific hook, click "More for this Hook ID." This action provides a comprehensive view of other deliveries associated with the same hook ID.

Branch Protection Rule

In GitHub Enterprise, branch protection rules are a crucial aspect of repository management that GitHub administrators use to enforce certain controls and policies on branches within a repository. These rules are designed to enhance code quality, enforce security measures, and prevent accidental or unauthorized changes to critical branches. GitHub administrators can configure branch protection rules for specific branches, typically the main or default branch, and define conditions that must be met before changes can be made. The key components of branch protection rules include

- **Required Pull Request Reviews:** GitHub administrators can mandate that a specific number of approving reviews from designated individuals or teams are required before any changes can be merged into a protected branch. This ensures that proposed changes undergo thorough review and meet the project's quality standards.

- **Dismissal of Stale Pull Request Reviews:** GitHub Enterprise allows administrators to set up rules to automatically dismiss stale pull request reviews. This ensures that reviews remain relevant and recent, encouraging timely and focused collaboration.

- **Branch Push Restrictions:** Administrators can restrict direct pushes to a protected branch, forcing contributors to make changes through pull requests. This helps maintain a structured and traceable development process, preventing accidental or uncontrolled modifications to critical branches.

461

- **Status Checks:** GitHub supports integration with various continuous integration (CI) and continuous deployment (CD) systems. Administrators can enforce the requirement for specific status checks to pass before allowing merges. This ensures that proposed changes pass automated tests and meet predefined criteria.

- **Required Commit Signatures:** To enhance security and traceability, administrators can enforce the requirement for commits to be signed with verified signatures. This helps maintain the integrity of the codebase and ensures that contributions come from trusted sources.

- **Restrictions on Branch Deletion:** GitHub administrators can impose restrictions on the deletion of protected branches, preventing accidental or unauthorized removal of critical branches.

- **Restrictions on Force Push:** Force pushing can overwrite the commit history of a branch, which might lead to data loss. Administrators can restrict force pushes to protected branches to maintain a stable and traceable version history.

- **Required Checks for Code Owners:** For projects with designated code owners, administrators can enforce the requirement for approval from these designated individuals or teams before changes are merged. This ensures that those responsible for specific areas of the codebase review and approve relevant changes.

By configuring branch protection rules, GitHub administrators can establish a secure and well-managed development workflow, ensuring that code changes undergo proper scrutiny, adhere to coding standards, and maintain the overall integrity of the codebase. These rules contribute to a more controlled and collaborative development environment within GitHub Enterprise.

Different Strategies for a Repository in an Enterprise

Organizing repositories effectively in GitHub Enterprise is crucial for streamlining development workflows, enhancing collaboration, and ensuring maintainability. Different strategies for repository organization cater to varying project structures and team needs. One common approach is to use a Monorepo, where multiple projects or components coexist within a single repository. This strategy simplifies dependency management and promotes shared code ownership. For instance, a Monorepo might contain folders for different microservices, libraries, or applications.

On the other hand, adopting a Multirepo approach involves creating separate repositories for each project or component. This strategy offers more granular control over versioning and releases. For example, a company with distinct front-end and back-end projects may choose Multirepo organization, allowing teams to manage and version each codebase independently.

Another organizational strategy involves using a combination of Mono- and Multirepo, known as a Hybrid approach. This allows teams to maintain separate repositories for independent projects while using a Monorepo for shared libraries or modules. For example, a company working on various applications might use a Monorepo for shared utilities and libraries, while individual applications reside in separate repositories.

When projects share common dependencies or are components of a larger system, Submodules can be employed. Submodules enable the inclusion of one repository within another. For instance, a repository for a web application might include a submodule referencing a shared authentication library.

GitHub organizations provide a hierarchical structure for repositories. Repositories within an organization can be categorized using Teams, which allows for fine-grained access controls. For example, an organization might have separate teams for front-end and back-end developers, each with access to their respective repositories.

In addition, GitHub Topics can be utilized to tag repositories with relevant keywords, making it easier to discover and categorize projects. For instance, repositories related to data analytics might be tagged with topics like "data science" or "analytics."

In summary, the choice of repository organization in GitHub Enterprise depends on factors such as project complexity, team collaboration preferences, and the need for code sharing. Whether opting for a Monorepo, Multirepo, or Hybrid approach or utilizing GitHub features like Submodules, Teams, and Topics, the goal is to create a structure that aligns with the development workflow and promotes efficiency within the organization.

Security and Compliance

Security and compliance are paramount considerations for GitHub Enterprise administrators to ensure the protection of code, data, and sensitive information. As a GitHub Enterprise administrator, your role involves implementing measures to safeguard repositories, managing access controls, and ensuring compliance with organizational and industry standards. Administrators of a GitHub Enterprise Server instance need to determine the method through which users will access the instance. Let's explore the requirements and configuration for this access.

Authentication Methods

GitHub Enterprise Server offers two primary authentication methods:

Built-In Authentication

- Users create personal accounts through invitations or by signing up.

- Each person authenticates with their account credentials to access the GitHub Enterprise Server instance.

- Configuration details for built-in authentication can be customized.

External Authentication

- Organizations using an external directory or identity provider (IdP) for centralized access to multiple web applications can integrate external authentication with GitHub Enterprise Server.

- External authentication can be implemented using various protocols such as CAS (Central Authentication Service), LDAP, or SAML.

- It's important to note that GitHub Enterprise Server supports either SAML or LDAP but not both concurrently.

- For users without accounts on the external authentication provider, fallback authentication can be configured. This allows access for individuals like contractors or machine users.

These authentication methods provide flexibility for organizations to choose the approach that best aligns with their security and access control requirements. The built-in authentication is user-centric, while external authentication enables integration with existing identity management systems. We will explore SAML authentication for enterprise IAM in the next section.

Note   When configured with built-in authentication, CAS, LDAP, or SAML, GitHub Enterprise Server implements a "just-in-time" (JIT) user account creation mechanism. This means that user accounts are automatically generated when an authorized person signs in to the instance. Additionally, for SAML configurations, there is an optional feature to provision user accounts directly from the IdP using System for Cross-domain Identity Management (SCIM). This JIT account creation ensures seamless onboarding of users, streamlining the user management process and providing immediate access to the GitHub Enterprise Server instance upon authentication.

SAML for Enterprise IAM

SAML Single Sign-On (SSO) provides a mechanism for individuals to authenticate and gain access to your GitHub Enterprise Server instance by leveraging an external system for identity management. This process adheres to the XML-based SAML standard, which governs authentication and authorization protocols. In the context of configuring SAML for your GitHub Enterprise Server instance, the external system responsible for authentication is referred to as the identity provider (IdP), while your instance functions as the SAML service provider (SP).

It's crucial to note that when utilizing SAML or CAS (Central Authentication Service), the GitHub Enterprise Server instance does not support or manage two-factor authentication. However, the external authentication provider may offer support for this security measure. Additionally, the enforcement of two-factor authentication on organizations is not an available feature. Following the configuration of SAML, individuals accessing your GitHub Enterprise Server instance are required to employ a personal access token for authenticating API requests.

In scenarios where you aim to permit authentication for individuals lacking an account on the external authentication provider, the option of enabling fallback authentication to local accounts on your GitHub Enterprise Server instance is available. GitHub Enterprise Server provides support for SAML Single Sign-On (SSO) with identity providers (IdPs) that adhere to the SAML 2.0 standard. GitHub officially supports and internally tests the integration with the following IdPs:

- Active Directory Federation Services (AD FS)

- Azure Active Directory (Azure AD)

- Okta

- OneLogin

- PingOne

- Shibboleth

For heightened security during the authentication process, you have the option to configure encrypted assertions on GitHub Enterprise Server if your IdP supports this feature. GitHub Enterprise Server does not support SAML Single Logout. To conclude an active SAML session, users are advised to log out directly on their SAML IdP.

You can refer to Chapter 4 for SAML SSO and SCIM configuration.

Enable Encrypted Assertions

To enhance the security of your GitHub Enterprise Server instance with SAML SSO, you can implement message encryption for the communications sent by your SAML IdP. Site administrators have the capability to configure encrypted assertions for the instance, which involves ensuring compatibility with your IdP's support for encrypted assertions.

Follow these steps to enable encrypted assertions for GitHub

Enterprise Server authentication:

- Confirm that your IdP supports the encryption of assertions.

- Provide the public certificate of your GitHub Enterprise Server instance to your IdP and configure encryption settings matching those of your IdP.

Note   It's crucial to verify any new authentication configuration in a staging environment to prevent potential downtime for your GitHub Enterprise Server instance.

- Optionally, enable SAML debugging for detailed entries in the authentication log to aid troubleshooting during failed authentication attempts.

  - Navigate to the "Site admin" page from the GitHub Enterprise Server instance.

  - In the "Management Console" under "Settings," access "Authentication."

  - Select "Require encrypted assertions."

  - To download a copy of your GitHub Enterprise Server instance's public certificate, click "Download" next to "Encryption Certificate."

  - Log in to your SAML IdP as an administrator.

- In the IdP application for your GitHub Enterprise Server instance, enable encrypted assertions and provide the public certificate downloaded in step 3.

- Note the encryption method and key transport method from the IdP.

- Return to the management console on your GitHub Enterprise Server instance.

  - Select the encryption method and key transport method matching your IdP from the previous step.

- Click "Save settings" and wait for the configuration run to complete.

- If you enabled SAML debugging for testing purposes, disable it once you've completed testing.

By implementing encrypted assertions, you contribute to securing the SAML SSO process for your GitHub Enterprise Server instance.

Update a User's SAML NameID

Updating a user's SAML NameID involves modifying the unique identifier associated with a user in the Security Assertion Markup Language (SAML) authentication process. The NameID is a critical element in SAML assertions, and changes may be necessary due to various reasons such as updates in the identity provider (IdP) or organizational changes. Here is a general guide on updating a user's SAML NameID:

- **Access GitHub Enterprise Server Management Console:**

  - Log in to the GitHub Enterprise Server instance with administrative credentials.

  - Navigate to the "Site admin" page.

- **Navigate to Authentication Settings:** In the "Management Console," go to "Settings" and select "Authentication."

469

- **Locate SAML Configuration:** Under "Authentication," find and select the SAML authentication settings.

- **Edit SAML Configuration:**

  - Look for the section related to SAML configuration where you can make adjustments.

  - There might be options to modify the SAML NameID or related attributes.

- **Save Changes:** After making the necessary updates, save the changes to apply the new SAML configuration.

- **Communicate Changes:** If required, inform users about the changes, especially if they need to take any actions such as reauthenticating.

- **Testing:** Test the SAML authentication to ensure that the updated SAML NameID is functioning as expected.

Please note that the exact steps and options for updating the SAML NameID may vary depending on the specific GitHub Enterprise Server version and the available configuration options.

Change the Authentication Method

Changing authentication methods on GitHub Enterprise Server is a process that involves transitioning from one method to another. Here are the key steps and considerations for changing authentication methods:

- **Preserving User Accounts:** User accounts on GitHub Enterprise Server will be preserved during the transition.

- **User Login Continuity:** Users will continue to log in using their existing accounts, as long as their usernames remain unchanged.

- **Handling Username Changes:**

  - If the new authentication method results in username changes, new accounts may be created.

  - Administrators have the ability to rename users through the site admin settings or the User Administration API.

- **Password Updates:** When switching to built-in authentication, users may need to set a password after the change is completed.

- **Administrative Privileges:** Administrative privileges are typically controlled by the identity provider when using SAML and can be managed by group membership in LDAP.

- **Team Membership:** LDAP allows control over team membership from the directory server.

- **User Suspension:** With LDAP authentication, access to GitHub Enterprise Server can be controlled through restricted groups. Existing users not in these groups may be suspended.

- **Group Membership Handling:** LDAP-based authentication automates user suspension and unsuspension based on restricted group membership and account status in Active Directory.

- **Git Authentication:**

  - SAML and CAS support Git authentication over HTTP/HTTPS using a personal access token. Password authentication over HTTP/HTTPS is not supported.

471

- LDAP supports password-based Git authentication by default, but it's recommended to disable this and use personal access tokens or SSH keys.

- **API Authentication:** SAML and CAS support API authentication using a personal access token. Basic authentication is not supported.

- **Two-Factor Authentication (2FA):** SAML or CAS does not manage 2FA on GitHub Enterprise Server. This is typically handled by the external authentication provider.

- **Fallback Authentication:** GitHub Enterprise Server allows inviting users to authenticate without adding them to the identity provider.

Administrators should carefully plan and communicate changes to users, considering the specific requirements and implications of the chosen authentication method. Testing in a staging environment is strongly recommended to avoid downtime and ensure a smooth transition.

Fallback Authentication

You have the flexibility to configure fallback authentication in GitHub Enterprise Server, allowing for built-in authentication for individuals without an account on your CAS, LDAP, or SAML authentication provider. By default, when external authentication is enabled, built-in authentication is disabled on your instance. However, if certain accounts, such as those for contractors or machine users, cannot be added to the external authentication provider, fallback authentication can be configured. This enables built-in authentication for external users and provides access to a fallback account if the primary authentication provider is unavailable. Enabling built-in authentication alongside external providers restricts the option for individuals who successfully authenticate with SAML or CAS to use a username and password. If LDAP is the chosen method, the credentials are no longer considered internal. A cautionary note is issued: if built-in authentication is disabled, individual user suspensions are necessary for revoking access to the instance.

To configure built-in authentication for external users, access the GitHub Enterprise Server Management Console from the site admin page. Navigate to Settings, select Authentication, and choose the desired authentication method. Enable "Allow creation of accounts with built-in authentication" after acknowledging the warning. When LDAP or built-in authentication is employed, two-factor authentication is supported. Organization owners have the option to mandate two-factor authentication for members.

To invite users outside your authentication provider to authenticate to your instance, follow these steps: sign in to your GitHub Enterprise Server instance, access the site admin page, and click "Invite user" in the left sidebar. Enter the username and email address for each user account, and generate a password reset link for them to sign in with a username and password.

Auditing Security Alerts

GitHub offers a suite of tools designed for security auditors and developers within an enterprise or organization to assess and analyze responses to security alerts. This comprehensive guide outlines these tools, encompassing historical timelines, security overviews, audit logs, the API, and webhooks. Security auditors leverage these tools to verify that proper measures are being implemented to address security alerts and to pinpoint areas where additional training might be required. Concurrently, developers utilize these tools to oversee and troubleshoot their own security alerts. It's important to note that access to data is restricted to repositories and organizations that the user already has permission to access.

Security Alert Timelines

The historical timeline for each security alert provides a detailed record of its creation and any subsequent changes, such as problem detection or closure. This timeline captures all status alterations, regardless of the initiator, whether it's Dependabot resolving a fixed issue or a developer reopening a previously closed alert. Accessible on the alert page, beneath the problem description, this timeline offers a comprehensive view of the alert's evolution. Furthermore, several events from this timeline are logged in the audit log, enabling users to query this data using the audit log UI or the API for in-depth analysis.

Audit Log

GitHub provides two methods for accessing and searching audit logs: using the API or the audit log UI. These logs document events arising from activities that impact your enterprise or organization, including specific interactions with security alerts. These interactions, whether initiated manually or automated (such as alerts generated by Dependabot), trigger events. In the context of security alerts

- **Secret scanning events** are logged when an alert is created, resolved, or reopened or when push protection is bypassed.

- **Dependabot events** are recorded when an alert is created, dismissed, or resolved.

Audit Log Events for Your Enterprise

GitHub's audit log provides detailed records of various events within your enterprise or organization. Some common audit log events related to security alerts include

- **Secret Scanning Events**

  - **secret_scanning_alert_created:** Triggered when a secret scanning alert is created

  - **secret_scanning_alert_resolved:** Generated when a secret scanning alert is resolved

  - **secret_scanning_alert_reopened:** Logged when a previously resolved secret scanning alert is reopened

  - **secret_scanning_push_protection_bypassed:** Indicates an event where push protection was bypassed during secret scanning

- **Dependabot Events**

  - **dependabot_alert_created:** Occurs when a Dependabot alert is created

  - **dependabot_alert_dismissed:** Generated when a Dependabot alert is dismissed

  - **dependabot_alert_resolved:** Triggered when a Dependabot alert is resolved

These events provide a comprehensive overview of interactions related to security alerts, enabling you to monitor and manage security incidents effectively within your enterprise. The GitHub audit log is a valuable resource for tracking the security posture of your organization and ensuring appropriate actions are taken in response to security alerts.

Audit Log Events for Your Organization

In the context of GitHub's audit log, various events can be logged for your organization, providing detailed insights into activities and changes within your GitHub organization. Some common audit log events for organizations include

- **Organization Settings Events**

    - **organization_settings_updated:** Recorded when organization settings are modified or updated

- **Membership Events**

    - **organization_member_added:** Occurs when a new member is added to the organization

    - **organization_member_removed:** Logged when a member is removed from the organization

- **Repository Events**

    - **repository_created:** Generated when a new repository is created within the organization

    - **repository_deleted:** Recorded when a repository is deleted

    - **repository_transferred:** Occurs when a repository is transferred to a different owner or organization

    - **repository_visibility_changed:** Indicates changes in the visibility settings of a repository

- **Team Events**

    - **team_created:** Recorded when a new team is created within the organization

    - **team_deleted:** Generated when a team is deleted

    - **team_member_added:** Occurs when a member is added to a team

    - **team_member_removed:** Logged when a member is removed from a team

- **Webhook Events**

  - **organization_webhook_created:** Recorded when a webhook is created for the organization

  - **organization_webhook_deleted:** Indicates the deletion of an organization webhook

These events, along with others not listed here, contribute to the audit log's comprehensive record of activities within your GitHub organization. Monitoring these events allows you to maintain a secure and well-managed GitHub environment for your organization.

Two-Factor Authentication for an Organization

Enforcing two-factor authentication (2FA) adds an extra layer of security to organization repositories and settings on GitHub Enterprise Server. This security measure helps protect against unauthorized access by requiring organization members and external collaborators to enable 2FA for their personal accounts. However, the availability and enforcement of 2FA depend on the authentication method in use:

For LDAP or Built-In Authentication

- Two-factor authentication is supported on GitHub Enterprise Server.

- Organization owners have the capability to mandate that members enable 2FA for their personal accounts.

- This ensures an additional level of security for accessing organization resources.

For SAML or CAS Authentication

- Two-factor authentication is not supported or managed directly on GitHub Enterprise Server.

- External authentication providers, such as SAML or CAS, may support 2FA, and users should configure it through their respective identity providers.

- Enforcement of 2FA specifically for organizations is not available on GitHub Enterprise Server in this context.

GitHub Enterprise Server administrators should communicate and coordinate with users, especially in organizations leveraging SAML or CAS, to ensure that 2FA is appropriately configured and enforced through the external authentication provider. Regularly educating users on the importance of 2FA and guiding them through the setup process contribute to a more secure development environment.

Prerequisites

Before GitHub administrators can enforce two-factor authentication (2FA) within GitHub Enterprise, several prerequisites must be addressed:

Enable 2FA for an Administrator's Personal Account: GitHub administrators need to enable 2FA for their personal accounts before implementing this security measure across the entire GitHub Enterprise instance.

Considerations and Requirements

- **Account Removal for Noncompliance:** Members and external collaborators, including bot accounts, who do not adopt 2FA will face automatic removal from the organization. This includes a loss of access to organization repositories and forks of private repositories. Individuals can reinstate their access privileges and settings by enabling 2FA within three months of removal.

- **Automatic Removal for Disabled 2FA:** Organization members or external collaborators who disable 2FA will be automatically removed from the organization.

- **Owner Limitations:** If the GitHub administrator is the sole owner of an organization mandating 2FA, disabling 2FA for the personal account is not possible without deactivating the 2FA requirement for the entire organization.

- **Notification and Preparation:** It is advisable for administrators to notify organization members and external collaborators before enforcing 2FA. Encouraging them to set up 2FA for their accounts is crucial. The 2FA status of members and collaborators can be verified on the organization's People tab.

Enabling 2FA

Before implementing the requirement for two-factor authentication (2FA), it is advisable to follow a notification and preparation process for organization members and external collaborators. Following this, the GitHub Enterprise Server administrator can proceed to enforce 2FA with the following steps:

- In the upper-right corner of GitHub Enterprise Server, select your profile photo, then click "Your organizations."

- Next to the organization, click "Settings."

- In the sidebar under the "Security" section, choose "Authentication security."

- Under "Two-factor authentication," select "Require two-factor authentication for everyone in your organization," then click "Save."

- If prompted, review the information provided regarding the potential removal of members and external collaborators who do not comply with 2FA.

- In the text field, type your organization's name to confirm the change, then click "Remove members & require two-factor authentication."

By following these steps, the GitHub Enterprise administrator can seamlessly implement the requirement for two-factor authentication while ensuring appropriate communication and awareness among organization members and collaborators.

View People Removed from Your Organization

To view individuals who were automatically removed from your organization due to noncompliance with the two-factor authentication requirement on GitHub Enterprise, follow these steps:

- In the upper-left corner of any page, click the GitHub logo.

- From an administrative account on GitHub Enterprise Server, in the upper-right corner of any page, click your profile photo.

- If you're not already on the "Site admin" page, navigate to it by clicking "Site admin" in the upper-left corner.

- In the "Archives" section of the sidebar, select "Security log."

- In the search field, enter the query "reason:two_factor_requirement_non_compliance" to retrieve a list of individuals who were removed for not complying with the two-factor authentication requirement.

- To narrow down the search, you can use additional filters like

  - For organization members removed: *action:org. remove_member* AND *reason:two_factor_ requirement_non_compliance*

  - For outside collaborators removed: *action:org. remove_outside_collaborator* AND *reason:two_ factor_requirement_non_compliance*

  - To view people removed from a specific organization (replace "octo-org" with your organization's name): *org:octo-org* AND *reason:two_factor_requirement_non_compliance*

- Click "Search" to retrieve the results based on your query.

This process allows GitHub Enterprise administrators to access detailed information about individuals who were automatically removed due to noncompliance with the two-factor authentication requirement. The security log provides transparency and helps administrators monitor and manage access within the GitHub Enterprise environment.

Helping Removed Members and Outside Collaborators Rejoin Your Organization

Upon enabling the mandatory use of two-factor authentication, individuals who are removed from the organization will receive an email notification of their removal. Subsequently, they are advised to activate 2FA for their personal accounts and get in touch with an organization owner to initiate the process of regaining access to the organization.

Viewing Whether Users in an Organization Have 2FA Enabled

You have the capability to monitor the status of two-factor authentication for organization owners, members, and outside collaborators. Here are the steps to access this information on GitHub Enterprise Server:

- In the upper-right corner of GitHub Enterprise Server, click your profile photo and then select "Your organizations."

- Choose the name of your organization from the list.

- Under your organization name, click "People."

- To check the status of two-factor authentication for organization members, including owners, navigate to the right side and select "2FA." You can then click "Enabled" or "Disabled" to see who has activated or deactivated 2FA. Figure 6-8 shows 2FA configuration.

Figure 6-8. *2FA configuration*

- For outside collaborators, go to the "Organization permissions" sidebar and click "Outside collaborators."

- To view the two-factor authentication status of outside collaborators, locate the 2FA dropdown menu above the list of collaborators. Select "Enabled" or "Disabled" to see which outside collaborators have activated or deactivated 2FA.

This information allows you to keep track of the security status of organization members and outside collaborators in relation to two-factor authentication. If needed, you can refer to the documentation on "Requiring two-factor authentication in your organization" for additional guidance.

Compliance Standards in GitHub Enterprise

GitHub administrators play a crucial role in ensuring that GitHub Enterprise aligns with compliance standards. Compliance standards typically encompass security, access control, auditability, and other factors to safeguard sensitive data and ensure the integrity of the development and collaboration processes. Here's how GitHub administrators can address compliance standards in GitHub Enterprise:

- **Access Control and Authentication:** GitHub administrators should configure access controls based on the principle of least privilege. This involves assigning roles and permissions to users and teams according to their responsibilities. Utilizing GitHub Enterprise's role-based access control (RBAC) features helps ensure that individuals have the appropriate level of access. Additionally, administrators should encourage or enforce strong authentication practices, such as two-factor authentication (2FA), for enhanced security.

- **Auditability and Logging:** GitHub administrators must enable and configure audit logs to capture relevant events on the platform. This includes user logins, code changes, repository access, and administrative actions. By regularly reviewing these logs, administrators can ensure that the platform is used in compliance with security policies and regulations.

- **Data Encryption:** Admins should configure GitHub Enterprise to use HTTPS for encrypted communication between clients and the server. Additionally, they may implement encryption at rest to secure data stored within the GitHub Enterprise instance. This helps meet compliance requirements related to data protection.

- **Code Review and Approval Workflows:** GitHub administrators play a role in establishing and enforcing code review and approval workflows. They can configure branch protection rules, set up required reviews, and define approval criteria. This ensures that changes to the codebase go through a controlled and documented process, aligning with compliance standards.

- **Secure Development Practices:** Administrators can integrate and configure security tools within GitHub Enterprise to support secure development practices. This includes enabling features such as dependency scanning, code scanning, and secret scanning to identify and address security vulnerabilities early in the development lifecycle.

- **Integration with CI/CD Pipelines:** GitHub administrators should facilitate the integration of GitHub Enterprise with CI/CD tools. By configuring and managing CI/CD pipelines, admins contribute to a consistent and automated software delivery process. This helps meet compliance requirements related to the reliability and traceability of the development pipeline.

- **Documentation and Collaboration:** Administrators should encourage the use of GitHub Enterprise's collaboration features, such as issues, wikis, and discussions. These tools support transparent communication and documentation of project-related activities, helping to maintain an auditable record of decisions and discussions.

- **Regulatory Compliance Features:** GitHub administrators should be aware of and leverage specific features designed to assist with regulatory compliance. This may include configuring retention policies for audit logs, setting up repository archiving, and staying informed about updates that address emerging compliance standards.

GitHub administrators should collaborate with other stakeholders, including security teams, developers, and compliance officers, to ensure that GitHub Enterprise is configured and used in a manner that aligns with regulatory requirements and organizational policies. Regular audits and reviews can help verify compliance and identify areas for improvement. Keeping abreast of GitHub Enterprise updates and best practices is also essential for maintaining a secure and compliant environment.

GitHub Enterprise Regulatory Requirements

The regulatory requirements that GitHub Enterprise needs to adhere to may vary based on factors such as the industry, geography, and specific use cases of the organizations deploying GitHub Enterprise. Here are some general considerations for regulatory requirements that organizations using GitHub Enterprise might need to address:

- **Data Protection and Privacy Regulations:** Organizations operating in regions like the European Union (EU) need to comply with the General Data Protection Regulation (GDPR). GitHub Enterprise must ensure the protection of personal data, and organizations may need to configure the platform to meet GDPR requirements, such as data encryption, user consent, and data access controls.

- **Financial Regulations:** For organizations in the financial sector, regulatory frameworks such as the Sarbanes-Oxley Act (SOX) or the Payment Card Industry Data Security Standard (PCI DSS) may apply. GitHub Enterprise should be configured to support controls related to financial reporting, data integrity, and secure handling of financial information.

- **Healthcare Regulations:** Healthcare organizations are subject to regulations like the Health Insurance Portability and Accountability Act (HIPAA) in the United States. GitHub Enterprise needs to be configured to meet HIPAA compliance requirements, including secure storage and transmission of protected health information (PHI).

- **Government Regulations:** Government agencies or organizations working with government contracts may need to comply with specific regulations and standards, such as the Federal Risk and Authorization Management Program (FedRAMP) in the United States. GitHub Enterprise must align with these regulations to support secure government operations.

- **Security Standards:** GitHub Enterprise should adhere to general security standards, including ISO/IEC 27001, which outlines best practices for information security management systems. Organizations may need to configure GitHub Enterprise to meet the security controls outlined in these standards.

- **Export Control Regulations:** Organizations dealing with software development and collaboration on a global scale must consider export control regulations.

GitHub Enterprise should be configured to prevent the inadvertent sharing of restricted technologies with individuals or entities subject to trade restrictions.

- **Accessibility Compliance:** Depending on the jurisdiction, organizations may be required to comply with accessibility standards to ensure that software applications are usable by individuals with disabilities. GitHub Enterprise should be configured and customized to support accessibility standards such as the Web Content Accessibility Guidelines (WCAG).

- **Regulations Specific to Industry Verticals:** Certain industries may have specific regulations that organizations must adhere to. For example, energy companies might need to comply with regulations like the North American Electric Reliability Corporation (NERC) standards.

GitHub Enterprise provides a set of features and tools that organizations can configure to meet various regulatory requirements. This includes access controls, audit logs, encryption options, and integrations with security tools. However, it's essential for organizations to work closely with compliance teams to understand specific regulatory requirements and implement the necessary configurations and practices. Additionally, staying informed about updates to GitHub Enterprise and related compliance best practices is crucial for maintaining a secure and compliant development environment.

Integration with CI/CD Pipelines

As a GitHub administrator, the integration with CI/CD pipelines plays a pivotal role in enhancing software development workflows and automating application delivery. Firstly, understanding CI/CD involves automating testing (CI) and deployment (CD) processes. GitHub seamlessly integrates with various CI/CD tools like Jenkins, Travis CI, GitHub Actions, and GitLab CI. GitHub Actions, GitHub's built-in CI/CD platform, facilitates customizable workflows defined using YAML configuration files. GitHub provides webhooks for real-time notifications, triggering CI/CD processes upon code changes or pull requests. Repository settings empower administrators to manage integrations, configure webhooks, and set environment variables. CI/CD configuration files, stored in repositories, outline steps for building, testing, and deploying code. For secure operations, GitHub enables the storage of sensitive information like API keys using secrets. Administrators monitor CI/CD workflows, review logs, and establish notifications for prompt issue resolution. Effective access control mechanisms ensure that only authorized individuals can trigger builds, deploy to specific environments, or modify configurations.

Scaling CI/CD becomes crucial as organizations expand, involving optimization of build processes and parallelizing tests. Compliance with standards and adherence to security best practices are essential considerations for administrators, prompting regular audits of CI/CD configurations. Documentation emerges as a key element for knowledge sharing and onboarding new team members, providing clarity on CI/CD processes and configurations. Let's take a look at concepts of continuous integration and continuous deployment.

Continuous Integration (CI)

Continuous integration (CI) is a fundamental software development practice that emphasizes the frequent submission of code changes to a shared repository. The act of committing code more regularly serves to identify potential errors at an earlier stage, significantly reducing the volume of code a developer must troubleshoot when pinpointing the source of an issue. The practice of regularly updating code also facilitates smoother collaboration within a software development team, making it simpler to integrate changes from various team members. This approach proves advantageous for developers as it allows them to allocate more time to writing code and less time grappling with debugging errors or resolving merge conflicts.

Upon committing code to a repository, it becomes essential to undergo continuous processes of building and testing to ensure that the commit does not introduce errors. These tests encompass various aspects, including code linting for style formatting, security checks, code coverage evaluations, functional tests, and additional custom checks. Effectively building and testing code necessitates the utilization of a server. Developers can opt to perform local testing before pushing updates to a repository, or they can leverage a dedicated CI server. The CI server actively monitors repositories for new code commits, automatically triggering the build and test processes to maintain the integrity and quality of the codebase. Let's explore how we can configure continuous integration with GitHub Actions.

Continuous Integration Using GitHub Actions

GitHub Actions provides a robust continuous integration (CI) solution that facilitates the building of code and execution of tests in your repository. Workflows in GitHub Actions can operate on GitHub-hosted virtual machines or on self-hosted machines. The configuration of CI workflows can be tailored to trigger on specific GitHub events, such as code pushes, on a predefined schedule, or in response to external events via the repository dispatch webhook. GitHub Enterprise Cloud conducts CI tests and furnishes the test results directly within the associated pull request. This immediate feedback allows you to assess whether the changes in your branch introduce any errors. Successful completion of all CI tests signals that the pushed changes are prepared for review or merging by team members. Conversely, a failed test indicates that a change in your code may have caused the failure. When initiating CI in your repository, GitHub Enterprise Cloud automatically analyzes the codebase and proposes CI workflows based on the programming language and framework used. For instance, if you utilize .NET, GitHub Enterprise Cloud suggests a starter workflow designed to install .NET packages and run associated tests. You have the flexibility to adopt the suggested CI starter workflow, customize it as needed, or craft an entirely bespoke workflow file to execute your CI tests.

Beyond facilitating CI, GitHub Actions extends its utility to enable the creation of workflows throughout the entire software development lifecycle. Actions can be employed to handle diverse tasks such as deployment, packaging, or releasing projects, providing a comprehensive automation solution for software development processes. Let's explore an example with building, testing, and publishing a .NET application.

GitHub-hosted runners come with a tool cache that features preinstalled software, such as the .NET Core SDK. This assumes you have a grasp of YAML syntax and its application in GitHub Actions, as well as a basic understanding of the .NET Core SDK.

Using a .NET Starter Workflow

For a swift start, incorporate a starter workflow into the .github/ workflows directory of your repository. GitHub conveniently offers a starter workflow tailored for most .NET projects. The subsequent sections in this guide provide examples illustrating how you can personalize this starter workflow. To initiate this process, follow these steps:

- Navigate to the main page of your repository on GitHub.com.

- Below your repository name, click "Actions."

- If you already have a workflow in your repository, select "New workflow."

- On the "Choose a workflow" page, peruse the recommended starter workflows and search for "dotnet."

Click "Configure" for the ".NET" workflow. Figure 6-9 shows an example of configuring a .NET workflow.

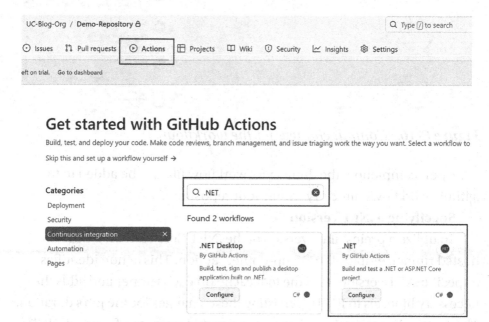

Figure 6-9. *Configure a .NET workflow*

- Customize the workflow as needed (e.g., altering the .NET version).

Commit the changes by clicking "Commit changes." Figure 6-10 shows the screen for committing changes.

Figure 6-10. *Commit changes for the workflow*

Upon completion, the dotnet.yml workflow file will be added to the .github/workflows directory within your repository.

Specifying a .NET Version

To utilize a preinstalled version of the .NET Core SDK on a GitHub-hosted runner, employ the "setup-dotnet" action. This action identifies a specific .NET version from the tool cache on each runner and adds the necessary binaries to PATH, persisting these changes for the job's duration. The "setup-dotnet" action is the recommended approach for using .NET with GitHub Actions, ensuring consistency across different runners and .NET versions. For self-hosted runners, manual installation and PATH configuration are necessary.

Using Multiple .NET Versions

```
name: dotnet package
on: [push]
jobs:
  build:
    runs-on: ubuntu-latest
    strategy:
```

```
matrix:
  dotnet-version: [ '3.1.x', '6.0.x' ]
steps:
  - uses: actions/checkout@v4
  - name: Setup dotnet ${{ matrix.dotnet-version }}
    uses: actions/setup-dotnet@v3
    with:
      dotnet-version: ${{ matrix.dotnet-version }}
  - name: Display dotnet version
    run: dotnet --version
```

Using a Specific .NET Version

You have the option to set up your job to utilize a particular .NET version, for instance, 3.0.22. Alternatively, you can employ semantic versioning syntax to acquire the latest minor release. In this instance, the example demonstrates the use of the most recent minor release for .NET 3:

```
- name: Setup .NET 3.1
  uses: actions/setup-dotnet@v3
  with:
    dotnet-version: '3.1'
```

Installing Dependencies

GitHub-hosted runners come with the NuGet package manager installed. Utilize the dotnet CLI to install dependencies, as demonstrated as follows, where the Swashbuckle.AspNetCore.Swagger package is installed:

```
steps:
- uses: actions/checkout@v4
- name: Setup dotnet
  uses: actions/setup-dotnet@v3
  with:
```

```
    dotnet-version: '3.1.x'
- name: Install dependencies
  run: dotnet add package Swashbuckle.AspNetCore.Swagger
--version 6.5.0
```

Caching Dependencies

You have the ability to cache NuGet dependencies by employing a unique key, enabling the restoration of these dependencies for subsequent workflows using the cache action. As an illustration, the following YAML code installs the Swashbuckle.AspNetCore.Swagger package:

```
steps:
- uses: actions/checkout@v4
- name: Setup dotnet
  uses: actions/setup-dotnet@v3
  with:
    dotnet-version: '3.1.x'
- uses: actions/cache@v3
  with:
    path: ~/.nuget/packages
    key: ${{ runner.os }}-nuget-${{ hashFiles('/*.csproj') }}
    restore-keys: |
      ${{ runner.os }}-nuget
- name: Install dependencies
  run: dotnet add package Swashbuckle.AspNetCore.Swagger
--version 6.5.0
```

Building and Testing Code

You have the flexibility to employ the same commands locally for building and testing your code. This example showcases the utilization of "dotnet build" and "dotnet test" within a job:

```
steps:
- uses: actions/checkout@v4
- name: Setup dotnet
  uses: actions/setup-dotnet@v3
  with:
    dotnet-version: '3.1.x'
- name: Install dependencies
  run: dotnet restore
- name: Build
  run: dotnet build
- name: Test with the dotnet CLI
  run: dotnet test
```

Packaging Workflow Data As Artifacts

Once a workflow is finished, you have the option to upload the generated artifacts for further analysis. This might include saving log files, core dumps, test results, or screenshots. The subsequent example showcases how you can utilize the upload-artifact action to upload test results:

```
name: dotnet package
on: [push]
jobs:
  build:
    runs-on: ubuntu-latest
    strategy:
      matrix:
        dotnet-version: [ '3.1.x', '6.0.x' ]
      steps:
        - uses: actions/checkout@v4
        - name: Setup dotnet
          uses: actions/setup-dotnet@v3
```

```
    with:
      dotnet-version: ${{ matrix.dotnet-version }}
  - name: Install dependencies
    run: dotnet restore
  - name: Test with dotnet
    run: dotnet test --logger trx --results-directory
    "TestResults-${{ matrix.dotnet-version }}"
  - name: Upload dotnet test results
    uses: actions/upload-artifact@v4
    with:
      name: dotnet-results-${{ matrix.dotnet-version }}
      path: TestResults-${{ matrix.dotnet-version }}
    if: ${{ always() }}
```

Publishing to Package Registries

You have the option to set up your workflow to publish your .NET package to a package registry upon successful completion of your CI tests. Repository secrets can be utilized to securely store any necessary tokens or credentials for publishing your binary. The provided example demonstrates the creation and publication of a package to GitHub Packages using the dotnet core CLI:

```
name: Upload dotnet package
on:
  release:
    types: [created]
jobs:
  deploy:
    runs-on: ubuntu-latest
    permissions:
      packages: write
      contents: read
```

```
steps:
  - uses: actions/checkout@v4
  - uses: actions/setup-dotnet@v3
    with:
      dotnet-version: '3.1.x'
      source-url: https://nuget.pkg.github.com/blog-uc/
      index.json
    env:
      NUGET_AUTH_TOKEN: ${{secrets.GITHUB_TOKEN}}
  - run: dotnet build --configuration Release blog-UC-Demo
  - name: Create the package
    run: dotnet pack --configuration Release blog-UC-Demo
  - name: Publish the package to GPR
    run: dotnet nuget push blog-UC/bin/Release/*.nupkg
```

Overall, continuous integration (CI) in GitHub Enterprise is a software development practice that involves automating the integration of code changes from multiple contributors into a shared repository. GitHub provides a robust CI environment with features like GitHub Actions, which enables the creation of custom workflows for building, testing, and deploying code. CI workflows can be triggered by various events, such as code pushes, pull requests, or external webhooks. The use of CI helps detect errors early in the development process, ensures code quality, and facilitates collaboration among team members by automating the testing and validation of code changes.

Note   Numerous continuous integration (CI) options are available based on the language and framework in your GitHub repository. As an example, we've utilized a .NET framework example among the available choices.

Continuous Deployment (CD)

Continuous deployment (CD) is a software development practice that leverages automation to seamlessly release and deploy software updates. In this iterative process, the code undergoes automated building and testing procedures prior to its deployment. Continuous deployment is commonly intertwined with continuous integration (CI), creating a cohesive pipeline where changes are not only integrated frequently but also automatically delivered to production environments, promoting efficiency and reliability in the software development lifecycle.

Continuous Deployment Using GitHub Actions

Setting up a GitHub Actions workflow for deploying your software product is a streamlined process. To ensure the functionality of your product, the workflow can initiate the build process in your repository and execute necessary tests before proceeding with the deployment. The configuration of your continuous deployment (CD) workflow can be tailored to specific events, such as a push to the default branch, scheduled intervals, manual triggers, or external events facilitated by the repository dispatch webhook on GitHub Enterprise Cloud. GitHub Actions provides robust features for enhanced control over deployments. For instance, utilizing environments allows you to mandate approval for a job to progress, restrict the branches capable of triggering a workflow, or control access to sensitive information. Additionally, concurrency management enables limiting the CD pipeline to a maximum of one in-progress deployment alongside one pending deployment.

Deploying with GitHub Actions

GitHub Actions provides capabilities for effective deployment control. Key features include

- **Event-Driven Workflow Triggering:** Initiate workflows based on a diverse set of events relevant to your project.

- **Environment Configuration:** Define environments with specific rules, ensuring that a job can only proceed after meeting predefined criteria. This includes managing access to sensitive information, such as secrets.

- **Concurrency Management:** Exercise control over the number of concurrent deployments, enabling efficient resource utilization and maintaining workflow stability.

It's essential to be acquainted with GitHub Actions syntax when working with deployment configurations.

Triggering Deployment

Deployment workflows can be triggered by various events, with common examples being pull_request, push, and workflow_dispatch. For instance, the following configuration triggers the workflow when

- There is a push to the main branch.

- A pull request is opened, synchronized, or reopened, targeting the main branch.

- It is manually triggered.

```
on:
  push:
    branches:
      - main
  pull_request:
    branches:
      - main
  workflow_dispatch:
```

This YAML configuration sets up the appropriate triggers for your deployment workflow.

Use Environments

Utilizing environments in GitHub Actions provides a way to specify a deployment target, such as production, staging, or development. When a workflow deploys to an environment, it is prominently featured on the main repository page. Environments offer various functionalities, including the ability to mandate approval for job execution, control workflow triggering by specific branches, enforce custom deployment protection rules, and restrict access to sensitive secrets.

Use Concurrency

Concurrency guarantees that only one job or workflow within the same concurrency group will execute at any given time. By employing concurrency, you can enforce a limit of one deployment in progress and one deployment pending for a specific environment. For detailed information on implementing concurrency, refer to the GitHub documentation on "Using concurrency." It's important to note that concurrency and environment settings are independent of each other. The value assigned to concurrency can be any string and is not restricted to an environment name. Additionally, if another workflow shares the same environment but does not explicitly define concurrency, that workflow will not be bound by any concurrency rules. This separation between concurrency and environment settings provides flexibility and control over the execution of workflows, allowing administrators to fine-tune deployment processes according to their specific requirements.

In the context of the following workflow, if any job or workflow using the "production" concurrency group is in progress, the execution of the following workflow will be temporarily paused with the status set to pending. Moreover, it will automatically cancel any job or workflow that shares the "production" concurrency group and is in a pending state.

This strict control mechanism ensures that, within the specified "production" concurrency group, there will be a maximum of one running and one pending job or workflow.

Example 1 – Concurrency at the Workflow Level:

```
name: Deployment
concurrency: production
on:
  push:
    branches:
      - main
jobs:
  deployment:
    runs-on: ubuntu-latest
    environment: production
    steps:
      - name: deploy
        # ...deployment-specific steps
```

Example 2 – Concurrency at the Job Level:

```
name: Deployment
on:
  push:
    branches:
      - main
jobs:
  deployment:
    runs-on: ubuntu-latest
    environment: production
    concurrency: production
    steps:
      - name: deploy
        # ...deployment-specific steps
```

You can also leverage the `cancel-in-progress` option to terminate any currently running job or workflow within the same "production" concurrency group.

```
name: Deployment
concurrency:
  group: production
  cancel-in-progress: true
on:
  push:
    branches:
      - main
jobs:
  deployment:
    runs-on: ubuntu-latest
    environment: production
    steps:
      - name: deploy
        # ...deployment-specific steps
```

These configurations provide administrators with precise control over deployment processes within GitHub Actions, ensuring a streamlined and controlled deployment environment.

View Deployment History

When a GitHub Actions workflow deploys to an environment, the deployment history is showcased on the main page of the repository.

Utilizing OpenID Connect for Cloud Resource Access in GitHub Actions

If your GitHub Actions workflows require access to resources from a cloud provider supporting OpenID Connect (OIDC), you can configure your workflows to authenticate directly with the cloud provider. This approach allows you to avoid storing these credentials as long-lived secrets, offering enhanced security benefits.

Starter Workflows and Third-Party Actions

In GitHub Enterprise, starter workflows and third-party actions play pivotal roles in enhancing automation and efficiency throughout the software development lifecycle.

Starter Workflows

GitHub Enterprise offers preconfigured starter workflows tailored to various popular services and frameworks. These starter workflows serve as foundational templates for CI/CD pipelines, reducing setup time and ensuring best practices. For example, GitHub provides deployment starter workflows for services like Azure Web App. Developers can quickly adopt these workflows by navigating to the Actions tab, selecting a new workflow, and choosing from the list of recommended starters. These workflows cover diverse scenarios, from building and testing to deployment, helping teams kickstart their automation journey.

Third-Party Actions

GitHub Marketplace hosts a rich ecosystem of third-party actions, offering a plethora of integrations and functionalities. These actions, contributed by the community and software vendors, extend GitHub's capabilities for diverse use cases. From code scanning and security checks to deployment and release automation, third-party actions empower users to tailor their workflows according to specific project requirements. Users can explore GitHub Marketplace to discover and integrate actions that align with their development stack and workflow preferences.

The following are some of the best practices:

- **Explore Starter Workflows:** Begin by exploring the available starter workflows provided by GitHub Enterprise for popular services and frameworks. These templates serve as valuable starting points for building robust CI/CD pipelines.

- **Customize Starter Workflows:** Tailor starter workflows to fit the unique requirements of your project. Customize steps, triggers, and environment configurations based on your development, testing, and deployment needs.

- **Leverage Third-Party Actions:** Explore GitHub Marketplace for third-party actions relevant to your development stack. Integrate actions that enhance code quality, security, deployment, and other aspects of your automation pipeline.

- **Contribute to the Ecosystem:** If you develop reusable automation scripts or actions, consider contributing them to the GitHub Marketplace. Sharing your workflows and actions can benefit the broader developer community.

- **Regularly Update Actions:** Keep third-party actions up to date to leverage the latest features, improvements, and security patches. Regularly review and update your workflows to align with evolving best practices.

- **Documentation and Sharing:** Document your workflows and actions comprehensively. This documentation aids collaboration within your team and serves as a valuable resource for others who might reuse or contribute to your automation processes.

By harnessing starter workflows and integrating third-party actions, GitHub Enterprise users can accelerate their automation initiatives, ensure code quality, and streamline software delivery pipelines effectively.

Additionally, many service providers offer dedicated actions on GitHub Marketplace designed for streamlined deployment processes to their respective services, like Deploy to Northflank, StackQL Studios – StackQL Exec, Deploy to IBM Cloud Foundry, etc.

Common Integrations for Automating Software Delivery Pipelines in GitHub Enterprise

Automating software delivery pipelines in GitHub Enterprise involves the integration of various tools and services to streamline development workflows. Notable integrations include continuous integration (CI) tools like Jenkins, which offers flexibility and extensive plug-in support for building, testing, and deploying code. Travis CI, a cloud-based service, seamlessly integrates with GitHub repositories for automated builds and tests, particularly suitable for open source projects. GitHub Actions, as GitHub's native CI/CD and automation tool, allows users to define workflows directly within repositories using YAML syntax, supporting building, testing, and deployment.

For code quality and analysis, integrations like SonarQube provide static code analysis insights, identifying code smells, bugs, and security vulnerabilities. Codecov measures code coverage and integrates with GitHub, offering visual reports. Containerization and orchestration tools such as Docker ensure consistent deployment, with GitHub Actions triggering deployments to Kubernetes clusters if required.

Deployment and release management integrations include AWS CodeDeploy for AWS-hosted applications, with GitHub Actions triggering deployments. Heroku integration automates deployments directly from GitHub repositories for those using Heroku for hosting. Testing automation tools like Selenium for web application testing and testing frameworks like JUnit or TestNG for automated unit testing can be seamlessly integrated into CI/CD pipelines.

Security scanning tools like Snyk and OWASP Dependency-Check identify security vulnerabilities in project dependencies, integrating smoothly into CI workflows. Collaboration and notifications are facilitated through Slack and Microsoft Teams integration, providing real-time notifications on pull requests, build statuses, and other events.

Monitoring and logging integrations like Prometheus and Grafana monitor application performance and infrastructure metrics. Artifact management tools such as JFrog Artifactory store and retrieve artifacts during the CI/CD pipeline.

These integrations enhance automation, collaboration, and quality assurance throughout the software delivery process, and the specific tools chosen depend on the project's requirements, technology stack, and desired outcomes of the CI/CD pipeline.

Best Practices for Automating Software Delivery Pipelines in GitHub Enterprise

Automating software delivery pipelines in GitHub Enterprise is crucial for enhancing efficiency, reliability, and consistency in the development process. Adopting a clear branching strategy, such as GitFlow, is fundamental for managing code changes effectively. For instance, creating a new feature branch and merging it into the develop branch follow a structured approach:

```
# Creating a new feature branch
git checkout -b feature/new-feature

# Merging feature into develop branch
git checkout develop
git merge --no-ff feature/new-feature
git branch -d feature/new-feature
```

Enforcing meaningful commit messages and adhering to a standardized commit message convention enhances traceability. Following a conventional commit format, like "git commit -m 'feat: implement new feature BLOGUC,'" ensures clarity and consistency in documenting changes.

In terms of CI/CD workflow design, breaking down workflows into modular steps improves manageability. A YAML configuration file can define a CI workflow with modular steps, facilitating easier understanding and maintenance:

```
# CI workflow defined in YAML
name: CI Workflow
on:
  push:
    branches:
      - main
jobs:
  build:
    runs-on: ubuntu-latest
    steps:
      - name: Checkout code
        uses: actions/checkout@v2
      - name: Build
        run: |
          # Your build commands here
      - name: Run Unit Tests
        run: |
          # Commands to run unit tests
```

Implementing a robust suite of automated tests, including unit, integration, and end-to-end tests, helps catch issues early in the development process. For example, running unit tests with "npm test," integration tests with "pytest integration_tests/," and end-to-end tests with "cypress run" contributes to a comprehensive testing strategy. Running tests in parallel, using tools like Jest or pytest, reduces build times and accelerates feedback loops.

Integrating static code analysis tools like SonarQube aids in identifying code smells and vulnerabilities while ensuring adherence to coding standards. Monitoring and improving code coverage using tools like Istanbul for JavaScript, with the command "npm test -- --coverage," is crucial for thorough testing.

Utilizing artifact repositories like JFrog Artifactory to store and manage build artifacts, dependencies, and release candidates is considered a good practice. Treating artifacts as immutable ensures reproducibility, as specific versions can be reproduced at any time.

Containerizing applications using Docker ensures consistency across different environments. A basic Dockerfile example might look like this:

```
# Dockerfile
FROM node:14

WORKDIR /app

COPY package*.json ./

RUN npm install

COPY . .

CMD ["npm", "start"]
```

Integrating with orchestration tools like Kubernetes for automated deployment and scaling ensures efficient container management. Deployment strategies such as blue-green deployments minimize downtime and enable quick rollbacks. For instance, Kubernetes can facilitate blue-green deployments. Feature toggles allow dynamic enabling or disabling of specific features, ensuring safe and incremental rollouts.

Regularly scanning dependencies for security vulnerabilities using tools like Snyk or OWASP Dependency-Check is essential. Managing sensitive information with GitHub secrets or a secure vault enhances security. Implementing robust monitoring using tools like Prometheus and Grafana helps track application performance and detect issues. Aggregating logs centrally using tools like the ELK stack aids in quick issue resolution and performance analysis. Integrating with collaboration tools like Slack or Microsoft Teams for real-time notifications, status updates, and interactive deployments enhances team communication. Configuring automation in pull requests to run pre-merge checks, tests, and code analysis ensures code quality before merging.

Maintaining clear documentation for CI/CD pipelines, including workflow steps, dependencies, and deployment processes, aids in onboarding and troubleshooting. Creating onboarding guides for new developers to quickly understand and contribute to the CI/CD setup fosters a smoother integration process. Encouraging feedback from developers and stakeholders helps identify areas for improvement in the CI/CD process. Using metrics and analytics to measure pipeline performance, identify bottlenecks, and refine workflows contributes to continuous improvement.

By adhering to these best practices and incorporating relevant examples, teams can establish reliable and efficient CI/CD pipelines, fostering collaboration, accelerating software delivery, and maintaining high-quality code.

Backup and Disaster Recovery

GitHub Enterprise Server Backup Utilities is a dedicated backup system designed to be installed on a separate host. This system takes regular backup snapshots of your GitHub Enterprise Server instance through a secure SSH network connection. The purpose of these snapshots is to enable the restoration of your GitHub Enterprise Server instance to a previous state from the backup host. The backup process is optimized to minimize the impact on performance. Only data added since the last snapshot is transferred over the network, occupying additional physical storage space. Notably, these backups are conducted online, and they operate under the lowest CPU/IO priority to avoid disruption. The advantage of this approach is that there is no need to schedule a maintenance window for the backup process.

It's important to note that major releases and version numbers for GitHub Enterprise Server Backup Utilities align with feature releases of GitHub Enterprise Server. Ongoing support is provided for the four most recent versions of both products. This ensures compatibility and effective backup functionality in alignment with the evolving features and updates of GitHub Enterprise Server.

To utilize GitHub Enterprise Server Backup Utilities, it is essential to set up a separate host system distinct from your GitHub Enterprise Server instance. This dedicated host facilitates the regular creation of backup snapshots for critical data preservation. The integration of GitHub Enterprise Server Backup Utilities into an existing environment provides a robust solution for the long-term and permanent storage of vital data. This ensures the availability of backups for recovery purposes, particularly in scenarios involving major disasters or network outages at the primary site. A key recommendation is to geographically separate the backup host from your GitHub Enterprise Server instance. This geographical distance adds an extra layer of resilience, guaranteeing that backups remain accessible even in the face of significant disasters or network disruptions at the primary site.

The physical storage requirements for the backup host are contingent on Git repository disk usage and anticipated growth patterns. The recommended hardware specifications include

- vCPUs: 4

- Memory: 8 GB

- Storage: Five times the allocated storage of the primary GitHub Enterprise Server instance

It's important to note that additional resources may be necessary depending on various factors such as user activity levels and the integration of selected tools and services. Tailoring the hardware specifications to your specific usage ensures optimal performance and reliable backup capabilities. Now let's see what is backup host and its requirement.

Backup Host and Backup Host Requirement

GitHub Enterprise Backup Utilities should be executed on a host dedicated to long-term permanent storage and must establish network connectivity with the GitHub Enterprise Server appliance. The software requirements for the backup host are modest, including a Linux or another modern Unix operating system (with Ubuntu being highly recommended), bash, git 1.7.6 or newer, OpenSSH 5.6 or newer, rsync v2.6.4 or newer (exceptions apply; see the following text), jq v1.5 or newer, and bc v1.0.7 or newer. Ubuntu is the preferred operating system for testing and is recommended for usage due to its compatibility. While alternative operating systems are supported, resolution of issues specific to those systems cannot be guaranteed. The use of Docker is encouraged, as it ensures compatibility with the required software versions. The parallel backup and restore feature necessitates the installation of GNU awk and more utils.

Network connectivity is essential, and the backup host must establish outbound connections to the GitHub appliance over SSH, using TCP port 122 for GitHub Enterprise Server backup. CPU and memory requirements are contingent on the size of the GitHub Enterprise Server appliance. A minimum of 4 cores and 8 GB of RAM is recommended for the host running GitHub Enterprise Backup Utilities. Continuous monitoring of CPU and memory usage on the backup host is advised to ensure adequacy for the specific environment.

As of April 2023, an update on rsync requirements is provided. The fix in rsync 3.2.5 for CVE-2022-29154 may cause performance degradation, which can be mitigated using the --trust-sender flag available in rsync >= v3.2.5. For backup-utils versions 3.9 or greater, --trust-sender is automatically applied if supported by the rsync version. If using an older rsync version, options include downgrading to a version before the CVE fix, upgrading to rsync v3.2.5 or newer, or manually downloading and building rsync v3.2.5 or newer if the operating system's package manager lacks access to it. This update ensures optimal performance and security in the backup process.

Storage requirements for GitHub Enterprise Backup Utilities depend on the current disk usage of Git repositories and the growth patterns of the GitHub appliance. It is advisable to allocate at least five times the storage amount assigned to the primary GitHub appliance to accommodate historical snapshots and accommodate future growth. Backup Utilities utilize hard links for efficient data storage, while GitHub Enterprise Server repositories use symbolic links. Therefore, the backup snapshots must be written to a filesystem that supports both symbolic and hard links. To confirm filesystem compatibility, run the following commands within your backup destination directory:

```
touch file
ln -s file symlink
ln symlink hardlink
ls -la
```

Using a case-sensitive filesystem is crucial to prevent conflicts. The performance of backup and restore operations is influenced by the storage system on the backup host. It is recommended to use a high-performance storage system with low latency and high IOPS. Avoid using an NFS mount for the data directory (where backup data is stored) to prevent performance issues and timeouts during backups.

GitHub Enterprise Server version requirements for Backup Utilities align with GitHub Enterprise Server upgrade requirements. Starting with Backup Utilities v2.13.0, support is limited to three versions of GitHub Enterprise Server: the version corresponding to Backup Utilities and the two releases prior to it. For example, Backup Utilities v2.13.0 can back up versions from GitHub Enterprise Server 2.11.0 to the latest 2.13 patch release.

Note   You can restore a snapshot at most two feature releases behind the target GitHub Enterprise Server version. For instance, to restore a snapshot of GitHub Enterprise Server 2.11, the target GitHub Enterprise Server appliance must run version 2.12.x or 2.13.x. Restoration from a newer version's backup to an older version is not supported.

Using multiple backup hosts or configurations is not recommended due to potential issues with components like MSSQL taking incremental backups. If using multiple instances for redundancy or different frequencies, ensure they share the same GHE_DATA_DIR backup directory.

Installing GitHub Enterprise Server Backup Utilities

To install GitHub Enterprise Server Backup Utilities on your backup host, begin by downloading the latest version compatible with your GitHub Enterprise Server instance from the github/backup-utils repository. Choose the version that corresponds to your GitHub Enterprise Server version, ensuring compatibility. For instance, if your GitHub Enterprise Server is version 3.8.4, download the latest GitHub Enterprise Server Backup Utilities version in the 3.10 series. GitHub Enterprise Server Backup Utilities maintains backward compatibility for two versions, allowing the 3.10 series to back up and restore instances running version 3.8, 3.9, or 3.10.

Once downloaded, follow these steps:

- Extract the repository using the following tar command:

  tar -xzvf /path/to/github-backup-utils-vMAJOR. MINOR.PATCH.tar.gz

- Change into the local repository directory using this command:

  cd backup-utils

- Copy the included backup.config-example file to backup.config:

  cp backup.config-example backup.config

- Customize your configuration by editing backup.config in a text editor. If you previously upgraded GitHub Enterprise Server Backup Utilities using Git, ensure you copy your existing configuration from backup.config into the new file.

Set the GHE_HOSTNAME value to your primary GitHub Enterprise Server instance's hostname or IP address. Note: If your GitHub Enterprise Server instance is deployed as a cluster or in a high-availability configuration using a load balancer, the GHE_HOSTNAME can be the load balancer hostname, provided the load balancer allows SSH access over port 122 to your GitHub Enterprise Server instance. To ensure a recovered instance is immediately available, perform backups targeting the primary instance even in a geo-replication configuration. Set the GHE_DATA_DIR value to the filesystem location where you want to store backup snapshots. It is recommended to choose a location on the same filesystem as your backup host.

- Grant your backup host access to your instance by opening your primary instance's settings page at http(s)://HOSTNAME/setup/settings and adding the backup host's SSH key to the list of authorized SSH keys.

- On your backup host, verify SSH connectivity with your GitHub Enterprise Server instance using the ghe-host-check command:

  ```
  ./bin/ghe-host-check
  ```

- To create an initial full backup, run the following command:

  ```
  ./bin/ghe-backup
  ```

Note   To prevent inadvertent overwriting of your data directory during upgrades of GitHub Enterprise Server Backup Utilities versions, it is recommended to ensure that your snapshots are not kept in a subdirectory of the GitHub Enterprise Server Backup Utilities installation directory.

Scheduling a Backup

To ensure data protection and disaster recovery preparedness, it's recommended to schedule regular backups on the backup host using the "cron(8)" command or a similar scheduling service. The frequency of your scheduled backups will determine the worst-case recovery point objective (RPO) in your recovery plan.

For example:

- A daily backup schedule at midnight may result in a worst-case maximum of 24 hours of potential data loss.

- Starting with an hourly backup schedule guarantees a worst-case maximum of one hour of data loss in a disaster scenario where primary site data is destroyed.

If backup attempts overlap, the "ghe-backup" command will abort with an error message indicating simultaneous backup existence. In such cases, it is advisable to decrease the frequency of scheduled backups. Refer to the "Scheduling backups" section in the GitHub Enterprise Server Backup Utilities README for more information.

Note   Restoring a backup crafted with GitHub Enterprise Server Backup Utilities version 3.7.0 or 3.8.0 may lead to login complications for users within the instance. Moreover, a bug existed, hindering the backup of secret scanning encryption keys. To overcome these challenges and ensure a seamless restoration, it is imperative to update your backup host to leverage GitHub Enterprise Server Backup Utilities version 3.8.1. Follow these steps to rectify the issues:

- Upgrade your backup host to GitHub Enterprise Server Backup Utilities 3.8.1.

- Generate a new full backup using the "ghe-backup" command.

For more comprehensive insights into utilizing an existing backup and addressing identified issues, consult the documentation on "Known issues with backups for your instance" (https://docs.github.com/en/enterprise-server@3.8/admin/configuration/configuring-your-enterprise/known-issues-with-backups-for-your-instance#users-cannot-sign-in-after-restoration-of-a-backup).

Restoring GitHub Enterprise Server Instance in Case of Extended Outage

In the event of a prolonged outage or a catastrophic incident at the primary site, the restoration of your GitHub Enterprise Server instance involves provisioning another instance and executing a restore operation from the backup host. Before initiating the restoration process, it is crucial to add the backup host's SSH key to the target GitHub Enterprise instance as an authorized SSH key. Several considerations apply during the backup restoration to your GitHub Enterprise Server instance. Firstly, you can only restore data from a backup that is at most two feature releases behind the current version. For instance, if you have a backup from GitHub Enterprise Server 3.0.x, it can be restored to an instance running GitHub Enterprise Server 3.2.x. However, attempting to restore data from a backup of GitHub Enterprise Server 2.22.x to an instance running 3.2.x is not feasible due to the three-version gap. In such cases, an incremental approach is necessary, where you restore to an instance running 3.1.x and subsequently upgrade to 3.2.x.

It is essential to note that network settings are not included in the backup snapshot, requiring manual configuration of networking on the target GitHub Enterprise Server instance post-restoration. The following are the prerequisites for restoration:

- Ensure that maintenance mode is enabled on the primary instance, and all active processes have concluded.

- Cease replication on all replica nodes in a high-availability configuration.

- Provision a new GitHub Enterprise Server instance designated for the restoration of your backup.

- If your GitHub Enterprise Server instance incorporates GitHub Actions, configure the external storage provider for GitHub Actions on the replacement instance. This will be covered as a part of GitHub Actions in this chapter.

Initiating the Restoration Process

To restore your GitHub Enterprise Server instance from the backup host using the last successful snapshot, utilize the "ghe-restore" command. Additional options can be employed to customize the restoration process:

- The "**-c**" flag allows overwriting of settings, certificate, and license data on the target host, irrespective of the existing configuration. Omit this flag when setting up a staging instance for testing, intending to retain the current configuration.

- The "**-s**" flag permits the selection of a different backup snapshot.

Upon executing "ghe-restore," the command conducts checks, confirms the restoration, and provides detailed status updates during the operation. Here is an example:

```
$ ghe-restore -c 169.154.1.1
> Checking for leaked keys in the backup snapshot that is being
restored ...
> * No leaked keys found
> Connect 169.154.1.1:122 OK (v2.9.0)

> WARNING: All data on GitHub Enterprise appliance 169.154.1.1
(v2.9.0)
>          will be overwritten with data from snapshot
20170329T150710.
> Please verify that this is the correct restore host before
continuing.
> Type 'yes' to continue: yes

> Starting restore of 169.154.1.1:122 from snapshot
20170329T150710
# ...output truncated
```

> *Completed restore of 169.154.1.1:122 from snapshot*
> *20170329T150710*
> *Visit https://169.154.1.1/setup/settings to review appliance*
> *configuration.*

For additional validation, you can configure an IP exception list to permit access to a specified set of IP addresses after the restoration. In cases of a high-availability configuration, post-restoration to new disks on an existing or empty instance may result in "ghe-repl-status" reporting Git or Alambic replication as out of sync due to stale server Universally Unique IDentifier (UUID). To address this, use "ghe-repl-teardown" after the restoration and before starting replication. If further assistance is needed, GitHub Enterprise Support is available.

Known Challenges with GitHub Enterprise Backups

- **Issues with GitHub Enterprise Server Backup Utilities 3.7.0 and 3.8.0 Restorations:** After restoring a backup created with GitHub Enterprise Server Backup Utilities version 3.7.0 or 3.8.0, users may encounter login problems. Additionally, a bug prevents the backup of secret scanning encryption keys. To address these concerns, it's crucial to upgrade your backup host to GitHub Enterprise Server Backup Utilities version 3.8.1. Follow these steps:

  - Upgrade your backup host to GitHub Enterprise Server Backup Utilities 3.8.1.

  - Generate a new full backup using the "**ghe-backup**" command.

- **Restoration Prerequisites and Version Compatibility:**

  - Before restoring your GitHub Enterprise Server instance, ensure maintenance mode is enabled on the primary instance, all active processes have completed, and replication is halted in high-availability setups.

  - A new GitHub Enterprise Server instance must be provisioned as the target for restoration.

  - GitHub Actions users should configure the external storage provider for GitHub Actions on the replacement instance.

- **Restoration Process and Options:**

  - Utilize the "ghe-restore" command for restoration, with options like "-c" to overwrite settings and "-s" to choose a specific backup snapshot.

  - Network settings are excluded from the backup snapshot, requiring manual configuration after restoration.

- **Version Compatibility Limitations:**

  - Restoration can only be performed for data at most two feature releases behind the target GitHub Enterprise Server version.

  - Network configurations must be manually configured after restoration.

- **Scheduled Backups and Overlapping Attempts:**

  - Schedule regular backups using "**cron**" or a similar command scheduling service on the backup host.

- Overlapping backup attempts result in an error message, signifying a simultaneous backup. Adjust backup frequencies to avoid conflicts.

- **Validation and IP Exception List:** For validation post-restoration, configure an IP exception list to allow access to specified IP addresses.

- **High-Availability Configuration Considerations:** In high-availability setups, after restoration, stale server UUIDs may cause Git or Alambic replication issues. Use **"ghe-repl-teardown"** to address this before starting replication.

For GitHub administrators, ensuring the safety and integrity of GitHub Enterprise data is paramount, and having robust backup and disaster recovery strategies is crucial. It involves utilizing reliable backup tools to regularly back up essential data, including repositories, configurations, and user data. Best practices include determining a suitable backup frequency, with considerations for the frequency of changes to the data. Regular backups, ideally performed daily, help minimize data loss in case of unforeseen events. It's essential to store backups in secure, off-site locations to guard against physical disasters or system failures. Validating the integrity of backups through periodic testing ensures they can be successfully restored when needed. Documentation of backup and recovery processes, as well as having a well-defined disaster recovery plan, is critical for a GitHub administrator to efficiently respond to unforeseen situations and maintain the resilience of the GitHub Enterprise environment.

Advanced Features and Customization

GitHub Enterprise provides advanced features that empower organizations to enhance collaboration, security, and efficiency in software development processes. These advanced features offer customization options and capabilities beyond basic version control. Let's delve into a range of sophisticated advanced features in GitHub Enterprise.

Fine-Grained Personal Access Tokens

Stolen or compromised credentials pose a significant threat to data security, and GitHub has a strong history of implementing security measures to protect developers and enterprises. These efforts include facilitating the adoption of two-factor authentication (2FA) through the GitHub mobile app, robust support for WebAuthn, and scanning for secrets at the point of push for GitHub Advanced Security customers. To enhance security further, GitHub is introducing a new type of personal access token (PAT) in public beta: fine-grained personal access tokens. Unlike the existing coarse-grained PATs, fine-grained PATs provide granular control over permissions and repository access. Developers and organization administrators can now exercise precise control, implement approval policies, and have full visibility into tokens accessing organization resources.

Key Features of Fine-Grained Personal Access Tokens

- Granular permissions with over 50 options controlling access to GitHub's APIs.

- Permissions can be granted on a "no access," "read," or "read and write" basis.

- Tokens expire, providing enhanced security.

- Limited access only to specified repositories or organizations, not all accessible repositories.

- Repository targeting, allowing tokens to be specific to a single repository in an organization.

Creating and Managing Fine-Grained Personal Access Tokens

- Fine-grained PATs can be created in the Developer Settings section of the account settings.

- They facilitate easier integration with GitHub Apps and script migration.

- Approval and auditing controls are available in the Personal Access Tokens tab of Organization Settings.

- Organization owners can approve, view, revoke, and set policies for fine-grained PATs.

- Enterprise owners can set policies across organizations through the Personal Access Tokens page in the Policies tab.

While existing personal access tokens (classic) remain fully supported, the introduction of fine-grained personal access tokens adds a new layer of security, control, and flexibility for developers and organizations using GitHub. Figure 6-11 shows the screen for creating a fine-grained personal access token.

Figure 6-11. *Creating a fine-grained personal access token*

GitHub Actions

GitHub Actions empowers members of your enterprise to enhance productivity by automating every phase of the software development workflow. This tool accelerates team efficiency at scale, leading to a significant increase in merged pull requests per day and faster merging of pull requests in large repositories. You have the flexibility to create custom automations or leverage workflows from a vast ecosystem of over 10,000 actions crafted by industry leaders and the open source community. Integrated seamlessly into the GitHub Enterprise Cloud experience, GitHub Actions is developer-friendly.

Enjoy the ease of GitHub-hosted runners, managed and updated by GitHub, or take control of your private CI/CD infrastructure using self-hosted runners. With self-hosted runners, you can define the specific environment and resources for your builds, testing, and deployments, ensuring a tailored development cycle without exposing it to the Internet. GitHub Actions offers enhanced deployment control, allowing you to implement features like requiring approval for job progression, restricting triggering workflows to specific branches, and managing access to secrets. For workflows requiring access to resources from a compatible cloud provider supporting OpenID Connect (OIDC), authentication can be configured directly, eliminating the need for long-lived secrets and providing security advantages. In addition, GitHub Actions provides tools to govern your enterprise's software development cycle and fulfill compliance obligations.

GitHub Actions serves as a comprehensive continuous integration and continuous delivery (CI/CD) platform, enabling the automation of your build, test, and deployment pipelines. This platform empowers your enterprise to automate, customize, and execute various software development workflows, including testing and deployments. However, before implementing GitHub Actions on a large scale within your enterprise, strategic planning is essential. Careful consideration and decisions must be made to ensure that GitHub Actions aligns with and effectively supports the unique requirements of your enterprise. Developing a comprehensive plan to govern your enterprise's utilization of GitHub Actions is crucial to meeting compliance obligations. Begin by determining the actions your developers will be permitted to use. Evaluate whether external access to actions will be enabled and configure options accordingly, especially if users require access to actions from GitHub.com or GitHub Marketplace.

Next, decide on the allowance of third-party actions not created by GitHub. Configuration options at the repository, organization, and enterprise levels can be utilized, and you have the flexibility to permit actions solely from GitHub or choose to include verified creators or specific actions from third parties. Consider integrating OpenID Connect (OIDC) with reusable workflows to ensure consistent deployments across repositories, organizations, or the entire enterprise. This involves defining trust conditions on cloud roles based on reusable workflows. Accessing information about GitHub Actions activity is possible through audit logs for your enterprise. If your business necessitates retaining this data beyond the default audit log duration, strategize how you will export and store this information externally from GitHub.

Refer to Chapter 5 for GitHub Actions and GitHub Packages.

Migrating Your Enterprise to GitHub Actions

To seamlessly transition your enterprise to GitHub Actions from an existing system, a well-structured approach involving planning, execution, and system retirement is essential. This guide provides specific insights into considerations crucial for a successful migration. For additional details on introducing GitHub Actions to your enterprise, refer to the previous section "GitHub Actions."

Planning Your Migration: Before initiating the migration to GitHub Actions, meticulous planning is paramount. Identify the workflows slated for migration, assess their impact on teams, and devise a strategic plan for execution. GitHub offers assistance in your migration process, and you may explore the advantages of GitHub Expert Services for enhanced support. Contact your dedicated representative or GitHub's Sales team for more information.

Identifying and Inventorying Migration Targets: To ensure a smooth migration to GitHub Actions, a comprehensive understanding of existing workflows in your current system is necessary.

- **Creating an Inventory**

  - Document existing build and release workflows across your enterprise.

  - Gather information on actively used workflows and those earmarked for migration or retirement.

- **Understanding Differences**

  - Familiarize yourself with disparities between your current provider and GitHub Actions.

  - Assess potential challenges in migrating each workflow and identify differences in features. Refer to "Migrating to GitHub Actions" for detailed insights.

Armed with this information, you can make informed decisions about which workflows are suitable for migration to GitHub Actions based on your enterprise's needs and preferences.

Evaluate Team Implications During Migrations

When transitioning to GitHub Actions, the alteration of tools within your enterprise has a profound impact on your team's workflow. Evaluating how this shift will influence the day-to-day tasks of developers is crucial. It necessitates a comprehensive analysis of processes, integrations, and third-party tools linked to your existing systems. Planning for necessary updates becomes imperative to facilitate a seamless migration. Additionally, the migration may trigger considerations regarding compliance. Assessing whether existing credential scanning and security analysis tools align with GitHub Actions or if new tools are required becomes a critical aspect. Furthermore, it is essential to identify the gates and checks inherent in your current system and ensure their effective implementation within GitHub Actions. Proactive planning in these areas is pivotal to a successful and harmonious integration of GitHub Actions into your enterprise workflow.

Identifying and Validating Migration Tools

To facilitate the transition of your enterprise's workflows to GitHub Actions, automated migration tools can be employed to translate the syntax from your existing system to the syntax required by GitHub Actions. It is advisable to identify suitable third-party tools or reach out to your dedicated representative or GitHub's Sales team for information on tools provided by GitHub. One example is the GitHub Actions Importer, which allows you to plan, scope, and migrate CI pipelines from various supported services to GitHub Actions. Once a migration tool is identified, it is crucial to validate its effectiveness by running it on test workflows and ensuring that the results align with expectations. While automated tools can handle the majority of workflows, there may be a need for manual intervention in a small percentage of cases. Therefore, it is recommended to estimate the extent of manual work required for a comprehensive migration.

Deciding on a Migration Approach

When determining the migration approach for your enterprise, the size of your teams plays a crucial role. Smaller teams may find success in migrating all their workflows at once, employing a "rip-and-replace" approach. On the other hand, larger enterprises may benefit from an iterative approach that involves active management combined with self-service options. You have the flexibility to choose between having a central body manage the entire migration or delegating the migration responsibility to individual teams. Our recommendation is to adopt an iterative approach that combines both active management and self-service elements. Begin with a small group of early adopters who can serve as internal champions. Identify a set of workflows that sufficiently represent the diversity of your business, and collaborate with early adopters to migrate these workflows to GitHub Actions, making necessary iterations along the way. This initial success will instill confidence in other teams that their workflows can also be seamlessly migrated. Subsequently, extend the availability of GitHub Actions to your larger organization. Offer resources to assist these teams in migrating their own workflows to GitHub Actions, and communicate the timeline for retiring the existing systems. Finally, notify any teams still using the old systems to complete their migrations within a specified timeframe. Highlight the successes of other teams to demonstrate that migration is not only feasible but also desirable.

Defining Your Migration Schedule

Once you've determined the migration approach, the next step is to develop a schedule outlining when each team will migrate their workflows to GitHub Actions. Start by setting a target completion date for your migration, such as aligning it with the expiration of your contract with the current provider. Collaborate with your teams to create a schedule that aligns with the deadline while accommodating their individual goals. Consider the cadence of your business and assess the workload of each team involved in the migration. Coordinate with each team to understand their delivery schedules, and formulate a plan that enables them to migrate workflows without compromising their ability to meet their objectives. When you're prepared to commence the migration, utilize the planned automated tooling and manual rewriting processes to translate your existing workflows to GitHub Actions. Additionally, you may want to devise a scripted process to archive old build artifacts from the existing system. This ensures a smooth transition while preserving relevant historical data.

Following the completion of your migration, the focus shifts to retiring your existing system. Consider running both systems concurrently for a certain duration to validate the stability of your GitHub Actions configuration. This allows you to ensure that there is no degradation in the experience for developers during the transition. Once you've verified the stability and functionality of GitHub Actions, proceed with decommissioning and shutting down the old systems. Take steps to ensure that no one within your enterprise can reactivate the old systems, marking the conclusive shift to GitHub Actions as the primary platform for your workflows.

Enforcing Policies for GitHub Actions in Your Enterprise

GitHub Actions facilitates the automation of software development workflows for members of your enterprise on GitHub Enterprise Server. Enabling GitHub Actions grants any organization within your GitHub Enterprise Server instance the ability to utilize GitHub Actions. To govern

529

the usage of GitHub Actions by members of your enterprise on GitHub Enterprise Server, you can establish and enforce policies. By default, organization owners have the authority to oversee and manage how GitHub Actions are utilized by members. You have the option to either deactivate GitHub Actions for all organizations within your enterprise or selectively permit its usage for specific organizations. Additionally, you can impose restrictions on the utilization of public actions, ensuring that individuals can only employ local actions available within your enterprise. Figure 6-12 shows the screen for enabling GitHub Actions policies.

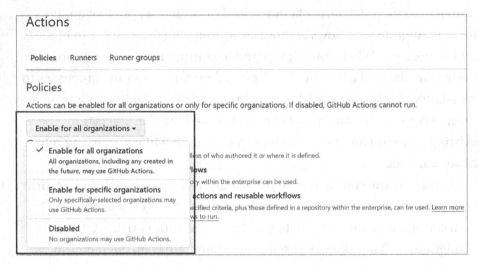

Figure 6-12. *Enabling GitHub Actions policies*

Allowing Select Actions to Run

When opting to "Allow select actions," you grant permission for the use of local actions, along with additional choices for permitting specific actions:

- **Allow Actions Created by GitHub:** Allowing GitHub-created actions for workflows. These actions are situated in the "actions" and "github" organizations.

- **Allow Marketplace Actions by Verified Creators:**
  This option is available with GitHub Connect enabled
  and configured for GitHub Actions. It enables the use
  of GitHub Marketplace actions created by verified
  creators, identified by the badge.

- **Allow Specified Actions:** Restricting workflows to use
  actions from specific organizations and repositories.
  The specified actions are limited to a maximum of
  1000 and can include tags or commit SHAs for precise
  identification.

  - To restrict access based on tags or commit SHAs,
    use the syntax OWNER/REPOSITORY@TAG-
    OR-SHA. For example, actions/javascript-action
    @v1.0.1 for a tag or actions/javascript-action
    @a824008085750b8e136effc585c3cd6082bd575f
    for a SHA.

  - The * wildcard character can be used for pattern
    matching. For instance, space-org*/* to allow all
    actions in organizations starting with "space-org"
    or */octocat'@* to allow all actions in repositories
    starting with "octocat." For more details on using
    the * wildcard, refer to "Workflow syntax for GitHub
    Actions."

Enforcing a Policy for Artifact and Log Retention in Your Enterprise

GitHub Actions allows for the storage of artifact and log files. The
default retention period for artifacts and log files created during workflows
is set to 90 days, after which they are automatically removed. You have the
flexibility to adjust this retention period within a range of 1 to 400 days. It's
important to note that any changes made to the retention period will only
affect new artifacts and log files; existing objects will not be retroactively

impacted. For repositories and organizations under management, the maximum retention period is subject to the limit set by the overseeing organization or enterprise. Figure 6-13 shows the Artifact and log retention screen.

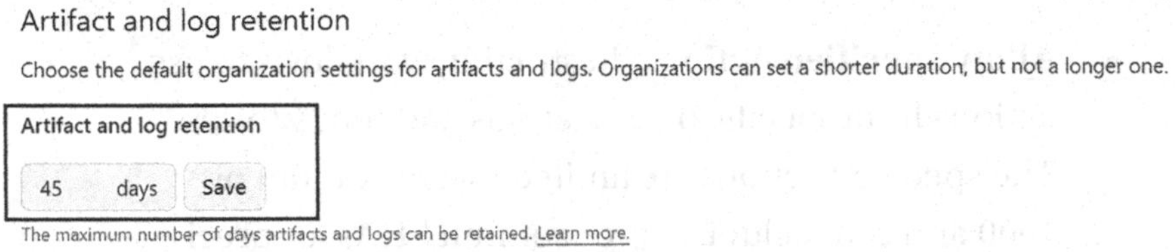

Artifact and log retention

Choose the default organization settings for artifacts and logs. Organizations can set a shorter duration, but not a longer one.

Artifact and log retention		
45	days	Save

The maximum number of days artifacts and logs can be retained. Learn more.

Figure 6-13. *Artifact and log retention*

Enforcing a Policy for Fork Pull Requests in Your Enterprise

You have the ability to implement policies that govern the behavior of GitHub Actions on your GitHub Enterprise Server instance, specifically when workflows are executed from forks by members of your enterprise.

Enforcing a Policy for Fork Pull Requests in Private Repositories

If your workflow involves utilizing forks of your private repositories, you have the option to configure policies that govern the execution of workflows triggered by pull_request events. These policy settings are applicable to private and internal repositories and can be configured at the enterprise, organization, or repository level. For enterprises, if a policy is enabled, it can be selectively disabled at the organization or repository level. Conversely, if a policy is disabled at the enterprise level, individual organizations or repositories cannot enable it. The available policies include

- **Run Workflows from Fork Pull Requests:** Permits users to execute workflows from fork pull requests using a GITHUB_TOKEN with read-only permission and without access to secrets

- **Send Write Tokens to Workflows from Pull Requests:**
  Allows pull requests from forks to use a GITHUB_
  TOKEN with write permission

- **Send Secrets to Workflows from Pull Requests:**
  Enables all secrets to be accessible to the pull request
  workflows

Figure 6-14 shows fork pull request workflows in private repositories.

Fork pull request workflows in private repositories

These settings apply to private repositories. Organization and repository administrators will only be able to change the settings that are enabled here.

☐ **Run workflows from fork pull requests**
This tells Actions to run workflows from pull requests originating from repository forks. Note that doing so will give maintainers of those forks the ability to use tokens with read permissions on the source repository.

Save

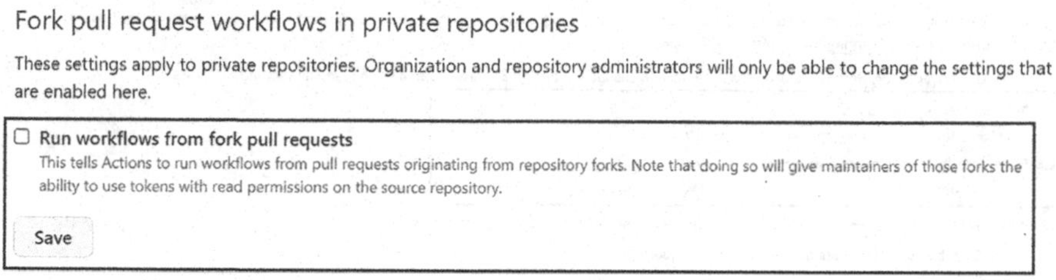

Figure 6-14. *Fork pull request workflows in private repositories*

Enforcing a Policy for Workflow Permissions in Your Enterprise

You have the ability to define the default permissions assigned to the GITHUB_TOKEN, offering the flexibility to opt for a more restrictive set of permissions or adopt permissive configurations. The default permissions for the GITHUB_TOKEN can be established in the settings of your enterprise, organizations, or repositories. If you opt for a restricted default setting at the enterprise level, it prevents the selection of a more permissive setting at the organization or repository level. Users possessing write access to a repository retain the authority to modify the permissions granted to the GITHUB_TOKEN. This can be achieved by editing the permission key in the workflow file, allowing the addition or removal of access as needed. To configure the default permissions for the GITHUB_ TOKEN, begin by navigating to the top-right corner of GitHub Enterprise Server. Click your profile photo and select "Enterprise settings." In the enterprise account sidebar, locate and click "Policies." Under the "Policies" section, find and click "Actions." Within the "Workflow permissions" settings, you have the option to determine whether the GITHUB_TOKEN should possess read and write access for all scopes (considered the permissive setting) or only read access for the content scope (referred to as the restricted setting). Once you've made your selection, click "Save" to apply the configured settings. Figure 6-15 shows the workflow permissions in your enterprise.

Workflow permissions

Choose the default permissions granted to the GITHUB_TOKEN when running workflows in this enterprise. You can specify more granular permissions in the workflow using YAML. Learn more about managing permissions.

Organization and repository administrators will only be able to change the default permissions to a more restrictive setting.

○ **Read and write permissions**
Workflows have read and write permissions in the repository for all scopes.

● **Read repository contents and packages permissions**
Workflows have read permissions in the repository for the contents and packages scopes only.

Choose whether GitHub Actions can create pull requests or submit approving pull request reviews.

☐ Allow GitHub Actions to create and approve pull requests

[Save]

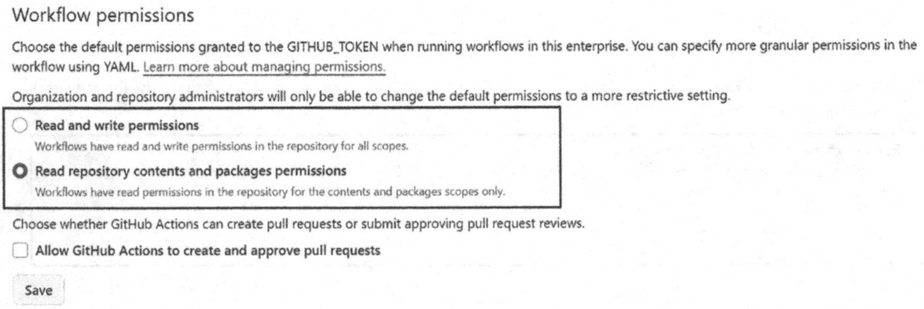

Figure 6-15. *Workflow permissions in your enterprise*

Preventing GitHub Actions from Creating or Approving Pull Requests

To control the ability of GitHub Actions workflows to create or approve pull requests, you have the option to either allow or prevent this functionality. Begin by navigating to the top-right corner of GitHub Enterprise Server and click your profile photo. From the dropdown, select "Enterprise settings." In the enterprise account sidebar, locate and click "Policies." Under the "Policies" section, find and click "Actions." Within the "Workflow permissions," you can specifically use the "Allow GitHub Actions to create and approve pull requests" setting to configure the permissions associated with the GITHUB_TOKEN for creating and approving pull requests. Once you've made the necessary adjustments, click "Save" to apply the configured settings. Figure 6-16 shows the screen for the workflow permission for GitHub Actions from creating or approving pull requests.

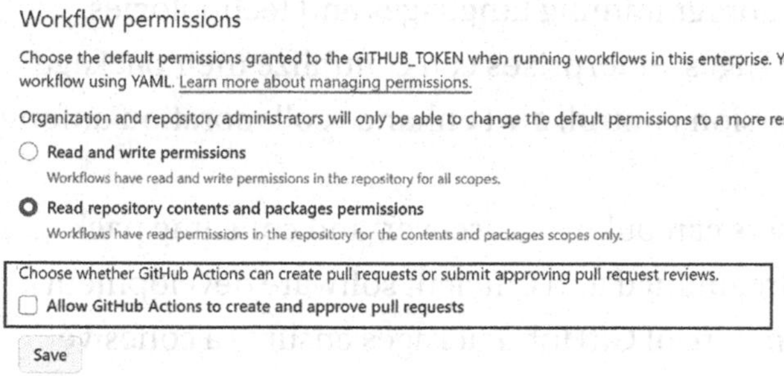

Workflow permissions

Choose the default permissions granted to the GITHUB_TOKEN when running workflows in this enterprise. You can specify more granular permissions in the workflow using YAML. Learn more about managing permissions.

Organization and repository administrators will only be able to change the default permissions to a more restrictive setting.

○ Read and write permissions
　　Workflows have read and write permissions in the repository for all scopes.

● Read repository contents and packages permissions
　　Workflows have read permissions in the repository for the contents and packages scopes only.

Choose whether GitHub Actions can create pull requests or submit approving pull request reviews.
☐ Allow GitHub Actions to create and approve pull requests

Save

Figure 6-16. *Workflow permission for GitHub Actions from creating or approving pull requests*

Enforcing a Policy for Cache Storage in Your Enterprise

By default, GitHub Actions on your GitHub Enterprise Server instance limits the total cache storage to 10 GB per repository, with a maximum allowed size of 25 GB. If this limit is surpassed, GitHub will save the new cache but start evicting older caches until the total size is below the repository limit. To customize these cache storage limits, you can establish an enterprise policy that defines both the default total cache size (e.g., 5 GB) for each repository and the maximum allowed total cache size (e.g., 15 GB). This allows repository administrators to configure cache sizes within the specified range, providing flexibility while maintaining control over cache storage. It's important to note that modifying the policy settings for GitHub Actions cache storage currently requires using the REST API.

GitHub Packages

GitHub Packages on GitHub Enterprise provides a powerful and integrated solution for managing and sharing software packages within an enterprise's GitHub environment. GitHub Packages allows organizations to host and publish packages directly within their GitHub Enterprise Server instance, facilitating seamless integration with their repositories and workflows. This feature supports a variety of package types, such as npm, Docker, Maven, NuGet, and more, enabling comprehensive package management for different programming languages and technologies. By leveraging GitHub Packages, enterprises can centralize their package management, improve version control, and enhance collaboration among development teams.

GitHub Enterprise users can publish, discover, and consume packages with ease, promoting a streamlined and efficient software development lifecycle. The integrated nature of GitHub Packages ensures a cohesive experience for developers, allowing them to access and utilize packages seamlessly within the GitHub Enterprise environment.

Note   GitHub Packages is accessible in GitHub Enterprise Server version 3.0 and above. If your GitHub Enterprise Server is running on an older version, you'll need to upgrade to at least version 3.0 to take advantage of GitHub Packages and its package management features. Upgrading your GitHub Enterprise Server ensures that you can leverage the benefits of GitHub Packages, enhancing your software development workflows with centralized package management capabilities. Refer to Chapter 5 for GitHub Packages.

Webhooks on GitHub

Webhooks on GitHub are a powerful feature that allow you to receive real-time notifications about events that occur in your repositories. Instead of constantly polling GitHub's servers to check for updates, webhooks provide an efficient way to get information instantly when specific actions take place. Here are some key points about GitHub webhooks:

- **Real-Time Notifications:** Webhooks deliver data immediately as events happen on GitHub. This ensures that you are always up to date with the latest changes in your repositories.

- **Event Based:** Webhooks are triggered by specific
  events, such as code pushes, pull requests, issues being
  opened or closed, and many others. You can choose
  which events you want to receive notifications for.

- **User-Defined Endpoints:** When you set up a webhook,
  you specify a URL (endpoint) on your server where
  GitHub should send the data. This endpoint is typically
  a route in your application that can handle the
  incoming webhook payload.

- **Customizable Payloads:** GitHub sends a JSON payload
  to your webhook endpoint. This payload contains
  information about the event, allowing you to customize
  your application's response based on the specific
  event type.

- **Wide Range of Use Cases:** Webhooks have numerous
  applications, including automating workflows,
  integrating with third-party services, triggering CI/CD
  pipelines, updating issue trackers, and more.

- **Security:** GitHub webhooks are secured using HMAC
  (Hash-based Message Authentication Code) to verify
  the authenticity of the payload, ensuring that the data
  comes from GitHub and has not been tampered with in
  transit.

- **Easy Configuration:** You can set up and manage
  webhooks for individual repositories or at the
  organization level. GitHub provides a user-friendly
  interface for creating and managing webhooks.

By leveraging GitHub webhooks, developers can create dynamic,
responsive, and highly automated workflows tailored to their specific
needs and use cases.

Types of GitHub Webhooks

Webhooks are limited to accessing events available within the repository, organization, GitHub Marketplace account, GitHub Sponsors account, or the specific GitHub App where they are installed. It's important to note that you cannot establish webhooks for individual user accounts or events specific to user resources, such as personal notifications or mentions. To create and manage webhooks, you must either own or possess admin access to the resource where the webhook is set up and listening for events. For instance, managing webhooks within an organization requires admin permissions for that organization. Additionally, certain webhook events are exclusive to specific types of webhooks. For instance, an organization webhook can subscribe to events unique to the organization level, events that a repository webhook cannot subscribe to.

Repository Webhooks

In a repository, you can set up webhooks that monitor events specific to that repository. To create and handle these webhooks within a repository, you need to either be the repository owner or have administrative privileges. It's important to note that you cannot create, modify, or remove webhooks in a repository unless you possess the necessary permissions. Within a single repository, you have the flexibility to establish multiple webhooks. However, there is a limitation: you can create a maximum of 20 webhooks for each individual event type. For instance, in one repository, you can set up up to 20 distinct webhooks, each tailored to subscribe to the push event.

Create Repository Webhooks

You can set up a webhook to receive notifications about specific events in a particular repository. To create a webhook in a repository, you need to be a repository owner or have admin access. Here is how you can create a repository webhook using either the GitHub web interface or the REST API:

- **GitHub Web Interface**

  - Go to the main page of the repository on GitHub.com.

  - Click "Settings" under your repository name. If you do not see the "Settings" tab, click the dropdown menu, and select "Settings."

  - In the left sidebar, click "Webhooks."

  - Click "Add webhook."

  - Enter the URL where you want to receive the webhook payloads under "Payload URL."

  - Optionally, choose the data format for the payload by selecting the appropriate Content type from the dropdown menu.

  - You can also provide a secret key under "Secret" to limit requests to those originating from GitHub.

  - Select the specific events that should trigger the webhook. Only subscribe to events that are necessary for your use case.

  - If you choose "Let me select individual events," pick the specific events you want to trigger the webhook.

  - To activate the webhook immediately after configuration, check the "Active" option.

  - Click "Add webhook."

After setting up the webhook, GitHub will send a ping event to confirm that the webhook is configured correctly.

Organization Webhooks

Within an organization, you can establish webhooks that monitor events occurring within that organization. Organization webhooks can observe events taking place in all repositories owned by the organization. Additionally, they can subscribe to events happening at the organizational level that extend beyond any repository, such as when a new member is added to the organization. To create and handle webhooks within an organization, you need to hold the position of organization owner. In a single organization, you have the option to create multiple webhooks. However, there is a restriction: you can create a maximum of 20 webhooks for each individual event type. For instance, within one organization, you can set up up to 20 distinct webhooks, each specifically tailored to subscribe to the push event. The management of organization webhooks can be carried out through either the GitHub web interface or the REST API.

Creating Organization Webhooks

You have the option to create a webhook to receive notifications about events within a specific organization. To create an organization webhook, you must be the owner of that organization. Here are the steps to create an organization webhook using either the GitHub web interface or the REST API:

- **Using GitHub Web Interface**

  - Click your profile photo in the upper-right corner of any GitHub.com page.

  - Select "Your organization."

  - Click the organization where you want to set up the webhook.

  - On the right side, click "Settings."

  - In the left sidebar, choose "Webhooks."

- Click "Add webhook."

- Enter the URL where you want to receive webhook payloads under "Payload URL."

- Optionally, choose the data format for the payload by selecting the appropriate Content type from the dropdown menu.

- You can provide a secret key under "Secret" to restrict requests to those originating from GitHub.

- Select the specific events that should trigger the webhook. Subscribe only to the events relevant to your use case.

- If you have chosen "Let me select individual events," pick the events that will activate the webhook.

- To activate the webhook immediately, check the "Active" option.

- Click "Add webhook."

Once you have created the webhook, GitHub will send a ping event to confirm that the webhook setup is correct.

GitHub Marketplace Webhooks

You can establish a webhook to monitor events associated with an application you have published on GitHub Marketplace. Each app in GitHub Marketplace can have only one webhook, and it can only be created and managed by the app owner or an app manager representing the organization that owns the app. Once created, a GitHub Marketplace webhook cannot be deleted; however, you can deactivate it to halt webhook deliveries and stop receiving event notifications. The management of a GitHub Marketplace webhook can be done through the GitHub web interface.

Creating a GitHub Marketplace Webhook

To subscribe to events related to an app you have published on GitHub Marketplace, the app owner or an organization's app manager can create a GitHub Marketplace webhook. Here is how you can set it up:

- **Navigate to GitHub Marketplace:** Go to your GitHub Marketplace listing page (`https://github.com/marketplace/manage`).

- **Access Webhook Settings:**

  - Next to the desired GitHub Marketplace listing, click "Manage listing."

  - In the sidebar, select "Webhook."

- **Configure Webhook:**

  - Provide the URL under "Payload URL" where you want to receive webhook payloads.

  - Optionally, select the Content type from the dropdown menu to specify the data format:

    - **application/json** delivers the JSON payload directly as the POST request body.

    - **application/x-www-form-urlencoded** sends the JSON payload as a form parameter called "payload."

  - Optionally, under "Secret," enter a string to use as a secret key. This key enhances security by allowing requests only from GitHub.

  - To activate the webhook immediately upon setup, check the "Active" option.

- **Create Webhook:** Click "Create webhook."

Upon creating the webhook, GitHub will send a ping event to confirm that the webhook setup is successful.

GitHub Sponsors Webhooks

You can set up webhooks to receive notifications about GitHub Sponsors events. For each GitHub Sponsors account, you are limited to creating a maximum of 20 webhooks. To manage sponsorship webhooks, you need to be either the account owner or have administrative access within the sponsored account. The management of GitHub Sponsors webhooks can be performed using the GitHub web interface. Here are the steps to create a webhook for your sponsorships on GitHub:

- **Access Your Sponsorship Dashboard:**

    - Click your profile photo in the upper-right corner of any page on GitHub.

    - Select "Your sponsors."

- **Choose the Sponsored Account:**

    - From the list of sponsored accounts, click the account for which you want to create a webhook.

    - Navigate to the "Dashboard" section.

- **Configure Webhook:**

    - In the left sidebar, click "Webhooks."

    - Click "Add webhook."

    - Under "Payload URL," enter the URL where you want to receive webhook payloads.

    - Optionally, select the Content type from the dropdown menu:

- **application/json** will deliver the JSON payload directly as the body of the POST request.

- **application/x-www-form-urlencoded** will send the JSON payload as a form parameter called "payload."

- Optionally, under "Secret," enter a string to use as a secret key. This enhances security by allowing requests only from GitHub.

- To activate the webhook immediately upon setup, check the "Active" option.

- **Create Webhook:** Click "Create webhook."

Upon creating the webhook, GitHub will send a ping event to confirm that the webhook setup is successful. This webhook will now subscribe you to events related to your sponsorships.

GitHub App Webhooks

You have the option to set up webhooks for a GitHub App, enabling it to receive notifications for specific events occurring in repositories or organizations it has access to. Each GitHub App is equipped with a default webhook, automatically generated by GitHub. Initially, this webhook is not subscribed to any events. However, you can customize the events it subscribes to based on your preferences. Although a GitHub App webhook cannot be removed entirely, you can deactivate it to halt webhook deliveries. Management of a GitHub App webhook can be done using either the GitHub web interface or the REST API.

Creating Webhooks for a GitHub App

Here are the steps to configure a webhook for an existing GitHub App registration:

For GitHub Apps Owned by a Personal Account

- Click your profile photo in the upper-right corner of any page on GitHub.

- Navigate to your account settings by clicking "Settings."

- In the left sidebar, click "Developer settings."

- Click "GitHub Apps."

- Next to the GitHub App you want to configure the webhook for, click "Edit."

- Under "Webhook," select "Active."

- Enter the "Webhook URL" where you want to receive payloads.

- Optionally, under "Webhook secret," enter a string to use as a secret key for added security.

- Click "Save changes."

For GitHub Apps Owned by an Organization

- Click your profile photo in the upper-right corner of any page on GitHub.

- Click "Your organizations."

- To the right of the organization, click "Settings."

- In the left sidebar, click "Developer settings."

- Click "GitHub Apps."

- Next to the GitHub App you want to configure the webhook for, click "Edit."

- Under "Webhook," select "Active."

- Enter the "Webhook URL" where you want to receive payloads.

- Optionally, under "Webhook secret," enter a string to use as a secret key for enhanced security.

- Click "Save changes."

Configuring Webhook Events

- In the sidebar, click "Permissions & events."

- Under "Repository permissions," "Organization permissions," and "Account permissions," select the appropriate permissions required for the events your app will subscribe to.

- Under "Subscribe to Events," select the specific webhook events you want your GitHub App to receive.

- Click "Save changes."

Remember, you can also use the GitHub REST API to create a webhook for your GitHub App if needed.

GitHub API

The GitHub REST API serves as a powerful tool for developers and integrators to interact programmatically with GitHub repositories and resources. Offering a straightforward and RESTful architecture, this API allows users to perform a wide array of actions, such as fetching repository details, creating issues, managing pull requests, and more. It follows standard HTTP methods and conventions, making it accessible through simple HTTP requests. Developers can use various programming languages to leverage the GitHub REST API, interacting with repositories, organizations, and users seamlessly. The API provides a standardized and well-documented interface, enabling the integration of GitHub functionalities into custom applications, automation scripts, and third-party tools. With its comprehensive scope, the GitHub REST API empowers developers to extend and enhance their workflows, fostering a dynamic and collaborative development environment. The REST API requests on GitHub comprise several essential elements. Each request includes an HTTP method, a path, headers, media types, authentication, and parameters. The HTTP method defines the action to be performed on a resource, with common methods like GET, POST, DELETE, and PATCH. The path, specified in the REST API reference documentation, identifies the endpoint's location, often including path parameters denoted by curly brackets. Headers offer additional information, such as the Accept header for media types and the User-Agent header for user identification. Media types, specified in the Accept header, dictate the format of data consumed from the API.

Each endpoint in the GitHub REST API is associated with a specific path, as detailed in the API reference documentation. For instance, the path for the "List repository issues" endpoint is /repos/{owner}/{repo}/ issues. The curly brackets {} within the path signify path parameters that must be specified. These parameters, such as {owner} and {repo} in the case of the "List repository issues" endpoint, are crucial modifications to the endpoint path and are mandatory in the request. To use this path effectively, replace {repo} with the desired repository name and {owner} with the account owning the repository. Headers play a significant role in conveying additional information about a request and the expected response. Notable headers used in GitHub REST API requests include

- **Accept:** Most GitHub REST API endpoints recommend including an Accept header with a value of application/ vnd.github+json, indicating the desired media type for the response.

- **X-GitHub-Api-Version:** This header allows users to specify the version of the REST API they intend to use in their request.

- **User-Agent:** Every API request must contain a valid User-Agent header, identifying the user or application making the request. While GitHub CLI automatically includes a valid User-Agent header, it is advisable to use your GitHub username or the application's name for improved contactability.

Media types, specified in the Accept header, determine the format of data to be consumed from the API. GitHub REST API supports common media types like application/vnd.github+json and application/json. Additionally, there are custom media types specific to certain endpoints, such as diff, patch, sha, full, raw, text, or html. These custom media types follow the format application/vnd.github.PARAM+json, where PARAM represents the media type name.

Authentication is a critical aspect of many endpoints, offering enhanced security and additional information for authenticated requests. While some REST API endpoints are accessible without authentication, GitHub CLI mandates authentication before utilizing the api subcommand for making API requests. The auth login subcommand is used to authenticate to GitHub, allowing users to benefit from increased request limits per hour. In GitHub REST API requests, various parameters play a crucial role in providing additional information to tailor the behavior of the request. There are three main types of parameters: path parameters, body parameters, and query parameters.

- **Path Parameters:** Path parameters serve to modify the endpoint path and are mandatory in a request. They directly influence the endpoint path, and users need to specify their values. For instance, in the "Create an issue" endpoint, path parameters might include elements like {owner} and {repo}.

- **Body Parameters:** Body parameters enable the transmission of supplementary data to the API, and their inclusion can be optional or mandatory based on the specific endpoint requirements. When creating a new issue, for example, the "Create an issue" endpoint necessitates specifying a title for the issue. Optionally, users can include additional details such as issue body text, assigned users, or labels.

- **Authentication for Body Parameters:** Authentication is a prerequisite for passing body parameters in a request. This ensures the security and integrity of the data being transmitted to the API.

- **Query Parameters:** Query parameters offer a means to control the data returned in response to a request. Typically optional, these parameters provide flexibility in refining the results based on specific criteria. For instance, in the "List public events" endpoint, the per_page query parameter allows users to adjust the number of issues returned, and the page query parameter facilitates fetching specific result pages.

In summary, understanding and appropriately utilizing these parameters in GitHub REST API requests empower users to customize their interactions with the API and retrieve or manipulate data according to their specific needs.

Making a Request with GitHub API

Making an authenticated request to the GitHub REST API using GitHub CLI involves a series of steps outlined as follows:

- **Setup:** To begin, install GitHub CLI on your operating system, whether it's macOS, Windows, or Linux.

- **Authenticate:** Proceed to authenticate with GitHub by executing the following command in your terminal:

  ```
  gh auth login
  ```

  You have the option to use the --scopes parameter to specify the desired scopes for authentication. If you prefer to authenticate with a preexisting token, you can utilize the --with-token option.

  Follow the on-screen prompts to complete the authentication process. GitHub CLI conveniently stores your Git credentials automatically. Choosing HTTPS as your preferred protocol for Git operations and affirming your willingness to authenticate to Git with your GitHub credentials during the prompts can be beneficial. This setup enables the use of Git commands like git push and git pull without the need for a separate credential manager or the use of SSH.

- **Choose an Endpoint for Your Request:** When preparing to make a request to GitHub's REST API, the first step is to select a specific endpoint relevant to the desired action. This choice involves exploring GitHub's REST API documentation to discover available endpoints suitable for interacting with GitHub's features and resources.

Once the endpoint is chosen, the next steps involve identifying essential details such as the HTTP method and path associated with that particular endpoint. For instance, when considering the "Create an issue" endpoint, the HTTP method used is POST, and the associated path is /repos/{owner}/{repo}/issues.

Moreover, it is crucial to recognize any mandatory path parameters for the chosen endpoint. These parameters are denoted within curly brackets {} in the endpoint's path. For the "Create an issue" example, the required path parameters are {owner} and {repo}. To execute the API request successfully, users must replace these parameter placeholders with specific values. For instance, {repo} should be substituted with the target repository's name, and {owner} should be replaced with the account name owning the repository. This meticulous identification and substitution process ensures the accurate and effective execution of the API request.

Here are examples of different request types:

- Example request for the "Get blog-uc" endpoint, returning the Bloguc as ASCII art:

```
gh api --method GET / Bloguc \
--header 'Accept: application/vnd.github+json' \
--header "X-GitHub-Api-Version: 2023-12-01"
```

- Example request for the "List stock symbols" endpoint, customizing the response:

```
gh api --method GET /getsymbols -F per_page=10 -F page=1 \
--header 'Accept: application/vnd.github+json'
```

- Example request for the "Create an enquiry" endpoint, generating a new issue in the / Bloguc/symbols:

```
gh api --method POST /repos/ Bloguc/symbols/enquiry \
--header "Accept: application/vnd.github+json" \
```

```
--header "X-GitHub-Api-Version: 2022-11-28" \
-f title=retrieved with the REST API' \
-f body='This is a REST API test'
```

These examples showcase the versatility of the `gh api` subcommand, allowing you to tailor your requests by specifying the required options based on the endpoint's characteristics.

Upon making a request, the API responds with the response status code, response headers, and potentially a response body.

Response Code and Headers

Every request results in an HTTP status code that signifies the success or failure of the response. Additionally, headers are provided to furnish more detailed information about the response. GitHub uses custom headers, often starting with X- or x-, to convey specific details. For instance, headers like x-ratelimit-remaining and x-ratelimit-reset inform you about the remaining number of requests allowed in a given time period.

To inspect the status code and headers, use the `--include` or `--i` option when sending your request. For example:

```
gh api \
--header 'Accept: application/vnd.github+json' \
--method GET /repos/Bloguc/symbols/enquiry \
-F per_page=10 --include
```

The response includes a status code (e.g., HTTP/2.0 200 OK) and headers providing additional context.

Response Body

Many endpoints return a response body, usually in JSON format unless otherwise specified. Blank fields are included as null instead of being omitted. Timestamps adhere to UTC time in ISO 8601 format: YYYY-MM-DDTHH:MM:SSZ.

While the GraphQL API allows you to specify the information you want, the REST API typically returns more information than necessary. If needed, you can parse the response to extract specific details. For instance, you can redirect the response to a file using the > operator. In the following example, replace REPO-OWNER with the account name owning the repository and REPO-NAME with the repository name.

Best Practices for Using the REST API

Avoid Polling: Subscribing to webhook events is a recommended practice to avoid unnecessary polling and ensure your integration operates efficiently within API rate limits. Webhooks provide a way for GitHub to notify your application when specific events occur, eliminating the need for continuous polling to check for updates.

Send Authenticated Requests: Making authenticated requests to the GitHub REST API is crucial for several reasons, including higher rate limits and better security.

Avoid Concurrent Requests: Avoiding concurrent requests is essential to prevent exceeding secondary rate limits on GitHub.

Pause Between Mutative Requests: To further avoid potential issues and adhere to rate limits, you can introduce pauses between mutative requests. This helps to prevent hitting rate limits and ensures a more stable interaction with the GitHub REST API.

Handle Rate Limit Errors: Absolutely, handling rate limit errors is crucial to ensure the proper functioning of your integration with the GitHub REST API. Here's a guide on how to handle rate limit errors:

- **Check for Rate Limit Headers:**

    - If the `Retry-After` response header is present, wait for the specified number of seconds before retrying the request.

    - If the `x-ratelimit-remaining` header is zero, wait until the time specified by the `x-ratelimit-reset` header before making another request. The `x-ratelimit-reset` header is in UTC epoch seconds.

- **Wait and Retry:**

  - If none of the rate limit headers are present, wait for at least one minute before retrying the request.

  - If your request continues to fail due to a secondary rate limit, implement an exponentially increasing amount of time between retries.

  - Consider setting a maximum number of retries to avoid indefinite retry loops.

- **Avoid Continuous Requests:**

  - Making requests while being rate-limited can lead to the banning of your integration. It's essential to respect the rate limits imposed by GitHub.

Follow Redirects: Handling HTTP redirection is an essential aspect when interacting with the GitHub REST API. Here's a guide on how to manage redirects:

- **Assume Any Request May Redirect:** Be aware that any request may result in a redirection. GitHub REST API may use redirection where appropriate.

- **301 Permanent Redirection**

  - If you receive a 301 status code, it indicates permanent redirection.

  - Repeat your request to the URL specified by the location header.

  - Update your code to use this new URL for future requests.

- **302 or 307 Temporary Redirection**

  - If you encounter a 302 or 307 status code, it indicates temporary redirection.

  - Repeat your request to the URL specified by the location header.

  - Do not update your code to use this URL for future requests. It might be a temporary redirection.

- **Other Redirection Status Codes**

  - Be aware that other redirection status codes may be used in accordance with HTTP specifications.

Do Not Ignore Errors: When making requests to the GitHub API, it is essential to handle errors appropriately. Ignoring errors can lead to unintended consequences and hinder the stability of your integration. Always check the response status code and handle errors according to the API documentation. Implement robust error-handling mechanisms to ensure the reliability and resilience of your application.

Exploring advanced features of GitHub Enterprise unlocks a range of capabilities for enhanced collaboration and automation. GitHub Actions enables customizable CI/CD workflows, GitHub Packages streamlines package management, and the GitHub API facilitates the creation of custom integrations and automation scripts. These features collectively empower teams to optimize development processes within the GitHub Enterprise environment.

Troubleshooting and Support

The GitHub admin role in GitHub Enterprise is responsible for overseeing troubleshooting and support activities, and they are typically involved in diagnosing and addressing problems related to repositories, permissions, integrations, and other aspects of GitHub functionality. If you encounter difficulties connecting to GitHub, troubleshooting your connection is crucial. Start by examining potential issues such as firewalls, proxy servers, corporate networks, or other network configurations that might be blocking access to GitHub. These elements are frequent culprits behind connection problems. To pinpoint and diagnose the issues, consider utilizing the GitHub Debug tool. This tool is designed to assist in identifying and resolving connectivity problems by providing detailed insights into the network and connection status. By systematically addressing these potential barriers, you can enhance your chances of resolving connection issues and ensure seamless access to GitHub.

Allowing GitHub's IP Addresses

If you want to allow GitHub's IP addresses through your network or firewall, you can do so by whitelisting the specific IP ranges associated with GitHub. This allows your systems to communicate with GitHub services without being blocked by firewalls or security measures. GitHub provides a list of IP addresses associated with their services, and you can find the most up-to-date information on their documentation. To allow GitHub's IP addresses, you typically need to

- **Obtain the List of GitHub IP Addresses:** GitHub provides a regularly updated list of IP addresses used by their services. You can find this information in the GitHub REST API documentation (`https://docs.github.com/en/rest?apiVersion=2022-11-28`) or on GitHub's status page.

- **Configure Your Network or Firewall:** Once you have the list of GitHub IP addresses, configure your network or firewall settings to allow incoming and outgoing traffic to and from these specific IP ranges.

It's important to note that GitHub's IP addresses can change, so it's recommended to regularly check for updates and adjust your configurations accordingly. Additionally, GitHub provides webhooks and other mechanisms that may be used as an alternative to IP whitelisting for certain scenarios. Always refer to GitHub's official documentation for the most accurate and up-to-date information on allowing GitHub's IP addresses. Let's find out what the IP addresses for GitHub are.

About GitHub's IP Addresses

GitHub's IP addresses are the specific numerical identifiers associated with the servers and infrastructure that make up GitHub's services. These IP addresses play a crucial role in facilitating communication between your systems and GitHub's platform. GitHub provides a list of IP addresses used for various purposes, such as accessing repositories, interacting with the GitHub API, and other services.

It's important to note that GitHub's IP addresses can change, and GitHub recommends regularly checking for updates to ensure that your configurations remain accurate. GitHub's IP addresses may be relevant in scenarios where you need to whitelist or allow traffic to and from GitHub through firewalls, proxies, or other network security measures.

To obtain the most up-to-date information on GitHub's IP addresses, you can refer to GitHub's official documentation, specifically the GitHub REST API documentation or GitHub's status page. This documentation provides details on the IP ranges associated with GitHub's services, enabling you to configure your network settings accordingly. Always rely on GitHub's official resources for accurate and current information regarding their IP addresses.

Using a Company or Organization's Network

In the event of connectivity issues within your company or organization's network, it is advisable to consult with your network administrator to determine if there are any network rules restricting specific traffic. If such rules are identified, it is recommended to request your network administrator to permit traffic to GitHub. This collaborative approach ensures that any network configurations align with the requirements of accessing GitHub, thereby resolving connectivity challenges and allowing seamless interaction with the platform. Open communication with network administrators helps address any potential restrictions and facilitates a more efficient and trouble-free connection to GitHub within the organizational network.

Troubleshooting Captcha

If encountering difficulties in verifying with the captcha on GitHub, follow these troubleshooting steps to address potential issues:

- **Enable JavaScript:** Confirm that JavaScript is enabled in your browser settings. Captcha functionality relies on JavaScript, and disabling it may impact the verification process.

- **Browser Compatibility:** Ensure that your browser is supported by GitHub. If not, consider upgrading your browser to a supported version. Refer to the "Supported browsers" documentation for a list of browsers compatible with GitHub.

- **Network Configuration:** Verify that your network configuration allows access to the captcha service domains, specifically https://octocaptcha.com/ and https://arkoselabs.com/. If you are behind a corporate firewall, contact your IT administrator to allow access to these domains. Confirm access by visiting https://octocaptcha.com/test and checking for the display of "Connection successfully made!" Also, visit the Arkose Labs Demo for a captcha test page to ensure successful loading of the captcha.

- **Browser Plug-Ins or Extensions:** Check for browser plug-ins or extensions that might interfere with GitHub's captcha verification. Disable these plug-ins temporarily during the captcha verification process to rule out any interference.

By systematically addressing these factors, you can troubleshoot and resolve captcha verification issues on GitHub. Ensuring JavaScript is enabled, using a supported browser, checking network configurations, and managing browser plug-ins contribute to a smoother captcha verification experience. If issues persist, reaching out to GitHub support or consulting with your IT administrator may provide additional assistance in resolving the problem.

Switching Cloning Methods

Switching cloning methods in GitHub Enterprise involves the process of transitioning from one protocol or URL scheme to another for cloning repositories. GitHub Enterprise supports multiple cloning methods, such as HTTPS and SSH, each with its own advantages. If switching from HTTPS to SSH, the first steps include generating an SSH key locally, adding the corresponding public key to the GitHub Enterprise account, and updating the remote URL of the local repository to utilize the SSH protocol. This allows users to perform cloning and pushing operations using SSH. Conversely, if transitioning from SSH to HTTPS, users need to remove the SSH key from their GitHub account and update the remote URL of the local repository to use the HTTPS version. In cases where HTTPS requires authentication, users may need to utilize a personal access token (PAT) instead of a password during operations. It's essential to update existing local repositories to align with the chosen authentication method, considering credentials, permissions, and potential security implications. Users are encouraged to refer to the GitHub Enterprise documentation for version-specific and precise guidance tailored to their configuration.

Best Practices for Enterprise Organization Management

In the ever-evolving landscape of software development, managing a GitHub Enterprise organization is akin to orchestrating a symphony of code collaboration and innovation. GitHub, as the epicenter of version control and collaborative development, demands a set of best practices to ensure harmony among teams, efficiency in workflows, and the security of your digital assets. This guide will walk you through the key principles and strategies that constitute best practices for GitHub Enterprise Organization Management. Whether you're a seasoned developer, a project manager, or an administrator, these practices serve as your compass, navigating the complexities of version control, collaborative coding, and project management within the GitHub ecosystem.

Picture this guide as a backstage pass to the GitHub theater – a place where repositories are the main characters, pull requests take center stage, and continuous integration and deployment dance in the background. As the curtain rises, we'll explore how to organize repositories effectively, establish secure access controls, streamline collaboration workflows, and embrace automation for seamless project management.

From branching strategies to code reviews, security scanning to documentation practices, each section unveils a crucial facet of GitHub Enterprise Organization Management. We'll delve into the nuances of project management, integration with third-party tools, and strategies for monitoring and maintaining optimal performance. In this symphony of best practices, we'll also emphasize the importance of education and community engagement, ensuring that your GitHub organization becomes not just a repository of code but a hub of knowledge sharing and collaboration. From fostering a positive collaboration culture to managing licenses and releases, every chapter contributes to the comprehensive playbook for GitHub success.

The journey through the best practices for GitHub Enterprise Organization Management promises to be both enlightening and empowering – a road map to transforming your GitHub organization into a beacon of efficient, secure, and collaborative coding.

Assign Multiple Owners

Let's assume where an enterprise has only one owner, there exists a potential risk of resources becoming inaccessible if the sole owner is unreachable. To ensure the continuity of access to critical resources, it is strongly advised that a minimum of two individuals within the enterprise be assigned the owner role. Managing administrators in GitHub Enterprise is a critical aspect of ensuring the smooth operation, security, and configuration of the GitHub platform within an organization. Administrators wield elevated privileges and play a pivotal role in overseeing various facets of GitHub Enterprise, ranging from access control to security configuration and system maintenance.

GitHub Enterprise administrators come in two primary types: site administrators and repository administrators. Site administrators possess overarching control over the entire GitHub Enterprise instance, allowing them to configure global settings, manage user access, and oversee the overall system functionality. On the other hand, repository administrators are assigned on a per-repository basis, enabling them to manage specific repositories, control access, and configure collaboration features within those repositories.

Adding administrators involves assigning users the appropriate roles, either as site or repository administrators. This process is crucial for ensuring that the right individuals have the necessary permissions to perform administrative tasks within the GitHub Enterprise environment. Fine-grained access control allows administrators to define specific permissions, dictating who can perform certain actions and collaborate on repositories. Security configuration is a paramount responsibility of GitHub Enterprise administrators. They manage SSL/TLS configurations to secure data transmission and determine authentication methods, including username/password, two-factor authentication, or single sign-on (SSO). Administrators are also tasked with monitoring the performance of GitHub Enterprise, utilizing audit logs to track user activities, logins, and any changes made to repositories or settings.

In addition to security and access control, administrators play a key role in troubleshooting and support. They assist users with technical issues, password resets, and access problems. During system upgrades, administrators ensure that GitHub Enterprise remains up to date with the latest features and security patches. This includes maintaining integrations with third-party tools and services used within the organization. GitHub Enterprise administrators contribute to documentation by outlining best practices, guidelines, and procedures. They often conduct training sessions to familiarize users and other administrators with GitHub Enterprise features and practices. Effective communication and collaboration with development, security, and operations teams are crucial aspects of administrator responsibilities to align GitHub Enterprise with organizational goals and ensure a cohesive software development environment.

Use the Best Authentication Method for GitHub Enterprise

The choice of the most suitable authentication method for your GitHub Enterprise instance involves a consideration of various factors, including security requirements, ease of use, and integration capabilities. GitHub Enterprise offers support for a range of authentication methods, each with its own strengths and considerations tailored to organizational needs. Username and password authentication, while simple to implement, may not be the most secure, particularly without robust password policies. SSH keys provide a more secure option, ideal for automation and command-line tasks, requiring users to generate and manage keys. OAuth enables authentication through third-party identity providers, enhancing security and simplifying user access, especially when integrated with Single Sign-On (SSO). Personal access tokens (PATs) offer token-based authentication with fine-grained permission control, suitable for automation and scripting. SAML Single Sign-On integrates with SAML identity providers, providing centralized authentication and authorization, enhancing both security and user experience. LDAP integration supports centralized user management, particularly for organizations with an existing LDAP infrastructure, and GitHub App installation access tokens are used for authenticating GitHub Apps, suitable for integrations and automation. Organizations often combine these methods based on their specific needs, considering factors like security, ease of use, scalability, and integration. Regardless of the chosen authentication method, implementing multifactor authentication (MFA) is recommended to fortify overall security measures.

Use Policies

The use of GitHub Enterprise policies is integral to establishing a structured and secure development environment while fostering collaboration and adherence to organizational standards. These policies encompass a range of features and configurations that organizations can leverage to govern their GitHub repositories effectively. Branch protection allows the enforcement of rules on branches, ensuring specific criteria are met before code merges into protected branches. Code owners, on the other hand, enable the assignment of responsibility for different codebase areas to individuals or teams, promoting accountability and targeted code review. Repository setting customization allows organizations to align features like issue tracking, project boards, and access permissions with their unique needs, maintaining control over the development environment. GitHub Actions and workflows empower automation for processes such as continuous integration, testing, and deployment, ensuring a streamlined development pipeline. Security and compliance policies involve scanning code for vulnerabilities, implementing security checks, and staying compliant with industry regulations through access controls and auditing features. Organization-wide policies extend the consistency of settings and integrations across multiple repositories, promoting standardized development practices.

Furthermore, defining review and approval processes, utilizing templates, and enforcing coding guidelines contribute to maintaining code quality and facilitating collaboration. In essence, GitHub Enterprise policies serve as a comprehensive toolkit for organizations to establish best practices, enhance security, and promote a collaborative and controlled development lifecycle.

To facilitate the enforcement of business rules and regulatory compliance, policies serve as a centralized management point for all organizations under an enterprise account. Each enterprise policy provides control over the configuration options available at the organization level. Organizations have the flexibility to either opt not to enforce a policy, allowing organization owners to tailor the policy settings, or to select from a predefined set of options for uniform enforcement across all owned organizations.

Take, for instance, the "base permission" policy. This policy allows the choice of granting organization owners the authority to configure it as per their organization's needs or, alternatively, enforcing a specific base permission level, such as "read," consistently across all enterprise-owned organizations. It's noteworthy that, by default, no enterprise policies are automatically enforced. The decision to enforce specific policies rests with the enterprise, and it is recommended to assess all available policies within the enterprise account. This evaluation should begin with a focus on repository management policies, ensuring that the chosen policies align with the unique business requirements of the enterprise.

Setting Up and Enforcing Repository Security Policies and Management

Setting up and enforcing security policies in GitHub repositories is crucial to maintaining the integrity, confidentiality, and availability of your codebase. GitHub provides various features and configurations to help you enhance the security of your repositories.

Note   GitHub provides several licensed features and tools to help organizations and developers manage their software projects effectively. Some of these features include code scanning, dependency insights, secret scanning, advanced security, security advisories, vulnerability alerts, dependency insights API, and licensing for GitHub Enterprise. Also, note that the availability of these features might vary based on your GitHub subscription plan (free, pro, team, enterprise, etc.) and the specific GitHub product you are using.

What Is GitHub Enforcing Repository Security Policies?

GitHub does not enforce security policies on repositories by default. Instead, GitHub provides tools and features that repository administrators and owners can use to set up security policies and best practices. Enforcing repository security policies involves configuring settings, access controls, and integrations to enhance the security of your codebase. Here is how you can enforce security policies in a GitHub repository.

Enforcing a Policy for Base Repository Permissions

Enforcing a policy for base repository permissions is crucial for maintaining the security and integrity of your GitHub repositories. GitHub provides several features and settings that allow you to enforce specific policies for base repository permissions. Here are the steps to enforce a policy for base repository permissions on GitHub:

- **Organization Level:** If you're managing repositories within an organization, you can set base permissions at the organization level. Go to your organization's settings on GitHub.

- **Repository Settings:** Navigate to the settings of the specific repository you want to enforce permissions for.

- **Branch Protection Rules**

  - Under the repository settings, look for the "Branches" or "Branch protection rules" section.

  - Add a new branch protection rule for the branches you want to enforce permissions on.

  - In the branch protection rule, you can enforce various policies such as requiring pull request reviews before merging, requiring status checks to pass, and requiring certain people or teams for code review.

- **Required Status Checks:** You can configure required status checks that must pass before a pull request can be merged. These checks can include code analysis, testing, and other automated processes.

- **Code of Conduct and Contributing Guidelines:** Enforce the presence of a code of conduct and contributing guidelines in your repositories. These files provide essential information for contributors and set the standards for behavior within the project.

- **Security and Dependency Scanning:** Integrate automated security scanning tools and dependency analysis into your repository. These tools can automatically identify vulnerabilities and alert maintainers.

- **Protected Branches:** Designate certain branches, such as **main** or **master**, as protected branches. Protected branches prevent force pushes and branch deletions, ensuring the commit history's integrity.

- **Access Control:** Review and manage user and team access regularly. Remove access for inactive or former contributors promptly.

- **Regular Audits:** Conduct regular audits of repository access, branch protection rules, and permissions to ensure compliance with organizational policies.

- **Documentation:** Document your repository policies and guidelines clearly. Ensure that all contributors are aware of these policies.

By enforcing these policies and settings, you can maintain a secure and well-organized GitHub repository, minimizing the risk of security breaches and ensuring a consistent and efficient collaboration process.

How to Enforce a Policy for Base Repository Permissions?

To enforce a policy for base repository permissions on GitHub, you can follow these steps:

For an organization

- **Navigate to Your Organization:** Go to your organization's GitHub page.

- **Access Settings:** Click the "Settings" tab, usually located on the right side of the organization's page.

- **Repository Defaults**

  - In the organization settings, find and click "Member privileges" or a similar option.

  - Here, you can set the default repository permissions for all repositories in the organization.

For a Specific Repository

- **Navigate to the Repository:** Go to the repository for which you want to enforce permissions.

- **Access Settings:** Click the "Settings" tab, usually located near the right side of the repository's page.

- **Branch Protection Rules**

  - Look for the "Branches" or "Branch protection rules" section in the repository settings.

  - Create a new branch protection rule for the branches you want to enforce permissions on.

- **Enforce Restrictions**

  - Within the branch protection rule, you can enforce restrictions such as

    - Requiring pull request reviews before merging

    - Requiring status checks to pass before merging

    - Requiring certain individuals or teams for code review

    - Restricting force pushes and branch deletions

    - Setting required commit signing

- **Required Status Checks:** You can configure required status checks that must pass before a pull request can be merged. These checks can include code analysis, testing, and other automated processes.

- **Access Control**

  - Manage user and team access under the "Access" or "Collaborators & teams" section in the repository settings.

  - Remove access for inactive or former contributors.

- **Security Scanning and Dependabot:** Integrate Dependabot or other automated security scanning tools into your repository to identify and fix vulnerabilities automatically.

- **Documentation**

  - Clearly document your repository policies, including contribution guidelines, code of conduct, and any other relevant information.

  - Ensure that contributors are aware of these policies.

By following these steps, you can enforce a policy for base repository permissions, ensuring a secure and organized development process on GitHub.

Enforcing a Policy for Repository Creation

Within all organizations under your enterprise, you have the flexibility to permit members to create repositories, limit repository creation solely to organization owners, or grant owners the authority to manage this setting at the organization level. If you opt to allow members to create repositories within your organizations, you can specify the types of repositories (public, private, and internal) they are permitted to create. For enterprises utilizing Enterprise Managed Users, there's an option to prevent users from creating repositories under their personal accounts. If this permission is granted, you can access these repositories temporarily and view them whenever necessary. More details can be found in the resources "Viewing user-owned repositories in your enterprise" and "Accessing user-owned repositories in your enterprise."

It's important to note that internal repositories serve as the default setting for all new repositories established within an organization linked to an enterprise account.

How to Enforce a Policy for Repository Creation?

To enforce a policy for repository creation on GitHub, you can follow these steps:

- **Organization Level**

  - If you are an organization owner, navigate to your organization's settings on GitHub.

  - Under the "Settings" tab, click "Member privileges."

  - Look for the "Repository settings" section.

  - Choose the appropriate option from the following:

    - **Allow Members to Create Repositories:** This allows all members to create repositories.

    - **Allow Only Organization Owners to Create Repositories:** Only owners of the organization can create repositories.

    - **Allow Owners to Change Repository Visibility:** This allows owners to manage the visibility settings (public, private, or internal) of repositories.

- **Enterprise Level (For GitHub Enterprise)**

  - If you are an enterprise owner, navigate to your enterprise account settings.

  - Under the "Settings" tab, click "Member privileges."

- Like the organization level, you will find options related to repository creation policies.

- Choose the appropriate settings to enforce the desired policy across all organizations owned by your enterprise.

- **Repository Templates (Optional)**

  - You can also enforce specific settings by creating repository templates. Repository templates allow you to define a standard repository structure, including files, directories, and default settings.

  - To create a repository template, go to your organization or user account settings, click "Repository templates," and create a new template repository.

  - When users create repositories from a template, they inherit the predefined structure and settings.

Remember, the exact steps and available options might vary slightly based on the type of GitHub account you have (GitHub.com, GitHub Enterprise Cloud, or GitHub Enterprise Server).

Enforcing a Policy for Forking Private or Internal Repositories

Enforcing a policy for forking private or internal repositories on GitHub means setting specific rules and restrictions regarding the process of creating copies (forks) of private or internal repositories within an organization. This policy helps maintain control over code access, security, and collaboration. Here are common aspects of such a policy:

- **Preventing Forks:** One option is to restrict users from creating forks of private or internal repositories. By preventing forks, you ensure that the codebase remains centralized and controlled.

- **Restricting Fork Destinations:** If forking is allowed, administrators can restrict the destination of forks. For instance, forks can be limited to specific teams or repositories within the organization, ensuring that code isn't forked to unauthorized places.

- **Approval Workflow:** Implementing an approval process means that before a fork is created, it needs approval from designated individuals or teams. This adds an extra layer of control, allowing only authorized forks.

- **Visibility Control:** You might want to enforce visibility settings on forks. For example, even if someone forks a private repository, the forked version should remain private and not become public without proper authorization.

- **Monitoring and Auditing:** Regularly monitor fork activities, track who is forking repositories, and ensure compliance with organizational policies. Detailed audit logs can help in reviewing these activities.

- **Integration with Access Control:** Ensure that the policy for forking repositories integrates well with overall access control mechanisms, including team permissions, user roles, and repository settings.

Enforcing such policies is crucial for maintaining data security, ensuring compliance with regulations, and preventing unauthorized distribution of sensitive code. Each organization might have unique requirements, so policies can be customized accordingly. Setting up these policies often involves using GitHub's administrative settings and features, such as repository settings, organization settings, and access control mechanisms.

How to Enforce Policy for Forking Private or Internal Repositories?

Enforcing a policy for forking private or internal repositories on GitHub involves configuring repository settings and access permissions to control who can fork repositories and under what conditions. Here is a step-by-step guide to enforcing such a policy:

- **Navigate to Repository Settings**

  - **Open the Repository:** Go to the main page of the private or internal repository that you want to enforce the policy for.

  - **Access Settings:** Click the "Settings" tab located near the right end of the menu bar.

- **Configure Forking Policies**

  - **Forking Restrictions**

    - **Restrict Forking:** Under the "Danger Zone" section, you might find an option to restrict forking. Enable this option to prevent forks of the repository.

    - **Destination Restrictions:** Some organizations have settings that allow forks only into certain teams or repositories. Configure these settings if available in your organization's policies.

  - **Branch Protection**

    - **Protect Important Branches:** Enable branch protection for important branches like **main** or **master**. In this, you can prevent force pushes and require status checks, ensuring that forks cannot disrupt the main branch.

- **Access Control and Collaborator Settings**

  - **Collaborator Access:** Review the list of collaborators and teams with access. Remove anyone who shouldn't have access to fork the repository.

  - **Team Permissions:** If your organization uses teams, review the permissions assigned to teams. Make sure only specific teams have permissions to fork repositories.

- **Approval Workflow (Optional)**

  - **Require Approval:** If you're allowing forks but want to enforce an approval process, enable protected branches for the repository. Require pull request reviews before changes can be merged, ensuring that changes from forks are reviewed and approved.

- **Regular Monitoring and Auditing**

  - **Audit Logs:** Regularly check audit logs on GitHub to monitor fork activities, including who is forking repositories and when. Investigate any unusual activities promptly.

By following these steps, you can enforce policies that control forking of private or internal repositories on GitHub, ensuring that your code remains secure and controlled within your organization.

Enforcing a Policy for Inviting Outside Collaborators to Repositories

Enforcing a policy for inviting outside collaborators to repositories on GitHub involves establishing rules and restrictions regarding who can invite external individuals or teams to collaborate on a repository. This policy is crucial for maintaining security and controlling access to sensitive code and projects. Here are the key aspects of enforcing such a policy:

- **Define Access Control:**

  - **Organization Owners:** Limit the privilege of inviting outside collaborators to organization owners or designated administrators. Only trusted individuals should have this authority.

  - **Team-Based Access:** Assign specific teams the responsibility to manage repository access. Team leaders can then invite collaborators on behalf of the team.

- **Authentication and Authorization**

  - **Two-Factor Authentication (2FA):** Encourage or enforce the use of two-factor authentication for all users, ensuring an additional layer of security.

  - **Access Permissions:** Clearly define the level of access external collaborators should have (read, write, admin). Assign permissions based on the specific needs of the collaboration.

  - **Approval Process:** Implement a workflow where users need to submit a request to invite an outside collaborator. This request should be reviewed and approved by designated personnel before access is granted.

- **Documentation and Training**

  - **Policy Documentation:** Clearly document the procedures for inviting outside collaborators, including who can approve requests and the criteria for approval.

- **User Training:** Educate users about the policy, including the importance of discretion when inviting external collaborators and potential security risks.

- **Regular Auditing and Review**

  - **Periodic Audits:** Regularly audit the list of outside collaborators across repositories. Remove any collaborators who no longer require access.

  - **Review Process:** Periodically review the access control policy to ensure it remains aligned with organizational security requirements.

- **Automated Tools and Integrations**

  - **GitHub Actions:** Use GitHub Actions to automate checks and notifications when new collaborators are added. Automate the validation process to ensure compliance with the policy.

  - **Third-Party Integrations:** Leverage third-party tools or GitHub integrations that provide additional access control and monitoring capabilities.

- **Integration with Identity Providers:** Integrate GitHub with your organization's identity provider for centralized user management. This integration ensures that only authorized users are allowed access.

- **Communication:** Maintain clear communication channels within the organization about the process for inviting outside collaborators. Encourage users to report any suspicious or unauthorized access attempts.

By enforcing these policies, organizations can maintain control over their repositories, prevent unauthorized access, and mitigate security risks associated with external collaborators. The specifics of policy enforcement may vary based on an organization's size, structure, and security requirements.

How to Enforce a Policy for Inviting Outside Collaborators to Repositories?

- **Access Enterprise Settings:**

  - Navigate to GitHub.com and click your profile photo in the top-right corner.

  - Select "Your enterprises" from the dropdown menu.

  - Choose the specific enterprise you want to manage.

- **Access Repository Policies:**

  - Within the enterprise account, locate the sidebar and click "Policies."

  - Under "Policies," find and click "Repositories."

- **Review Current Settings:**

  - In the "Repository outside collaborators" section, you'll find information about changing the settings.

  - Optionally, you can click "View your organizations' current configurations" to see the current setup for all organizations in the enterprise account.

- **Modify Repository Outside Collaborators Policy:**

  - Under "Repository outside collaborators," click the dropdown menu to reveal the available policies.

  - Choose the specific policy from the list by clicking it to apply the desired settings.

By following these steps, you can access and modify the policy for repository outside collaborators within the specified enterprise account on GitHub.

Enforcing a Policy for the Default Branch Name

Within your enterprise on GitHub, you have the capability to define the default branch name for every new repository initiated by members. You have the flexibility to either mandate this default branch name uniformly across all affiliated organizations or permit individual organizations to set their own preferences. This ensures consistency and aligns the default branch naming conventions across the enterprise's repositories. Here are the steps to enforce a policy for the default branch name:

- **Access Enterprise Settings:**

    - Go to GitHub.com and click your profile photo in the top-right corner.

    - Select "Your enterprises" from the dropdown menu.

    - Choose the specific enterprise you wish to configure.

- **Access Repository Policies:**

    - Inside the enterprise account, locate the sidebar and click "Policies."

    - Under "Policies," find and click "Repositories."

- **Set Default Branch Name:** In the "Default branch name" section, enter the desired default branch name that new repositories should utilize.

- **Optional – Enforce Default Branch Name Across the Enterprise:** If you want to enforce the default branch name for all organizations within the enterprise, select "Enforce across this enterprise."

- **Apply Changes:** Once you've configured the settings, click "Update" to save your changes.

By following these steps, you can specify and enforce the default branch name for new repositories across the entire enterprise on GitHub.

Enforcing a Policy for Changes to Repository Visibility

Enforcing a policy for changes to repository visibility refers to setting rules and regulations within an organization or enterprise on how repository visibility settings can be altered. This policy determines who has the authority to change the visibility of a repository, whether it's public, private, or internal. By enforcing this policy, organizations can maintain control over their data and ensure that sensitive information is not inadvertently exposed to the public.

For example, an organization might enforce a policy where only designated administrators or owners have the ability to change a repository's visibility. This ensures that changes to visibility settings are deliberate and comply with the organization's security and privacy standards. Enforcing such policies helps organizations maintain a secure and controlled environment for their repositories.

Enforcing a Policy for Repository Deletion and Transfer

Enforcing a policy for repository deletion and transfer involves setting specific rules and restrictions within an organization or enterprise regarding the removal or transfer of repositories. This policy outlines who has the authority to delete or transfer repositories, as well as the conditions under which such actions can be performed. By enforcing this policy, organizations can maintain control over their repositories, prevent data loss, and ensure that repository transfers are conducted securely and transparently.

For example, an organization might enforce a policy where repository deletion is restricted to designated administrators or owners to prevent accidental or unauthorized removal of important codebases. Similarly, the policy could specify conditions under which repository transfers are allowed, ensuring that ownership changes are documented and approved according to organizational protocols.

Enforcing a Policy for Deleting Issues

Enforcing a policy for deleting issues involves establishing rules and guidelines within a GitHub organization or repository that dictate who has the authority to delete issues and under what circumstances issues can be removed. Enforcing such a policy helps organizations maintain a structured approach to issue management, ensuring that issues are deleted responsibly and in accordance with established protocols. This helps prevent accidental or unauthorized removal of valuable information while promoting a secure and accountable environment for issue tracking.

For example, an organization might enforce a policy where only specific team members or administrators are allowed to delete issues to maintain data integrity. Alternatively, they could specify that issues can only be deleted if they contain sensitive information or violate community guidelines.

Minimize the Number of GitHub Organizations

Minimizing the number of GitHub organizations within an enterprise is often recommended for several practical reasons. Firstly, consolidating organizations helps streamline management and administration. With fewer organizations, it becomes more straightforward to oversee and maintain consistent policies, permissions, and configurations. This centralized approach facilitates better control over access, security, and compliance measures. Secondly, reducing the number of organizations promotes collaboration and knowledge sharing. Teams and individuals within the enterprise can benefit from a unified environment, making it easier to discover and contribute to relevant projects. This cohesion fosters a sense of community and enhances cross-team collaboration.

Furthermore, consolidating organizations simplifies the implementation of organization-wide policies. It becomes more efficient to enforce and manage policies uniformly across a smaller number of organizations, ensuring consistent security practices, compliance standards, and development workflows.

Another consideration is cost optimization. GitHub pricing is often based on the number of users and private repositories within an organization. By minimizing the number of organizations, enterprises can potentially reduce licensing costs, making resource allocation more efficient.

In summary, minimizing the number of GitHub organizations within an enterprise streamlines administration, encourages collaboration, facilitates policy enforcement, and can lead to cost savings. It's a strategic approach that aligns with effective organizational management and enhances the overall efficiency of the development and collaboration processes on the GitHub platform. Let's now explore some recommended best practices for organizing GitHub Enterprise organizations.

Best Practices for Organizing GitHub Enterprise Organizations

Establishing effective organizational structures within a GitHub Enterprise environment involves adopting best practices that contribute to streamlined workflows and enhanced collaboration. First and foremost, consider creating a clear hierarchy of organizations that mirrors the organizational structure of your enterprise. This hierarchy ensures that repositories are logically organized, making it easier for teams to locate and collaborate on projects. Another key practice is to implement consistent naming conventions for organizations and repositories. This fosters clarity and standardization, aiding in the quick identification of projects and promoting a cohesive development environment. Additionally, leverage teams within organizations to group users with similar responsibilities, facilitating efficient access management and code review processes. Encourage the use of README files and documentation to provide essential information about each repository, enhancing visibility and onboarding for new contributors. Regularly review and update access permissions to maintain security, ensuring that users have appropriate levels of access based on their roles. Lastly, consider implementing cross-organization collaboration by using features like cross-repository teams, enabling seamless cooperation between teams in different organizations. These practices collectively contribute to a well-organized, secure, and collaborative GitHub Enterprise environment tailored to the specific needs of your enterprise.

About Organizational Number

In general, GitHub advises against creating an excessive number of organizations. Encouraging collaboration and inner sourcing is more feasible with fewer organizations, contributing to increased efficiency. Many businesses find that a single organization serves them best due to several reasons. Firstly, locating resources is simpler within a single organization as there is a unified search space. Communication is streamlined within a single organization, as @-mentions only function among members of the same organization. The cohesion and collaboration fostered within a single, expansive organization contribute to a sense of loyalty, whereas fragmentation into smaller organizations may lead to teams feeling isolated. While organization owners inherently have access to all organization-owned repositories, in larger companies, it might be prudent to consider multiple organizations if no single owner should have access to all repositories.

The primary advantage of creating multiple organizations lies in the ability to configure distinct policies, settings, and requirements for each. For instance, each organization can have its unique SAML configuration. However, it's advised against establishing a one-to-one relationship between organizations and structural entities like individual teams or business units. Instead, grouping entities that can share policies into a single organization maximizes collaboration while still meeting regulatory requirements.

Starting with a small number of organizations provides flexibility in the future. Adding organizations is easier than removing them, as removal often involves migrations and a reduction in the flexibility teams have grown accustomed to. Many customers regret creating numerous organizations after facing the challenging and time-consuming process of reducing their number. Establishing fixed and transparent rules for creating new organizations within your enterprise is recommended. This approach enhances understanding regarding the purpose of each organization and the location of assets, contributing to a more organized and efficient structure.

About Organizational Structure

There are five primary archetypes for organizational structure, characterized by two key decisions:

- The choice between using a single organization or multiple organizations

- The decision on whether to provide all members with access to every repository or to employ teams for more granular management of repository access

Single Organization with Direct Repository Access

A single organization with direct repository access is an organizational structure where all members within the organization have direct access to every repository. In this archetype, there is no intermediate layer, such as teams, managing repository access. Each member of the organization has the same level of access to all repositories, simplifying the access management structure. While straightforward, this approach may be less suitable for larger organizations with complex access requirements or the need to implement more fine-grained permissions.

Single Organization with Teams for Repository Access

In a single organization with teams for repository access, all members belong to the same overarching organization, but access to repositories is managed through the use of teams. Instead of granting direct access to every repository for all members, teams are created within the organization, and members are assigned to specific teams based on their roles or responsibilities. Each team is then granted access to specific repositories, allowing for more granular control over who can contribute to and access particular codebases. This structure is beneficial for larger organizations or projects with diverse access requirements, as it provides a hierarchical and organized way to manage repository access permissions.

Multiple Organizations with Direct Repository Access

In the context of multiple organizations with direct repository access, this organizational structure involves the creation of distinct organizations, and members within each organization have direct access to the repositories associated with that organization. Each organization operates independently, and there is no shared access to repositories across organizations. This approach is useful when different teams or departments within an enterprise require autonomy over their repositories, and there is no need for a centralized structure to manage repository access. While it provides isolation and independence for each organization, it may lead to challenges in terms of visibility and collaboration across organizational boundaries.

Multiple Organizations with Teams for Repository Access

In a scenario of multiple organizations with teams for repository access, an organizational structure is established where distinct organizations exist, and access to repositories is managed through the implementation of teams within each organization. Instead of granting direct access to all repositories for every member within an organization, teams are created, and members are assigned to specific teams based on their roles or responsibilities. Each team is then given access to particular repositories within the organization, allowing for a more nuanced control over repository access. This approach is beneficial for larger enterprises or projects with diverse access requirements, as it maintains the autonomy of separate organizations while providing a structured and organized means to manage repository access through teams.

Multiple Organizations with Different Access Methods

In the context of multiple organizations with different access methods, this organizational structure involves the creation of distinct organizations, each employing varied approaches to managing repository access. Each organization may choose a different access method, such as direct repository access for its members or the use of teams for more granular access control. This flexible model allows organizations within an enterprise to adopt access methods that align with their specific needs and preferences. It accommodates diverse access requirements, enabling autonomy and customization at the organization level. However, it may introduce complexity in terms of coordinating access methods across the enterprise and requires clear communication and documentation of the chosen access approaches within each organization.

Minimize Collaborative Efforts Within User-Owned Repositories

It is strongly advised to prioritize collaboration within organization-owned repositories whenever feasible and to limit collaborative efforts in user-owned repositories. Organization-owned repositories offer advanced security and administrative features, providing a more robust and controlled environment for collaborative work. Additionally, these repositories remain accessible even when there are changes in enterprise membership, ensuring continuity and consistency in the development process. By centralizing collaboration in organization-owned repositories, teams can take full advantage of the enhanced capabilities and long-term stability offered by this structured and secure environment.

Opt for Easily Understandable and Human-Readable Usernames

When managing usernames for enterprise members, opt for human-readable usernames rather than machine-generated IDs that may be challenging for humans to interpret. This choice enhances user-friendliness and simplifies identification. Additionally, you have the capability to oversee the display of usernames within your enterprise's private repositories, allowing for a customized and user-centric experience. This practice not only improves clarity but also contributes to a more accessible and comprehensible environment for collaboration within your enterprise.

Summary

The GitHub administrator's guide commenced with an exploration of GitHub Enterprise, emphasizing a comprehensive understanding of its unique features and distinctions from the standard GitHub platform. This initial exploration established a foundational overview, providing a context for the subsequent chapters. As administrators progress, the chapter delved into the intricacies of setting up a GitHub Enterprise instance, offering detailed insights into configuration steps, hardware and software requirements, installation procedures, and initial setup considerations. The focus then shifted to user management and access control, covering the entire lifecycle of user accounts, from creation to suspension and deletion. This chapter went on to explore the implementation of role-based access control, the formation of teams, and the management of permissions to facilitate collaborative development.

The repository management segment introduced administrators to best practices for creating and managing repositories within the GitHub Enterprise environment. It addressed repository settings, branch protection rules, and effective organizational structuring strategies. Subsequently, the chapter delved into security and compliance considerations, highlighting features such as two-factor authentication, SAML Single Sign-On, and audit logs. Special attention was given to GitHub Enterprise's role in meeting regulatory compliance standards. Integration with CI/CD pipelines was the next focus, providing administrators with insights into how GitHub Enterprise seamlessly integrates with continuous integration and continuous deployment tools. The chapter included examples and best practices for automating software delivery pipelines.

Crucial for administrators, this chapter provided backup and disaster recovery guidelines, covering aspects such as data backup, disaster recovery strategies, backup tools, frequency, and the maintenance of data integrity. Following this, the chapter explored monitoring tools and performance tuning techniques to ensure the health and optimal performance of GitHub Enterprise instances across various workloads. Advanced features and customization options, including GitHub Actions, GitHub Packages, and the utilization of the GitHub API for custom integrations and automation, were also discussed.

Troubleshooting and support constituted a critical aspect of the chapter, offering insights into common GitHub Enterprise issues and effective troubleshooting methods. Additionally, guidance on accessing and utilizing GitHub's support resources was provided. Best practices for managing large-scale GitHub organizations were then discussed, encompassing strategic advice on governance, policy enforcement, and the cultivation of a collaborative culture. Real-world examples and case studies were incorporated to illustrate successful GitHub Enterprise deployments and management strategies. Finally, the chapter looked forward, keeping administrators informed about future trends, upcoming features, and strategies to stay updated with the latest developments in GitHub Enterprise.

Resources

- About GitHub for enterprises: `https://docs.github.com/en/enterprise-cloud@latest/admin/overview/about-github-for-enterprises`

- Best practices for enterprises: `https://docs.github.com/en/enterprise-cloud@latest/admin/overview/best-practices-for-enterprises`

- Known issues with backups for your instance: `https://docs.github.com/en/enterprise-server@3.8/admin/backing-up-and-restoring-your-instance/known-issues-with-backups-for-your-instance`

- Customer stories: `https://github.com/customer-stories/all`

- About Identity and Access Management: `https://docs.github.com/en/enterprise-cloud@latest/admin/identity-and-access-management/understanding-iam-for-enterprises/about-identity-and-access-management`

- Access roles in an enterprise: `https://docs.github.com/en/enterprise-cloud@latest/admin/managing-accounts-and-repositories/managing-users-in-your-enterprise/roles-in-an-enterprise`

- Best practices for structuring organizations in your enterprise: `https://docs.github.com/en/enterprise-cloud@latest/admin/managing-accounts-and-repositories/managing-organizations-in-your-enterprise/best-practices-for-structuring-organizations-in-your-enterprise`

- About the audit log for your enterprise: `https://docs.github.com/en/enterprise-cloud@latest/admin/monitoring-activity-in-your-enterprise/reviewing-audit-logs-for-your-enterprise/about-the-audit-log-for-your-enterprise`

- Access permissions on GitHub: `https://docs.github.com/en/enterprise-cloud@latest/get-started/learning-about-github/access-permissions-on-github`

- About the REST API: https://docs.github.com/en/
  rest/about-the-rest-api/about-the-rest-api?apiV
  ersion=2022-11-28

- Best practices for using the REST API: https://docs.
  github.com/en/rest/using-the-rest-api/best-
  practices-for-using-the-rest-api?apiVersi
  on=2022-11-28

- GitHub Actions: https://docs.github.com/en/
  enterprise-cloud@latest/admin/github-actions

- About enterprise policies: https://docs.github.
  com/en/enterprise-cloud@latest/admin/policies/
  enforcing-policies-for-your-enterprise/about-
  enterprise-policies

- Managing accounts and repositories: https://docs.
  github.com/en/enterprise-cloud@latest/admin/
  managing-accounts-and-repositories

- Accessing the administrative shell (SSH): https://
  docs.github.com/en/enterprise-server@3.11/
  admin/configuration/configuring-your-
  enterprise/accessing-the-administrative-
  shell-ssh

- Upgrading GitHub Enterprise Server: https://docs.
  github.com/en/enterprise-server@3.11/admin/
  enterprise-management/updating-the-virtual-
  machine-and-physical-resources/upgrading-
  github-enterprise-server#taking-a-snapshot

CHAPTER 7

GitHub Copilot Management

This chapter delves into GitHub Copilot, an AI-powered coding assistant that helps developers write code more efficiently. It provides a thorough understanding of the tool, how to use it effectively, and its best practices.

Topics covered in this chapter include

- Introduction to GitHub Copilot

- GitHub Copilot Plan and Licensing

- Setting Up and Using GitHub Copilot

- Understanding the Capabilities of GitHub Copilot

- Copilot for Different Programming Languages and Frameworks

- Best Practices for Using GitHub Copilot

Introduction to GitHub Copilot

GitHub Copilot is a groundbreaking code assistance tool developed by GitHub in collaboration with OpenAI. It is designed to significantly enhance coding experience by using machine learning and artificial

© Balu Nivrutti Ilag, AjayKumar P. Baljoshi, Ganesh J. Sangale and Yogesh Athave 2024
B. N. Ilag et al., *Mastering GitHub Enterprise Management and Administration*,
https://doi.org/10.1007/979-8-8688-0369-7_7

intelligence (AI) to assist developers in writing code more efficiently and effectively. In this chapter, we will delve into the intricacies of GitHub Copilot, exploring what it is, how it functions, and the various benefits it offers to developers and development teams.

What Is GitHub Copilot?

GitHub Copilot revolutionizes the coding experience by serving as an AI-powered ally embedded within familiar coding environments like Visual Studio Code. Unlike conventional tools that offer auto-completion and syntax checks, Copilot takes a leap by generating entire code blocks, presenting code snippets, and offering real-time coding aid. Its versatility spans multiple programming languages and frameworks, catering to an extensive array of development needs.

Trained comprehensively in languages found in public repositories, Copilot suggestions' effectiveness may vary based on the breadth and depth of available training data for a particular language. For instance, JavaScript, abundant in public repositories, stands as one of Copilot's most robustly supported languages. Conversely, languages with limited representation in these repositories might yield fewer or less refined suggestions.

The extension for GitHub Copilot is accessible across a suite of coding platforms including Visual Studio Code, Visual Studio, Vim, Neovim, JetBrains' suite of IDEs, and Azure Data Studio.

How Does GitHub Copilot Work?

GitHub Copilot relies on a powerful AI model that has been trained on a vast dataset of publicly available code repositories. This model leverages machine learning techniques, including deep learning and natural language processing, to understand and predict the context of your code. As you type, Copilot analyzes your code in real time, identifies patterns, and offers relevant code suggestions. It can generate code for a variety of purposes, such as defining functions, writing conditionals, and even creating complex data structures.

The key to Copilot's effectiveness lies in its ability to understand not only the programming syntax but also the intent behind your code. It can interpret comments, documentation, and even natural language descriptions in your code comments, allowing it to provide contextually relevant suggestions. For instance, if you write a comment describing the functionality you want, Copilot can generate the corresponding code based on that description.

Benefits of GitHub Copilot

GitHub Copilot offers several compelling benefits to developers and development teams:

- **Increased Productivity:** Copilot significantly accelerates the coding process by automating repetitive tasks and providing instant code suggestions. This allows developers to write code faster and more efficiently.

- **Improved Code Quality:** With Copilot's assistance, developers can reduce the likelihood of introducing bugs and errors in their code. The tool helps maintain consistent coding standards and practices.

- **Learning Aid:** Copilot serves as a valuable learning tool for both novice and experienced developers. It provides insights into best practices, coding patterns, and language-specific conventions, helping developers improve their skills.

- **Code Consistency:** Copilot promotes code consistency within a project by suggesting code that aligns with the existing codebase. This is particularly valuable for collaborative development efforts.

- **Reduced Cognitive Load:** Developers can offload some cognitive burden onto Copilot, allowing them to focus more on solving complex problems and architecting software solutions.

- **Cross-Language Support:** Copilot supports multiple programming languages and frameworks, making it versatile for a variety of development tasks, from web development to data science.

In conclusion, GitHub Copilot is a powerful tool that leverages AI and machine learning to assist developers in writing code more efficiently and effectively. By understanding context and providing relevant suggestions, Copilot enhances productivity, code quality, and collaboration within development teams. In the subsequent sections, we will explore Copilot's features in greater detail and learn how to make the most of this innovative coding assistant.

GitHub Copilot Plan and Licensing

GitHub Copilot is available under different plans, including business and enterprises. The paid plans could offer additional features, higher usage limits, or other benefits compared to the free version. Specific details about the plans, such as pricing, usage limits, and included features, would be available on the GitHub Copilot plans page.

Integrating Copilot into Your Coding Workflow

- **Pricing:** $19 per user/month.

- **Code Completions:** Enhance your coding efficiency with intelligent code suggestions.

- **Chat in IDE and Mobile:** Communicate and collaborate directly within your integrated development environment and on mobile devices.

- **CLI Assistance:** Get command-line interface support for streamlined operations.

- **Security Vulnerability Filter:** Automatically filter out code that may introduce security vulnerabilities.

- **Code Referencing:** Easily reference and integrate existing code snippets.

- **Public Code Filter:** Filter suggestions from public code repositories for unique code generation.

- **IP Indemnity:** Protect your intellectual property with indemnification coverage.

- **Enterprise-Grade Security, Safety, and Privacy:** Ensure the highest standards of security and privacy in your coding environment.

- **Availability:** Came out in 2022.

GitHub Copilot for Enterprise
Tailoring Copilot to Your Organization's Needs Throughout the Software Development Lifecycle

- **Pricing:** $39 per user/month.

- Includes Everything in Copilot Business.

- **Chat Personalized to Your Codebase:** Get chat support that's customized to your specific codebase.

- **Documentation Search and Summaries:** Quickly search and summarize technical documentation for efficient reference.

- **Pull Request Summaries:** Simplify code reviews with concise summaries of pull requests.

- **Code Review Skills:** Enhance code quality with advanced code review capabilities.

- **Fine-Tuned Models:** Benefit from models that are finely tuned to your organization's coding practices and requirements.

- **Requirement:** Requires GitHub Enterprise Cloud subscription.

Figure 7-1. *Copilot plan*

Setting Up and Using GitHub Copilot

GitHub Copilot is compatible with various editors, including Azure Data Studio, JetBrains IDEs, Vim/Neovim, Visual Studio, and Visual Studio Code. Let's take a closer look at an example using Visual Studio Code (VS Code), a popular and versatile code editor that seamlessly integrates with GitHub Copilot. VS Code is preferred for its user-friendly interface and seamless integration. Supporting a wide range of programming languages, it offers versatility for developers. The active community and extensive library of extensions enhance the development experience. With built-in version control and cross-platform compatibility, developers can efficiently manage GitHub repositories. The performance and responsiveness of VS Code complement GitHub Copilot, providing a smooth coding experience.

Installing GitHub Copilot Extension in Visual Studio Code

Let's walk through the process of adding the GitHub Copilot extension to Visual Studio Code. It's straightforward:

1. **Find GitHub Copilot in the Visual Studio Code Marketplace**

    - Go to the GitHub Copilot extension page in the Visual Studio Code Marketplace (`https://marketplace.visualstudio.com/items?itemName=GitHub.copilot`).

    - Click the "Install" button.

2. **Open Visual Studio Code**

    - A pop-up will show up, asking you to open Visual Studio Code. Click "Open Visual Studio Code."

3. **Install GitHub Copilot**

- Inside Visual Studio Code, go to the "Extension: GitHub Copilot" tab.

- Click the "Install" button.

4. **Authorize Visual Studio Code**

- If you haven't authorized Visual Studio Code in your GitHub account before, you might be prompted to sign in to GitHub within Visual Studio Code.

5. **Automatic Authorization (If Already Authorized)**

- If you've already authorized Visual Studio Code for your GitHub account, GitHub Copilot will be automatically authorized.

6. **Authorize Manually (If Not Prompted)**

- If you don't see the authorization prompt, click the bell icon in the bottom panel of the Visual Studio Code window.

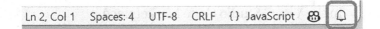

Figure 7-2. Bell icon in Visual Studio Code

7. **Web Authorization**

- Your browser will open, and GitHub will request the necessary permissions for GitHub Copilot.

- Click "Authorize Visual Studio Code" to approve these permissions.

8. **Confirm Authentication**

- Back in Visual Studio Code, in the "Visual Studio Code" dialog box, click "Open."

And there you have it! GitHub Copilot is now integrated into your Visual Studio Code, ready to assist you as you code.

Understanding the Capabilities of GitHub Copilot

Exploring Your First GitHub Copilot Suggestion

Before we begin, a quick heads-up: If you've enabled duplication detection in GitHub Copilot, you might get fewer or no suggestions when using provided code examples. Alternatively, try typing your own code to see GitHub Copilot's suggestions. To learn more about duplication detection, check out "Configuring GitHub Copilot settings on GitHub.com" in the GitHub documentation.

GitHub Copilot is versatile, offering suggestions for many languages and frameworks. It shines particularly well with Python, JavaScript, TypeScript, Ruby, Go, C#, and C++. Additionally, it can help with generating queries for databases.

Let's get started in Visual Studio Code by creating a new test (*.js) file.

In this test file, type the function header as shown in Figure 7-3.

```
JS test.js    2  ●

C: > Users > yogesh > JS test.js > ⊕ createLinkedList
  1  function createLinkedList(arr) {
         let head = new ListNode(arr[0]);
         let node = head;
         for (let i = 1; i < arr.length; i++) {
             node.next = new ListNode(arr[i]);
             node = node.next;
         }
         return head;
     }
```

Figure 7-3. Offering suggestion for the createLinkedList function

GitHub Copilot will jump in and suggest the entire function body in grayed text, just like this. Keep in mind that the exact suggestion may vary.

To accept the suggestion, simply press the "Tab" key.

Important Note   If you don't see any suggestions, make sure GitHub Copilot is enabled. Look for the Copilot icon at the bottom right of your Visual Studio Code window.

If a file has been set to exclude content for GitHub Copilot, the icon in the status bar will have a diagonal line through it. Hover over the icon to see a tooltip explaining which settings are restricting suggestions.

Figure 7-4 shows a snapshot of the Copilot icon in VS Code with a tooltip indicating content exclusion.

Figure 7-4. *Github Copilot icon disabled in the status bar*

Setting Rules for GitHub Copilot to Ignore Some Files

You have the power to tell GitHub Copilot which files to ignore when suggesting code. This helps you focus on the files that matter most. If you don't want Copilot to provide suggestions from specific files, you can easily configure these exclusions. This ensures that Copilot won't interfere with certain files, giving you control over your coding environment.

Who Can Use This Feature?

This feature is available to repository administrators and organization owners with a Copilot Business subscription. Those with a "Maintain" role can view exclusion settings but cannot modify them.

Important Information

This feature is exclusive to organizations with a Copilot Business subscription. Please note that excluding content is currently in public beta.

How to Configure Content Exclusions

You may want to exclude certain files from Copilot's suggestions. This can be done by specifying paths to exclude content in the settings for your repository or organization.

- The excluded content won't be used for suggestions in other files.

- Copilot suggestions won't be available in the excluded files.

Changes to exclusions may take up to 30 minutes to take effect in IDEs where settings are already loaded. You can force changes in your IDE by reloading content exclusion settings.

Limitations

- Excluding content currently only affects code completion, not Copilot Chat.

- Content exclusion doesn't prevent Copilot from deriving information from excluded files indirectly.

What Can You Exclude?

When specifying content exclusion in repository settings, you can only exclude files within that repository. For organization settings, you can exclude files in any Git-based repository accessible through specific syntaxes.

Reviewing and Propagating Changes

Organization owners can review changes to content exclusions in the "Audit log" page. To check the effect of settings changes, open a file in the editor and start typing. The Copilot icon in supported IDEs indicates if Copilot is disabled by content exclusion.

How to Configure Exclusions

For repositories

- Go to your repository settings on GitHub.com.

- Navigate to "Code & automation" ➤ "Copilot."

- Under "Paths to exclude in this repository," enter paths to files for exclusion.

For organizations

- On GitHub.com, go to your profile photo ➤ "Your organizations."

- Select your organization and navigate to "Copilot" ➤ "Content exclusion."

- Under "Repositories and paths to exclude," enter details for exclusion.

Exploring Different Ideas with GitHub Copilot

GitHub Copilot isn't just a one-trick pony – it often gives you multiple suggestions for a given input. Here's how you can check them out:

1. Open Visual Studio Code and create a new test (*.js) file.

2. In test.js file, type the function header as shown in Figure 7-3.

   GitHub Copilot will jump in with a suggestion.

3. Now, if you want to explore alternative ideas, here's how you can do it based on your operating system:

   - **macOS:** Use Option Alt+] to see the next suggestion, and Option Alt+[to see the previous suggestion.

   - **Windows:** Press Alt+] to see the next suggestion, and Alt+[to see the previous suggestion.

   - **Linux:** Press Alt+] to see the next suggestion, and Alt+[to see the previous suggestion.

Alternatively, you can hover over the suggestion to bring up the GitHub Copilot command palette, giving you more options.

To accept a suggestion, just press "Tab." If you want to say no to all suggestions, hit "Esc." It's your call!

Shortcut Keys to Enhance Your GitHub Copilot Experience

Using GitHub Copilot with Visual Studio Code is flexible. You have the option to stick with the default keyboard shortcuts or customize them to match your preferences. If you want to change the shortcuts, it's easy to do so in the Keyboard Shortcuts editor. This way, you can use the commands in a way that feels most comfortable for you.

Shortcuts for Windows: Boosting Your Efficiency in Visual Studio Code

You can access the keyboard shortcuts by navigating to "File" ➤ "Preferences" ➤ "Settings" ➤ "Keyboard Shortcuts."

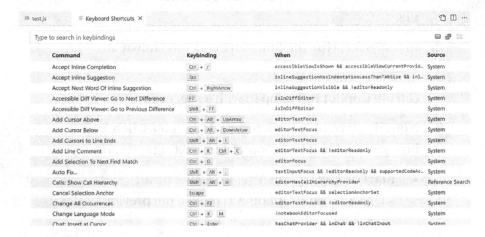

Figure 7-5. *Keyboard shortcuts*

Rebinding Keyboard Shortcuts

If you prefer different keyboard shortcuts than the default ones in Visual Studio Code for GitHub Copilot, you have the option to customize them. Use the Keyboard Shortcuts editor to assign your preferred shortcuts for specific commands.

To modify keyboard shortcuts on Windows, follow these steps:

- Click the File menu, then select Preferences, and finally, click Keyboard Shortcuts.

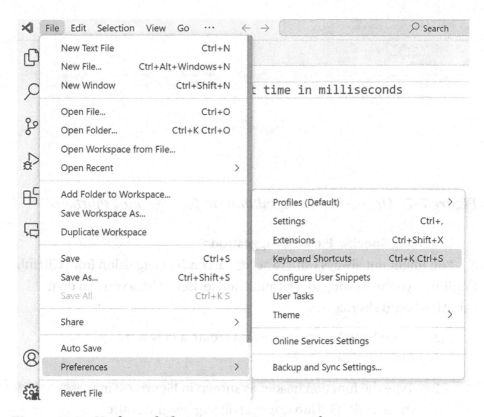

Figure 7-6. Keyboard Shortcuts option in preferences

- In the Keyboard Shortcuts editor, find the command name associated with the keyboard shortcut you wish to alter.

- Next to the command you want to adjust, click the pencil icon.

- Enter the keystrokes you desire for the command, and then press Enter/Return.

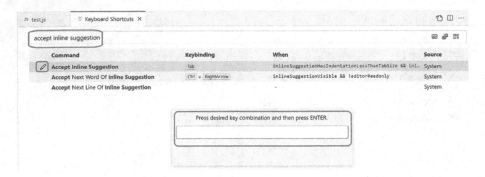

Figure 7-7. Use desired key combination for keyboard shortcuts

Choosing Specific Parts of Suggestions

You might not always want to accept an entire suggestion from GitHub Copilot. If you're looking to pick and choose, here's how you can do it using keyboard shortcuts:

1. Open Visual Studio Code and create a new test (*.js) file.

2. Type the function header as shown in Figure 7-3 in the test file. GitHub Copilot will suggest the entire function body in grayed text.

   Please note that the exact suggestion may vary.

3. Now, if you only want to accept the next word of the suggestion, use one of these keyboard shortcuts based on your operating system:

   • **macOS:** Command + →

   • **Windows:** Control + →

   • **Linux:** Control + →

4. If you prefer to accept the next line of the suggestion, you'll need to set a custom keyboard shortcut for the command "editor.action.inlineSuggest. acceptNextLine." For guidance on custom keyboard shortcuts, check out "Configuring GitHub Copilot in your environment" in the GitHub documentation.

Alternatively, you can hover over the suggestion to reveal the GitHub Copilot command palette, providing more options for choosing specific parts of the suggestions.

Exploring More Options with GitHub Copilot in a New Tab

If you're not thrilled with the initial suggestions from GitHub Copilot, no worries! You can ask GitHub Copilot to give you more options in a new tab using a simple keyboard shortcut.

Here's what you need to do:

1. Open Visual Studio Code and create a new test (*.js) file.

2. Type the function header as shown in Figure 7-3 in the test file. GitHub Copilot will provide you with a suggestion.

3. Now, to open a new tab with several additional options, press Ctrl+Enter.

```
JS test.js   2 ●                                    □ ···   JS GitHub Copilot Suggestions for test.js 4 ×
C: > Users > yogesh > JS test.js > ⊕ createLinkedList              1   Synthesizing 10/10 solutions (Duplicates
 1   function createLinkedList(arr) {          — 1    2
       let head = new ListNode(arr[0]);
       let node = head;                               Accept Solution
       for (let i = 1; i < arr.length; i++) {    3   ========
         node.next = new ListNode(arr[i]);       4   Suggestion 1
         node = node.next;                       5
       }                                         6   function createLinkedList(array) {
       return head;                              7     const linkedList = new LinkedList();
     }                                           8     array.forEach(item => linkedList.appen
                                                 9     return linkedList;
                                                10   }
                                                11
                                                     Accept Solution
                                                12   =======
                                                13   Suggestion 2
                                                14
                                                15   function createLinkedList() {
                                                16     const linkedList = new LinkedList();
                                                17     linkedList.append(1);
                                                18     linkedList.append(2);
```

Figure 7-8. Offering multiple suggestions in a new tab

4. If you find a suggestion you like, just click "Accept Solution" above the suggestion. If none of them work for you, simply close the tab to reject all suggestions.

That's it! You've got a new tab full of possibilities to choose from with GitHub Copilot.

Receiving Code Recommendations Through Comments

Here's a cool trick: you can tell GitHub Copilot what you want to do in plain English within a comment, and it will offer suggestions on how to write the code.

Let's try it out in Visual Studio Code:

1. Open Visual Studio Code and create a new test (*.js) file.

2. Type the comment as shown in Figure 7-9 in the test file. GitHub Copilot will then suggest an implementation of the function.

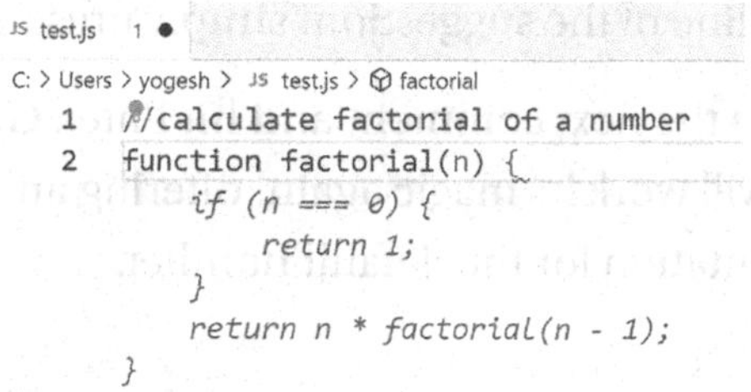

```
JS test.js  1 ●
C: > Users > yogesh > JS test.js > 𝔐 factorial
  1   //calculate factorial of a number
  2   function factorial(n) {
          if (n === 0) {
              return 1;
          }
          return n * factorial(n - 1);
      }
```

Figure 7-9. *Receiving suggestions from a comment*

That's it! You've just used a comment to communicate your intention, and GitHub Copilot has smartly suggested the code to achieve your goal.

Leveraging GitHub Copilot with Frameworks

What are the benefits of leveraging GitHub Copilot with frameworks?

Here's another neat trick with GitHub Copilot – you can use it to come up with suggestions for APIs and frameworks. In this example, we'll use GitHub Copilot to effortlessly create a basic Express server that gives back the current time.

Let's walk through it in Visual Studio Code:

1. Open Visual Studio Code and create a new test (*.js) file.

2. In that test file, type the comment as shown in Figure 7-10 and hit Enter. GitHub Copilot will then propose a ready-made implementation for your Express app.

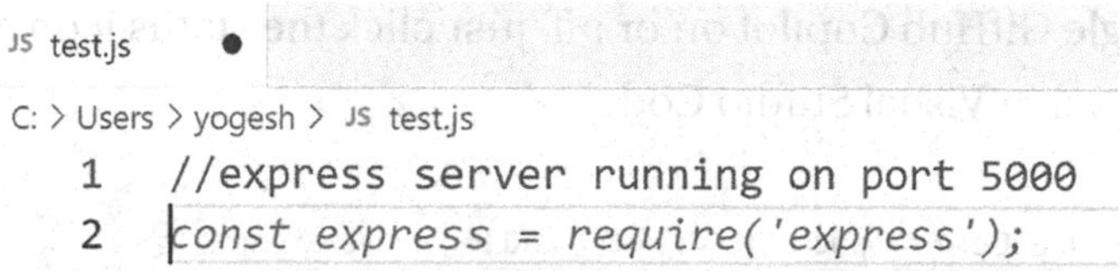

```
JS test.js     ●
C: > Users > yogesh > JS test.js
  1   //express server running on port 5000
  2   const express = require('express');
```

Figure 7-10. *Receiving ready-made implementation*

To accept each line of the suggestion, simply press Tab and then Enter.

3. Now, type the next comment and hit Enter. GitHub
Copilot will work its magic again, offering an
implementation for the default handler.

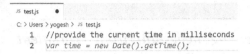

Figure 7-11. *Offering an implementation for the default handler*

To accept each line of this suggestion, just press Tab.

There you have it! GitHub Copilot has effortlessly helped you set up a basic Express server that returns the current time. Easy as pie, right?

Turning GitHub Copilot On or Off

Why you need to turn on and off github copilot?

Enabling or disabling GitHub Copilot in Visual Studio Code is a breeze. Keep an eye on the GitHub Copilot status icon at the bottom panel of your Visual Studio Code window – it tells you if GitHub Copilot is currently active or not.

- When it's turned on, the icon's background color matches the status bar.

- When turned off, the icon's background color stands out from the status bar.

To toggle GitHub Copilot on or off, just click the status icon at the bottom panel in Visual Studio Code.

Figure 7-12. *Visual Studio Code screenshot with the GitHub Copilot icon highlighted in dark orange*

If you decide to turn off GitHub Copilot, you'll be prompted to choose whether you want to disable suggestions globally (for all languages) or just for the specific language of the file you're currently working on.

- If you want to disable suggestions from GitHub Copilot everywhere, click "Disable Completions."

- If you only want to disable suggestions for the language of your current file, click "Disable for LANGUAGE."

Figure 7-13. *Screenshot displaying the option to disable GitHub Copilot either globally or for the current language*

Copilot for Different Programming Languages and Frameworks

GitHub Copilot is an incredibly versatile coding assistant that can be used across a wide range of programming languages and frameworks. In this chapter, we will explore how Copilot adapts to various programming ecosystems, demonstrating its versatility and ability to assist in diverse coding scenarios.

1. **Multi-language Support**

   Copilot supports numerous programming languages, making it accessible to developers in various domains. Some of the prominent languages supported include

   - **JavaScript and TypeScript:** Copilot can assist with web development, including front-end and back-end JavaScript and TypeScript code. It can generate React components, Node.js server code, and much more.

   - **Python:** Copilot is adept at generating Python code for tasks like data analysis, machine learning, web development with Django or Flask, and automation scripts.

   - **Java:** Copilot can assist with Java development, including Android app development, enterprise applications, and back-end services.

   - **C++:** Copilot is proficient in generating C++ code, suitable for systems programming, game development, and high-performance computing tasks.

   - **Go:** Developers working with the Go programming language can benefit from Copilot's assistance in writing efficient, concurrent code.

   - **Ruby:** Copilot supports Ruby, making it valuable for web development, automation, and scripting tasks.

   - **C# and .NET:** Copilot can generate C# code, which is commonly used for Windows applications, game development, and web services using .NET.

- **PHP:** Copilot can assist with PHP development for web applications and server-side scripting.

- **Swift:** Swift developers can utilize Copilot for iOS and macOS app development.

These are just a few examples, and Copilot supports many more languages, ensuring its usefulness across a wide spectrum of programming domains.

2. **Frameworks and Libraries**

In addition to supporting different programming languages, Copilot can also assist with various frameworks, libraries, and platforms:

- **Web Development:** Copilot can help with popular web development frameworks like React, Angular, Vue.js, Django, Ruby on Rails, Express.js, and more. It can generate code for components, routes, and database interactions.

- **Machine Learning and Data Science:** Copilot can assist data scientists and machine learning engineers by generating Python code for tasks such as data preprocessing, model training, and evaluation.

- **Mobile App Development:** For mobile app development, Copilot supports Android (Java/Kotlin) and iOS (Swift/Objective-C). It can generate code for UI components, navigation, and app logic.

- **Game Development:** Copilot can generate code for game engines like Unity (C#) and Unreal Engine (C++), helping game developers create game mechanics and features.

- **Cloud Services:** Whether you're using Amazon Web Services (AWS), Microsoft Azure, or Google Cloud Platform (GCP), Copilot can assist in generating code for cloud infrastructure and services.

3. **Project-Specific Patterns**

   Copilot's ability to learn from your coding style extends to project-specific patterns and conventions. It adapts to your coding standards, making it an asset for maintaining consistency within a development team, regardless of the language or framework you're using.

4. **Cross-Language Integration**

   Copilot's cross-language support is particularly beneficial when working on projects that require multiple programming languages. It can assist in generating code that integrates seamlessly between different parts of your project.

In conclusion, GitHub Copilot is a remarkably versatile tool that adapts to different programming languages, frameworks, and development scenarios. Its multi-language support, familiarity with various libraries, and adaptability to project-specific patterns make it an invaluable asset for developers in diverse domains. Whether you're building web applications, mobile apps, or games or working on machine learning projects, Copilot can significantly enhance your coding experience and productivity, regardless of the technology stack you choose to use.

Best Practices for Using GitHub Copilot

GitHub Copilot is a powerful tool that can significantly enhance your coding experience. However, it's essential to use it judiciously and in conjunction with your developer skills. This chapter outlines best practices for leveraging Copilot effectively while maintaining code quality and developer discretion.

1. **Complement, Don't Replace**

   GitHub Copilot is a coding assistant, not a replacement for a developer's judgment. It can assist you in writing code faster and more efficiently, but it should not be relied upon blindly. Always review Copilot-generated code to ensure it aligns with your project's requirements, coding standards, and best practices.

2. **Understand the Code It Generates**

   Take the time to understand the code generated by Copilot. This is crucial for debugging, maintenance, and ensuring that the code aligns with your project's logic and design. If you encounter code that you don't fully grasp, research and learn from it to improve your skills.

3. **Use Descriptive Comments**

   When writing comments, be descriptive about the functionality you intend to implement. Copilot can understand and generate code based on your comments, so clear and detailed comments can lead to more accurate code suggestions.

4. **Regularly Review Code Suggestions**

   Copilot provides code suggestions in real time as
   you type. Review these suggestions carefully before
   accepting them. Ensure that they are relevant to
   your current coding task and that they follow your
   project's coding standards.

5. **Customize Copilot to Your Needs**

   GitHub Copilot allows you to customize its behavior
   to match your coding style and preferences. Explore
   the settings in your code editor to fine-tune Copilot's
   suggestions and code style.

6. **Don't Blindly Accept Suggestions**

   While Copilot can generate code quickly, it's
   important not to blindly accept its suggestions
   without understanding the context. Ensure that the
   code aligns with your project's architecture and
   requirements.

7. **Keep Learning**

   Use Copilot as a learning tool. It can provide
   valuable insights into coding best practices,
   patterns, and language-specific conventions.
   Continuously seek to improve your coding skills by
   learning from Copilot-generated code.

8. **Maintain Code Quality**

   Even with Copilot's assistance, adhere to best
   practices for maintaining code quality. Perform
   regular code reviews, conduct testing, and follow
   proper software development methodologies.

9. **Collaborate Effectively**

If you're working in a team, ensure that your colleagues are aware of your use of Copilot. Collaborate to establish coding standards and practices that everyone can follow consistently.

10. **Encourage Discussion**

Promote discussions within your team about the use of Copilot. Share your experiences, tips, and challenges to collectively improve how you integrate Copilot into your development process.

11. **Be Mindful of Security**

Pay special attention to security when using Copilot-generated code. Avoid exposing sensitive data or vulnerabilities inadvertently. Conduct thorough security reviews of any code generated by Copilot, especially if it deals with authentication, data handling, or external APIs.

12. **Maintain Code Ownership**

While Copilot can generate code, it's essential to maintain code ownership and accountability. Developers should take responsibility for the code they produce, whether it's manually written or generated with Copilot.

Summary

In conclusion, GitHub Copilot is a powerful tool that can boost developer productivity and code quality. However, it should be used thoughtfully and in conjunction with human judgment. By following these best practices, you can maximize the benefits of Copilot while ensuring that the code it produces aligns with your project's needs and standards. Copilot should be viewed as a valuable assistant that augments your coding skills, not as a substitute for them.

Resources

- GitHub Copilot getting started: `https://docs.github.com/en/copilot/using-github-copilot/getting-started-with-github-copilot`

- Setting up and using GitHub Copilot `https://docs.github.com/en/copilot/using-github-copilot/getting-started-with-github-copilot?tool=vscode`

- GitHub Copilot: `https://github.com/features/copilot/plans`

## CHAPTER 8

Automate Development Tasks and Workflow with GitHub Actions

This chapter focuses on using GitHub Actions to automate repetitive tasks and workflows, ultimately helping to streamline development processes and enhance productivity along some examples of automating GitHub administration.

Topics covered in this chapter include

- Introduction to CI/CD
- Using GitHub Actions for CI/CD
- Accessing GitHub Data Programmatically
- Automating GitHub Administration Tasks with GitHub Actions
- Reusable Workflows
- GitHub Actions Integration with Notification Tools
- Best Practices for Using GitHub Actions for CI/CD

© Balu Nivrutti Ilag, AjayKumar P. Baljoshi, Ganesh J. Sangale and Yogesh Athave 2024
B. N. Ilag et al., *Mastertng GitHub Enterprise Management and Administration*,
https://doi.org/10.1007/979-8-8688-0369-7_8

Introduction to CI/CD

Before we start creating our CI/CD workflow, let us understand about CI/CD; it is like having a magical code assistant which helps us build, test, and release our code automatically.

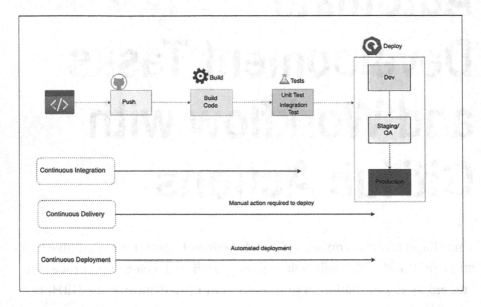

Figure 8-1. *CI/CD flow*

It is a software development practice that aims to improve the efficiency, quality, and agility of the software development and release processes.

Continuous Integration (CI)

- CI is a development practice where code changes are integrated into a shared repository frequently, often multiple times a day.

- The primary goal of CI is to detect and address integration issues and bugs early in the development cycle.

- Developers use automated build and testing tools to validate code changes, ensuring that the software remains in a deployable state.

- CI helps teams collaborate more effectively, maintain code quality, and reduce the risk of integration problems.

Continuous Delivery (CD)

- CD is an extension of CI that focuses on automating the process of deploying code changes to production or staging environments.

- In CD, code changes that have passed CI tests are automatically prepared for deployment to production at any time.

- CD ensures that the software is always in a state where it can be released, reducing the time and effort needed to make releases.

- It provides greater flexibility and enables quicker, more reliable releases.

Continuous Deployment (CD)

- Continuous deployment takes CD a step further by automatically deploying code changes to production as soon as they pass CI and CD tests.

- CD ensures that every code change that passes the testing phase is automatically released to production without manual intervention.

- It allows for rapid, frequent updates to applications and services.

Some of the commonly used tools are Jenkins, GitHub Actions, GitLab-CI, AWS CodePipeline, and Azure DevOps.

Next up, we will explore how to make the most of GitHub Actions for CI/CD and will cover some of the most used use cases along with optimization tips that will help to use GitHub Actions efficiently.

Using GitHub Actions for CI/CD

Before we start using GitHub Actions for CI/CD, we need to understand one more thing about branching strategy.

Need a Branching Strategy for Branching Strategy

In collaborative software development, multiple developers work on the same codebase simultaneously. A branching strategy helps manage this collaboration efficiently, allowing developers to work on features or bug fixes without disrupting the main codebase. It also helps in parallel development, testing, and deployment.

Commonly Used Types of Branching Strategies

In the world of software development, branching strategies play a crucial role in managing code changes and ensuring a smooth workflow. GitHub, as a platform, supports various branching strategies that cater to different development needs. These strategies help teams collaborate more effectively, allowing for isolated development, easier code reviews, and quick fixes to production issues. Let's delve into some of the commonly used types of branching strategies on GitHub.

Feature Branching

Feature branching is a widely adopted strategy that involves creating a separate branch for each new feature or enhancement. This approach isolates development work from the main codebase, typically referred to as the main or master branch. By working in a dedicated feature branch, developers can focus on their tasks without disrupting the ongoing work of others or the stability of the main branch. Once a feature is complete, it undergoes testing and code review before being merged back into the main branch. This strategy enhances collaboration and minimizes conflicts, making it easier to integrate new features.

Release Branching

Release branching comes into play when a team is gearing up for a new software release. This strategy involves creating a branch off the main codebase specifically for the upcoming release. The release branch serves as a stabilization phase, where the focus is on bug fixes, performance enhancements, and ensuring that only the intended features make it to the release. This separation from the main development work allows teams to freeze feature development for the release, providing a clear cutoff point for what is included. After the release is finalized and deployed, changes from the release branch can be merged back into the main branch and any development branches as needed.

Hotfix Branching

Hotfix branching is a critical strategy used to address urgent issues that arise in the production environment. When a critical bug or security vulnerability is identified in a live release, a hotfix branch is created from the affected release branch or the main branch to quickly address the issue. This allows for a focused effort on resolving the problem without interfering with ongoing development activities. After the fix is implemented and tested, the hotfix branch is merged back into both the main branch and any relevant release branches, ensuring that the fix is propagated across all necessary parts of the codebase.

623

Each of these branching strategies serves a specific purpose in the software development lifecycle, offering a structured approach to feature development, release preparation, and issue resolution. By leveraging these strategies, teams can maintain a high level of code quality and stability while efficiently managing multiple streams of work.

The following are some of the best practices for branching:

1. **Keep Branches Short-Lived:** Minimize the time branches exist to reduce the chance of conflicts.

2. **Regularly Update Local Branches:** Fetch the changes from the remote repository to keep your branches up to date.

3. **Code Reviews:** Before merging, have your code reviewed to ensure quality and adherence to coding standards.

4. **Continuous Integration:** Integrate changes often to identify and fix issues early in the development process.

5. **Meaningful Branch Names:** Use clear and concise branch names that reflect the branch's purpose.

Tools Used in the GitHub Workflow

When creating workflow for an application, follow the below best practices which can include below steps:

- **Code Quality and Static Code Analysis:** This will ensure our code follows best practices for readability, maintainability, and correctness; it can also be called static code analysis.

- **Test Case:** Depending on the use cases, there can be integration tests, functional tests, or both. They ensure that different parts of the code work together as intended and perform their functions correctly.

- **Code Coverage:** It provides a way to measure how much of the code is tested to find potential issues or hidden bugs.

The following table covers a list of most used tools and frameworks:

Programming Language	Code Quality/Static Code Analysis	Test Case Framework	Code Coverage
Python	Pylint, Flake8	unittest, pytest	Coverage.py (coverage), pytest-cov
Java	Checkstyle, SonarQube	JUnit, Selenium	JaCoCo, Cobertura
Node Js	ESLint, JSHint	Mocha, Cypress	Istanbul, Jest

Implementation Steps

Implementing a continuous integration/continuous deployment (CI/CD) pipeline within GitHub can significantly enhance the development process, ensuring that code is automatically tested, built, and deployed with each change. By leveraging Python-based code and GitHub Actions, developers can automate these workflows, streamlining the path from code commit to deployment. This discussion will elaborate on the steps required to create a comprehensive CI/CD pipeline, focusing on Python applications.

1. **Code Quality Checks Using Pylint**

   The first step in the CI/CD pipeline involves ensuring that the code adheres to quality standards. Pylint is a widely used tool for analyzing Python code, identifying coding errors, enforcing a coding standard, and looking for code smells. It can be integrated into the GitHub Actions workflow to automatically review every commit or pull request. This step helps maintain high code quality and consistency across the project. To implement this, you would add a step in your GitHub Actions workflow that installs Pylint and runs it against your codebase, reporting any issues back to the developer.

2. **Run Code Coverage**

   After ensuring the code quality is up to par, the next step is to measure how much of your code is covered by tests. Code coverage is an important metric that helps developers identify untested parts of the codebase. Tools like Coverage.py can be used for this purpose. Integrating code coverage into your CI/CD pipeline involves adding steps in your GitHub Actions workflow to execute your test suite with Coverage.py, then generating a report that highlights the covered and uncovered lines of code. This step is crucial for maintaining a reliable and robust codebase.

3. **Build and Test Docker Image**

For applications destined for containerized
environments, building and testing a Docker image
is a key pipeline stage. This involves creating a
Dockerfile that specifies how to build the image
of your application, then using GitHub Actions to
automate the Docker build process. Following the
build, you can run automated tests to verify that the
containerized application behaves as expected. This
ensures that any issues are caught early before the
image is pushed to a registry or deployed.

4. **Test the Changes on a Kubernetes Cluster**

For applications deployed to Kubernetes, it's
important to test changes in an environment that
closely mirrors production. This can be achieved
by deploying the application to a test Kubernetes
cluster. GitHub Actions can automate the
deployment of your Docker image to a Kubernetes
cluster, where integration and end-to-end tests can
be run. This step verifies that the application works
correctly in a Kubernetes environment, catching
configuration and compatibility issues early in the
development cycle.

5. **Deploy Using Helm Charts**

Helm is a package manager for Kubernetes that
simplifies the deployment and management of
applications. Helm charts define a set of resources
needed for running an application on a Kubernetes
cluster. In the final step of the CI/CD pipeline,
GitHub Actions can be used to automate the

627

deployment of your application using Helm charts. This involves updating the Helm chart with the new version of your application, then executing a Helm upgrade command to roll out the changes to the production environment. This step ensures a smooth and consistent deployment process.

GitHub Actions Component Overview

Understanding the components of GitHub Actions is essential for setting up your CI/CD pipeline. Workflows, triggered by specific events like a push to the main branch or a pull request, automate your development and deployment processes. Each workflow consists of jobs that run on runners – virtual environments provided by GitHub. Jobs are made up of steps, which are individual tasks such as checking out your repository or executing a script. By combining these components, you can create powerful automation tailored to your project's needs. Each to-do list, or "**job**," is done by a helper, called a "**runner**." The job is made up of smaller tasks called "**steps**," and these steps do specific actions, such as checking out the project or running custom commands like "python app.py". It is all explained in more detail in Chapter 5.

In summary, implementing a CI/CD pipeline using Python-based code and GitHub Actions involves automating code quality checks, test coverage measurement, Docker image building and testing, Kubernetes cluster testing, and deployment with Helm charts. Each step is crucial for ensuring that the code is production-ready, adhering to quality standards, and capable of being deployed seamlessly to a Kubernetes environment.

Implementation Workflow

Stepwise Workflow

Step 1: Code Quality Checks Using Pylint

Let's clone the repo and create a branch called github-workflow-setup, then create a directory to store the workflows and name our file as lint-test. yml; the following are the steps:

```
git clone <repo-url>
git checkout -b github-workflow-setup
mkdir -p .github/workflows/
touch .github/workflows/ lint-test.yml
```

Here is the directory structure of the repository:

.github/: Contains workflow-related files

src/: Application code and test case–related code

requirements.txt: File with Python requirements

.gitignore: File which contains files, directories, and extensions that need to be ignored

Now let's start adding jobs to the workflow.

Our goal is to improve code visibility by running pylint on the application code. We'll create a shell script called py-lint.sh, that executes pylint and fails if the score is below 7. This script will help ensure code quality by enforcing a minimum pylint score.

As the first step, we need to check out the code; it can be achieved using **actions/checkout@v3**, which is a GitHub-provided action that can be called in the workflow. The next step is to install Python and packages required to run pylint; this can be accomplished by using **actions/setup-python@v3** and using **run** to install the package.

629

Figure 8-2 shows the official link for checkout and Python action.

```
1    name: Python-Lint-Test
2    on: [push]
3    jobs:
4      lint_and_test:
5        runs-on: ubuntu-latest
6        steps:
7        - name: Checkout code
8          uses: actions/checkout@v3
9        - name: Set up Python
10         uses: actions/setup-python@v3
11         with:
12           python-version: 3.8
13           cache: 'pip' # caching pip dependencies
14       - run: pip install -r requirements.txt
15       - name: Run pylint
16         run: |
17           bash ci-scripts/py-lint.sh
```

Figure 8-2. *Pylint workflow [Refer to the lint-test.yml file for code]*

Details

- In the preceding workflow, **name** is the workflow name.

- **on: [push]:** This is the trigger which will trigger the workflow.

- **jobs:** This is where the actual job definition starts.

- **lint_and_test:** This is the job name.

- **runs-on:** This is the runner's name.

- **steps:** From here, we will define the steps which will be executed as part of workflow.

  - **Step 1 – Checkout Code:** Code will be checked out to the runner, using actions/checkout@v3.

  - **Step 2 – Set Up Python:** It will install Python with the version defined in the step.

  - **Step 3:** Using the run statement, we will install all requirements.

  - **Step 4 – Run pylint:** Here, using the shell script, we will execute pylint.

Once all these steps are added, we can commit the code and push it to the branch using the following commands:

```
git add -A
git commit -m "added workflow"
git push origin github-actions-workflow
```

Once we successfully push the changes, it will trigger the workflow; now to check the workflow status, we can check it under Actions.

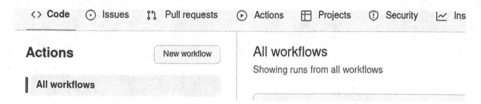

Figure 8-3. *Actions options*

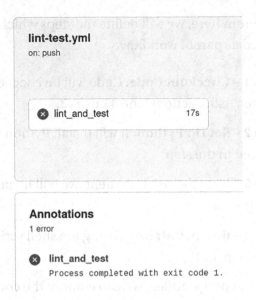

Figure 8-4. Workflow summary

It looks like a job has failed. Let us dig deeper to see which job failed and why.

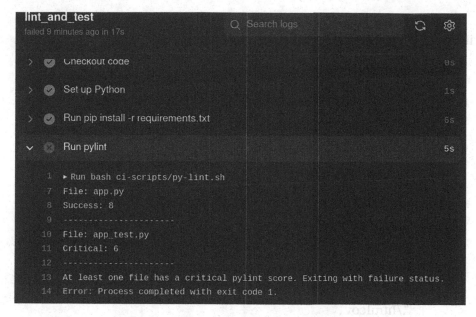

Figure 8-5. *Failed job*

On checking, we can see it has failed in the Run pylint job; let us fix it and push the changes; as changes fix the lint errors, let's add one more step that will perform code coverage.

Step 2: Code Coverage and Reporting

In this step, we will run test cases and generate a code coverage report; add coverage in requirements.txt, which is the package required to run code coverage; and then add steps to run coverage, generate a report, and save it as artifacts.

- **Running Code Coverage**

    We will use the following command to execute tests while measuring code coverage:

    ```
    coverage run --omit 'venv/*' src/app_test.py
    ```

Here, we are specifying a test file; we can also use the --source= option if we want to run test cases that are in different directories.

- **Generating a Report**

  After running the tests with coverage, the **coverage html** command is used to generate an HTML-based coverage report.

- **Uploading an Artifact**

  GitHub Actions provides a prebuilt action called actions/upload-artifact@v4. Using it, we can upload the generated HTML coverage report as an artifact; we will name the artifact "coverage-report," and it requires a path where the report will be saved; the path is "./htmlcov".

Once all these steps are added, our workflow file will look like Figure 8-6.

```
1    name: Python-Lint-Test
2    on: [push]
3    jobs:
4      lint_and_test:
5        runs-on: ubuntu-latest
6        steps:
7        - name: Checkout code
8          uses: actions/checkout@v3
9        - name: Set up Python
10         uses: actions/setup-python@v3
11         with:
12           python-version: 3.8
13           cache: 'pip' # caching pip dependencies
14       - run: pip install -r requirements.txt
15       - name: Run pylint
16         run: |
17           bash ci-scripts/py-lint.sh
18       - name: Runing code coverage
19         run: |
20           coverage run --omit 'venv/*' src/app_test.py
21       - name: Generating report
22         run: |
23           coverage html
24       - name: Upload Artifact
25         uses: actions/upload-artifact@v4
26         with:
27           name: coverage-report
28           path: ./htmlcov
29           if-no-files-found: error
```

Figure 8-6. *Artifact workflow [Refer to the lint-test.yml file for code]*

Step 3: Build and Test the Docker Image

In this step, we will build a docker image and run a functionality test. On successful testing, we will push the image.

When we build a docker image, we should be able to track the build. There are multiple ways of achieving it; some of the commonly used options are as follows:

1. Image-registry:date-version

2. Image-registry:jon_id-date

3. Image-registry:commit-id

In our use case, we will use the third option; instead of using the entire commit, we will use the short version of the commit; we can achieve it as follows:

```
- name: Add SHORT_SHA env property with commit short sha
  run: echo "SHORT_SHA=`echo ${GITHUB_SHA} | cut -c1-5`" >>
  $GITHUB_ENV
```

In this step, we create an environment variable called "SHORT_SHA" and then use it for the docker image.

As we are using a GitHub runner, it comes with a docker installed, so we can directly use the docker build command once the image is built; Since the GitHub runner comes with Docker installed, we can directly use the docker build command to build the image. Once the image is built, we can run it locally using docker run to test it. Steps looks as below:

```
- name: Build and Run docker container
  run: |
      docker build -t ghcr.io/ajay253517/flask-app:v-
      ${SHORT_SHA} .
      docker run -d -p 8080:8080 ghcr.io/ajay253517/flask-app:v-
      ${SHORT_SHA}
```

Once the container has started running, we will validate whether
the container is running or not; then we can perform some functionality
testing like whether the application returns an HTTP status 200; if we have
any health check path, we can use it. The step looks as follows:

```
- name: Runing test on container
  run: |
      docker ps -a && sleep 30
      status_code=$(curl -o /dev/null -w "%{http_code}"
      localhost:8080) && [ "$status_code" -eq 200 ] || {echo
      "Request failed with status code $status_code."; exit 1;}
        curl localhost:8080/api | grep test || {echo "app is not
        working"; exit 1;}
```

Based on above step test results, we can push the image to the docker
registry in this workflow we are using GitHub Packages, similar steps can
be followed other registries as well, to push we need to authenticate to the
respective registry; it can be done by using a GitHub-provided action and
GitHub secrets to provide an authentication token and then using a docker
push command to push the image. All this can be done using the following
commands.

Here, we are creating a secret called "GHPAT_TOKEN", which is a
GitHub personal access token with written access to the GitHub registry,
and the username is available in the GitHub environment; it can be
directly referred to using github.actor.

```
- name: Login to GitHub Container Registry
  uses: docker/login-action@v3
  with:
  registry: ghcr.io
  username: ${{ github.actor }}
  password: ${{ secrets.GHPAT_TOKEN }}
- name: Pushing docker image
  run: |
  docker push ghcr.io/ajay253517/flask-app:v-${SHORT_SHA}
```

Step 4: Test the Changes on the Kubernetes Cluster

Here, we will use helm charts to deploy an application into the Kubernetes cluster; before we deploy, we will check whether the template is currently configured by using a helm lint and template. As part of workflow at inital step we will check whether all the required tools are installed or not, once we add these steps the workflow looks as below:

```
- name: check tools version
  run: |
      kubectl version –short
      helm version –short
- name: lint and generate template
  run: |
        helm lint . -f dev-values.yaml
        helm template . -f dev-values.yaml
working-directory:
      flaskapp-chart
```

Once charts templates are validated, then we will have different values for develop and prod which has environment-specific values based on that we will create workflow steps. Here, we can use a self-hosted runner that will ensure execution is executed securely; it looks as follows:

```
- name: install-upgrade on dev
    if: github.ref == 'refs/heads/develop'
    run: |
        helm upgrade --install dev-flask-app . --dry-run -f dev-
        values.yaml
    working-directory:
        flaskapp-chart
- name: install-upgrade on prod
    if: github.ref == 'refs/heads/master'
```

```
run: |
    helm upgrade --install prod-flask-app . --dry-run -f
    prod-values.yaml
working-directory:
    flaskapp-chart
```

GitHub Actions supports the ability to check conditions, such as verifying if a preceding statement is true, with our workflow now configured, it is time to optimize it.

Optimize Workflow

Modularizing the Workflow

Instead of adding all the steps to a single workflow, we will break them down, for example, pylint and coverage can be ignored on master [main] or develop, so we can create separate files and add conditions as follows:

```
push:
    branches-ignore:
        - "master"
        - "develop"
```

Using Conditional with Path

Also, we can add an additional condition in the workflow; it should run only when source files get changed, so we can add one more condition under push as follows:

```
paths:
    - src/**
```

Note   We can also use the "paths-ignore:" option if we want to ignore based on some path in the repository.

Artifact Management

If the artifact file is not found, this can be achieved by adding a condition in the upload. Then we can set a retention period so that artifacts get cleaned and frequently updated. The action looks as follows:

```
- name: Upload Artifact
  uses actions/upload-artifact@v4
  with:
        name: coverage-report
        path: ./htmlcov
        if-no-files-found: error
        retention-days: 5
```

As a next step, we build a docker image and push it to the registry, but it should be executed only on develop and main, so the workflow with the condition will look as follows:

```
push:
branches:
      - "master"
      - "develop"
```

Workflow – Condition

In the last step, we need to deploy an application using the helm tool, but it should be executed after the image build is completed, and it should be successful; it can be achieved by setting the condition as follows:

```
workflow_run:
    workflows: ["Docker-Build-Push"]
    branches:
        - "master"
        - "develop"
    types:
        - completed
```

These are some of the optimization techniques that can help to effectively manage a workflow.

Release Management

There will be some applications or some cases where we can run a workflow. When a tag is created as a release, it can be achieved by using the following workflow; once the release is created, it will be visible in repositorics on the main page.

A tag is a reference that points to a specific commit in your Git history. Tags are often used to mark specific points in your project's history, such as a release version, a stable point, or a significant milestone; use the following commands to create and push tags:

```
git tag -a v1.0.0 -m "App Release"
git push --tags
```

Once the push tag command is executed, the workflow in Figure 8-7 is executed.

```
1    name: Create release
2    on:
3      push:
4        tags:
5          - v*
6    permissions:
7      contents: write
8    jobs:
9      release:
10       name: Release pushed tag
11       runs-on: ubuntu-22.04
12       steps:
13         - name: Create release
14           env:
15             GITHUB_TOKEN: ${{ secrets.GITHUB_TOKEN }}
16             tag: ${{ github.ref_name }}
17           run: |
18             gh release create "$tag" \
19                 --repo="$GITHUB_REPOSITORY" \
20                 --title="${GITHUB_REPOSITORY#*/} ${tag#v}" \
21                 --generate-notes
```

Figure 8-7.   *Release workflow [Refer to the release.yml file for code]*

On successful execution, a release will be created, and it looks like
Figure 8-8.

Figure 8-8.   *Tag output*

Accessing GitHub Data Programmatically

GitHub offers multiple options for programmatically accessing its data, providing developers with the flexibility to integrate GitHub functionality into their applications, automate workflows, and gather insights into repositories, organizations, and enterprise-level information.

Some of the options are discussed as follows:

GitHub REST API

- **Overview:** The GitHub REST API is a way to allow developers to interact with GitHub resources using standard HTTP methods.

- **Authentication:** It requires authentication using either personal access tokens or OAuth tokens.

- **Endpoints:** Various endpoints are available for different actions, such as creating issues, fetching repository details, or managing workflows.

- **Example:** Here is an example that uses cURL to make a GET request to the GitHub REST API to fetch details about a specific repository.

```
curl -H "Authorization: token YOUR_ACCESS_TOKEN"
https://api.github.com/repos/username/repository
```

GitHub GraphQL API

- **Overview:** GitHub's GraphQL API offers a more flexible and efficient way to request data. It allows developers to request only the specific data they need and supports batch operations.

- **Authentication:** It requires authentication like the REST API, using personal access tokens or OAuth tokens.

- **Queries:** Developers can define custom queries to retrieve the exact data they need, reducing the amount of data transferred over the network.

- **Example:** This example uses cURL to make a POST request to the GitHub GraphQL API to fetch specific details about a repository.

```
curl -H "Authorization: bearer YOUR_ACCESS_
TOKEN" -X POST
-d @query.graphql https://api.github.com/graphql
query.graphql
query {
  repository(owner:"username",
name:"repository") {
    name
    description
    stargazers {
      totalCount
    }
  }
}
```

- **Options Used**

  - Authorization: bearer YOUR_ACCESS_TOKEN: Authenticates the request using a personal access token

  - -X POST: Specifies that it is a POST request

  - -d @query.graphql: Sends the GraphQL query defined in the file query.graphql

Octokit Libraries

- **Overview:** Octokit is a set of client libraries for the GitHub API, available in various programming languages such as JavaScript, Ruby, .NET, and more.

- **Abstraction:** Octokit abstracts away some of the complexities of working directly with the raw API, providing a more convenient interface for developers.

- **Octokit Library Example (JavaScript)**

  ```
  const { Octokit } = require("@octokit/rest");

  const octokit = new Octokit({auth: "YOUR_ACCESS_
  TOKEN"});

  // Get repository details

  const repoDetails = await octokit.repos.get({owner:
  "username", repo: "repository"});
  ```

  This example uses the Octokit library in JavaScript to fetch details about a GitHub repository.

  - Octokit({auth: "YOUR_ACCESS_TOKEN" }): Initializes the Octokit instance with authentication using a personal access token

  - octokit.repos.get({owner: "username", repo: "repository" }): Uses the Octokit API to get details about a specific repository

GitHub CLI

- **Overview:** The GitHub CLI (command-line interface) provides a command-line interface to GitHub features, enabling developers to interact with repositories, issues, pull requests, and more directly from the terminal.

- **Integration:** It can be used in scripts or automation tasks to perform GitHub Actions from the command line.

- **Example**

  gh issue create -R username/repository -t "New Issue" -b "Description of the issue"

  Here is an example that uses the GitHub CLI to create a new issue in a GitHub repository; the options used in the command are explained as follows:

  - gh issue create: Initiates the command to create a new issue

  - -R username/repository: Specifies the repository where the issue should be created

  - -t "New Issue": Sets the title of the new issue

  - -b "Description of the issue": Adds a description to the new issue

Automating GitHub Administration Tasks with GitHub Actions

There are some GitHub administration tasks which can be automated using GitHub Actions; some of the most common use cases are listed here.

User Management

Example 1: Enabling SAML Single Sign-On (SSO) and team synchronization for your GitHub organization

There are different ways of accomplishing it. Here, we will use one of the popular IaC tools called Terraform, and the code looks like the following; it is future optimized based on the requirements:

```
provider "github" {
    token = "YOUR_GITHUB_TOKEN"
}
# Create a new SAML SSO organization credential
resource "github_organization_saml_sso" "sso_config" {
  organization = "your-org"
  enabled      = true
  auto_start   = true
  sync_teams   = true
}
# Create a team for team synchronization
resource "github_team" "sync_team" {
                name     = "SyncTeam"
                privacy  = "closed"
                auto_init = true
                organization = "your-org"
        }
# Add members to the team for synchronization
    resource "github_team_membership" "team_members" {
        for_each = {
```

```
                        "member1" = "your-username1",
                        "member2" = "your-username2"
                        # Add more members as needed
                    }
    team_id  = github_team.sync_team.id
            username = each.value
        }
    # Output the SAML SSO configuration details
output "sso_configuration" {
            value = github_organization_saml_sso.sso_config
                }
```

- **github_organization_saml_sso** is used to enable and configure SAML SSO for your organization.

- **github_team** creates a team that will be synchronized with your identity provider.

- **github_team_membership** adds members to the team for synchronization.

After running the preceding Terraform script, you should be able to see the SAML SSO and team synchronization configuration in your GitHub organization settings.

Note   The script provided here is a basic example and may need adjustments based on your specific requirements or GitHub Enterprise Cloud features.

All the scripts are saved in gh-admin-scripts/tf-scripts directory.

Example 2: Sending an invite to users

Here is another use case, where if we want to send invites to users for GitHub, this can be achieved by using the REST API and creating a Python script; it looks as follows:

```python
import requests
import sys
organization = 'YOUR_ORG'
access_token = 'YOUR_ACCESS_TOKEN'
team_ids = [TEAM_ID_1, TEAM_ID_2]
# Check if username_to_invite is provided as a command line
argument
if len(sys.argv) < 2:
    print("Usage: python invite_user.py <username_to_invite>")
    sys.exit(1)
username_to_invite = sys.argv[1]
url = f'https://api.github.com/orgs/{organization}/invitations'
headers = {
    'Authorization': f'token {access_token}',
    'Accept': 'application/vnd.github.v3+json'
}
data = {
    'invitee_id': username_to_invite,
    'role': 'direct_member',
    'team_ids': team_ids
}
response = requests.post(url, headers=headers, json=data)
if response.status_code == 201:
    print (f'Successfully sent an invitation to {username_to_
    invite}.')
else:
```

```
print (f'Failed to send an invitation to {username_to_
invite}. Status code: {response.status_code}, Response:
{response.text}')
```

Before executing the script, make sure to install requests package, use the pip install requests command, and execute the script as follows:

python invite_user.py USERNAME

On executing the script, the user will get an invite to the GitHub organization; above script can be scheduled as a GitHub workflow and integrated with some ticketing system use api to call this script; a similar script can be created to remove users.

The script is saved in gh-admin-scripts/admin-py-scripts/send-invite.py.

Usage Reports

On a organization level, there are some use cases where we need to visibility on GitHub components, some of examples are like total members in organization, GitHub actions minutes usage.

Example 1: Script for getting the count of members in the organization

```
import requests
organization = "your-organization"
access_token = "your-github-access-token"
# GraphQL query to get the list of users in the organization
query = """
{
    organization(login: "%s") {
    members(first: 100) {
        nodes {
            login
```

```
            }
        }
    }
}
""" % organization
url = https://api.github.com/graphql
headers = {
    "Authorization": f"Bearer {access_token}",
    "Content-Type": "application/json",
}
response = requests.post(url, headers=headers, json=
{"query": query})
if response.status_code == 200:
    data = response.json()
    users = data["data"] ["organization"]["members"]["nodes"]
print (f"Users in the {organization} organization:")
    for user in users:
        print(user["login"])
else:
print (f"Failed to fetch user list. Status code: {response.
status_code}, Response: {response.text}")
```

Here, we are using graphql to get the list of users in the organization; this script can be scheduled as a workflow in GitHub Actions; also, ensure the requests library is installed.

This is saved in gh-admin-scripts/admin-py-scripts/get-members.py

Example 2: Getting Actions minutes usage

To get the usage of Actions minutes, we can schedule this script as the GitHub workflow and send the usage as a report as per the requirements; see the following script for reference:

```
import requests
```

```
organization = "your-organization"
access_token = "your-github-access-token"
url = f"https://api.github.com/orgs/{organization}/settings/
billing/actions"
headers = {
    "Authorization": f"Bearer {access_token}",
    "Accept": "application/vnd.github.v3+json",
}
response = requests.get(url, headers=headers)
if response.status_code == 200:
    data = response.json()
    usage = data.get("total_minutes_used", 0)
    print (GitHub Actions minutes used by {organization}:
    {usage} minutes")
else:
    print (f"Failed to fetch GitHub Actions usage. Status code:
    {response.status_code}, Response: {response.text}")
```

Now we can adjust the script to get the usage per operating system; this can also schedule as a workflow to get the report based on requirements.

This is saved in gh-admin-scripts/admin-py-scripts/actions-minutes-usage.py

Example 3: When we want to get list of total members at enterprise level and then breakdown members at organization level, script looks as follows:

```
import requests
access_token = "github-personal-access-token" ## Ensure it has
access for enterprise
# Replace 'enterprise-name' with your actual GitHub Enterprise
hostname
enterprise_name = "enterprise-name"
```

```
# Get total consumed licenses for the GitHub Enterprise
url = f"https://api.github.com/enterprises/{enterprise_name}/
settings/license"
headers = {
    "Authorization": f"Bearer {access_token}",
    "Accept": "application/vnd.github. v3+json",
}
response = requests.get(url, headers=headers)
if response.status_code == 200:
    total_licenses = response.json(). get ("total_all_
    users", 0)
    print (f"Total consumed licenses for the GitHub
    Enterprise: {total_licenses}")
else:
    print (f"Failed to fetch total consumed licenses. Status
    code: {response.status_code}, Response: {response.text}")
  exit ()
# Get license breakdown per organization
orgs_url = fhttps://api.github.com/enterprises/{enterprise_
name}/organizations
orgs_response = requests.get(orgs_url, headers=headers)
if orgs_response.status_code != 200:
print (f"Failed to fetch organizations. Status code: {orgs_
response.status_code}, Response: {orgs_response.text}")
exit ()
organizations = orgs_response.json()
print ("\nLicense breakdown per organization:")
for org in organizations:
org_name = org["login"]
url = f"https://api.github.com/enterprises/{enterprise_name}/
organizations/{org_name}/settings/license"
```

```
org_response = requests.get(url, headers=headers)
if org_response.status_code == 200:
org_licenses = org_response.json(). get ("total_users", 0)
print (f"Organization: {org_name}, Consumed licenses: {org_
licenses}")
else:
print (f"Failed to fetch license usage for {org_name}.
Status code: {org_response.status_code}, Response: {org_
response.text}")
Saved in gh-admin-scripts/admin-py-scripts/ent-license-usage.py
```

Common Automation Use Cases

The following are some of the common automation use cases which can help GitHub administrators to work efficiently:

- Closing stale issues and pull requests

- Labeling and categorizing issues

- Enforcing code quality

- Scheduled tasks

- Issue and pull request templates

- Automated releases

- Branch protection

- Security scanning

- Dependency updates

- Documentation updates

- User access management

- Custom workflows for code review

- Issue triage

- Branch cleanup

- Metrics and reporting

- Environment provisioning

- Custom notifications

These are some of the use cases that demonstrate how GitHub Actions can be used to automate repetitive tasks, improve workflow efficiency, and maintain the health and organization of GitHub repositories. Automation allows development teams to focus more on coding and collaboration, reducing manual intervention in routine administrative processes.

As we have seen multiple examples of workflows, if we notice some of the use cases that are repeated or have similar steps, or require the same inputs, there is a feature in GitHub Actions called reusable workflow.

Where we can templatize the workflow and call it into other workflows will be discussed in the next section in detail with all examples.

Reusable Workflows

GitHub Actions provides a feature called reusable workflow, where we can create a workflow and reuse it in other workflows; concepts will be explained in detail.

Instead of copying and pasting the same set of instructions from one workflow to another, GitHub Actions allows you to create reusable workflows. This means that you can define a set of automated steps once and then use it in different workflows whenever needed, it can also be shared with other users.

The main advantage of reusing workflows is that it helps you avoid redundancy. Instead of duplicating the same code across multiple workflows, you can centralize it in a reusable workflow. This not only makes your workflows easier to manage but also speeds up the creation of new workflows. It's like building on others' work, like how you use existing actions.

Example: Imagine a scenario where a workflow is in progress, consisting of three build jobs. Once these build jobs are successfully completed, a subsequent job called "Deploy" is triggered. This "Deploy" job, instead of containing the deployment instructions directly, calls for a reusable workflow. This reusable workflow has three jobs: "Staging," "Review," and "Production."

Notably, the "Production" deployment job only runs after the "Staging" job has been successfully completed. The progress of the jobs targeting different environments is visualized with a progress bar. For instance, the "Production" job may have multiple steps, with the diagram indicating that it is currently processing step 6.

Figure 8-9. *Workflow flow [Image source: https://docs.github. com/assets/cb-34427/mw-1440/images/help/actions/reusable- workflows-ci-cd.webp]*

By using reusable workflows for deployment jobs, you can execute these jobs for each build without duplicating code in individual workflows. This modular approach simplifies maintenance, fosters collaboration, and ensures that your deployments are consistent and reliable across various projects.

Components of Reusable Workflows

Caller Workflow

- A **caller workflow** is like a director in a play. It initiates the action, calling upon another workflow to perform specific tasks; think of it as the main script that orchestrates various parts of your project.

- To summarize, a workflow that uses another workflow in its execution steps is called a "caller" workflow.

Called Workflow

- The **called workflow** is like an actor that gets its cues from the director (caller workflow). It contains the specific tasks or actions that need to be performed; this workflow is reusable and can be summoned by different caller workflows.

- We can have **multiple called workflows**, each serving a different purpose.

Managing Access to Reusable Workflows

Accessing reusable workflows can be divided into three different ways; they are as follows.

Same Repository

- If both workflows are in the same repository, they can easily be used interchangeably.

- We can use it for testing the functionality, where the caller and called functions will be saved in the same repository.

657

Public Reusable Workflow

- If the called workflow is stored in a public repository, and your organization allows it, you can use it.

- There are some readily available actions, which are already discussed at the beginning of the chapter, like installing Python.

- Also, while using public reusable workflow, you can filter based on publish; it is recommended to use creators who are verified so we get updates frequently.

Private Reusable Workflow

- If the called workflow is stored in a private repository, you can still use it if the repository settings allow access.

- It is like a shared resource in your organization that you can access with the right permissions.

To summarize, the idea is that workflows can be shared and reused within the same repository or across repositories, depending on their accessibility (public or private) and organizational policies. This flexibility encourages collaboration and efficiency in managing automation across different projects.

Note   To improve security, GitHub Actions restricts redirects for actions or reusable workflows, preventing successful execution if there are changes to the repository owner, name, or action name.

Runners in Reusable Workflows

When a reusable workflow is created, whatever runner is defined in the workflow will be used in the caller workflow; there is no option to override or modify it, so while creating a reusable workflow we need to keep that in mind.

If we use GitHub-hosted runners, it will always be evaluated using only the caller's context.

Billing for GitHub-hosted runners is always associated with the caller.

If we use self-hosted runners, it should be owned by the same user or organization as the caller workflow can access self-hosted runners from the caller's context.

Reusable Workflow in Action

Defining Triggers

Reusable workflows use YAML-formatted files, like any other workflow file; here, also, workflow files are stored in the .github/workflows directory; for a workflow to be reusable, the values for on must include workflow_call, as follows:

```
on:
    workflow_call:
```

Secrets and Variables in a Reusable Workflow

Defining and using secrets and variables through a reusable workflow, it can be done as follows:

- **Defining Secrets and Variables in the Reusable Workflow**

  While using secrets and variables in the reusable workflow, you will use the inputs and secrets keywords to define inputs or secrets that will be passed from a caller workflow, and it looks as follows:

```
on:
    workflow_call:
        inputs:
                app-name:
                required: true
                type: string
        secrets:
                api-key:
                required: true
```

- **Adding Steps to the Workflow**

  Once we define the input variables and secrets that are required for our workflow, the next step is where we define actual run statements which will be executed when it is called, and it looks as follows:

```
jobs:
                Deploy-App:
                    runs-on: ubuntu-latest
                    steps:
                        - run: echo "Started
                        deployment of application
                        ${{ app-name }}."
                        - run: echo "Validated
                        application deployment using
                        ${{ api-key }}"
```

The complete file looks as follows:

```
on:
    workflow_call:
        inputs:
            app-name:
            required: true
            type: string
        secrets:
            api-key:
            required: true
    jobs:
        Deploy-App:
            runs-on: ubuntu-latest
            steps:
                - run: echo "Started deployment of
                application ${{ app-name }}."
                - run: echo "Validated application
                deployment using ${{ api-key }}"
```

- **Using It in the Caller Workflow**

  In the above section we have two steps, using it we have
  created a resuable workflow, to call a reusable workflow
  by using the "uses" keyword, to use reusable workflow
  it will be called directly within a job, and not from
  within job steps.

To reference reusable workflow files using one of the following syntaxes:

- {owner}/{repo}/.github/workflows/{filename}@{ref} for reusable workflows in public and private repositories

- ./.github/workflows/{filename} for reusable workflows in the same repository

In the first option, {ref} can be a SHA, a release tag, or a branch name; in case a release tag and a branch have the same name, then the release tag takes precedence over the branch name.

Using the commit SHA is the safest option for stability and security.

The following is an example for a caller workflow:

```
jobs:
     deploy-app:
     uses: org-name/repo-name/.github/workflows/workflow-file-
     name.yml@branch-name
     with:
                app-name: ${{ vars.dev_app_name }}
     secrets:
                api-key: ${{ secrets.app_api_key }}
```

In the preceding example, we can see the inputs are passed using the "with" keyword in a job; to pass the api_key value, which is saved in secerts we have to use keyword "secrets".

Note   Workflows that call reusable workflows in the same organization or enterprise can use the inherit keyword to implicitly pass the secrets.

Using Multiple Reusable Workflows

We can call multiple workflows, referencing each in a separate job, and it looks as follows:

```
jobs:
                  call-workflow-1-in-local-repo:
        uses: org/local-repo/.github/workflows/workflow
        1.yml@172021f7ba04fe7327647b213799853a9eb89
                  call-workflow-2-in-local-repo:
                    uses: ./.github/workflows/
                    workflow-2.yml
    call-workflow-in-another-repo:
                    uses: org/another-repo/.github/
                    workflows/workflow.yml@v1
    call-workflow-in-another-repo-branch:
                    uses: org/another-repo/.github/
                    workflows/workflow.yml@main
```

Using Matrix Strategy for Workflows

Imagine you have a task that needs to be done in different environments like development, staging, and production. Instead of manually running the task for each environment, you can use something called a "matrix strategy."

Here's how it works:

1. You create a list of different environments (in this case, dev, stage, prod).

2. You set up a job (a task to be done) that uses this list as a variable.

3. The matrix strategy automatically runs the job for each environment on the list.

So, if you have a reusable set of instructions (a workflow) that can be used in each environment, you can make the job call that workflow with the different environments using the matrix strategy.

The following is an example for the workflow:

```
jobs:
  ReuseableJobDeployment:
    strategy:
      matrix:
          target: [dev, stage, prod]
    uses: org/org-repo/.github/workflows/deployment.yml@main
    with:
        target: ${{ matrix.target }}
```

There are some of the use cases where we can use nested workflows; it is explained in detail as follows.

Nested Reusable Workflows

Imagine you have a set of tasks that need to be done, and you've organized them into different workflows. In this system, it will be used as follows:

Explaining the Nested Reusable Workflows

1. **You Can Connect Workflows in a Certain Way:**

   - You have the main workflow; let's call it caller-workflow.yml.

   - This main workflow can call another workflow; let's call it called-workflow-1.yml.

   - That second workflow can call yet another workflow, called-workflow-2.yml.

- And finally, the third workflow can call one more workflow, called-workflow-3.yml.

- So, it's like a chain of workflows, but you can only have up to three levels in this chain.

2. **Important Limitation**

- You can't create loops in this chain. A loop would be like Workflow A calling Workflow B, and Workflow B calling Workflow A – that's not allowed.

3. **Special Case**

- If you are inside one of these workflows, let's say called-workflow-1.yml, you can call another reusable workflow from there.

An example for a nested workflow looks like this:

```
name: Reusable workflow
on:
    workflow_call:
jobs:
    call-another-reusable:
    uses: org/org-repo/.github/workflows/another-reusable.yml@v1
```

Passing Secrets for Nested Reusable Workflows

Managing secrets in a nested resuable workflows, are explained in detail below.

- **Passing Secrets Directly**

  If you have Workflow A and it calls Workflow B, Workflow A can send specific secrets to Workflow B. It's like passing a note directly.

- **Passing All Secrets**

  Alternatively, if Workflow A wants to share all its secrets
  with Workflow B, it can use the "inherit" keyword. It's like
  saying, "Hey, Workflow B, you get access to all my secrets!"

- **Important Note on Passing Secrets Down the Chain**

  Secrets are only passed directly from one workflow to the
  next. So, if you have a chain of workflows (like A > B > C),
  secrets from A can only reach C if they're passed from A
  to B and then from B to C.

- **Example Scenario**

  In a specific example, let's say Workflow A shares all its
  secrets with Workflow B. However, Workflow B decides
  to pass only one of those secrets to Workflow C. Any
  other secrets that Workflow A shared with Workflow
  B don't automatically go to Workflow C. It's a bit like
  sharing a secret with your friend, and your friend
  decides which secrets to share with someone else.

The following is an example for using secrets in nested workflows:

```
jobs:
    workflowA-calls-workflowB:
        uses: org/repo/.github/workflows/B.yml@main
        secrets: inherit # pass all secrets

jobs:
    workflowB-calls-workflowC:
        uses: different-org/example-repo/.github/
        workflows/C.yml@main
        secrets:
        envPAT: ${{ secrets.envPAT }} # pass just
        this secret
```

Managing Access and Permission for Nested Reusable Workflows

- **Nested Workflows and Accessibility**

  If you have a series of tasks (workflows) and some of them are inside others (nested), the whole process will fail if any of the inner workflows can't be accessed by the first one.

  It's like trying to follow a set of instructions, but if you can't get to one of the steps, everything stops. You can learn more about reusable workflow using GitHub offical documentation link https://docs. github.com/en/actions/using-workflows/reusing-workflows#overview.

- **GITHUB_TOKEN Permissions**

  There's a special key (GITHUB_TOKEN) that allows workflows to do certain things. If you have a chain of workflows (like A > B > C), the permissions of this key in B and C can only be the same or more restrictive than in A.

  For example, if A can read a package, B and C can't have the ability to write to that package.

- **Tracking Workflow Files**

  If you're curious about which files were used in a particular set of tasks, you can use the API to find out. It's like checking a record of which documents were consulted during a specific project.

Managing Outputs from a Reusable Workflow

- **Using Data from Reusable Workflows:**

  Imagine you have a set of tasks that can generate useful information, and you want to use that information in another set of tasks. In GitHub Actions, these sets of tasks are called workflows.

  If you want to use the data generated by one workflow in another, you need to specify what that data is.

- **Output Handling in Matrix Strategy**

  Now, if you're running these tasks with a strategy that involves multiple variations (a matrix strategy), and each variation can set some data, here's a key point:

  The data that gets passed on is from the last successful variation that actually set a value. So, if the last variation sets an empty value and the one before it sets a real value, the real value is what gets passed on.

- **Example Scenario**

  Let's take a simple example. You have a reusable set of tasks (workflow) that has a job with two steps. Each step sets a word as an output: "hello" and "world."

  These outputs are then labeled as output1 and output2. In the workflow itself, you define two overall outputs, first-word and second-word, and map them to output1 and output2, respectively.

An example for a workflow looks like this:

```
name: Deploy App Workflow
on:
   workflow_call:# Map the workflow outputs to job outputs
   outputs:
      build_name:
         description: "The build name"
         value: ${{ jobs.deploy_job.outputs.build_name }}
jobs:
   deploy_job:
      name: Deploy Application
      runs-on: ubuntu-latest
   outputs:
      build_name: ${{ steps.generate_build.outputs.
      build_name }}
steps:
   - id: generate_build
     name: Generate Build Name
     run: |
        # Simulate generating a unique build name, e.g.,
        based on timestamp
        build_name="app-$(date +%Y%m%d%H%M%S)"
        echo "build_name=$build_name" >> $GITHUB_ENV
        echo "::set-output name=build_name::$build_name"
   - id: deploy_step
     name: Deploying the Application
     run: |
        # Use the generated build name in deployment step
        echo "Deploying application with build: ${{ needs.
        deploy_job.outputs.build_name }}"
        # Actual deployment commands will start here
```

The preceding workflow can be explained as follows:

- The workflow now generates a unique build name (e.g., based on the timestamp) in the generate_build step.

- The generated build name is then used in the deploy_ step to provide information about the deployment process.

- The build name is made available as an output variable (build_name) for the deploy_job job.

- You would replace the placeholder deployment commands in the deploy_step with your actual deployment commands.

This setup allows you to pass the generated build name from the generation step to the deployment steps in a reusable way.

Monitoring Reusable Workflows

We can use the GitHub REST API to track reusable workflows. When a workflow job starts, a specific action called **prepared_workflow_job** is triggered. This action records important information in an audit log, including the following fields:

- **Repository Information**

  repo: This tells you which organization and repository the workflow job belongs to. If a job is calling another workflow, this info reflects the organization/repository of the caller workflow.

- **Timestamp**

  @timestamp: This gives you the date and time when the job was started, represented in Unix epoch format.

- **Job Details**

  job_name: This the name of the job that was executed.

- **Caller Workflow Information**

  calling_workflow_refs: This is an array containing file paths of all the caller workflows involved in this job.

  The array is ordered in reverse, showing the order in which they were called. For instance, in a sequence A > B > C, the array for a job in C would be ["organization/repository/.github/workflows/B.yml", "organization/repository/.github/workflows/A.yml"].

- **Caller Workflow SHAs**

  calling_workflow_shas: Another array, but this one holds the SHAs (unique identifiers) for all the caller workflows involved. The order of items in this array corresponds to the order in the calling_workflow_ refs array.

- **Workflow Reference**

  job_workflow_ref: It identifies the workflow file used for the job. It's in the format {owner}/{repo}/{path}/{filename}@{ref}. For a job calling another workflow, this pinpoints the called workflow.

Rerunning Workflows and Jobs with Reusable Workflows

If you want to rerun workflows or jobs that use reusable workflows from public repositories, you can reference them using a SHA (a unique identifier), a release tag, or a branch name. This is helpful for reusing predefined workflows. Here's what you need to know:

671

- **Choosing a Reference**

  When you rerun a workflow that uses a reusable workflow, and you didn't use a specific SHA as a reference, you need to be aware of how it behaves.

- **Rerunning All Jobs in a Workflow**

  If you choose to rerun all jobs in a workflow, it will use the reusable workflow from the specified reference (like a release tag or branch name). This is useful if you want to rerun the entire workflow with the latest changes from the reusable workflow.

- **Rerunning Failed Jobs or a Specific Job**

  If you're specifically rerunning failed jobs or a single job in a workflow, it will use the reusable workflow from the same commit SHA (a unique identifier) as the first attempt. This ensures consistency and helps address issues that may have occurred in the previous run.

As we understood various aspects of reusable workflow, while using GitHub reusable workflows, there are some of the limitations listed as follows.

Limitations of Reusable Workflow

The following are some of the limitations of a reusable workflow:

- You can connect to four levels of workflows, the top-level caller workflow and up to three levels of reusable workflows.

  For example: *caller-workflow.yml* → *called-workflow-1. yml* → *called-workflow-2.yml* → *called-workflow-3.yml*. Loops in the workflow tree are not allowed.

From within a reusable workflow, you can call another reusable workflow.

- Only a maximum of 20 reusable workflows from a single workflow file is allowed; it includes a limit of any trees of nested reusable workflows.

- Caller workflow environment variables set in an "env" context that are defined at the workflow level will not be propagated to the called workflow.

- We can use outputs of the reusable workflow, where we need to use env.

- We can reuse variables in multiple workflows by setting them at the organization, repository, or environment level and reference them using the "vars" context.

- When reusable workflows are called directly within a job and not from within a job step, you cannot pass values, therefore use "GITHUB_ENV" to pass values to job steps in the caller workflow.

Types of Workflows

In the realm of GitHub Actions, workflows play a pivotal role in automating the software development processes, with composite workflows and reusable workflows standing out for their efficiency and flexibility. Composite workflows allow users to combine multiple actions into a single action, enabling a more streamlined and concise approach to defining CI/CD processes. This is particularly useful for encapsulating a set of steps that are frequently repeated across different jobs or workflows, thereby reducing redundancy and simplifying maintenance. On the other hand, reusable workflows take modularity and efficiency a step further by allowing entire workflows to be reused across different projects within an organization. This not only promotes best practices by sharing well-defined processes but also significantly cuts down on the effort required to set up CI/CD pipelines for new projects. Both composite and reusable workflows underscore GitHub Actions' capability to enhance automation, encourage code reuse, and facilitate a more organized and efficient development workflow. In GitHub Actions workflows, there are two types of workflows; they are as follows:

1. Composite workflows

2. Reusable workflows

Composite Workflows

In this workflow type, it allows you to combine multiple steps within one action. For example, you can use this feature to combine multiple run commands in a workflow as an action and then have a workflow that executes all the commands as a single step using that action.

When you run a workflow, the steps might have multiple run commands which reduce the visibility, and they will be logged together.

When a composite action is executed, it exclusively calls a single step in a job, which means there can be other steps, which can exist before or after the composite action.

Reusable Workflows

It is a type of workflow which is used to avoid duplication as you can reuse the same workflow in multiple other workflows and which can be centrally maintained.

When a job executed using resuable workflow, you will have clear visibility about what is happening, and as a single job and step is logged independently in real time.

When a workflow with reusable workflows executes, it will be called directly within a job definition, and not from within a job step, as it uses only steps defined in the reusable workflow and no extra steps can be added to it. Based on the use case, you can use either the composite or reusable workflow.

GitHub Actions Integration with Notification Tools

GitHub.com allows users to stay informed about activities on the platform through a customizable notification inbox. Users can subscribe to repositories or other users to receive updates. The notification inbox provides a way to manage and prioritize these updates, allowing users to stay informed about changes, issues, and other activities relevant to their subscriptions. It enables efficient tracking and organization of GitHub activities, ensuring users can stay connected and engaged with the repositories and users they are interested in.

Default Notifications and Subscriptions

Managing Subscriptions

If you want to keep updated on what's happening on GitHub.com, you can sign up to get notifications about specific activities. These notifications fill you in on the stuff you've subscribed to, like discussions in issues, pull requests, or gists.

You can even choose to get updates about all the action in a whole repository, including things like workflow statuses with GitHub Actions, or specific events such as issues, pull requests, releases, security alerts, or discussions (if they're turned on).

There's also a neat feature that automatically watches all the repositories you can push changes to, except for forks. And if you want to keep an eye on any other repository you have access to, you can do it manually by clicking the "Watch" button.

If your interests shift and you're no longer keen on getting updates for a specific conversation or repository, you have options. You can unsubscribe, stop watching, or tweak the kinds of notifications you want to receive going forward. For example, if you're done with notifications from a particular repository, just hit "Unsubscribe." If you need more info on managing your subscriptions, check out the "Managing your subscriptions" section in the GitHub documentation.

Default Notifications

By default, GitHub ensures you stay in the loop by automatically subscribing to various conversations. This happens when you haven't disabled the automatic watching feature for repositories or teams you've joined in your notification settings – a setting that's turned on by default.

You're also automatically subscribed when you've been assigned to an issue or pull request, opened one yourself, commented on a thread, manually subscribed by clicking "Watch" or "Subscribe," had your username mentioned with "@", changed the state of a thread (like closing an issue or merging a pull request), or had a team you're a part of mentioned.

In addition, GitHub takes care of keeping you updated by automatically watching all repositories that you create and that are owned by your personal account.

If you find yourself automatically subscribed to conversations you'd rather not follow, you have options. You can tweak your notification settings to change the default behavior, or you can directly unsubscribe or stop watching specific activities on GitHub.com. More details on managing your subscriptions can be found in the "Managing your subscriptions" section in the GitHub documentation, here is the GitHub official

documentation link `https://docs.github.com/en/account-and-profile/
managing-subscriptions-and-notifications-on-github/managing-
subscriptions-for-activity-on-github/managing-your-subscriptions`.

Exploring Personalized Alerts and Subscriptions for GitHub Events

You've got options when it comes to checking your GitHub notifications – whether it's through the notification inbox on the website (`https://github.com/notifications`), the GitHub Mobile app, via email, or a mix of these.

Make your notification experience your own by setting things up in a way that suits you. Decide on the types of updates you want and where you want to see them by tweaking your notification settings. Keep your subscriptions tidy by going through your subscribed and watched repositories regularly. Unsubscribe from ones you're not interested in anymore.

For a more tailored approach to specific pull requests or issues, fine-tune your preferences right within the issue or pull request itself.

If you're using the GitHub Mobile app, you can take it a step further and customize and schedule push notifications to fit your routine.

GitHub Actions Integration with Notification Tools

We can use GitHub Actions workflow to send notifications on a specific event, with custom messages; some of the example uses case are as follows:

- **Build Success Notification**

  Scenario: Your team just pushed a significant update, and the GitHub Actions workflow successfully builds the project.

- **Test Failure Alert**

  Scenario: After a code change, the automated tests in your GitHub Actions workflow detect a failure; this instant notification will help the development team, allowing for a quick response and resolution.

- **Deployment Status Update**

    Scenario: A deployment workflow is triggered, and you want to keep the operations team informed about the deployment status; by implementing this integration, it provides a real-time information on the deployment progress, any issues encountered, or successful deployment completion.

- **Code Review Request**

    Scenario: A pull request is opened, and you want to notify the relevant team members for code review; we can use this integration to send a notification in a designated Slack channel mentioning the pull request details and requesting code review from specific team members.

- **Security Scanning Alerts**

    Scenario: Security scans are part of your GitHub Actions workflow, and a critical security issue is detected; using this integration, we can immediately alert the security team through Slack, providing details about the security vulnerability and triggering the necessary response actions.

- **Scheduled Maintenance Notification**

    Scenario: A GitHub Actions workflow is scheduled for routine maintenance tasks, such as database backups; this integration will help to notify the operations team in advance through a Slack message, ensuring awareness and minimizing disruptions during the maintenance window.

These use cases demonstrate how integrating GitHub Actions with notification tools can enhance communication, collaboration, and overall workflow efficiency within a development team.

GitHub Actions Integration Using Microsoft Teams

To make sure our GitHub Actions workflow gets the attention on failure or any event which requires attention, we're going to explore how to seamlessly integrate with popular notification tools like Microsoft Teams and Slack.

Before we dive into crafting the workflow, let's ensure we've got everything set up. Here are a few simple steps to get started with Microsoft Teams; the following are the prerequisites:

- **Microsoft Teams Account**

  - You should have access to a Microsoft Teams account, and you should be an administrator or have the necessary permissions to configure incoming webhooks.

- **Create an Incoming Webhook in Microsoft Teams**

  - Set up an incoming webhook in your Microsoft Teams channel. This webhook will provide the URL that the GitHub Actions workflow uses to send notifications.

  - To create an incoming webhook, go to the desired Teams channel, click the ellipsis (…) next to the channel name, select "Connectors," and then search for and configure the "Incoming Webhook" connector. Follow the prompts to create the webhook and obtain the URL.

- **GitHub Repository Access**

  - You need administrative or collaborator access to the GitHub repository where you want to implement this workflow.

- **GitHub Actions Secret**

  - Store the Microsoft Teams Incoming Webhook URL as a secret in your GitHub repository. This ensures the sensitive information is securely managed.

  - Go to your GitHub repository, navigate to "Settings" ➤ "Secrets," and add a new repository secret named MS_TEAMS_WEBHOOK_URL with the value being the Microsoft Teams Incoming Webhook URL obtained in step 2.

- **GitHub Actions Workflow Configuration**

  - Modify the GitHub Actions workflow file (e.g., .github/workflows/main.yml) to include the steps provided in the workflow example.

  - Customize the workflow file by replacing <YOUR_WEBHOOK_URL> with the actual secret reference (${{ secrets.MS_TEAMS_WEBHOOK_URL }}).

By ensuring these prerequisites are met, you can seamlessly integrate GitHub Actions with Microsoft Teams to receive notifications on workflow failures. This setup enhances collaboration and facilitates prompt responses to potential issues in your development pipeline.

The workflow looks as follows.

To send a notification to Microsoft Teams using the Microsoft Teams Incoming Webhook API, you can use the curl command within your GitHub Actions workflow. The following is an example workflow that sends a notification to a Microsoft Teams channel when the workflow fails:

```
notify:
    runs-on: ubuntu-latest
    needs: build
    if: failure()
    steps:
    - name: Send Microsoft Teams Notification
      run: |
        curl -H "Content-Type: application/json" -d '{
          "title": "GitHub Actions - Build Failed",
          "text": "The GitHub Actions workflow encountered a
          failure. Check the workflow run for more details.",
          "themeColor": "FF0000"
        }' ${{ secrets.MS_TEAMS_WEBHOOK_URL }}
      env:
        MS_TEAMS_WEBHOOK_URL: ${{ secrets.MS_TEAMS_
        WEBHOOK_URL }}
```

In this example, replace <YOUR_WEBHOOK_URL> with your actual Microsoft Teams Incoming Webhook URL. Make sure to add this URL as a secret named MS_TEAMS_WEBHOOK_URL in your GitHub repository.

This workflow has a notify job that runs only if the build job fails. The curl command is used to make an HTTP POST request to the Microsoft Teams Incoming Webhook URL with a JSON payload containing the notification details.

Below is the Github repository link, it provides additional information about integrating GitHub Actions with teams and also details about some example use cases.

```
https://github.com/integrations/microsoft-teams
```

GitHub Actions Integration Using Slack

Before setting up the GitHub Actions workflow to send notifications to Slack on the creation of a new issue, there are a few prerequisites you need to take care of. Let's ensure everything is in order for a seamless integration:

- **Slack Workspace**

  - Ensure you have access to a Slack workspace where you want to receive notifications. If you don't have a workspace, create one on the Slack platform.

- **Create a Slack App**

  - Create a Slack app in your workspace. This app will act as the bridge between GitHub Actions and Slack. Follow Slack's documentation on creating a new app: Create a Slack App, `https://api.slack.com/start/quickstart`.

- **Incoming Webhook Integration**

  - Set up an incoming webhook integration for your Slack app. This will generate a unique webhook URL that GitHub Actions will use to send notifications to your Slack channel. Follow Slack's documentation on setting up incoming webhooks: Incoming Webhooks, `https://api.slack.com/messaging/webhooks`.

- **Slack Channel**

  - Decide on the Slack channel where you want to receive GitHub issue creation notifications. Ensure your Slack app has access to post messages to this channel.

- **GitHub Repository Access**

  - Ensure you have the necessary permissions to configure GitHub Actions in the repository where you want to implement this workflow.

- **GitHub Actions Secret**

    – Store the Slack Incoming Webhook URL as a secret in
      your GitHub repository. To add a secret, go to your
      GitHub repository, navigate to "Settings" ➤ "Secrets,"
      and add a new repository secret named SLACK_
      WEBHOOK_URL with the value being the Slack
      Incoming Webhook URL obtained in step 3.

With these prerequisites met, your GitHub Actions workflow will
be all set to send notifications to your Slack channel; now let's create a
GitHub Actions workflow that sends a notification to Slack when an issue is
created; you can use the Slack Incoming Webhook API. The following is an
example workflow in YAML format. Make sure to replace <YOUR_SLACK_
WEBHOOK_URL> with your actual Slack webhook URL:

```yaml
name: Notify on Issue Creation
on:
    issues:
        types:
            - opened
jobs:
    notify:
    runs-on: ubuntu-latest
    steps:
    - name: Send Slack Notification
        run: |
            curl -X POST -H 'Content-type: application/json'
            --data '{"text": "New issue created in the
            repository: \nTitle: ${{ github.event.issue.title }}\
            nAuthor: ${{ github.event.issue.user.login }}\nURL:
            ${{ github.event.issue.html_url }}"
```

```
    }' ${{ secrets.SLACK_WEBHOOK_URL }}
  env:
      SLACK_WEBHOOK_URL: ${{ secrets.SLACK_WEBHOOK_URL }}
```

In this example

- The workflow is triggered on the "opened" event of an issue.

- The notify job runs on an Ubuntu environment.

- The curl command is used to make an HTTP POST request to the Slack Incoming Webhook URL with a JSON payload containing the issue details.

- The workflow uses a secret named SLACK_WEBHOOK_URL, where you should store your Slack Incoming Webhook URL.

Remember to add the Slack webhook URL as a secret in your GitHub repository. To do this, go to your GitHub repository, navigate to "Settings" ➤ "Secrets," and add a new repository secret named SLACK_WEBHOOK_URL with the value being your Slack webhook URL.

This example provides a basic notification, and you can customize the JSON payload within the curl command to include more information or formatting based on your preferences and the capabilities of the Slack Incoming Webhook API.

Best Practices for Using GitHub Actions for CI/CD

Using GitHub Actions for continuous integration (CI) and continuous deployment (CD) can significantly streamline your development workflows. Here are some best practices to make the most out of GitHub Actions for CI/CD:

Organize Workflow Files:

- Maintain a clean and organized structure for your workflow files. Group related workflows and name files descriptively. This makes it easier for contributors to understand and locate specific workflows.

Parallelize Jobs:

- If your project has multiple test suites or tasks that can run concurrently, use parallel jobs to speed up the overall workflow execution. This takes advantage of GitHub Actions' scalability.

Use Matrix Builds for Testing:

- Leverage matrix builds to test your project across multiple versions of programming languages, dependencies, or operating systems. This ensures compatibility and identifies issues early on.

Cache Dependencies:

- Cache dependencies to avoid redundant installations and speed up workflow execution. Utilize the caching mechanism provided by GitHub Actions to store and retrieve dependencies between workflow runs.

Secret Management:

- Store sensitive information, such as API keys or deployment credentials, using GitHub Actions secrets. Avoid hardcoding sensitive data directly in workflow files.

Environment Variables:

– Use environment variables for configuration parameters that may vary between environments (e.g., development, staging, production). This promotes flexibility and avoids hardcoding values.

Conditional Workflows:

– Implement conditional workflows to trigger specific actions based on branch names, tags, or other criteria. This allows you to customize workflows for different scenarios.

Approval Workflows for Deployment:

– Implement approval steps for deployment workflows. Require manual approval before deploying to production to ensure a controlled release process.

Logging and Debugging:

– Include comprehensive logging in your workflow steps. Use the GitHub Actions console and artifacts to troubleshoot and debug any issues that may arise during the CI/CD process.

Notifications:

– Set up notifications to alert your team about workflow status, especially failures. Use built-in GitHub Actions notifications or integrate with external communication tools like Slack or Microsoft Teams.

Automated Testing:

- Implement thorough automated testing in your workflows. Ensure that all critical aspects of your application
  are covered by tests, including unit tests, integration
  tests, and end-to-end tests.

Regularly Review and Update:

- Periodically review and update your workflows to incorporate new GitHub Actions features or optimizations.
  GitHub regularly introduces improvements, and staying
  up to date ensures you benefit from the latest
  enhancements.

Version Control for Workflow Files:

- Version control your workflow files along with your
  codebase. This helps in tracking changes, understanding
  historical context, and ensuring that workflow changes
  align with code changes.

By following these best practices, you can create efficient and robust
CI/CD workflows using GitHub Actions, ultimately enhancing your
development process and code quality. As we conclude GitHub reusable
workflows, in the next chapter we will discuss GitHub Advanced Security
to help secure the entire software development lifecycle.

Summary

The concept of continuous integration/continuous deployment (CI/CD)
serves as a cornerstone in modern software development practices,
streamlining the process from code commit to deployment in a seamless,
automated fashion. GitHub Actions emerges as a powerful tool in this
landscape, enabling developers to automate their CI/CD pipelines directly

within GitHub's ecosystem. It not only facilitates the automation of testing and deployment tasks but also extends its capabilities to accessing GitHub data programmatically, thereby enhancing the efficiency of managing project resources. Moreover, GitHub Actions proves instrumental in automating GitHub administration tasks, further reducing the manual overhead for developers. The introduction of reusable workflows marks a significant advancement, allowing for the sharing of common processes across projects, thereby fostering efficiency and consistency. Integration with notification tools through GitHub Actions ensures real-time alerts and updates, keeping teams informed about the status of their CI/CD pipelines. Adhering to best practices for using GitHub Actions for CI/CD, such as optimizing workflow triggers and managing secrets securely, organizations can leverage this powerful automation tool to its fullest potential, ensuring robust, efficient, and streamlined software development processes.

Resources

- GitHub Actions checkout: `https://github.com/actions/checkout`

- Setup Python: `https://github.com/actions/setup-python`

- GitHub Marketplace: It is the list of available tools in GitHub Marketplace for developers to use or purchase. `https://github.com/marketplace?type=actions`

- Understanding GitHub Actions: Here is the link, which is provided by GitHub, to understand in detail about GitHub Actions. `https://docs.github.com/en/actions/learn-github-actions/understanding-github-actions`

- Below is the list of available actions created and managed by GitHub, which can be directly used in the workflow. https://github.com/actions

- Executing Script: There is a readily available action, which can be used to execute some GitHub script; here is the link for it, and there are also some other options which will be discussed in detail. https://github.com/actions/github-script

- Official Link: https://docs.github.com/en/rest?apiVersion=2022-11-28

- Rate Limit: Note when we use the REST API, there is a rate limit, which is explained in this link. https://docs.github.com/en/rest/using-the-rest-api/rate-limits-for-the-rest-api?apiVersion=2022-11-28

- The GraphQL API: https://docs.github.com/en/graphql/overview/about-the-graphql-api

- Rest JS information: https://octokit.github.io/rest.js/v20/

- Slack GitHub Action: https://github.com/slackapi/slack-github-action

- GitHub CLI: https://cli.github.com/manual

- Managing team sync for the organization and best practices: https://docs.github.com/en/enterprise-cloud@latest/organizations/managing-saml-single-sign-on-for-your-organization/managing-team-synchronization-for-your-organization

- GitHub workflow: https://docs.github.com/en/
actions/using-workflows/workflow-syntax-for-
github-actions#onworkflow_callinputs

- Supported keywords for jobs that call a reusable
workflow: https://docs.github.com/en/actions/
using-workflows/reusing-workflows#supported-
keywords-for-jobs-that-call-a-reusable-workflow

- Workflow information: https://docs.github.
com/en/actions/using-workflows/reusing-
workflows#overview

- Managing subscriptions and notifications on GitHub:
https://docs.github.com/en/account-and-profile/
managing-subscriptions-and-notifications-on-
github/setting-up-notifications/configuring-
notifications

- Managing subscriptions for activity on GitHub:
https://docs.github.com/en/account-and-profile/
managing-subscriptions-and-notifications-on-
github/managing-subscriptions-for-activity-
on-github

- Triaging a single notification: https://docs.
github.com/en/account-and-profile/managing-
subscriptions-and-notifications-on-github/
viewing-and-triaging-notifications/triaging-
a-single-notification#customizing-when-to-
receive-future-updates-for-an-issue-or-pull-
request " for a step-by-step guide

- Configuring and managing your notification settings with GitHub Mobile: `https://docs.github.com/en/account-and-profile/managing-subscriptions-and-notifications-on-github/setting-up-notifications/configuring-notifications#managing-your-notification-settings-with-github-mobile`

- Microsoft Teams and GitHub integration: `https://github.com/integrations/microsoft-teams`

CHAPTER 9

Secure Software Development Lifecycle Through GitHub Advanced Security

This chapter's focus is on using GitHub Advanced Security to help secure the entire software development lifecycle. The chapter discusses the tools and features available through GitHub Advanced Security, including code scanning and secret scanning.

Topics covered in this chapter include

- Introduction to GitHub Advanced Security
- Understanding the Cost of GitHub Advanced Security Licenses
- Understanding and Implementing Code Scanning
- Understanding and Implementing Secret Scanning

- Understanding and Enabling Dependabot and Alerts

- GitHub Advanced Security in the SDLC

- Effective Response to Security Alerts

- Configuring GitHub Advanced Security

- Best Practices for Managing Environment Secrets
  on GitHub

Introduction to GitHub Advanced Security

The introduction of GitHub Advanced Security comes as a fundamental development in the landscape of software development and cybersecurity. In an era where digital transformation is at the forefront of enterprise strategy, the security of development environments has never been more critical. The necessity for robust security measures within GitHub, a leading platform for software development, is underscored by the increasing sophistication of cyber threats and the high-profile data breaches that have impacted millions of individuals and businesses worldwide.

GitHub Advanced Security represents a significant leap forward in securing software development processes within organizations, especially for those facing the ever-evolving landscape of cybersecurity threats. As a security administrator for an enterprise organization, the introduction of GitHub Advanced Security into your cybersecurity toolkit can be a game changer in protecting your development environment from both external threats and internal vulnerabilities.

GitHub Advanced Security offers a suite of enhanced security features, available through an Advanced Security license, designed to bolster the security posture of organizations managing extensive software repositories. For public repositories hosted on GitHub.com, certain features are automatically activated, providing a foundational level of security.

694

Envision yourself as a security engineer tasked with overseeing application security within a sprawling organization that operates thousands of repositories. Given the vast scale of your software ecosystem, ensuring robust application security has emerged as a critical priority. Recognizing the importance of this, your organization has recently invested in GitHub Advanced Security licenses. This strategic move is aimed at integrating security practices earlier in the software development lifecycle, a concept known as "shifting security left." By adopting GitHub Advanced Security, your company aims to minimize technical debt and proactively identify vulnerabilities, thereby enhancing the overall security of its software development processes.

GitHub, as a central hub for over 65 million developers to collaborate and share code, is inherently a target for malicious actors. The platform hosts a vast amount of proprietary and open source code, making it a gold mine for hackers looking to exploit vulnerabilities. The introduction of GitHub Advanced Security is a response to this evolving threat landscape, aiming to provide enterprise organizations with the tools and capabilities to secure their code, detect vulnerabilities early, and automate security protocols.

Your mandate involves developing a comprehensive plan for the phased implementation of GitHub Advanced Security across all development teams within the organization. To achieve this, you must familiarize yourself with the array of features offered by GitHub Advanced Security, understanding how each can be effectively integrated into different stages of the software development lifecycle. This knowledge will enable you to leverage these advanced security features to their fullest potential, ensuring a smooth and successful rollout across the organization.

What Is GitHub Advanced Security?

GitHub Advanced Security is a comprehensive suite of tools and functionalities designed to enhance the security of your codebase and development environment throughout the entire software development

lifecycle. This suite is not limited to safeguarding your production
environment but extends its protective measures to every phase of
development, ensuring that your code is secure from inception to
deployment. By integrating GitHub Advanced Security, you gain the
upper hand against potential security threats and breaches, tapping into
the collective knowledge and expertise of the global security community.
This proactive approach allows for the safe utilization of open source
software, mitigating risks associated with vulnerabilities. Moreover, GitHub
Advanced Security plays a pivotal role in fostering a culture of security
within your organization by implementing and promoting security best
practices. This initiative not only guards against the immediate threats
posed by malicious actors but also builds a foundation for a security-
conscious mindset among your development teams, ensuring that security
considerations are an integral part of the development process. GitHub
Advanced Security mainly focuses on protecting organizations in three
areas: supply chain, code, and environment. Refer to Figure 9-1, which
shows the GitHub Security features.

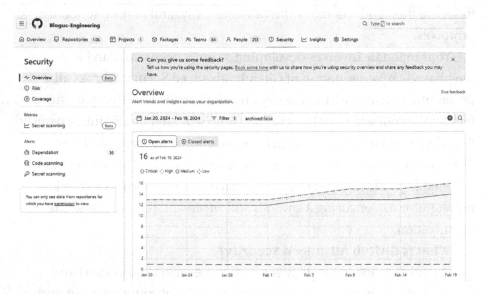

Figure 9-1. *Security features*

GitHub Advanced Security is an enhancement to GitHub's existing security features, designed to provide enterprise teams with advanced tooling to improve the security of their code right from the initial stages of development. It integrates directly into the GitHub workflow, making it easier for developers and security teams to collaborate on identifying, addressing, and preventing security vulnerabilities.

Capabilities of GitHub Advanced Security

GitHub Advanced Security addresses these challenges by offering a suite of tools designed to improve the security posture of development projects. Key features include

- **Code Scanning:** Utilizes static analysis to automatically scan every git push to detect vulnerabilities in code before it is merged and deployed. This feature supports a wide range of programming languages and frameworks, making it versatile for diverse development projects.

- **Secret Scanning:** Identifies and alerts on secrets accidentally pushed to repositories, such as API keys and tokens, preventing potential unauthorized access to external systems and data breaches.

- **Dependency Scanning:** Automatically scans dependencies for known vulnerabilities and suggests updates or patches. Given the widespread use of open source libraries, this feature is crucial for maintaining the security integrity of software projects.

- **Security Policies and Insights:** Provides a dashboard for tracking and managing security issues across the organization, enabling security administrators to enforce security policies and gain insights into the security posture of their entire development ecosystem.

Why Is Security Needed on GitHub?

The necessity for robust security measures like GitHub Advanced
Security can be underscored by reflecting on recent cybersecurity
incidents:

- **Equifax (2017):** A delay in applying a known patch
  led to a massive data breach. This incident highlights
  the importance of timely vulnerability management, a
  process that GitHub Advanced Security can streamline
  through its automated scanning and alerting
  capabilities.

- **Marriott Hotels (2018):** The breach of personal data
  of millions of users underscores the need for stringent
  security measures at all levels of software development
  and data storage. GitHub Advanced Security's secret
  scanning can prevent the exposure of sensitive
  information that could lead to such breaches.

- **Log4j Vulnerability (2021):** The widespread impact of
  this vulnerability across millions of servers worldwide
  illustrates the critical need for dependency scanning
  to identify and mitigate vulnerabilities in third-party
  libraries and frameworks.

GitHub Advanced Security offers a comprehensive suite of tools
designed to fortify the software development lifecycle against the backdrop
of increasing cybersecurity threats. For enterprise organizations, adopting
GitHub Advanced Security means not only protecting their development
environment but also safeguarding their business and customer data
against the far-reaching impacts of cyber incidents. This proactive
approach to security is essential in today's digital age, where the cost of
negligence or delay in addressing vulnerabilities can be devastating.

**Using GitHub Advanced Security to Secure Your Software
Supply Chain**

In software development, the concept of a supply chain extends
beyond the physical production of goods in an industrial setting
to encompass the entire lifecycle of software development. This
lifecycle involves producing, reviewing, and refining code, much like
manufacturing goods, with added protections and guidelines to ensure
the production of a high-quality software product. A critical aspect of
this software supply chain is the integration of third-party or open source
software, which constitutes a significant portion of modern software
projects. Studies suggest that up to 94% of active repositories utilize open
source code, highlighting the reliance on external dependencies that may
not be directly produced by your team.

The significance of managing these dependencies became starkly
apparent with the 2021 Log4j vulnerability, which underscored the
potential risks associated with third-party software components. Such
vulnerabilities can introduce weaknesses into your project, making
effective dependency management a cornerstone of secure software
development.

GitHub Advanced Security offers automated tools designed to identify
and address these vulnerabilities, streamlining the process of securing
your project's dependencies. These tools include

- **Security Overview:** GitHub's security overview
  provides a centralized dashboard for monitoring
  your software supply chain, offering insights into the
  state of your project's dependencies. It enables you to
  identify vulnerable repositories and assess the impact
  of dependencies on your code's security. From this
  overview, you can activate security features, view
  and manage automated security alerts, and prioritize
  responses based on the risk level of each alert. The

dashboard also features icons representing different
types of alerts, giving you a quick visual summary of
potential issues.

- **Dependency Graphs:** Dependency graphs offer
  a visual representation of your project's package
  dependencies, both direct and indirect, and their
  security status. These graphs summarize the manifest
  and lock files in your project's ecosystem, providing
  a clear view of whether dependencies are up to date
  and secure. By activating the dependency graph
  feature, you gain access to dependency reviews for
  repositories within your organization, helping prevent
  the introduction of vulnerabilities.

- **GitHub Advisory Database:** The GitHub Advisory
  Database serves as a comprehensive resource for
  tracking vulnerabilities in third-party packages. It
  allows you to search for and browse information on
  security vulnerabilities affecting your dependencies.
  Curated by a dedicated team, the database lists
  vulnerabilities ranked from low to critical severity,
  ensuring you have access to up-to-date information
  sourced from authoritative databases like The National
  Vulnerability Database and the npm security advisory
  database.

- **Dependabot for Automated Dependency
  Management:** Dependabot automates the monitoring
  and updating of your project's dependencies. By
  examining your project's manifest files and consulting
  the GitHub Advisory Database, Dependabot identifies
  out-of-date or vulnerable dependencies. It then alerts

authorized team members to these issues and any
changes in the dependency graph of a repository. This
automation facilitates efficient maintenance and helps
avoid potential security oversights.

In outline, GitHub Advanced Security provides a robust set of tools
for securing your software supply chain, from centralized monitoring and
visual insights to automated dependency management. By leveraging
these features, you can ensure that your project remains secure against
vulnerabilities in third-party components, thereby safeguarding your
software development lifecycle against potential security threats.

Creating a Culture of Security Within Your Organization

This topic explores how leveraging GitHub Advanced Security features
can significantly enhance your organization's security posture. It delves into
the concept of "shifting left" in the software development lifecycle (SDLC)
and illustrates how this approach can fortify your development processes
against security vulnerabilities. Additionally, it examines various security
workflow models, highlighting best practices that can be adopted to foster a
security-centric organizational culture.

Adopting a Security Mindset

Cultivating a security-focused culture within an organization ensures
that security considerations become an integral part of every action,
decision, and piece of work. This mindset shift is crucial for achieving
superior outcomes in software development and strategic planning.
Beyond the deployment of security tools, it's essential to recognize and
mitigate human error, which can inadvertently facilitate security breaches.
Whether it's a user unknowingly enabling an attack or a developer
writing insecure code, the human element cannot be overlooked. Many
security incidents begin with the exploitation of an individual within the
organization, highlighting the need for a comprehensive security strategy.

The Shift Left Philosophy

The term "shift left" refers to integrating security practices early
in the SDLC, moving away from treating security as an afterthought.
Traditionally, security reviews were conducted late in the development
process, often by a specialized team, separate from the developers.
Shifting left means embedding security considerations into the design
phase, encouraging developers to prioritize security from the outset.
This approach facilitates the development of secure code and policies,
streamlining the entire development process.

Identifying Faulty Security Models

Common pitfalls in organizational security models often stem from
treating security as a siloed concern. This can lead to inefficiencies, such
as the need to revisit and repair code after moving on to new projects,
resulting in duplicated efforts and wasted resources. Characteristics of
ineffective security models include limited team involvement in security,
treating security reviews as a final step, lack of comprehensive security
documentation, and development environments that do not align with
security guidelines.

Characteristics of an Ideal Security Model

An effective security model involves comprehensive team
involvement, where security is a priority at every stage of development.
Key elements include

- **Broad Scope of Team Involvement:** Security is
  everyone's responsibility, with all team members
  engaged in securing the project within their roles.

- **Prioritization of Security:** Security measures are
  embedded throughout the development lifecycle,
  ensuring continuous protection.

- **Comprehensive Documentation:** Clear, written
  standards and guidelines inform team members of
  security expectations and reporting processes.

- **Tooling and Automation:** Development platforms and
  tools enforce security standards, automating checks to
  maintain secure code and environments.

Security Policies and Enforcement

A robust security culture is underpinned by well-defined policies that
outline permissible actions within repositories or branches. GitHub facilitates
this through the SECURITY.md file, which details the organization's security
policies and reporting procedures. However, policies alone are not sufficient;
they must be actively enforced. GitHub Advanced Security's compliance
and policy management features enable administrators to implement these
policies effectively, using protected branches and other controls to ensure
adherence to organizational security requirements.

By integrating these practices, organizations can create a secure,
efficient, and collaborative development environment, significantly
reducing the risk of security vulnerabilities and fostering a culture of
security awareness and responsibility.

Understanding the Cost of GitHub Advanced Security Licenses

GitHub Advanced Security offers enhanced security features for enterprise
accounts on both GitHub Enterprise Cloud and GitHub Enterprise Server,
with certain functionalities also accessible for public repositories on
GitHub.com. To leverage GitHub Advanced Security for private or internal
repositories, an organization must have a GitHub Advanced Security
license. This license is included with subscriptions to GitHub Enterprise
Cloud or GitHub Enterprise Server.

For organizations interested in exploring the capabilities of GitHub Advanced Security, GitHub offers trial periods for both GitHub Enterprise Cloud and GitHub Advanced Security. These trials provide a risk-free opportunity to evaluate how GitHub Advanced Security can benefit your organization. Detailed guidance on initiating these trials can be found in the GitHub Enterprise Cloud documentation.

It's important to note that GitHub Advanced Security features are automatically available for public repositories on GitHub.com without the need for an additional license. However, should the visibility of a repository change from public to private, GitHub Advanced Security features will be deactivated for that repository unless the organization possesses a GitHub Advanced Security license. This policy ensures that advanced security measures are consistently applied across all private and internal repositories within an enterprise account, provided the necessary licensing is in place. Figure 9-2 shows GitHub Advanced Security pricing.

Additional add-ons

GitHub Copilot	Codespaces	Large File Storage	GitHub Advanced Security	Enterprise Only
Starting at $10/month after a 30 day trial.	Starting at $0.18 per hour of compute and $0.07 per GB of storage.	$5 per month for 50 GB bandwidth and 50 GB for storage.	$49 per month per active committer.	
Compare plans >	Learn more >	Learn more >	Learn more >	

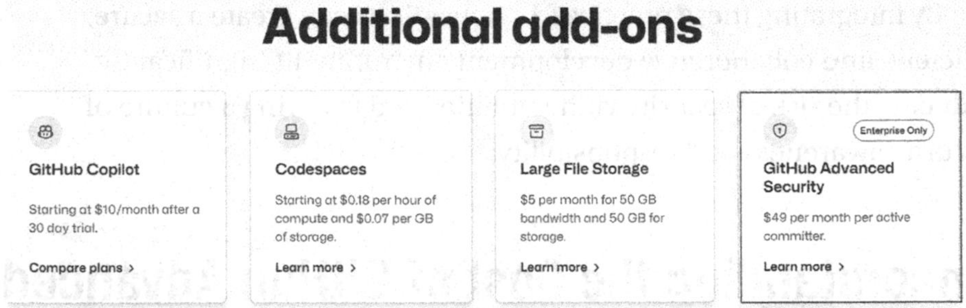

Figure 9-2. *GitHub Advanced Security pricing*

Initiating a Trial of GitHub Advanced Security

As an administrator, you have the opportunity to explore GitHub Advanced Security at no cost. This suite of tools is designed to enhance the security and quality of your code through features like code scanning, secret scanning, and dependency review, all pivotal for maintaining high standards in your projects.

If your organization subscribes to GitHub Enterprise Cloud and payments are made via credit card or PayPal, you're eligible to start a trial of GitHub Advanced Security. This opportunity is also available if you're currently engaged in a free trial of GitHub Enterprise Cloud. For those who handle billing through invoices, a discussion with GitHub's Sales team is necessary to explore trial options for your enterprise.

A notable advantage of this trial is the flexibility it offers; you can add an unlimited number of committers and activate GitHub Advanced Security across as many organizations as you wish. Typically, the trial spans 30 days, but if you're already participating in a GitHub Enterprise Cloud trial, the GitHub Advanced Security trial will align with the remaining duration of that trial.

Prerequisites for the Trial

To set up your trial, you must hold an owner role within an enterprise account. Further details about enterprise accounts and the specific roles within an enterprise can be found on GitHub's documentation.

How to Set Up Your Trial

To begin, navigate to your profile photo at the top-right corner of GitHub.com, select "Your enterprises," and then choose the enterprise account you wish to manage. From the enterprise account sidebar, select "Settings," then "Enterprise licensing." Here, you'll find the option to "Start free trial" next to GitHub Advanced Security. Simply click "Start trial" to commence.

Concluding Your Trial

Should you decide to continue benefiting from GitHub Advanced Security after the trial, you can transition to a paid plan at any point during the trial period. If a purchase isn't made by the end of the 30-day trial, the trial will automatically conclude.

To purchase GitHub Advanced Security, return to the "Enterprise licensing" section under "Settings" in your enterprise account. There, you'll find the "GitHub Advanced Security trial" section. Click the "Manage" dropdown and select "Purchase." You'll then be prompted

to specify the number of committers for which you're buying licenses,
confirm your billing information, and choose your payment method before
finalizing the purchase by selecting "Purchase Advanced Security."

Understanding and Implementing Code Scanning

Securing your software supply chain is a critical step, but GitHub
Advanced Security doesn't stop there. It extends its protective measures
to the very heart of software development: the code itself. Human errors,
such as inadvertently inserting vulnerabilities into the codebase, pose
significant risks to project security. GitHub Advanced Security addresses
these risks through a trio of features: code scanning, secret scanning, and
push protection, each designed to find and fix security issues as you write
your code.

Even the most skilled developers can introduce errors into their code,
necessitating a process for detection, triage, and remediation. GitHub's
code scanning feature integrates seamlessly into the development
workflow, performing static analysis with each git push. This real-time
scanning identifies common misconfigurations, errors, and vulnerabilities,
enabling developers to address issues before they reach production.
GitHub notifies relevant developers within the repository about detected
problems, offering detailed guidance and suggestions for remediation.
This process not only helps in maintaining code quality but also educates
your team on secure coding practices.

To activate code scanning

1. Go to the Security tab of your repository.

2. Under Code scanning alerts, click Set up code
    scanning.

3.   Choose Set up this workflow under CodeQL
     Analysis. Figure 9-3 shows the code scanning alert
     option. However, GitHub Advanced Security is not
     enabled, and it says Contact sales to enable the code
     scanning alerts.

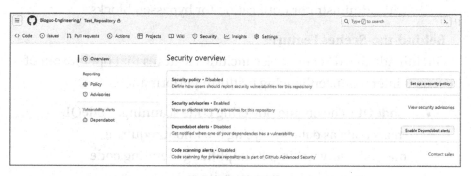

Figure 9-3. *Code scanning alerts*

Supported languages include C, C++, C#, Java, JavaScript, TypeScript,
Python, and Go. The default workflow triggers scans on code pushes, pull
request creations, and according to a schedule, ensuring comprehensive
coverage.

Secret Scanning and Push Protection

Applications often authenticate with external systems using secrets,
such as API keys, which developers might accidentally commit to
repositories. Exposed secrets are a significant security vulnerability.
GitHub Advanced Security mitigates this risk through

- **Secret Scanning:** Automatically scans all branches
  of your GitHub repository for secrets. Configurable
  alerts notify designated users upon detection, enabling
  prompt remediation actions, such as key rotation or, if
  necessary, ignoring false positives.

- **Push Protection:** Adds a proactive layer by scanning
  for secrets in code before it's committed to the
  repository. This feature prevents the exposure of
  secrets, offering developers options to remove the
  secret, declare it a false positive, or bypass the alert
  with administrator notification for bypassed blocks.

Behind-the-Scenes Features

GitHub Advanced Security also includes features that operate out of
direct user interaction, enhancing platform performance:

- **CodeQL:** The engine powering code scanning, CodeQL
  treats code as data, analyzing it without requiring
  manual query writing. It simplifies generating code
  scanning results for your repository.

- **Third-Party Tool Integration:** GitHub supports the
  integration of third-party analysis tools that produce
  SARIF (Static Analysis Results Interchange Format)
  data, offering flexibility in how you approach code
  security.

Together, these features of GitHub Advanced Security form a
comprehensive approach to identifying and resolving security issues
directly within the development process, ensuring that your code is not
only functional but secure from the ground up.

**Configuring the Default Setup for Code Scanning in Your
Repository**

For repository administrators or those with the security manager
role, setting up code scanning with GitHub Advanced Security is a
straightforward process designed to enhance your code's security and
quality. This feature is pivotal for identifying security vulnerabilities and
coding errors, ensuring your repository maintains high standards.

Who Can Use This Feature

If you have admin permissions or hold the security manager role for
a repository, you're equipped to configure code scanning. This capability
extends to all public repositories on GitHub.com and private repositories
within organizations subscribed to GitHub Enterprise Cloud, provided
they have a GitHub Advanced Security license.

About Default Setup

Opting for the default setup is the most efficient way to get started with
code scanning in your repository. This method automatically tailors a code
scanning configuration based on your repository's code, covering CodeQL-
supported languages. It activates scans on each push to the default or any
protected branch, during pull request creations or commits against these
branches, and on a weekly basis. However, if the repository remains inactive for
six months, the weekly scans will pause to conserve GitHub Actions minutes.

Bulk Enablement and Granular Control

You can enable the default setup across multiple or all repositories
within an organization simultaneously, offering a streamlined approach
to broad implementation. For those requiring more detailed control over
code scanning configurations, an advanced setup option is available.

Requirements

Your repository qualifies for the default setup if GitHub Actions are
enabled and it's publicly visible. It's recommended to activate the default
setup for any repository likely to include CodeQL-supported languages in
the future. If a repository doesn't currently contain supported languages,
enabling the default setup won't consume any GitHub Actions minutes
until such languages are added.

Customizing and Configuring

Starting with the default setup is advised. After initial configuration,
you can assess its effectiveness and make adjustments to better align
with your security needs. To configure the default setup, navigate to
your repository's settings, select "Code security and analysis" under the
"Security" section, and then choose "Set up" next to "Code scanning"

to enable the default setup. This process automatically generates a configuration, which you can review and modify, such as selecting different query suites for more comprehensive scans.

Finalizing Your Setup

Upon enabling the default setup, a workflow initiates to test the new configuration. Should you switch from an advanced setup, be aware that the default setup will supersede existing configurations. You can review and adjust your setup anytime to ensure it meets your repository's evolving needs.

By following these steps, you can swiftly implement code scanning to safeguard your codebase, streamline your security processes, and maintain the integrity of your software development lifecycle.

Understanding and Enabling Secret Scanning

GitHub's secret scanning feature is a critical tool for enhancing the security and integrity of code within GitHub repositories. It's designed to automatically detect known types of secrets, such as tokens or private keys, that might have been inadvertently committed to a repository. This capability is crucial for preventing unauthorized access to external services and safeguarding sensitive information.

Secret Scanning for Partners and Users

For public repositories and *npm packages*, GitHub automatically runs secret scanning to notify service providers about potential secret leaks, helping mitigate risks promptly. Additionally, secret scanning alerts are freely available for all public repositories, offering immediate feedback to repository owners and organization members. For private and internal repositories within organizations subscribed to GitHub Enterprise Cloud and equipped with a GitHub Advanced Security license, secret scanning alerts can be enabled, extending protective measures across all repository types.

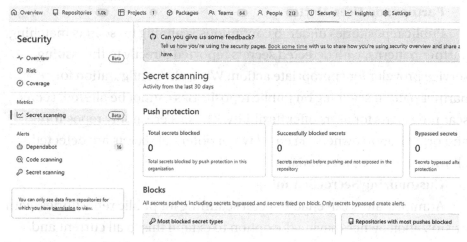

Figure 9-4. Security scanning

The Importance of Secret Scanning

When a project interacts with external services, using secrets for
authentication is common. However, if these secrets are checked into
a repository, they become accessible to anyone with read permissions,
posing a significant security risk. GitHub recommends storing secrets
outside the repository in a secure location to prevent unauthorized access.
Secret scanning covers the entire Git history across all branches, including
issue descriptions, comments, pull requests, and discussions, ensuring
comprehensive protection.

Managing Secret Scanning Alerts

GitHub provides tools for auditing actions taken in response to
secret scanning alerts, allowing for thorough oversight of security
measures. Additionally, GitHub offers push protection for repositories
and organizations, preventing code containing detected secrets from
being pushed. This feature can be customized with a link to resources
specific to organizational needs, guiding contributors on how to address
blocked pushes.

Partner and User Alerts

Public repositories undergo continuous scanning for secrets matching partner patterns, with detected secrets reported directly to the issuing service provider for appropriate action. While the configuration for partner pattern scanning on public repositories cannot be altered, secret scanning alerts for users offer flexibility. These alerts notify repository and organization owners via email when potential secrets are detected, allowing for prompt remediation.

Customizing Secret Scanning

Administrators can enable secret scanning for public repositories, with organization owners having the option to extend this to all current and future public repositories within an organization. Custom secret scanning patterns can also be defined for a repository, organization, or enterprise, tailoring the scanning process to specific needs. Detected secrets are securely stored, encrypted both in transit and at rest, ensuring the highest level of security.

Accessing and Responding to Alerts

Upon detecting a secret, GitHub generates an alert visible in the repository's Security tab and sends email notifications to relevant parties. These alerts enable quick identification and resolution of security issues, maintaining the integrity of the codebase and protecting external service access.

In summary, GitHub's secret scanning is an indispensable feature for maintaining code security, offering automated detection of secrets, comprehensive scanning capabilities, and flexible management options to ensure that repositories remain secure and compliant.

Configuring Secret Scanning for Your Repositories

GitHub offers a secret scanning feature that helps safeguard your repositories by detecting leaked secrets, such as tokens or private keys, within your code. This feature is crucial for maintaining the security of your projects and preventing unauthorized access to external services.

Enabling Secret Scanning Alerts

Secret scanning is automatically active for all public repositories, providing alerts for leaked secrets to both repository owners and service providers. For organizations with GitHub Enterprise Cloud and a GitHub Advanced Security license, secret scanning can also be enabled for private and internal repositories, extending this protective measure across all repository types.

To activate secret scanning for your public repositories, simply navigate to the repository's settings, then to the "Code security and analysis" section. Here, you can *enable secret scanning*, which will then monitor your entire Git history across all branches, including issue descriptions, comments, pull requests, and discussions for any secrets.

Secret scanning   Enable

Receive alerts on GitHub for detected secrets, keys, or other tokens.

GitHub will always send alerts to partners for detected secrets in public repositories. Learn more about partner patterns.

Figure 9-5. Enable secret scanning

Bulk Enabling and Push Protection

Organizations can enable secret scanning across multiple repositories simultaneously, enhancing security measures organization-wide. Additionally, GitHub provides the option to enable push protection, which prevents the pushing of code containing high-confidence secrets, further securing your repositories.

Personal Account Settings for Secret Scanning

For individual users, secret scanning alerts can be managed through personal account settings, allowing you to enable or disable alerts for all your public repositories with a single action. You also have the option to automatically activate secret scanning for any new public repositories you create, ensuring continuous protection.

Excluding Directories from Secret Scanning

GitHub allows for the customization of secret scanning through the creation of a *secret_scanning.yml* file in your repository. This file can specify directories to exclude from scanning, useful for directories containing tests or randomly generated content. However, there are limitations to the number of entries and the file size that can be excluded.

Implementing Secret Scanning

To implement secret scanning

1. Go to your repository's settings and select *"Code security and analysis."*

2. Enable secret scanning and, if desired, push protection.

3. For personal accounts, manage secret scanning alerts through the *"Security"* section in account settings.

4. Optionally, use a *secret_scanning.yml* file to exclude specific directories from scanning.

Secret scanning

Receive alerts on GitHub for detected secrets, keys, or other tokens.

GitHub will always send alerts to partners for detected secrets in public repositories. Learn more about partner patterns.

| | Disable |

Push protection

Block commits that contain supported secrets.

| | Disable |

Access to alerts

Admins, users, and teams in the list below have permission to view and manage code scanning, Dependabot, or secret scanning alerts. These users may be notified when a new vulnerability is found in one of this repository's dependencies and when a secret or key is checked in. They will also see additional details when viewing Dependabot security updates. Individuals can manage how they receive these alerts in their notification settings.

Choose the people or teams you would like to grant access

> Q Search for people or teams

People and teams with access

Organization administrators, repository administrators, and teams with the security manager role
These members always see code scanning, Dependabot, and secret scanning alerts.

Save changes

***Figure 9-6.** Secret scanning*

By configuring secret scanning for your repositories, you're taking a significant step toward securing your code and protecting your projects from potential security breaches. This feature not only enhances the security of your repositories but also supports compliance with security best practices.

Understanding and Enabling Dependabot and Alerts

Dependabot is a valuable tool integrated into GitHub that helps you maintain the security and up-to-dateness of your software dependencies. This quickstart guide is designed to introduce you to Dependabot's capabilities, guiding you through the process of enabling it for your repository and navigating the alerts and updates it provides.

Understanding Dependabot

- Dependabot enhances your repository's security posture through three key features:

- **Dependabot Alerts:** Notifies you of any vulnerabilities within your repository's dependencies

- **Dependabot Security Updates:** Automatically generates pull requests to update dependencies flagged for having known security vulnerabilities

- **Dependabot Version Updates:** Automatically generates pull requests to ensure your dependencies remain current, reducing the risk of security vulnerabilities

Getting Started with Dependabot

To show Dependabot's functionality, we'll use a demo repository. Here's how to get started.

Fork the Demo Repository: Navigate to the Dependabot demo repository at `https://github.com/dependabot/demo` and fork it to your account by clicking the "Fork" button. Choose your personal account as the owner and give your repository a name.

Enabling Dependabot in Your Repository

After forking the demo repository, follow these steps to activate Dependabot:

> **Access Repository Settings:** On your repository's main page, click "Settings." If the "Settings" tab isn't visible, use the dropdown menu to find it.

> **Navigate to Code Security:** In the sidebar, click "Code security and analysis."

> **Enable Dependabot Features:** Next to Dependabot alerts, security updates, and version updates, click "Enable" to activate these features for your repository.

Configure Version Updates (Optional): If you're
interested in Dependabot version updates, navigate
to the .github/dependabot.yml file to create or
edit the Dependabot configuration file. This file
allows you to customize how Dependabot version
updates are handled, tailoring it to your project's
needs. Figure 9-7 shows Dependabot alerts; security
updates enable options.

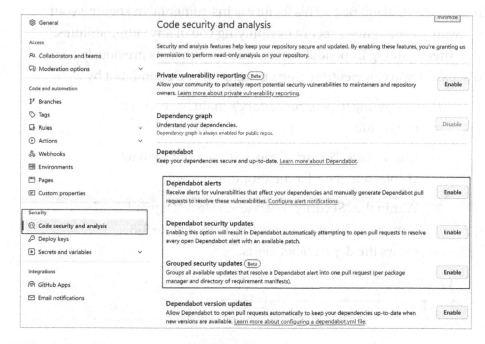

Figure 9-7. *Enable Dependabot alerts*

Note   If your repository hasn't already activated the dependency
graph, GitHub will do so automatically upon enabling Dependabot,
ensuring that your project benefits from comprehensive dependency
tracking and security analysis.

By following these steps, you'll not only secure your project against known vulnerabilities but also ensure that your dependencies are always up to date. Dependabot is an essential tool for any developer looking to automate the maintenance of their project's dependencies, thereby enhancing the project's overall security and reliability.

How to View Dependabot Alerts?

If you've enabled Dependabot alerts for your repository, you can easily monitor and address these alerts through the "Security" tab on your repository's GitHub page. This feature is instrumental in keeping your software dependencies secure by notifying you of any vulnerabilities.

After enabling Dependabot for your repository, as previously discussed, you can view any alerts generated by Dependabot by

1. Navigating to your repository's main page on GitHub.

2. Clicking the "Security" tab. If it's not immediately visible, find it under the dropdown menu.

3. Within the "Security" overview, select "Dependabot" from the sidebar to access the alerts. Figure 9-8 shows the dependabot alerts.

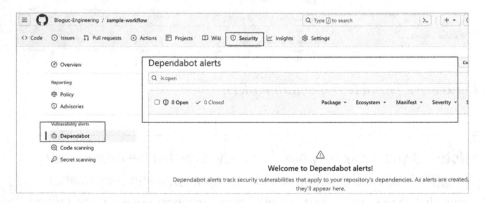

Figure 9-8. *Dependabot alerts*

The Dependabot alerts page will list all current alerts under the "Open" tab, with an option to view "Closed" alerts as well. These alerts can be filtered using various criteria to help you prioritize and manage them effectively.

Detailed Alert Information

Clicking an alert, such as the "Command Injection in lodash" example, will bring up detailed information, including

- If a pull request has been created by Dependabot to fix the vulnerability

- The package involved and the versions affected

- A brief description of the vulnerability

Additional details like the severity, Common Vulnerability Scoring System (CVSS) metrics, and any related Common Vulnerabilities and Exposures (CVE) or GitHub Security Advisory (GHSA) IDs will also be displayed, providing comprehensive insight into the nature and severity of the vulnerability.

Fixing or Dismissing an Alert

To address an alert, you can

1. Review and merge the pull request generated by Dependabot, which contains the necessary security fix. This process involves reviewing the commits in the pull request and, when satisfied, merging it to update your dependency and resolve the vulnerability.

If you decide the alert is not relevant or poses no risk to your project, you can dismiss it by

1. Returning to the alert's detail page

2. Clicking "Dismiss alert" in the top-right corner

3. Choosing a reason for dismissal and optionally adding a comment for justification, which is useful for audit and reporting purposes

After dismissal, the alert will move from the "Open" to the "Closed" tab, clearing your active alerts list while still allowing you to access and review dismissed alerts.

By following these steps, you can effectively manage Dependabot alerts, ensuring your repository remains secure against known vulnerabilities in dependencies. This proactive approach to security helps maintain the integrity of your software projects and protects against potential threats.

Securing Your Automated Workflow Environment Within GitHub

Securing your automated workflow environment within GitHub is crucial for maintaining the integrity and security of your software development process. GitHub Actions and Microsoft Azure are popular tools for automating or customizing software development workflows. When setting up a workflow, developers define an environment where their code will run. These environments, which may include runners akin to virtual machines, are distinct from repositories and are designated targets for executing workflow jobs. To ensure these environments remain secure while providing necessary access controls, GitHub employs several security measures including protection rules, environment secrets, and wait timers.

Security Measures for Automated Workflows

- **Protection Rules:** Administrators can implement rules requiring specific reviewers to approve workflow runs in an environment. These reviewers, with read-only access to the repository, can approve or reject workflow runs, ensuring that changes are scrutinized without granting them code editing permissions.

- **Environment Secrets:** For workflows executed in environments, such as those managed by GitHub Actions or Azure, access to environment-specific secrets is essential. These secrets enable workflow jobs to interact with the environment securely. Approval from a designated reviewer may be required to access these secrets for a job.

- **Wait Timers:** To control when code deployments occur, administrators can set timers that delay deployment for up to 30 days. This feature provides additional oversight and timing control over deployment processes.

GitHub Advanced Security in the SDLC

Integrating GitHub Advanced Security (GHAS) into your software development lifecycle (SDLC) fundamentally transforms how security is woven into your projects. To better understand this transformation, let's compare traditional security practices with the GHAS-enhanced approach.

Traditionally, security in the SDLC has been treated somewhat like a checkpoint or a gate – often positioned toward the end of the process, typically during the quality assurance (QA) phase. Here, security testing acts as a final hurdle to clear before the software can be released. While this method does ensure that security assessments are conducted, it often leads to significant bottlenecks. Discovering vulnerabilities at this late stage can delay releases, creating a rush to patch issues, which, in turn, can introduce more errors or lead to shortcuts in testing. Essentially, this "security as a gate" approach can make security a hindrance rather than a helpful, integrated aspect of software development.

The GHAS Approach to Security in the SDLC

Now, envision a different scene with GitHub Advanced Security enhancing every phase of your SDLC. Instead of a single checkpoint, security becomes a continuous, integrated process that begins at the very start and actively participates throughout the lifecycle.

- **At Project Configuration:** Security policies are established, setting the stage for a secure development process right from the get-go.

- **During Development:** As developers work, GHAS features such as code scanning and secret scanning actively monitor every commit and merge for potential vulnerabilities and accidental exposure of sensitive information like tokens and private keys. This immediate feedback loop allows developers to address issues as they arise, significantly reducing the accumulation of technical debt.

- **At Every Pull Request:** The dependency review feature shines by analyzing changes in project dependencies. It compares updates or additions against databases of known vulnerabilities, providing a clear assessment of how these changes might impact the project's security posture. This ensures that vulnerabilities can be caught and addressed before they are integrated into the main codebase.

- **High-Level Oversight:** The security overview feature offers project administrators a comprehensive view of the project's overall security health. This dashboard highlights areas of concern and helps prioritize interventions in repositories that may pose a higher risk.

The Impact of GHAS on Your SDLC

By embedding security practices throughout the development process, GHAS shifts the paradigm from security being a bottleneck to an enabler of faster, safer software releases. This approach not only streamlines the QA phase – since many potential issues have already been identified and resolved – but also fosters a culture of security within the development team. Developers become more aware of security best practices and can write more secure code from the outset.

In essence, GitHub Advanced Security transforms the SDLC by making security an integral, empowering aspect of software development. This leads to more secure products, happier teams, and a smoother, more efficient path from development to deployment.

Leveraging GitHub Advanced Security in Your SDLC

Integrating GHAS features into your SDLC allows you to address security concerns at the earliest stages of development, effectively minimizing the risk of vulnerabilities in your final product. Here's how these features can be leveraged:

- **During Development:** Code scanning and secret scanning can be integrated into your development workflows, automatically scanning your code for vulnerabilities and secrets as changes are made. This integration ensures that security issues can be identified and remediated by developers in real time, without waiting for a separate security review.

- **Before Merging:** The dependency review feature plays a crucial role before merging changes, especially when updating or adding new dependencies. It provides a clear view of the security implications of these changes, allowing developers and security teams to make informed decisions about incorporating new code.

- **Organization-Wide Security Posture:** The security overview feature is instrumental for security and development teams to gain insights into the overall security health of their projects. It allows for

prioritizing remediation efforts based on the risk
profile of each repository, ensuring that resources
are allocated effectively to mitigate the most critical
vulnerabilities first.

In summary, GitHub Advanced Security provides a robust framework
for integrating security into every phase of the software development
lifecycle. By enabling these features, organizations can significantly
enhance their ability to detect and respond to security issues, fostering a
culture of security and compliance across all development activities.

Effective Response to Security Alerts

Understanding the critical nature of security breaches is essential, as
demonstrated by significant incidents like the 2017 Equifax breach, where
inadequate dependency management played a critical role. This topic
emphasizes the importance of promptly addressing security alerts and
outlines GitHub's features designed to facilitate swift responses.

Evaluating Security Alerts

Timely responses to security alerts are crucial for minimizing risks.
Delayed actions can leave your systems vulnerable to attacks, potentially
leading to data breaches that could harm your brand's reputation and
customer trust. By acting quickly on security alerts, you can mitigate these
risks effectively.

Triage of Security Alerts

GitHub's code scanning feature plays a vital role in identifying
vulnerabilities within your codebase. Upon detecting an issue, it generates
alerts to notify your team, enabling rapid identification and analysis of the
problem.

For instance, if a code scan misinterprets your code, you have the option to dismiss the alert, specifying the reason for dismissal, such as a false positive or code used solely for testing purposes. This level of control ensures that you can manage alerts efficiently, focusing on genuine vulnerabilities.

Managing Security Alerts

GitHub offers a comprehensive overview of all security alerts for your repository, streamlining the triage process. This functionality allows you to prioritize alerts effectively, ensuring that critical vulnerabilities are addressed promptly. You can access this overview by navigating to the security tab of your repository and selecting "Code scanning alerts." Filters and free-text search options are available to help you sort through alerts efficiently.

Moreover, GitHub can suggest fixes for identified vulnerabilities, significantly reducing the time required to address issues. This feature not only enhances convenience but also supports your objective of rapidly mitigating security risks.

Utilizing Security Advisories

In scenarios where a vulnerability is discovered, security advisories provide a confidential platform for code maintainers to discuss and address the issue without public exposure. This approach prevents premature disclosure of vulnerabilities, allowing maintainers to resolve issues discreetly.

Once a vulnerability is fixed, the details are then published to the GitHub Advisory Database, informing the wider community and enabling affected parties to take necessary precautions.

In summary, the ability to effectively respond to security alerts is a critical component of maintaining a secure development environment. GitHub's features for evaluating, triaging, and managing security alerts, along with the use of security advisories, empower teams to address vulnerabilities efficiently and discreetly, safeguarding their projects against potential security threats.

Availability of GitHub Advanced Security Features

GitHub Advanced Security (GHAS) offers a suite of features designed to enhance the security posture of software development projects, whether they are housed in public or private repositories. These features are fundamental for organizations aiming to integrate security practices early in the software development lifecycle (SDLC), often referred to as "shifting left." By adopting GHAS, companies can proactively identify and mitigate vulnerabilities, thereby reducing technical debt and enhancing the overall security of their applications.

The availability of GHAS features varies based on the type of repository (public or private) and whether the repository is covered under a GitHub Advanced Security license. Here's a detailed look at the availability and functionality of GHAS features:

- **Code Scanning:** Available for both public and private repositories with Advanced Security. This feature automatically detects common vulnerabilities and coding errors in your codebase, helping to catch potential security issues early in the development process.

- **Secret Scanning:** While limited functionality is available for public repositories, full functionality, including the ability to exclude files from scanning and define custom patterns, is reserved for private repositories with Advanced Security. Secret scanning alerts you when secrets, such as API keys or credentials, are exposed in your code, preventing unauthorized access to your services.

- **Dependency Review:** This feature is enabled for public and private repositories with Advanced Security. It allows you to review the impact of changes to dependencies within your pull requests, providing insights into any vulnerable versions before merging. This proactive approach ensures that dependencies do not introduce security vulnerabilities into your codebase.

- **Security Overview:** Exclusive to private repositories with Advanced Security, the security overview offers a comprehensive view of an organization's security posture. It enables teams to review the security configuration and alerts across all repositories, identifying those at the highest risk and necessitating immediate attention.

Configuring GitHub Advanced Security

You as an admin can enable GitHub Advanced Security for Enterprise Cloud and Enterprise Server.

Activating GitHub Advanced Security for Enterprise Cloud

Integrating GitHub Advanced Security into your organization's software development lifecycle marks a fundamental step toward enhancing your security posture. As we've discussed the role and features of GitHub Advanced Security in various GitHub plans, it's time to focus on activating this powerful tool for your enterprise.

Activating GitHub Advanced Security at the organization level is a straightforward process that extends its benefits across all private and internal repositories within your organization. It's important to note that activating this feature will allocate seats from your GitHub Advanced Security license to committers in your organization's repositories.

Here's how you can enable GitHub Advanced Security for your
organization:

1. **Access Organization Settings:** Start by navigating
   to your organization's settings page. Look for the
   "Settings" option, then proceed to "Code security
   and analysis."

2. **Enable GitHub Advanced Security:** Within the
   "Configure security and analysis features" section,
   you'll find the option to enable GitHub Advanced
   Security. Click the "Enable all" button adjacent to
   the GitHub Advanced Security listing. If this option
   is grayed out, it may be due to a lack of available
   seats on your GitHub Advanced Security license.

3. **Confirm Activation:** After clicking "Enable all,"
   you'll be prompted to review the implications of
   activating Advanced Security across all repositories.
   Take a moment to understand the impact, then
   confirm by clicking "Enable all" again.

To ensure that GitHub Advanced Security is also automatically
activated for any new private and internal repositories added to your
organization in the future:

Automatic Activation for New Repositories: Locate the option for
automatically enabling GitHub Advanced Security on new private and
internal repositories. Check the box to select this feature, review the
implications for activating Advanced Security on all new repositories, and
confirm by clicking "Enable for new repositories."

By following these steps, you'll have successfully enabled GitHub
Advanced Security for your organization, bolstering the security of
your development projects. This proactive measure not only secures

your existing codebase but also ensures that any new additions to your
organization benefit from GitHub Advanced Security features from
the outset.

Activating GitHub Advanced Security for the Enterprise Server

To harness the full potential of GitHub Advanced Security across your
organization's repositories on GitHub Enterprise Server, initial activation
on your server instance is required. This foundational step ensures that
your development environment benefits from enhanced security features,
including code scanning, secret scanning, and Dependabot alerts. Here's a
guide to smoothly integrating GitHub Advanced Security into your GitHub
Enterprise Server environment.

Prerequisites

Before proceeding with the activation, ensure the following
prerequisites are met:

- Your GitHub Enterprise Server license includes GitHub
  Advanced Security, and it has been uploaded to your
  server instance.

- Familiarize yourself with the prerequisites for the
  specific features you intend to enable:

- Code scanning prerequisites

- Secret scanning prerequisites

- Dependabot prerequisites

Important Note   Activating GitHub Advanced Security features
will necessitate a restart of user-facing services on your GitHub
Enterprise Server. Plan this operation to minimize disruption to
your users.

Activation Steps

GitHub Advanced Security can be enabled through two main
pathways, the GitHub user interface or the administrative shell (SSH),
depending on your preference for graphical or command-line operations.

Via the GitHub User Interface

1. Access the Site admin dashboard of your GitHub
    Enterprise Server account and navigate to the
    Management Console.

2. In the sidebar, select "Security" to view available
    security features.

3. Choose the security features you wish to activate.

4. Save your settings and allow the configuration
    process to complete. This step will restart
    the necessary services on your GitHub
    Enterprise Server.

After the server restarts, proceed to enable GitHub Advanced Security
for your organization's repositories by following the guidelines provided
for Enterprise Cloud environments.

Via the Administrative Shell

For those who prefer or require a command-line approach, such as
when using infrastructure-as-code tools for staging or disaster recovery
deployments, GitHub Advanced Security features can be enabled via SSH:

1. SSH into your GitHub Enterprise Server instance.

2. Execute the following commands to enable the
    desired features:

- **For Code Scanning:** ghe-config app.minio.enabled
  true and then ghe-config app.code-scanning.
  enabled true

- **For Secret Scanning:** ghe-config app.secret-
  scanning.enabled true

- **For the Dependency Graph:** ghe-config app.
  dependency-graph.enabled true

3. Apply the configuration changes by running ghe-
   config-apply.

Once your GitHub Enterprise Server has restarted, finalize the
activation by enabling GitHub Advanced Security for all organization
repositories, mirroring the process outlined for Enterprise Cloud setups.

This comprehensive approach ensures that your GitHub Enterprise
Server instance and all associated repositories are fortified with GitHub's
cutting-edge security features, aligning your organization's development
practices with best-in-class security standards.

Configuring GitHub Advanced Security for Your Projects

After enabling GitHub Advanced Security in line with your enterprise
plan, the next step involves configuring access and establishing security
policies for your projects. This topic will help you manage access to
security alerts and set up comprehensive security policies at both the
organization and repository levels.

Managing Access to Security Alerts

Ensuring that the appropriate team members have access to security
alerts is crucial for maintaining the security integrity of your project.
Access to various types of security alerts within GitHub Advanced Security
is role dependent:

- **Code Scanning Alerts:** Require write permission on
  the repository to view and manage.

- **Secret Scanning:** Accessible by repository
  administrators and organization owners. Repository
  administrators and organization owners can extend
  access for managing secret scanning.

- **Dependabot Alerts:** Dependabot alerts to users and
  teams with write permissions on the repository through
  the repository's security and analysis settings.

With the correct permissions, team members can effectively manage
security alerts by committing code fixes, dismissing unnecessary alerts, or
updating dependencies flagged by Dependabot.

Setting a Security Policy at the Organization Level

Implementing a security policy across your organization ensures
uniform use of GitHub Advanced Security features. You might, for
instance, allow all repository administrators within your organization to
activate Advanced Security features for their repositories.

To establish a security policy for your organization, follow these steps:

1. Go to your enterprise account's sidebar; select
   Policies ➤ Advanced Security.

2. Choose a policy for your enterprise-owned
   organizations from the GitHub Advanced Security
   dropdown menu.

3. You can also specify policies for individual
   organizations, allowing or disallowing Advanced
   Security features as needed. Note that restricting
   Advanced Security for an organization limits
   repository administrators from enabling new
   Advanced Security features but does not deactivate
   already enabled features.

Implementing a Security Policy at the Repository Level

Documenting how to report security vulnerabilities is equally vital at
the repository level. This is typically done through a SECURITY.md file
placed in the root, docs, or .github folder of your project's repository. This
file should outline supported project versions and the process for reporting
vulnerabilities, providing clear guidance for contributors.

To add a security policy to your repository, follow these steps:

1. Navigate to Security ➤ Security policy in your
   repository settings.

2. Click Start setup to create a new SECURITY.md file.

3. Fill in the file with details on supported versions and
   vulnerability reporting instructions.

4. Commit the SECURITY.md file to your repository.
   Figure 9-9 shows the security policy.

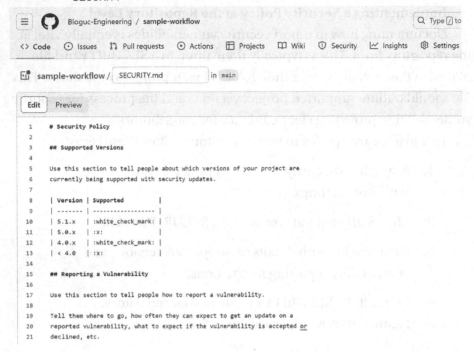

Figure 9-9. *Security policy*

This approach not only streamlines the vulnerability reporting process but also leverages GitHub Security Advisories to manage the disclosure and remediation of security issues effectively.

By carefully managing access to security alerts and establishing clear security policies at both the organization and repository levels, you can enhance the security posture of your projects and ensure a proactive stance against potential vulnerabilities.

Monitor and Manage GitHub Advanced Security Features

As a GitHub administrator, it's crucial to stay informed and proactive about the security of your projects. This guide will walk you through the essentials of monitoring and managing security risks using GitHub's Advanced Security features and alerts. By leveraging the security overview and understanding the GitHub Advanced Security endpoints, you can ensure your projects are well protected.

Utilizing the Security Overview

The security overview is a powerful tool currently in beta, designed
to give you a comprehensive view of your project's security posture.
Accessible via the Security tab in both organizations and repositories, it
serves multiple levels of analysis:

- **Organization Level:** Here, you'll find aggregated
  security data across all repositories within your
  organization, alongside repository-specific insights.
  This level allows for filtering by security feature,
  enabling you to pinpoint areas needing attention.

- **Team Level:** For teams with admin privileges, the
  security overview presents security information
  specific to their repositories. This feature is invaluable
  for managing security within specific segments of your
  organization.

- **Repository Level:** At this granularity, the overview
  highlights active security features for each repository
  and suggests configuration options for unutilized
  security measures. Its interactive nature and filtering
  capabilities make it an excellent resource for both
  broad overviews and detailed investigations into your
  security status.

Whether you're assessing the rollout of GitHub Advanced Security
across your enterprise or scrutinizing specific types of alerts and their
severity across your organization, the security overview is your go-to tool.

GitHub Advanced Security Endpoints

To further enhance your security management, GitHub provides
several Advanced Security endpoints, each tailored to different security
features. Here's a breakdown:

- **Code Scanning:** Manage code scanning alerts
  within a repository, automate alert reports for your
  organization, and upload offline scanning results.
  Access these functionalities through the code
  scanning API.

- **Secret Scanning:** Activate or deactivate secret scanning
  for repositories, and manage secret scanning alerts
  for private repositories via the Repos API and secret
  scanning API.

- **Dependency Review:** Control dependency alerts,
  the dependency graph, and security fixes for your
  repositories. View dependency details through the
  Repos API and GraphQL API.

Managing GitHub Actions Permissions

When automating security workflows with GitHub Actions, setting
the correct permissions for the GITHUB_TOKEN is essential. This token's
default permissions vary, offering different levels of access based on the
scope. You can adjust these permissions in your workflow files to ensure
your actions have the necessary access without compromising security.
Remember, the goal is to provide the least access required, enhancing your
project's security posture.

For comprehensive workflow or job-specific permission
configurations, utilize the permission key in your workflow files. This
approach ensures that only the required permissions are granted, with
all others defaulting to no access, except for the metadata scope, which
retains read access.

Effectively monitoring and managing GitHub Advanced Security
features and alerts is pivotal for maintaining the security integrity of
your projects. By utilizing the security overview for strategic insights and
configuring Advanced Security endpoints and GitHub Actions permissions

appropriately, you can safeguard your projects against potential threats. This proactive stance on security management not only protects your code but also fosters a culture of security within your organization.

Understanding and Implementing Code Scanning

Here, readers learn about code scanning, a feature that scans code for potential security vulnerabilities. The chapter explains how to enable code scanning, how it works, and how to interpret and respond to the results.

Understanding and Implementing Secret Scanning

This section covers secret scanning, a feature designed to prevent the accidental exposure of sensitive information, such as passwords and tokens. The chapter provides guidance on enabling secret scanning, understanding the scan results, and remediation strategies.

Best Practices for Managing Environment Secrets on GitHub

Managing environment secrets securely is crucial for maintaining the integrity and security of your software development lifecycle. Here are some best practices to consider:

- **Avoid Structured Data As Secrets:** Structured data, such as JSON objects, can complicate the redaction process in logs, potentially exposing sensitive information. Stick to simple key-value pairs for secrets to ensure they can be securely redacted.

- **Register Secrets Used in Workflows:** Always register secrets that are used within GitHub Actions workflows, particularly if a secret is used to generate another sensitive value. This ensures that all sensitive information is accounted for and protected.

- **Implement Required Reviewer Approvals:** To safeguard environment secrets, configure your workflows to require explicit approval from designated reviewers before accessing secrets. This adds an additional layer of security, ensuring that only authorized personnel can use these secrets in workflow jobs.

Safely Using Runners

Use Self-Hosted Runners with Caution: Self-hosted runners should ideally be used within private repositories to minimize the risk of unauthorized access. When using self-hosted runners in both private and internal repositories, it's vital to implement strict security measures to protect the runner environment and prevent potential access to secrets by unauthorized users.

Licensing Considerations for GitHub Advanced Security

GitHub Advanced Security (GHAS) offers a suite of features designed to enhance the security of your projects. While dependency review, code scanning, and secret scanning are available at no additional cost for public repositories, private repositories require a GHAS license. This license, obtainable through GitHub Enterprise Cloud or GitHub Enterprise

Server, covers a specific number of seats, allowing organizations to tailor
their security measures to their needs. When strategizing your security
approach, prioritize repositories with high commit activity and those
critical to your organization's operations to ensure they benefit from
GitHub Advanced Security's comprehensive protection.

Benefits of GitHub Advanced Security

- **Proactive Vulnerability Management:** GitHub
  Advanced Security integrates seamlessly into the
  development process, enabling teams to detect and
  address vulnerabilities early. This proactive approach
  significantly reduces the window of opportunity for
  potential exploitation.

- **Enhanced Collaboration:** By bridging the gap between
  development and security teams, GitHub Advanced
  Security fosters a culture where security is prioritized
  from the start. This collaborative environment ensures
  that security considerations are integrated into the
  development process, enhancing the overall security
  posture of projects.

- **Compliance and Risk Management:** For organizations
  subject to regulatory requirements, GitHub Advanced
  Security provides essential tools for compliance and
  risk management. With comprehensive security
  insights and audit trails, teams can easily demonstrate
  compliance and manage risks effectively.

- **Developer Efficiency:** Automating security checks
  within the development workflow frees developers to
  focus on feature development rather than on identifying
  and fixing security issues. This efficiency not only
  accelerates the development process but also ensures
  that security is a built-in aspect of the product lifecycle.

In outline, by adhering to best practices for managing environment secrets and leveraging the features offered by GitHub Advanced Security, organizations can significantly enhance the security and efficiency of their development processes. These measures not only protect sensitive information but also promote a security-first culture, ensuring that projects are developed with the highest security standards in mind.

Summary

This chapter provided a comprehensive guide to enhancing software security within an organization's development processes using GitHub's powerful tools. It began with an introduction to GitHub Advanced Security, highlighting its role in identifying, addressing, and mitigating security risks in codebases. The chapter emphasized the importance of embedding security practices within organizational culture, ensuring that every team member is aligned with security objectives. Through detailed discussions on code scanning and secret scanning, it offered insights into how these features can automatically detect vulnerabilities and exposed secrets within code, significantly reducing the potential for security breaches. The integration of GitHub Advanced Security within the software development lifecycle (SDLC) was thoroughly examined, showcasing how continuous security checks can be seamlessly incorporated into every stage of development, from initial coding to deployment. The chapter also covered strategies for an effective response to security alerts, ensuring that teams can quickly address and remediate identified issues. Configuration guidelines provide a road map for setting up GitHub Advanced Security features, tailored to meet specific organizational needs. Finally, the chapter concluded with best practices for utilizing GitHub Advanced Security, advocating for a proactive, informed approach to software security. This holistic view underscores the pivotal role of GitHub Advanced Security in fostering a secure, efficient, and resilient development environment, ultimately contributing to the creation of safer software products.

Resources

- You can check the GitHub Advanced Security
  license pricing: `https://github.com/
  pricing#compare-features`

- Configuring Dependabot alerts: `https://docs.
  github.com/en/code-security/dependabot/
  dependabot-alerts/configuring-dependabot-alerts`

- Dependabot quickstart guide: `https://docs.
  github.com/en/code-security/getting-started/
  dependabot-quickstart-guide`

- Code scanning: `https://docs.github.com/en/code-
  security/code-scanning`

- Secret scanning: `https://docs.github.com/en/code-
  security/secret-scanning`

- Troubleshooting secret scanning: `https://docs.
  github.com/en/code-security/secret-scanning/
  troubleshooting-secret-scanning`

- About GitHub Advanced Security: `https://docs.
  github.com/en/get-started/learning-about-
  github/about-github-advanced-security`

CHAPTER 10

GitHub Troubleshooting, Monitoring, and Reporting

In the dynamic and collaborative world of software development, GitHub stands as a crucial platform for code management and collaboration. However, navigating through its complexities can sometimes be challenging, leading to a need for effective troubleshooting, monitoring, and reporting strategies. This chapter is particularly crafted to address these aspects, offering a comprehensive guide for developers, project managers, and teams who rely on GitHub for their development needs.

This chapter begins by exploring common issues encountered on GitHub, from merge conflicts to authentication errors, providing clear, step-by-step solutions to resolve them. It then delves deeper into advanced troubleshooting techniques tailored for complex scenarios that go beyond everyday use, including strategies for debugging CI/CD pipelines and handling large repositories. Recognizing the importance of proactive measures, the chapter also focuses on monitoring GitHub operations, discussing tools and practices essential for maintaining repository health and performance.

© Balu Nivrutti Ilag, AjayKumar P. Baljoshi, Ganesh J. Sangale and Yogesh Athave 2024
B. N. Ilag et al , *Mastering GitHub Enterprise Management and Administration*,
https://doi.org/10.1007/979-8-8688-0369-7_10

Effective reporting is crucial in a collaborative environment, and this chapter provides insights into creating meaningful reports on repository metrics and workflow efficiency. It guides readers through leveraging GitHub's API for custom reports and integrating with external tools for enhanced data visualization. Additionally, the chapter emphasizes the importance of regular maintenance, offering best practices to keep repositories optimized and secure.

A unique feature of this chapter is the emphasis on setting up a GitHub Health Dashboard, a vital tool for real-
time monitoring of key metrics and system status. This not only aids in immediate issue detection but also in strategic planning and resource allocation. Lastly, the chapter addresses incident management, underscoring the importance of learning from past incidents to improve future practices.

Overall, this chapter serves as an essential resource for anyone looking to enhance their proficiency in managing GitHub environments. It provides the tools and knowledge needed to navigate challenges, optimize workflows, and maintain a high standard of efficiency and security in GitHub operations.

Topics covered include

1. Understanding GitHub Monitoring and Reporting

2. Learning GitHub Audit Logs

3. Understanding Common GitHub Issues

4. Advanced Troubleshooting Techniques

5. Monitoring GitHub Operations

6. Best Practices for GitHub Maintenance

7. Setting Up a GitHub Health Dashboard

8. Handling and Learning from Incidents

Understanding GitHub Monitoring and Reporting

The topic is crucial for organizations leveraging GitHub Enterprise Cloud for their software development needs. This area focuses on the tools, features, and practices that enable enterprises to monitor their GitHub environment and generate insightful reports effectively. Here's a detailed breakdown.

Monitoring in GitHub Enterprise Cloud

Understanding GitHub monitoring and reporting within GitHub Enterprise Cloud encompasses a comprehensive suite of tools and features designed to provide real-time insights, ensure system health, enhance security, and optimize performance. This multifaceted approach to monitoring and reporting is crucial for maintaining operational efficiency, ensuring security compliance, and facilitating transparent and effective management of GitHub environments.

Real-Time Monitoring

GitHub Enterprise Cloud offers an Activity Dashboard that serves as a real-time window into the activities occurring within the GitHub environment. This dashboard tracks and displays various actions such as push, pull, and merge activities across all repositories, offering immediate visibility into the development workflow. Additionally, system health checks are conducted regularly to assess the overall health of the system. These checks cover server status, response times, and uptime metrics, ensuring that any system issues can be promptly identified and addressed to maintain continuous operation.

Audit Logs

A key component of GitHub's monitoring capabilities is the comprehensive audit logs it maintains. These logs capture detailed records of user actions, repository changes, and administrative activities, providing a granular view of operations within the GitHub environment. This level of detail is invaluable for security purposes, compliance auditing, and operational transparency. Audit logs are retained for a specified period, allowing organizations to conduct historical analysis and retrospective investigations when necessary.

Security Monitoring

Security is a paramount concern, and GitHub addresses this through automated security scans that integrate with security tools to perform code scanning, vulnerability assessments, and dependency checks. This proactive approach to security monitoring helps identify and mitigate potential vulnerabilities before they can be exploited. Additionally, real-time alerts and notifications are generated in response to security incidents, such as potential breaches or unauthorized access attempts, enabling swift action to protect sensitive data and maintain the integrity of the GitHub environment.

Performance Metrics

To ensure that GitHub Enterprise Cloud operates at peak efficiency, performance metrics related to resource utilization are closely monitored. This includes tracking CPU, memory, and storage usage to prevent performance degradation. Traffic analysis further complements this by examining web traffic, API usage, and other relevant metrics. Understanding these usage patterns helps in identifying potential bottlenecks and optimizing resource allocation to meet the demands of the GitHub environment effectively.

GitHub's monitoring and reporting capabilities within the Enterprise Cloud platform provide organizations with the tools and insights needed to manage their GitHub environments effectively. From real-time activity monitoring and comprehensive audit logs to robust security measures and performance optimization, GitHub equips administrators with the necessary resources to ensure operational excellence, security compliance, and efficient resource management.

Understanding GitHub Reporting in GitHub Enterprise Cloud

GitHub Enterprise Cloud offers a comprehensive suite of reporting tools designed to enhance visibility into various aspects of software development projects. These tools are pivotal for teams aiming to optimize performance, ensure compliance, and make data-driven decisions.

Customizable Reporting Tools: GitHub provides a range of customizable reporting options to suit diverse needs.

- **Activity Reports:** These reports are invaluable for assessing team performance, tracking repository activity, and measuring contributions across projects. By analyzing these metrics, teams can identify areas of high productivity as well as opportunities for improvement.

- **Compliance Reports:** For organizations subject to regulatory requirements, GitHub offers tools to generate compliance-related reports. These are crucial during audits, helping organizations demonstrate adherence to legal and industry standards.

Integration with Analytics Tools: GitHub's flexibility in data integration allows for a more in-depth analysis.

- **API Access:** GitHub's API opens the door to extracting detailed data from your repositories, which can then be integrated with external analytics and reporting tools. This capability enables teams to tailor their analysis to specific requirements.

- **Third-Party Integrations:** By leveraging integrations with leading business intelligence tools, GitHub users can enhance their data analysis and visualization efforts. These integrations facilitate advanced analytics, offering deeper insights into project metrics and trends.

Insights and Dashboards: GitHub provides intuitive insights and dashboards for real-time project monitoring.

- **Project Insights:** These visual dashboards offer a snapshot of project progress, issue resolution rates, and team collaboration dynamics. They serve as a central hub for monitoring the health and progress of projects.

- **Trend Analysis:** By examining data trends over time, teams can make informed strategic decisions to enhance workflow efficiency and project outcomes. Trend analysis helps in identifying patterns that could indicate potential issues or opportunities for optimization.

Custom Reporting: For tailored data analysis, GitHub offers robust custom reporting features.

- **Query Builder:** GitHub's query builder and API endpoints allow for the creation of custom reports that meet the unique needs of an organization. This flexibility ensures that teams can focus on the metrics that matter most to them.

- **Export Capabilities:** With the ability to export data in various formats, GitHub facilitates further analysis or presentation outside the platform. Whether for internal reviews or external presentations, this feature ensures that key data is accessible and usable in the desired format.

GitHub Enterprise Cloud's reporting capabilities provide organizations with the tools they need to monitor performance, ensure compliance, and derive actionable insights from their data. By utilizing these features, teams can enhance their project management, streamline workflows, and ultimately drive better outcomes for their software development projects.

Monitor GitHub Events by Using a Webhook with Azure Functions

Monitoring GitHub events with Azure Functions involves setting up webhooks to receive real-time notifications from GitHub repositories. Azure Functions, a serverless computing service by Microsoft, allows developers to create event-driven functions triggered by these webhooks. These functions can be customized to perform specific actions based on GitHub events, such as code commits or pull requests. The integration enhances efficiency by automating tasks like updating databases or sending notifications. The combination of webhooks and Azure Functions enables agile responses to repository activities. Overall, this integration enhances the overall development lifecycle by facilitating automated, event-driven actions in response to GitHub events.

Learning GitHub Audit Logs

GitHub Audit Logs in GitHub Enterprise Cloud

GitHub Audit Logs for the Enterprise: Enhancing Debugging and Compliance

GitHub Enterprise Cloud offers comprehensive audit logs, a crucial tool for debugging and adhering to both internal and external compliance requirements. These logs meticulously record a range of user, organization, and repository events, providing a transparent view of activities within your enterprise.

Understanding Audit Logs

For certain scenarios, webhooks might be a more efficient alternative to audit logs or API polling. GitHub's webhooks notify your server about specific events in repositories, organizations, or the entire enterprise. They can be particularly effective for tracking specific occurrences without the need to constantly poll the API or search the audit log. More details are available in the "Webhooks documentation."

Audit logs in GitHub Enterprise Cloud capture events for the current month and up to six previous months, with Git events being retained for seven days. By default, the logs display events from the past three months. To access older events, you need to specify a date range using the "created" parameter. Each entry in the audit log is identified by a combination of an event category and an operation type. For instance, "repo.create" denotes the creation operation in the repository category.

Details Captured in Audit Log Entries

- Enterprise or organization where the action occurred

- User (actor) who performed the action

- Affected user

- Repository involved in the action

- Nature of the action

- Country of the action

- Date and time of the action

- SAML SSO identity of the actor (in public beta)

- Authentication method for actions outside the web UI

- Source IP address of the actor (optional)

Additional Monitoring Tools: Beyond the audit log, you can monitor enterprise activities through global webhooks and other tools, especially for actions related to security alerts. More information is available in the GitHub documentation on "Exploring user activity in your enterprise."

- **Interacting with Audit Logs:** As an enterprise owner, you have several ways to engage with your audit log data.

- **Viewing the Audit Logs:** Access detailed logs for your enterprise.

- **Searching and Exporting Data:** Search for specific events and export audit log data.

- **Identifying Events by Access Token:** Trace events back to specific access tokens.

- **Displaying IP Addresses:** Opt to show IP addresses associated with events.

- **Streaming Audit and Git Events:** Stream data to external systems for comprehensive data management.

- **Using the Audit Log API:** Access actions performed in your enterprise via the API.

GitHub Common Issues and Troubleshooting

GitHub Enterprise Cloud users often encounter a range of common issues that can impact their workflow and productivity. These challenges include difficulties with authentication and permissions, problems with repository access, integration glitches with third-party tools, and challenges in managing CI/CD pipelines using GitHub Actions. Additionally, users sometimes face issues related to rate limiting, especially when dealing with large-scale operations or data migrations.

Troubleshooting these issues effectively requires a systematic approach. For authentication and permission-related problems, verifying the user's role and permissions within the organization, along with checking any third-party identity providers' configurations, is crucial. When repository access issues arise, ensuring that the repository settings and access controls are correctly configured can often resolve the problem. For integration issues, reviewing the application logs and the configuration settings of the third-party tool, as well as consulting the tool's documentation for known compatibility issues with GitHub, can provide valuable insights.

CI/CD pipeline challenges in GitHub Actions can often be addressed by examining the workflow files for errors, checking the GitHub Actions runner's status, and reviewing the execution logs for specific error messages that can guide troubleshooting efforts. To mitigate rate limiting issues, optimizing API usage, leveraging caching, and considering the use of GitHub's recommended best practices for large-scale operations are effective strategies.

Moreover, GitHub provides extensive documentation, community forums, and, for enterprise customers, dedicated support channels that can be invaluable resources for troubleshooting. Staying informed about the latest updates and features released by GitHub can also help users anticipate and adapt to changes that might affect their workflows.

Monitor GitHub Events

GitHub events refer to various actions or changes that occur within a GitHub repository. These events include activities like code commits, pull requests, issues, and more. GitHub provides a mechanism known as webhooks, which allows users to receive real-time notifications about these events.

When these events happen, we can monitor these events and perform some actions using GitHub Actions, which is discussed in Chapter 5. Here, we will explain how to use third-party tool like Azure Functions and perform some action using webhooks.

Webhooks are personalized HTTP callbacks that get activated by specific events, like pushing code to a repository or modifying a wiki page. When these events happen, the originating site sends an HTTP request to the designated URL set up for the webhook. Using Azure Functions, we can establish customized operations within a function that executes in response to receiving a webhook message. This means we can create tailored responses and actions based on the specific triggers defined by these events, offering a flexible and automated way to handle various scenarios within our application or system. Once we understand GitHub events and webhooks, we will understand about Azure Functions.

Azure Functions are a serverless computing service provided by Microsoft, enabling developers to write, deploy, and run event-driven functions without managing infrastructure. These functions are triggered by various events, such as HTTP requests, database changes, or timer schedules. One key advantage is the ability to scale automatically, as Azure Functions allocate resources dynamically based on demand. They support multiple programming languages, allowing developers to choose the language that best suits their needs; it has the following components.

In simple terms, a trigger initiates the execution of a function by defining how it is invoked. Each function must have precisely one trigger, and triggers often come with associated data, commonly presented as the function's payload. On the other hand, a binding serves to link a resource to a function, allowing the definition of both input and output bindings. Input bindings provide data to the function as parameters, facilitating seamless integration with external resources. For instance, connecting a database to Azure Functions can be achieved through a binding, eliminating the need for additional connection code. It is important to note that bindings are optional, and a function may incorporate one or more input and/or output bindings based on its requirements.

Monitor GitHub Events by Using a Webhook with Azure Functions

Here, we will discuss initiating your function through a webhook, allowing it to be triggered by external events. Examine the information conveyed in the webhook's message to gather insights and process relevant data. Ensure the security of webhook payloads by implementing a secret, safeguarding the communication between the webhook and your function. This process involves fortifying the integrity of the data exchange and contributes to a more secure and reliable execution of your function in response to external triggers.

One of the practical use cases will be if you want to keep an eye on changes in your company's GitHub wiki, so you are using Azure Functions. The first step is making an Azure Functions app with a function that kicks in when there is an update, thanks to a webhook. This helps you tap into the benefits of webhooks and ensures your function runs smoothly each time there is a wiki update.

Later, this use case will be discussed; you will find out why webhooks are handy and learn how to make your Azure Functions respond to them. This way, you can easily catch details like when the wiki was updated and who made the changes, making it simpler to stay on top of things.

As we have discussed about Azure Functions functionality in the earlier part of the chapter,now we will see it in action.

Steps to Create a Function App

Perform the following steps to create a function in the Azure portal.

To set up your Azure Functions app, begin by signing in to the Azure portal using your MS Learn account. Navigate to "Create a resource," and under Categories, choose "Compute." In the search box, look for and select "Function App." Click "Create," and on the Basics tab, provide the necessary details. Ensure your Function App Name is unique, and for Subscription, choose "Subscription."

Under Instance Details, enter your chosen Function App Name, select "Code" for Publish, and opt for "Node.js" as the Runtime stack with the default version. Choose the region nearest to you from the allowed Sandbox regions and set the operating system to "Windows." For Hosting, select "Consumption (Serverless)."

Move to the Storage tab, where you will create a new Storage account with the default name. After inputting these details, click "Review + create." Azure will verify your entries, and once confirmed, select "Create" to initiate the creation of your Function App.

Steps to Create a Webhook-Triggered Function

Once your deployment is finished, click "Go to resource" to access the Overview pane for your Function App. Under the Functions section, choose "Create in Azure portal." This action opens the Create function pane. In the template selection, opt for "HTTP trigger," and then click "Create." This leads you to the HttpTrigger1 pane, providing essential information about your newly created trigger.

Now, on the left menu, go to Developer and select Code + Test. This action opens the Code + Test pane for your Function, revealing the JavaScript file generated from the chosen template. The code file should resemble the provided example. This step allows you to review and test the code associated with your HTTP trigger, providing insights into its functionality and structure.

```javascript
module.exports = async function (context, req) {
    context.log('JavaScript HTTP trigger function processed a
    request.');
    const name = (req.query.name || (req.body && req.
    body.name));
    const responseMessage = name
        ? "Hello, " + name + ". This HTTP triggered function
        executed successfully."
        : "This HTTP triggered function executed successfully.
        Pass a name in the query string or in the request body
        for a personalized response.";
    context.res = {
        // status: 200, /* Defaults to 200 */
        body: responseMessage
    };
}
```

The JavaScript function found in the index.js file, generated through the portal, handles incoming requests. Specifically, it processes the "name" parameter, which can be provided either as part of the query string or within the request body. The function then generates a response, delivering a "Hello" message based on the provided name. This code is designed to handle and respond to requests by customizing a greeting based on the input parameter.

Navigate to the dropdown list above the code where you can choose the file name. Select "function.json," and the corresponding JSON file, generated by the template, will be displayed. The content of this file outlines the configuration details for the function. It typically includes information such as the trigger type, input/output bindings, and other settings. In this case, the structure of the file should resemble the provided example, offering a clear representation of how the function is configured and what inputs and outputs it expects or produces:

```
{
    "bindings": [
        {
            "authLevel": "function",
            "type": "httpTrigger",
            "direction": "in",
            "name": "req"
            "methods": [
                "get",
                "post"
            ]
        },
        {
            "type": "http",
            "direction": "out",
            "name": "res"
        }
    ]
}
```

The JSON bindings define that the function responds to both HTTP GET and POST requests targeted at the function app's URL.

Once we have created the required function, we can test by using the following steps.

Testing Function Triggers

To test the Function, first we need identify the Function url and then use it for testing, follow below step to test a Function.

Accessing the Function URL

Access the top menu bar and choose "Get function URL." In the ensuing dialog box, pick "default" from the Key dropdown list under Function key. Copy the URL, which resembles

https://<your-functionapp-name>.azurewebsites.net/api/HttpTrigg er1?code=azseddaaaaasesdedaw==.

Testing the Function

Paste the copied URL into a browser, and to the end of the URL, add the query string parameter: &name=<yourname> (e.g., &name=Dick and Jane). Press Enter to run the request. The function's response, like "Hello Dick and Jane. This HTTP triggered function executed successfully," will be displayed in the browser.

By following these steps, you've successfully created a functional HTTP-triggered Azure Functions that can be activated via a URL.

As our function is ready, we will configure the webhook in the GitHub repository.

Overview of a Setup Webhook for a GitHub Repository

Before we set up a webhook for a GitHub repository, here is a summary of the steps:

- **Setting Up GitHub Webhooks:** GitHub webhooks can be configured for an entire organization or a specific repository, triggering events subscribed to by the user. An example is the Gollum event, ideal for monitoring wiki updates, including page creations and modifications.

- **Two-Step Webhook Setup Process:** The process involves specifying webhook behavior and subscribed events on GitHub, followed by configuring the Azure Functions to handle the payload. This module focuses on setting up a repository-specific webhook. On GitHub, navigate to Settings, select Webhooks, and click Add webhook.

- **Configuring Webhook Options:** Webhooks require several configuration options. The Payload URL is crucial, specifying the server's URL for receiving webhook POST requests. The Content type can be either application/json, delivering the JSON payload directly in the POST request body, or application/x-www-form-urlencoded, sending the JSON payload as a form parameter named payload.

- **Managing Webhook Events:** Events play a central role in webhooks, triggering actions when repository activities occur. Configure events to call the specified URL upon occurrence. For instance, to respond to raised issues, select the Issues checkbox under Let me select individual events. Ensure the Active checkbox is selected, and then Add webhook to activate the trigger. For wiki updates, choose the Wiki checkbox, representing the Gollum event.

- **Exploring Webhook Event:** A comprehensive list of webhook events and their triggers can be found in the GitHub webhook event documentation. Refer to the "Resources" section for the link.

Step-by-Step Process of Setting Up a Webhook for a GitHub Repository

Repository Setup

Begin by signing in to your GitHub account and creating a new repository named, for instance, "ghWebhook." Activate the wiki module by selecting "Public" and create the first wiki page, adding some text to serve as the Home page.

– **Setting Up a Webhook for Gollum Events**

Gollum is a GitHub event triggered upon the creation or update of a wiki page. Navigate to the Home page, select Settings, and then Webhooks. Add a new webhook with the specified settings: the payload URL pointing to your Azure Functions app, content type as application/json, and selecting the Wiki checkbox for events. Ensure the webhook is marked as active.

– **Testing the Webhook**

Edit the Home page in the wiki, adding a text like "Testing Webhook." Save the page, then go to Settings ➤ Webhooks, and select the top delivery entry under Recent Deliveries. Examine the Headers and Payload sections to verify the webhook's trigger event and confirm that the wiki page was edited. Additionally, check the Response tab to see the message generated by the Azure Functions, confirming the successful execution of the HTTP-triggered function.

Request URL: `https://testwh123456.azurewebsites.net/api/HttpTrigger1?code=aUjXIpqdJOZHPQuBOSzFegxGJuOnAXmsQBnmkCpJ6RYxleRaoxJ8cQ%3D%3D`

Request method: POST

Accept: */*

content-type: application/json

User-Agent: GitHub-Hookshot/16496cb

X-GitHub-Delivery: 9ed46280-6ab3-11e9-8a19-f1a14922a239

X-GitHub-Event: gollum

X-GitHub-Hook-ID: 312141005

X-GitHub-Hook-Installation-Target-ID: 394459163

X-GitHub-Hook-Installation-Target-Type: repository

Sample headers look like these.

```
"pages": [
    {
        "page_name": "Home",
        "title": "Home",
        "summary": null,
        "action": "edited",
        "sha": "04d012c5f92a95ae3f7721173bf9f2b1b35ea22f",
        "html_url": https://github.com/.../wiki/Home}
    ],
"repository" : {
    "id": 176302421,
    "node_id": "MDEwOlJlcG9zaXRvcnkxNzYzMDIOMjE=",
    "name": "tieredstorage",
    ...
  },
  "sender" : {
    ...
  }
```

A section contains information indicating that your wiki page was edited. The payload contains **pages**, **repository**, and **sender** sections, which should look something like before.

By following these steps, you've successfully set up and tested a webhook for Gollum events in your GitHub repository, integrated with your Azure Functions.

Triggering an Azure Function with a GitHub Event
Understanding the Gollum Event

The GitHub Gollum event allows you to track updates to your wiki. When triggered, your Azure HttpTrigger function is activated, enabling you to retrieve and process the sent data by parsing the payload.

In the preceding section, we have already configured a webhook for Gollum events on your company's GitHub repository. Additionally, you have illustrated the capability of Azure Functions apps to execute code in response to webhook requests; let us examine the Gollum event payload.

Examining the Gollum Event Payload

The payload for the Gollum event encompasses essential details such as updated pages, repository information, and details about the event-triggering user. For instance, a payload might include data on the page name, title, action (created or edited), HTML page URL, repository name, owner details, repository URL, and information about the event-raising user, for example, a payload might look like the following code:

```
"pages": [
    {
        "page_name": "Home",
        "title": "Home",
        "summary": null,
        "action": "edited",
        "sha": "562362bc141b9e2db1fb971e1ecb4fd0b7457f68",
        "html_url": "https://github.com/testrepo/Hello-World/
        wiki/Home
    }
],
"repository": {
```

```
  ...
  "name": "testrepo",
  ...
"owner": {
    ...
  },
  "html_url": "https://github.com/...",
  ....
},
"sender": {
    "login": "..."
.....
}
```

Preparing for Payload Parsing

This payload, transmitted as the body of an HTTP POST request, needs to be correctly parsed and processed by your function. The logic in your function should be updated to extract relevant information, like retrieving the repository name from the payload. The event type is identified in the x-github-event request header. The example response provided showcases how the function can output data, indicating the repository name and the event type, and it looks as follows:

```
if (req.body.repository.name){
    context.res = {
        body: "Repository is: " + req.body.repository.name + ",
        Event Type is: " + -req.headers['x-
        github-event']
    };
}
```

The next steps will be updating function code to effectively handle incoming Gollum events, ensuring accurate parsing and processing of the associated payload.

Updating Function Code

Navigate to the Azure portal, locate your Function App, and access the HttpTrigger1 you created. In the Code + Test pane, select index.js from the dropdown list. Replace the last three lines of code in the function body with the provided JavaScript code. This updated code extracts information from the payload, including the page title, action, and event type, constructing a response summarizing the action. Save your changes.

```javascript
module.exports = async function (context, req) {
    context.log('JavaScript HTTP trigger function processed a
    request.')
    // Existing code..
    if (req.body.pages[0].title){
        context.res = [ body: "Page is " + req.body.pages[0].
        title + ", Action is " + req.body.pages[0].action + ",
        Event Type is " + req.headers['x-github-event']
        };
    }
    else {
        context.res = {
            status: 400,
            body: ("Invalid payload for Wiki event")
        };
    }
}
```

Triggering the Function

In GitHub, access your repository's Settings, go to Webhooks, and select Edit for your webhook. Navigate to the Recent Deliveries tab and select the latest entry. Choose Redeliver, confirm the redelivery in the dialog box, and then check the Response tab. Verify that the webhook successfully triggered your function, parsing the information and responding with details like the page, action, and event type, which looks as follows:

The page is home, the action is edited, and the event type is gollum.

By following these steps, you have effectively updated your Azure Functions to parse Gollum event payloads and tested its functionality with a simulated wiki page change.

Securing Webhook Payloads with GitHub

After configuring your function to receive payloads, it actively listens for any payload sent to the designated endpoint. To enhance security, it's crucial to restrict requests to those originating from GitHub. One approach is approving requests from GitHub's IP address, but a more straightforward method involves setting up a secret token and validating requests using this token.

Scenario Overview

In the given scenario, your IT department's management is pleased with the webhook-triggered function in the Azure Functions app. This function effectively parses information about updates to the company wiki, sending it to the business every time the Gollum event occurs. However, management is concerned about the security of the information transmitted from GitHub and has tasked you with finding a way to secure and verify that GitHub is indeed the source of updates.

Webhook Secrets

Setting a webhook secret provides a layer of verification, ensuring that POST requests to the payload URL originate from GitHub. Upon setting a secret, GitHub includes the x-hub-signature header in the webhook POST request. This signature is essential for validating the authenticity of requests.

Validation Process

Once the secret token is established, GitHub utilizes it to generate a hash signature for each payload. This hash signature, along with the request, is sent in the headers as x-hub-signature. When your function receives a request, it must compute the hash using the secret and ensure it matches the hash in the request header. GitHub employs an HMAC SHA1 hexdigest for this computation, and you must calculate the hash in the same manner, using your secret key and the payload body. Notably, the hash signature begins with the text sha1=.

In the next section, you will learn how to set the secret field on GitHub and implement the validation process to secure webhook payloads effectively. This additional layer of security ensures that the information received by your function is authenticated and originates from GitHub, mitigating potential security risks.

Here are the steps to be followed to implement securing a webhook:

Step 1: Accessing the Azure Function

- Navigate to the Azure portal and locate your Function App created in the initial exercise.

- In the Functions section, choose the HttpTrigger1 function, and enter the Code + Test pane.

Step 2: Integrating the crypto-js Library

- Include a reference to the crypto-js library at the beginning of the index.js:

```
const Crypto = require('crypto');
```

Step 3: Generating and Saving a Secret Key

- Save the function after incorporating the library, triggering the appearance of the Logs pane.

- Under Developer, go to Function Keys, reveal the default key, and copy it for later use.

Step 4: Implementing Payload Validation

- In the Code + Test pane, after the context.log statement, add code to compute the hash using the secret key:

```
const hmac = Crypto.createHmac("sha1",
"<default key>");
```

```
const signature = hmac.update(JSON.stringify
(req.body)).digest('hex');
```

Step 5: Preparing Signature for Comparison

- Append sha1= to the hash to match the x-hub-signature
  format in the request header:

```
const shaSignature = `sha1=${signature}`;
```

Step 6: Retrieving GitHub Signature

- Fetch the GitHub signature from the request header:

```
const gitHubSignature = req.headers
['x-hub-signature'];
```

Step 7: Comparing Signatures and Processing the Request

- Compare the computed and GitHub signatures,
  proceeding if they match:

```
if (!shaSignature.localeCompare(gitHubSignature)) {

    // Existing code

    if (req.body.pages[0].title) {

        ...

    } else {

        ...

    }

} else {
```

```
// Return HTTP 401 response for mismatched
signatures

context.res = {

    status: 401,

    body: "Signatures don't match"

};

}
```

Once the preceding changes are completed, the code looks as follows:

```
const Crypto = require('crypto');

module.exports = async function (context, req) {
    context.log('JavaScript HTTP trigger function processed a
    request.');

    const hmac = Crypto.createHmac("sha1", "<default key>");
    const signature = hmac.update(JSON.stringify(req.body)).
    digest('hex');
    const shaSignature = `sha1=${signature}`;
    const gitHubSignature = req.headers['x-hub-signature'];

    if (!shaSignature.localeCompare(gitHubSignature)) {
        if (req.body.pages[0].title) {
            context.res = {
                body: "Page is " + req.body.pages[0].title +
                ", Action is " + req.body.pages[0].action + ",
                Event Type is " + req.headers['x-github-event']
            };
        }
        else {
```

```
            context.res = {
                status: 400,
                body: ("Invalid payload for Wiki event")
            }
        }
    }
    else {
        context.res = {
            status: 401,
            body: "Signatures don't match"
        };
    }
};
```

Step 8: Saving and Confirming Connection

Save the modified function and observe the Logs pane displaying a "Connected!" statement; the next steps are to update the webhook secret and perform testing it.

Update the Webhook Secret

To configure your GitHub webhook with the newly added security, follow these steps:

- **Access GitHub Settings:**

    Open your GitHub account in the GitHub portal.

    Navigate to your specific repository.

- **Access Webhook Settings:**

    From the top menu, click "Settings" to open the Settings pane.

    In the sidebar, choose "Webhooks" to access the Webhooks pane.

- **Edit Webhook Configuration:**

  Locate and select "Edit" next to the webhook
  associated with your Azure Functions.

- **Enter the Secret Key:**

  In the provided "Secret" text box, input the default
  key obtained from your Azure Functions during the
  previous steps.

- **Update Webhook Configuration**

  Scroll down to the bottom of the page.

  Click "Update webhook" to save and apply the changes.

Upon completion, the Webhooks/Manage webhooks pane will appear,
confirming the successful update of your webhook configuration.

Testing the Execution

To validate the integration of your webhook and Azure Functions,
perform the following steps:

- **Access Recent Deliveries:**

  Navigate to the "Recent Deliveries" tab in the webhook
  settings on GitHub.

- **Choose the Latest Delivery Entry:**

  Click the ellipses (…) button to select the most recent
  delivery entry.

- **Redeliver the Payload:**

  Opt for the "Redeliver" option in the subsequent dialog
  box by choosing "Yes, redeliver this payload."

- **Simulate a Wiki Page Edit:**

  This step emulates the process of editing your
  wiki page.

- **Review the Headers Section:**

  Once the redelivery is complete, choose the latest
  delivery entry again.

  Inspect the Headers section to verify the presence of
  the x-hub-signature.

- **Check Response Code:**

  Confirm that the response code is 200, signifying the
  successful processing of the request.

Example Request Details
Request URL: `https://testwh123456.azurewebsites.net/api/Http`
`Trigger1?code=aUjXIpqdJOZHPQuBOSzFegxGJuOnAXmsQBnmkCpJ6RYxleRao`
`xJ8cQ%3D%3D`
Request Method: POST
Content Type: application/json
Expect:
User-Agent: GitHub-Hookshot/16496cb
X-GitHub-Delivery: ce122460-6aae-11e9-99d4-de6a298a424a
X-GitHub-Event: gollum
X-Hub-Signature: sha1=<hash of default key>
To validate the handling of an invalid signature, follow these steps:

- **Access Webhooks Settings:**

  Navigate to the "Settings" tab in the GitHub portal on
  the webhooks page.

- **Change the Secret:**

  In the "Secret" text box, select "Change Secret."

  Enter a random string, scroll down, and update the webhook.

- **Mismatched Key:**

  Confirm that the key used by the webhook no longer matches the expected key by the Azure Functions.

- **Recent Deliveries:**

  Go to the "Recent Deliveries" tab.

- **Choose the Latest Delivery Entry:**

  Select the most recent delivery entry by clicking the ellipses (...) button.

- **Redeliver with Invalid Signature:**

  Opt for "Redeliver"; in the ensuing dialog box, select "Yes, redeliver this payload."

- **Observe Unauthorized Response:**

  Notice that the response code is 401, indicating that the request was not authorized.

- **Inspect Response Details:** Examine the latest delivery entry (redelivery) by selecting its ellipse button. Navigate to the "Response" tab and verify the presence of the message "Signatures don't match" in the "Body" section.

Now, use this learning to modify the code to monitor events happening in a repository or organization or even at the enterprise level.

Understanding Common GitHub Issues

Handling Merge Conflicts in the GitHub Repository

Here, we will discuss and understand merge conflicts, effective ways of handling them, and some best practices to avoid them.

Overview of Merge Conflicts

- **Understanding Merge Conflicts on GitHub:** Merge conflicts on GitHub arise when there are conflicting changes in different branches of a repository. This typically occurs when two or more contributors modify the same lines of code or related sections independently, leading to conflicts during the merge process.

- **Causes of Merge Conflicts:** Merge conflicts can be triggered by various situations, such as simultaneous edits to the same line or lines of code, conflicting changes in different branches, or when one branch is ahead of another in terms of commits. These conflicts arise when Git cannot automatically reconcile the changes.

- **Effective Strategies to Reduce Merge Conflicts:** To minimize merge conflicts, it's crucial to encourage a collaborative workflow and regular communication among team members. Breaking down tasks into smaller, more manageable units can reduce the chances of conflicting changes. Additionally, regularly pulling the latest changes from the main branch into feature branches helps maintain synchronization and identifies potential conflicts earlier in the development process.

Best Practices for Avoiding Merge Conflicts

- **Branching Strategy:** Adopt a clear branching strategy, such as feature branching, where each developer works on a specific feature in an isolated branch. This minimizes overlap and reduces the likelihood of conflicts.

- **Regular Pulls and Updates:** Regularly pull changes from the main branch into your working branch to stay up to date with the latest codebase. This practice helps identify and resolve conflicts early.

- **Communication:** Foster effective communication within the team to ensure everyone is aware of ongoing changes. This reduces the chances of multiple developers unintentionally modifying the same code simultaneously.

- **Code Reviews:** Implement thorough code reviews before merging changes. This allows team members to catch potential conflicts, provide feedback, and ensure code quality.

- **Use of .gitignore:** Utilize a comprehensive .gitignore file to exclude unnecessary files and directories from version control. This reduces the chances of conflicts arising from nonessential files.

- **Atomic Commits:** Make atomic commits that focus on specific changes. Breaking down changes into atomic commits not only simplifies the project's history but also diminishes the chances of conflicting modifications within a single commit.

Effective User Access Management

Effectively managing user access on GitHub at the organization and enterprise levels is vital for upholding security, fostering collaboration, and streamlining workflows. This process revolves around utilizing GitHub users and teams strategically to ensure that individuals possess the necessary permissions for repositories and resources. Simultaneously, it aims to safeguard against any unauthorized access to maintain the integrity of the platform.

Identifying Authentication Errors and Permission Issues

To identify authentication errors and permission issues, organizations should regularly conduct audits and reviews of user access. Paying attention to authentication logs and permission settings can help detect anomalies. Authentication errors may arise from incorrect login credentials or issues with two-factor authentication. Permission issues often occur when users have inadequate access rights to repositories or when there are discrepancies in the defined access levels.

Steps to Identify Authentication Errors and Permission Issues

- **Regular Audits:** Conduct routine audits of user access, reviewing authentication logs and permission settings.

- **Monitoring Authentication Attempts:** Keep an eye on failed authentication attempts, which can signal potential errors or unauthorized access.

- **Utilizing Access Logs:** Leverage access logs to track user interactions and identify any unusual or suspicious activities.

- **Collaborative Reviews:** Foster collaboration between security teams and repository administrators to cross-verify user access against organizational policies.

To promptly address authentication errors and permission issues on GitHub, it is advisable to set up alert mechanisms that notify relevant stakeholders when such incidents occur. These alerts can be configured to trigger based on specific events or patterns indicative of authentication errors or permission discrepancies. By implementing proactive alerting systems, organizations can ensure quick detection and timely resolution of issues related to user authentication and access permissions in their GitHub repositories. This enhances security measures and contributes to maintaining a seamless and secure development environment.

Best Practices for User Access Management

- **Role-Based Access Control (RBAC):** Implement RBAC to assign specific roles and permissions to users based on their responsibilities and needs.

- **Least Privilege Principle:** Adhere to the principle of least privilege, granting users the minimum access necessary to perform their tasks.

- **Regular Training:** Educate users about access management best practices and the importance of secure authentication methods.

- **Two-Factor Authentication (2FA):** Encourage or enforce the use of 2FA to add an extra layer of security to user authentication.

- **Access Reviews:** Conduct periodic reviews of user access rights to ensure alignment with organizational changes and policies.

- **Documentation:** Maintain clear documentation of user access policies, roles, and permissions to facilitate effective management and troubleshooting.

In the next section, we will discuss managing repositories, also covering some of the most common issues and fixing them.

Effective Repository Management

Managing repository access on GitHub is crucial for smooth collaboration, but it can sometimes lead to challenges. Here are common problems related to repository access, examples of errors, and steps to efficiently handle access management:

1. **Access Denied Errors:** The problem is users encounter "Access Denied" errors when trying to perform specific actions. For example, a contributor is unable to push changes to a repository. The resolution is to ensure the user has the appropriate permissions. Check branch protection settings, repository settings, or organization-level access.

2. **Permission Issues:** The problem is users may have insufficient permissions to create branches, merge pull requests, or perform other actions. For example, a team member cannot create new branches in a repository. The resolution is to adjust repository or branch permissions for the user. Confirm they are part of the required teams or have explicit access.

3. **Collaborator Invitation Failures:** The problem is that inviting collaborators to a private repository fails. For example, a project manager tries to add a new team member as a collaborator but encounters issues. The resolution is to check if the user has accepted the invitation. Ensure they have a GitHub account and the email used for the invitation is associated with their GitHub account.

4. **Branch Protection Rules:** The problem is the inability to force-push or delete branches due to branch protection rules. An example is that the developers are restricted from force-pushing to a protected branch. The fix is to adjust branch protection rules, allowing or restricting specific actions based on the team's workflow.

5. **Two-Factor Authentication (2FA) Issues:** The problem is that the users with 2FA enabled face difficulties accessing repositories via Git. For example, a developer encounters authentication errors when pushing changes. The fix generates a personal access token for Git operations or uses SSH keys. Update remote repository URLs with the token.

Efficient Repository Access Management

- **Organize Teams:** Create teams based on roles (e.g., developers, managers) for streamlined access assignment.

- **Leverage Branch Protections:** Implement branch protection rules to prevent accidental data loss or unwanted changes.

- **Regular Access Audits:** Conduct periodic reviews of repository access to remove inactive users and ensure the right people have appropriate permissions.

- **Documentation:** Clearly document access control procedures and guidelines for contributors.

- **Training:** Provide training for team members on repository access management and best practices.

Addressing these challenges and adopting effective access management practices is essential for GitHub repositories to uphold security, encourage collaboration, and ensure a smooth development workflow. Now, let's delve into the exciting realm of GitHub Actions, exploring common issues faced by users and tackling more intricate problems in the next section.

Advanced Troubleshooting Techniques

As part of the advanced troubleshooting techniques in GitHub Actions, we then handle large repositories and security vulnerabilities. In the domain of software development, mastering GitHub Actions is pivotal for automating your workflows to enhance efficiency, maintainability, and reliability. Starting with the basics, employing a YAML linter is crucial for identifying syntax errors and formatting issues, ensuring your workflow files are correctly structured. This can be achieved through extensions in code editors or the GitHub web editor itself. Organizing your workflow into logical segments, using descriptive names for jobs and steps, and adopting reusable workflows for repetitive tasks can significantly streamline your process.

It's essential to document your workflows, adding comments to elucidate complex steps or decisions, thereby improving code readability while keeping comments concise and meaningful. For handling sensitive information, GitHub secrets or environment variables should be utilized instead of hardcoding, with careful attention to prevent exposing this data in logs.

Matrix builds are a powerful feature, allowing you to test your code across various dependencies or platforms, ensuring broad compatibility and early detection of potential issues. Caching, when used correctly, can expedite workflow execution, particularly for stable dependencies. Additionally, implementing conditional statements enables customized workflow actions based on specific triggers like branch names or event types, enhancing the workflow's adaptability.

Setting appropriate timeouts for jobs and steps is crucial to avoid indefinite workflow runs, with adjustments made based on the workflow's nature. Error handling and recovery mechanisms should be robust, with workflows triggered by specific events to minimize unnecessary executions. Testing workflows locally, when feasible, using tools like "act," can help identify errors early, streamlining the development process.

Documentation is key; clearly outlining the workflow's purpose, any necessary secrets, and result interpretation guidelines is invaluable. Explicitly specifying the version of GitHub Actions used can safeguard against unexpected behavior changes. The GitHub Actions Marketplace is a treasure trove of existing actions that can save time and effort, though it's important to assess the source and maintainability of third-party actions.

Configuring notifications for workflow outcomes and incorporating status badges in your README provides transparency and immediate feedback on the build status. Ultimately, simplicity is paramount. A straightforward, easily understandable workflow not only facilitates current project needs but also ensures future adaptability and optimization.

GitHub Actions Workflows: The following are the best practices to ensure that your workflows are efficient, maintainable, and reliable.

> **Use a Linter:** Use a YAML linter to catch syntax errors and formatting issues early on. This helps ensure that your workflow file is valid YAML.
>
> It can be used in two way either by using extensions in code editor or GitHub web editor also has the functionality to check the format and syntax.
>
> **Organize Your Workflow:** Split your workflow into logical steps and jobs. Use job and step names that are descriptive and easy to understand. Identify repetitive jobs and replace them with reusable workflows.

Comments: Add comments to explain complex steps or decisions in your workflow. Use comments sparingly but effectively to improve code readability.

Secrets and Environment Variables: Avoid hardcoding sensitive information in your workflow. Use GitHub secrets or environment variables. Be cautious about exposing sensitive information in logs. Use the set-env command or secrets for sensitive data.

Matrix Builds: Use matrix builds to test your code across multiple versions of dependencies or platforms. This helps ensure compatibility and catches potential issues early on.

Caching: Utilize caching to speed up workflow execution, especially for dependencies that don't change frequently. Be mindful of the cache key to avoid unexpected issues.

Conditional Steps: Use conditional statements to run certain steps or jobs based on specific conditions (e.g., branch names, event types). This allows you to customize workflow behavior based on the context.

Timeouts: Set appropriate timeouts for your jobs and steps to prevent workflows from running indefinitely. Consider the nature of your workflow and adjust timeouts accordingly.

Error Handling: Implement proper error handling and recovery mechanisms. Use the on clause to trigger workflows only on specific events to avoid unnecessary executions.

Testing Locally: Whenever possible, test your workflow locally using tools like act. This helps catch errors early and speeds up the development process.

Documentation: Document your workflow. Provide information on the purpose of the workflow, any required secrets, and how to interpret the results.

Versioning: Be explicit about the version of GitHub Actions you're using to prevent unexpected changes in behavior.

Use Actions Marketplace: Leverage existing GitHub Actions from the Actions Marketplace to avoid reinventing the wheel. Verify the source and maintainability of third-party actions.

Notifications: Configure notifications to alert you of workflow failures or other important events. Use status badges in your README to display the current build status.

Keep It Simple: Avoid unnecessary complexity. Keep your workflow simple and easy to understand. Refactor and optimize workflows as needed.

Runners

As you are already aware, there are two types of runners; the following will discuss about some common issues and using different types of runners.

GitHub-Hosted Runners: Using GitHub Actions runners can be generally smooth, but there are some common issues that users may encounter. Here are some of them:

Permissions and Access: Ensure that the GitHub Actions runner has the necessary permissions to access repositories, install dependencies, and perform other required tasks. Double-check the permissions of any tokens or credentials used in your workflow.

Customize Software and Packages: Here is the link for the software and package lists (`https://github.com/actions/runner-images`) that are available as part of an image. It can be customized based on requirements.

Token Expiry: If you're using personal access tokens or other credentials, they may expire. Make sure to update them in your workflow or use GitHub Actions secrets.

Resource Constraints: GitHub provides a certain number of resources for each runner. If your workflow requires more resources than available, it might fail. Consider optimizing your workflow or splitting it into smaller jobs.

Network Issues: Network interruptions can cause workflow failures. Ensure that your network connection is stable, and there are no firewalls or network restrictions preventing communication with GitHub.

Job and Step Failures: Jobs or individual steps within a job may fail due to issues such as incorrect commands, missing dependencies, or unexpected errors in your code. Check the logs and error messages for details on why a specific step or job failed.

Caching Problems: Caching is a powerful feature in GitHub Actions, but it can lead to issues if not configured correctly. Verify your cache setup and consider clearing the cache if needed.

Runner Self-Update Issues: Runners need to be kept up to date to benefit from the latest features and fixes. However, the self-update process can sometimes encounter problems. Check for runner updates and follow GitHub's documentation on updating runners.

Docker Image Pull Failures: If your workflow uses Docker images, failures in pulling the required images can occur due to network issues, image unavailability, or authentication problems. Check the Docker image references and ensure that they are correct and accessible.

GitHub Actions Service Outages: Like any service, GitHub Actions may experience outages or degraded performance. Check GitHub's status page for any ongoing issues.

Environment Variable Issues: Incorrectly set or missing environment variables can lead to failures in your workflow. Ensure that your workflow relies on accurate environment variable values.

Concurrency Limits: GitHub Actions has concurrency limits for free and public repositories. If you exceed these limits, your workflows may be queued or fail to run. Consider adjusting workflows or upgrading your plan if necessary.

Third-Party Actions: If you're using third-party actions, be aware that they may be updated by their maintainers. Incompatibility issues or changes in behavior may arise.

GitHub Self-Hosted Runners: GitHub self-hosted action runners can be a powerful tool, but like any technology, they come with their own set of potential issues. Here are some common issues users may encounter with self-hosted action runners:

- **Runner Registration Issues:** Failure to properly register the self-hosted runner with the repository can lead to workflow failures. Check the registration token and ensure that the runner is correctly registered on the GitHub repository.

- **Runner Connectivity Problems:** Network issues or firewalls may prevent the self-hosted runner from connecting to GitHub. Ensure that the runner machine has proper Internet access, and there are no network restrictions.

- **Runner Permissions:** Verify that the user account running the self-hosted runner has the necessary permissions to perform actions specified in the workflow, such as pulling code or pushing artifacts.

- **Runner Token Expiry:** The runner registration token used during the setup process expires. If a runner is failing to start, check if the registration token has expired and re-register the runner if necessary.

- **Runner Offline:** If the self-hosted runner machine is turned off or experiences issues, workflows depending on that runner will fail. Regularly monitor the status of your self-hosted runners.

- **Resource Constraints:** Inadequate resources on the runner machine, such as low memory or disk space, can lead to failures during workflow execution. Ensure that the runner machine meets the resource requirements of your workflows.

- **Runner Self-Update Issues:** The self-hosted runner needs to be kept up to date to ensure compatibility with GitHub Actions. Sometimes, the self-update process may encounter problems.

- **Runner Configuration Errors:** Incorrect configuration of the self-hosted runner can lead to issues. Double-check the configuration, including repository associations, labels, and any environment variables.

- **Authentication Issues:** If your workflows interact with external services or repositories, ensure that the self-hosted runner has the necessary authentication credentials. Use GitHub Actions secrets or other secure methods.

- **Runner Environment Variables:** Be aware of any environment variables set on the self-hosted runner. In some cases, conflicts or misconfigurations of environment variables can cause unexpected issues.

- **Caching Problems:** If you're using caching on the self-hosted runner, ensure that it is properly configured. Incorrect caching configurations can lead to unexpected behavior.

- **Repository Permissions:** Check if the repository permissions for the self-hosted runner are still valid. If permissions are changed or revoked, it may result in workflow failures.

- **Security Scanning Software:** Some security scanning tools or antivirus software on the self-hosted runner machine might interfere with workflow execution. Whitelist GitHub Actions processes or adjust security settings accordingly.

- **Logs and Debugging:** Review the runner logs and workflow output for error messages. This can help identify the root cause of failures.

- **Update Dependencies:** If your workflows rely on specific tools or dependencies, ensure they are up to date. Outdated dependencies might cause compatibility issues.

- **GitHub Service Outages:** Check GitHub's status page for any ongoing service outages that might affect the GitHub Actions infrastructure.

By being aware of these common issues and regularly monitoring your self-hosted runners, you can maintain a reliable GitHub Actions setup. Periodic checks and updates help prevent potential problems and ensure smooth workflow execution.

GitHub Large Repositories

A large repository on GitHub is characterized by factors such as an extensive codebase with numerous files and directories, the inclusion of large binary assets like images or compiled binaries, a complex commit history marked by frequent and extensive changes, and a substantial number of contributors in collaborative projects.

The decision to use large repositories is contingent on specific scenarios. For instance, in the case of monolithic applications where different system components are tightly integrated, it may be pragmatic to maintain all aspects within a single repository. Large repositories also find applicability in shared libraries, frameworks, or components that are intended for reuse across multiple projects. Enterprises might opt for large repositories to efficiently manage extensive codebases encompassing multiple projects and applications. Additionally, repositories housing historical or legacy code tend to accumulate over time, resulting in larger repositories.

However, large repositories present challenges, including performance issues during tasks like cloning and fetching, the need for meticulous maintenance and organization, complexities in collaboration due to a multitude of contributors, and potential delays in continuous integration workflows, necessitating optimization efforts.

To mitigate these challenges, some teams opt for alternative strategies. They might embrace a microservices architecture, breaking down a monolithic repository into smaller, more manageable repositories that align with microservices principles. Another approach involves using Git submodules or Git Large File Storage (LFS) to manage large binary files separately. Additionally, organizing code into smaller, reusable components enables independent development and versioning. These strategies help address the complexities associated with large repositories, providing more efficient and streamlined development workflows.

Handling Large Repositories

Handling large repositories on GitHub can introduce various challenges. Here are some common issues associated with large repositories and potential ways to resolve or mitigate them:

1. **Cloning and Fetching Performance**

    Issue: Cloning or fetching from a large repository can be slow, especially when dealing with a large number of files.

    Resolution: Use shallow clones ('--depth') to fetch only the latest commit history.

    Leverage Git LFS (Large File Storage) for managing large binary files separately.

787

2. **Pushing Performance**

   Issue: Pushing changes to a large repository can be time-consuming, impacting development speed.

   Resolution: Use Git's '--force-with-lease' option cautiously when force-pushing, ensuring you don't unintentionally overwrite changes. Consider splitting large repositories into smaller, more manageable ones.

3. **Merging and Pull Requests**

   Issue: Merging branches or creating pull requests can become complex and error-prone in large repositories.

   Resolution: Encourage feature branching and smaller, focused pull requests to make merges more manageable. Use tools like "git rebase" to keep commit histories cleaner.

4. **GitHub Web Interface Performance**

   Issue: Browsing the repository on the GitHub web interface might be slow.

   Resolution: Utilize Git's sparse-checkout feature to clone only the necessary directories. Consider using Git submodules for large, independent components.

5. **Repository Size Limit**

   Issue: GitHub has a repository size limit (currently 100 GB).

   Resolution: Use Git LFS for large binary files to reduce the actual size of the repository. Offload large files or artifacts to external storage or package registries.

6. **Continuous Integration (CI) Performance**

   Issue: CI workflows can take a long time to run on large repositories.

   Resolution: Optimize CI configuration to run only necessary tests. Use caching to speed up build processes. Consider parallelizing CI jobs.

7. **Branch Protection Rules**

   Issue: Adding or updating branch protection rules can be challenging in large repositories.

   Resolution: Leverage automation tools or scripts to manage branch protection rules consistently. Consider having specific teams or individuals responsible for rule management.

8. **Git History Size**

   Issue: Over time, the Git history can become extensive, making certain operations slower.

   Resolution: Periodically clean up and prune unnecessary branches. Consider using 'git gc' (garbage collection) to optimize the repository.

9. **Collaboration Challenges**

   Issue: Collaborating on a large repository with many contributors can be complex.

   Resolution: Establish clear contribution guidelines. Use code reviews and communication channels effectively.

10. **Third-Party Integrations**

    Issue: Some third-party tools and integrations may not perform optimally with large repositories.

    Resolution: Verify the compatibility of integrations with the repository size. Explore alternative integrations that better handle large repositories.

11. **Git Submodule Complexity**

    Issue: Git submodules can introduce complexity, especially for new contributors.

    Resolution: Provide thorough documentation on working with submodules. Consider alternatives like Git subtrees if submodule complexity is a concern.

By addressing these common issues with thoughtful practices and optimizing workflows, teams can work more efficiently with large repositories on GitHub. It's essential to balance repository structure and size with the requirements of the project and the development team.

Handling Security Vulnerabilities

GitHub, a widely used platform for hosting and collaborating on software projects, faces security vulnerabilities that need attention from both GitHub itself and its users. One type of vulnerability involves code issues like SQL injection or Cross-Site Scripting (XSS) found within repositories. To tackle these issues, it's important to conduct regular code reviews and use automated security scanning tools.

Another vulnerability comes from third-party dependencies, and GitHub offers tools like Dependabot to automatically identify and suggest updates for outdated or vulnerable dependencies. Issues related to access control may arise due to misconfigured settings, potentially leading to unauthorized access and exposure of sensitive information. It's advised for users to review and update access permissions regularly, following the principle of least privilege.

Authentication weaknesses, often caused by weak or compromised credentials, are another concern. GitHub promotes strong authentication practices like multifactor authentication (MFA) to address this. Ongoing education about phishing attacks and social engineering attempts is essential, stressing the importance of staying vigilant.

Insecurely configured integrations can introduce vulnerabilities, prompting users to regularly review and audit integration permissions. GitHub's security advisory platform helps in reporting and managing security vulnerabilities, urging users to stay informed about advisories related to their dependencies and promptly address reported issues.

Handling sensitive data within repositories, like API tokens or private keys, requires care to prevent data exposure. GitHub encourages users to use secrets and GitHub Actions securely to avoid unintentional disclosure. Security risks also include insecure file uploads, emphasizing the need to regularly scan and restrict file types that pose potential threats.

Using outdated software, including Git and GitHub clients, exposes users to known security vulnerabilities. Regular updates to tools and software are vital for maintaining a secure development environment. Equally important is incident response planning, ensuring an efficient approach to addressing security incidents when they occur.

GitHub actively addresses security concerns through features like security advisories, Dependabot, and Actions for continuous security monitoring. Users play a crucial role by staying informed about best practices, actively participating in the security of their repositories, and collaborating with the GitHub security community. This collective effort contributes to a safer and more secure development environment on GitHub.

Common Issues and Fixes

Handling security vulnerabilities on GitHub involves addressing common issues to ensure a secure development environment. Here are some common issues related to security vulnerabilities and ways to resolve them:

- **Code Vulnerabilities**

  Issue: Security vulnerabilities in the code, such as SQL injection or Cross-Site Scripting (XSS).

  Resolution: Conduct regular code reviews, use static code analysis tools, and employ automated security scanning tools to identify and address vulnerabilities.

- **Dependency Vulnerabilities**

  Issue: Outdated or vulnerable third-party dependencies.

  Resolution: Use tools like Dependabot to automatically identify and suggest updates for outdated dependencies. Regularly review and update dependencies to patch security vulnerabilities.

- **Access Control Issues**

  Issue: Misconfigured access settings leading to unauthorized access.

  Resolution: Regularly review and update access permissions, follow the principle of least privilege, and implement proper access controls to prevent unauthorized access.

- **Authentication Weaknesses**

  Issue: Weak or compromised credentials.

  Resolution: Promote strong authentication practices, such as multifactor authentication (MFA). Educate users about the importance of creating and maintaining secure credentials.

Issue: Users falling victim to phishing attacks or social engineering attempts.

Resolution: Provide ongoing education on phishing risks, encourage users to remain vigilant, and report suspicious activities promptly.

- **Insecure Integrations**

  Issue: Insecurely configured integrations introducing vulnerabilities.

  Resolution: Regularly review and audit integration permissions. Ensure that third-party integrations adhere to security best practices.

- **Handling Sensitive Data**

  Issue: Improper handling of sensitive data within repositories.

  Resolution: Encourage the use of secrets and GitHub Actions securely to prevent unintentional disclosure of sensitive information. Implement encryption and access controls for sensitive data.

- **Insecure File Uploads**

  Issue: Repositories allowing insecure file uploads.

  Resolution: Regularly scan for and restrict file types that pose security threats. Implement content security policies to prevent insecure file uploads.

- **Outdated Software**

  Issue: Using outdated software, including Git and GitHub clients.

Resolution: Regularly update tools and software to the latest secure versions. Follow GitHub's recommendations for updating Git and GitHub clients.

- **Incident Response Planning**

  Issue: Lack of a well-defined incident response plan.

  Resolution: Establish and document an incident response plan. Ensure that the plan covers the reporting, investigation, and mitigation of security incidents effectively.

GitHub actively provides features and tools to address security concerns, such as security advisories, Dependabot, and Actions for continuous security monitoring. Users should actively participate in the security of their repositories, stay informed about best practices, and collaborate with the GitHub security community to collectively enhance security measures. In the next section, we discuss monitoring GitHub operations, where we will cover why and how monitoring GitHub is important.

Monitoring GitHub Operations

Maintaining the health and performance of GitHub repositories and workflows is crucial for smooth software development. Think of it as keeping your workspace organized and efficient. Monitoring plays a key role in this by helping teams catch issues early on. It's like having a radar for potential problems, allowing for quick and proactive solutions. This is especially important in the fast-paced world of coding where small issues can escalate if not addressed promptly.

Monitoring also helps in optimizing workflow. It's like having a GPS for your development process, pointing out where things might be slowing down. This optimization not only makes the work smoother but also improves collaboration among team members. Everyone's on the same page, and tasks get done more efficiently.

Another aspect is resource utilization. Just like you'd keep an eye on your computer's storage and memory, teams need to monitor server capacity, bandwidth, and storage on GitHub. This ensures that resources are used effectively and helps in planning for future needs.

Security is a big deal in software development, and monitoring is like having a security guard for your code. Regular checks identify vulnerabilities and outdated dependencies. This proactive approach ensures compliance with security standards and keeps your code safe.

Performance metrics, such as how often code is committed or the time it takes for pull requests, give a clear picture of the repository's health. It's like having a fitness tracker for your codebase, helping teams set goals and continuously improve. Collaboration is at the core of GitHub, and monitoring tools shed light on how contributors interact. It's like having a team-building exercise, but for your virtual workspace. Understanding collaboration patterns helps in creating a more transparent and cooperative development environment.

Automated alerts are like having an assistant that taps you on the shoulder when something needs your attention. They ensure that the team is quickly notified of critical issues, minimizing downtime and keeping the development pipeline running smoothly.

Briefly, monitoring is like having a set of tools that help you maintain a healthy and high-performing GitHub environment. It is about catching problems early, optimizing processes, ensuring security, and fostering a collaborative and efficient development workflow.

GitHub Native Monitoring Tools

GitHub provides a suite of native monitoring tools that empower developers and teams to efficiently oversee and manage their repositories. These tools are integral to maintaining the health, security, and performance of projects hosted on the platform.

GitHub Audit Log provides a native solution within the GitHub platform. This tool records and displays a comprehensive list of activities taking place in a repository, including push events, pull request actions, and modifications to access permissions. Users can access the Audit Log through the GitHub web interface, applying filters to narrow down activities based on date, user, or event type. Also, we can use the GitHub API to download the required logs and filter them as per requirement.

GitHub Actions enables the automation of workflows, including continuous integration and deployment. It can be configured to trigger in response to specific events such as code pushes, pull requests, or the creation of issues. This automation capability allows users to set up custom workflows for notifications or other actions tied to repository events.

For security-focused monitoring, **GitHub Security Alerts** automatically notifies repository maintainers about known vulnerabilities in project dependencies. By enabling this feature in the repository settings, teams receive timely notifications regarding any security risks associated with their dependencies, enhancing proactive vulnerability management.

Dependabot serves as an automated dependency manager native to GitHub. This tool creates pull requests automatically to update project dependencies whenever new versions become available. By activating Dependabot in repository settings, developers can ensure that their projects are always using the latest, secure versions of libraries.

For real-time notifications and external integrations, **GitHub Webhooks** can be configured. Webhooks allow external services to be notified instantly about specific repository events, facilitating the triggering of external scripts, services, or notifications in platforms such as chat applications.

796

To gain insights into repository history and contributor patterns, tools like **GitStats** or **Gitinspector** come into play. These tools offer detailed analysis of repository history, including statistics on contributors, code changes over time, and commit frequency. Integration of these tools into the development environment aids in identifying unusual trends or irregularities in coding practices.

For advanced security analysis, **GitHub Advanced Security** provides features like code scanning and secret scanning. By activating this feature in repository settings, teams benefit from automated analysis of their codebase, identifying security vulnerabilities and sensitive information during the development process.

In conclusion, a combination of native GitHub features and external tools enhances the monitoring of GitHub repositories. Whether through audit logs, automation with GitHub Actions, security alerts, dependency management with Dependabot, webhooks for real-time notifications, historical analysis tools, or advanced security features, these tools collectively contribute to a robust and secure GitHub repository management strategy.

Alerting for GitHub Events

Setting up alerts for unusual activities on GitHub involves using a combination of native features and external tools. The following is a step-by-step guide to help you configure alerts for detecting unusual events in your GitHub environment:

GitHub Audit Log: To access your GitHub Enterprise or Organization audit log and enhance security measures, start by navigating to your Enterprise or Organization and selecting the "Settings" tab. Once in the settings, scroll down to the "Audit log" section located on the left sidebar. Here, you can tailor your audit log settings to capture specific activities relevant to your project. Customize filters based on your unique requirements, ensuring that the log captures the information crucial to your security monitoring. It's advisable to routinely review the audit log to promptly identify any unusual or unexpected activities, allowing for swift response and maintenance of a secure development environment, monitoring events for adding users to organization is one of common use case where we want to make sure no outside collaborator is added unless there is a expection.

The following is a sample code using Python to get the event whenever an outside collaborator is added to the organization:

```python
import requests
def get_audit_log(org_name, token):
    url = f"https://api.github.com/orgs/{org_name}/
    audit-log"
    headers = {"Authorization": f"token {token}", "Accept":
    "application/vnd.github.v3+json"}
    response = requests.get(url, headers=headers)
    if response.status_code == 200:
        return response.json()
    else:
        print(f"Error: {response.status_code}")
        print(response.text)
        return None
def filter_outside_collaborator_added_events(audit_log):
    if not audit_log:
        return None
    outside_collaborator_events = [
        event for event in audit_log
            if event.get('action') == 'outside_
            collaborator_added']
    return outside_collaborator_events

def main():
    org_name = "<YOUR_ORG_NAME>"
    token = "<YOUR_PERSONAL_ACCESS_TOKEN>"
```

```
    audit_log = get_audit_log(org_name, token)
   if audit_log:
      outside_collaborator_events = filter_outside_
      collaborator_added_events(audit_log)
      if outside_collaborator_events:
            print("Outside Collaborators Added:")
            for event in outside_collaborator_events:
                print(event)
      else:
            print("No events of outside collaborators being
            added.")
   else:
      print("Failed to fetch the audit log.")
if __name__ == "__main__":
   main()
```

This script defines three functions:

- **get_audit_log(org_name, token):** Fetches the organization's audit log using the provided organization name and personal access token.

- **filter_outside_collaborator_added_events(audit_log):** Filters the audit log events to include only those where outside collaborators are added.

- **main():** The main function that orchestrates the execution of the script. It fetches the audit log, filters the relevant events, and prints them.

Now the script is ready, we can schedule a workflow and combining it sending notification on the workflow to notify whenever there is outside collaborator add event happens.

GitHub Workflow Alerting

To establish an effective alert system for your GitHub repository, initiate the process by generating a new workflow file. Name the file, for instance, alerts.yml, and place it within the .github/workflows directory in your repository. Within this workflow file, define triggers based on events that signify unusual activities, such as code pushes, pull requests, or the creation of issues.

Configure the job steps within the workflow to execute specific actions tailored to your requirements, such as sending notifications, running scripts, or interfacing with external services. Ensure the customization of the workflow aligns precisely with your unique alerting needs, creating a responsive and tailored system for monitoring and addressing potential issues.

- **GitHub Security Alerts:** To fortify the security of your GitHub repository, navigate to the repository page and access the "Security" tab. In the repository settings, activate both "Automated security fixes" and "Vulnerability alerts." Enabling these features empowers GitHub to automatically notify you about any recognized vulnerabilities present in your project's dependencies. This proactive approach enhances your ability to promptly address and mitigate potential security risks within your repository.

- **Dependabot:** To streamline dependency management within your GitHub repository, access the "Settings" tab of the repository and proceed to "Security & analysis." Within these settings, enable Dependabot and set up configurations to generate pull requests for updates to project dependencies. By activating Dependabot, the system automatically generates alerts for any outdated dependencies, ensuring that your repository stays current and secure. This integration simplifies the process of keeping software components up to date and aligned with the latest versions.

- **GitHub Webhooks:** To establish real-time notifications and external integrations for your GitHub repository, start by accessing the repository settings through the "Settings" tab. Navigate to the left sidebar and select "Webhooks," then proceed to add a new webhook. Specify the payload URL, designating the endpoint where you wish to receive alerts. Choose the specific events, such as pushes, pull requests, or issues, that should trigger the webhook.

Ensure the webhook is active and perform a test to confirm that it successfully sends alerts as expected. This setup enhances your repository's communication capabilities, allowing for seamless integration with external systems or services based on specified events.

External Monitoring Tools

Enhance the surveillance of your GitHub repository by incorporating external monitoring tools with expertise in anomaly detection, such as security information and event management (SIEM) solutions. Establish connections between these tools and your GitHub repository through APIs or integrations to facilitate seamless communication. Within the external monitoring tool, establish rules or queries designed to identify abnormal patterns or activities within the repository.

Configure alerts within the monitoring tool to promptly notify relevant stakeholders whenever anomalies are detected. Notable examples of external monitoring tools include popular SIEM solutions like Splunk, ELK Stack (Elasticsearch, Logstash, Kibana), and open source platforms like Prometheus for advanced analytics and alerting based on repository activities. These integrations bolster your repository's security infrastructure, providing a comprehensive approach to anomaly detection and response.

GitHub Advanced Security

Elevate the security measures of your GitHub repository by visiting the "Security" tab within the repository settings. Activate GitHub Advanced Security features, encompassing functionalities such as code scanning and secret scanning. Tailor security policies to clearly define criteria for identifying what is considered unusual or insecure within your codebase. Further, establish a system of notifications to promptly alert relevant stakeholders of any security alerts generated by these advanced features. Examples of security alerts could include the detection of vulnerable code patterns, exposed credentials, or potential security threats. This integration of GitHub Advanced Security ensures a proactive and vigilant approach to identifying and mitigating security risks within your repository.

As we have understood the need and different options available for alerting, the next step is to understand the repository metrics, contribution statistics, and workflow efficiency for the implementation of effective reporting strategies.

GitHub Monitoring Using Third-Party Tools

There are several third-party tools accessible for monitoring crucial GitHub components such as repositories, organizations, workflows, and other elements; here, we will use some of the key reasons for enabling monitoring.

Performance optimization is a key aspect facilitated by monitoring tools such as Prometheus and Grafana. GitHub administrators leverage these tools to evaluate the performance of repositories, workflows, and other components. Through the tracking of metrics and visualization of data, administrators can pinpoint bottlenecks, optimize resource usage, and ensure the seamless operation of GitHub.

The swift identification and resolution of issues are paramount for maintaining a healthy GitHub environment. Monitoring tools like Prometheus and Datadog play a crucial role in this regard by providing real-time insights into potential problems. This capability enables administrators to promptly address issues such as downtimes, high resource consumption, or workflow failures, ensuring the overall health of the GitHub ecosystem.

Resource planning and scaling is another vital function facilitated by monitoring tools. GitHub administrators utilize these tools to analyze historical data and trends, empowering them to make informed decisions regarding resource allocation and scalability. This proactive approach ensures that the GitHub infrastructure is adequately provisioned to handle increasing workloads, contributing to overall system stability.

Security monitoring is significantly enhanced through monitoring tools, contributing to GitHub's robust security posture. By tracking access patterns, identifying unusual activities, and implementing alerting mechanisms, administrators can swiftly respond to security threats. This proactive approach helps enforce access controls, ultimately enhancing the overall security of GitHub repositories and organizations.

Understanding and improving user experience is a crucial goal for GitHub administrators. Monitoring tools assist in achieving this by gauging user behavior and experience. By tracking response times, user interactions, and overall system performance, administrators gain valuable insights. This information enables them to make enhancements that align with user expectations, ultimately improving the overall GitHub user experience.

Compliance and audit trail are addressed through the implementation of monitoring tools. GitHub administrators can track changes, access logs, and monitor workflows, ensuring that GitHub activities comply with regulatory standards and internal policies. This not only aids in meeting compliance requirements but also establishes a robust audit trail for accountability.

Customization and integration are facilitated by tools like Prometheus and Datadog. These tools offer customization options and seamless integration with other systems. GitHub administrators can tailor monitoring configurations to align with specific organizational needs. Additionally, the integration of monitoring data with other platforms provides comprehensive insights into GitHub operations.

Data-driven decision-making is a key benefit of leveraging monitoring tools. GitHub administrators can base their decisions on real-time and historical data, enhancing decision-making processes. This data-driven approach enables administrators to align GitHub management strategies with performance metrics and organizational goals, fostering efficient and effective GitHub management.

Using Prometheus for Monitoring GitHub

There are two different ways of sending data to Prometheus, either using an existing Prometheus exporter or using a Prometheus client.

1. **Using a Prometheus GitHub Exporter**

   Configuring GitHub monitoring using Prometheus involves several steps. The following is a simplified guide on how to set up Prometheus to monitor GitHub repositories. Note that this guide assumes you have a working knowledge of Prometheus and GitHub. Also, keep in mind that GitHub's API rate limits apply, so be mindful of your API usage.

   • **Clone the GitHub Exporter Repository:** *git clone* `https://github.com/githubexporter/github-exporter.git`

   `cd github-exporter`

   • **Build a GitHub Exporter:** *go build*

   This command will create an executable binary named github-exporter.

- **Create a Configuration File:**

Create a configuration file named config.yml
to specify the GitHub repositories you want to
monitor. Here is a simple example:

```
github:

    repositories:

        - owner: your-username

        name: your-repo

        - owner: another-username

        name: another-repo
```

Adjust the owner and name fields according to
the GitHub repositories you want to monitor.

- **Run the GitHub Exporter:**

Run the GitHub Exporter with the created
configuration file:

```
./github-exporter -config.path=config.yml
```

This will start the exporter, and it will expose
metrics on the default port 9171. You can
access the metrics by navigating to http://
localhost:9171/metrics in your browser.

- **Integrate with Prometheus:**

Edit your Prometheus configuration file
(prometheus.yml) to include the GitHub Exporter
as a target:

```
scrape_configs:

- job_name: 'github'

      static_configs:

          - targets: ['localhost:9171']
```

This configuration tells Prometheus to scrape metrics from the GitHub Exporter on localhost:9171.

- **Restart Prometheus:**

Restart Prometheus to apply the new configuration.

- **Query GitHub Metrics in Prometheus:**

Access the Prometheus web UI (typically at http:// localhost:9090) and use PromQL queries to explore GitHub metrics. For example, you can query the total number of pull requests:

```
github_pull_requests_total
```

- **Grafana Integration:**

If you are using Grafana, you can integrate Prometheus as a data source and create dashboards to visualize GitHub metrics.

Important Notes

- **GitHub API Token**

  - If you encounter rate limiting issues with GitHub's API, consider using a GitHub API token by setting the GITHUB_TOKEN environment variable.

  - export GITHUB_TOKEN=your-github-token ./github-exporter -config.path=config.yml

  - Replace your-github-token with your actual GitHub token.

- **Security Considerations:**

  When using GitHub Exporter in a production environment, consider securing it, especially if it is exposed to the public Internet. You can use tools like reverse proxies or firewalls to restrict access.

- **Documentation:**

  Refer to the GitHub Exporter GitHub repository for any additional configuration options or updates.

2. **Using Custom Script**

   Let's take an example of getting a list of users in each team for a GitHub organization. To achieve this task, you can use the GitHub REST API to fetch the organization's members and their teams. Then, you can send this information to Prometheus using the **prometheus_client** library. Make sure to install the library using

   pip install prometheus_client

Here's a sample Python script to get you started. Note that you'll need to replace "YOUR_GITHUB_TOKEN", "YOUR_ORGANIZATION_NAME", and "YOUR_PROMETHEUS_METRIC_NAME" with your actual GitHub token, organization name, and Prometheus metric name:

```python
import requests
from prometheus_client import start_http_server, Gauge
from requests.auth import HTTPBasicAuth

# GitHub API URL
GITHUB_API_URL = "https://api.github.com/orgs/{org}/teams"

# Prometheus metric name
PROMETHEUS_METRIC_NAME = 'github_organization_users'

# Replace with your GitHub organization name
ORGANIZATION_NAME = 'YOUR_ORGANIZATION_NAME'

# Replace with your GitHub personal access token
GITHUB_TOKEN = 'YOUR_GITHUB_TOKEN'

# Replace with your desired Prometheus metric labels
PROMETHEUS_LABELS = ['organization', 'team']

# Prometheus metric initialization
github_organization_users_metric = Gauge(
    PROMETHEUS_METRIC_NAME,
    'GitHub organization users grouped by team',
    labelnames=PROMETHEUS_LABELS
)

def get_github_organization_teams():
    headers = {
        'Authorization': f'token {GITHUB_TOKEN}',
        'Accept': 'application/vnd.github.hellcat-
        preview+json'  # Enable team discussions API preview
    }
```

```python
    url = GITHUB_API_URL.format(org=ORGANIZATION_NAME)
    response = requests.get(url, headers=headers)

    if response.status_code == 200:
        teams = response.json()
        return teams
    else:
        print(f"Failed to fetch teams. Status code: {response.
        status_code}")
        return None

def get_github_team_members(team_id):
    headers = {
        'Authorization': f'token {GITHUB_TOKEN}',
    }

    url = f"https://api.github.com/teams/{team_id}/members"
    response = requests.get(url, headers=headers)

    if response.status_code == 200:
        members = response.json()
        return members
    else:
        print(f"Failed to fetch team members. Status code:
        {response.status_code}")
        return None

def main():
    teams = get_github_organization_teams()

    if teams is not None:
        for team in teams:
            team_id = team['id']
            team_name = team['name']

            members = get_github_team_members(team_id)
```

```
    if members is not None:
        # Set Prometheus metric
        github_organization_users_metric.labels(
            organization=ORGANIZATION_NAME,
            team=team_name
        ).set(len(members))

# Start Prometheus HTTP server
start_http_server(8000)

# Run indefinitely
while True:
    pass
if __name__ == "__main__":
    main()
```

As the script is ready now, we run this script as a service; here, we will see two options using supervisord or systemd. The following are the high-level steps.

Using a Process Manager (Supervisord)

Install Supervisord (if not installed):

```
pip install supervisor
```

Create a Supervisord configuration file (e.g., my_script.conf):

```
[program:my_script]
            command=/path/to/your/python /path/to/your/
            script.py
            autostart=true
            autorestart=true
            stderr_logfile=/var/log/my_script.err.log
            stdout_logfile=/var/log/my_script.out.log
```

Adjust the **command, stderr_logfile**, and **stdout_logfile** paths accordingly.

Start Supervisord:

supervisord -c /path/to/your/my_script.conf

Using systemd (Linux)

Create a systemd service file (e.g., my_script.service):

```
[Unit]
Description=My Script Service
After=network.target
[Service]
ExecStart=/path/to/your/python /path/to/your/script.py
Restart=always
User=your_username
WorkingDirectory=/path/to/your/script_directory
[Install]
WantedBy=default.target
```

Adjust the **ExecStart, User,** and **WorkingDirectory** fields accordingly.

Copy the service file to the systemd system directory:

```
sudo cp my_script.service /etc/systemd/system/
```

Reload systemd:

```
sudo systemctl daemon-reload
```

Enable and start the service:

```
sudo systemctl enable my_script
sudo systemctl start my_script
```

Choose the method that best fits your system and requirements. Both methods allow your Python script to run as a background service and automatically restart in case of failures.

Once our script starts executing now, we will need to make configuration changes in Prometheus which looks as follows:

```
scrape_configs:
  - job_name: 'github_organization_users
    static_configs:
      - targets: ['localhost:8000']
```

Replace 'localhost:8000' with the appropriate address if your script is running on a different host or port; once configuration changes are completed, restart the Prometheus service.

The script increments the metric with the number of members in each GitHub team, and the data will be exposed at the /metrics endpoint on the HTTP server started by the prometheus_client library.

Here's an example of what the data could look like when Prometheus scrapes the /metrics endpoint:

```
# HELP github_organization_users GitHub organization users
grouped by team
# TYPE github_organization_users gauge
github_organization_users{organization="YOUR_ORGANIZATION_
NAME",team="Team1"} 5.0
github_organization_users{organization="YOUR_ORGANIZATION_
NAME",team="Team2"} 7.0
github_organization_users{organization="YOUR_ORGANIZATION_
NAME",team="Team3"} 3.0
```

In this example

- github_organization_users is the name of the metric.

- organization and team are labels representing metadata associated with each time series.

- The values (5.0, 7.0, 3.0) represent the number of members in each team.

812

When querying in Prometheus or visualizing in Grafana, you can use PromQL queries like

```
sum(github_organization_users) by (team)
```

This query sums the metric values based on the team label, providing a breakdown of the total number of members per team.

Using Datadog for Monitoring GitHub

To enhance your GitHub experience, setting up the GitHub integration with Datadog involves configuring GitHub Apps and GitHub Actions, ensuring secure repository access, and gathering advanced telemetry like audit logs, vulnerability reports, secret scanning, and repository statistics.

In the Repository Configuration tab of the GitHub integration tile, you can conveniently manage various aspects of your integration. This includes utilizing Datadog's source code integration to visualize code snippets within your stack traces. Additionally, you can establish a connection between stack traces and source code on GitHub, specifically beneficial for Lambda functions. This integration allows you to display test result summaries directly in pull request comments through CI visibility. Moreover, it provides access to multiple service definitions on GitHub via the Service Catalog. Overall, these features contribute to a more streamlined and efficient development process by seamlessly connecting and optimizing your GitHub workflows through Datadog.

Steps to Configure Integration Between Datadog and GitHub

To link a repository in your GitHub organization or personal account and configure GitHub Apps, start by going to the GitHub integration tile and accessing the Repo Configuration tab. Click "Link GitHub Account" to create a new GitHub App. In the configuration step, either choose Organization and provide a name or select Personal Account. Optionally, you can specify the URL for your GitHub Enterprise Server instance and ensure Datadog servers can connect to it.

In the Edit Permissions section, grant Datadog read permissions for issues, pull requests, and contents – at least one permission must be selected. After that, click "Create App in GitHub" and enter a name for your GitHub App. Complete the process by clicking "Create GitHub App."

Move to the Configuration tab and select "Install GitHub App" followed by "Install & Authorize." Your GitHub App will now be visible in the integration tile. To enable inline code snippets in stack traces, refer to the instructions for setting up source code integration. This step-by-step guide ensures a smooth connection between Datadog and your GitHub repositories, enhancing collaboration and visibility in your development workflows.

Monitoring Audit Logs

Audit logs on GitHub provide a comprehensive record of all activities and events within a GitHub organization. To initiate the collection of these logs through an application's installation, it is crucial to grant read access to organization administration permissions. By doing so, the application gains the necessary permissions to capture GitHub's audit stream, effectively functioning as logs for the entire GitHub organization. This ensures that all significant actions and events are recorded for monitoring, analysis, and maintaining a transparent and accountable development environment.

Metric Collected by Datadog

The GitHub integration includes the collection of Code Scan Alert and Secret Scan Alert metrics, offering a comprehensive overview of the organization's alert status. These metrics categorize alerts based on their state, repository, and secret type, providing valuable insights into the overall security posture. By tracking alert trends and progress over the long term, these metrics contribute to a better understanding of the organization's security landscape. This data not only helps in promptly addressing current issues but also aids in making informed decisions to enhance the organization's overall security measures and practices.

The metrics '*github.code_scan_alert*' and '*github.secret_scan_alert*' are gauges that provide insights into Code Scan Alerts and Secret Scan Alerts on GitHub, respectively. These gauges function as visual indicators, offering a snapshot of the current alert status within the GitHub environment. Specifically, 'github.code_scan_alert' keeps track of the number of Code Scan Alerts, while 'github.secret_scan_alert' focuses on Secret Scan Alerts. These metrics are valuable for teams as they enable a clear visualization of alert levels, allowing for real-time monitoring of security status. By providing information on the severity and urgency of alerts, these metrics empower teams to promptly assess and respond to potential security threats. In essence, they play a crucial role in enhancing the organization's security monitoring and response efforts.

Integrating for GitHub Events

To configure webhooks for GitHub and Datadog and ensure events appear in the Events Explorer, follow these steps. In your GitHub project, go to Settings ➤ Webhooks, then click "Add webhook." Enter the following URL in the Payload URL field: `https://app.datadoghq.com/intake/webhook/github?api_key=<DATADOG_API_KEY>`. Replace <DATADOG_API_KEY> with your Datadog API key. Choose "application/json" in the Content type dropdown menu and optionally add a secret in the Secret field.

In the "Which events would you like to trigger this webhook?" section, select "Let me select individual events" and choose from supported options such as Branch or tag creation, Commit comments, Issue comments, Issues, Pull request review comments, Pull requests, Pushes, Repositories, Security and analysis, and Team adds. Specify the desired actions within each event category.

Activate the webhook by selecting "Active" to receive event details when triggered, then click "Add webhook" to save the configuration. This setup ensures that relevant events are transmitted to Datadog, allowing you to explore and monitor them effectively in the Events Explorer.

Adding a Webhook in Datadog

To configure webhooks in the GitHub integration, follow these steps in the Webhooks tab. Specify the repositories and branches you want to monitor, using wildcards (*), if necessary, for broader coverage. For instance, if you wish to capture events related to the master branch of the DataDog/documentation repository, enter "DataDog/documentation" in the Repository field and "master" in the Branches field.

For a more extensive setup, like gathering events from all master branches in the DataDog organization, input "DataDog/*" in the Repository field and "master" in the Branches field. Note that when using wildcards for the repository name, it's essential to specify the user or organization.

Select the checkboxes for Commits and Issues to receive alerts for these events. Once configurations are in place, click "Update Configuration" to save the webhook settings. With these webhooks set up, events from the specified GitHub repositories will begin appearing in the Events Explorer, providing a streamlined way to monitor and track relevant activities within your repositories.

Once data becomes accessible, it can be leveraged to construct customized dashboards or alerts. These tools prove invaluable for GitHub administrators and other stakeholders, offering insights into GitHub's functionality and performance, thus facilitating a better understanding of its overall effectiveness.

GitHub Service Monitoring

GitHub provides a link, `www.githubstatus.com`, which is crucial for monitoring the operational health of GitHub services. It provides real-time information about the platform's status, including ongoing incidents, past incidents, and general performance updates. Regular monitoring of this page is essential for users, administrators, and stakeholders relying on GitHub for development and collaboration.

By checking the GitHub Status page, users can quickly ascertain if there are any ongoing issues or disruptions that may impact their ability to work on projects, push code, or collaborate with team members. The page provides transparency regarding incidents, their severity, and the affected components. This information is valuable for planning and mitigating potential disruptions to development workflows.

GitHub's commitment to maintaining a transparent and up-to-date status page demonstrates their dedication to providing a reliable and efficient service. Users can make informed decisions based on the status updates, ensuring a smoother development process and minimizing downtime. Overall, the GitHub Status page serves as a vital tool for proactive monitoring, helping users stay informed and responsive to any service-related issues.

Same data is available in the API (`www.githubstatus.com/api#status`), using which we can programmatically access and get response in JSON and send data to other monitoring tools. The following is an example script where we get a service name where the status is not equal to "All Systems Operational." We will use the Python library request and json to get output in JSON:

```
import requests
import json
def check_github_status():
    # GitHub Status API endpoint
    api_url = "https://www.githubstatus.com/api/v2/status.json"

    try:
        # Make a GET request to the GitHub Status API
        response = requests.get(api_url)
        response.raise_for_status()  # Raise an exception for
        4xx and 5xx status codes
```

```
    # Parse JSON response
    status_data = response.json()

    # Check if all systems are operational
    if status_data["status"]["indicator"] != "none":
        # If not, create a report
        report = {
            "status": status_data["status"]["description"],
            "last_updated": status_data["page"]
            ["updated_at"]
        }

        # Print the report (you can customize this to send
        the report via email, Slack, etc.)
        print("GitHub Status Report:")
        print(json.dumps(report, indent=2))

except requests.exceptions.RequestException as e:
    # Handle request exceptions (e.g., network issues)
    print(f"Error: {e}")

if __name__ == "__main__":
    check_github_status()
```

In this script, the check_github_status function sends a GET request to the GitHub Status API, parses the JSON response, and checks if all systems are operational. If not, it creates a report and prints it. You can modify the script to send the report in a preferred way (e.g., email, Slack, etc.); make sure to install the requests library before running the script.

As the output is available in JSON format, most of the monitoring provides a way to accept JSON, so we can use it to enable service monitoring and create a dashboard or alerts as per requirements.

GitHub Reporting Strategies

Ensuring effective reporting strategies for GitHub repository metrics, contribution statistics, and GitHub Actions workflow efficiency is paramount for GitHub administrators seeking valuable insights and making well-informed decisions at both organizational and enterprise levels. Let's delve into the breakdown of reporting strategies for each aspect.

Firstly, concerning GitHub repository metrics, administrators can leverage overview reports, offering a comprehensive summary of the repository's health, encompassing issues, pull requests, and codebase changes. Branch and release reports are instrumental in highlighting progress and stability across different branches and the success of releases. Additionally, code quality metrics, encompassing code complexity and test coverage, ensure code maintainability, while collaboration reports track team interactions, fostering a collaborative development environment.

Moving on to contribution statistics, administrators can utilize individual and team reports to evaluate contributions at both levels, recognizing achievements and pinpointing areas for improvement. Code review metrics aid in assessing the effectiveness of code reviews, contributing to overall code quality, and commit frequency and size reports analyze patterns and contribution sizes, providing insights into development pace and potential bottlenecks.

In terms of GitHub Actions workflow efficiency, administrators can monitor workflow execution time, enabling identification of bottlenecks for optimization. Failure analysis allows tracking and analyzing workflow failures, facilitating quick resolutions and continuous improvement. Resource utilization reports help optimize resource usage by examining how workflows utilize CPU, memory, and storage resources.

At the organizational and enterprise levels, administrators can benefit from consolidated dashboards, providing an overarching view of multiple repositories and workflows, aiding in identifying trends and patterns.

Cross-repository analysis enables the comparison of metrics across various repositories, identifying best practices and areas for improvement. Customized alerts play a crucial role in drawing attention to critical metrics, ensuring prompt action. Integration with project management tools streamlines decision-making processes and aligns development efforts with organizational goals. Regular periodic review meetings further foster collaboration and proactively address challenges.

These reporting strategies are important in offering a holistic view of the development process. They empower administrators with data-driven insights, facilitate collaboration, and optimize workflows, ultimately enhancing productivity at both organizational and enterprise levels.

Let's explore various methods for generating reports on GitHub repository metrics and contribution statistics. Firstly, GitHub Insights offers a built-in tool accessible through the Insights tab on your GitHub repository. This tool provides data on code frequency, contributors, and traffic, allowing you to capture screenshots or export data for inclusion in your reports.

Another approach involves using custom dashboards. Employ tools like GitHub Actions to automate metric collection and contribute to custom dashboards. Integration with visualization tools such as Grafana or Power BI enables the creation of visually appealing and interactive reports. GitHub Actions can be scheduled to trigger data collection and update dashboards regularly.

For automated dissemination of information, set up email reports using services like GitHub Actions or third-party tools. Schedule these reports to be sent to relevant stakeholders, ensuring regular updates on project metrics and contributions.

When creating reports, it is crucial to tailor them to the specific needs and goals of your organization or project. Regularly reviewing and updating reports allows for adaptation to changing requirements, providing ongoing insights into the health and progress of your GitHub repositories.

Sample Report Format

For generating report for GitHub usage we can use repository metrics, contribution statistics , and workflow efficiency to generate this report we can use GitHub Api and schedule as workflow and report it in html or generate it in json format and the send it tools like power bi for better visualization.

Based on requirement other metrics like self-hosted runners count, license usage and other metrics can also be added.

Script in Python

Let us create a script which is used to generate a report in html format to get total number of repositories, users count and repositories statistics, we will be using GitHub Api and script looks as below.

```python
import requests
from jinja2 import Template
from datetime import datetime
# Define GitHub organization and access token
organization = 'Org-Name'
access_token = 'ACCESS_TOKEN'
# Token with admin access
# Define function to get organization details
def get_organization_details():
    url = f'https://api.github.com/orgs/{organization}'
    headers = {'Authorization': f'token {access_token}'}
    response = requests.get(url, headers=headers)
    if response.status_code == 200:
        org_data = response.json()
        total_repositories = org_data['public_repos'] + org_
        data['total_private_repos']
        return {
            'organization_name': organization,
            'total_repositories': total_repositories,
        }
    else:
```

```
        print(f"Failed to fetch organization details:
        {response.status_code}")
        return None

# Define function to get total members in the organization
def get_total_members():
    url = f'https://api.github.com/orgs/{organization}/members'
    headers = {'Authorization': f'token {access_token}'}
    response = requests.get(url, headers=headers)
    if response.status_code == 200:
        members_data = response.json()
        total_members = len(members_data)
        return total_members
    else:
        print(f"Failed to fetch organization's members:
        {response.status_code}")
        return None

# Define function to get repository metrics
def get_repository_metrics(repo_name):
    url = f'https://api.github.com/repos/{organization}/{repo_
    name}/stats/contributors'
    headers = {'Authorization': f'token {access_token}'}
    response = requests.get(url, headers=headers)
    if response.status_code == 200:
        contributors_data = response.json()
        total_commits = sum(contributor['total'] for
        contributor in contributors_data)
        total_additions = sum(sum(week['a'] for week
        in contributor['weeks']) for contributor in
        contributors_data)
        total_deletions = sum(sum(week['d'] for week
```

```
        in contributor['weeks']) for contributor in
        contributors_data)
        workflow_status = 'Completed'  # Placeholder, you can
        replace this with actual workflow status retrieval
        return {
            'repo_name': repo_name,
            'total_commits': total_commits,
            'total_additions': total_additions,
            'total_deletions': total_deletions,
            'workflow_status': workflow_status
        }
    else:
        print(f"Failed to fetch data for repository {repo_
        name}: {response.status_code}")
        return None

# Define function to get all repositories in the organization
def get_all_repositories():
    url = f'https://api.github.com/orgs/{organization}/repos'
    headers = {'Authorization': f'token {access_token}'}
    response = requests.get(url, headers=headers)
    if response.status_code == 200:
        repos_data = response.json()
        repository_metrics = []
        for repo in repos_data:
            metrics = get_repository_metrics(repo['name'])
            if metrics:
                metrics['members'] = get_total_members()  # Add
                total members info to each repository metrics
                repository_metrics.append(metrics)
        return repository_metrics
    else:
```

```python
        print(f"Failed to fetch organization's repositories:
        {response.status_code}")
        return None

# Call the function to retrieve organization details
organization_details = get_organization_details()

# Call the function to retrieve statistics for all repositories
repository_metrics = get_all_repositories()

# HTML template for the report
template = """
<!DOCTYPE html>
<html>
<head>
    <title>GitHub Organization Report</title>
    <style>
        body {
            font-family: Arial, sans-serif;
            margin: 20px;
            padding: 20px;
        }
        h1 {
            color: #0366d6;
        }
        table {
            border-collapse: collapse;
            width: 100%;
            margin-bottom: 20px;
        }
        th, td {
            border: 1px solid #dddddd;
            text-align: left;
```

```
        padding: 8px;
    }
    th {
        background-color: #f2f2f2;
    }
    </style>
</head>
<body>
    <h1>GitHub Organization Report</h1>
    <h2>Organization Details</h2>
    <table>
        <tr>
            <th>Organization Name</th>
            <td>{{ organization_details.organization_
            name }}</td>
        </tr>
        <tr>
            <th>Total Repositories</th>
            <td>{{ organization_details.total_
            repositories }}</td>
        </tr>
        <tr>
            <th>Total Members</th>
            <td>{{ total_members }}</td>
        </tr>
    </table>

    <h2>Repository Statistics</h2>
    <table>
        <tr>
            <th>Repository Name</th>
            <th>Total Commits</th>
```

```
            <th>Total Additions</th>
            <th>Total Deletions</th>
            <th>Workflow Status</th>
        </tr>
        {% for repo in repository_metrics %}
        <tr>
            <td>{{ repo.repo_name }}</td>
            <td>{{ repo.total_commits }}</td>
            <td>{{ repo.total_additions }}</td>
            <td>{{ repo.total_deletions }}</td>
            <td>{{ repo.workflow_status }}</td>
        </tr>
        {% endfor %}
    </table>
</body>
</html>
"""

# Render the HTML template with organization details and
repository metrics data
html_report = Template(template).render(organization_
details=organization_details, repository_metrics=repository_
metrics, total_members=get_total_members())

# Save the HTML report to a file
with open('github_organization_report.html', 'w') as f:
    f.write(html_report)

print("HTML report generated successfully.")
```

The script begins by importing necessary modules like requests for HTTP requests and jinja2.Template for HTML template rendering. It then proceeds to retrieve information about the GitHub organization through the get_organization_details() function, querying the GitHub API for details such as the organization's name and total repository count. Another function, get_total_members(), fetches the total number of members in the organization by querying the GitHub API endpoint specifically for organization members. Following this, the script retrieves repository statistics using the get_repository_metrics(repo_name) function. This function gathers data such as total commits, additions, deletions, and a placeholder for workflow status for a given repository by querying the GitHub API endpoint for repository contributors. The get_all_repositories() function compiles repository metrics for all repositories within the organization. It iterates through each repository, collecting metrics via the get_repository_metrics() function. Utilizing Jinja2 syntax, the script constructs an HTML template stored in the template variable, featuring placeholders for organization details, repository statistics, and member count. Subsequently, the HTML template is rendered via the jinja2.Template.render() method, incorporating organization details, repository metrics, and total members as context. Finally, the rendered HTML report is saved to a file named github_organization_report.html, with a success message printed upon completion of the report generation process, and it looks like Figure 10-1.

GitHub Organization Report

Organization Details

Organization Name	Bloguc-Engineering
Total Repositories	5
Total Members	4

Repository Statistics

Repository Name	Total Commits	Total Additions	Total Deletions	Workflow Status
GitHub-Permissions	3	28	0	Completed
demo-repository	1	44	0	Completed
sample-workflow	5	280	0	Completed
python-ci-cd	7	416	138	Completed

Figure 10-1. *Sample report*

Now this script can be scheduled as a workflow and send mail to required users; you can use these APIs to generate data visualization and optimize the performance. The following is a sample workflow for sending data to Power BI.

Data Visualization Using Power BI

When we run a script or API, we will receive a response from APIs or modify the script to get the data in JSON format. Once we have this JSON data, we can use it to send information to Power BI. Here are the steps to accomplish this.

The process of sending JSON data to Power BI involves several steps, including authentication, preparing the data, and pushing it to Power BI service using its API. Here's a detailed explanation of each step:

1. **Authentication**

   - To interact with the Power BI service programmatically, you need to authenticate using the OAuth 2.0 authentication flow. This involves obtaining an access token that grants your application permission to access Power BI service APIs.

   - In the provided script, authentication is achieved by making a POST request to the Azure AD token endpoint (`https://login.microsoftonline.com/common/oauth2/token`) with the client ID, client secret, username, password, and resource details.

2. **Preparing JSON Data**

   - Before sending JSON data to Power BI, you need to format it according to the requirements of Power BI datasets.

- The script prepares the JSON data by defining the dataset's structure, including the dataset name, default mode, tables, and columns. You can customize the JSON data based on your specific dataset structure and data requirements.

3. **Sending Data to Power BI**

   - Once the access token is obtained and the JSON data is prepared, the script sends a POST request to the Power BI REST API endpoint (`https://api.powerbi.com/v1.0/myorg/groups/{workspace_id}/datasets`) to create a dataset in Power BI.

   - The request includes the access token in the Authorization header and the JSON data in the request body.

   - If the request is successful (status code 201), it indicates that the dataset has been created in Power BI successfully. Otherwise, an error message is printed indicating the failure.

4. **Handling Errors**

   - The script checks the HTTP response status code to determine whether the dataset creation was successful.

   - If the status code is 201 (Created), it prints a success message indicating that the dataset was created successfully.

   - If the status code indicates an error, it prints an error message along with the status code and the response text, providing information about the failure.

Overall, this process allows you to programmatically create datasets in Power BI and push JSON data to them, enabling you to visualize and analyze your data within the Power BI environment.

The following is a sample script in Python:

```python
import os
import requests

# Get Power BI credentials from environment variables
power_bi_credentials = {
    'username': os.getenv('POWER_BI_USERNAME'),
    'password': os.getenv('POWER_BI_PASSWORD'),
    'client_id': os.getenv('POWER_BI_CLIENT_ID'),
    'client_secret': os.getenv('POWER_BI_CLIENT_SECRET'),
    'workspace_id': os.getenv('POWER_BI_WORKSPACE_ID')
}

# Define the URL for obtaining an access token
token_url = 'https://login.microsoftonline.com/common/
oauth2/token'

# Get access token
token_data = {
    'grant_type': 'password',
    'client_id': power_bi_credentials['client_id'],
    'client_secret': power_bi_credentials['client_secret'],
    'resource': 'https://analysis.windows.net/powerbi/api',
    'username': power_bi_credentials['username'],
    'password': power_bi_credentials['password']
}
response = requests.post(token_url, data=token_data)
access_token = response.json().get('access_token')
```

```python
# Define the URL for creating a dataset in Power BI
create_dataset_url = f'https://api.powerbi.com/v1.0/myorg/
groups/{power_bi_credentials["workspace_id"]}/datasets'

# Prepare your JSON data
json_data = {
    "name": "Your Dataset Name",
    "defaultMode": "Push",
    "tables": [
        {
            "name": "Your Table Name",
            "columns": [
                {"name": "Column1", "dataType": "String"},
                {"name": "Column2", "dataType": "Int64"},
                {"name": "Column3", "dataType": "DateTime"}
                # Add more columns as needed
            ]
        }
        # Add more tables as needed
    ]
}

# Send the JSON data to create a dataset
headers = {
    'Content-Type': 'application/json',
    'Authorization': f'Bearer {access_token}'
}
response = requests.post(create_dataset_url, json=json_data,
headers=headers)

# Check the response
if response.status_code == 201:
    print("Dataset created successfully.")
```

```
else:
    print(f"Failed to create dataset. Status code: {response.
    status_code}, Response: {response.text}")
```

This script is used to create a dataset in Power BI using JSON data. Let's break down how it works:

1. **Import Necessary Libraries:** The script imports the os and requests modules.

2. **Get Power BI Credentials from Environment Variables:** It retrieves Power BI credentials (username, password, client ID, client secret, and workspace ID) from environment variables using the os.getenv() function.

3. **Define the Token URL:** It defines the URL for obtaining an access token from the Azure AD token endpoint.

4. **Get the Access Token:** It prepares the data needed to obtain an access token (including grant type, client ID, client secret, resource, username, and password) and sends a POST request to the token URL to get the access token. The access token is extracted from the response JSON.

5. **Define the Create Dataset URL:** It defines the URL for creating a dataset in Power BI. The URL includes the workspace ID obtained from environment variables.

6. **Prepare JSON Data:** It prepares the JSON data for the dataset, including the dataset name, default mode, and table details (name and columns).

7. **Send JSON Data to the Create Dataset:** It sends a POST request to the create dataset URL, including the JSON data in the request body and the access token in the Authorization header.

8. **Check Response:** It checks the response status code. If the status code is 201 (Created), it prints a success message indicating that the dataset was created successfully. Otherwise, it prints an error message with the status code and response text.

This script provides a straightforward way to create datasets in Power BI using JSON data and can be customized to fit specific dataset requirements.

Best Practices for GitHub Maintenance

Maintaining a GitHub organization or enterprise-level repository involves several regular tasks like repository cleanup, dependency updates, and security audits. Here's a guide on how to effectively handle these best practices:

Overview of Performing GitHub Maintenance

1. **Repository Cleanup**

   - **Regular Review:** Perform periodic reviews of repositories to identify outdated or unused projects, branches, or files, add topics with team name example team-sapdev to repositories which helps to easily identify teams associated with repository, once repository are identified you can reachout to respective team using teams name in topics.

   - **Archiving:** Archive or delete obsolete repositories or branches to declutter the organization.

- **Documentation:** Document repository organization and cleanup procedures to ensure consistency across teams.

2. **Dependency Updates**

- **Automated Tools:** Utilize tools like Dependabot or Renovate to automatically identify and update outdated dependencies.

- **Scheduled Reviews:** Conduct periodic manual reviews to identify dependencies that require manual intervention or have breaking changes.

- **Testing:** Always test dependency updates in a separate branch or environment to ensure compatibility and stability.

3. **Security Audits**

- **Automated Scans:** Integrate automated security scanning tools like GitHub's CodeQL or third-party services to regularly scan repositories for vulnerabilities.

- **Security Policies:** Define and enforce security policies for code contributions, such as requiring code reviews, enforcing coding standards, and implementing secure coding practices.

- **Incident Response Plan:** Develop an incident response plan to address security incidents promptly, including procedures for vulnerability disclosures and patch management.

4. **Enterprise-Level Considerations**

- **Access Control:** Implement granular access controls and permissions to ensure that only authorized individuals can access and modify repositories.

- **Compliance:** Ensure compliance with relevant regulations and standards by implementing necessary controls, such as data encryption, access logging, and audit trails.

- **Monitoring and Logging:** Set up monitoring and logging to track repository activities, identify security incidents, and ensure compliance with organizational policies.

- **Training and Awareness:** Provide training and awareness programs to educate employees about security best practices, including secure coding, phishing awareness, and incident response.

5. **Documentation and Communication**

- **Documentation:** Maintain comprehensive documentation for maintenance procedures, including step-by-step instructions, troubleshooting guides, and best practices.

- **Communication Channels:** Establish clear communication channels, such as mailing lists, chat platforms, or forums, for discussing maintenance tasks, sharing updates, and addressing issues collaboratively.

6. **Continuous Improvement**

- **Feedback Mechanism:** Encourage feedback from team members to identify areas for improvement in maintenance processes and tools.

- **Iterative Approach:** Continuously iterate on maintenance processes based on feedback, emerging threats, and changes in organizational requirements.

By following these practices, you can effectively handle regular maintenance tasks for GitHub organizations and enterprise-level repositories, ensuring security, efficiency, and compliance with organizational standards.

Performing Maintenance of Self-Hosted Runners

Performing maintenance activities on self-hosted runners on GitHub with minimal or no impact on pipelines, following a rolling update approach, involves updating each runner individually while ensuring continuous workflow. Here's a detailed guide on how to achieve this:

1. **Prepare for Maintenance:**

- Schedule a maintenance window during off-peak hours to minimize the impact on pipeline activity.

- Notify relevant teams and stakeholders about the scheduled maintenance window and the planned rolling update process.

2. **Identify Runner Groups:**

- If you have multiple self-hosted runners, categorize them into groups based on factors such as hardware specifications, operating system, or geographical location.

- This segmentation allows you to update runners in batches, reducing the risk of disrupting pipeline runs.

3. **Disable a Runner Group:**

   - Begin by disabling one group of self-hosted runners in the GitHub repository or organization settings.

   - This prevents new pipeline jobs from being assigned to the disabled runners while allowing existing jobs to complete on other active runners.

4. **Drain Existing Jobs:**

   - Allow ongoing pipeline jobs assigned to the disabled runner group to finish executing.

   - Monitor the progress of these jobs and ensure they are completed successfully before proceeding with the update.

5. **Perform a Rolling Update:**

   - Start updating the disabled runner group one by one, ensuring that only one runner is taken offline at a time.

   - Perform necessary maintenance tasks such as software updates, system patches, or hardware maintenance on each runner.

   - Follow best practices for system administration to minimize downtime and ensure a smooth transition.

6. **Verify Runner Status:**

   - After updating each runner in the disabled group, verify its status to ensure it is back online and available for use.

   - Monitor for any unexpected errors or issues during the update process and address them promptly.

7. **Enable the Runner Group:**

   - Once all runners in the disabled group have been successfully updated and verified, re-enable them to allow new pipeline jobs to be assigned to them.

   - Ensure that the updated runners are properly integrated with GitHub Actions and ready to accept incoming jobs.

8. **Monitor Pipeline Activity:**

   - Monitor the pipeline activity closely after re-enabling the updated runner group to ensure they are functioning properly and handling incoming jobs without issues.

   - Validate that pipelines run successfully and without any unexpected errors or failures.

9. **Repeat for Remaining Groups:**

   - Repeat the process for each subsequent runner group, disabling and updating them one at a time until all self-hosted runners have been updated.

   - Ensure there is enough capacity on the active runners to handle pipeline jobs during the rolling update process.

10. **Post-Maintenance Review:**

- Conduct a post-maintenance review to evaluate the effectiveness of the rolling update process and identify any areas for improvement.

- Gather feedback from stakeholders and teams involved to refine future maintenance procedures.

11. **Documentation:**

- Document the rolling update process performed, including any issues encountered and their resolutions, for future reference.

- Update documentation with any changes or lessons learned from the maintenance process.

By following these steps and best practices, you can perform maintenance activities on self-hosted runners on GitHub with minimal impact on pipelines, ensuring continuous workflow and reliability of your CI/CD processes. In the next section, we will discuss about setting up health dashboard for GitHub Health.

Setting Up a GitHub Health Dashboard

Here is an approach where a dashboard that contains organization members, license information, GitHub service status, and workflow status is a centralized interface designed to provide a comprehensive overview of various aspects related to a GitHub organization or repository. Here's an explanation of each component:

1. **Organization Members:** This section typically displays a total count of members associated with the organization or repository. It may include details such as usernames, roles, and permissions within the organization. This allows administrators to easily manage and monitor the contributors involved in the project.

2. **License Information:** This component provides details about the GitHub user licenses, which will have information about licenses consumed, available, and total; this will help procurement team to buy licenses at a very early stage.

3. **GitHub Service Status:** This section indicates the current status of GitHub's services. It may include any ongoing incidents or maintenance activities. Monitoring the service status is crucial for ensuring the reliability and availability of the GitHub platform, which directly impacts the development workflow.

4. **Workflow Status:** This component displays the status of automated workflows or pipelines configured within the repository. This could include information about continuous integration (CI) builds, automated tests, code quality checks, deployment pipelines, and more. Monitoring workflow status helps teams identify issues early in the development process and ensures that changes are properly integrated and deployed.

5. **Self-Hosted Runner:** This component indicates the status and utilization of self-hosted runners configured within the repository. Self-hosted runners are custom execution environments used to run GitHub Actions workflows. Monitoring their status ensures that there are enough resources available for running workflows efficiently and that they're properly maintained.

Overall, this dashboard serves as a central hub for monitoring and managing various aspects of a GitHub organization or repository, providing stakeholders with valuable insights into member contributions, platform availability, and development workflow status, and it looks like Figure 10-2.

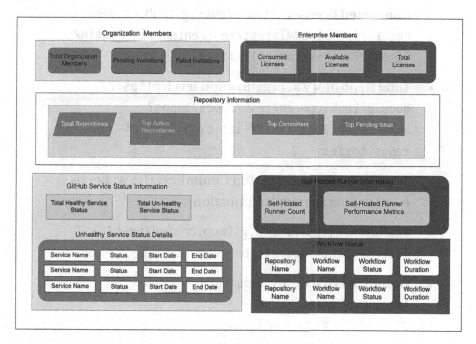

Figure 10-2. *Sample GitHub dashboard*

To get this view, we must write custom scripts and use webhooks as data is in JSON which can be used with tools Prometheus and other tools where it supports send the data in JSON format; here is a list of APIs that can be used to convert to a script and send it to the respective tool:

- **Get users list at organization level:** `https://docs.github.com/en/rest/users/users?apiVersion=2022-11-28#list-users`

- **Pending Invitations:** `https://docs.github.com/en/rest/orgs/members?apiVersion=2022-11-28#list-pending-organization-invitations`

- **Failed invitations:** `https://docs.github.com/en/rest/orgs/members?apiVersion=2022-11-28`

- **Consumed license:** `https://docs.github.com/en/enterprise-cloud@latest/rest/enterprise-admin/license?apiVersion=2022-11-28`

- **Total Repository at organization level:** `https://docs.github.com/en/rest/repos/repos?apiVersion=2022-11-28#list-organization-repositories`

- **Top Active Repoitories, Top Commiter:** Use webhook event to filter required information

- **Top issue:** `https://docs.github.com/en/rest/issues/labels?apiVersion=2022-11-28`

- **Github Service status:** Refer GitHub Service Monitoring section

- **Self-Hosted runner:** `https://docs.github.com/ en/enterprise-cloud@latest/rest/actions/self- hosted-runner-groups?apiVersion=2022-11-28`

- **Workflow Status:** Use webhook event and filter it by workflow execution.

Third-Party Dashboards

If you are using third-party tools like Grafana and Datadog, there is a built-in dashboard which can be used and future customized as per requirements; the following are the links for the dashboard:

- **Datadog:** `https://docs.datadoghq.com/ integrations/rapdev_github/`

- **Grafana:** `https://grafana.com/grafana/ dashboards/14000-github-default/`

Handling and Learning from Incidents

Here are some of the common user access issues and some insights into the reasons for workflow and repository access issues, along with best practices to avoid these problems:

Common Issues and Best Practices

1. **Security Vulnerabilities**

    - **Reasons for the Incident:** Security vulnerabilities can stem from outdated dependencies, improper input validation, lack of encryption, or insecure coding practices.

    - **Best Practices to Avoid:** Regularly update dependencies, follow secure coding practices, conduct security audits, and implement security measures such as encryption and access controls.

2. **Workflow Failures**

- **Reasons for the Incident:** Workflow failures can occur due to misconfigurations, environmental issues, dependency problems, or integration errors.

- **Best Practices to Avoid:** Conduct thorough testing of workflows, monitor for errors and failures, implement automated testing, use version control for configurations, and document workflows clearly.

3. **Repository Access Issues**

- **Reasons for the Incident:** Access issues may arise from misconfigured permissions, accidental changes to access settings, or unauthorized access attempts.

- **Best Practices to Avoid:** Regularly review and update access permissions, implement least privilege principles, use groups or teams for access management, enforce two-factor authentication, and monitor access logs for suspicious activity.

4. **Service Disruptions**

- **Reasons for the Incident:** Service disruptions can result from maintenance activities, infrastructure issues, DDoS attacks, or software bugs.

- **Best Practices to Avoid:** Plan maintenance activities in advance, implement redundancy and failover mechanisms, monitor for unusual traffic patterns, and have incident response plans in place.

5. **User Access Issues**

- **Reasons for the Incident:** User access issues may arise from onboarding/offboarding processes, role misconfigurations, or permission conflicts.

- **Best Practices to Avoid:** Implement clear onboarding/offboarding procedures, regularly review and update user roles and permissions, provide training on access management, and automate access provisioning/deprovisioning where possible.

6. **Data Loss or Corruption**

- **Reasons for the Incident:** Data loss or corruption can occur due to accidental deletions, data breaches, software bugs, or hardware failures.

- **Best Practices to Avoid:** Implement regular backups, enforce version control for critical data, implement access controls to prevent unauthorized modifications, and train users on data protection best practices.

7. **Compliance Violations**

- **Reasons for Incident:** Compliance violations may result from failure to adhere to licensing requirements, data protection regulations, or industry standards.

- **Best Practices to Avoid:** Stay informed about relevant regulations and standards, conduct regular compliance audits, implement controls to enforce compliance, and provide training on compliance requirements to organization members.

8. **Communication Breakdowns**

- **Reasons for the Incident:** Communication breakdowns can occur due to misunderstandings, conflicts, or lack of clarity regarding project requirements or deadlines.

- **Best Practices to Avoid:** Foster open communication channels, encourage regular team meetings and updates, document project requirements and expectations clearly, and address conflicts or misunderstandings promptly.

By addressing these common issues and implementing best practices to mitigate them, GitHub organizations can maintain a secure, efficient, and collaborative development environment. Regular monitoring, proactive management, and ongoing training are key to ensuring the smooth operation of GitHub repositories and workflows.

Response Strategies and Post-Incident Reviews

Some of the immediate response strategies, post-incident reviews, and the importance of learning from incidents are listed as follows:

1. **Immediate Response Strategies**

- **Establish Clear Communication Channels:** Ensure that there are clear communication channels in place to notify relevant stakeholders immediately when an incident occurs.

- **Activate Incident Response Plan:** Follow the organization's incident response plan to address the incident promptly. This may involve assembling an incident response team, isolating affected systems, and implementing mitigation measures.

- **Containment and Mitigation:** Take immediate actions to contain the incident and mitigate its impact. This may include shutting down compromised systems, deploying patches or fixes, or activating backup systems.

- **Regular Status Updates:** Provide regular updates to stakeholders on the status of the incident and the steps being taken to resolve it. Transparency and communication are key during incident response.

2. **Post-Incident Reviews**

- **Conduct a Post-Incident Review (PIR):** After the incident has been resolved, conduct a thorough post-incident review to analyze what happened, why it happened, and how it was handled.

- **Involve Key Stakeholders:** Include representatives from relevant teams and departments in the post-incident review to gather diverse perspectives and insights.

- **Identify Root Causes:** Identify the root causes of the incident, including any underlying issues or vulnerabilities in processes, systems, or practices.

- **Document Lessons Learned:** Document the findings from the post-incident review, including key takeaways, lessons learned, and recommendations for improvement.

- **Implement Changes:** Implement corrective actions and improvements based on the lessons learned from the incident. This may involve updating policies, procedures, or systems, as well as providing additional training or resources to team members.

3. **Learning from Incidents**

    - **Emphasize Continuous Improvement:** Emphasize
      the importance of continuous improvement
      and learning from incidents to prevent future
      occurrences.

    - **Promote a Culture of Learning:** Foster a culture
      where incidents are viewed as opportunities for
      learning and growth rather than as failures or
      setbacks.

    - **Encourage Knowledge Sharing:** Encourage
      knowledge sharing and collaboration among
      team members to disseminate insights gained
      from incidents and prevent similar incidents in
      the future.

    - **Document Incidents and Changes:** Maintain
      detailed records of incidents, post-incident
      reviews, and changes implemented as a result of
      lessons learned. This documentation serves as a
      valuable resource for future incident response and
      prevention efforts.

By integrating immediate response strategies, post-incident reviews,
and a culture of learning from incidents into their incident management
processes, GitHub organizations can effectively respond to incidents,
minimize their impact, and prevent future occurrences. Continuous
improvement and proactive measures based on lessons learned are
essential for maintaining the security, reliability, and efficiency of GitHub
repositories and workflows.

Summary

This chapter offered a comprehensive guide for navigating the complexities of managing GitHub environments effectively. It began by addressing common GitHub issues, such as merge conflicts and authentication errors, providing readers with straightforward solutions to overcome these challenges. The chapter progressed to cover advanced troubleshooting techniques, equipping users with the skills needed to tackle complex scenarios, including debugging CI/CD pipelines and managing large repositories.

A significant portion of the chapter was dedicated to proactive measures, emphasizing the importance of monitoring GitHub operations. It discussed essential tools and practices for ensuring repository health and performance, highlighting the critical role of effective reporting in a collaborative setting. The guide instructs on creating impactful reports on repository metrics and workflow efficiency, utilizing GitHub's API for custom reports, and integrating with external tools for superior data visualization.

Maintenance practices are also a focal point, with the chapter offering insights on keeping repositories optimized and secure through regular upkeep. An innovative aspect introduced was the setup of a GitHub Health Dashboard, a pivotal tool for real-time monitoring of key metrics and system status, aiding in swift issue detection, strategic planning, and resource allocation.

Furthermore, the chapter delved into incident management, stressing the value of learning from past incidents to refine future practices. This approach not only helps in immediate problem resolution but also contributes to the development of more resilient GitHub operations.

Covering topics from understanding GitHub monitoring and reporting and learning GitHub audit logs to implementing effective reporting strategies and setting up a GitHub Health Dashboard, this chapter stands as a vital resource. It concluded by underscoring best practices for GitHub maintenance and the importance of handling and learning from incidents, providing readers with a holistic view of maintaining efficiency and security in GitHub operations. This chapter is an indispensable guide for anyone aiming to enhance their GitHub management skills, offering the knowledge and tools necessary to navigate challenges, optimize workflows, and uphold a high standard of operational excellence.

Resources

- Organization members: `https://docs.github.com/en/rest/orgs/members?apiVersion=2022-11-28`

- Enterprise members: `https://docs.github.com/en/enterprise-cloud@latest/rest/enterprise-admin/license?apiVersion=2022-11-28#list-enterprise-consumed-licenses`

- Repository: `https://docs.github.com/en/rest/repos/repos?apiVersion=2022-11-28#list-organization-repositories`

- Issues: `https://docs.github.com/en/rest/issues?apiVersion=2022-11-28`

- Service status: `www.githubstatus.com/api`

- Self-hosted runner information: `https://docs.github.com/en/rest/actions/self-hosted-runners?apiVersion=2022-11-28`

- Workflow status: `https://docs.github.com/en/rest/actions/workflows?apiVersion=2022-11-28`

- GitHub webhook event documentation: `https://docs.github.com/en/webhooks#events`

Index

A

© Balu Nivrutti Ilag, AjayKumar P. Baljoshi, Ganesh J. Sangale and Yogesh Athave 2024   851
B. N. Ilag et al., *Mastering GitHub Enterprise Management and Administration*,
https://doi.org/10.1007/979-8-8688-0369-7

B

C